# The LION & the LILY

Also by Ira Mukhoty

*Song of Draupadi: A Novel*
*Akbar: The Great Mughal*
*Daughters of the Sun: Empresses, Queens and Begums of the Mughal Empire*
*Heroines: Powerful Indian Women of Myth and History*

# The LION & the LILY
## THE RISE & FALL OF AWADH

## IRA MUKHOTY

ALEPH BOOK COMPANY
An independent publishing firm
promoted by *Rupa Publications India*

First published in India in 2024
by Aleph Book Company
7/16 Ansari Road, Daryaganj
New Delhi 110 002

Copyright © Ira Mukhoty 2024
The Image Credits on p. 393 constitute an extension of the copyright page.

Border on cover from 5005 folio 12. Courtesy Staatliche Museen zu Berlin, Museum für Asiatische Kunst / Martin Franken Public Domain Mark 1.0.

All rights reserved.

The author has asserted her moral rights.

The views and opinions expressed in this book are the author's own and the facts are as reported by her, which have been verified to the extent possible, and the publishers are not in any way liable for the same.

The publisher has used its best endeavours to ensure that URLs for external websites referred to in this book are correct and active at the time of going to press. However, the publisher has no responsibility for the websites and can make no guarantee that a site will remain live or that the content is or will remain appropriate.

No part of this publication may be reproduced, transmitted, or stored in a retrieval system, in any form or by any means, without permission in writing from Aleph Book Company.

ISBN: 978-81-19635-97-9

1 3 5 7 9 10 8 6 4 2

Printed in India

This book is sold subject to the condition that it shall not, by way of trade or otherwise, be lent, resold, hired out, or otherwise circulated without the publisher's prior consent in any form of binding or cover other than that in which it is published.

*To my grandmothers,*
*Berthe Lintant and Bijeswari Devi.*

# CONTENTS

| | |
|---|---:|
| *Cast of Characters* | xi |
| *Select Chronology of Major Events* | xxv |
| *Prologue* | xxix |
| *Introduction* | xxxiii |

**THE FISH OF HINDUSTAN: (1720–1775)**

| | |
|---|---:|
| 1764: Somewhere Between Bihar and Bengal | 3 |
| When Awadh Was a Hardship Posting | 12 |
| Shuja-ud-Daula, Warrior King, and Nawab Begum | 26 |
| A Battle at Buxar | 39 |
| A City is Born | 54 |
| A Frenchman at Faizabad | 72 |
| Tinker Tailor Soldier Spy | 85 |
| A Portrait of a Nawab | 98 |
| Fathers and Sons | 106 |
| A Nabob in Delhi | 111 |
| The World on Fire | 117 |

**THE LIONS OF GOD: (1775–1785)**

| | |
|---|---:|
| The Road to Lucknow | 125 |
| All Frenchmen Must Leave | 137 |
| The Begums and a Raja | 141 |
| Punishing a Begum | 154 |
| From Yorktown to Awadh | 170 |
| The Ghost of the Mughal Empire | 180 |
| Zoffany and a Mughal Zenana | 193 |
| The Chameleons of Lucknow | 202 |

**THE TIGER AND THE FISH: (1785–1794)**

| | |
|---|---:|
| The Glory of Lucknow | 213 |
| The Bara Imambara and a Light Divine | 227 |

| | |
|---|---|
| Art in Chaos | 239 |
| Courtesans and Poets | 248 |
| The Rooster and the Tiger | 262 |
| Claude Martin in Mysore | 269 |
| De Boigne and the Armies of Hindustan | 277 |
| The Age of Splendour | 287 |

THE LION OF BRITAIN: (1794–1803)

| | |
|---|---|
| Men of Empire | 299 |
| The Golden Age of Awadh | 311 |
| Little England in Awadh | 315 |
| Making an Ethiopian White | 322 |
| Death of a Nawab | 333 |
| The Secrets of the Zenana | 343 |
| Tumult In Benaras | 356 |
| A Trap For a Tiger | 363 |
| The Fall of Seringapatam | 368 |
| The Battle of Delhi | 382 |
| | |
| *Epilogue* | 388 |
| *Acknowledgements* | 391 |
| *Image Credits* | 393 |
| *Notes* | 395 |
| *Bibliography* | 421 |
| *Index* | 427 |

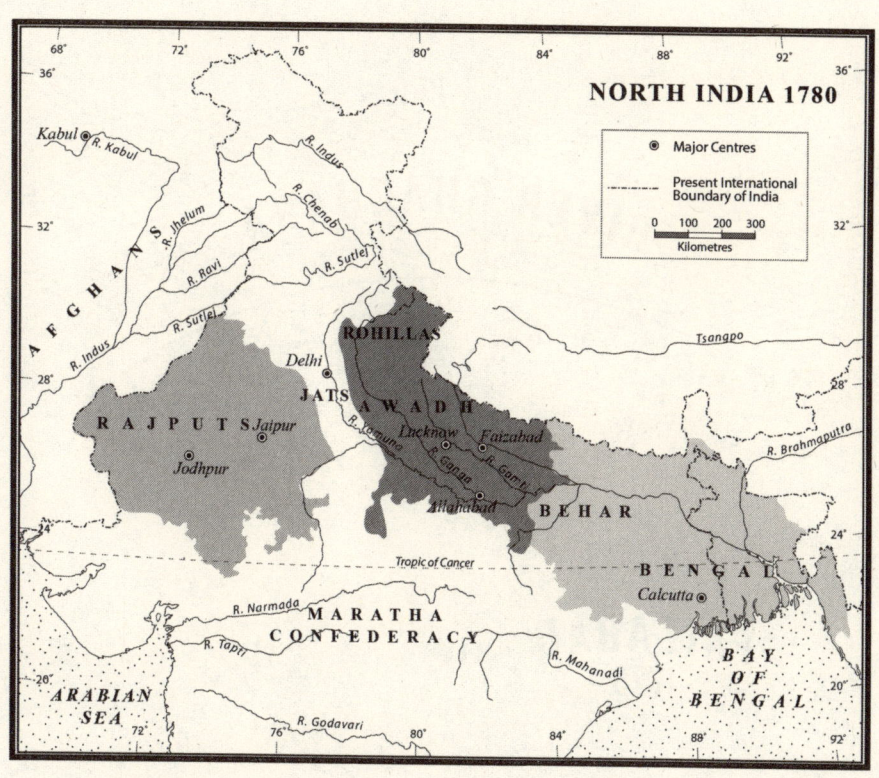

This map has been prepared in adherence to the 'Guidelines for acquiring and producing Geospatial Data and Geospatial Data Services including Maps' published vide DST F.No. SM/25/02/2020 (Part-I) dated 15th February, 2021.

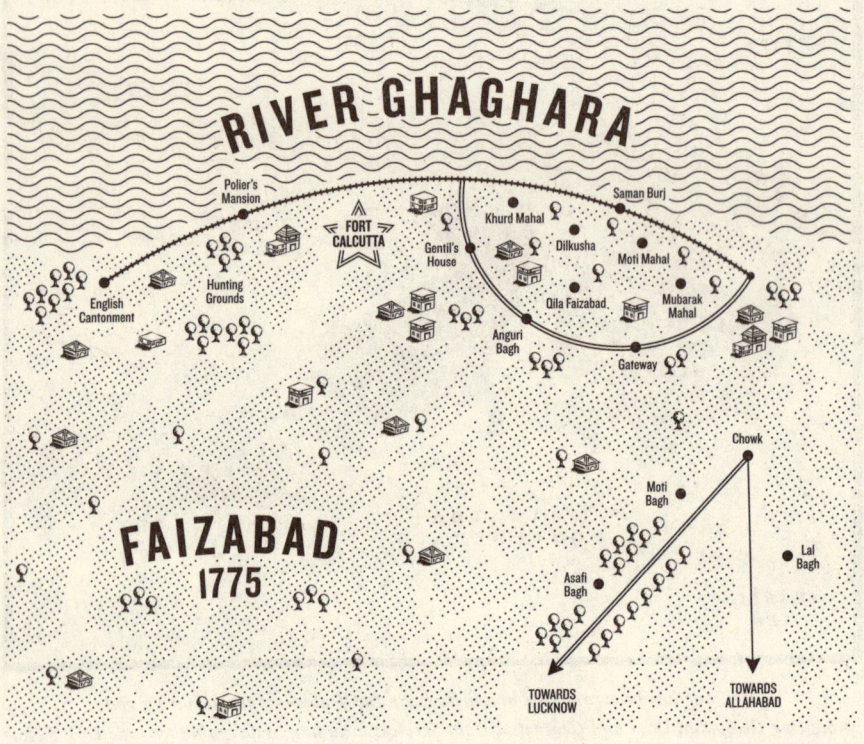

# CAST OF CHARACTERS

## THE NAWABS OF AWADH

**Saadat Khan (c. 1680–1739):** A Persian immigrant from an aristocratic family of Sayyids from the city of Nishapur, Mir Muhammad Amin joined the service of Emperor Muhammad Shah 'Rangeeley', and was soon rewarded with the titles Saadat Khan and Burhan-ul-Mulk, as well as the insignia of the Mahi Maratib—the Order of the Fish—for his bravery in battle. Later exiled to Awadh as punishment for failing to quell a Jat rebellion, Saadat Khan showed ambitious energy in settling the province. He called for four nephews from Persia, one of whom, Safdar Jang, he married to his daughter Sadr-un-Nisa Begum, the future Nawab Begum. Outplaying his hand when trying to parlay with the vicious Persian warlord, Nadir Shah, in 1739, Saadat Khan died by suicide.

**Safdar Jang (1708–1754):** A famously temperate man, his only wife was the formidable Nawab Begum, the daughter of Saadat Khan. Safdar Jang was made wazir of the Mughal empire but in the 1750s got caught up in the faction politics and civil unrest wracking Delhi. In a fatal misjudgement, he earned the abiding enmity of the Mughal queen mother Qudsiya Begum by having her khwajasara (elite eunuch) Javed Khan murdered. Safdar Jang left Delhi at this point, never to return, and remained in Awadh. His son Shuja-ud-Daula would later build the famous Safdar Jang tomb for his father in Delhi.

**Shuja-ud-Daula (1732–1775):** The only son and heir of Safdar Jang and Nawab Begum, Shuja began his career on a less than promising note, displaying his tempestuous, impulsive nature, solely occupied with kite-flying and womanizing. However, guided by his iron-willed mother, Shuja very quickly reformed his ways to become one of the great generals of India by the time of the Battle of Buxar (1764). His well-managed lands were amongst the richest in the country, his army was formidable, and his own personal valour unmatched. This led to his sense of unassailability, and he was utterly devastated by his defeat at this battle. With the help of his wife Bahu Begum, and the advice of French advisers like Jean-Baptiste Gentil, Shuja regained his lands. He relocated to Faizabad after his defeat at Buxar and began the process of transforming the city into one of enormous prosperity and culture.

**Asaf-ud-Daula (1748–1797):** Perhaps the most infamously maligned of all the nawabs of Awadh, Asaf-ud-Daula was criticized as a debauched, obese, profligate, quivering puddle of a man, whereas he fought to assert himself from the time his father died unexpectedly, using his generosity, charm, skill, and guile to smooth away obstacles. Immediately upon the death of Shuja, Asaf had to face the incessant demands for more money from venal Company men as well as greater interference in the management of his domains. His distracting, loquacious charm hid his gauging intelligence, and he was able to checkmate most of his enemies. His buoyant charm won over Warren Hastings with whom he shared his kebab recipe, and he later stood firm when Cornwallis sought more aid. However, Governor General John Shore's rigid, puritanical intransigeance would be the end of Asaf, who could not fathom such inflexibility. During his two decades in Lucknow, Asaf fostered a Shia renaissance and a glorious, syncretic culture that would continue to be celebrated by all future nawabs of Awadh.

**Wazir Ali Khan (1780–1817):** Asaf's adopted son and recognized heir, Wazir Ali was brought up as a prince and had a fabulously extravagant wedding. Proclaimed nawab of Awadh at just seventeen when Asaf died unexpectedly, Wazir Ali resented the excessive interference by the pro-British adviser Tafazzul, and refused to abide by his dictates, increasingly worrying the EIC officials. His grandmother, Bahu Begum, also withdrew her support when she realized he would not be as malleable as she had hoped. John Shore used the trumped-up excuse of Wazir Ali's questionable parentage to depose the young man and install his uncle Saadat Ali Khan instead. Wazir Ali was banished to Benaras, where he rose in revolt and was involved in the killing of George Cherry.

**Saadat Ali Khan (1752–1814):** Having organized a rebellion when his half-brother, Asaf-ud-Daula, became nawab of Awadh, Saadat Ali Khan was exiled to Benaras where he cultivated the friendship of

Company officials and adopted many English ways. When Wazir Ali was found wanting by the Company men in 1798, Saadat Ali was the perfect choice to replace him and he was made to sign a treaty that was practically 'a treaty of vassalage' whereby he agreed to a far larger subsidiary than had ever been agreed upon by an Indian state before.

## THE DELHI COURT

**Muhammad Shah 'Rangeeley' (1719–1748):** Cultured and beloved Mughal emperor who brought some stability to the throne after a period of chaos following Aurangzeb's death in 1707. The destruction wrought by the Persian warlord Nadir Shah when he invaded Delhi in 1739 exposed the fragility of the Mughal throne, and traumatized the emperor till the end of his life.

**Shah Alam II (1728–1806):** Cultured, erudite, scholarly, and pious, Shah Alam was always criticized by Europeans as lacking a certain force of character to accomplish truly great things. Nevertheless, the events of the eighteenth century conspired against Shah Alam who had shown considerable panache and vim when as Mirza Ali Gauhar he had escaped the confinement of the Red Fort to try and raise an army to fight the British and reclaim Bengal. The defeat of the Mughal forces at the Battle of Buxar, however, began the process of servitude to the British which the emperor was never really able to extricate himself from, and the course of his life would be a steady crumbling of his power to the EIC as well as to the other powerful local rulers like the Marathas.

**Mirza Jawan Bakht (1749-1788):** The eldest son of Mughal emperor Shah Alam, the prince made a rather daring escape from the Red Fort of Delhi to try and raise an army to come to his father's help. He arrived in Lucknow at the court of Asaf-ud-Daula in 1784 where Hastings was utterly captivated by the charm of the situation, writing that he found Jawan Bakht 'gentle, lively, possessed of a high sense of honour...' Antoine Polier, more realistic, added that the prince was 'very fond of pleasure and women and much inclined to indulge himself freely in the pursuit of them'. Mirza Jawan Bakht never did return to Delhi, dying in Benaras of a fever in 1788.

**Najaf Khan (1723–1782):** Persian Shia commander of the Mughal forces at Delhi, Najaf Khan was a celebrated general and military genius. Beloved by his men, he was always able to win their undying loyalty. A vigorous, charismatic, and relentless warrior, he was instrumental in keeping Delhi peaceful in the 1770s, right up till his death in 1782. He was related by marriage to Nawab Begum of Awadh, and maintained close links with her till his death.

AWADH COURTS OF FAIZABAD AND LUCKNOW

**Hasan Reza Khan:** Hasan Reza Khan, affectionately known as Mirza Hasnu, had begun his career as an illiterate attendant of Shuja-ud-Daula but as he made his way up through the ranks, he became extremely powerful. He was finally appointed khan-e-saman—superintendent of the kitchens—for Shuja-ud-Daula and later became Asaf-ud-Daula's minister. He lived in grand style in the imposing home he built across the river, called Hasangary. Went over to the British when he saw their star rising.

**Haider Beg Khan:** Powerful minister of Asaf-ud-Daula and deputy to Hasan Reza Khan. An intelligent, determined man, he was sent as the nawab's ambassador to Cornwallis in Calcutta in 1786, where he stoutly defended the nawab's interests. Later went over to the British, to further his cause.

**Maharaja Tikait Rai:** Deputy minister to Hasan Reza Khan after the death of Haider Beg Khan, he was from a Kayastha family that had a long history of service with the nawabs. Infamous for promoting a very large number of his family and dependents to posts under his authority, he was mistrusted by Asaf and did, in fact, go over to the British.

**Jhau Lal:** A Kayasth from an undistinguished family, Jhau Lal was Asaf's favourite minister. He adopted the Shia lifestyle of the Lucknow elite, and Asaf gave him the honorific title 'maharaj'. Hard-working and entirely loyal to the nawab, he was suspect to the British because of this unwavering loyalty. His banishment from Lucknow by John Shore effectively spelled the beginning of the end for the devastated Asaf.

**Jawahar Ali Khan and Bahar Ali Khan:** The elite eunuchs—or khwajasaras—of Bahu Begum and Nawab Begum of Awadh. Very influential men, they served as intermediaries between the powerful begums of Awadh and their interests in the outside world, and were assiduously courted by the gentry who, it was said, greeted their every pronouncement with loud shouts of 'Wah Wah' and 'Subanallah'. Since they were extensions of the begums' households, they conducted themselves with great reserve and dignity, maintaining a sober but grand and cultured lifestyle, and were prodigiously generous. They were imprisoned by the orders of Hastings during the infamous 'despoliation of the begums' episode in the 1780s.

**Allama Tafazzul Hussain Khan Kashmiri:** Popularly known as the Khan-i-Allama, Tafazzul had studied at the Firangi Mahal of Lucknow and was a scholar of some repute, being a master of debate, mathematics, astronomy, and Aristotelian logic as well as a fluent speaker in Persian, Arabic, Latin, Greek, and English. He began his career with the nawabs of Awadh, but then became very close to various Company men after he was appointed ambassador of the court of Awadh to the EIC at Calcutta. He was genially loathed by Asaf who quite rightly suspected his loyalties of lying with the British.

**Almas Ali Khan:** This most famous and powerful of all the khwajasaras of Awadh began his career as a humble cup-bearer to Bahu Begum, accompanying her when she married Shuja-ud-Daula. He ended up as manager of all Bahu Begum's lands and would prove to be a supremely capable administrator, becoming fabulously wealthy in the process. By the time Asaf-ud-Daula became nawab, he controlled a quarter of the revenue generated by Awadh. He was deemed a judicious and able ruler even by the critical Company men.

**Bahu Begum:** Khaas Mahal, or chief wife, of Shuja-ud-Daula, Bahu Begum earned the lasting respect and affection of her husband when she offered up part of her fortune to repay the debt he owned the EIC. The mother of Asaf-ud-Daula and a forceful and powerful woman, Bahu Begum presided over her independent court at Faizabad after Asaf became nawab and moved to Lucknow.

**Nawab Begum:** The only wife of Safdar Jang and the mother of his only heir, Shuja-ud-Daula. Pious and discrete, she was also a woman of great strength and courage. She defended her home and family against enemy Mughal troops in Delhi during the absence of Safdar Jang, and once even proposed to Bahu Begum that they ride out together to fight against the troops of Asaf-ud-Daula who were threatening them. Maintained a dignified court at Faizabad, supporting many elite women refugees from the chaos of Delhi.

**Noor Begum:** Sister of Faiz Begum, the bibi of Palmer, she became the bibi of the powerful military commander of the Maratha brigades, the Savoyard Benoit de Boigne. Unusually for the time, de Boigne took Faiz Begum and their two children back to England with him when he left India in 1795. However, he proceeded to leave her in a village outside London and returned to France, where he would marry a young French aristocrat, Adèle d'Osmond. Faiz Begum would live alone in England, looking after the interests of her children, and leading a fairly quixotic existence. Her fascinating letters to de Boigne survive in the Chambery archives of the de Boigne family.

OTHER INDIAN LEADERS

**Tipu Sultan (and Hyder Ali):** Hyder Ali became ruler of Mysore when he overthrew the Wodeyar raja of Mysore, and actively sought French help to fight the British EIC. This policy was continued by his son, Tipu Sultan, who even sent an embassy to the court of Louis XVI in 1788. This preference for the French was increasingly exploited by the British—as global tensions with France increased—to justify violence and aggression against Tipu. Governor General Cornwallis seized half of Tipu's lands, effectively shackling the ruler, while Wellesley finished the job by besieging Seringapatam during which Tipu was killed and the city sacked.

**Mahadji Scindia:** Maratha warlord who became the most powerful force in northern India in the last quarter of the eighteenth century. Genuinely loyal to Mughal emperor Shah Alam, a battle injury had left him limping for the rest of his life for which Claude Martin nicknamed him 'le boiteux' (he who limps). His most important general was Benoit de Boigne, whose Brigades of Hindustan fought many battles alongside him. Scindia was considered by the French to be one of the great men of Hindustan.

**Daulat Rao Scindia:** Came to power at the age of only fifteen after the death of Mahadji in 1794. He clashed with the British in 1803 and, young and inexperienced, suffered many reversals.

**Raja Chait Singh:** When his father died in 1770, the seventeen-year-old Chait Singh, of 'handsome features and engaging manners', became raja of Benaras. In 1775 pressure was put on him by the EIC to increase the subsidy he paid them to fund their overseas wars and when he refused yet another additional subsidy in 1778, he incurred the furious wrath of Hastings. Hastings had the raja imprisoned in his own palace, setting off a violent insurrection in the country which was also encouraged by the begums of Awadh, and from which Hastings barely escaped alive. Chait Singh was never allowed back on the throne of Benaras.

## THE ROHILLAS

**Zabita Khan Rohilla:** The son of Rohilla chieftain Najib-ud-Daula, Zabita Khan was made governor of Delhi in 1768 when still very young, inexperienced, and unruly. Rumours of his depredations against the Mughal family caused Shah Alam to return from Allahabad, where he had been in exile for twelve years, to Delhi. Zabita Khan would be defeated by the Maratha and Mughal forces in 1772.

**Ghulam Qadir:** He was the son of Zabita Khan, and had been captured and brought back to Delhi when his father was defeated in 1772. Shah Alam grew very fond of the charming, good-looking boy and raised him like a son. There were rumours of an unnatural interest of the emperor in the boy, but it was more likely that Ghulam Qadir harboured ideas of revenge for the death of his father and other atrocities committed against the Rohillas for, in 1787, he attacked Delhi and unleashed an orgy of violence against the Mughal family and blinded the emperor.

## THE EUROPEANS

**Comte Louis Federbe de Modave:** Modave was a French aristocrat who arrived in India for the second time at the age of fifty. A brilliant yet impractical man, he had a peculiar knack for failing spectacularly at every enterprise he undertook. He was of the old order of military men who believed only aristocrats could be officers and the highly informative and entertaining memoirs of his adventures in India are liberally peppered with his prejudices towards the French adventurers he encountered in India as well as his incisive and intuitive analysis of the political situation in the country.

**Antoine Polier:** Born to Swiss Protestant parents of French descent in Lausanne, Polier's allegiances always remained a bit of a mystery. He arrived in India at the age of sixteen and immediately joined the EIC army at Madras as an engineer. His Protestantism made it easy for him to integrate the EIC but as tensions between France and England escalated globally, it became harder for Polier to advance within the Company and he asked to be deputed to the prosperous court of Nawab Shuja-ud-Daula instead. With several Indian bibis and children, and a fluency with languages, Polier was something of a chameleon. He was at times a Persianate nobleman in Awadhi muslin, a clipped English officer in his smart red jacket, and a suave Frenchman plying his trade for the nawab. In Faizabad, and then Lucknow, Polier would patronize a painting atelier headed by the artist Mehr Chand. With an assured sense of aesthetics, he influenced the creation of the art he patronized, and left behind one of the great collections of muraqqas, or albums, of the late eighteenth century.

**Jean-Baptiste Gentil:** From a distinguished but impoverished French family, Gentil joined the army and was sent to India as an officer in an infantry regiment in 1752 where he served alongside famous French leaders like Joseph François Dupleix and the Marquis de Bussy. After the French factories were finally destroyed by the EIC, Gentil offered his services first to Mir Qasim in Bengal and then to Shuja-ud-Daula of Awadh. He was instrumental in brokering peace for Shuja after his defeat at the Battle of Buxar, and returned to Faizabad with the nawab where he was a steadfast and loyal presence, and a generous friend to many needy Frenchmen wandering the country. Shuja was very grateful to Gentil, whom he used to improve his arms and ammunition. He also encouraged Gentil to create a corps of French soldiers. In Faizabad, Gentil also set up an art atelier that would produce some of the very first examples of European-influenced Indian art that would later become famous as 'Company Paintings'. He married an Indo-Portuguese woman and returned with his wife to France in 1778 where he would die in poverty, having lost his pension due to the French Revolution.

**Claude Martin:** Born in Lyon, France, to a humble family, Martin enlisted as a simple soldier with the French Compagnie des Indes in 1751 as a teenager. He initially fought for the French in India but after the 1760 Siege of Pondicherry, deserted to the Bengal army of the British EIC. He was eventually posted to Awadh where he would spend twenty-five years, hanging on to this most lucrative province despite many attempts by the British to dislodge him from there. He used bribery, corruption, and extortionate usury to amass a truly gobsmacking fortune. Despite his decades in India, and his many bibis and Indian servants, Martin remained something of an outsider, described by a historian as being a 'border crosser, social climber, chameleon and collector'.

**René Madec:** Madec escaped a poverty blighted childhood in Quimper, France, to sail to India at the age of twelve and joined the French EIC under Dupleix. When captured at the fall of Pondicherry by the British along with compatriot Claude Martin, Madec chose to escape to the Mughals and fought with valour at the Battle of Buxar. A hard-living grifter of a man, Madec was determinedly anti-British, and stoutly patriotic, carrying the banner of the French fleur-de-lys into battle. He showed himself to be so outrageously brave and steadfast in battle that he made a real name for himself and was courted by many Indian rulers. He fought at various times for Shuja-ud-Daula, the Jats, and the Rohillas, and was truly devoted to Shuja, weeping when the nawab died unexpectedly. Madec returned to France with his Indo-Portuguese wife a fabulously wealthy man—the first of the 'Indian Nabobs' to return to France. He died in France in a riding accident.

**Benoit de Boigne:** A French-speaking son of a trader from the Chambéry region of Savoy before it became part of France, de Boigne left home at seventeen to join the French army. After a complicated journey, he arrived in India in 1778 where he met Hastings and was introduced to the court of Lucknow in the 1780s. Here he would meet William Palmer's bibi's sister, Noor Begum, who would become his concubine. 'More than six feet tall with piercing blue eyes', de Boigne was a giant of a man and a force of nature. He found great fame and fortune fighting for the Maratha warlord, Mahadji Scindia, for whom he raised the legendary 'Brigades of Hindustan'. He eventually returned to Europe with Noor Begum and his children, but abandoned them in England before returning to France and marrying a sixteen-year-old impoverished but beautiful aristocrat, Adèle d'Osmond.

## THE COMPANY MEN

**Robert Clive:** Clive would later admit that he had been inspired by Dupleix's example in South India to use European trained forces to acquire territory in India. Unstable, ruthlessly arrogant, and venal, but also a brilliant military leader, Clive effected a real coup when after the Battle of Plassey, the EIC acquired a territory three times the size of England, and he personally became one of the richest men in the world. His actions at Plassey and then at Buxar, after which he dragooned Mughal emperor Shah Alam II to hand over the diwani of Bengal to the EIC, would lead inexorably to British rule in India.

**Warren Hastings:** A cerebral, austere, and frigidly reserved man, Hastings arrived as the first governor of Bengal just before Britain got involved in the ruinously expensive and deeply humiliating American War of Independence in 1775. This would propel in Hastings an obsessive drive to extract as much wealth from Indian powers as possible. This brought him into conflict with the begums of Awadh with whom he showed himself to be coldly furious and violently retributive. Despite a reputation for incorruptibility, there is enough evidence to show that he was, in fact, corrupt and he returned to Britain to face a protracted trial of impeachment for corruption and for his role in the 'despoliation of the begums'.

**Charles Cornwallis:** A veteran of the American Revolutionary War where he had had to surrender to George Washington, the blunt and soldierly Cornwallis was sent to India in 1786 to sort out the fracas caused by Hastings's handling of the begums of Awadh. He was strongly opposed to interference in Awadh's affairs, and reduced Asaf-ud-Daula's financial burden. He was, however, far less placatory with the warrior sultan

Tipu—an ally of the French—and attacked Seringapatam during the Third Anglo-Mysore War and personally oversaw the dismemberment of Tipu's country.

**John Shore:** When Shore arrived in India as Governor General in 1793, it was his second posting in the country. Whereas during his first stay as a young Writer he had enjoyed a rambunctious, libertine lifestyle, Shore had become a new man and he landed in 1793 as a fervent and austere Protestant evangelical and attempted to promote Christianity as the religion of the state. Plagued by vague aches and pains during his entire stay in India, these mysterious illnesses seemed to get worse when he dragooned the young Nawab Wazir Ali of Awadh out of his legitimate country and brought in Saadat Ali Khan instead.

**Richard Wellesley:** Wellesley was an Anglo-Irish Governor General of India. An avowed enemy of the French, Wellesley was arrogant, 'staggeringly vain', and ambitious. He followed rapacious policies of aggrandizement against the nizam of Hyderabad and Tipu Sultan of Mysore.

**George Cherry:** Part of a new crop of Company men, Cherry came to India as a teenager. Due to his excellent language skills, especially Persian, and his command therefore of the intelligence network, Cherry quickly climbed the Company ladder. Resident at Lucknow at just thirty-two years of age, he could be brutish and bullying with the nawab in pursuing his ambitions. Wazir Ali blamed Cherry for his humiliation at Benaras, and for wanting to exile him even further to Calcutta, and murdered him during an insurrection in Benaras.

**Neil Benjamin Edmonstone:** Erudite and scholarly, Edmonstone came to India as a teenager and became a Writer and Translator with the EIC. Like his closest friend George Cherry, Edmonstone was intransigent about the need for the EIC to be more aggressive in India, finding a willing listener especially in Richard Wellesley. He became Wellesley's chief intelligence officer in Calcutta, amongst the first of the shadowy British spymasters.

**John Bristow:** Resident in Lucknow in 1775, Bristow was famously corrupt. He was the protégé of Hastings's sworn enemy, Philip Francis. When told to streamline Asaf-ud-Daula's finances, he took to the task with such heavy-handed gusto that the usually good-natured nawab left Awadh in disgust, challenging Bristow to rule in his lieu.

**Alexander Hannay:** One of Hastings's protégés and the most violent of the extractive revenue farmers of Awadh. Hastings allowed him to illegally take over the revenues of the rich, timber-producing districts of Gorakhpur and Bahraich, and it was said that he 'dropped off gorged' having made some 300,000 pounds. He was detested for the violent means by which he terrorized the country as a tax collector, allegedly beheading recalcitrant landowners. Caught up in the insurrection of Benaras in the 1780s, he would be stripped of his post and disgraced.

**William Palmer:** The confidential agent of Warren Hastings in Lucknow, Palmer lived with an Indian bibi, Faiz Begum, to whom he was truly devoted, and his Anglo-Indian children. This unique family was immortalized by an unfinished Zoffany painting. Palmer was part of a tight-knit circle of Europeans in Lucknow, and Benoit de Boigne is believed to have met his bibi, Noor Begum, the sister of Faiz Begum, when visiting Palmer in Lucknow.

**Gerard Lake:** Legendary British general and a veteran of the American War, Lake was known to be fastidious about his appearance and had a reputation for always appearing in full uniform, buttons done up, powdered wig in place. Lake led the British forces in the Battle for Delhi in 1803, took control of the Mughal emperor and appointed the very first Resident of Delhi, David Ochterlony.

## THE ARTISTS

**Johann Zoffany:** Anglo-German artist with a louche reputation who became famous for his 'conversation piece' paintings. Zoffany settled in Lucknow where he became friends with Claude Martin and lived in Indo-Persianate style, with bibis and children, and painted famous scenes of Asaf and his court.

**William Hodges:** British artist who arrived in India in 1779 and stayed for six years. He painted many landscape scenes of the country which became very popular. In 1781 he accompanied Hastings to Benaras and got caught up in the fracas with Raja Chait Singh of Benaras.

**Ozias Humphrey:** English portrait painter and miniaturist who arrived in Lucknow in 1786 hoping to make a fortune. Despite obtaining commissions to paint Nawab Asaf-ud-Daula and some of his courtiers, he was never paid and was constantly tormented by the climate in India.

**Mehr Chand:** From a family of hereditary artists in Delhi, Mehr Chand left the chaos of the capital to look for patronage under the wealthy and art-loving nawab of Awadh, Shuja-ud-Daula, at Faizabad. Here he encountered Antoine Polier in 1773, and would remain in his atelier for the rest of his career. Polier was a discerning and exacting patron, and Mehr Chand would produce some of the finest of the late Mughal works of this period.

**Khanum Jan:** Khanum Jan was a celebrated courtesan whose soirees in Calcutta were the toast of the town. She was part of an elite troupe of courtesans who travelled through the major north Indian towns, including Lucknow, where Khanum Jan performed for Asaf-ud-Daula.

## THE TRAVELLERS AND WITNESSES

**Abu Talib:** Abu Talib came from an aristocratic family who had a tradition of service to the nawabs of Awadh, but he decided to join the EIC instead. In Calcutta, an EIC agent convinced him to open a Persian language school in London, where he was celebrated as 'the Persian Prince'. He then wrote a lively account of his travels through England, France, and the Middle East.

**Muhammad Faiz Baksh:** Faiz Baksh served as munshi, or secretary, for Bahu Begum, often rephrasing the illiterate begum's letters. He later wrote a history of Faizabad, which provides a unique glimpse into the lost world of the late eighteenth-century Awadhi zenana. In his account he is fiercely protective of the begums, often assigning blame to Asaf-ud-Daula and the eunuchs.

# SELECT CHRONOLOGY OF MAJOR EVENTS

**1723:** Saadat Khan's daughter Sadr-un-Nisa Begum is married to his nephew, Safdar Jang, who is appointed deputy subedar of Awadh.

**1739:** Nadir Shah invades North India in the reign of Emperor Muhammad Shah 'Rangeeley'. Saadat Khan dies by suicide.

**1740-1748:** *War of the Austrian Succession.*

**1753:** Safdar Jang is driven out of Delhi due to his enmity with Qudsiya Begum, queen mother, and her khwajasara, Javed Khan.

Civil war in Delhi.

**1754:** Death of Safdar Jang; Shuja-ud-Daula becomes nawab of Awadh.

**1756:** Siraj-ud-Daula of Bengal throws the English out of Calcutta.

Afghan chieftain Ahmad Shah Abdali (Durrani) terrorizes Delhi.

*The Seven Years' War begins.*

**1757:** Robert Clive takes back Calcutta, places Mir Jaffar on the throne and defeats the Mughals at the Battle of Plassey.

Clive also seizes Chandernagore from the French.

Ahmad Shah Durrani invades North India.

**1758:** The Marathas take control of Delhi.

Mirza Ali Gauhar, son and heir to Emperor Alamgir II, escapes the Red Fort and seeks refuge with Shuja in Awadh.

Antoine Polier arrives in India and joins the EIC.

**1761:** The Afghans win the Battle of Panipat alongside Shuja and destroy the Maratha forces.

The English seize Pondicherry, Jean-Baptiste Gentil and René Madec are forced out of the French trading posts.

Claude Martin defects to the EIC.

**1763:** *The Treaty of Paris brings to an end the Seven Years' War.*

**1764:** The Mughal forces including Jean-Baptiste Gentil and René Madec are beaten by the EIC at the Battle of Buxar.

**1765:** Emperor Shah Alam is forced to sign over the diwani of Bengal to Robert Clive.

Awadh is given back to Shuja after an enormous war subsidy is paid by his wife, Bahu Begum.

Shuja moves his capital to Faizabad and begins large-scale construction works.

Shah Alam remains at Allahabad.

**1769:** Shah Alam is a guest at Faizabad where he meets Frenchman Gentil.

Gentil sets up an early atelier in Faizabad employing Nevasi Lal among others.

**1771:** The Marathas return to North India and escort Shah Alam back to Delhi.

**1772:** Warren Hastings appointed Governor of Bengal.

**1773:** Comte Louis Federbe de Modave arrives in India for the second time.

Antoine Polier arrives in Faizabad as architect engineer sent by Warren Hastings. Sets up an atelier employing Mehr Chand.

**1775:** Death of Shuja-ud-Daula.

Asaf-ud-Daula becomes nawab and shifts his capital to Lucknow.

The EIC renegotiate a treaty with Asaf, forcing him to expel most of the Frenchmen in his service, including Gentil and Madec, and cede Benaras to them.

Claude Martin arrives in Lucknow.

*The American Revolutionary War begins.*

**1776:** Rebellion of Saadat Ali Khan.

France begins surreptitiously aiding the American Revolutionary forces.

**1778:** The English seize all the French trading posts.

Anglo-French war declared over America.

**1780:** The EIC forces are decisively beaten by Hyder Ali and Tipu Sultan of Mysore at the Battle of Pollilur.

**1781:** Hastings imposes war subsidy on Raja Chait Singh of Benaras.

Revolt in Benaras and countryside, supported by the begums of Awadh.

*Cornwallis surrenders to Washington.*

**1782:** The EIC imprison the khwajasaras, Jawahar Ali Khan and Bahar Ali Khan to put pressure on the begums to give up their treasure.

Hyder Ali of Mysore dies.

Corrupt John Bristow appointed Resident of Lucknow by Hastings.

Death of Najaf Khan.

**1783:** Tipu Sultan becomes ruler of Mysore.

Pondicherry returned to the French.

*Treaty of Versailles brings to an end to hostilities between the French and the English.*

**1784:** Hastings arrives in Lucknow to resolve the fracas caused by his handling of the begums, meets Mirza Jawan Bakht.

Founding of Asiatic Society of Bengal by William Jones. Founding members include Hastings, Martin, and Polier.

**1785:** Hastings recalled to England to give an account of his handling of the affairs of Benaras and Awadh.

**1786:** Tentative start date of the Great Imambara of Lucknow by Asaf.

British artists Ozias Humphrey and Charles Smith arrive in Lucknow. Johann Zoffany is already in residence.

Charles Cornwallis arrives in India as Governor General.

Tipu takes the title Padshah.

**1787:** Ghulam Qadir attacks Delhi.

**1788:** Ghulam Qadir blinds Shah Alam II.

Mahadji Scindia and de Boigne come to the rescue of Shah Alam, and execute Ghulam Qadir.

Hastings's impeachment trial begins.

Tipu sends an embassy to the court of Louis XVI of France.

**1789:** *Beginning of French Revolution as Bastille prison is seized.*

**1790:** EIC signs tripartite treaty with the nizam of Hyderabad and the Marathas against Tipu.

**1791:** Tipu defeats the EIC at Coimbatore.

**1792:** Cornwallis personally leads his troops at Seringapatam and Tipu surrenders. He is forced to cede half his territories and two of his sons as hostages.

**1793:** Governor General John Shore arrives in India.

*Louis XVI is guillotined.*

**1793–1794:** *Reign of Terror in France.*

**1794:** Asaf seizes Rohilkhand with the help of the EIC.

**1796:** Mutiny of the Bengal army officers.

Shore asks Asaf for money and aid.

Death of Nawab Begum.

De Boigne returns to Europe with Noor Begum and children.

*Napoleon has great success in battles across Europe; beginning of Napoleonic Wars.*

**1797:** John Shore arrives in Lucknow with Neil Edmonstone in February.

Death of Asaf in September.

Wazir Ali Khan becomes nawab of Awadh.

So-called Revolutionary force under François Ripaud lands in India and arrives at Tipu's capital, Seringapatam.

**1798:** John Shore arrives in Lucknow and deposes Wazir Ali who is exiled to Benaras.

Saadat Ali Khan is made nawab by John Shore.

Richard Wellesley arrives as Governor General of India.

*Napoleon lands in Egypt.*

**1799:** Insurrection by Wazir Ali at Benaras, George Cherry is murdered.

Tipu is attacked in his capital by EIC forces under Wellesley and he dies in battle.

*Napoleon seizes power in France in a bloodless coup.*

**1801:** *French forces left behind in Egypt by Napoleon surrender to British forces which include an Anglo-Indian contingent.*

**1803:** The last French defenders at Delhi are beaten by the EIC forces at the Battle of Delhi and Lord Lake marches into the city to take control of Emperor Shah Alam.

David Ochterlony becomes the first Resident of Delhi.

*1815: Napoleon defeated at the Battle of Waterloo.*

# PROLOGUE

In the early dawn of 2 November 1746, French commander Jean-Jacques Duval d'Eprémesnil had decided upon a most dangerous plan. Fort St. George in Madras that he had recently captured from the British was being besieged by Mahfuz Khan, son of the elderly nawab of the Carnatic, Anwaruddin. Starved and harassed, the small French garrison in the fort was now being deprived of drinking water, which Mahfuz Khan's forces had commandeered. Desperate, d'Eprémesnil had decided upon a dawn sortie with a small force of 400 French infantry to recover the freshwater spring. Hidden in the centre of this small body of marching soldiers were two field guns. As the men moved rapidly towards the small spring, the large army of Mughal* soldiers guarding that water source quickly jumped onto their war horses and galloped towards the advancing soldiers. The sudden shouts of the men and the thudding hooves of the rearing horses broke through the early morning peace and the Mughal force, some 10,000 horsemen strong, would have been serenely confident of smashing the small French corps to bits. But as the galloping horses thundered towards them, the French soldiers kept moving steadily in disciplined lines towards the horsemen. Just as the hot breath of the Mughal horses was almost upon them, the French soldiers moved aside to reveal the two field guns hidden behind them. As the field guns and the soldiers simultaneously opened deadly fire, the effect upon the Mughal horsemen was devastating. The horses reared, screaming with fear at the explosive sound of the cannons, while cavalrymen were blown off their horses in a nightmare of smoke, noise, and fury. Even as the Mughal horses kept charging, the French guns reloaded and fired continuously, at a terrifying rate never before witnessed by Mahfuz Khan's men.† The soldiers, meanwhile, kept up a steady fusillade of musket fire and, within minutes, seventy Mughal cavalrymen lay dead on the ground in an orgy of bloodied limbs and the entire force turned

---

*In this context and time, Mughal refers to the forces of the local leader appointed who was part of the Mughal hierarchy.
†According to most sources, the French guns could fire fifteen shots per minute compared to the Indian guns' rate of four or five shots per hour.

around and fled the site. Mahfuz Khan hastily mounted his war elephant and escaped.

A day later, Mahfuz Khan gathered his scattered and shocked troops, determined to vanquish these infuriating firangi soldiers once and for all. News had arrived that the French governor of Pondicherry, Joseph François Dupleix, had sent a force of some 1,000 men to strengthen the besieged French garrison at Madras. Mahfuz Khan stationed his men south of Madras near the town of St Thome, on the banks of the Adyar River. The French contingent marching from Pondicherry consisted of 230 Europeans and 700 trained Indian sepoys led by a Swiss engineer, Paradis. Arriving at the Adyar River at dawn on 4 November, the French party saw a most sobering sight—the entire Mughal army massed in an immense line upon the far shore in neat ranks of horses, foot soldiers, and cannon, firing across the river towards them with their artillery. Paradis decided upon a lightning strike and, turning around to gather his men, plunged into the river and up towards the gathered Mughal troops, followed by all his soldiers. The French troops fired one deadly round with their highly accurate guns and then charged the Mughal soldiers with their bayonets, screaming, causing such mayhem amongst the Mughals that they abandoned their guns and fled into the town of St Thome, 'with dishevelled hair and dress'. The French soldiers continued to advance upon the Mughal troops, firing in sections, wave upon wave of highly disciplined troops firing with superior flintlock muskets and bayonets. Even as the Mughal soldiers tried desperately to assume defensive positions, the speed and deadly firepower of the French soldiers decimated the Mughal troops, with dead and dying men and horses blocking the lanes and causing utter chaos. Mahfuz Khan mounted his elephant and this time rode all the way back to Arcot, the capital of the Carnatic. His soldiers, in St Thome, abandoned 'baggage, horses, oxen, rams, even hope itself' as they tried to escape the carnage. 'The rout was so general', noted translator and diarist Ananda Ranga Pillai, 'that not a fly, not a sparrow not a crow was to be seen in all Mylapore'.

The two consecutive battles of Adyar and St Thome in November 1746 would be the first time in India that a foreign power with a small force would decisively rout what until then had been the fearsome quasi-legendary power of the great Mughal forces. With these two battles the French demonstrated that a well-drilled and well-equipped infantry force could quite easily defeat a vastly larger but ultimately ineffective Mughal or Indian style cavalry. This would have enormous consequences for the history of India for the next 200 years, and would ultimately completely upend the power dynamic that existed in the beginning of the eighteenth century. What is astonishing also is that the Mughal forces of the nawab of the Carnatic were collateral damage in what was essentially the beginning of an armed global struggle between two foreign powers on Indian soil—the British and the French and that, at this point, it was the French who had the upper hand.

# INTRODUCTION

When the British were finally quitting India with such unseemly haste and annoyed pique in 1947, journalists recording these historic moments were distracted and entertained by a 'pall of smoke' that spread over Delhi. The origin of the noxious smoke was a fire in which the last civil servants of the British empire were destroying countless documents deemed too sensitive to remain in newly independent India. This pall of smoke would swirl into the sky time and again over the next decades, in the various capitals of the newly independent countries which were once part of the largest global empire ever spawned. Instructions were issued that waste from the bonfires was to be reduced to ashes, and the ashes further broken up. In Kenya, documents were loaded into crates and dropped into the deep ocean. When simply destroying these documents was not enough, 'Operation Legacy' was implemented in which only civil servants 'of European descent' would identify sensitive documents to be removed to murky archives in Britain and all trace of their existence was then wiped clean in their countries of origin. In *The History Thieves*, writer Ian Cobain identifies this need for secrecy as a 'very British disease' and argues that the mass obliteration and hiding of these documents was deemed necessary so that 'the British way of doing things' would be remembered with 'fondness and respect'.

In India, the mass destruction of documents in 1947 was not the first time that precious documents relating to India's history, its memories, and its countless voices, were destroyed. The 1857 Uprising was similarly followed by a carnage of violence when the centres of the uprising were re-conquered by the British, and documents, paintings, and archives were destroyed in great smouldering masses in Delhi and Lucknow. All of this destruction, elision, rewriting, and confabulation means that we have inherited a largely tainted and skewed version of history, especially with regard to the tumultuous eighteenth century, and in particular pertaining to Lucknow and the province of Awadh. And so the multiplicity of truths and voices that make up the complex and intertwined world of that century comes to us largely in bland soliloquy.

A particularly tenacious result of the monochrome recording of Indian history is a sense of the inevitability of British expansion, accompanied by a certain sighing acquiescence or, worse still, a simpering ineptitude on the part of many Indian rulers to this takeover by a foreign behemoth. But the modern retrospective assumption that British dominance in India was somehow inevitable, inexorable, and smoothly linear is misleading. As historian Maya Jasanoff argues, 'British expansion was hotly contested both by indigenous powers and by European rivals, notably France.' The trajectory of the EIC's dominance in India stuttered and stumbled, driven by the ambition of individual personalities. The trajectory was also very often waylaid by the ambition and vision of Indian rulers, who reacted in varied and inventive ways to the bullying incursions of the EIC. One of the states which reacted with great ambition and imagination to the churning events of the eighteenth century was the so-called 'buffer state' of Awadh and its nawabs and begums.

By focusing on the subah of Awadh, *The Lion and the Lily* seeks to understand the fine-grained texture of the culture of the region and the finesse with which the nawabs and begums navigated a constantly changing world. As regards the nawabs of Awadh and the British encounter, certain enduring myths remain. The most famous nawab in cultural memory is Wajid Ali Shah (r. 1847–1856). The powerfully resonant themes associated with his nawabi percolate through the decades and colour all his predecessors so that, in a sense, a certain essence of Wajid Ali Shah is what is remembered, and celebrated even in the modern era like in Satyajit Ray's *Shatranj ke Khiladi* (1977), or in the fables of excessive Lucknawi politesse. In this ideal, the nawab is a doomed man, haunted by his powerlessness, sinking into a gorgeous but helpless aestheticism.

The truth, however, was quite different. From the time of the founder, Saadat Khan Burhan-ul-Mulk, the nawabs were redoubtable warriors as well as patrons of the arts. They were canny and intelligent diplomats, playing myriad warring factions against each other to establish Awadh as the richest province of Hindustan*. Saadat Ali's grandson Shuja-ud-Daula (r. 1754–1775) was widely considered the most powerful and intimidatingly courageous of all the rulers in the

---

*Hindustan refers to North India; India refers to the subcontinent as a whole.

country. It is the story of the rise and fall of the nawabs and begums of Awadh that we will follow in this narrative, with the East India Company (EIC) simply one of the many competing forces operating at the time. The story of Awadh will be used as a lens through which to demonstrate the chicanery and guile that the EIC consistently resorted to, and the enduring myths that were subsequently perpetuated. Particularly fraught encounters will be described during which local power bases, including the women of the zenana and elite khwajasaras*, repeatedly challenged and terrorized the EIC forces. These include Warren Hastings's involvement in the uprising of Raja Chait Singh of Benaras in 1781, the begums of Awadh's prolonged and violent resistance of the 1780s, the imperial eunuchs' armed militarization and resistance during the same time period, and Wazir Ali's insurrection of 1798.

For while it is generally assumed that Awadh became essentially a British protectorate after the Battle of Buxar (1764), this is very far from the complicated reality. Instead, for Nawab Shuja-ud-Daula, the English were simply one of many potential allies and enemies whom he effortlessly parried, by turns charming or staunch, genial or fierce. All the while the nawab poured his endless energy and wealth into building a vibrant and distinctive culture, while also maintaining his independence from the Mughal court at Delhi. This book will therefore bring to centre stage the lives of the nawabs, the begums, the eunuchs, and other lesser-known players, in addition to the perspective provided by the involvement of certain French adventurers and soldiers.

As for Asaf-ud-Daula (r. 1775–1797), who can be said to be the founder of Lucknawi culture, even modern historians continue to propagate tired old British calumnies. Asaf-ud-Daula is systematically described as being an overweight, simpering fool, while his mother, Bahu Begum, is criticized for being venal and strident. The reputation of Asaf is full of contradictions, as the British tried to manipulate his image and simultaneously denigrate any talent or proclivity he may have shown. And so Asaf was derided as being both ridiculously pious and simply godless; a raunchy womanizer and an effete homosexual; a profligate wastrel and a miserly ruler. His powerful and ambitious

---

*In Hindustan, elite eunuchs were called khwajasaras, and held important roles as military commanders, or in political or intelligence gathering capacities.

mother was relentlessly derided and ridiculed for wishing to rule, this desire being considered 'unwomanly', while Asaf himself was too effete. This British character assassination was not innocent, instead its aim was to justify taking over the administration of Awadh entirely. More than half a century before the annexation of Awadh in 1856, this was already being planned by EIC men at the highest levels, and the propaganda was used by the EIC to paint Asaf as a debauched, corrupt, and ineffectual ruler. The questioning of his sexuality would be particularly pernicious, ending in the accusation of impotency so as to justify the deposition of his recognized heir, Wazir Ali Khan, a tactic that would much later be used by Governor General Dalhousie. The character of one of the most powerful women in Hindustan at that time—Bahu Begum—was similarly misunderstood. This book will look closely at one of the seminal clashes of personalities of that time—between the austere Warren Hastings and the fiery Bahu Begum. For Bahu Begum refused to operate within the idealized framework Hastings imagined, which would make of her a helpless brown woman who would require saving by the gallant white man. She would never become, literally or figuratively, the white man's burden. Instead, she became Warren Hastings's albatross.

*The Lion and the Lily* will show Asaf-ud-Daula to have been a visionary and an exemplary diplomat, and Bahu Begum a formidable force of nature. Asaf created a Shia renaissance that outshone any other in the world at the time. In contrast to British descriptions of his decadent city and suspect aestheticism, what Asaf was creating was a challenge to both Mughal Sunni power and the increasing parochialism of the EIC. It was once fashionable to lament the degeneration of what had once been the glorious Mughal legacy in art and architecture from the eighteenth century onwards. Master artists who migrated from 'Mughal' Delhi to seek new patronage in nascent towns used to have their art sniffily described as 'provincial' or 'sub-imperial'. Now, however, a whole host of younger scholars[*] have demonstrated that, instead, art and culture flourished—they simply evolved in new and innovative ways, reacting with verve and originality to the chaos of the eighteenth century. French players also contributed to this cultural legacy, including in the field of art, architecture, and dance, sometimes

---

[*] Yuthika Sharma and Malini Roy amongst others.

decades before their much more famous British counterparts.

In the cities of Faizabad and then Lucknow, Shuja, Asaf, Bahu Begum, Nawab Begum, their eunuchs, and their elite entourage created a visible and extravagant culture of Shia remembrance to rival any in the world at the time. The expression of Shiism has been described by scholar Simonetta Casci as celebrating the martyrdom of religious heroes who fought until death against a stronger enemy. In that context it is piquant to wonder if the building of extravagant imambaras and the fostering of a high-octane Shia culture was not simply a confident proclamation of their independence from the Sunni Mughals at Delhi but also an intimation of Awadh's struggles against the foreign and powerful EIC.

In India, Islam was never a monotheistic entity as imagined by the West, with a fixed and rigid set of ideologies. As pointed out by scholar Deepa Kumar, Islam is not only practised in many ways—Sunnism, Shiiasm, Sufism etc.—but its practice has evolved over the centuries as Islam has spread to different regions of the world, incorporating strands of local cultural practices. In this narrative we will discover how the nawabs and begums created a luminescent and vibrant identity for Faizabad and Lucknow that elegantly wove together the strands from different cultures. For the Shiism of Awadh used codes that were familiar not only to Muslims, but to Hindus too, and would unite the population of these cities through the fervour of the rituals that would come to define them. Whether it was the structure of the imambara that would echo that of the baradari, the Muharram processions that would recall the Hindu processions such as Durga Puja, the Jagannath festival, and Dussehra, or the annual collective ritual fasting and the visible demonstrations of piety that would bring together different castes and communities. The British, meanwhile, would find the Shia remembrance rituals increasingly alienating, mystifying, and horrifying.

In the eighteenth century, the primary reason for the particularly fraught and volatile nature of Indo-British encounters was the presence of another firangi nation—the French. Indeed, one of the most compelling of the lost threads that runs through the eighteenth century is the story of French involvement in India. Though largely forgotten today both in India and in France, Franco-British rivalry exerted enormous influence on British policies and actions in the eighteenth century. In fact, the French presence was paramount to British actions throughout this century, both locally in India and globally through their century-long wars of empire, right up to the Battle of Waterloo in 1815. Because Britain did eventually succeed in ruling India, the privilege of writing the story of conquest was theirs, as was the elision of uncomfortable encounters, especially vis-à-vis the French. A key moment in the conquest of India by the EIC, for example, is usually believed to be the Battle of Plassey in 1757, in which Robert Clive and his army of EIC troops defeated the Mughal forces of Siraj-ud-Daula, the nawab of Bengal. This is understood to be the moment when the dream of a British territorial empire was conjured, clearly marking a move away from a purely trading enterprise. In reality, this process was foretold almost two decades earlier, in a different corner of India altogether, and as part of the imperial dreams of a different European nation.

Joseph François Dupleix, the most brilliant and ambitious Governor General that France would ever send to India, had arrived in Pondicherry in 1742, having already transformed the fortunes of the French trading post of Chandernagore in Bengal. Within months of his arrival in Pondicherry, Dupleix had received an unprecedented honour from the Mughal emperor at Delhi—the title of 'nawab' and 'panj-hazari' (commander of 5,000 horses), thus becoming the first European nawab in India, and officially part of the Mughal hierarchy. Dupleix had also begun recruiting local soldiers, or sepoys, trained and kitted out in the European manner. In a few years, Dupleix would have two regiments of sepoys whose deadly effectiveness was about to be demonstrated. Pierre Benoît Dumas, the French governor before Dupleix, had already successfully petitioned the Mughal emperor for the right to mint coins in Pondicherry. And all these energetic French shenanigans were making the British in India very nervous indeed.

The swashbuckling, swaggering French trading posts at Chandernagore and Pondicherry were vastly different from the European trading centres of the past century. The early trading posts had remained largely hunkered along the coast of India, often small, inconsequential enclaves on the huge, fertile fields of India. The reason these trading posts remained timidly perched along the edge of India was the fearsome presence of one of the greatest empires in the world—the Mughal empire. Founded by Babur in 1526, by the mid-seventeenth century, the Mughal empire was generating a quarter of the world's manufacture, and was home to 100-120 million people, 20 per cent of the world's population, with the ability to raise a truly astounding army of 4 million infantry.

Every time a European country wanted to establish a trading post, they had to ask permission first from the Mughal emperor, plumed hat in hand, and 'could conduct business only on Mughal terms'. For the Mughals themselves, the presence of these curious foreigners was usually not even a momentary distraction. In 1617, the first official English ambassador to the Mughal court of Jahangir (r. 1605–1627), the famously prickly Thomas Roe, was mortally offended when the emperor's son, Mirza Khurram, who would later reign as Shah Jahan (r. 1628–1658), refused even to allow him entry into the durbar, and told him to present himself like any other supplicant, at the jharoka window. Emperor Jahangir, meanwhile, when he saw the tattered gifts that the English ambassador presented to him, wondered sotto voce if Roe's monarch could really be worthy of that appellation at all.

By the early eighteenth century, however, the enormous juggernaut of the Mughal edifice was beginning to crumble. By the time the sixth Mughal emperor Aurangzeb (r. 1658–1707) died in 1707, the fault lines were stark. A humourless, austere, and relentlessly driven man, Aurangzeb had spent the last twenty-five years away from the Mughal heartland, trying and failing to subdue the Marathi-speaking chieftains of the western Deccan, and bankrupting the Mughal state. By the time of Aurangzeb's death, the Marathas were extracting the chauth, a fourth of the revenue normally paid to the Mughal exchequer, in territories including Khandesh, Malwa, and Gujarat. The situation for the Mughals became immeasurably worse upon the death of Aurangzeb at the age of nearly ninety. Aurangzeb had been morbidly suspicious of his sons, haunted till the end that they might do to him what he had done to his own father, Shah Jahan\*. So by the time he died, Aurangzeb's sons were unproven middle-aged men who

---

\*Aurangzeb had imprisoned his father, the reigning emperor Shah Jahan, and had murdered all his brothers including the heir apparent, Dara Shukoh. So heinous was his regicide that the Sharif of Mecca would not acknowledge him as emperor of India till after Shah Jahan had died, a full eight years after Aurangzeb declared himself Padshah.

had never been given the resources nor the responsibilities to allow them to establish loyal entourages and power bases. Instead, powerful Mughal noblemen found they could better serve their individual cause by propping up weak puppet emperors whom they could control for their own advancement. After the death of Aurangzeb, talented and ambitious governors began to realize that Mughal service was less rewarding than establishing fiefdoms of their own. But even when governors set up hereditary dynasties in Bengal, Hyderabad, and Awadh in the early eighteenth century, they held power, at least nominally, in the name of the Mughal emperor to whom they owed allegiance and for whom they raised troops and under whose banner they fought their battles. They also sent revenue back to Delhi, with Bengal's annual revenue amounting to some 10 million rupees. All of this, however, was about to change.

The remnant of the Mughal emperor's tattered dignity would be forever lost in 1739 when an ambitious and ruthless Persian warlord, Nadir Shah (r. 1736–1747), gauged that the power of the Mughals was crumbling and rode right through the Khyber Pass and up to Delhi with his 150,000 strong cavalry. Nadir Shah's shockingly easy defeat of the Mughal army and the ferocity of the violence he unleashed against the Mughal family and the people of Delhi would bring about an existential crisis in the Mughal world. The warlord's invasion had shown the Mughal empire's might to be a mirage, and the consequences would be catastrophic. Nizam-ul-Mulk of Hyderabad and Safdar Jang of Awadh,* whose forces had suffered this ignominious defeat on behalf of the Mughal emperor, now stopped sending tax revenue to Delhi, exacerbating the financial ruin of the empire. 'Ever since the invasion of Nader Shah', agreed French aristocrat and adventurer Louis Federbe de Modave, 'this great country, once so flourishing, has descended into complete anarchy'.

And it was this anarchy that Dupleix was to take advantage of in Pondicherry in 1746. Nor was the timing of Dupleix's actions against the British trading post at Madras arbitrary, for, in Europe, Britain and France had declared war against each other as all of Europe got embroiled in the War of the Austrian Succession (1740–1748). Following the declaration of war, the Royal Navy in Britain sent a

---

*Saadat Khan's son-in-law.

squadron of ships to India in 1745 which immediately began attacking French ships trading off the coast of Madras and, in a short while, had almost decimated French trade in India. A desperate Dupleix finally asked for military help from the French East India Company and by the summer of 1746, a French fleet consisting of nine frigates arrived in Pondicherry. Dupleix meticulously prepared an attack upon Fort St George and Madras was captured in September 1746 after a siege of only four days. The English residents, including a young EIC man called Robert Clive,* were expelled from Madras.

These muscular actions by the French in Madras had greatly annoyed the nawab of the Carnatic†. The Carnatic, with its capital at Arcot, was made up of the southern part of the Deccan and was ruled by a subsidiary ruler, Anwaruddin, who was dependent upon the nizam of Hyderabad. This was an area of special diplomacy with the Europeans since both French Pondicherry and British Madras lay within the territory of the Carnatic. When towards the end of October 1746 Dupleix learnt that Anwaruddin's son, Mahfuz Khan, was making preparations to march towards Madras, he sent a letter to Anwaruddin in a distinctly altered tone to his earlier, cordial interactions.

> It is surprising that standing as (Mahfuz Khan) does in the relation of an elder brother to us...he should seek to assist the cause of the English. The French have always been a warlike race, and it is impossible to subdue them. It grieves us much that they should be compelled to turn upon your son, and bring to bear against him the courage which overthrew the English. If you, however, should act without due caution, we are determined to give you a proof of the power of our valour. We will then raze the fort and town of Madras to the ground, and will work out our own policy as circumstances may dictate.

And so it was that Mahfuz Khan attacked the French at Madras twice, at Adyar and St Thome, and was both times decisively routed, propelling European and Indian troops into open aggression for the first time. Meanwhile, in Europe, in October 1748, the War of the

---

*Robert Clive at this point was a twenty-one-year-old minor Company employee.
†This region refers roughly to the area occupied by the Kannada-speaking people, in the area corresponding to modern-day Karnataka.

Austrian Succession ended with the Treaty of Aix-la-Chapelle, officially bringing to an end the First Carnatic War. But war between Britain and France in India, once sparked, would continue to burn for a long while. The death of the nizam of Hyderabad in 1748 and then that of Anwaruddin of the Carnatic in 1749 brought about succession disputes in the Deccan which Dupleix was now confident enough to meddle in. In Hyderabad, Dupleix also had the support of the brilliant young French Company officer, the Marquis de Bussy-Castelnau. De Bussy, with his 'deceptive manner of a little marquis from a pantomime with his angelic face', was enormously successful in Hyderabad. An earnest young French infantry ensign, Jean-Baptiste Gentil, also joined de Bussy's Hyderabad campaign immediately upon landing in India. Under the influence of the urbane and sophisticated de Bussy, Gentil would cultivate a sensitive appreciation for Hindustani art and culture that he would later bring to Awadh. So successfully did de Bussy train his superbly disciplined forces that he was granted land concessions in the shape of the Circars (coastal Andhra Pradesh) by the nizam of Hyderabad in return for the support of his army, a precursor of the subsidiary alliance system which the British would use so relentlessly a few decades later.

For Britain, however, these French victories in South India were the stuff of nightmares. In the mid-eighteenth century, Britain had every reason to be extremely wary of France. Britain was a small island, with a risible population of 8 million people, only half that of France's, 'an imbalance', writes Jasanoff, 'that provoked tremendous national anxiety'. France also had a far greater economy, double that of Britain's, and the largest army in Europe. Both Britain and France were also vigorously engaged in empire building across the world, including in North America, the Mediterranean, and the Middle East. Nonetheless, the French Company did not want to enter into ruinous wars in India which were so disruptive to trade, and the directors sent a letter to Dupleix baldly saying 'we do not wish to become a political power in India, we only want a few small factories. No victories, no conquests, just a lot of trade goods and dividends.' Dupleix was recalled to France by Louis XV in 1754 and would die in 1766, uncelebrated and disgraced.*

---

*Dupleix was found to have made a fortune for himself through private trade, all of which he was charged to have done at the expense of the Company's fortunes.

The Anglo-French peace was a mirage, however, and in 1756 these two powers would clash again, this time taking the war to five continents in what would later be described by Winston Churchill as 'the first world war'. The Seven Years' War (1756–63) began a long way away from India, in the far north of the American continent along the volatile border between the French and British colonies there. In India this conflict would drive the Carnatic Wars—a series of battles between the French EIC and the English EIC throughout the Carnatic. Galvanized by the declaration of war, France sent a huge expeditionary force of 2,000 of the king's best regiments to the Carnatic. Included in this expedition was the brilliant young aristocrat Modave, whose previously untranslated memoirs* would greatly enliven the history of Awadh.

After a few spectacular victories, the tide turned against the French, and the English were ultimately able to win key battles, some notably under the leadership of the young Robert Clive. Dupleix's old desire for a French commercial monopoly in India would instead lead to a much greater militarization of the English EIC and retaliatory struggles so that by 1757, it would be the English who effectively controlled the Carnatic and Pondicherry would be razed. The spectre of the French menace would also drive the EIC to strengthen Fort William at Calcutta, which in turn would lead to Siraj-ud-Daula's aggressive reaction and then to his defeat at the Battle of Plassey. Robert Clive would later write admiringly that Dupleix had been the first to 'discover the superiority of European discipline, and hence led into the idea of acquiring a territorial sovereignty in India'. The wars of territorial conquests had been launched, and the nature of colonial rivalry in India had been changed forever. The age of purely mercantile empires was over, and it was now the dawn of capitalist imperialism.

The destruction of Pondicherry would lead to the exodus of many French officers and soldiers all over India, looking to sell their services to Indian rulers who were increasingly aware of the deadly efficiency of European-trained troops. One of these soldiers was a scrappy and showily courageous cavalry grenadier called René Madec, who escaped Pondicherry and was captured by the British. Another

---

*The memoirs were translated during the writing of this book by G. S. Cheema as *Soldier of Misfortune: The Memoirs of the Comte de Modave*.

was the timelessly spry Claude Martin, who deserted the French and joined the British army right away. The dispersal of all these French soldiers and adventurers would explain the bemusing presence of a number of European players in what would soon become one of the crucial battles of the eighteenth century—the Battle of Buxar in 1764.

For in the backdraft of these conflagrations, the Mughal rulers at Delhi had also conclusively been shown to no longer be the sacrosanct power they had once been. By the mid-eighteenth century, Delhi had seen a dizzying succession of Mughal emperors, made and unmade by various kingmakers. So febrile was the atmosphere at the Red Fort of Delhi that in 1759 Emperor Alamgir II's eldest heir, Ali Gauhar, escaped from Delhi altogether, fearing assassination. When Emperor Alamgir II was assassinated instead, Ali Gauhar proclaimed himself Emperor Shah Alam II, and made his way to Bengal to recruit an army and reclaim Bengal from the EIC. By 1764, an enormous cohort had gathered under the couchant lion and sun standard of the young Shah Alam. They would include the famously ferocious army of the nawab of Awadh, Shuja-ud-Daula*, as well as that of the aggrieved nawab of Bengal, Mir Qasim, who had been deposed by the EIC. French officers fighting on the side of this Mughal force would include Jean-Baptiste Gentil and René Madec and his company of French troops. Fighting on the side of the EIC, meanwhile, was a French-speaking Swiss Protestant officer called Antoine Polier†. Unlike the Battle of Plassey, which was less a battle and more a sleight of hand performed by Clive, the Battle of Buxar in October 1764 was a desperately fought ferocious and bloody encounter whose outcome hung in the balance the entire time. In the end, the Mughal emperor's enormous army was defeated by a much smaller EIC army and the following year Shah Alam was forced to sign the infamous Treaty of Allahabad, whereby Robert Clive strong-armed the emperor into allowing the EIC to collect the taxes of Bengal. 'An international corporation,' writes historian William Dalrymple, 'was transforming itself into an aggressive colonial power', and the pillage of Bengal had begun in earnest.

It is often believed that after the defeat of the French in the Seven Years' War and the signing of the Treaty of Paris in 1763, France

---

*The only son of Nawab Safdar Jang.

†Polier was from a protestant French family who had settled in Switzerland. He arrived in India as a seventeen-year-old in 1758 and joined the English EIC as a cadet.

abandoned her ambitions in India around the time of the Battle of Buxar. Instead, France would undertake a new form of offensive against her old enemy, Britain. Under the leadership of King Louis XV and his minister Étienne François de Choiseul, the French began a global 'guerre de revanche' or 'war of revenge', to restore France's prestige at a time of debilitating debt for the British after the crushing expense of the Seven Years' War. The most successful outcome for France of this strategy was across the Atlantic Ocean, in the American colonies. French support for the 'Americans' of the thirteen colonies against their 'motherland' Britain would lead to the American Revolutionary War (1775–83). This global, militarized, and highly destructive war would lead to the greatest loss Britain ever suffered in her global empire—with America winning its independence—and it would be mirrored by vicious proxy wars between France and Britain in India as well.

French players in India would continue to hustle and intrigue throughout the last quarter of the eighteenth century in the various courts of India. As for the situation between France and Britain, after the outbreak of the French Revolution in 1789 there would be decades of almost continuous, industrialized, and bloody violence through the French Revolutionary Wars (1792–99), segueing into the Napoleonic Wars which would only end at Waterloo in 1815. These wars would lead to even greater volatility in India, with EIC men, and especially Governor General Richard Wellesley, using the bogey of the French threat as justification for outright aggression and plunder at the turn of the nineteenth century. The most infamous incidence of this egregious and violent attitude would be used by the EIC in dealing with the ruler of Mysore, Tipu Sultan.

Tipu Sultan and his father Hyder Ali before him cultivated the longest alliance between an Indian state and the French, one that would involve the participation of Louis XVI and Napoleon Bonaparte in the affairs of India. For many Indian rulers, one sweaty, periwigged foreigner was much like another, much to the despair of the French. Tipu Sultan would be the only Indian ruler who would get accurate and timely updates about the political situation in Europe, and he never abandoned the hope that the French would one day come to his aid. Tipu would be viewed most consistently as a fanatical, unreliable despot precisely because he embodied that most loathed nightmare—a militarily aggressive Muslim ruler who was allied to the French. In 1799 Tipu was attacked by Wellesley using intrigue, lies, and deceit, and his defeat and death would be described with obscene gloating. A contemporary young French surgeon would note that 'The English papers said many horrible things about Tipu, representing him as a violent and possessive man, a tyrant, a sort of general impression that they use rather often against all countries who oppose them or who try and unmask them.'

Of all these Franco-British encounters, the French victory which would have the most devastating effect on British morale, and would propel their subsequent actions, was the Franco–American win during the American Revolutionary War. Many British veterans of the American revolution—the gruff military man Charles Cornwallis, for example—were then sent to India where, in a sense, they exorcized the demons of their American defeat at the hands of the Americans and their French allies. The loss by the British of their American colonies would profoundly affect the national psyche, followed by events like the French Revolutionary Wars which would then impact the very nature of British nationalism itself. In the last decades of the eighteenth century, British nationalism would come to be more explicitly defined, most particularly in opposition to events in France, and so Britain would become the exemplar of sober Protestantism as against outlandish French Catholic excess. All of which effects would then translate into a violent and aggressive 'defence' of their Indian territories against French threat. For the British, their Indian colonies would now provide the resources and manpower to combat French power in its most frightening avatar till then—Napoleon Bonaparte. In the last decades of the eighteenth century, the rise of Protestant Evangelicalism in direct opposition to French Catholicism would radically transform the attitudes of the Company men, fostering a spirit of moral superiority, and justifying political transgressions vis-à-vis the Indian rulers. Ideas of racial superiority would enter the discourse and the French presence would be used to justify and initiate countless British atrocities as well as to validate deceit and lies against Indian powers.

The last decades of the eighteenth century also describe one of those liminal moments when the notion of the Muslim as the feared and despised 'other' was born. In the 1990s a think tank called the Runnymede Trust in the UK coined the term 'Islamophobia' to describe the discrimination faced by Muslims in the UK, a term that would soon become widespread. In the late eighteenth century in India, the first tiny poisonous seeds of Islamophobia were already being sown, swept along the tide of European imperialism, alongside racism. These ideas were first whispered in the dark recesses of imperial corridors, by invisible policy makers and shadowy advisers like Neil Edmonstone, into the ears of eager and wanton imperialists like Wellesley. The ruling elite who had been traitorously displaced became the 'Muslim enemy', to be feared and, therefore, destroyed. Long before Hindutva ideology luxuriated in the ahistorical but virulent idea of 1,000 years of rule by Muslim aggressors, they were outperformed by Western Orientalists who were claiming a 'clash of civilizations' between Christianity and Islam having lasted 1,400 years, showing a deep amnesia about discomfiting realities like Al-Andalus, when Muslims ruled the Iberian Peninsula for 800 years, bringing knowledge and culture into the Dark Ages of Europe. Similarly, this was also the moment in India when biology and race were linked in a manner to exclude those considered 'impure', like Anglo-Indians. The notion of biological racism had been introduced by the blood purity laws of modern Spain, so as to expulse the Jews from Spain where they occupied high office. Now in India, through Cornwallis's 1791 law, similarly 'impure' Anglo-Indians would be excluded from lucrative civil and naval careers within the EIC.

To the victor go not just the spoils, but also the music, for it is to their glory that the bards sing their songs. And so the history of the British in India has dominated the narrative, with beguiling stories, expertly wielded prejudice, and hidden truths. Historian Sujit Sivasundaram has said, in the context of the global history of science, that, 'If we are to de-centre from Europe, we need to use radically new kinds of sources'. In that spirit, this book has sought to balance English language sources with extensive use of French sources such as Modave's memoirs, the French archives at the ANOM (Archives Nationales d'Outre Mer), the family archives of the Count de Boigne at Chambery, France, the Bibliothèque Nationale de France, the Islamic Museum of Berlin, the memoirs of René Madec and Jean-Baptiste Gentil, amongst others. The world of the zenana of Bahu Begum and

Nawab Begum has been described thanks to the treasure trove that is Faiz Baksh's first-hand account of the Faizabad zenana. Other non-traditional sources were also emphasized. A 'kebaub recipe' in Warren Hastings's tiny scrawl within a palm-size leatherbound diary at the British library brought him to life more vibrantly than the reams of official letters he wrote. And then there is the architecture, the endlessly intriguing miniature paintings, the multilingual letters, the songs and dance, and all the paraphernalia of a gorgeous, disappearing culture, proudly called the Ganga-Jamuni tehzeeb.

'Until lions learn to write', the African proverb tells us, 'the stories will always glorify the hunter.' And so *The Lion and the Lily* joins the growing tribe of books that seeks to challenge the monochrome recording of Indian history, and introduce a larger chorus of voices to tell the stories. Some of the silenced and forgotten voices are resurrected so that a horde of glorious lions walk into the stories: from Antoine Polier's crafty Arsalan-e-Jang (Lion in Battle), Claude Martin's eccentric 'Lyon' in Chateau de Lyon, Tipu Sultan's ferocious Assad Allah ul-Ghalib (The Victorious Lion of God) to Imam Ali's 'Lion of God' which pervaded so much of the nawabs of Awadh's imagery through their Shia legacy. In the end, of course, the rampant British lion would trample over so many of these destinies. Braiding through these stories is the jaunty and eccentric 'fleur-de-lys' lily of the French adventurers, that would itself soon burst into flames to be replaced by the red, white, and blue rosette of the French Republic. With these textured stories, perhaps some of that forbidden legacy may yet be recovered from the fires that burnt as the sun finally set on the British empire in India.

BOOK I

THE FISH OF HINDUSTAN
(1720–1775)

# 1764: SOMEWHERE BETWEEN BIHAR AND BENGAL

On a cool February morning, surgeon and translator in the English East India Company* Archibald Swinton was greatly alarmed by the cacophonous and untimely beating of army drums. The Company's camp had been pitched in the borderlands of Hindustan—at the very edge of the known world where Bengal ended and Awadh† began. Now suddenly, a great, boisterous melee of European soldiers, many French, stormed around the camp, grabbing guns and fixing bayonets, preparing to abscond. 'We were not leaving the English like vile deserters,' one of the Frenchmen later sniffed. 'We left in broad daylight, with our arms and baggage, like a corps that is changing camps.'

Some 250 European soldiers left the English camp on that day, despite Company officers desperately alternating between threats and supplications. The atmosphere was febrile, admitted an officer, with Indian sepoys‡ joining the deserters and cannons being seized. 'Had one firelock gone off by accident or otherwise,' wrote the officer, 'it would certainly have been the destruction of the whole army and the loss of almost, if not quite all, the Europeans and the total loss of Bengal.' These European mutineers had been unwilling soldiers,§ press-ganged into fighting for the Company after having been made prisoner years before at the fall of Pondicherry.¶ Now, finding themselves close to the territory of the independent nawab of Awadh, and unpaid for many months, they decamped. Their leader, Frenchman René Madec, later

---

*Henceforth, the 'Company'.
†In 1580, under Emperor Akbar's reign, Ayodhya and neighbouring cities became one of the twelve subahs of the Mughal empire and came to be known as Awadh, spelled Oudh in colonial accounts. Some 24,000 sq miles of the Gangetic plain lay within the province of Awadh. Lucknow was made the capital of Awadh, evidence of its importance even in the sixteenth century.
‡Indian soldiers who were recruited and trained to fight for the Company.
§In the early years of the EIC, their infantry was recruited in Britain, attracting notoriously mediocre specimens—'criminal riff-raff' and the like, and so they supplemented their forces by locally recruited white or mixed-race mercenaries, French prisoners of war, and Swiss and Germans from the French service.
¶Many French soldiers had been captured after the fall of Pondicherry in 1761. French prisoners were submitted to harsh mistreatment, including starvation, to induce them to join the EIC in Bengal. Madec and 400 of his compatriots had made a pact to desert together as soon as they got the opportunity.

wrote to the Company officers to say that 'they had always behaved like good soldiers...(but) they had been ill used...and that as they were Frenchmen (they) would always find them as good Frenchmen still.'

By 1764, René Madec had already spent considerably more than half his twenty-eight years on foreign shores. One of ten children born to an impoverished Breton family, he had brawled through his bruising childhood, trying to escape the mist-bound town of Quimper in western France. The traits he had shown as a child—aggression, volatility, and a flighty and obdurate refusal to be educated—had made of him a scrappy, brash, and hard-living man, with a prickly sense of honour. It had also made him supremely courageous and physically impulsive to the point of madness. But these were traits that were valued in the French Compagnie des Indes[*] and that would make of him one of the 'great men' of Hindustan in the eighteenth century. In February 1764, Madec found himself entirely in his element, bellowing almost joyously to his fellow mutineers: 'Let all those who love me, follow me!' The English, meanwhile, would blow from their cannons some twenty sepoys who had wanted to follow the European deserters.

Madec and his ragtag band of French soldiers crossed into Awadh through forced marches. As the days grew warmer, the heat baffled these men who had never been so deep into this vast country, far from the lush beguilement of Bengal and Pondicherry. In Benaras they were disoriented by the rising smoke of incense and burning pyres, and the riotous gongs of endless bells reminded them that they were very far from the relative comfort of the European settlements. The villagers they crossed en route, meanwhile, scuttled away from these strange foreign men and their dangerous red uniforms[†]. Finally, after twenty days they reached the war camp of Nawab Wazir[‡] Shuja-ud-Daula, south of Lucknow on the banks of a river. The French soldiers quickly got

---

[*]The French East India Company (henceforth French EIC) was founded in 1664. Like all the European trading companies, it also had an ignominious link to the African slave trade. In 1720, the French king gave the monopoly for the African slave trade on the African coast to the French EIC. Between 1719 and 1770 the EIC armed 190 slave ships and 56,800 black slaves were transported from Africa to the West Indies.
[†]In the eighteenth century, battles were fought over small areas with short range weapons. Red was the colour of choice for uniforms so that commanders could see them easily on the smoke-filled battlefields.
[‡]Shuja had recently received the acknowledgment by the Mughal emperor that he would be the wazir but he was yet to be formally invested with this office.

rid of their filthy coarse red Company uniforms and exchanged them for the lightweight clothes of the local soldiers. Madec wore the long, flared tunic, voluminous salwar, and flat turban of the local noblemen and settled into the spacious tents that Nawab Shuja-ud-Daula had graciously sent for him. The turban gave some character to Madec whose bland, pale face was dominated by a long, narrow nose and hooded blue eyes. As he grew older in Hindustan's harsh light, his skin darkened and his high cheekbones and appraising gaze lent him the air of a particularly intractable Kabuli merchant. In Shuja's camp Madec met an old acquaintance and a Frenchman of a rather different mettle. Almost ten years older than Madec, Jean-Baptiste Gentil[*] was an infantry colonel in the French army from a distinguished family. A slim and elegant man, dressed smartly in his French officer's uniform, Gentil's benignly bulging eyes gave him a distracted, slightly pained air. After serving under French officers during campaigns of questionable success and glory, he now found himself after the destruction of the French trading post at Chandernagore by the EIC in the service of one of the most powerful Indian rulers and was eager to recruit Madec to the same cause.

When Madec went to present his nazr[†] to Shuja, the nawab was reclining in state in his huge war tent, leaning against silk bolsters laid upon an embroidered carpet. Madec knelt down to place his gold coins at the feet of the nawab, who immediately bestowed a khillat[‡] upon him. Indeed Shuja was delighted to add the Breton mercenary and his French followers to his growing band of European soldiers and promised Madec a salary of 12,000 rupees per month. Madec, who had never personally met any other great Indian ruler, was overwhelmed. 'The prince was gracious, kind, and gifted with a great elegance of speech', he would later confess in his memoirs. For the brusque, pugnacious Breton this was an education in refinement with

---

[*]Like Madec, Gentil too was chased out of Pondicherry and then Chandernagore by the Company. He then joined the service of the deposed nawab of Bengal, Mir Qasim, before finally joining Shuja-ud-Daula's forces in 1763. Before that he had served with distinction under the likes of Dupleix, de Bussy, Law de Lauriston, and was knighted with the Order of the Cross of Saint-Louis.
[†]An offering or tribute that is made to a superior, who may or may not accept it. The nazr could be something quite humble, like a small coin, or a grand present like an elephant and trays of jewelry. The nazr seals the supplicatory position of the offeror.
[‡]Ceremonial robe.

strength, and his tenacious admiration would not falter for the rest of the nawab's life. Much later, when all was lost, he would weep over the nawab's grief for the loss of his lands. For Shuja was a towering man both in size and personality and was deemed outstanding in a time and place fairly bristling with extraordinary characters. Even a foe was moved to admit that he was 'the most handsome person I have ever seen in India' while a Scots officer, Alexander Dow, said that he was 'extremely handsome in his person, about five feet eleven inches in height and so nervous and strong that with one stroke of the sabre he could cut off the head of a buffalo'. This officer tempered his effusions somewhat by clarifying that the nawab was, nonetheless, the 'dastardly son of a Persian flea market salesman'.

So seductive was this combination of martial prowess and charismatic manners that another French adventurer, the Comte de Modave, no slouch in terms of aristocratic elegance himself, admitted that the nawab's 'strength and skill in all physical exercise had something of the romantic'.

Madec also spied another figure in the nawab's camp, a man 'of average height, quite dark, with fine features, full of grace and dignity'. This was the young Mughal emperor Shah Alam II,* driven out of his own capital of Delhi upon the assassination of his father, an errant and increasingly unhappy figure, desperate to regain his beloved capital city. Also present in this camp was Mir Qasim, the aggrieved, recently deposed nawab of Bengal, determined to wrest back Bengal from the Company. 'The English had made of him their enemy,' wrote Modave, 'because he did not want to be their slave.' Modave added that Mir Qasim was 'the man of Hindustan who has the most depth of character, and who is a master of durbar politics...the most skilfully deceptive man in the Mughal empire'. When Mir Qasim had first sought refuge with Shuja the previous year, there had been a degree of posturing and a show of opulence between the two nawabs, noblesse oblige. Mir Qasim had set up a magnificent tent and canopy, and had arranged for his troops, all magnificently dressed, to line the road outside his camp. When the nawab arrived to greet him, he was presented with twenty-

---

*Born in 1728, Shahzada Ali Gauhar was just thirty when his father Alamgir II was assassinated in Delhi by kingmaker Imad-ul-Mulk. Ali Gauhar sought sanctuary with Shuja-ud-Daula and claimed the title Shah Alam II as the next emperor.

one trays of cloths, six elephants, and fourteen horses. The next day when Mir Qasim returned the visit, the nawab had brought out his Mughal cavalry in their scarlet uniforms armed with muskets to line the road to an ostentatiously much longer distance. 'Sweet friendly talk' was exchanged, we are assured, but Mir Qasim must have returned to his camp somewhat sobered.

Resentful about the refuge that Shuja had given to Mir Qasim, a man they considered their own puppet, a thing to make and unmake,* the English now sent the nawab a warning against marching towards Bengal to fight his cause, threatening retaliation. But Shuja was prickly about questions of honour and he was piqued enough to send the following reply to the Company:

> Former Kings of Hindustan...bestowed greater kindness and honour upon (the English) than either upon the country merchants or any other Europeans; you have interfered with the King's (Shah Alam) country, possessed yourself of districts belonging to the Government...and turned out and established Nabobs at pleasure without the consent of the Imperial court...and since you have ruined the trade of the merchants of the country, granted protection to the King's servants, injured the revenue of the Imperial court, and crushed the inhabitants by your acts of violence...to what can all these proceedings be attributed but to an absolute disregard of the court and wicked design of seizing the country for yourselves.

For what the grifter Madec had unwittingly stumbled upon was no errant scrum or upstart rabble. This was a gathering of some of the most powerful and charismatic men in Hindustan. These were rulers with ancient pedigrees and brand-new grievances. Into this mix the Frenchman Madec brought his own personal sense of vengeance when he described 'the hope that I entertained to contribute to the downfall of a nation (Britain) that had ruined mine, I worked with all my heart to bring about their complete defeat'. Three days after Madec's arrival at the camp, this gathering of soldiers, rulers, and refugees set off towards

---

*The English had installed Mir Qasim as nawab of Bengal after having defeated the hereditary nawab, Siraj-ud-Daula. When Mir Qasim proved less amenable to their cause than they expected, they replaced him with his father-in-law, Mir Jafar.

Patna, where Madec had rebelled from the Company at the edge of the Bihar-Awadh border. The purpose of the confrontation was to restore Mir Qasim to the nawabi of the wealthy province of Bengal and Bihar, secure revenue for the desperately impoverished Mughal emperor, and teach the grasping Company a severe lesson, perhaps expel them out of the country altogether. Seeing this enormous army on the march, Captain John Carnac, who was commanding the Company forces, smartly turned around and headed for the relative safety of Patna.

In the months that followed there were sharp skirmishes and desultory sieges, lengthy waiting, and complicated negotiations as both parties used diplomacy and threats, bribes and promises to entice different factions to come over to their side. Jealousies, avarice, and paranoia beset both camps, but especially the large, unwieldly gathering led by Nawab Shuja-ud-Daula. By October 1764, the nawab had been encamped through the monsoon at a small, fertile plain called Buxar, between Benaras and Patna. By now this was not so much a camp as a temporary city, stretching out far into the green fields all around. The force consisted of 200,000, of whom only 40,000 were fighting soldiers. Madec* left a description of this Mughal war camp, which reflected his overwhelmed horror at the conditions in this immense, teeming encampment:

> A veritable temporary city made of reeds and clay, endless, you came and went as you pleased, and everyone wallowed in deep mud in the midst of elephants, camels, horses, bullock carts and dogs in endless numbers. The camps were like ovens, and malaria was rampant, but this in no way lessened all sorts of debauchery. There were not only the lodgings of soldiers and the official looters, as well as gardens, but also the stores of a bazaar, jugglers, astrologers, dancers with their orchestras; and also large, luxurious tents for the princes and their generals, comprising compartments for their concubines and their treasures, surrounded by the miserable huts of their slaves. And finally, a few hundred golden cages for Shuja's beloved doves.

---

*Madec and Gentil were not the only Europeans leading forces at Buxar for there was also Walter Reinhardt, an Austrian mercenary of recent infamy, who had come to Hindustan to join the French forces and who ended up, through a fairly circuitous route, in the employ of Mir Qasim.

Shuja commanded forces at Buxar that could strike terror in the enemy simply by their fearsome appearance. He had in his army 6,000-7,000 Persian Qizilbash (red hat) cavalry, who had once belonged to Nadir Shah's armies. Then he also had a large contingent of Naga Gossains, some 10,000 strong, 'who were a race of most valiant and reckless fighters, and whose leaders were popularly believed to be expert in witchcraft and proof against bullets and cannonballs.' Perhaps most intimidating to the enemy was the fact that the Naga troops fought stark naked, their bodies smeared with ash and their long matted hair streaming past their shoulders, attacking with swords and arrows, fuelled by opium. The nawab could take comfort also in the righteousness of their cause and the magnitude of the aura of legitimacy that swept men up in its wake. The most potent of these symbols was the Mughal emperor himself, proud inheritor of the immense legacies of his ancestors Akbar and Shah Jahan. The young Shah Alam II himself had charm and determination and 'had often proved that he lacked neither courage nor intelligence; more than once his faith and his energy were put to the test and he always conducted himself with honour'.

Among the many different banners fluttering in the warm air, some bearing the sun, the lion, the fish, and many more, one was particularly startling, for it had never been flown as part of a Hindustani force before. This was the royal banner of the 'fleur-de-lys', the lily flower which had long been part of the French kings' heraldry. This was the banner that marked Madec's band, for he had formed the first French 'parti' (corps) of the country, which would continue to fight under the colours of France till Madec left India more than a dozen years later. This potent and quirky symbolic gesture certainly reflected Madec's assurance that 'I had always fought in this country under the banner of France, despite the fact that we (the French) no longer had holdings here, to the great displeasure of the English.' Madec now commanded a considerable force of twenty-two companies consisting of sixty men each that he had recruited from all over Hindustan*. He bought horses and bullock carts, organized his train, hired dispersed Europeans, and

---

*This was a considerable number. The great French commander de Bussy never had more than 6,000 men under him. Indian armies, for their part, rarely numbered more than 20,000 fighting men.

even cast some pieces of cannon in a foundry set up by Gentil. At Buxar, Madec set up his encampment a little apart from that of the Indian chiefs and it was scarce cleaner and here, too, could be found the accompanying courtesans, merchants, and prostitutes. But there was better order and discipline in Madec's camp and, most crucially, the Breton insisted on regular training exercises for his recruits, using the techniques he had picked up in Pondicherry and Fort Williams.

The confounding presence of French troops in the fields of Buxar, and indeed scattered throughout Hindustan, would not have been seen by the local rulers for what they really were*—the consequence of a global war between France and Britain which had begun a few decades earlier and would last another half century. As these ancient enemies grappled like two insatiable behemoths across time and continents for global empires in the eighteenth century, the shockwaves would be felt all the way from the St. Lawrence River in Quebec† to the storied cites of Egypt and all the way to the nondescript fields around Buxar. They would stoke paranoia, greed, jealously, and obsession and they would be used, also, as coldly calculating means to incite devastation and justify plunder.

The Company forces facing this glittering and fearsome gathering were altogether more pedestrian. Accompanying Major Carnac, the Company officer, was the elderly nawab of Bengal, Mir Jafar, 'an uneducated Arab soldier of fortune', who was an unhappy participant 'intimidated by the Wazir's numbers and by his personal character for valour and prowess'. Between them, the Company and Mir Jafar had mustered a rather paltry 19,000 somewhat fatigued and dispirited troops.

Waiting impatiently in the grand stone fort of Allahabad, meanwhile, were two women who would also play a crucial and extraordinary role in the years to come. These two purdah-bound aristocratic women had close connections to the Mughal court and enormous personal legitimacy. Sadr-un-Nisa Begum (known as Nawab Begum) was Shuja's mother and the other, Ummat-ul-Zohra Begum (known as Bahu Begum), was about to become his favourite wife. Until the Battle of

---

*Of all the Indian rulers, only Tipu Sultan of Mysore had a realistic grasp of the global wars being fought between these two empires.
†The deciding battle of the Seven Years' War between France and Britain (1756–1763) in Quebec took place on the banks of the St. Lawrence River.

Buxar, Bahu Begum was simply the khaas mahal,* or chief consort in the famously libertine Shuja's harem. But events following the denouement of the battle would make Shuja so extravagantly grateful to Bahu Begum, when she would assure his life and his honour, that it would change forever her status and influence at his court.

The Battle of Buxar is often overlooked, bookended as it is between the more glamorous battles of Plassey, Panipat, and the Anglo-Mysore Wars. But this was the seminal moment in which the Mughal emperor handed over all tax collection rights to the three wealthiest provinces of India—Bengal, Bihar, and Orissa—to a foreign trading company, and thereby relinquished his authority as the only legitimate ruler of India. This battle, in turn, would initiate a skein of lies and generate a cauldron of forces that would shape the country for a hundred years.

---

*Both Sadr-un-Nisa and Ummat-ul-Zohra were the only 'mankuha' wife of their husbands, meaning that they married by nikah rites, despite a maximum of four wives by nikah being permitted. The status of khaas mahal 'generally conferred upon the Nawab's chief consort recognised prerogatives to manage her husband's household finances and his children's marital unions, in addition to her own personal property'. See Nicholas J. Abbott, '"It All Comes from Me": Bahu Begam and the Making of the Awadh Nawabi, circa 1765–1815.' *Modern Asian Studies*, Vol. 57, 2023.

# WHEN AWADH WAS A HARDSHIP POSTING

On 2 November 1721, the young Mughal emperor Muhammad Shah\* rode triumphantly on a giant elephant called Shah-Pasand, back into the Qila-e-Mualla (the exalted fortress, today known as the Red Fort) of Delhi. 'The prince, adorned by all the graces of youth and beauty,' wrote the aristocratic historian Ghulam Hussain Khan admiringly, 'made his appearance on a gigantic elephant, and seated upon a throne that literally blazed with a profusion of jewels and rich ornaments.' Amidst the frenetic beating of large drums, the discordant wailing of trumpets and the joyous acclamation of the onlookers, the train of elephants made its stately way through the Ajmer gate into the fort. Following the elephants were troops of resplendent noblemen on their shimmying horses, clad in full battle armour, banners fluttering in the golden dust. Running ahead were 'beautiful slave-boys and young men clad in cloth of gold,' while from his elephant the delighted emperor threw gold coins down to the clamouring crowd.

As the thirteenth emperor of the illustrious Mughal dynasty, Muhammad Shah had inherited a troubling legacy. Since the death of the last of the so-called Great Mughals, Aurangzeb†, in 1707, there had been a breathlessly rapid succession of emperors, three having been murdered, as the empire convulsed through the changes of the early eighteenth century. Obsessed with notions of treason and betrayal, Aurangzeb had jealously protected his own power and had never allowed his sons to create patronage-based households of their own and all the Mughal emperors from this time forward would be fatally dependent on the whims of kingmakers and puppet masters. Muhammad Shah himself had been installed as emperor through the dangerous power of the Sayyid brothers,‡ who belonged to the old military aristocracy from the time of Aurangzeb.

---

\*Born Roshan Aktar in 1702, the emperor was only nineteen years old at this time. He took the regnal name Muhammad Shah when he ascended the throne in in 1719, and is better known by his sobriquet 'Rangeela' or 'Rangeeley'.
†The first six Mughal emperors—Babur, Humayun, Akbar, Jahangir, Shah Jahan, and Aurangzeb—are usually referred to as the Great Mughals.
‡After the death of Aurangzeb, brothers Syed Hassan Ali Khan and Syed Hussain Ali Khan became very influential at the Mughal court, helping overthrow emperors and instate new ones.

As the power of the Mughals slowly folded in on itself, drawing away from the Deccan and Bengal to settle around the capital of Delhi, the governors of these distant provinces began to dream of independence. The huge swathe of land in northern India around Delhi grew increasingly fractious, as the Rajputs, the Jats,* and the Sikhs all began rising up sporadically and growing increasingly militarized. In the Punjab, especially, the Khalsa Sikhs had organized themselves into war bands, after the brutal execution of their charismatic leader, Banda Bahadur, in 1716. These war bands or misals used guerrilla tactics to challenge Mughal sovereignty in the region while also contending with the Maratha incursions and the Afghan presence. As for the Maratha state in the western Deccan, they were sending plundering parties ever further north, undermining Mughal power by demanding the 'chauth'†. For other important groups in Hindustan like the Rajputs and the Jats, meanwhile, both the Afghans and the Marathas were plundering foes, and equally alien. Not long after Muhammad Shah became emperor, Shehzaadi Zinat-un-Nisa Begum,‡ Aurangzeb's daughter and the last of the great Padshah Begums of the Mughal harem, died, almost like a premonition of the arrival of more calamitous times.

In Muhammad Shah's train in 1721 was a distinguished Persian Shia nobleman, an immigrant from the celebrated city of Nishapur in Persia, Saadat Khan§. Saadat Khan had participated in the emperor's recent campaigns to neutralize the power of the Sayyid brothers and had been rewarded with the title Bahadur Jang—Lion in Battle—and with the exalted insignia of the Mahi Maratib, the Order of the Fish.¶

---

*The Jats belong to the north Indian agricultural peasant community, and first rebelled against Mughal emperor Aurangzeb in the seventeenth century in the Delhi, Mathura, and Agra region. They established a kingdom at Bharatpur in the eighteenth century.
†From the Sanskrit term meaning a quarter, this referred to the tax of 25 per cent of the total revenue that the Marathas demanded from all kingdoms under them.
‡Zinat-un-Nisa Begum was Aurangzeb's unmarried daughter. She remained Padshah Begum, or most senior woman, of the Mughal harem even after the death of her father.
§Emperor Muhammad Shah had recently given the title Saadat Khan to Mir Mohammad Ameen, the Persian immigrant, and two years later he would further award him the title Burhan-ul-Mulk, or Proof of the Realm. He belonged to an aristocratic family of Sayyids and his father was a qazi in the Safavi empire. In 1707, his father migrated to Hindustan and settled in Patna. His son followed him to India a year later.
¶The Mahi Maratib has somewhat mysterious origins, with many theories to explain its genesis, but is most likely an old Mongol tradition. It was the highest honour that could be conferred in the Mughal empire. It consisted of a giant face of a catfish, with scales and teeth, mounted on a high pole, carried in processions. In popular legends, a fish jumped out of the water and

Saadat Khan was forty-two at this time, a skilled warrior and a barrel-chested man with a blunt wedge of a beard hiding his neck. But very soon, having been unable to quell a Jat rebellion, Saadat Khan was demoted and exiled to the badlands of Awadh, which produced only half the revenues of his previous subedari* of Agra and which was, moreover, teeming with refractory zamindars. To underline his displeasure, the emperor refused Saadat Khan access to the court, a most grievous punishment, and instead had the robes of his new posting sent to him by a lowly messenger.

Thus chastised, Saadat Khan removed himself to Awadh, where he would return several times, either upon incurring royal displeasure or in a show of pique. Saadat Khan never considered Awadh an independent territory or in any way separate from the Mughal empire. He would build no capital city and instead simply constructed a wooden hut with a thatched roof for shelter in Faizabad in the monsoon season, the remainder of the time living in his tented encampments.† Nevertheless, perhaps musing upon the vagaries of royal fortunes at such a time of extreme volatility, it seems Saadat Khan was thinking of the future of his line when he sent for four of his nephews from Nishapur. Saadat Khan had no sons himself so now in 1723 he married his daughter, Sadr-un-Nisa, to one of his nephews, Safdar Jang,‡ a strapping young man with a face barred by a dense black beard, and nominated him deputy subedar, with the emperor's approval, thus quietly making of the nawabi of Awadh a hereditary assignation. The 1720s would be a dismaying decade for the Mughal emperor, with Hyderabad, Awadh, and Bengal all slipping out of the grasp of Mughal authority by claiming hereditary status to what had simply been temporary governorships of subahs, whose governors were frequently transferred.

From this time on, Saadat Khan spent a great deal more time

---

fell into the lap of Saadat Khan when he was crossing the Gomti. This was interpreted as an auspicious sign and Saadat Khan adopted the symbol of the fish.
*A province in the Mughal empire was called a subah, and the governor the subedar. At this time, the Mughal emperor was constantly rotating his subedars every three to four years amongst provinces to prevent them from forming strong ties to the regions and developing power bases.
†This humble dwelling was surrounded by a mud wall and there were large enclosures with rooms for the cavalry, infantry, artillery stables, and zenana--all made of mud. These structures came to be known as Bangla.
‡Mirza Abu'l Mansur Mohammad Mukeem, later known as Safdar Jang, was the son of Saadat Khan's eldest sister.

consolidating and enlarging his territories around Awadh, boldly subduing challengers.* Indeed while Awadh was a prosperous,† strategically located province, it was plagued with notoriously unruly taluqdars (landholders) and peasants, always ready to arm themselves and their clansmen to fight against imperial revenue collectors. The most nefarious of these Rajput taluqdars was Bhagwant Singh, who had long flouted imperial authority by the simple if bloody expedient of murdering the Mughal governors sent to the region. Finally, in 1735, Saadat Khan engaged the zamindar in a viciously fought battle at the end of which, in a gesture worthy of Babur himself, the heads of Bhagwant Singh and his son were stuffed with straw, impaled on spikes, and sent to Delhi to be displayed in the Urdu Bazar near the Police kotwal,‡ where the urbane citizens of Delhi must have been dismayed at this grisly augury of change for their genteel and refined capital.

Far worse, however, was in store for the beleaguered people of Delhi. For in the fatally weakening empire of neighbouring Persia, a coup d'etat had taken place and a talented military officer, Nadir Shah, imposingly tall with flashing black eyes and a voice like thunder, had seized power and turned his malevolent eye towards Hindustan. Now, in 1739, calamitously, invaders from the north-west had overrun Mughal forces at the border and were thundering towards Delhi. Indeed so distracted was the Mughal court at this time that the first indication of the inferno at their doorstep was when a scattering of grass-cutters rushed back to camp wailing about the hard blows they had just received from some 'Moghul' foreigners. Reacting far too late, the emperor scrambled to recall his scattered Mughal forces, and Saadat Khan left Safdar Jang in charge of Awadh while he galloped back to the capital,

---

*Over the course of the next few years, Saadat Khan would thus incorporate Benaras, Jaunpur, Ghazipur, and Chunargarh into Awadh, always with imperial approval. To see the details of how Saadat Khan subdued the refractory Awadh countryside, see Violette Graff, *Lucknow: Memories of a City*, Oxford University Press, 1997, pp. 22-25.

†Awadh produced calico, other cotton cloths, embroidery, archery bows. Straddling the fertile plains between the Yamuna and the Ganga, it also controlled the river trade in goods across these plains.

‡According to Swapna Liddle in *Shahjahanabad: Mapping a Mughal City*, the Urdu Bazar terminated in the square known as Kotwali Chowk, which was infamous for the severity of the punishments meted out there. There was a tall pole called Lal Khan ka Lakkad on the raised platform of the chowk, to which criminals were tied and beaten.

450 km away, with his 40,000 strong army. Lured into attacking Nadir Shah's Persian cavalry at the gates of Delhi, Saadat Khan sent his men into a disastrous frontal attack. 'The Indian warriors, sayyids, shaikhs, Afghans and Rajputs, so fought with their cruel swords,' wrote a witness about this suicidal encounter, that 'the (Persians), dreading the swords of these brave men, left the field, and firing their guns from a distance... made heaps of the corpses of Indians, who preferred death to flight.' Captured and brought before Nadir Shah, Saadat Khan answered the Persian's questions with enough aplomb and bravura to convince him of the great military strength of the Hindustani emperor, as well as his noblemen and rajas. Evidently more circumspect now, Nadir Shah engaged in genial negotiations, with dinners and entertainments on both sides, involving Saadat Khan and another important Mughal officer, the veteran Nizam-ul-Mulk*. The men might have witnessed the surprising agility of the huge, hulking Nadir Shah as he expertly practised his battleaxe manoeuvres, slicing and thrusting the heavy, deadly weapon through the air from his audience tent.† At the end of a few days, a decidedly modest war indemnity of 50 lakh rupees was agreed upon, and it seemed like catastrophe had been averted. Almost immediately, however, Saadat Khan found out that the coveted post of Mir Bakshi he had long hankered after had gone to his great rival Nizam-ul-Mulk, and in his fury and rage he informed Nadir Shah that there was a great deal more wealth to be extricated from the emperor yet.

The consequences of Nadir Shah's entry into Delhi were catastrophic for the citizens of Delhi. Almost immediately the Persian conqueror began behaving with arrogance, venality, and boorish vulgarity. Saadat Khan was humiliated and realizing he had outplayed his hand and no longer had any future in imperial service in Hindustan, died after swallowing poison. Nadir Shah proclaimed himself emperor of Hindustan and for two months he unleashed an apocalypse of violence and pain on the people of Delhi. The city was set on fire and Nadir

---

*Nizam-ul-Mulk had served under Aurangzeb himself and was summoned to court by Emperor Muhammad Shah in 1722 from the Deccan, where he was governor, and was made the wazir of the empire.

†This fondness for the battleaxe, which had fallen from use in Persia till it was resuscitated by Nadir Shah, earned him the sobriquet the Axe Khan. Many battleaxes were made for the shah in Lahore, one of which can be admired at the National Museum, Delhi. One was also made for Saadat Khan, who was clearly impressed with the shah's handling of the weapon.

Shah's soldiers roamed the streets plundering, raping, and killing the inhabitants indiscriminately. According to one Dutch account, 100,000 people were killed. The Dutch report further chillingly stated that 'Nader Shah gave orders to kill anyone who defended himself. As a result it seemed as if it were raining blood, for the drains were streaming with it.' After two months, having annihilated the very fabric of Mughal imperial authority, Nadir Shah dispensed some fairly gratuitous advice on running an empire and returned to his country 'carrying the pick of the treasures the Mughal Empire had amassed over its 200 years of sovereignty and conquest' and leaving behind a Persian ambassador at the Mughal court.* The paltry present of seven horses and a few trays of jewels and clothes that he gave Mohammad Shah in return must have seemed like a terrible insult to the emperor, who never recovered from this trauma. 'For the ten years that he survived this disaster,' wrote the Comte de Modave, travelling just a few decades later† through Hindustan, 'he never overcame the memory of this event.':

> (the Mughal Empire) had lasted until the 39th year of this century in a state of apparent splendour despite a long series of internal troubles. But the invasion of the Persian King precipitated its ruin. Never has any state suffered so much as Hindustan did after this fatal invasion. Even though by then the empire was surviving more on the weight of its past glory than on its real worth. It seemed somewhat recovered from the troubles of the early century following the death of Aurangzeb in 1707. Mohammad Shah brought some peace to this great crumpling empire, seeming to give it some vigour and life. But Nadir Shah... gave renewed urgency to all the vicissitudes that the empire was still managing to contain, and brought down the empire less by his devastations, his massacres and his extortions—even though he surpassed himself in all this—than in the contempt in which he threw Mughal imperial power. When this terrible conqueror returned to Persia, Mohammad Shah, dazed by all that he had undergone, did not have the courage to surmount his tragedy. He used to tell everyone that Nader Shah had degraded and debased

---

*Nawab Munir-ud-Daula stayed on even after Nadir Shah's assassination and served three successive Mughal emperors.
†Modave came to Hindustan in 1773.

him to such an extent that he no longer deserved to be called a king. This painful humiliation influenced his conduct entirely.

In this new, starless night in the city there would be upheavals that would be felt in every thread of the courtly fabric of Mughal Delhi, and down to the ordinary townsfolk. Most notoriously, the illusion of Mughal power had been viciously laid bare not only through the bloody mayhem of Delhi's devastation, but through the carting away of what had been mythical and quasi-divine symbols of Mughal legitimacy—the Peacock Throne, the exquisite gold and silver objects, the talismanic glittering jewels carrying the charisma of past emperors. The effects of the shattering of Mughal influence would be felt by even the most humble of Delhi's citizens. Emperor Mohammad Shah had been a discerning and enthusiastic patron of the arts—dance, music and painting—earning him the affectionate sobriquet of 'Rangeeley'(Colourful). He was the last Mughal emperor to preside over a substantial atelier that employed talented painters of Mughal miniatures. There are many fine paintings of Mohammad Shah, often in the zenana or holding court with his favourite officials.* Court painters experimented with light and shadows for the first time, their inexperienced enthusiasm showing in the solid cones of dark colours meant to depict shadows. But the chaos and uncertainty seeded by Nadir Shah's sacking of Delhi would cause a steady exodus of painters, poets, musicians, and dancers to more affluent and stable courts, one of the most attractive being the court of Awadh at Faizabad and Lucknow.

Meanwhile, in the years following his father-in-law's suicide, Safdar Jang remained largely in Awadh, strengthening his position.† He had already gathered 2 crore rupees to give to Nadir Shah in return for the confirmation of his nawabi of Awadh and Mohammad Shah, with not much say in the matter, confirmed the appointment and awarded him the imperial title of 'Safdar Jang'—Lion in War. He also managed to lure away 6,000-7,000 of the dreaded Qizilbash cavalry from Nadir Shah's army with the substantial offer of 50 rupees a month.

It was only in 1743 that the new nawab of Awadh, Safdar Jang,

---

*One painting, however, utterly inexplicably shows the emperor sitting companionably with his hated nemesis, Nadir Shah.
†Safdar Jang acquired the important forts of Rohtas and Chunar by promising to help the nawab of Bengal, but never did exert himself on that occasion.

finally arrived at the Mughal capital and presented himself to the emperor from the banks of the Yamuna, in some style, on a crisply cool day in November:

> (Safdar Jang) had with him over ten thousand horse, all well-mounted and well-armed, the Hindustanis upon horses of value of their own country, while the Mughals dressed in scarlet uniforms were upon Persian horses adorned with silver trappings. Besides, there were some elephants caparisoned with clothes worked in threads of silver and gold plaitings. Of the elephants, three bore the nawab's standards. When Safdar Jang reached opposite to the Musaman Burj of the (diwan e khaas) which, being richly gilt, was shining like the sun, he alighted from his elephant, bowed low according to custom and stood awhile in a respectful posture.

Much pleased with this show of martial splendour, elegance, and obedience from his most important officer and not to be outdone, Mohammad Shah sent a bunch of fragrant roses through a khwajasara to the chivalrous nawab of Awadh. A few days later Safdar Jang crossed the river on a bridge of boats, accompanied by all his troops and his fourteen-year-old son, Jalaluddin Haidar. He presented himself to the emperor at court and then took up residence in his Delhi home, in the Dara Shukoh mansion*. Safdar Jang soon found himself embroiled in court politics, where there was a fairly bitter ongoing power tussle between the Sunni Turani† factions and the Shia Persian ones. As a Persian officer of outstanding pedigree, Safdar Jang was soon nominated to the post of Mir Atish (superintendent of the imperial artillery) with duties to protect the imperial family and so he shifted into the Qila-e-Mualla itself. The young Jalaluddin would have often

---

*The Dara Shukoh mansion was a huge and splendid establishment which had served as the Delhi residence of the Mughal prince, son of Shah Jahan. It was assigned to the nawabs of Awadh from the time of Saadat Khan himself and is today largely destroyed, though historian Swapna Liddle has identified a few extant structures. In addition to the Dara Shukoh mansion, the nawabs of Awadh would acquire at least two more mansions for their use in Delhi, described by Banmali Tandon as 'among the greatest Indo-Islamic style domestic architecture ever commissioned during the history of Mughal architecture'. Swapna Liddle has identified the sites and structure in her book *Shahjahahanabad: Mapping a Mughal city*, as being in the Guzar Lahori Darwaza Thana and Guzar Etiqad Khan thana, towards the north-west of the Red Fort.

†The Mughal family was Sunni, and of Turki/Turani origins, but Persian immigrants were often greatly promoted at the Mughal court, both as a counterweight to the powerful Turani group and for their own cachet as bearers of Persian language and culture.

attended the imperial durbar along with his father and it was this favour that led to one of the most spectacular celebrations of Mohammad Shah's reign.

The emperor was particularly fond of the daughter of a deceased Persian nobleman, a young girl of perhaps eleven or twelve called Ummat-ul-Zohra Begum*. Zohra Begum was doted upon by the emperor and had been raised at court. The emperor now proposed to cement the fortunes of this family by marrying this young girl, the future Bahu Begum, to the teenage son of Safdar Jang.† The nawab of Awadh was clearly pleased with this match too, for he would make the wedding celebrations the grandest that the Mughal court had known since the famously glorious displays at Dara Shukoh's wedding. On the day of the sachaq,‡ streams of splendidly dressed relatives walked from the Ajmeri gate of the Qila to Feroz Shah Kotla, bearing trays of sweets, fruits, shimmering clothes, bottles of perfumes, furniture, and one thousand and one dishes of silver, while the appreciative onlookers jostled to get a view and murmured their approval. Zohra Begum was given a rich dowry, while Safdar Jang organized celebrations and illuminations rumoured to have cost 46 lakh rupees, the most ever spent on a Mughal wedding. The wealth and power that Bahu Begum§ and Nawab Begum, two high-born Shia Persian women with connections to the Mughal court, would bring with them would substantially influence the fate of Awadh and its nawabs in the years to come.

In 1748, as Nizam-ul-Mulk,¶ Safdar Jang's great rival, lay dying at Burhanpur, he had written a letter to his old enemy: 'You are now the most promising of the children of these days. Take that office (wazir) upon yourself and exert yourself in recovering the affairs of the Empire and bringing them to some order.' And so it was that a

---

*Her brother was the nobleman Mirza Muhammad, later given the title Najm-ud-Daula.
†Bahu Begum's brothers would gain prominence at the Awadh court and, in addition, Safdar Jang took into his service the husbands of his brothers' daughters. Nikah marriages were thus used to strengthen and grow alliances at the Awadh court.
‡A Turki word to denote the ceremony during which gifts, especially wedding clothes, were sent from the bridegroom to the bride's home, along with sugar and dried nuts.
§Bahu Begum was also given a jagir consisting of a number of parganas with yearly revenue of 9 lakh rupees.
¶Nizam-ul-Mulk had been given the title Asaf Jah, and he carved out the state of Hyderabad from the Mughal Deccan. His descendants would be known as the nizams of Hyderabad, once the capital was moved from Aurangabad to Hyderabad after 1763.

few days later, but out of respect only once Nizam-ul-Mulk had died, Safdar Jang accepted a khillat consisting of seven pieces of clothing, four plates glittering with gems and jewels, and finally assumed the title of wazir of the empire. As he wore the intricately woven robes of honour and stepped into the durbar of the Delhi palace, all the noblemen bowed to salute him as the long, fulsome list of his titles was read out.* The emperor who conferred these honours on him was not Muhammad Shah, who had also recently died, but the son of his favourite concubine Udham Bai now styled Qudsiya Begum. This new emperor, Ahmad Shah, was described rather tartly by Ghulam Hussain as a man 'full of levity, and (who) carried a head without brains' while another historian sighed that he 'was not a man of great intellect (for) all the period of his youth...had been spent in the harem.' And it was into the tentative hands of Ahmad Shah that the fate of the already fragile Mughal empire now fell.

As for Safdar Jang, he found that the wazirat that he had so longed for no longer held the lustre it once did. There were factions at court that opposed him, the most obdurate of whom was Queen Mother Qudsiya Begum's fifty-year-old illiterate khwajasara, Javed Khan. Contemporary historians are fairly breathless in their description of the hold Javed Khan had over Qudsiya Begum and her son. 'Javed Khan', thundered the author of the *Tarikh-i Ahmad Shah,* 'who had in the days of the former sovereign carried on a secret intimacy with Ahmad Shah's mother, who was originally a dancing girl, now openly governed the realm in concert with her, and contrary to the custom of all harems, where no male domestics are allowed at night,† he always remained in the women's apartments all night.' That the noblemen of the time deeply resented the influence of a courtesan and her eunuch is clear, but the times had changed in Mughal India in the eighteenth century. No longer would it be possible for elite princesses to exercise the power their earlier sisters had. In the scrappy, hardscrabble, and

---

*Principal of the Kingdom, Centre of all Business, Hero of the Age, Trustworthy of all the Provinces of the Empire, The Father of Victory, The Hercules in Battles, and the Generalissimo of the Imperial Forces.
†This is a curious accusation. Khwajasaras not being considered sexually male were in fact, often allowed into the women's inner apartments. We will later encounter just such a situation with Bahu Begum in Faizabad, in which her most respected khwajasara, Jawahar Ali Khan, considered it his honour and privilege to sleep at night in his mistress' quarters.

constantly shifting sands of a new age, it was the courtesans, cultured and sophisticated in the arts of manipulating men, who would claim the greater glory.*

What is incontestable is that Javed Khan, endlessly greedy, with his unreasonable influence over the emperor and his mother, hustled to gather power to himself and it was not long before the khwajasara and the wazir clashed. In one instance, when Safdar Jang was away from Delhi, Javed Khan spread rumours about the wazir's death and plotted to take over his establishment and property at the Dara Shukoh haveli near Kashmiri Gate. It was Safdar Jang's wife, Sadr-un-Nisa Begum, 'a woman of uncommon genius and courage' who refused to be dismayed by the rumours and instead rallied her son and dependents, organized 10,000 troops, and prepared for the defence of her home and honour with enormous temerity.† When Safdar Jang reached Delhi, he wrote angrily to Qudsiya Begum and Javed Khan that even dead, his body was worth more than another man's living one. But the breach was now irreparable between the wazir and the imperial family and in a politically disastrous move, Safdar Jang had the khwajasara murdered in 1752. His dismembered head was thrown down from Dara Shukoh's mansion into the midst of the khwajasara's wailing attendants who ran away screaming in horror.

The murder of the infuriating but essentially self-serving and politically isolated khwajasara only exacerbated Safdar Jang's problems at court because it allowed the rise of far more vicious and powerful enemies.‡ Safdar Jang now found himself dangerously exposed at the Mughal court, with nobles who resented his actions as self-aggrandizement and with the imperial family now irrevocably set against him. Indeed by scheming so openly to increase his lands and revenues at the expense of powerful factions, he alienated both the Turani nobles and the Rohilla and Bangash Afghans of Hindustan. The Turani nobles also accused Safdar Jang of favouring Hindu officials at

---

*The examples of Udham Bai, Mahlaqa Bai Chanda, Begum Sombre, amongst others, is telling.
†The great mansions of the elite at Shahjahanabad were built to be self-sufficient and defended. They had high, encircling walls, guarded gates often equipped with cannon, and huge interlocking courtyards which could house all the military, equipment, and provisions required to defend itself.
‡The two most dangerous were Intizam-ud-Daula, the head of the Turani faction, and Imad-ul-Mulk, grandson of Nizam-ul-Mulk.

court, as, for example, his vakil at the Mughal court, Raja Lakshmi Narayan. For the Turani faction, fiercely proud of their Central Asian lineages, this was entirely unacceptable.

In the end, however, Safdar Jang was bundled out of Delhi not by any grizzled Mughal warlord, or some unctuous nobleman, but a woman. 'Every business was transacted by (Qudsiya Begum)', noted a historian about the Begum's power. 'All the high officers used to sit down before her audience chamber and she would discuss affairs with them from behind a screen.' One day, finding the guns of the Qila-e-Mualla ominously facing the direction of his haveli, Safdar Jang decided this was an insult he could no longer accept. On a cold, wet day in March 1753, Safdar Jang left the Dara Shukoh haveli on his elephant, leaving the Qila forever. Reaching the Lahori gate of the Qila-e-Mualla, Safdar Jang dismounted from his elephant, turned in the direction of the Diwan-e-khas, and bowed low to the emperor, hidden from sight, as the rain settled like pearls on his robes and his black beard, and wet his face like tears*.

For a few weeks after leaving Shahjahanbad, Safdar Jang roamed the warren of streets outside the fort, wracked by indecision over his next course of action, and waiting for a summons from the emperor which never came. Loath to leave the capital entirely, but baulking at the idea of outright aggression against the Mughal emperor himself, Safdar Jang frittered away the advantage of a large force. This long prevarication also allowed the imperial party to win over the support of the Maratha forces camped at Delhi, promising them the nawab's rich provinces. Finally, Safdar Jang called for his ally, Surajmal Jat,† to come to his assistance. By then, however, a veritable fury of mercenaries and rebels had joined their forces to that of the imperial army.‡ And the most implacable of Safdar Jang's enemies in Delhi was a talented and charming but murderously ambitious teenager whose fortunes he

---

*The fact that the begum was able to give orders to train the Qila's cannons upon Safdar Jang's haveli point to the possibility that the wazir would have been staying at this time at his home in Dara Shukoh's haveli, adjacent to the Qila, rather than at his haveli near Lahori Darwaza, which would have been too far away to the north-west to be visible from the Qila-e-Mualla.
†Jat power reached its apogee with Surajmal Jat, who brought together the different tribes and established an administrative structure that encompassed the subahs of Agra, Meerut, and Aligarh. After his death in 1763, Jat power slowly faded.
‡For details of what became a civil war, see *Ashirbadi Lal Srivastava, The First Two Nawabs of Awadh*, New Delhi: Life Span Publishers and Distributors, 2022, pp. 207–34.

had once bolstered. 'Imad-ul-Mulk', admitted French officer Jean Law de Lauriston, 'combined the most subtle intelligence to a charming appearance'. Law de Lauriston further claimed that this was a double betrayal for the nawab because Safdar Jang 'had regarded him as his own son...and had never imagined that he nursed a serpent at the breast.' For six months in 1753 Safdar Jang and Imad-ul-Mulk, the seventeen-year-old grandson of Nizam-ul-Mulk, fought for the streets of Delhi* as battles raged between factions in Delhi and the Feroz Shah Kotla neighbourhood which Safdar Jang controlled. Law de Lauriston described the carnage:

> Imad ul Mulk needed allies and using his natural talents, with which he had gained the trust of the Badshah, he brought over the Marathas to whom he was willing to sacrifice his honour, his benefactor, and even his country. In no time at all, a furious war broke out which destroyed Delhi and its suburbs.

The greatest loss for Safdar Jang personally was the death of his old Gossain† warlord, Rajendra Giri. This Hindu Naga had a most eccentric and terrifying style of fighting, leaping into the fray naked with his long, matted hair twisting down his back whenever 'the lust of battle fired his blood', followed by his chaotic Naga troops, with no previous intimation or coordination with other generals. So often had he survived these deadly skirmishes 'that a notion prevailed that he had some piece of witchcraft about his body, or some talisman about his person.' But at last a musket ball found its mark and this fearsome warrior lay dead. After the death of Rajendra Giri 'Safdar Jang became heart-broken and never went personally into battle again' wrote the anonymous writer of the *Tarikh-i Ahmad Shah*. The worst sufferers of this bloody civil war, however, were the beleaguered citizens of

---

*Delhi at this time, and in this book, refers to Shahjahanabad, today known as Old Delhi. Built by emperor Shah Jahan in the mid-seventeenth century, it was a planned city, and remains the only living Mughal city still largely extant in its original form. Large parts of Shahjahanabad were destroyed by the British post 1857, and then it was upstaged as a centre of power when the British shifted their capital from Calcutta to Delhi in 1911, and built a 'New Delhi', today sometimes known as Lutyens' Delhi, from which to rule India.

†Gossains were Dasnami Shaivites, one of the largest groups of orthodox Indian sadhus. Warrior ascetics like the Gossains were a unique feature of pre-colonial warfare in India. They were held together by personal loyalty to their leader, fighting for mercenary reasons and personal display rather than well-articulated political goals.

Delhi. Both the Jat supporters of Safdar Jang and the Maratha allies of the imperial forces plundered, looted, and destroyed with an almost insatiable hunger. So thorough was the Jat destruction of the poorer sections of the city that the term Jat gardi (Jat affliction), entered the Urdu vocabulary. For the objective of this bizarre and senseless battle was not land or power, but the ability to own and control the symbols of Mughal legitimacy, and the Mughal emperor himself. After six months of ruinous yet indecisive carnage, both sides lost the will to fight and Safdar Jang broke up his war camp and marched away to Awadh.

Even cast out of the Mughal capital, Safdar Jang was far from homeless, however, unlike Imad-ul-Mulk who had no other fiefdom. Safdar Jang had been carefully managing his subedari of Awadh in the past few years* and had been keeping the revenues of his prosperous lands instead of sending tax revenues to Delhi.† He had also obtained the title of Shuja-ud-Daula for his son Jalaluddin, and the subedari of Awadh had now become clearly hereditary. He may have lost the title of wazir, but he had already extracted all the use he could make of that jaded old Mughal symbol. The nawab now returned to his base at Awadh, where a new order had proclaimed itself. No longer would the nawabs put the interests of the Mughal emperor above and beyond all personal considerations. Instead, these new kingmakers were ready to claim their destiny and shine with the light of their newly forged ambitions.

---

*The nawab had added the contiguous subedari of Allahabad to his domains, and had annexed the territory around Farrukhabad from Ahmad Khan Bangash.
†Other leaders who were also taking steps to shed their obligations to the Mughal empire were Nizam-ul-Mulk and his descendants in Hyderabad, Alivardi Khan in Bengal, and the Marathas in a swathe from Gujarat to Orissa.

# SHUJA-UD-DAULA, WARRIOR KING, AND NAWAB BEGUM

No sooner had the young Shuja become nawab of Awadh upon the unexpected death* of his father in 1754 than he committed a crime so offensive to the people of Awadh that he was almost deposed the very same year. And yet it had been a gilded start for the twenty-two-year-old nawab, confirmed immediately in his position as subedar of Awadh and Allahabad, with a complete acquiescence by the emperor to the fact that this was now a hereditary title†. Having confirmed his father's officers in their posts, the tall, strapping Shuja then turned to the decidedly more frivolous pastimes of kite-flying and pigeon-flying. One day, infatuated with a Hindu Khatri woman whose beauty he had glimpsed, Shuja had her abducted from her house by his Naga soldiers, Umrao Giri and Anoop Giri, and brought to his palace in Faizabad. By the time the young woman was sent back to her house early the next morning, there was clamorous pandemonium in the town. The relatives of the young woman marched to the home of the diwan of Awadh, Ram Narayan, where they laid their turbans at his feet in humiliation and grief. By now thousands of Khatri townsfolk had gathered, dangerous in their simmering anger. Ram Narayan and his brother, Jagat Narayan, decided to walk to the home of Ismail Khan, commander of the nawab's forces. Behind them trailed a mob, their bare feet and the turbans in their hands proclaiming their outrage to the hushed, watching townsfolk.

When Shuja angrily refused to hand over his Naga chieftains for retribution, some of the Mughal commanders decided to quietly send for Mohammad Quli Khan,‡ the nawab's cousin, from Allahabad and proclaim him subedar instead. This was a precarious moment for Shuja. For the previous nawabs, successful political integration had meant

---

*Safdar Jang died in October 1754 of a tumorous wound on his leg which did not heal and became gangrenous.
†The emperor sent him a handwritten note accompanied by the customary robes of honour and Shuja-ud-Daula became the third nawab of Awadh.
‡Muhammad Quli Khan was the son of Safdar Jang's elder brother, Mirza Mohsin. His step-mother was Khadija Begum, Najaf Khan's elder sister. Muhammad Quli Khan was thus both Shuja-ud-Daula's first cousin, and Najaf Khan's nephew.

employing dominant Rajput zamindars, as well as Muslim and non-Rajput Hindu elite in their armies and in their administration and Shuja had catastrophically stumbled from this delicate balance.

But just as the suddenly hopeful Mohammad Quli Khan had jumped onto his horse with great alacrity heading towards Faizabad, the fevered uproar over her son's high-handed and scandalous behaviour had reached the zenana and Nawab Begum was furious. She immediately gave orders for Ram Narayan to be brought to the zenana mahal and, from behind a screen, she used the full force of her stature as daughter of the great Saadat Khan Burhan-ul-Mulk himself. She demanded from Ram Narayan the recognition and loyalty that was owed to the son of Safdar Jang, the rightful ruler of Awadh. She reminded Ram Narayan of all that Safdar Jang had done for him, and for the other officers, and bitterly complained that they had connived together to steal Shuja's inheritance from him and had created such a furore over a complaint by an inconsequential Hindu. Considerably chastened, Ram Narayan promised to handle the matter with the complainant, and asked Nawab Begum to also speak to the Mughal officers so as to contain a potentially volatile situation. Nawab Begum called for the Mughal officers and reminded them harshly of the duty of loyalty towards 'him whose salt they had eaten', gave them suitable presents, and thus won over these proud, fearsome soldiers. Mohammad Quli Khan unexpectedly found himself in the awkward position of pretending to arrive in Faizabad simply to visit Shuja while the young nawab, tight-lipped, went along with the charade and accepted his cousin's offering of nazr.

This incident would have been quite a lesson in diplomacy and propriety for Shuja. He learnt that there would be no question of him behaving like a rapacious despot and there were lines that could not be crossed and his own Mughal officers would not tolerate the blurring of those lines. He would have appreciated also the forthright, courageous manner with which his mother had claimed the right to intercede and the ballast of these claims she was able to articulate, as the daughter and wife of nawabs who had not faltered in their duty to their people.

Nawab Begum had once reacted in a very different manner when Shuja had been embroiled in a similar situation. Almost ten years prior, as a young teenager, Shuja had been caught in an almost farcical manner, halfway up a ladder to a young girl's window in Benaras. When asked by the kotwal of the town about what was to be done with the illustrious miscreant, Safdar Jang and Nawab Begum were furious and gave orders that their only son and heir was to be treated like a common criminal. Beaten and starved, Shuja was brought before his father a week later. Safdar Jang continued with the game of chess he was engrossed in, glanced up to see his son cowering before him in his filthy clothes, humiliated in front of a group of elite noblemen, and raised an eyebrow to say: 'So, huzoor, it is you', before calmly returning to his game and sending the boy back to prison. The punishment continued for six months and finally Nawab Begum and the entire court had to plead his cause before Safdar Jang would allow his son to be reinstated.

It is easy to imagine the abject humiliation and ignominy of the situation. Safdar Jang in his immaculate and perfumed jama, the disregard of his cold fury, and Shuja in his stinking and soiled clothes bowing to his father while the noblemen looked on in baffled embarrassment. Perhaps Shuja's trespass when he became nawab was an angrily deliberate violation of his father's legacy, the reaction of a boy who had once been powerless. For Safdar Jang was a famously temperate man, who only had one wife at a time when having several wives was a sign of affluence and prestige among the elite. Indeed, his reputation for sobriety was such that Safdar Jang was said to be unique for being a man 'whose private life was marked by a high standard of morality, extremely rare in the class in which he belonged to and in the age in which he lived.' During the earlier incident, Nawab Begum had been just as implacable as her husband in her determination to punish her son but now, in 1755, the stakes had changed entirely. Now it was the nawab of Awadh whose power was threatened, just when the sudden death of Safdar Jang had exposed the fragile fault lines upon which loyalties were carefully balanced.

Shuja was thus initially loath to get involved in the administration of Awadh after his deeply embarrassing debacle in 1755. Law de Lauriston describes the conundrum he found himself in at this point in his career:

> The reasonable thing for Shuja-ud-Daula was to curtail any expansive plans so as to recover from the huge losses incurred by his father during his last war. He saw himself condemned to a quiet life which did not suit his fiery temperament. And so he left

all the day to day affairs to the begum, his mother, who, helped by a few faithful ministers, carried out these essential duties. The nawab was only interested in entertaining himself, in hunting, and in extremely demanding physical exercise.

As for Shuja himself, it appears that whatever contrary urges he may have harboured towards the memory of his father, he realized very quickly that he would only end up destroying himself. Modave described the nawab he knew, a couple of decades later, as the veritable model of equanimity:

> He was of a kind and generous nature. I have been told that he has never lost his temper, and has never used the sort of obscene language that is so very common among the elite in this country. His style of ruling was no doubt tainted by the prejudices of his religion and his country, but these were balanced by a great love of order and justice.

Nawab Begum continued to guide the affairs of her son in these early years, whenever she felt the irrepressible nawab slide back into his old habits, especially his love of beautiful courtesans. In 1757, the Maratha envoy at the nawab's court, admitted that the Nawab Begum tried to persuade Shuja to dismiss thirty of his courtesans from his service, but he refused to part with four or five of them whom he then took on as wives or concubines.

But even at this early stage, Shuja could not long afford to ignore his duty as there were constant dangers to the integrity of the territory of Awadh. These were years during which, throughout Hindustan, groups and factions postured, jostled, and threatened, made alliances and then unmade them, as they all scrambled to take advantage of crumbling Mughal power and local opportunities. And so Shuja quickly learnt to control his tempestuous nature and direct his energies towards subduing these many threats. He parlayed with the raja of Benaras, Balwant Singh, expertly skirmished with the Afghan Rohillas and kept diplomatic channels open with the Marathas. And then one day in 1759 the most famous individual in the country arrived in Awadh seeking refuge, the emperor of Hindustan himself.

After Safdar Jang left Delhi for the last time in 1753, the city had entered a dark season of chaos and terror. Plunderers from different factions roamed the streets, seizing whatever goods they could, while in the Qila, the Mughal family lived in an atmosphere of increasing penury and fear as revenues to the court dried up completely. Finally, on a hot night in June, in that moment of quickening just before dawn, Imad-ul-Mulk walked into the palace with his Maratha allies. They swaggered into the salatin quarters* where all the sons and grandsons of the former emperors lived lives of genteel squalor and brought out a grandson of Bahadur Shah I and crowned him Alamgir II, the new emperor of Hindustan. The hapless Ahmad Shah and his mother, Qudsiya Begum, were found cowering behind some trees in the gardens of the Khaas Mahal, from where they were dragged out and thrown into prison, united in the final unravelling of their unlikely destinies. With Alamgir II, utterly controlled by the increasingly volatile and unpredictable Imad-ul-Mulk and the Mughal treasury empty,† the fate of the once-glorious Mughal empire was as fragile as the morning dew.

There were several powerful factions swirling around the court of Delhi, eager to control the Mughal emperor, a terribly diminished but enduring symbol of Mughal legitimacy. And Imad-ul-Mulk wanted to try and control this symbol himself, while containing and directing the energies of these many clashing forces. The two most fearsome forces eddying around the region of Delhi at this time, however, were the Marathas and the Afghans. The Marathas had by now roamed far from their Deccan homeland to plunder and then control large areas in the plains of Hindustan. Their forces had also mutated from the light, mobile guerrilla units of their earlier incarnation to become, by the 1750s, huge lumbering armies 40,000 strong with trains of baggage and artillery. Indeed, by the late 1750s, the Marathas had reached the very apogee of their power in India.

The Afghans, however, challenged Maratha hegemony in North India and would pose a regular and violent menace to the region

---

*The extended members of the Mughal family were kept by this time in an informal sort of 'house arrest' in the Red Fort since they were considered too dangerous to be allowed to roam freely and potentially pose a challenge to the ruler. They could socialize and even leave their quarters during the day, returning at night. From the late eighteenth century onwards, they would be kept in much stricter confinement.
†From 1707 to 1720, the treasury at Agra dropped from 90 million rupees to just over 10 million rupees. By the time of Muhammad Shah's death in 1748, even Bengal, the only revenue for a few decades to send money, had stopped sending revenue to the court. See Eaton, *India in the Persianate Age*.

after Nadir Shah's bloody example in 1739. The Mughals had ceded territory in North India to Nadir Shah and the Afghans would claim these territories as legitimately theirs to extract revenue from. Though Nadir Shah himself would not survive for very long in Persia and was murdered by his own Qizilbash soldiers in 1747, he had an equally ferocious successor. And Ahmad Shah Abdali* also considered the lands in the Punjab, west of the Indus, legitimately his to control, just as Nadir Shah had done. It was in pursuit of the revenues from these frequently troublesome lands that Abdali then mounted almost yearly excursions into these territories. In 1756, annoyed by constantly shifting loyalties among various governors, he marched up to Delhi itself, had coins struck in his name and married a daughter of the deceased emperor, Mohammad Shah, took a daughter of the reigning emperor Alamgir II, as a wife for his son Timur, before reinstating the unhappy Mughal emperor upon the takht of Delhi and returning to Afghanistan. The Afghans were thus another powerful force contending for control of the Mughal emperor. Their natural allies in Hindustan were their clansmen, Rohilla and Bangash ethnic Afghans who had acquired vast tracts of land in northern India along the horse trade routes which they had established over many years, and where they had founded Rohilkhand in the eighteenth century.

A poet of Delhi, Mir Taqi Mir, captured the bemusement of the people of Delhi, benumbed spectators to the constant chaos in their city and the bewildering succession of emperors and their allies.

> Every day there is a new master of the world
> Is power a beggar, going from door to door?

Meanwhile, in the Qila-e-Mualla in Delhi in 1758, Emperor Alamgir II decided to send his son and heir, Ali Gauhar, far away from the murderous intrigues of the court and the unlovely care of Imad-ul-Mulk. Ghulam Hussain describes the poignant scene that took place as the young prince left the Qila, which had once been his jail, and to which he would return only after a long, arduous separation of thirteen years. His mother, Zeenat Mahal, accompanied him to the

---

*Ahmad Shah took the title Shah Durr-i-Durran (Pearl of Pearls) and changed the name of his Abdali tribe (a confederation of Afghans) to 'Durrani', after himself. He is referred to as the father of modern Afghanistan.

door of the zenana where she entrusted him into the care of historian Ghulam Hussain's father, weeping as she put her son's hand in the nobleman's, and implored him with all the force of the grief and misery in her heart to look after the gentle prince. Hidayat Ali Khan was so shaken by the entreaties of the sobbing queen that he 'was overcome by such an unexpected scene, and from that moment resolved firmly to support him with all the vigour and fidelity in his power'.

The soft-spoken, sensitive Ali Gauhar had only recently been released from the salatin quarters on a whim by Imad-ul-Mulk after he had deposed Emperor Ahmad Shah and replaced him with Alamgir II. For almost the duration of the prince's first twenty-five years, he had lived in the suffocating, cloistered quarters in which all the princes of royal blood, uncles, nephews etc. were confined. Modave has described these miserable habitations which he visited a few years later:

> These unfortunate victims of a stupid and unhealthy tradition which wants them to be locked up in a quarter of the fort which has recently been given over to this sad purpose. Here they live a deplorable life and most of them die of poverty and stupefaction. They are given a stipend for their food, which the emperor decides upon... They are allotted just one room, a kitchen, and a few tiny hutments in which they are very crowded. The door to the quarters is guarded by sepoys, who answer to a khwajasara who reports to the Padshah himself.

So it was from this stifling prison that Ali Gauhar was first released, and then escaped entirely in May 1758 as he hurried out of Delhi with just a few hundred followers, evading the fury of Imad-ul-Mulk. For the next few years, Ali Gauhar wandered the land, desperately seeking resources and allies. He finally reached Awadh in early 1759 where Shuja marched out of Lucknow to receive his royal visitor, to whom he presented 101 gold coins, palanquins, elephants, seven horses, a trayful of jewels, weapons, tents, vessels of gold and silver and ten wagons. Despite the respectful reception, Shuja was leery about committing himself in any substantial way to the itinerant prince's cause. Many local chieftains had a similar reaction—outwardly deferential but, in effect, serving only themselves. In December 1759, the unstable and murderous Imad-ul-Mulk assassinated Alamgir II in Delhi, suspecting him of being too malleable by the Afghans, and placed yet another hapless salatin prince on the throne. But Ali Gauhar, still in exile, proclaimed himself the rightful emperor and took the title Shah Alam II. Orphaned and reduced to pitiable means, Shah Alam was now eager to recover the rich province of Bengal and Bihar, which the EIC had recently seized themselves, after deposing the nawab of Bengal, Siraj-ud-Daula.* After an ultimately unsuccessful incursion into Bihar and Patna by Shah Alam, ominous news arrived that the king of Afghanistan, Ahmad Shah Durrani, was back in Hindustan.

By the 1750s, the Martha forces had realized that the greatest threat to Hindustan was not the Mughal empire after all, whose power and legitimacy they continued to quietly subvert, but the Afghans under Ahmad Shah Durrani and their control of the Punjab territories. In the late 1750s, therefore, the Marathas seized control of territories in the Punjab, and the reaction from Ahmad Shah Durrani was immediate. But before these two fierce adversaries would meet at the Battle of Panipat, there was one nobleman whom both sides were desperate to win over to their cause—Shuja-ud-Daula of Awadh.

Shuja was in a uniquely powerful position at this time. Still only twenty-nine years old, he ruled over the most extensive and fertile lands in the country, apart from Bengal. His army was widely considered the best in the country, with its Qizilbash regiments from Nadir Shah's army, his terrifying Naga Gossains, part warriors part alchemists, his excellent European artillery, the enormous financial resources of his subahs, and the reputation of his own charismatic personal valour. The Marathas pleaded their cause by reminding the nawab of his duty to the Mughal empire against the greedy foreign invaders, the hereditary connection between the nawab's family and the Marathas, as well as through assurances of great gains for the nawab himself. Ahmad Shah Durrani, meanwhile reminded Shuja of the terrible threat posed by the Marathas, and then sent an extraordinary envoy to Awadh in the form of the revered widow of Emperor Muhammad Shah—Malika Zamani.

---

*When the EIC began strengthening Fort Williams in Calcutta, as part of the ongoing global hostilities against the French during the Seven Years' War, Siraj-ud-Daula considered this an act of hostility and seized the fort from the British. Robert Clive not only seized Calcutta back from the nawab, but also captured French Chandernagore and then, urged on by the powerful brokers, the Jagat Seths, attacked and defeated the forces of Siraj-ud-Daula at the Battle of Plassey in 1757.

When even this elderly widow could not persuade Shuja, the Afghans sent their most talented ambassador, the Rohilla chieftain Najib-ud-Daula*. This supremely sophisticated and subtle man spent days with the nawab, carefully defusing every objection Shuja could think of till, finally, in an ultimate act of gallant bravado, he placed the nawab's sword upon his own neck, declaring he would die as a pledge for the nawab's safety. Invigorated by this swashbuckling gesture, Shuja agreed to march to the Durrani camp. He first sent his family to Lucknow, appointed Mirza Amani,† his eldest son, in charge of Awadh and Raja Beni Bahadur as adviser, and left for Anupshahar‡ with 10,000 cavalry.

When Shuja arrived at the Afghan camp and strode into the Durrani's tent, he was greeted and embraced by Timur Shah, the Afghan king's son. An avuncular-looking man, imposing and round-cheeked with a short black beard peppered with grey, Ahmad Shah Durrani himself remained reclining. Perhaps this subtle but sure sign of diplomatic posturing rankled with the prickly young nawab, for at the end of this visit he brusquely asked for permission to have his naubat (orchestra) and drums play their music in the Durrani camp. When Ahmad Shah Durrani objected mildly, pointing out that this was most irregular, the tall nawab spun around to say 'it may be so for other music, but mine is the gift of the emperor of Hindustan, and not of your Majesty's; nor am I your subject, but only your hearty well-wisher.' Perhaps silently wondering if his noble ally was worth all this trouble, Ahmad Shah nonetheless graciously agreed and Shuja's drums and music would strike up a tune the minute the Afghans had finished their own music.

It appears that Shuja was never entirely comfortable while at the Durrani camp and almost seemed to go out of his way to provoke the Afghans and proclaim his own sense of independence. Barely a month after his arrival, Shuja and his followers were found showily participating in a Muharram§ procession. In August 1760, the mournful procession of the nawab and his followers, all dressed in long black

---

*Najib-ud-Daula, sometimes known as Najib Khan, was a noted Rohilla chieftain who founded Najibabad in Bijnor district where he carried out many architectural commissions.
†The future Asaf-ud-Daula.
‡In modern-day Uttar Pradesh, 170 km from Delhi.
§A commemoration of the Battle of Karbala and the death of the Prophet's grandson Hussain, observed by Shia Muslims.

robes, barefoot and bare-headed, passed noisily in front of the Afghan king's tents, all the while proclaiming their grief with loud, piercing shouts and wails, thumping their chests. The Sunni Durrani soldiers, quite unsurprisingly, found this a gratuitous provocation and proposed beating up their allies, but Ahmad Shah hastily controlled them. A few months later, at the Battle of Panipat, Ahmad Shah was shocked to see the nawab's infamous Naga troops. The Afghan king was so horrified by the sight of these naked, armed sadhus that he gave the nawab a lecture on 'the impropriety of unrestrained kafirs, naked in front and behind.... Parading and lounging in front of Muslims*,' and ordered them off the field before his own soldiers attacked them. Indeed, there was a great deal about the composition of Shuja's Hindustani forces that would have been disquieting for the Afghan king, who was claiming also to be leading a holy war against infidels. For two of the three top generals in the nawab's troops were Naga Gossains, his chief interlocutor with the Afghan king during the entire contest was a Marathi-speaking Brahmin, Kashiraj Shivdev, and his chief minister or diwan was the Brahmin, Raja Beni Bahadur.

The details of the Battle of Panipat† of January 1761 are well known. The Marathas under the command of Sadashivrao Bhau had captured Delhi, where Ahmad Shah Durrani besieged and starved them. Surajmal Jat, an ally of the Marathas, had already deserted the Marathas and returned to his own lands after he witnessed the plundering of the Qila-e-Mualla and Nizamuddin Auliya's tomb by the Marathas. 'They had stripped the (Diwan-e-Aam) of its wainscoting, which was of silver, elegantly enamelled,' wrote Ghulam Hussian, 'and had sent it to the mint.' They also stole the gold and silver vessels at the shrine of Nizamuddin Auliya and stripped Mohammad Shah's mausoleum of its gold and silver candelabras, lamps and other utensils, all melted down in the mint. In 1761, the Marathas finally broke out of the siege and arrived at Panipat to face the Afghans one final time. On the one hand were the Durrani Afghans, 40,000 strong, whose officers in heavy, glinting armour rode superb Khurasani horses while a contingent of

---

*Barnett in his translation of the Persian original intriguingly remarks that the original is so direct as to be untranslatable. See Jadunath Sarkar, *A History of Dasnami Naga Sanyasis*, India: P.A. Mahanirvani, 1959. It is translated as follows: 'how could the Kaffirs have so much liberty as to walk with their things and buttocks exposed before the Moslems.'
†The city of Panipat is 90 km north of Delhi.

2,000 camels carried two soldiers apiece, armed with swivel guns, called zamburaks, which formed 'the finest mobile artillery of that age in Asia'. Opposite them were the Marathas, 60,000 strong, but described by historian Jadunath Sarkar as 'a starving army mounted on sorry famished nags'. At this final battle at Panipat, the Maratha army was routed.*

After the battle, when the Durrani soldiers were dragging out survivors and massacring them, Shuja intervened to rescue 'eight thousand miserable Maratha refugees and four hundred of their officers' whom he sent with a strong escort to Surajmal's lands. Surajmal behaved with exemplary gallantry, handing out rations and hospitality to every Maratha refugee, some 50,000 men and women. Indeed Surajmal, 'a man of middle stature and of a robust frame, very black in complexion and very fat...with two extremely sparkling eyes' was an exceptionally competent ruler, described by a Jesuit as being 'prudent, politic, valiant and noble above his birth'.

Shuja was also very anxious to obtain the bodies of the fallen Maratha generals, so they could be cremated with honour according to the Hindu rites. This was a challenging task, for the Durranis 'very much wanted to stuff these officers' corpses for trophies'. The Durrani troops gathered in angry, blood-smeared mobs and Shuja appealed to the Afghan king for the corpses to be released. He explained to the king that it was an ancient, sacred custom for defeated enemies to be handed over to their families and anything else would bring grave dishonour upon the victors. He added that it would be difficult for himself and his allies, 'the permanent Muslim residents of India who had to deal with the Hindus all through their lives', if they were to be dishonoured in such a heinous way. Finally Shuja was able to recover the bodies of Viswas Rao and Sadashiva Bhau and a few other officers, which were entrusted to Anoop Giri and Kashiraj for the Hindu last rites.

On 24 January 1761, Ahmad Shah and Shuja triumphantly entered Delhi. The Afghan king confirmed Shah Alam II as Mughal Badshah, but as he was still away in Bengal at this time, his twelve-year-old son, Mirza Jawan Bakht, was appointed emperor in lieu. The Afghan

---

*Mahadaji Scindia, a Maratha leader whom we will encounter later, was wounded in this battle and would hereon walk with a limp.

ambassador, Najib-ud-Daula, was left in charge of court affairs at Delhi, where he would control the Mughal emperor and the Delhi court for the next ten years. In the tumult of the Durrani soldiers plundering the city of Delhi, many families fled their once green and cultured city, seeking the safety of Lucknow or Faizabad. 'Thousands of wretches, in the midst of that raging fire, scarred their hearts with the mark of exile,' wrote Delhi poet Mir about the carnage, 'and ran off into the wilderness and like lamps at dawn, died in the cold air... It was a reign of tyrants.'

One such family was the Indo-Portuguese Velho clan, with its hereditary connection to the Mughal court. When Sebastian Velho, patriarch of the family, was murdered by Durrani soldiers, his widow and her daughter fled to Faizabad, where Shuja would give them shelter and a pension till the end of his life. Many others—artists, singers, poets*, merchants, courtesans, and more—would follow suit, carrying on the exodus that had begun decades ago. It was at around this time that some of the famous names from Mohammad Shah Rangeeley's atelier moved to Awadh. Nidha Mal, Hunhar, Faqirullah Khan, Mir Kalan Khan, Chitarman, and others would bring their classical Mughal miniature training away from the chaos of Delhi and transform it in the cauldron of Awadh's cultural renaissance.

As for Shuja, after finding out he was not to be given the wazirat he had been promised, and having been involved in some desultory skirmishes with the Durrani soldiers, he packed his camp and abruptly departed for Awadh early in March 1761 without formally informing the Afghan king. After a short stay at Lucknow Shuja would join the emperor near Bengal where, despite the lack of the wazirat, he would have been well satisfied. He had emerged from the Battle of Panipat as the one Hindustani leader of the greatest consequence, whom every other faction hankered to have on their side. He had steadfastly maintained the illusion of only ever acting for the Mughal emperor, covert about his true intentions. And the outcome of the battle was the most profitable for the nawab in the long run. It was never the Afghan king who was the real threat to autonomous powers in Hindustan, focused as the Afghan was on his Punjab territories where the Sikh

---

*The famous Delhi poets Mirza Muhammad Rafi Sauda, Mian Hasrat, and Ashraf Ali Khan moved to Faizabad at this time.

warriors would very soon escort him out of Hindustan altogether. It was the Maratha forces who posed the greatest threat, spreading out from the Deccan in violent waves, demanding the chauth, bringing devastation upon the local peasantry in their train. For Shuja, as for the British watching nervously from Bengal, the subjugation of the Maratha forces was the most desirable of all outcomes.

# A BATTLE AT BUXAR

From 1759 onwards, for the first time in the history of the Mughal empire, the emperor of Hindustan was homeless. At the very same time, the grasping 'firangis' were making themselves quite at home in Calcutta. As France and Britain began hostilities against each other in Europe over the War of the Austrian Succession (1740–48), the effects ricocheted through to their trade companies in India. The most audaciously aggressive player at this time was the brilliant French Governor General Joseph Dupleix who, in the 1740s, used French troops and French-trained Indian sepoys to fight local rulers and conquer territory for the French EIC for the first time on the Coromandel Coast. A moody and fractious young British EIC employee at Madras, Robert Clive, was so galvanized by these examples that when he was sent to Calcutta to deal with the nawab of Bengal Siraj-ud-Daula's aggressive new policies, he did a great deal more. So much more, in fact, that he would seize treasures that would make him the richest man in Europe, for which he would then be impeached on charges of corruption, eventually leading to his death by suicide. For Clive not only seized Calcutta back from the nawab but connived to overthrow the nawab altogether and installed a puppet nawab in his place. On 23 June 1757, at the Battle of Plassey, the elderly Mir Jafar was made nawab of Bengal by Clive, effectively transforming the EIC into the rulers of Bengal.

For the French EIC in Hindustan, the British had become a deadly menace. Their old enemy had gone from being a relatively insignificant player in the earlier part of the eighteenth century, when Portugal, France, and Spain had sprawling empires, to having something like a global empire by 1763. The Seven Years' War from 1756–1763 had been fought between Britain and France over their North American colonies, but by forcing France out of Quebec and conquering Canada, and depriving France of most of her Indian and West African possessions, and then driving Spain out of South America, Britain suddenly became a global force. Indeed, a scholar has called this war 'the most dramatically successful war the British ever fought'. Britain then intensified its efforts against the French in India, attacking and destroying French factories at Pondicherry and Chandernagore, which would lead to an exodus of French officers like René Madec, Law de Lauriston, and Jean-Baptiste Gentil, desperate to seek opportunities with local rulers and avenge themselves against 'perfidious Albion'.

While the cataclysmic changes of the Battle of Plassey were taking place in Bengal, in Delhi, the emperor of what had once been the most powerful empire in the world was struggling to gather men to his doomed cause. 'It is notorious,' bemoaned a historian,* 'that on the (Shahzaada's) coming out of Delhi, his circumstances were so distressful and his poverty so complete, that not one man of character would think of either assisting him or following his fortunes.' The refugee prince Ali Gauhar, now Shah Alam II after the murder of his father, was a desperate man. Having escaped the dangerous control of Imad-ul-Mulk and the Marathas in Delhi, the emperor now struggled to raise the forces he would need if ever he dreamed of returning to Delhi. The reaction of the governor of Bihar, Raja Ram Narain, to the emperor's presence in his territory in 1760, was an example of the troubling dissonance between the quasi divine aura the emperor of Hindustan was meant to carry and the utter ruination of his actual condition. Initially, when the governor had heard of the approaching imperial army 'he was overawed by the very name of an Emperor and intimidated by the fame of his Mogul troops.' When offering his nazr, 'he advanced with limbs trembling and lips dried up by fear.' But once he was admitted into the imperial presence, the ludicrously excessive deference demanded of him despite the sadly frayed condition of the Mughal party meant that 'he reflected in his mind, on that air of wretchedness and misery that pierced through all the flimsy gaudiness which was intended to disguise the Emperor's condition, and that of his famished courtiers...he wished himself gone, and out of the clutches of those famished vultures.' The young emperor even found himself insulted and mistreated by his own generals, as witnessed by Law de Lauriston. 'The various generals behaved towards him in the most dishonourable manner, not providing for the most basic needs for Shah Alam and his family, and even allowing him to be insulted by the Marathas.'

Law de Lauriston also tried to dissuade Shah Alam from what was clearly a futile attempt to invade Bengal, which the prince was anxious

---

*Ghulam Hussain.

to do after his initial escape from Delhi. The unfortunate young prince's answer was poignant in the self-awareness and humility he displayed: 'Alas! It is all the same for me. Wherever I go, I will only find pretenders, nawabs or rajas, now used to an independence which is too beguiling for them to abandon. And yet, I have no other means but them, unless Providence comes to my rescue. Moreover,' added the prince with unexpected gallantry, 'what face could I show if, at the moment of entering the battlefield, I should go away—my subjects would feel only contempt for me, in addition to their current indifference.'

Jean Law de Lauriston was a fairly flamboyant man himself, from an illustrious French family and ex-governor of one of the five French trading posts[*] in India—Chandernagore. The razing of Chandernagore by Robert Clive[†] in 1757 had made an errant fugitive of Law de Lauriston too, and he attached himself and his soldiers for some years to the train of the wandering emperor, determined to use his forces against his loathed British foes in whatever manner possible. While Law de Lauriston was with the imperial forces, he received disquieting news about the French loss at the Battle of Wandiwash (1760)[‡] and it only strengthened his resolve to march on with the emperor's troops because, as he wrote glumly in his memoirs, 'I was still serving my nation by engaging the British forces in Bengal which would otherwise be used against Pondicherry.' But Pondicherry was about to fall to the British too, and Law de Lauriston would bitterly regret not having joined Shuja's forces instead. For, with the fall of Pondicherry, France's power on the Coromandel Coast would now be severely curtailed.

Indeed Law de Lauriston,[§] was frustrated and appalled by the fact that Hindustani rulers and noblemen seemed to be blissfully ignorant of the threat posed by the British and their EIC:

---

[*]The others were Pondicherry, Mahe, Karaikal, and Yanam.
[†]Robert Clive began his career as a Writer in the EIC's civil service in Madras. He then joined the military as an ensign in 1747 despite no formal military training. By 1757 he was commanding the Company army. Chandernagore was the administrative centre of the French EIC. When hostilities broke out between France and Britain in Europe during the Seven Years' War, Clive bombarded and razed Chandernagore as a step towards driving the French out of Bengal entirely.
[‡]A battle between the French, under the Comte de Lally and the British, under Sir Eyre Coote. It was the decisive battle in the Anglo-French struggle in southern India during the Seven Years' War.
[§]Law de Lauriston was defeated alongside Shah Alam II at the Battle of Elsa in January 1761, imprisoned for a year in Bengal, then allowed to return to France in 1762.

> What surprised me the most when I was in Delhi was the absolute lack of knowledge about the English. I had thought that after the revolution that had taken place in Bengal, the city would have been abuzz about the English. There was indeed talk of the revolution, but the blame was put on the Jagat Seths, and Rae Doloram. They knew the name of Clive, a great captain, apparently, that the Jagat Seths had called for from far away, at great expense, to deliver Bengal from the tyranny of Siraj ud Daula, just like Salabat Jang had asked M de Bussy to keep the Marathas in check. Many notables even asked me what country he came from. Others think all Europeans are one, asking me if I was a deputy of Mr Clive. I tried to tell them that we were enemies, that the English were behind all that had happened in Bengal, more than what even the Seths would have wanted, that they were in fact ruling the government and not Mir Jaffar. They would start laughing. Indeed how to convince people who only know others like themselves, that a force of two or three thousand Europeans at the most, could direct affairs in a country as large as Bengal.

As for the simple village folk, who had never seen Europeans before, they wondered if they were a certain type of 'Musulmaun' and 'if so were we Arabs, Tartars, Pathans or Mughals?'

At the conclusion of the Seven Years' War, the Treaty of Paris was signed in 1763, effectively dividing up the world* all the way from Canada across to the Philippines, between Britain and France and their respective allies.† And yet, though France lost the Seven Years' War, it was in no way the end of her imperial ambitions. France's Indian factories were all re-instated‡ at the end of the war, and

---

*In more recent events, we can see the deadly results of another such arbitrary line: in 1916, the Great Powers Britain and France decided to divide up the Middle East, using Mark Sykes' appallingly flippant phrase suggesting a division of the map 'from the E of Acre to the K of Kirkuk', resulting in the infamous Sykes-Picot Agreement (1915), which has had repercussions to this day.

†In North America, Britain gained all French territory east of the Mississippi, while French territories west of the Mississippi became Spanish, along with the port of New Orleans. Britain was also ceded territory in Africa and India, and retained Cuba, while France would regain the commercially lucrative Caribbean islands of Martinique, Guadeloupe, and St Lucia. For the French, retaining the islands' enormously profitable sugar industry was much more attractive than vast territories in Canada.

‡France traded principally on 'luxury goods', of which cloths (calicos, Bengal silks, cottons,

her lucrative Caribbean islands restored. France's ambitions would mutate after the Treaty of Paris and French forces in India would now dedicate themselves to thwarting British power wherever they could. Many French officers and soldiers who escaped the destruction of Pondicherry and Chandernagore by the British found employment in the court of Indian rulers. For Jean-Baptiste Gentil and René Madec, the cauldron they found themselves in was Bengal. And this was how Gentil and Madec came to be at Buxar, surrounded by the glittering and cacophonous army of the nawab of Awadh in 1764, fighting with the Mughal army against the British. Driven out of the French trading posts, their covert and determined aim would be to block British ambitions and they gambled that the Mughal emperor's cause against the British in Bengal was their most likely chance for success.

When Nawab Mir Qasim* of Bengal was deposed by the British in December 1764, he had sought refuge with the itinerant Emperor Shah Alam II, himself sorely in need of a secure stronghold. And so it was that the two most venerated names in Hindustan found themselves appealing for help to Shuja. The nawab, wrote Modave, 'was a man of a great deal of intelligence and knew all that a man of his standing and education could know.' His deadly failure, realized Modave, as had Law de Lauriston earlier, was that he did not fully appreciate the threat posed by the British. 'All that he had heard about the Europeans,' wrote Modave: 'was through bazar gossip, all of which seemed to him to be monstrous exaggerations.

> His own great successes against noble enemies, his glorious role at the Battle of Panipat, an army of more than 80,000 men, whom he believed to be much stronger than they were in reality, and his own wealth which was considerable, all prevented him from seeing the English for what they were—redoubtable enemies. He disdainfully rejected Mir Qasim's advice on the way in which to fight against the English. He imagined that he would crush this band of foreign outlaws who were trying to dictate to him, at the very door of his capital city.

---

muslins) constituted 50%, the rest being spices, incense, tea, coffee, indigo, opium, saltpetre and other products.
*Mir Qasim would die in abject penury and obscurity, in 1777. According to Polier, his last shawl was sold to pay for his winding sheet.

It appears incontrovertible that Shuja, with his recent successes still flickering like a halo around him, having been courted by the king of the Afghans himself, felt complacently sure of himself at the thought of facing these inconsequential foreign pretenders. Indeed, the nawab had controlled his earlier tempestuous nature and forged a forceful new personality now tempered with intelligence and charm. 'Like all men of rank in Asia,' wrote civil servant George Forster, 'he was courteous and genial. He had a lot of skill, charm and polish. These qualities, along with a striking figure, put him at a great advantage in his dealings with foreign agents.' Ghulam Hussain, however, was predictably more critical. The nawab 'was so full of himself, and so proud to have fought by the side of the Abdali king, whom he had taken for his model,' wrote Ghulam Hussain bitterly, 'that whenever anyone made bold to propose any advice upon the mode of carrying on the war, he used to cut him short with a "do not trouble yourself about that; you shall fight as I shall bid you."' And indeed the nawab seems to have admired not only Ahmad Shah Durrani's forceful and peremptory style of command but also his sartorial sense, for it was whispered that the nawab preferred to appear at court wearing Persian-inspired clothes with a fur stole (image 1) and swinging a gorgeously worked battleaxe in his hand.

But if Shuja seemed not to understand British pretensions it was perhaps because the British themselves at this stage were thoroughly conflicted about their plan of action. Intense correspondence between different parties showed that the British were, on the one hand, morbidly suspicious of Shuja's aspirations but also intimidated by his strength. 'The Vizier crossed the karmnasa with the most formidable army that any nabob has commanded for many years,' admitted an EIC officer (Captain Archibald Swinton) while Ghulam Hussain also pointed out another discordant note—the fact that this British trading company was now raising arms against the legitimate Mughal emperor himself. 'The English themselves, affected by the shame and disgrace of fighting against the legitimate possessor of the throne, were desirous of some accommodation, provided it could be obtained without endangering their trade.' A further concern, real or imagined, would be the presence of French forces, scattered like debris throughout Hindustan, which the British would skilfully use to justify increasingly harsher measures against local rulers who employed French troops.

In Buxar, meanwhile, in October 1764, the battle seemed to be concluding rapidly in favour of Shuja's Mughal forces. 'I fancy that had but one or two thousand of the enemy's cavalry behaved as well as those few that attacked the Grenadiers,' wrote an EIC officer, 'we should have lost the day... The chance was more than once against us.' René Madec and his European troops fought with deadly accuracy and determined courage, 'and even though my troops were inferior to the English battalion' wrote Madec, 'we fought with such success that they were obliged to fall back in complete disorder upon the main battlefield, where the English were contemplating retreat.' The battle was a scrappy, bloody affair with the British losing a quarter of their troops. But in the end, despite some desperate skirmishes, the battle was lost just as it was being won by Shuja's forces. The main reason for the debacle of the imperial forces was that they were composed of so many different factions,[*] each with their own conflicting motives and loyalties, many also bought off or otherwise disarmed by the British. As for Ghulam Hussain, he singled out the French commanders for praise writing that 'the whole army of the Nawab was a heterogeneous crowd of men, animated by little loyalty either to the person of the Wazir or to the cause that they professed to serve, the only exceptions being the two French officers (Madec and Gentil) and their comrade Samru[†] and some Hindu and Indian Muslim (Shaikhazada) troops in the Nawab's service.' The Naga Gossains conducted themselves with their usual chaotic bravery and their leader, Anoop Gossain, was badly wounded.

Emperor Shah Alam himself was in communication with the British throughout the months leading up to Buxar. 'The (Shahzaada), who was sick of his dependence on Shuja-ud-Daula,' wrote Ghulam Hussain, 'as well as tired with his obstinacy and his airs of superiority, was desirous likewise to shake off the yoke that had insensibly slipped upon his neck.' The Mughal and Durrani troops, utterly mercenary, did the most damage to their own side by stopping to plunder retreating parties and sabotaging Shuja's forces as a result. Modave would later

---

*Only the nawab's cavalry—consisting of Qizilbashes, Persians, Turanis, and Gossains—was relatively well performing. The infantry, though huge in number, was ill-equipped and badly motivated as they were poorly paid, 10 or 12 rupees per month. Artillery was old-fashioned and lacked discipline.

†Austrian mercenary Walter Reinhardt also known as 'Sombre' or Samru.

rail that 'it is a truly unbelievable thing to see 3000 inferior English soldiers, lacking either discipline or military spirit, scattered along the two shores of the Ganga...commanding Hindustan.'

Shuja himself rallied what remained of his troops, including his Gossain chieftain, Anoop Giri, and sped away with René Madec, now effectively a refugee in his own lands. 'For a time,' wrote Madec sadly, 'he was sick with grief that he had lost the battle.' After a few desperate but futile engagements, Shuja retired to Lucknow with his remaining forces, including the Frenchmen Madec and Gentil. The nawab was particularly pleased with the Breton Madec, who had acquitted himself with exemplary courage, especially when compared to the shambolic efforts of his own Mughal and Durrani troops. He was also pointedly grateful to those who stood by him in trying times and bestowed upon Madec the honorific title 'Himmat Bahadur'. He increased Madec's pay to 20,000 rupees per month, and also persuaded him to get engaged to the daughter of one of his courtiers, a man named Augustin Barbette, from an old Indo-Portuguese family driven out of Delhi at the time of Nadir Shah's invasion. The daughter, a girl named Marie-Anne Barbette, was only twelve years old and the engagement was simply an alliance, and no doubt Shuja hoped that this would keep Madec close to him. As for the raffish Madec, he sheepishly admitted to having been 'blinded by the pomp and glory of the great station in life he had attained, but that he was now tired of his bachelor's existence and needed order in his life.' Finally Shuja heard the dreaded news that the British forces were marching towards Allahabad, and then on to Lucknow itself and, despair in his heart, he abandoned his provinces entirely. Thoroughly unnerved by a defeat he had thought inconceivable, when the British had tried to negotiate a peace settlement after the battle, the proud nawab had 'thought it derogatory to his dignity, and dishonourable to his name, family and pedigree'. Instead, he had tried for seven months after Buxar to broker alliances to raise an army,* determined to ride into battle again and railing furiously against the prospect of utter defeat. 'I was beyond consolation,' wrote a heartbroken Madec, 'to witness the utter ruination of a prince who had loved me so well, and who I had

---

*From the end of the Battle of Buxar in October 1764 till the summer of 1765, Shuja tried to forge alliances with the Rohillas, Najib-ud-Daula and Malhar Rao Holkar, refusing to accept the prospect of defeat.

hoped to use to recover what my country had lost to the English in Bengal,' he added with pragmatic candour. But Madec was leery about the chances of success for the nawab's army for 'troops who have once been beaten over here', he wrote, 'lose hope entirely.' To ensure the nawab's entire humiliation, Carnac marched a force into Faizabad, tore down the nawab's pennants, had the kotwal beaten up, and took up residence in Shuja's palace where he held a durbar for a month during which he accepted nazr from the cowed gentry.

Finally in the summer of 1765 Shuja sent another French officer, the urbane and genteel Jean-Baptiste Gentil, to negotiate a peace settlement with Captain Carnac and the British forces. Gentil described in his memoirs his meeting with Carnac, positively brimming with bonhomie and good-humour:

> 'I have a lot to discuss with you about this war' Gentil said to Carnac 'But first tell me, do you consider me your friend or are you suspicious of me?'
>
> 'No, by God!' answered Carnac genially, grabbing Gentil by the hand in his enthusiasm. 'I consider you my friend, speak freely.'

With this warm encouragement, Gentil went on to tell Carnac that he should not fight with Shuja, and instead 'make a friend of him by giving him back his two provinces (Awadh and Allahabad), rather than make an enemy of him because all of Hindustan would rise up with him.' René Madec agreed that '(Gentil) had demonstrated to the English how important it was for them to keep a barrier between Patna and the upper reaches of the Ganga, this barrier being Awadh, and for Awadh to be ruled by its legitimate Nawab.' Since the British did not want to manage these provinces themselves, reinstating the nawab was in fact precisely what the British wanted to do.* Carnac was also keen to show appropriate consideration for an illustrious enemy. 'It will in my opinion,' he wrote to a select committee in Calcutta, 'greatly add to the credit of the English name throughout the country our behaving with generosity towards a person who has all along borne so high a reputation in Hindustan.'

---

*According to historian Michael Fischer, referring to the lands they had now 'conquered', the Company 'lacked the funds or the manpower to garrison, the expertise or power to administer, and the inclination or authority from Parliament or its Court of Directors to annex them.'

'It is known all over the world that the illustrious chiefs of the English nation are constant and unchangeable in their friendship,' Shuja now wrote to Carnac, surrendering unconditionally. 'I now see things in their proper light and have a strong desire to come to you alone and I am persuaded you will treat me in a manner befitting your own honour.' Carnac, quite delighted with this change of heart, wrote back to the nawab to say that 'you (were) before unacquainted with our customs and dispositions. Thanks be to god that you are now become sensible of the justice and upright intentions of the English...you may depend on the best reception in my power suitable to our customs.'

And so on a warm summer's afternoon at 4 p.m., rising dust in the distance alerted the British camp* to the nawab approaching them, accompanied by just 200 soldiers. The British officers were sitting in a tent, still at the dining table and, redolent with food, passing around the post lunch drinks. When they saw the cloud of hazy dust, they all scrambled to their posts, hurriedly putting aside their drinks and napkins, while Carnac embraced Gentil warmly for having brought about such a happy conciliation. Carnac and his officers rushed over to receive the nawab personally, while the nawab stepped down from his palanquin and embraced Carnac in the Indian manner.† Carnac pointed out to the select committee 'that he had received the wazir with all possible marks of distinction, at which he expressed much satisfaction. He appears, however, a good deal dejected at his present condition, which must bear very hard upon him, and he must find himself without resources or being as he undoubtedly is the most considerable man in the empire and of an uncommon high spirit, he would not have submitted to such a condescension.' Shuja was reassured to learn that he would be given back his lands and indeed 'Gentil assured Shuja-ud-Daula that the need of the English to return in Bengal to assure their control there would allow him to obtain as good a deal from them in defeat as he would have obtained in a victory.' But before any final arrangement could be decided upon, news arrived that a very different sort of man entirely, Governor and

---

*At Jajmau, just outside Lucknow, on the banks of the Ganga.
†Jean-Baptiste Gentil would produce a most extraordinary document of these events, in the illustrations that would accompany his memoirs, copies of which lie at the Bibliotheque Nationale de Paris and the Victoria and Albert Museum.

Commander-in-Chief Robert Clive, was on his way to Allahabad to oversee the final treaty concluding the Battle of Buxar.

A bell-shaped and carnelian-complexioned man, Robert Clive's complicated legacy would not stand the test of time. Now described by historians variously as a 'vicious asset-stripper' and 'an unstable sociopath and a racist', Clive, at the time of Buxar, was a celebrated military general and the man who had almost single-handedly halted French General Dupleix's ambitions in the Carnatic. Indeed, it was the Anglo-French wars in the Carnatic, that spanned the period 1740–1763, that first alerted the EIC and Clive to the huge fortunes to be made from the economic resources and treasures of Indian states, once they were able to oppose them with their trained sepoys. Clive took this knowledge with him back to Bengal where, in the Battle of Plassey, the EIC acquired a territory three times the size of England itself and 'almost overnight (Clive) became one of the richest men in the world.'

In Allahabad, meanwhile, the aim of Clive and the EIC was to rapidly restore peace and order, so that trade could resume most profitably for the Company, and substantial war indemnity extracted as England had incurred crippling debts during the recently concluded Seven Years' War against France. Clive and Shuja first met at Benaras, where terms were agreed. The nawab would retain Awadh in return for duty-free trade concessions throughout eastern India. The nawab himself was to pay a war indemnity of 50 lakh rupees and he was to promise not to harbour English enemies[*] or deserters ever again.

From Benaras, the party moved on to Allahabad to meet with the emperor and obtain his final approval, for appearance's sake. Shuja would have been gratified by the English reception at Allahabad, where all the officers were waiting to honour him. 'The English gentlemen took off their hats, and showed all marks of respect, according to the custom of their country, and behaved with great affability.' The minute the nawab strode in before them, the English officers burst into a thunderous round of applause, and then led him with every show of deference into the fort of Allahabad. Carnac had quickly gauged the nawab's character and had warned the Council[†] at Calcutta that

---

[*] Mir Qasim was banished from the nawab's territories and sought refuge with the raja of Gohad.
[†] The EIC was governed initially by three councils, or 'presidencies', of leading merchants at

'every appearance of insult and violence to a person of Shuja-ud-Daula's character ought to be carefully avoided.' This deferential behaviour towards the nawab rankled with Shah Alam, who felt he had been used in a cavalier way by the proud nawab for his own gains. 'Shah Alam changed colour,' agreed a witness. 'What passed in his mind he knew alone...all this honour and respect which the English showed to the Nawab were very disgusting to Shah Alam.'

But Shah Alam did not have much room to manoeuvre, having become a gilded symbol to be used by whoever controlled him. On 12 August 1765, it was the EIC who had the emperor firmly in its grasp. Clive was ruthless, duplicitous, and venal in the final negotiations he carried out between the Company and the emperor. The previous agreement between Shah Alam and the EIC was that the whole of the Awadh domains would be awarded to him and Clive had moreover given him his word that he would be escorted back to Delhi. Now, however, realizing the extent of Clive's duplicity the emperor 'expressed warmth,' admitted a historian, 'and even resentment, upon the hardness of these arbitrary conditions; but the necessities of the humbled monarch left him without means of relief.'

The English hastily brought out their dining table and placed an armchair on it, all of which they covered in some drapery, thereby smartly transforming their dining room into a diwan-e-aam. The makeshift throne 'did not stand like the famous throne of his ancestors, on six massive feet of gold inlaid with rubies, emeralds and diamonds', but Shah Alam had to clamber on to this travesty of a throne, while Clive, Carnac, and the other officers stood before him in a parody of the gatherings at the diwan-e-aam in the Qila-e-Mualla, feigning a reverence that they increasingly smirked at (image 2). And so it was that the emperor of Hindustan signed over the diwani\* of Bengal, Bihar, and Orissa to the EIC, lending much needed gloss and legitimacy to what was the violent usurpation of the emperor's powers by a trading

---

Bombay, Madras, and Calcutta. Each council had its own small military force designed to defend the Company's 'factories', or trading posts, and each was run more or less independently. By the end of the eighteenth century, Calcutta would emerge as the most important Presidency.
\*The EIC thus became entitled to gather all taxes in Bengal, the Bengal revenues provided an indirect subsidy to the British treasury. From this point onwards, England no longer needed to send bullion to India, since Bengal's revenues were largely sufficient not only to pay for merchandise to send back to England, but to finance a large standing army made up of 90 per cent of Indian sepoys.

company. For the first time, the EIC was being treated on a par with an indigenous ruler. In return, Shah Alam was promised 26 lakh rupees as royal tribute from Bengal. Clive had felt 20 lakh rupees would have sufficed but sneeringly agreed that 'as we intend to make use of his Majesty in a very extraordinary manner for obtaining nothing less than a sanad for all the revenues of the country, 6 lakhs of rupees will be scarce worth our disobliging the King'. Perhaps the most despicable of Clive's behaviour towards the fallen emperor was his appalling lie in implying that he would conduct Shah Alam to Delhi himself if the King of England gave his consent. A grotesque charade was then encouraged in which a trusting Shah Alam was to send a letter, along with costly presents, through a nobleman called Aitisam-ud-Daula who would travel to England along with Archibald Swinton to present this petition to King George III. Instead, Clive withheld the emperor's letter and presents, some of which he would present to King George III later as if coming from himself*. In England, Aitisam-ud-Daula was never allowed to approach the British monarch and he would accuse Clive of treason, and both Aitisam-ud-Daula and Swinton charged Clive with 'breach of faith'. Shah Alam, meanwhile, remained in Allahabad, a prisoner of the Company's whims.

The most pressing matter for Shuja, meanwhile, was to pay the war indemnity imposed by the British, without which his lands would not be restored to him. 20 lakh rupees of the total sum were due immediately, and with his treasury entirely depleted by his long battle against the British, the nawab now cast about desperately for allies to send him money or jewellery. But all the people he reached out to—his brothers-in-law, his mother, and other court officials—all of whom had grown rich in his service, prevaricated, and sent miserly sums. It was the nawab's wife, Bahu Begum, who quite unexpectedly came forward with her enormous dowry, generously offering it up to Shuja. Bahu Begum gathered all that she had immediately at hand—cash, jewels, gold and silver plates, expensive furniture, and the jewels she was wearing. She even removed her nose-ring with its bunch of pearls and when her horrified entourage rushed up to her to stop her, she replied with assured gallantry that 'whatever I have is of use to me so long as Shuja-ud-Daula is safe. If he ceases to live, all these

---

*It has never been entirely clarified as to what happened to all of the emperor's presents.

things (wealth and ornaments) would also cease to be of value to me.' With the treasure that his wife gave him, Shuja was able to gather the sum owed to the Company and in fact the alacrity with which Shuja was able to collect such a large sum alerted the Company to the possibility of the endless wealth to be extracted from Awadh. It was also at this time that some luxurious Mughal manuscripts, owned by Shuja, entered into the possession of Robert Clive and it is not impossible to imagine that these manuscripts were offered, along with the tribute demanded, to further facilitate the recuperation of Awadh by the nawab.* The Small Clive Album, with its numerous images of delicate single flowers and groups of women, may even have belonged to Bahu Begum,† and been part of her famous trousseau. The album lacks folios of calligraphy, unusual in a Mughal album but since Bahu Begum was illiterate, this could account for the specific absence of calligraphic pages too.

After the disaster of Buxar, Shuja would follow the 'friendly advice' of Ahmad Khan Bangash of Farrukhabad, to the effect that if he now recovered the government of the province, not to trust the Mughals, but to make use of his own dependents and eunuchs and make Faizabad his capital. And indeed the nawab would relocate to Faizabad, where he was endlessly grateful to Bahu Begum, who had reacted with so much grace and generosity at the time of the nawab's bleakest hour. He never would forget the great debt he owed her, entrusting the seals of his government into her custody and, on a more personal note, dining both times of the day at her palace with her, despite his tenacious wandering ways. Bahu Begum would always remain till the end of his days 'his best friend and his confidant, the guardian of all his secrets and his treasures'.

Shuja would also return to Faizabad a considerably sobered man. From the wreckage of Buxar, the nawab would re-evaluate all his alliances, his friends, and his soldiers. But Shuja was a man of ferocious and almost limitless energy, drive, and self-belief and he would successfully reinvent himself and his place in the world once again. The one thing that would torment him till the day he died was

---

*The so-called Large and Small Clive Albums, that today lie at the Victoria and Albert Museum.
†Art historian Emily Hannam, at the Polier Symposium at the Museum of Islamic Arts Berlin, 2021.

his forced alliance with the British for, as he would confess ominously to Modave, and though he had successfully parlayed with notoriously volatile and unbridled allies such as Nadir Shah, the Marathas, the Jats, the Rohillas, and more—how could he ever control allies who were 'so greedy, so powerful and so paranoid'.

## A CITY IS BORN

In 1767, the English travel writer Jemima Kindersley had this to say about Nawab Shuja-ud-Daula: 'The nabob...is the most formidable nabob in Hindustan, active, enterprising, deceitful and unprincipled, bound by no laws divine or human, which can interfere with his interest; supple to the greatest meanness to those he fears; a tyrant in power, in short a true oriental Great Man.' The candour with which Kindersley excoriated both the nawab and the 'Great Men of the Orient' is breathtaking in itself but, prejudice apart, it is in its own way a rather glowing testament to Shuja's temperament and talents. Indeed, General Richard Smith, British commander at Allahabad, and churlishly critical of Indian rulers, was astounded that 'Shuja-ud-Daula bred up in all the luxury of the east and ever much addicted to pleasures should now so totally change his manners as to adopt this system of conduct which in time must infallibly render him truly formidable. I own I cannot but admire the man for the great progress he has already made in his new system.' The bewilderment, one senses in these colonial recordings, stems not so much at the expected 'Oriental' tyranny, debauchery, and despotism, but rather that this particular Oriental potentate overcame adversity with rather more 'English' verve and courage.

For, after the shocking debacle of Buxar, Shuja did not allow himself to slump into a paralysing stupor of despair but instead instantly turned his insatiable energy and ambition into strengthening his city and province. A Company officer wrote with alarm about the nawab's renewed interest in governing his country; 'Till of late he gave little attention to business,' he grumbled. 'He was up before the sun, mounted his horse, rushed into the forest, and hunted down tiger or deer till the noon of day. He then returned, plunged into the cold bath and spent his afternoons in the harem among his women. Such was the state of Shuja-ud-Daula's mind till the late war.' But, after Buxar, the nawab would make Awadh, and Faizabad in particular, the focus of his work. Up until this time, Lucknow and Faizabad had both been alternating centres of power for Shuja, while for the earlier nawabs, the lure of imperial Delhi had been irresistible. But after 1765, it was Faizabad that would become the vortex of Shuja's passion and energy, and he would completely alter its topography and culture.

In light of the humiliation the nawab had suffered due to the fecklessness and greed of his troops, it is not surprising that his attention first turned towards the reorganization of his army. His Mughal troops, entirely mercenary, were completely disbanded, to be replaced by new troops and officers hired from among his Rajput, Brahmin, and Shaikhazada* subjects as well as from the armies of other regional rulers. 'Within eighteen months,' writes historian Richard B. Barnett, 'he had brought together more than 30,000 troops, both cavalry and infantry, training and organizing them after the European model with the assistance and advice of the French, Armenian, and Abyssinian officers....' Shuja moved away from the practice of Safdar Jang and Saadat Khan of hiring wholesale contingents of Persian and Afghan troops, instead replacing them with heterogenous local troops. Other officers were recruited from amongst old family retainers who had been elevated by the nawabs and therefore owed absolute loyalty to Shuja. Raja Beni Bahadur, the Brahmin Naib of Awadh since 1757, had proved a man of such slippery fealty† during the Battle of Buxar that Shuja would later have him arrested and blinded. The raja was replaced with an illiterate Afghan retainer called Ilich Khan who had begun his career as a carpet spreader and was entirely in thrall to the nawab. And a final feature was the appointment of khwajasaras as important military leaders. Khwajasaras were deracinated troops without their own ties of blood, who therefore considered the nawab their surrogate parent, serving him with complete loyalty. These measures betrayed a man obsessed with the need to create a fighting corps of men who would lay down their life for him, immune to corruption or poaching. The infamously unreliable feature of Hindustani armies had become rampant by this time, as described by Modave:

> In India there are many chieftains who lend themselves to different princes along with their followers. They serve either a raja, or a soubedar, can often wage war against a prince whose salt they

---

*Descendants of a courtier, supposedly from the time of Emperor Akbar, Abdur Rahim, who settled in Awadh.
†The journals of Archibald Swinton describe the raja being willing to collude with the British after Buxar, and desert to the Company along with the majority of the nawab's troops. When the English asked him to first leave his wife and daughters with them as safeguard for his good conduct, he hurriedly returned to the nawab.

have long eaten, as we say in this country. These chieftains are great looters and destroyers. If the prince who is keeping them does not have the money to give them their entire pay, he tells them—'here is this province which belongs to me, and which my enemies have taken over. Try to establish yourself there'... This leads to unhappiness and tyranny.

Indeed, according to an EIC merchant, George Foster, the debacle of Buxar was quite simply a blessing in disguise for the nawab. 'The defeat of Buxar delivered the Nawab from a turbulent and undisciplined cavalry' wrote the merchant. 'With the utmost energy he created an infantry corps, armed with artillery, on the European principles. It was a challenging endeavour, one which very few Asian princes were in a position to carry out. But through his talent, his energy and his perseverance, Shuja-ud-Daula overcame all the obstacles of deep-rooted prejudices and habit due to the physical and moral limitations of these people.'

The nawab would have remembered, too, the bloody mayhem that had resulted from the lack of coordination and the frankly riotous actions of his many units. 'Another great failing,' agreed Modave about the Hindustani forces, 'is that the armies are not part of a regular whole like they are with us. In addition to the slowness and the waste of time that results, there is never any secrecy that can be maintained and so every project ends in failure.' Contrasting this with the disciplined EIC troops, Shuja was determined to modernize his army along European models. He recruited European officers, notably French ones, and established factories for the manufacture of muskets and cannons 'almost as good as those produced in European factories' wrote Modave, who pointed out that by hiring French mercenaries the nawab 'hoped to overcome the English by confronting them with a mass of Frenchmen loyal only to him'. Shuja supervised the training of his infantry personally, 'spending several hours every day in overseeing the troops at drill, parade and military review.' And in the eighteenth century, as it is today, knowledge was power and the nawab reinforced his spy network, striving to be kept informed of all doings in the different regions of the country. 'He had also 22,000 messengers and spies who brought tidings every 7th day from Punah...and on every 15th day from Kabul', wrote contemporary historian Mohammad Faiz

Baksh, who also pointed out that at the nawab's court at Faizabad, there were emissaries from every sizeable court in Hindustan including the Marathas and the Delhi court.

And if the warriors were at the nawab's court at Faizabad, with their retinues, followers, and servants, then so were the rest of the populace. 'As soon as it was known that Shuja-ud-Daula had decided on Faizabad for his headquarters,' wrote Lucknow historian Abdul Sharar, 'crowds flocked in that direction, the entire population of Delhi seemed to be making preparations to move there. In no time persons of every race and creed, literary men, soldiers, merchants, craftsmen, individuals of every rank and file had gathered there.' Faiz Baksh has described the veritable scrum of merchants, tradespeople, food stalls, artists, poets, and sundry citizens who sprang up almost miraculously once it was known that the wealthy nawab was to reside in Faizabad. Faiz Baksh encountered them himself when he arrived at the city for the very first time. 'Four miles outside Faizabad,' he wrote, 'various kinds of sweet meats, hot viands, kebabs and curries were being cooked and chapatis and parathas baked under the shade of trees. Stalls for distributing cold drinking water. Different sorts of sherbets and faluda with hundreds of people buying.' When Faiz Baksh had asked if this appetizing gathering represented Faizabad, the scoffing response was: 'Huzoor! The city gate is four miles from here! What are you thinking of?' In the city of Faizabad itself, the air was dense with the sound of drums, laughter, and singing: 'There was not a moment from morning until evening when one could not hear the army or the beat of the regimental drums. From sunrise to sunset the noise of the drums, and kettle drums of the regiments never ceased, and the sounds of the gongs which told the hours and the watches deafened the ears. Well-dressed young men, the sons of nobles of Delhi, physicians of the Greek school, singers and dancers of both sexes and of every land, were in the enjoyment of large salaries. In every street and market, artisans and scholars flocked hither from Dhaka, Bengal, Gujarat, Malwa, Hyderabad, Delhi, Lahore, Peshawar, Kabul, Kashmir and Multan.'

To accommodate all his ambitions, and the soldiers, craftspeople, and sundry populace that came along with them, the nawab commissioned architectural activities at a frenetic pace. No longer distracted and burdened by the need to bolster the Mughal cause, the nawab could instead direct all his resources towards Awadh. He began by razing various sundry 'Mughal' houses—these homes presumably tainted by the shameful behaviour of their owners in battle. The nawab then built mud forts and a series of defensive walls on a large scale, to enclose both the nawabi residences and the city itself. To modern notions, a mud construction sounds whimsically impermanent, but eighteenth-century mud forts were no such thing. Popular with the landed aristocracy of Awadh from before the time of the nawabs, these forts were constructed of well-beaten mud, as strong as Lakhori bricks*. They had walls of great thickness, with entrances fortified by large, guarded gateways. In 1771, the nawab would begin work on a fortress described by scholar Banmali Tandon as 'the greatest fortress erected up to then in the eighteenth century in not only Hindustan but the whole Gangetic basin', with a design that was 'at once revolutionary and traditional'.

In addition to the military and defensive structures, the nawab began work on palaces, gardens, and two large hunting parks. The most beautiful of the gardens, the Lal Bagh, had a splendid ornamented gateway, while the menagerie included all sorts of unusual creatures—gazelles, tigers, leopards, nilgai, Kabul sheep famous for their fine, white wool, Tibetan goats and more. The two large hunting parks on the outskirts of the city provided recreation for the nobility and also for the English and French contingents which had settled in Faizabad since 1764. The ponds in the parks 'were stored with a variety of curious fishes, both exotic and domestic, with their fins and tails adorned with small golden rings', whom the nawab delighted in feeding by hand, watching them leap above the water to catch the grains of rice. The expansive hunting grounds were also where the Meena bazars were held. The women of the zenana set up stalls, selling a variety of goods and sweets they had sourced, while the begums and noblewomen of Faizabad strolled through, their odhanis light as clouds, delighted as much by the bonhomie and chivvying good humour as by the items on offer. On one occasion, Nawab Begum was so delighted with the charm of a Meena bazar that she distributed 5,000 rupees amongst

---

*Thin, flat, burnt clay red bricks that became very widely used in the architecture of Lucknow and Faizabad. These slim bricks, not more than 20 mm wide, could be used with great versatility and flexibility in innovative ways

the nawab's household. The English cantonment was on the western edge of the city while the French were companionably closer to the nawab's palace, with Gentil having built a house next to the Anguri Bagh of the Qila itself.* Next to the palace of the nawab was a foundry, set up under the charge of Gentil, exclusively for the manufacture of a wide range of high-quality small arms as well as artillery pieces for Shuja's army. 'Employing some 500 persons, no armaments industry had ever been set up on such a scale in the history of the Mughal empire,' writes Tandon, 'and never had a native state produced such sophisticated European armaments.' Outside Faizabad, the fields were neatly hedged by mud walls, laced with canals, while the horizon was dotted with groves of mango and tamarind trees, providing shade as well as a barrier against the blustery winds.

All this swirling activity made of Faizabad a bustling commercial hub at this time, second only to Calcutta, with at its heart the Chowk Bazar 'from the south gate of the fort to the Allahabad gate of the city' and 'so broad that "nearly ten bullock carriages can run abreast it."' Merchants from all over Hindustan and beyond sold their goods at Chowk Bazar, including merchants from Persia, Turkey, China, and Europe. 'There is such a great crowd here' agreed Modave, 'from ten in the morning to four in the afternoon that it is difficult to pass by. In the evenings, the scene changes entirely as little lamps are lit on both sides, and all the merchant stalls are replaced by so many wooden beds than you think you have wandered into some large hospital dormitory.' The shops along Chowk Bazar were a microcosm of life in Faizabad itself. There were the bazar cooks, 'basting kababs over a charcoal fire with one hand, and beating off the flies with a bunch of date-leaves in the other', assistants kneading dough for bread, goldsmiths with furnace and crucible, muslin weavers at their loom, hookah makers, tobacco mixers, sellers of toys made of clay or wood, medicine men with their bags of herbs, milk and cream sellers, and yet more sellers of the mundane and the magical.

According to Modave, Faizabad owed its growing prosperity to the fact that 'it is the residence of one of the greatest officers of the Mughal empire.' Shuja himself took part in the re-imagining of his capital.

---

*These English and French cantonments were a new innovation to the Hindustani urban layout, and would become standard in many colonial era towns.

He 'would ride out each morning and evening to inspect the streets and houses', wrote Faiz Baksh. And much like a strict surveyor, 'he would take workmen armed with mattocks and spades and whenever he saw houses out of alignment or encroaching, he would start diggers immediately.' Despite the nawab's best efforts, however, the streets of the city apart from the wide Chowk Bazar were a warren of hustling merchants, lumbering animals, and appraising shoppers, all jostling for precedence with bullocks, cows, buffaloes, horses, camels, and elephants.

The most stunning of the buildings built by Shuja and his family in the decade between 1765 and 1775 was a series of eight palaces, most along the Ghaghara, of which seven were entirely new.* The old nawabi Dilkusha palace was extensively remodelled by Shuja while the new palaces included Bahu Begum's Moti Mahal, the lesser wives' Khurd Mahal, a free-standing building called the Samman Burj, and Mubarak Mahal. These structures, enclosed within a protective mud wall, were collectively called Qila Faizabad. Nawab Begum's palace was outside the Qila, some distance away and within the city proper, and finally there was Bahu Begum's brother Salar Jang's palace, probably near the Lal Bagh.† From what remains of Dilkusha palace today (image 3) one can admire the great ingenuity with which its topography was shaped to harness the very best conditions for an expansive and peopled life in a hot, dry climate. The palace is on an incline, gently sweeping towards the Ghaghara, the course of which the nawab changed so that it would flow below the palace. The orientation of the enormous width of the palace over a north-east axis funnelled the breeze, first cooled as it blew over the river. A profusion of riverfront openings and octagonal corner pavilions further enhanced this effect while chambers built partly under the cool earth of the riverfront functioned as a tehkhana‡. Since Faizabadad was far from the quarries that provided the red sandstone and white marble of Delhi's imperial buildings, Faizabad's buildings were made of Lakhori brick, covered in resplendent white lime stucco with walls painted in gold and silver designs. The stucco could be manipulated with great elegance, creating floral shapes, emblems, and

---

*The seventh new palace was the fort and palace complex begun in 1771 but never completed.
†Of all these structures, only parts of Dilkusha and Moti Mahal, in ruins, remain today.
‡Underground chambers, popular with the Mughal palaces too.

cusps which gleamed in the blazing sunshine. With its cusped arches, elegant spaces, noble proportions, and decorations floor to ceiling on its wall faces, the artist William Hodges deemed it 'certainly the most splendid Monument to the Arts in Hindostan at the Time'. At the entrance to Dilkusha was a large gate, above which was the naubat whose enormous drums beat out the sombre intimation of the nawab's presence, at sunrise and sunset.

Bahu Begum's adjacent Moti Mahal was similarly splendid, built in a haveli style series of horizontally spaced interlocking courts. This palace was for the exclusive use of Bahu Begum and the other highborn begums. As for the lesser wives and concubines who were living in the Khurd Mahal, Bahu Begum had forbidden anyone from even mentioning their names or the names of their children in front of her and resolutely refused to acknowledge their presence as long as Shuja was alive. The Moti Mahal had a huge garden with a central well, a mosque, and rooftop terraces for sleeping during the hot season. This was also where the nawab kept his enormous surplus treasure, and all the cash offerings he received, thereby delegating to Bahu Begum more power than to any other single person. For the nawab was faithful to the grateful promise he had made to his wife when she had handed over her dowry to secure his freedom. And as promised, the nawab ate both his meals in the Moti Mahal, and this was a serious commitment indeed for the preparing and serving of meals in Awadh was no flippant affair.

The delicate and refined art of gastronomy would reach great heights in Awadh, especially during the reign of the nawab's son. But even in the time of Shuja, it would have been an elaborate and refined affair. Every day, food for the nawab and the begum arrived in the Moti Mahal from six separate kitchens. The collective name for dishes sent to others was tora,* and would include 'pulao muzaffar, a sweet saffron-flavoured rice dish; mutanjan, meat, sugar and rice with spices; shirmal; safaida, a simple sweet rice dish; fried aubergine; shir birinj, a sweet dish of rice boiled in milk; qorma, pieces of meat slowly braised in spices and yoghurt or cream gravy; arvi cooked with meat; shami kebabs (ground meat and chickpea patties); and as condiments, murabba, pickles and chutney' (image 4).

---

*From the Persian for basket, according to food historian Colleen Taylor Sen.

Each kitchen would have been the fiery domain of chefs called rakabdars*, who only cooked small quantities of food for select audiences. The large-scale cooking was left to the lowly harried bawarchis, or ordinary cooks, who often specialized in a particular food item, such as meat, bread, kebabs or desserts. First, there was food from the nawab's own kitchens, whose darogah-i-bawarchikhana† was Mirza Hasnu‡. Mirza Hasnu had a budget of 2,000 rupees to spend on food every day. He brought the dishes from the kitchen to the door of the begum's zenana, where he would hand them over to her maids, who had whimsical and rhyming names like Dhaniya, Paniya, and Maniya. The maids would then present the food to Bahu Begum for inspection, before placing the trays on the gleaming white dastarkhwan§. According to Faiz Baksh, the begum's maids, though endowed with skittish names, held quite a bit of power, and Mirza Hasnu was careful to slip them money regularly. A fly once found its way into the dishes sent over by the nawab's kitchens and when the nawab asked about the provenance of the tainted food, the maids were quick to attribute the offending dish to Salar Jang's kitchens, knowing that the nawab would not wish to embarrass his brother-in-law and thus saved Mirza Hasnu from a stinging punishment.

Then there was food sent from the subsidiary royal kitchen supervised by the khwajasara Ambar Ali Khan, who spent 300 rupees a day on the kitchen. The third kitchen, supervised by the khwajasara Bahar Ali Khan was Bahu Begum's own kitchen, while food was also sent from Nawab Begum's kitchens, and two of Bahu Begum's brothers' kitchens—Salar Jang and Mirza Ali Khan. Salar Jang's kitchens were especially renowned, his specialty being a particularly complicated pulao so heavy that only Salar Jang was ever allowed to eat it, presumably having the necessary iron-clad digestive system. Each kitchen would probably have had a few dishes they specialized

---

*One of Asaf's chefs was paid rupees 1,200 per month (equivalent today to about 5,000 pounds). The chefs were in high demand at other important courts in India, Hyderabad and elsewhere, and thus helped to take Lucknawi cuisine to all the great courts of the country.
†Superintendent of the kitchens.
‡Hasan Reza Khan was presented to Shuja and appointed superintendent of the kitchen and audience chamber. He was affectionately called Mirza Hasnu.
§The gleaming white of cloths was produced through the art of the bleachers, who used lime, chalky soil, dung, and sunshine to make the rough cotton bright white. Dastarkhwans would sometimes have blessings, or poems, inscribed on them.

in, specially chosen for the nawab. Qorma had long been a beloved dish of the nawabi, moving patrons to great lengths of emotion and poetry in its practice. A great chef, when asked what he could cook, answered with succinct panache: 'O Mian! What is there to eat besides qorma and chapati?'

When the towering nawab strode into the Moti Mahal accompanied by his entourage, he would have been wearing a style of clothes that was essentially Mughal, though highlighted by a few flourishes that recalled his Persian origins. The tunic-like garment called the jama was popularized by Akbar in the sixteenth century, when it fell just below the knees but by the eighteenth century, the jama reached the ankle, in soft folds of fine white muslin which was particularly favoured by Shuja. Over the jama the nawab often wore a Persian style coat with a fur tippet, or stole, around his neck while on his head he would have worn a small fitted cap with a jewelled band, or goshpech. For a particularly dashing effect, the nawab sometimes wore boots to complement his Persian-style robe. These simple yet expensively detailed clothes would enhance the nawab's elegant stature and famously bristling moustaches. About muslin, poet Amir Khusrau had sighed evocatively that 'one could compare it with a drop of water...it is so transparent and light that it looks as if one is in no dress at all but has only smeared the body with pure water.'

After the meal, the nawab would be presented with water in a besandani, the coarse corn flour being useful to scrub the grease from the liberal use of ghee off one's fingers. The gold or silver basins were covered with a sieve, so that the offending used water was hidden from sight while a further layer of grass prevented the water from splashing out. Next, the increasingly popular paan would be presented, each ingredient of this fragrant and intoxicating court favourite carefully prepared and presented. To the usual lime, catechu, cardamom, and supari were added gold, silver, and pearl powders. The paan was then wrapped in silver leaf and presented on silver plates. The afternoon could then be spent in pleasant torpor, smoking hookahs, which were popular with men and women alike, and murmured conversations. The hookahs of the nawabs were intricately fashioned, the base made of bidri work in silver, and the cords made of silk and silver-gilt kalabattun threads. Though the ever-restless nawab was just as likely to go for a swim in the Ghaghara—he was such a strong swimmer that when the river was in spate in the monsoon, he insisted on swimming across the river and back, unaccompanied. While the nawab was in residence, the palaces and gardens trilled to the sound of his pigeons' muted cooing and their feathery, fluttery movements, for Shuja was devoted to his birds. According to Modave, he kept tens of thousands of pigeons, which he took with him when he went on tours, carried in eight to nine thousand cages by countless porters.

This frenzy of activity and entertainment was mostly confined to the four months of the monsoon season during which the nawab was in residence in Faizabad, as the rest of the year he spent touring his country. And it was in the monsoon, or saawan, that Faizabad and the Moti Mahal was at its most beguiling. The rain would begin, first in large, fat drops that fell like stones on to the dusty earth and then in sweeping curtains of water that drifted across the huge courtyards of the Mahal as the green leaves on the trees and the bushes unfurled seemingly overnight. The corridors of the palaces would have been distractingly rich with the perfume of rose and kewra water, produced especially in this season. In the begum's huge gardens, jhoolas (swings) would have been suspended from the branches of the trees, and they would have glinted as they swayed in the breeze against the stone-grey skies, from the metallic kalabattun and silk threads that made up the ropes of the swings. The clothes of the begums and their attendants would also have appeared particularly enticing on the swings, the glittering jewellery shining from behind the transparent folds of the women's shifting, fine odhanis. The women would have been wearing the high-waisted, full-length peshwaj over a shorter tunic and a short tight bodice called the angiya. The use of gold embroidery zardozi work would become increasingly popular, with clothes being studded with sequins, sitara (star shapes), katori (small domed sequins) and badla (gilt-strips) work which Awadh became famous for. Elements like seed pearls and glass beads added to the magnificence of the clothes. The use of the dupatta or odhani by these elegant women was poetry itself, best described by an Englishwoman, Fanny Parkes, a few decades later:

> The dupatta is so transparent it hides not; it merely veils the form, adding beauty to the beautiful by its soft and cloudlike folds. The jewellery sparkles beneath it; and the outline of this

drapery is continually changing according to the movements or the coquetry of the wearer.

And it wasn't just the clothes that were gorgeously embellished, even the coverings for hookahs, the mats, the cushions, the little purses, the shoes, were all similarly exquisitely embroidered and decorated. Artisans called mughlanias had their own quarters in the palace in which to dye and embroider cloth. To the natural colours* used for dyeing cloth, real flowers were added to perfume the clothes—rose, harsingar, and khas in the summer, bela, chameli, and champa in the monsoon, musk, and amber in the winter. In addition to the dyers of cloth, there was a great demand for artisans and workers of all sorts—weavers, embroiderers, and tailors for the increasingly elaborate clothes; acrobats, naqqals (imitators), bhands (comedians), dancers, and musicians for the entertainments; bird trainers for the nawab's beloved pigeons and roosters; betel sellers; water carriers, and a great deal more.

The nawab had also promised to spend his nights in the begum's palace and whenever his tempestuous nature got the better of him, tradition has it he had to pay Bahu Begum 5,000 rupees per transgression, as agreed. No doubt Bahu Begum would have made a tidy sum from these dalliances of the nawab but a more secure source the begum owned was the perquisite the nawab allowed her of a tax of a 24th part of the yearly pay of every officer and soldier of cavalry. She also had a jagir consisting of a number of parganas including Salone, from which she earned an income of 9 lakh rupees, in addition to the considerable dowry that still remained with her. At the time of Shuja's death in 1775, Bahu Begum's wealth was estimated at 2 million pounds, making of her an extremely wealthy and powerful woman, so wealthy, in fact, that it would prove irresistible to an EIC Governor General and would lead to his trial for impeachment. Faiz Baksh had this to say about the power of Bahu Begum:

> This lady of ladies...passed the whole of her long and noble life in splendour and state.... There was not a woman left of so great distinction and rank, bearing and dignity; and no one woman in all the 32 subahs of India can be held up in these days as her

---

*Walnut was used for black, indigo for blue, pomegranate rinds for green, etc.

rival in either the grandeur of her surroundings or the respect she could command. When at the zenith of her glory she had 10,000 troops, horses and foot, scores of elephants and countless horses. The people who earned their bread directly or indirectly through her bounty must have been more than a hundred thousand and all felt as happy and secure as though they were in a mother's arms.

Though Nawab Shuja-ud-Daula was a vastly different man at thirty-five than he had been as a youth, scaling the walls of a young woman's home, he remained entranced by the company of beautiful, talented, and cultured women and the courtesans of Faizabad became the refined symbol of the city as a result. The nawab patronized them with gifts and money, and his example was followed by the discerning elite of the city. These women became extravagantly wealthy,* and accompanied the nawab and his entourage, even when touring the country. They owned several sumptuous tents each, and when the nawab left Faizabad after the monsoon, their tents 'would be loaded with stately grandeur on to bullock carts along with those of the Nawab and guarded by a party of 10 or 12 soldiers'. Other chieftains also emulated the nawab and this glittering cortege of women, musicians, dancing girls, and servants would bring the flavour of Faizabad glamour and charm wherever they went.

Many of the courtesans of Faizabad had impeccable pedigrees, escaping the devastation of imperial Delhi where once Muhammad Shah Rangeeley had been their discerning patron, and following in the trail of the poets, singers, musicians, and artists, wave upon wave of vulnerable talent carrying the poetry and music of Delhi to the lavish patronage of the elite of Awadh. In Faizabad they created worlds of refinement and beauty, and their grateful patrons laid at their jewelled and hennaed feet priceless gifts of brocade shawls, cashmere stoles, caps, and shoes glinting with jewels, fly whisks of silver, gold and jade, alongside their endless longing. For the best of the courtesans, two of whom were Dilruba and Ujagar, had perfected the art of seductive bashfulness, each graceful gesture and demure glance conjuring up an entire world. Their enchanting shyness was captured by a poet:

---

*See Veena Oldernburgh's essay, 'Lifestyle as Resistance: The Case of the Courtesans of Lucknow, India'—The courtesans of Lucknow were amongst the highest taxpayers in 1857.

> I had barely opened my lips to speak
> That she cast down her eyes and blushed.

Even Jemima Kindersley was moved to exclaim that 'many of the Eastern women have so much beauty in their fine long black eyes, eyebrows, and long black eye-lashes', before sighing that they would have been even more alluring 'if they were set off by a fine red and white complexion' like that of European women. Through the generous patronage of the nawab and the elite of Faizabad, the city thrummed with the glamour of their presence and the music of their accompanists. 'There was such a multitude of bazar beauties and dancers in the town', agreed Sharar, 'that no lane or alley was without them'.

But if these courtesans had perfected the fine art of demure seduction, they remained feisty and spirited women. On one occasion, Shuja and his retinue were enjoying a day of entertainment with musicians and mimics in one of the nawab's large gardens, when the nawab teased one of the particularly attractive courtesans by asking her whether she thought she could ride his horse and make him gallop. The courtesan replied with aplomb that she most certainly believed she could, in which case she asked that she be given the horse. If she fell and died, the charming woman added, she would consider her life an offering to her master the nawab. The terms were accepted by the nawab and the courtesan successfully controlled the galloping horse.

The other powerful woman of Faizabad was Shuja's mother, Nawab Begum, who presided over a vast establishment of 1,000 persons in her palace in the city. She had 400 soldiers to guard her palace while her entourage included noblemen, physicians, scholars, religious men, and cognoscenti from Delhi families, many fallen on hard times since the crumbling of Mughal power at Delhi, and whom she employed at Faizabad. Her coterie also included a large number of khwajasaras, with Muharram Ali Khan being one of the most powerful, along with the khwajasaras' friends, companions, and servants, all of whom formed their own vibrant court at the begum's palace. Nawab Begum was a famously pious woman, spending her days in prayer and penance. 'She followed the style and fashion of the days of Alamgir and Bahadur Shah' wrote an approving Faiz Baksh, and when she went out of the palace she was 'escorted by macebearers decently dressed, and elephants with flags and drums, all moving in good order and slowly, not like the nobles these days, hurrying along unnecessarily so footmen are bathed in perspiration' added the irritated historian. It appears that in the eighteenth century like in the twenty-first, the older generation were unsettled by the scandalously fast-paced life of the younger lot, rushing about with unbecoming haste. Since Nawab Begum was rather more conservative in her dress, she may have favoured clothes in delicate, pastel shades made from natural dyes which were worn by the discerning Delhi elite, and which had replaced the earlier robust indigenous reds, indigos, and ochres.*

Nawab Begum's discretion and generosity are exemplified in the coded way in which her maid would ask her for money, when in need. Sukh-Vachan, the maid in charge of the keys of the treasury, would tell the begum that she needed to collect the bags of money to dry them of moisture in the sun. The begum, immediately divining the reason for such a strange request, would at once agree with the maid, who thus obtained her money and bypassed any need for demeaning requests.

Nawab Begum also commissioned a magnificent mosque and an imambara behind the Moti Bagh. When Safdar Jang had died at Paparghat in 1753 Nawab Begum had brought his body in a coffin to Faizabad and interred him in the middle of a garden planted with roses called the Gulab Bari. Here his body lay in state while Nawab Begum remained in mourning at the head of his grave. Later on, the remains were sent to Delhi where Shuja built a memorial to his father, today known as Safdarjang's Tomb.

The majority of the population (11 million by the beginning of the nineteenth century) of Awadh, including the landholding class, was Hindu, with its own distinctive cultural identity and its own language—Awadhi. The Hindu landholders, Rajputs and Brahmins, predated the arrival of the nawabs by centuries and claimed divine sanction for their right to power in the region. The Muslim community made up about 10 per cent of the population, a large proportion of which were Sunni, like the Mughal emperors. The nawabs being of Iranian origin, however, were Shia and soon enough, as they established a powerful and vibrant court at Faizabad, the ostentatious display of Shia rituals and practices

---

*The palette included badami (almond), firozi (turquoise), gul e anar (pomegranate red), tarbuji (watermelon red), zafrani or kesariya (saffron), narangi (orange), pistai (pistachio green), dilbahar (purple), kishmishi or sultania, etc.

became synonymous with elite culture among the nobility. Not only did a large number of Shia families and scholars migrate to Faizabad and Lucknow from Delhi, they started arriving from Bengal after 1760 too, as a result of the decline of nawabi rule there.

As a result of the patronage of the nawabs, some of the elite Sunni Muslims, the courtesans, and even Hindu families converted to Shiism, while others adopted some of the visible cultural markers of the Shia identity. The begums of Awadh, with their enormous wealth and their political visibility, became significant influences in the way Shia rituals and practices developed in Faizabad, and later in Lucknow. With time and wealth at their disposal, and often a thorough knowledge of the Shia religious practices, the begums began an audacious elaboration of their Shia identity that proclaimed their piety and their elite status, and made these purdah-bound women formidably 'visible' presences.

The feminine voice had a compelling part to play in the practice of Shiism.* The very first majlis, or lamentation assembly, for Imam Hussain† was held by his sister, Zainab. Zainab and her sister Umm Kulthum were captured after the great massacre at Karbala and brought to Caliph Yazid's‡ court in Damascus, where they were paraded through the streets of Kufa. The hushed and shamed crowds tried to offer the sisters gifts of bread and dates but the sisters, untouchable in their soaring grief, refused any help. This defiance of Zainab even in her utter vulnerability would resonate through the long and arid centuries in the Shia community. The elegiac pain of the majlis—the enactment of the catastrophic suffering of the disinherited martyrs, the thirsting for water in a desert far away, the unbearable pain of the

---

*Shia Muslims hold Hazrat Ali, the Prophet's son-in-law, Hazrat Ali's wife, Fatima, and his two sons Hussain and Hasan, and all his descendants (known as Ahl al-Bayt, or People of the House) as particularly beloved and the legitimate successors to Prophet Muhammad. The word Shia is derived from Shiat Ali—followers of Ali, Shia for short. Shias believe that religious authority should have been solely invested in Hazrat Ali and his descendants after the Prophet, whereas the Sunnis selected a caliph as successor by election.
†Imam Hussain, the grandson of Prophet Muhammad, through his daughter Fatima and son-in-law Ali, is revered by Shia Muslims as the third Imam (after Ali, and his elder brother, Hasan). He was martyred at the Battle of Karbala.
‡Yazid was the Umayyad Khalifa, or ruler, who demanded allegiance from Imam Hussain, leading to the exodus of Imam Hussain and his entourage from Mecca. This small band of 72 persons including women and children, was engaged in battle en route, at Karbala, and martyred. The commemoration and remembrance of this battle is the most visible manifestation of Shia identity.

dying children—these exquisite griefs that occurred in a foreign land a millennium earlier were channelled by the begums in the majlis of Faizabad, where they would be followed by the elite of the city and the townsfolk, till Faizabad thrummed with the ecstasy of this divine recollection. Through the bleak and saturated days of Muharram, as the suffering of the martyrs was remembered, the hours became sparse and shorn of all luxury and excess. The beds were put away, replaced by date-palm mats, the paan was banished, no doubt with a sigh, and the food was pared down. The fragrant pulaos and kebabs were replaced by coarse foods such as barley bread and khichdi minus ghee, seasoning or spices. Also banished were the gorgeous clinking jewellery—the seven-stringed 'satlara' necklaces, the earrings in the form of fish called machalia, the armbands studded with rubies, the tinkling anklets and a galaxy of rings for every finger and toe. All the colourful odhanis, payjamas, and angiyas were put aside, to be replaced by stark black clothes. The exquisite jhoomar, which the begums usually wore on the left side of their head, was put aside, and their long, black hair remained loose and unadorned, a powerful statement of mourning in India.

The chanting of dirges during Muharram known as soz khwani became very popular at this time and were also patronized by Bahu Begum. Elite women themselves sometimes performed these dirges, the emotion and the beauty of the women's voices gaining them great respect. Soon enough, professional female soz khwan singers flourished, gaining access into the zenana where male singers were not allowed and in this cloistered, intimate space of the women, a separate universe unfurled, where women were the chosen participants.

And what the begums enacted in the seclusion of their private imambaras (a place where people gather for majlis), the nawab would recreate with panache in the streets of Faizabad. A few years previously, Shuja had already marked Muharram as an act of provocation in front of Ahmad Shah Durrani but now, in Faizabad, he would honour the memory of Imam Hussain and his sacrifice with all the resplendence in his power. Jean-Baptiste Gentil had written about the month of Muharram that 'everyone makes a space according to their means and one visits each other to commemorate this death. Every night, there are grand illuminations and food for all those who need it. The poorer people distribute lemonade to everyone.' An extraordinary painting exists depicting the Muharram procession in Faizabad in 1774, commissioned by Gentil. An endless serpentine throng of men, horses, and elephants stretch into the distance. The men are all dressed in black and march sombrely, with some chanting marsiya and others thumping their chests in fierce grief. Banners flutter, the alams* are raised proudly while countless tazias, depicting the ceremonial shrines of the martyred imams, are held high. In the centre of the painting is a circle of men, including the nawab. Shuja, as he commemorates this Muharram procession, is surrounded by his liegemen and his followers, while the spectacle of his great wealth and power glitters off the gold of the banners, the elephants' trimmings and the double-edged sword of Ali, dhul fikar. The scale and ostentation of the procession was the proud proclamation of the nawab's Shia identity, which he and his successors would carefully nurture as they forged a place and identity for themselves far from the decadence and ruin of the Mughal empire.

---

*Alams represent the banners carried by the martyrs of Karbala.

## A FRENCHMAN AT FAIZABAD

In 1778, the honest citizens of the somnolent medieval town of Bagnols-sur-Cèze in Southern France were watching a most astonishing spectacle—a local man from an ancient but somewhat impoverished noble family was returning to his native home after twenty-five years, entirely transformed. 'Mossu Gentil,' they murmured to one another, now looked almost like one of the Indians in whose company he had spent the past quarter of a century. Even more intriguingly, he was surrounded by the objects and people of his exotic life in India—his Indo-Portuguese wife and her family,* his large retinue of Indian servants, his effects, and all the habits he had assimilated during his lifetime in a foreign country. 'They said,' wrote his son Leon Alegre, 'that his family continued to live in the manner and customs of the Orient, which greatly piqued the curiosity of the local inhabitants.' The Governor of Chandernagore had written a letter of introduction for Gentil the previous year, saying that 'he has so well adopted the habits of the Asian peoples, after his long stay among them, that he has practically forgotten his own country's habits. He would not charm anyone by an overly seductive appearance,' he added rather damningly, 'but he will speak the truth, and will not deviate from it.' But in just a few years, Gentil would lose whatever small fortune he had brought back with him from Awadh, would give away his astounding collection of manuscripts and objects to the king and the peoples of France in return for scant recognition and would die in penury. For it was his greatest virtue—honesty—which was of no value at all in the late eighteenth century, and certainly not in the world of grifters in India that the British thrived in.

And yet, just a decade earlier, after the Battle of Buxar, Jean-Baptiste Gentil seemed poised to become one of the most influential players on the slithering sands of Indian politics. When Shuja had first met Gentil, 'he was delighted', wrote Gentil later, 'to find a Frenchman who spoke his language'. Gentil's fluency in Urdu and his steadfast,

---

*This included his mother-in-law, Lucia Mendec, his brother-in-law, Louis Francois Velho, his three children—two daughters, Jeanne-Marie Therese and Jeanne-Marie Agnes, and a fifteen-month-old son.

competent presence endeared him to the nawab and he became the trusted commander of arguably the most powerful and talented of rulers in India. By Modave's assessment, Shuja by this time 'was a famous man in all of Hindustan due to his important wars, due to his worth, and especially due to his wealth and strength...a wise and skilful political career had greatly increased the inheritance he had received from his father'. Gentil, meanwhile, had increased the number of French soldiers he had gathered at Faizabad from 200 to 600, their salaries costing the nawab 960,000 pounds, not including the salaries of the main officers. He had been awarded a torrent of grandiose titles: 'Raised in Honour', 'Commander in Battle', 'Valiant', 'Counsellor of the Emperor',* and the nawab himself never addressed him as anything other than Nawab Bahadur. Modave simply bemoaned the fact that '(Gentil) was an intelligent man who needed only greater strength of character to play the most satisfying and brilliant role in Hindustan that any foreigner with no title and no standing could hope to achieve.' And in 1769, Gentil had received a mark of great distinction, one that few Indian men, far less a foreign man, could have hoped to receive—a visit from the emperor of Hindustan himself.

Four years after he had begun the transformation of the city of Faizabad, Nawab Shuja-ud-Daula had invited the emperor to visit his sparkling new capital. In February of 1769, the nawab rode out several miles outside Faizabad to formally greet his distinguished visitor, who was travelling in a sedate, lumbering retinue with his harem and his court. Forty years old now, Shah Alam had spent the last ten years in exile in Allahabad, parsing his patience and gauging the intentions of the EIC. Still slim and elegant, his face was shadowed by worry, his earlier vigour and his confidence slowly ravaged by the relentless forces that now ruled Hindustan. Now in Faizabad, Shuja presented the emperor with 125,000 rupees in cash, 'besides several trays full of jewels, rare wearing apparel, some elephants and horses', all of which presents were estimated at 11 lakh rupees. Both parties entered Faizabad well pleased with themselves, and the emperor was lodged in gracious style in the sprawling Lal Bagh for three days of festivities, ceremonies, and hunts. By February, Faizabad would have been at its most alluring—the Lal Bagh fragrant with roses and marigolds,

---

*Rafi-al-Daula, Nizam-i-Jang, Bahadur, Tadbir-al-Muluk.

the new havelis and palaces sparkling in the dense sunlight, and the Ghaghara bright with the pennants of many boats as the gathering heat of summer was kept at bay just a while longer. It was during one such excursion that the emperor, who knew of Gentil by reputation, learnt that his cortege was passing in front of the Frenchman's house*. Sensing the emperor's interest, Shuja sent for Gentil, who must have rushed out in some agitation, hurriedly straightening his red coat, to present his nazr to the emperor of Hindustan, who was sitting in an open palanquin, followed by four of his sons, also in palanquins. Shah Alam spoke kindly to Gentil, and even proposed that the Frenchman join his service, but Gentil sensibly preferred to remain at the court of Shuja-ud-Daula, 'because he was very attached to him and because he felt he would be more useful to the French at the court of Shuja-ud-Daula', though he would certainly not have admitted this to the emperor. Just a few years later Gentil would note that 'the Emperor began placing his hopes on the French nation, certain that an alliance with the French would help him free himself from the guardianship of his rebellious subjects and from the English'. Gentil's assessment of Shah Alam was that 'this prince lacked the force of character necessary to execute such a formidable project...and my presence could only prove detrimental to him because I would not be able to rid him of English control.'

Shuja organized several spectacular hunts† for the emperor's amusement in the hunting grounds of Faizabad during his stay, hunts being one of the greatest pastimes of the nobility, and of the nawab in particular. He kept 200 falcons specially for hunting birds—pheasants, geese, and ducks essentially, but also herons, who would put up so valiant a fight that it could take up to half an hour for the falcon to kill them. Tiger hunts were popular too, and the nawab kept thirteen elephants and a troop of cavalry and infantry just for this purpose. On one occasion during a tiger hunt, a particularly ferocious specimen launched itself with desperate courage at one of its tormentors, the English captain Gabriel Harper. The powerful beast had almost reached

---

*Gentil's house was within Qila Faizabad itself, opposite the nawab's vine garden, or Anguri Bagh.

†According to Gentil's *Receuil sur l'Indoustan*, animals hunted included boars, bears, tigers, buffaloes, wild bulls, rhinos, elephants, as well as pheasants, roosters, wild hens, and black and grey partridges.

the terrified captain on his elephant when the nawab, with astonishing sangfroid and accuracy, killed the animal with a single shot. Gentil noted many instances of the nawab's truly astounding expertise with the bow and arrow, as well as the musket, writing that he had witnessed him killing a peacock in flight, strike a turtle on the opposite side of a river with an arrow, and shoot at a clay pot bobbing by in a river with a single musket shot. Shuja would spend the entire season every year from the end of November to the end of June touring his lands, collecting revenue, and hunting every time the army marched. The nawab's travelling sarai was a magnificent sight. The fighting corps was led by Mirza Amani, at the head of the cavalry, followed by the infantry and then the artillery, the equipment and the kitchen.

For Shah Alam, however, the nawab organized the rather more sedate deer hunts, with the emperor upon an elephant and the nawab in the place of honour sitting behind him. Riding beside the royal elephant was Gentil himself. All around them were officers on horses, and huntsmen on foot. Cheetahs, which would have been used to hunt the deer, would have risen from the boxes that were carried on bullock carts when prey was sighted and they were released, their power uncoiled in a fury of sinew and blood.

Shah Alam would have been particularly appreciative of the nawab's gallant hospitality given that his stay at Allahabad, under the unlovely care of the British, was increasingly taking on the humiliating guise of servitude. 'The King resides now with his court and zanana and several children,' wrote Jemima Kindersley, 'in a few bungalows a short distance from the fort on the banks of the Yamuna, a dwelling very unworthy of the imperial dignity—where he keeps up a shabby fort of grandeur and parade, and has a few sepahis in his own pay, just sufficient to attend him when he appears abroad. They are clothed after the English custom, but are ill-disciplined and as ill-paid.' The emperor was dark-complexioned, Kindersley noticed, and 'of a grave deportment, bordering upon sadness.' At least she had the good grace to conclude that the 'indolent and inactive life' she accused him of leading was 'the consequence of repeated disappointments which have at last left him perhaps without even the hope of ever recovering the possession of his empire, or ever being seated on the throne of his ancestors at Delhi' (image

5). The British, meanwhile, struggled to keep up even a semblance of respect for the unfortunate emperor. In an infamous incident, the swaggering General Richard Smith, who had taken over from Robert Clive, and now strove to outdo him in violent megalomania, forbade the musicians of the naubat at Allahabad fort from playing the morning reveille, since it woke him up. When the musicians continued to play their music, loyal to the emperor whose special privilege the naubat remained, Smith sent soldiers with orders to fling the musicians from the top of the naubat khana. Luckily the musicians ran away nimbly, leaving behind a clatter of drums and trumpets, which were then thrown down the fort's gateway in lieu of the musicians. Smith would later holler at another offending soldier: 'Do you know, Sir, who is master here? It is I, because I am stronger.'

Unsurprisingly, Shah Alam was desperately keen to get back to his own beloved capital city. Ever since the disaster at Buxar, it had become chillingly clear that none of the forces at play were willing to risk money and lives for the sake of the Mughal emperor. Moreover, disquieting rumours had reached the imperial camp at Allahabad. The Rohilla chieftain Najib-ud Daula—who had been appointed by Ahmad Shah Durrani after the Battle of Panipat, had given up the governorship of Delhi in 1768 installing instead his dangerously inexperienced son, Zabita Khan*. It was being whispered that the sisters of the emperor had been molested, and Shah Alam was haunted by the danger in which his heir, the prince Jawan Bakht, his mother, and the other imperial ladies, now found themselves. But for the British, it was a great deal more politically expedient for the emperor to remain under their control at Allahabad and they prevaricated endlessly until one day, gathering the remains of his ragged dignity around him, Shah Alam summoned General Smith. Holding out his arms towards him crossed at the wrist, as if bound, Shah Alam implored him that it was no longer possible for him to remain like a prisoner at Allahabad. Though the EIC gave their grudging acquiescence, they were in no mood to send troops to accompany the emperor safely back to his capital. With the territories around Delhi still extremely volatile, the emperor needed soldiers to protect him so he turned to the other great power who had once stood by him at the Battle of Buxar—Shuja-ud-Daula. But the nawab

---

*Najib-ud-Daula died soon after, in 1770.

was loath to commit himself any longer to the unhappy emperor's threadbare cause. He gave Shah Alam many grandiose assurances of his support, but in the end managed to extricate himself from any such immoderate enterprise. A British traveller had marvelled about the nawab that because he was 'blessed with an eloquent tongue, he could calm the most violent tempers. Even though one doubted the sincerity of all his promises, it was nonetheless difficult to resist the seduction of his conversation.' The unhappy emperor would need to look elsewhere for a power to lead him back to Delhi.

In Faizabad, meanwhile, right through the decade following the Battle of Buxar, Gentil was a steady and loyal presence, assiduously courting the nawab so that the French cause might one day be bolstered. Indeed following the Seven Years' War and the Treaty of Paris of 1763, this was official French policy—to thwart British ambitions all over the world, so as to maintain a balance of power in Europe between France and Britain. French officers overseas were encouraged to participate covertly against British interests in their global empire, using whatever means they could. In Awadh, Gentil's salary was increased to 32,000 rupees per annum and in addition he received some 10,000 rupees in gifts every year. Even so, Gentil was not able to amass the sort of staggering fortune that his English colleagues and 'nabobs' like Madec were beginning to make. He was generous to a fault, forever ready to help out any compatriot fallen upon hard times with money, advice, and goods. As French Resident to the court of Shuja-ud-Daula, he attracted a large number of impecunious French citizens, some of dubious merit, but all of whom Gentil paid a stipend to until they were gainfully employed. Moreover, styling oneself a courtier at the lavish court of Faizabad was an expensive business. As a well-wisher would write in a letter years letter, when petitioning for a pension for the impoverished Gentil:

> To keep the nawab well disposed towards the French[*] he was obliged, as per the practice at the courts in India, to present to the nawab every year rare and precious presents that he ordered from Europe, at a considerable cost to himself. These expenses, attributable to his great zeal for his country, took up all the salary

---

[*]In a letter, Gentil writes that he needed to incur these expenses so that the French were allowed to import and export goods from Awadh without paying taxes.

of 50 thousand livres that the nawab paid him during his stay at Faizabad so that he was not able to save any money to bring back to France. He estimates at 200,000 livres the sum thus spent to further the cause of the French nation.

In his house opposite the Anguri Bagh,* Gentil would have led the capacious life of an Indian courtier, with attendants and servants. He kept pigeons, as did the nawab, in dovecotes with wire mesh on the windows, and he kept sheep and lambs. He would have kept company with the large number of Frenchmen in Faizabad, many of whom he lured to the service of the nawab.† Aside from training the nawab's European soldiers, and overseeing the foundry, Gentil accompanied the nawab on his hunts and excursions, and was a keen observer and participant in Faizabadi festivities, such as weddings and the Muharram processions. And, in 1772, Gentil contracted an alliance that placed him within the very fabric of elite Mughal-Awadhi society. A decade earlier, among the many refugees who had fled Delhi following the terror unleashed by the army of Ahmad Shah Durrani, there was an Indo-Portuguese widow called Lucia Mendec and her two small children who also sought refuge with Shuja. Lucia Mendec was no ordinary woman, and held the hereditary title of 'Juliana', which her ancestor Juliana Dias da Costa had acquired from Emperor Bahadur Shah‡, for her great services to the Mughal empire. Bahadur Shah had said of the original Juliana, 'if Juliana was a man, I would have made her Wazir'.§ In 1761, after the murder of her husband Sebastien Velho by Ahmad Shah Durrani's soldiers, Lucia Mendec was welcomed to Faizabad by Shuja and given a generous pension. Gentil was greatly moved by the tragic and romantic story of this once influential Indo-Portuguese family, and made great efforts to further their cause with the nawab. In 1772, 'thinking to further help them out', Gentil married Lucia's

---

*Frustratingly, we don't have details about the actual house, whether it was a haveli-style building or something different. It had an enclosure wall adorned with rustication and horizontal mouldings on its gate posts, in a European neo-classical type.
†These included Rene Madec, and also Daniel du Jardin, Michael Filose who wrote Persian poetry, and his son, Jean Baptiste de la Fontaine.
‡Also known as Shah Alam I, r. 1707–1712.
§For details of the fascinating story of Juliana, see Gentil, *Memoires sur L'indoustan*, p. 373. The family was gifted the haveli of Dara Shukoh, which was later bought from them for a nominal sum by Safdar Jang.

daughter, Therese Velho, who would have been a young teenager at this time while the Frenchman was forty-six (image 6).

Gentil's marriage to a family with connections to the Mughal court would no doubt have gained him access to the inner circles of the nawabi court. After all, both Nawab Begum and Bahu Begum had strong links to the Mughal imperial family and would certainly have known of the 'Juliana' legacy. In an earlier age, Emperor Bahadur Shah had witnessed Juliana extinguish a blazing fire using a palm branch previously blessed by Jesuit priests at Easter, and was so impressed with this proof of her piety that he entrusted her with the education of some of his sons. Eventually, Bahadur Shah would reward her tenacious loyalty to the royal family with various honours, the right to sit on the same battle elephant as him, and the titles of Khanum and Fidwi Duago Juliana.

Because Gentil had begun his career in the Deccan under the great French commander the Marquis de Bussy who was something of a connoisseur of Indian paintings, he was able to acquire an expertise in Indian art, culture, and history quite unique for a European of his time. According to Modave, Gentil far surpassed his mentor when it came to appreciating Indian history and architecture. About the great cave temples of Ellora, Modave railed with his usual acerbic irritation that 'among the mass of Frenchmen who visited (the caves), not one appreciated them for the marvel that they are. I found that only M Gentil understood them for the treasures that they represent.' Gentil showed discernment in the manuscripts he obtained too and we find his incongruous and sparse figure in that vaulting chain of knowledge that brought the Upanishads, untranslated from the original Sanskrit before then, from the seventeenth century to the attention of Western scholars in the nineteenth century. Gentil obtained manuscripts for Anquetil-Duperron, one of which was a copy of the *Sirr-i-Akbar*, the translation of the Upanishads into Persian undertaken by Dara Shukoh, Emperor Akbar's grandson. Anquetil translated the Persian into French and Latin, finally bringing these ancient texts to a wider Western audience, a moment that is considered a 'watershed in the history of western Indology'.

It may not be purely coincidental, therefore, that Gentil began writing his memoirs in 1772, also the year of his marriage, called

*Mémoires sur l'Indoustan: Ou Empire Mogol*, in which he rather felicitously added a chapter on 'Some Great Women of Hindustan' which allowed him to segue into a chapter on Juliana, and thereby the illustrious history of his own young wife. This might have been a way for Gentil, always more doleful than debonair, to claim a place of more flamboyant legitimacy now that he found himself constantly in the company of emperors, princes, and noblemen. In his memoirs Gentil would include details and anecdotes often not mentioned in any other histories of the time, which would carefully place him within the charmed circle of nawabi life.* To further underline the exalted circles he moved in, Gentil's memoir was dedicated to 'Shuja-ud-Daula, the constant friend and protector of the French.'

It was also around this time, in the decade between 1765–1775, that Gentil indulged in that most elite of Mughal pastimes—the setting up of a small art atelier. In Faizabad, Gentil would have had access to artists trained in the imperial Mughal style, as well as their descendants and pupils, and he would use them to create arguably the earliest and largest collection of art assembled by a single patron in Awadh.† Indeed, although there are no records of paintings being produced in Lucknow in the first half of the eighteenth century, in the second half of the century, all of Awadh was in an effervescence of cultural activity—the refugee poets, dancers, musicians, and artists creating new worlds of beauty and poetry for wealthy patrons, away from the churn and fire of a ravaged Delhi. Gentil would use the paintings he commissioned in his atelier to illustrate episodes from his memoirs, as well as the histories of India that he would write.‡

The artists involved in the production of these gorgeous paintings have always remained elusive, but we do know that two of Gentil's painters included Mohan Singh, son of the Delhi imperial painter Govardhan II, and Nevasi Lal.§ And in most of these works, Gentil's own earnest presence is unmistakable, both conceptually and literally.

---

*The details of Gentil's involvement in the peace proposals between Carnac and Shuja, for example, take up several pages in the memoirs, but are entirely missing in the British accounts of the same events.

†Indologist Jean-Marie Lafont proposed that the atelier set up by Gentil be recognized as the Faizabad School of Art.

‡During his twelve years in Faizabad, Gentil commissioned fifteen volumes of art.

§A letter in the ANOM mentions 'three painters working for ten years' to produce Gentil's works.

Scholar Dhir Sarangi writes of 'rigorous planning in the conception of both the whole, and of its constituent parts' in Gentil's collection, betraying a desire in the Frenchman to capture as much of the essence of this enigmatic country in a form that could be transmitted and translated to an elite, scholarly audience in France. This was no slipshod, haphazard collection of random images, prettily strung together to represent a 'life and times' of peoples and places of the exotic Orient. Rather, as scholars have now shown, there was instead a deep engagement of the Frenchman with the old Mughal traditions of artistic interpretation, using local sources such as Abu'l Fazl's *Ain-i Akbari*, in conversation with local painters steeped in the venerable Mughal miniature traditions, to create a new hybrid style tinged with the hues of many sources. Gentil would have shown his artists a range of different manuscripts to examine for ideas—perhaps the *Padshanamah* that Shuja had in his collection, the *Ain-i Akbari*, which Gentil possessed, and European works too.* Gentil's albums covered such diverse subjects as the history and mythology of India, the geography, the habits and costumes of the people, religion and philosophy, and the coins of India.

Perhaps one of the most beguiling of the works created by the Frenchman was a geographical work called the *Gentil Atlas*, made in 1770. Using both local and European sources,† Gentil created a visual cartography of the Mughal empire, dividing it into twenty-one subahs. At a time when there was no local school of map-making, Gentil used the descriptions written by Abu'l Fazl in the *Ain-i Akbari* to create European style maps with a great many more place names on the maps than any that had been created until then.‡ Gentil included geographical information on the regions and, in addition, each region had marginal drawings, with historical and cultural information relating to the province being mapped. The very first subah in the atlas is the subah of Delhi. Unlike the following folios which teem with the life of agitating minuscule figures and animals, the folio of Delhi is eerily quiet.

---

*Including, possibly, Bernard Picart's *Illustrations de Ceremoies et Coutumes Religieuses de Tous les Peuples du Monde*, published in 1737.
†According to Susan Gole, Gentil used the maps of Jean-Baptiste Bourguignon d'Anville.
‡*Gentil Atlas* contained more place names, and covered more area, than any other map of the eighteenth century. Mughal maps that existed were based on route marches while Hindu, Buddhist, and Jain cosmographies were not realistic geographical maps. Maps made by the British based on route marches were made with little accuracy until triangulation surveys began in the nineteenth century.

While all the signs of imperial life are present—banners, the Peacock Throne, naubat instruments—the emperor himself is conspicuously absent, as though he had simply stepped out of the page. Instead, it is in the margins of the subah of Ajmer that the emperor Shah Alam II is shown, receiving the pirzada of Ajmer, while in another corner the naubat noisily rings out the emperor's presence (image 7). In the folio on subah Aurangabad, there is a detailed drawing of the Ellora caves, from the survey that Gentil had personally conducted. The *Atlas*, then, is not a bland recording of Indian places, but is actively engaged with Mughal and nawabi life, with Gentil acting as interpreter. According to art historian Mildred Archer, the marginal paintings closely resemble works that would be made by artists Sital Das, Gobind Singh, and Ghulam Reza for an English patron—Richard Johnson, in 1780–1782. They would use the same palette developed in Gentil collections— grey, pink, mauve, pale yellow, and green. 'Adjustments to European tastes', writes Mildred Archer, 'had in fact begun at Faizabad at least ten years before Johnson went to Lucknow. It is also significant that in *Gentil's Atlas*, subjects which were later to become the stock-in-trade of "Company's painters" were already present in miniature form. Hitherto, the early date of this phenomenon in northern India has not been fully recognized, but as proof of it there is no more vivid testimony than Gentil's private copy of the illustrated atlas in the Library's collection'.

Despite being a fluent Persian speaker, Gentil's notes in his albums were written in French, so his prospective audience were French speakers—an elite gathering of scholars and researchers. Clearly Gentil hoped that much use would be made of the unique and precious information gathered so painstakingly by him in India. There is even a sharp injunction written in Gentil's inelegant scrawl, to any future sloppy readers of his beloved manuscripts, sternly forbidding them 'from touching the paintings with their fingers'. In a letter to the French king in 1778, Gentil wrote about his efforts in India: 'I spared no effort to attach the Indians to the French nation. They consider France first amongst all the nations,' he added perhaps somewhat wishfully. 'They love France. Despite the diminished French holdings in India, they expect that France will one day break their chains*.'

---

*The theme of 'breaking of chains' from British rule would crop up again and again in the writings of Frenchmen.

When Gentil finally returned home to Bagnols-sur-Cèze in 1778, he would take back 183 Indian manuscripts in Persian, Arabic, and Sanskrit. He also had an additional fifteen bound albums as well as a collection of armaments—swords, daggers, helmets, shields, muskets, axes, and more. He scorned an English offer to buy his entire collection for what would have been a huge sum—120,000 rupees, preferring to gift his collection to French king Louis XVI instead. But the king was in an unenviable position himself, soon to be swept up in the inferno of the French Revolution, and Gentil's collection would go largely unnoticed. Gentil's young wife, Therese Velho, would be dead within three months of landing in France, and Gentil would be left with three children to raise. He would be deprived of his pension post the French Revolution, and would be reduced to writing pitiable letters pleading for allowances for his three children. 'I was rewarded by the glory and the good name that I left behind in India,' he wrote humbly in 1778, 'but my poor children are right in accusing me of giving away to others what was theirs by right.' Perhaps most galling for Gentil would have been the fact that it was the English who would claim the rewards for being the originators of the 'Company'* school of European patronized paintings, while his immense legacy would be almost entirely forgotten. Gentil had already written with prescient bitterness tinged with fatalism about the military situation of the British in 1772 when he wrote that 'despite all their setbacks, it all works out well for the English. The storm gathers, but never comes crashing down upon them. Mark my words...all our plans will come to nought and the English will prosper.' His words were echoed in 1777 by Jean-Baptiste Chevalier, director of the French trading post at Chandernagore: 'I have lost all courage and energy in my incessant fractious dealings with the English, and in my dealings with the local chiefs who are instigated by them' he wrote glumly. 'We are clothed in opprobrium and humiliation. Every day is marked

---

*Paintings made by Indian artists for the English have for a while been called 'Company' paintings, a name first coined by art historian Mildred Archer in the 1970s, from an Urdu term used in Patna, 'Kampani Kalam'. Many art historians today hesitate to use this term, as it draws attention away from the indigenous artists and the variety of the material produced. It has been difficult to find a suitable alternative term. Jean-Marie Lafont proposes the Firangi School which, while including Europeans, still retains the other problematic implications.

by ever more dastardly behaviour by the English against the people of the French king, and his honour.'

But appearing on the hazy, gold-flecked horizon of Faizabad was a man of uncertain background and chameleon-like changeable mien, who would deal with a great deal more ruthlessness, cynicism, talent, and finesse with the nawabs, the noblemen, and the English, dastardly or otherwise.

# TINKER TAILOR SOLDIER SPY

The swaggering, somewhat jowly, man sitting in a sumptuous Mughal travelling tent was in a highly querulous mood in 1773 as he dictated a letter to his long suffering munshi, Kishan Sahai. 'The embroiderer is a bastard,' he snapped angrily at the munshi, who obediently scribbled down the words intended for the man's agent in Lucknow. 'He said he would finish the work within twenty to thirty days but he has not yet completed it!' Spread out in front of him were gorgeous swatches of cloths, with names that were poetry itself—Gulbadan (light-textured cloth made of a mix of silk and cotton), suzani (Tajikistan-inspired cloths), and qarmizi in nawabi green, badami white, gul-i-anar (pomegranate flower) red, or saffron yellow. But the sample of embroidery had failed to be delivered, yet again. Another complaining letter he dictated was to his agent in Faizabad: 'I do not like the spiceless pickle of the gourd, it is fit for poor people.' As for the sugar candy that he ate in alarming quantities, the verdict was succinct: 'too oily and not white.' Indeed, his agent in Faizabad was kept busy running errands and dispensing punishment to various suppliers and workers. A particularly errant employee was the man's gardener. 'Ask the gardener,' he wrote to his agent in fury, 'why he accepted (the job) in the first place…now that he is up to mischief and is negligent in his duty, beat him with a stick ten to twenty times and dismiss him.'

These furious letters were speedily delivered, for the man kept an impressive retinue of messengers using a relay system of horses, harkaras (couriers, literally har-kara—do all) and dak-bearers (post bearers) who jogged or galloped across the land, letters tucked into their turbans for safety. At one point, the man employed four dak-bearers and a masalchi (torch-bearer) at every 8 kos* of the road between Lucknow and Faizabad. And these letters were not simply the petulant outbursts of an irascible employer, but rather the detailed, if somewhat obsessive, instructions of a perfectionist for whom every aspect of his gargantuan household and business was equally important. Even the richly textured tents in which he lived while on campaign had been made according

---

*Approximately 1.8 km, working out to roughly 32 dak-bearers and 8 masalchis stationed on just this section of road.

to his precise instructions. The canopied howdah for his elephant was singularly wide, to accommodate his larger proportions, and had cushions to match the colour of the lining of the canopy. In fact, every aspect of the lacquered world of the Mughal nobleman was buffed to glowing perfection (image 8). In the evenings the man sometimes leafed through his collection of exquisite manuscripts, the miniature paintings jewel-bright. 'I relished the murabba (sweet fruit preserve) and enjoyed reading the book and going through the album,' he wrote one day graciously to a canny contact who had gifted him a fine copy of the *Gulistan*. Other evenings he lounged against silk bolsters and watched graceful kathak dancers, his dark eyes appraising under arched eyebrows, the scene lit by the flickering light of dozens of candles in silver candelabras. He would have been at his ease in the evenings in a jama made of the finest white muslin, with a turban in the Awadhi style. His hookah, made entirely of bidri-ware,* would have been placed by his side, filled with his favourite Multani tobacco while paan would have been served to him from his silver paan-daan. On his finger was a spectacularly beautiful table-cut, rectangular emerald signet ring, engraved with the finest nastaliq script bearing his title—Arsalan-e-Jang (Lion in Battle), a title bestowed upon him by Emperor Shah Alam himself (image 9).

Perhaps the one area of his life that constantly defied all attempts at good order and rectitude was his household at Faizabad. Here he had a large haveli filled with the usual paraphernalia of a busy Awadhi life. The spacious haveli was well furnished with carpets and purdahs of kamkhwab,† white farsh-e-chandani‡ on the floor, and there were different quarters for the unruly retinue of male and female servants, palki bearers, midwives, and kitchen staff. And it was from the zenana that the greatest disruptions to the man's life arose. One blistering day in May 1774, the man's haveli in Faizabad was the scene of a most scandalous fracas—the man's senior wife stormed into the quarters of the junior wife and dragged the pregnant and sobbing younger woman out, all the while bellowing at her that she was nothing but her slave. The senior wife's two young sons looked on in abashed horror while

---

*Made of a zinc, copper, and lead tin alloy.
†Indian brocade, embroidered with silver, gold, and silk threads.
‡A type of soft, white floor covering popularized by Noor Jahan.

Lal Khan, the khwajasara in charge of their care, stood helplessly by. 'This was not in the fitness of things and I am extremely pained,' wrote the man to his mother-in-law, mortified by this latest debacle. 'Imagine what honour will be left, if I call your daughter her slave,' he continued. 'It is loathsome for women to come out of their seclusion, not to speak of running out from their own house, to that of others and raising a commotion. Shame!'

But for all his thundering talk of shame and honour, and despite the priceless jewellery, fine muslin, and riotous attendants, this was no Mughal nobleman at all. Indeed, not only was he not a nobleman, he was not even a Hindustani. For bookended between the superb titles on his emerald ring proclaiming him Imtiyaz-al-Dawla Iftikhar-al-Mulk and Arsalan-e-Jang, was a rather more pedestrian appellation—Anthony Polier 'Bahadur'. For Anthony Polier was a 'firangi' man, born to Swiss Protestant parents of French descent in Lausanne, who arrived in Hindustan in 1757 at the age of sixteen as an engineer and joined the English army at Madras as a cadet. Youth, and a somewhat suspect background as a man of French origins, was no deterrent to the ambitions of the young Antoine who quickly anglicized his name to Anthony. He learnt languages with admirable fluency including English, Urdu, and Persian, and cultivated contacts with a self-interested focus that went quite beyond the limitations of country and religion. 'I had the happiness of unmaking their intrigues,' he wrote in 1766 about the Europeans he had denounced to his English superiors—soldiers who were planning a mutiny against pay cuts brought about by Robert Clive. 'The brilliant success that this expedition had is known in Europe', he continued. But despite Polier's satisfaction with his own brilliance, he was denied the promotions he was hoping for, blaming it on xenophobia towards him because he 'was not born English'.

Polier would languish for a few more years in Company service before he was able to use the favours of one of his patrons, the first governor of Bengal Warren Hastings*, to seek a more lucrative post with the nawab of Awadh. 'I felt the slight deeply,' confessed Polier about his lack of promotions within Company service. 'I hesitated no more to profit from the goodwill of Mr Hastings, and from the credit

---

*Hastings first arrived in India as a seventeen-year-old in 1750 where he joined the EIC as a clerk, or 'writer'.

that he had with the nabads, who had become allies of the English.' And thus began a three-way, high-stakes dance between Hastings, Polier, and Shuja, propelled by desire, fear, and greed, ending in an impeachment.

Warren Hastings was a man who enjoyed the doubtful blessing of looking ageless—his portraits all show a self-consciously pensive man with a long nose, pale and gaunt, a vaguely dreamy expression and an increasingly high forehead. According to Modave he had 'a polite but cold exterior' and was 'exceedingly reserved'. In his notes to the Seir Mutakherin, Haji Mustapha[*] wrote of Hastings that 'he always wore a plain coat of English broad-cloth, and never anything like lace or embroidery. His table (was) sometimes neglected; his diet sparing and always abstemious; his address and deportment very distant from pride, and still more so, from familiarity.' An austere, bookish, and cerebral man then, whose claims to frugality were somewhat belied by the huge sums of money he sent home to England,[†] by his later trial for impeachment on charges of corruption, by the speed and ostentation with which he spent the first fortune he made from India in 1765 which landed him in debt, and by the reputation of his second wife, Marian Hastings. Indeed, when the Hastingses returned to England in 1788, Marian presented herself wearing so much ostentatious silk and jewellery that she could boast of a personalized limerick in the satirical work *The Rolliad*:

> 'Tis Mrs Hastings' self brings up the rear!
> Gods! How her diamonds flock
> On each unpowdered lock!
> On every membrane see a topaz clings!
> Behold!—her joints are fewer than her rings!

One of the above-mentioned rings Marian possessed was, in fact, a rectangular cut emerald with exquisite calligraphy, extremely

---

[*] Haji Mustapha was the alias of a Frenchman, M. Raymond, who had converted to Islam. He translated Vol. 2 of *The Seir Mutaqherin* into English and provided footnotes.

[†] 'It has been shown that Hastings, in his thirteen years of office from 1772 to 1785, remitted to England at least 218,527 pounds. This sum was nearly ten times his annual salary, nearly ten thousand times the annual income of a poor gentleman.' See John T. Jr Noonan, 'The Bribery of Warren Hastings: The Setting of a Standard for Integrity in Administration,' *Hofstra Law Review*: Vol. 10, Iss. 4, Article 5. 1982.

reminiscent of Polier's own emerald ring.* Moreover, when Hastings returned to England, he would buy back the ancestral property which had once belonged to the Hastings family, Daylesford Estate, with over a thousand acres, and stuff it full of exquisite and priceless solid ivory furniture 'gifted' to him by Munni Begum, widow of Mir Jafar, once puppet of the British†. Nevertheless, ostentatiously plain and sober in appearance at least, Hastings had been sent to Bengal to sort out an administration that was plagued with corruption and excess ever since Clive had so unexpectedly secured a complete victory and amassed a colossal fortune. Modave's assessment of the state of affairs in Bengal was that 'when the English acquired Bengal...their first instinct was to extract as much profit as possible from an acquisition which could easily slip out of their hands, rather than to think of its prosperity. This corrupted the administration. Everyone thought about their own personal affairs and nobody worried about public affairs. A number of prodigious personal fortunes were made at many people's expense.' Polier would court Hastings assiduously, and finally in 1773 was able to write that he had 'accepted the post of architect engineer that he (Hastings) procured for me with Shuja-ud-Daula. I thus quit Calcutta to go to Faizabad where this nabab lived and on establishing myself there, I took on the customs and the usages of the Indians with whom I lived.'

And so it was that in Awadh, Polier 'went native' and took on the iridescent plumage of the Indo-Persianate culture that was spreading in opulent waves through Awadh. He corresponded with high-status Iranians, Afghans, as well as the Kayasthas and Khatris who had all adopted the language and the etiquette that was to become synonymous with the elegance of Awadh. While on tours outside the cities he would send for endless quantities of candles to light up his evenings, demand mango pickles, mango murabba, and falsa sherbet to have along with his meals, as well as coffee, tea, Madeira wine,

---

*Comparisons by experts would be required to ascertain if these rings were indeed engraved by the same engraver, thereby supporting the theory that the ring may have been gifted to Marian by Polier.
†Outside the scope of this book is the case of Raja Nand Kumar, a zamindar who accused Hastings of corruption, and in turn was accused of forgery, a crime which carried the death sentence at the time. He was tried by Hastings' friend Chief Justice Elijah Impey, found guilty, and hanged.

and brandy. There was an urgency in the way in which he wrote: 'send ¼ ser each of hot spices like darchini, choti elaichi, jaifal, and laung. Also if the Indian chef and bread-maker has reached, send him here quickly.' But Polier did not content himself with simply enjoying the spicy food and the delicious sweets, he was also a connoisseur, who confidently altered and moulded his world to his taste. 'Since the mango season has arrived,' he wrote one day to his overworked factotum, Gora Mistri, 'you should acquire two to three mans of pulpy raw mangoes and get first rate pickle prepared with white vinegar and the following ingredients: dry garlic, ginger, nigella seeds, aniseed etc and use these ingredients generously so that the pickles in the vinegar get thoroughly tender.'

At his haveli in Faizabad (image 10) he kept a bewildering number of birds and animals, including imported turkeys, ducks, partridges, waterfowl, all in elaborate birdhouses, and Barbari goats for milk. He grumbled when the alien turkeys died, admonishing Gora Mistri and telling him to feed the sturdy survivors 'wheat bran soaked in water; once in a week they should also be given onion pieces and dry garlic'. He attempted experiments in crossing the birds, and wrote excitedly about a letter 'containing information about the turkey ducklings and the waterfowl chicks and the possibility of getting their eggs roosted by Indian birds.' In his large gardens he planted both local and exotic species of bulbs and flowers, and kept his clearly harassed gardeners busy with his detailed instructions. He sourced plum, peach, and cherry saplings, planted grape vines, and had flower beds filled with cypress plants, narcissus, calendula, tulips, and jasmine. There was also a badar khana, or ice house, in which ice was produced in the broiling summer by means of salt crystals brought to Faizabad on camels. Polier's aesthetic sensibility was highly polished, unique to him, and supremely confident, and he did not hesitate to influence even the embroidery patterns of the cloths he traded in. He was critical of the Karchobi sample—raised metallic thread embroidery work—that was sent for approval from Faizabad. It was 'ten times inferior' to the ones made at Agra, he grumbled sniffily, and ordered embroidery made without borders, only a flower design. And while he would influence every aspect of the Indo-Persianate world he inhabited—the colours of the clothes, seal engravings, house and tent constructions, embroidery patterns, even letter-writing—perhaps his single most influential contribution would be to the art of the Mughal muraqqa, or album. For like his friend and fellow Francophone firangi, Jean-Baptiste Gentil, Polier also patronized a painting atelier. And at the head of his atelier was a painter who is now considered by scholars to be one of the most outstanding and prolific of the late Mughal masters—a man called Mehr Chand.*

Mehr Chand too had fled the chaos of Delhi and by 1765 had followed Shuja to Faizabad. Though Mehr Chand is now considered a master painter, Polier's relationship with this extraordinary artist appears to have been fairly imperious. Polier gave Mehr Chand detailed instructions on what and how to paint, and scolded him like he would his son, wife, carpenter, or clerk. There was certainly no special consideration for the loftier status, or indeed the finer feelings of this extraordinary artist. 'I fail to understand why you are sitting idle', he once wrote in reply to Mehr Chand's request for payment. 'Prepare some more similar portraits if you have finished the ones you were engaged with so far. Making portraits is your work, and it is meaningless to sit idle…you will receive the money and not be in distress anymore.' Later, when trying to lure Mehr Chand to Delhi, he was slightly wheedling (Rest assured that in all cases I will be considerate towards you) and untruthful (The climate here is good).

Polier also wrote regularly to his Indian wives, except that they were not really his wives at all, simply his 'bibis',† whose status would have been fragile, and as evanescent as the mist that sometimes rolled over the Ghaghara. This would explain the senior bibi's‡ fury when she found out her younger co-wife was pregnant. Despite her own sons, she would have known that a younger, favoured bibi with a son of her own could have threatened her position in Polier's household. And when Polier found out about the unseemly incident, he wrote to his senior bibi's mother in alarming language: 'you have not understood my

---
*For more information on the career and art of Mehr Chand, see Malini Roy, *Idiosyncrasies in the Late Mughal Painting Tradition: The Artist Mihr Chand, Son of Ganga Ram*, University of London, PhD, 2009.
†European men, especially in the mid- to the end of eighteenth century, formed temporary liaisons with local women, who were called their bibis.
‡Polier's bibis have been named Jawahar and Khward in the translation of the *Ijaz-i-Arsalani* (The Wonders of Arsalan, from his Mughal title Arsalan Jang). Elsewhere, Claude Martin will refer to them as Jugnu and Zinnat.

nature', he said threateningly. 'I swear that if there is any harm done to junior bibi or to her pregnancy, I will finish both of you (the bibi and her mother) there and then and will never see your faces again.' For these were ultimately transactional relations, with Polier buying the girls, sometimes as young as nine or ten. He appointed a trusted woman, Sayyid Begum, to look after them and supplied them with copper utensils, clothes, and some carpets, and gave instructions for them to always be clean and for their hair to be dressed and combed. Some of the girls he kept, and trained in song and dance, hiring qawwals for their musical instruction. To the khwajasara Lal Khan he wrote: 'Insist upon the singers to work hard in the training so that I enjoy the fruits of their labour when they reach here.' Some of these girls became his concubines, and in turn were assimilated in the training machinery. 'I do not know what is the state of preparation of dance and music there these days,' Polier wrote to his senior bibi. 'What are the kind of songs and dance being taught? This is your responsibility, and you should take care of this and write.'

For there was an unsavoury side to Polier's suave and cultured Persian nobleman persona. Some of the young girls he bought he then sent to European men. In 1775, he was somewhat doubtful when he learnt the age of a girl whom he had just bought in Farrukhabad. A girl, moreover, euphemistically referred to as a 'gift'. 'Earlier I had learnt that the gift from Farrukhabad is 11 to 12 years old. Now I gather from your letter that she is 8 to 9 years old', he wrote. But the age of the child was no deterrent to Polier, who intended her as a gift for one Mr Louis Perceret, his chargé d'affaires. He tracked her movements from Farrukhabad relentlessly, furious when the child's father seemed to have a change of heart, and refused to send her. 'You had acquired the deed (razinama) with the seal of the qazi from her father,' he railed to his agent, and ordered that all dissenting persons be punished severely. Ultimately, the clearly unwilling child, along with two other 'slaves' from Srinagar, one boy and one girl, were successfully handed over to Mr Perceret.

Though he was deputed to Shuja as an architect and engineer, he was also primarily a hawker of that most precious of commodities—information. Polier's mastery over the flow of information through Awadh was explicitly visible through the exceptionally large network of harkaras and dak posts he maintained. These dak posts were vital to relaying information throughout Mughal India—the EIC had only established regular posts between Calcutta, Patna, and Benaras at this time. Their knowledge of the hinterland, meanwhile, was sketchy. And so Polier spied for Hastings in Awadh and Delhi, informing him about the movements of the nawab but also about the activities of other Frenchmen in the region. 'The French have machinated much more than I had even thought of, and may again do it should they have an opportunity,' he wrote to Hastings in 1776 from Delhi. 'Three battalions with English officers, in their quarters, will secure that point, particularly if influence is used to drive or extirpate those two chicks—Sombre and Madec.'

To keep his lines of communications running smoothly between his numerous multi-lingual contacts, Polier sent bribes and 'gifts' to concerned parties, ranging from the pedestrian—essence of darchini for the young Raja Chait Singh of Benaras\* for example; to the more luxurious—a watch for Mughal nobleman Nawab Murid Khan, engraved emerald rings for Europeans; to the outright bizarre—aphrodisiacs ('medicines to enhance your vigour and vitality') for a zamindar of Srinagar; and finally the troubling 'gifts' of young girls and slave children.

Though he spied for Hastings and the British, this did not deter Polier from carefully gathering information that could be passed on to whoever would be most grateful. And so Polier kept a colossal network of informants and contacts that spread out like a spiderweb over the land. He kept separate entourages at the courts of Faizabad, Lucknow, and, later, Delhi. Information fizzed through the region, tucked into the turbans of the harried runners. 'No new letters have been received (in Faizabad). I know nothing about the developments (at Etawah, at Shuja's court) he wrote irritably in 1775 to an employee of the nawab's. 'You must under all circumstances be present at M Gentil's and keep recording the daily news so that the information is available here.' And while he owed his position in Awadh to Hastings's favours, Polier did not even complete the surveying work that was required of him,

---

\*Upon the death of Balwant Singh of Benaras in 1770, his seventeen-year-old son, Chait Singh, with 'handsome features and engaging manners' was made raja, as noted by Ashirbadi Lal Srivastava.

and instead undertook many building assignments for the nawab and engaged in trading and commercial activities with gusto. Polier was something of an entrepreneur, along the lines of another Frenchman, his good friend Claude Martin, and he also made a fortune trading in goods, including indigo. He sourced luxury European goods for the court, and when he sold goods for Europeans, he charged them 50 per cent of the profit. For all his mercantile preoccupations, Polier also remained a man of action and gamely followed Shuja, whom he described as having a 'warrior temper', on a campaign, and ended up spearheading the siege of Agra against the Jats on behalf of great imperial warlord Najaf Khan.

Polier wrote letters* in Persian, French, and English, depending on the interlocutor and he was by turn, a refined Persian scholar, appreciatively commenting on the calligraphy or painting of a precious manuscript, a Mughal nobleman speaking authoritatively to imperial courtiers, a Frenchman plying his trade for the nawab, or a clipped English soldier, genial and accommodating. A shape-shifter, he could be many men at once, to different people. Writing to his diwan in 1776 about the need to find a good agent to manage his affairs he airily said: 'I need a Bengali here to take care of my work at the court. This place (Delhi) is full of Kashmiris. However, to me there is no distinction between a Bengali and a Kashmiri.' In the same year, writing to Hastings about some money he was trying to recover from an employee, he wrote that he was hopeful of obtaining the money and that 'to get this from a sircar, and a Bengali to boot, I know is not an easy task', clearly echoing sneering prejudices he would have heard in Calcutta among the English employees. Scholar Maya Jasanoff has called men like Polier and Claude Martin 'border crossers, social climbers, chameleons and collectors.' And while for Polier the façade of the chameleon mostly held true—he was generally well liked by his peers and Europeans, and Modave called him 'a good man, full of honour and integrity (who) enjoys good company'—very rarely the façade seems to have slipped, with one contemporary noting that his appearance was 'uncouth...and his address ungainly'.

---

*Polier's Persian letter-book was put together by his munshis, upon his instructions, and some 2,000 of his Persian letters were included in the *Ijaz-i-Arsalani*. (M. Alam and S. Alavi, *A European Experience of the Mughal Orient: The I'jāz-i Arsalānī (Persian Letters 1773–1779) of Antoine-Louis Henri Polier*, Oxford University Press. 2001)

For all Polier's braggadocio confidence, it appears that Shuja had his reservations about Polier when Hastings sent him to Faizabad as his engineer. Though an earlier letter had betrayed his eagerness at employing a Persian-speaking firangi, by 1773 the nawab had become a great deal more circumspect, perhaps more leery now about these grasping foreigners. 'I am here alone in a country of strangers courtesy your kindness,' wrote Polier to the nawab piteously in 1773. 'It will be difficult for me to live in your court if you do not take proper care of me.' Polier was playing fast and loose with the truth considering he had a full zenana and a clutch of Franco-Indian children and was hardly a stranger in a strange land. But the nawab kept him waiting for at least six months before allowing him a visit to his court. The nawab had reason to be very wary, for many of the Europeans in Shuja's employ owed their positions to Polier, and were indebted to him. They included Khwaja don Pedrose de Silva, who was fluent in Persian and English, and had translated Persian books into English for Polier. Gora Mistri was also in the nawab's employ, while simultaneously looking after Polier's commercial interests and another nawabi employee, the French Jesuit Padre Wendel, was also a spy and a close friend of Polier's.

The question of Polier's own sense of identity and belonging is an intriguing one. On the one hand, having arrived in the country as a young teenager, the beguiling customs, language, and aesthetics of his adopted country were clearly second nature to Polier. At the same time, his keen sense of ambition meant he instantly aligned himself with the English, his Swiss Protestant background providing him enough ground cover to enter service with the EIC. He avowedly supported the British aversion to Frenchmen in Awadh and was vociferous in his animosity towards men like René Madec, for example, but was entirely genial towards Gentil and towards some other Frenchmen whom he even housed clandestinely on his estates. While Hastings was relentlessly supportive of Polier, other EIC agents were much more suspicious of him, given the climate of antipathy towards the French in India, and his position always remained ambiguous. In a letter to an Indian chieftain, Polier referred to the Frenchman Claude Martin as 'Sardar I Angrez', a foreigner in English service. And while Polier was proud of his Persianate lifestyle—his art, his manuscripts, his exquisite and elegant objects—he was often peremptory and high-handed in his dealings with local men. In the hundreds of letters he wrote to Indian artisans, clerks, noblemen, and emperors, not one betrays real warmth and empathy. At best they are businesslike, polite, and condescending.

Ultimately, the person that Polier owed the greatest allegiance to was Polier himself. To the advancement of his own cause and his personal fortune, Polier was determined, focused and tenacious. Notions like patriotism and loyalty appear like veils of gold dust when applied to Polier—beautiful but ephemeral, scattered with a single breath. If there ever was a core of vulnerability in Polier's somewhat dissolute grifter's heart it may have been in his love for his sons. He wrote tender letters to his two young boys in Faizabad, Bare Baba and Chote Baba,* and sent them pomegranates and oranges, and embroidered caps and slippers. He clothed them in the garb of little Persianate gentlemen and wrote to them in Urdu but instructed them in the ways of being firangi: 'it is necessary that you go for horse riding and for strolls in the garden to enjoy the greenery and the beautiful flowers', he wrote to 'Anthony Babajaan',† who seemed to show rather more inclination to lounge indoors, away from the roasting sun, eating pomegranates. 'You should visit Captain [Claude] Martin two or three times a day without fail. Sit with him for some time and introduce yourself to whoever comes there so that you get used to interacting with people.' He sent them milk, oranges, and vegetables from his gardens, horses to ride, and indulged their requests for money.

And then dismayingly, in May 1775 he wrote: 'I was shocked to learn about the sad demise of my younger son. Since we are helpless and have to abide by the will of God, we can only be patient. Please take utmost care of the elder son.' Then in the same letter, almost in the same breath, he tells his interlocutor to 'be careful about the copying of the *Ain-i Akbari* because it has not been ready for quite some time.' It can appear baffling to the modern reader, that a father would spare no more than a line to acknowledge the death of a beloved child, and be equally concerned with a matter of scholarly interest. But not long after this tragic occurrence, Polier wrote a letter to his master painter Mehr Chand: 'I have learnt ...that you are preparing a painting of the

---

*Bare Baba was also known as Anthony 'Babajaan'. Perhaps also Didar Baksh. Chote Baba, perhaps Qadir Baksh.
†It is not known if Anthony survived into adulthood.

dance. I instruct you to suspend this work for the moment. Instead prepare a half-size portrait of Didar Baksh.' The identity of Didar Baksh has long remained a mystery, and scholars cannot even be sure if the name referred to a male or a female. Might this, therefore, have been the name of Polier's younger son, in whose name he also earlier asked for a small spade, possibly as a plaything. Perhaps, ruminating over the loss of his child, Polier thought to have a memento of him in the way he loved best, through art.*

For all Polier's obsessive interest in his art collection, when he was finally to leave Hindustan in 1788 he put away his soft muslin robes and embroidered shawls, and abandoned his bibis, leaving no provision for them. For Polier, in the end, there was a price for everything. Even, and especially, for beauty.

---

*This painting, a half-sized portrait of Didar Baksh, has never been identified by scholars among the many paintings attributed to Mehr Chand for Polier.

# A PORTRAIT OF A NAWAB

When, in 1772, Shuja first saw the portrait that was painted of him, he must have been somewhat startled. There had been portraits painted of him before by his court painters, naturally, but they were always in the familiar side profile of the Mughal miniature, the features indistinguishable from any other except for a distinctive, jaunty moustache—a coy clue to the identity of the minuscule figure. A couple of centuries earlier when Jesuit priests had unveiled an oil painting of the Madonna in Agra, it had caused pandemonium, the agitated townsfolk rushing to prostrate themselves before this apparently divine apparition. And now before Shuja was an enormous image (image 11) in which the nawab, captivatingly human, looked out of the painting just past the viewer's gaze, with magisterial power and dignity certainly, but also a certain haunting thoughtfulness. The material of his jamdani jama fell in gorgeous, soft folds and the brocade effect of his kamkhwab Persian jacket glittered like gold. Perhaps the nawab might have felt uncertain about a painting which betrayed his humanity all too clearly. Might the nawab have been troubled, also, to see how the painter had captured the expression of his oldest son, Mirza Amani, who was looking up at his father with an expression that was at the same time anxious and admiring, but with a tiny pucker of amusement in his small, full mouth.

The painting that brought to life the nawab in such textured and troubling detail was the work of the first major British artist to travel to India—Tilly Kettle. As art historian Mildred Archer has written, 'in the beginning at least, artists were lured to India by visions of splendid Maharajas, loaded with rupees and anxious to divest themselves of riches in return for portraits in the British manner'. Tilly Kettle, with the earnest brown eyes of a spaniel in a plain face, was thirty years old when he arrived in India, propelled by an urgent desire to make his fortune. This would explain why he had barely grazed the shores of India when he rushed with unseemly haste, not to some picturesque backwater, but to the court of the fabulously wealthy nawab of Arcot. From there he hurried to Calcutta and then on to Faizabad, to the court of Nawab Shuja-ud-Daula, clutching his letters of recommendation from the governor of Fort Williams. It was to Kettle's great good fortune that his novelty value earned him the commissions of both Shuja and some British residents including General Robert Barker. Later European painters would not be so lucky, the nawabs disinclined to be treated as gullible fools to be parted from their money.

At Faizabad, Kettle painted a number of full-length portraits of Shuja, either alone, or alongside his sons and some of the English residents. In all these portraits the figure of the nawab, forty years old now, and in the prime of his life, dominates the paintings, towering head and shoulders above the other figures, captivating the audience with the easy confidence of his steady, warm gaze. Kettle also painted some of the court personages, and the dancing girls and bibis of Faizabad, but it was his oil portraits of the nawab which were the most influential. These portraits immediately caused something of a frisson amongst the art cognoscenti of Faizabad for, after all, never had this most powerful figure in Awadh been painted with such shocking candour and recognizable immediacy. Patrons like Polier and Gentil urged their painters to copy these oils, and a brand-new idiom for the physiognomy of the nawab, somewhat like a blueprint, now came into circulation.*ℹ Not all these studies were equally felicitous. Painters trained in the Mughal tradition of the side profile, struggled visibly with the full-frontal format, the subjects often ending up with an unfortunate squint.

Kettle's successful dalliance at the court of Shuja-ud-Daula would have important repercussions for the trajectory of the visual representation of Awadh. Following his example, a number of European painters would arrive in a modest wave in Awadh—Johann Zoffany, Charles Smith, Ozias Humphry and, later, the Daniells—Thomas and his nephew, William. These painters, and the way in which they interpreted Faizabadi and Lucknawi buildings, people, and culture, would powerfully mould European imaginings of Awadh. Kettle himself stayed three years in India, living with an Indian bibi and fathering two daughters, christened Anne and Elizabeth. He then returned to England sans bibis or daughters, but with a tidy fortune, which he proceeded to spend speedily.†

---

*Even in future generations, many portraits 'in the style of Kettle' came to be made.
†So ruined did Kettle find himself within a few years that he decided to return to India, but fell ill and died en-route at Aleppo in 1786.

In 1774, Gentil borrowed four of Kettle's portraits of the nawab, wanting to have miniatures made of them to take back with him to France. One of his Indian painters made such a fine painting based on Kettle's, of the nawab and his son, that Gentil proudly showed it to Shuja, who in turn liked it so well that he kept it. When Gentil found out the following day that the nawab had then gifted the miniature to the British Resident, Nathaniel Middleton, who had also greatly admired it, he quite understandably felt aggrieved and protested bitterly to the nawab. 'What need have you of this painting,' the nawab questioned Gentil smilingly. 'Have you not my image engraved upon your heart?' 'Yes, indeed,' replied Gentil, well versed by now in Persian pleasantries, 'but how might I show it to my friends in France, not being able to remove it from my heart? Since you have kept my beautiful miniature, I shall keep the original.' And so it was that Kettle's painting of the nawab found its way to France, and hangs today at Versailles.

Scholars are uncertain when it comes to evaluating the legacy of Shuja as a patron of art.* Unlike earlier emperors and patrons, there is a scarcity of clearly signed and attributable albums, and an identifiable stylistic imprint for Awadh in the second half of the eighteenth century. What is clear, however, is that the eighteenth century in northern Hindustan was often a very violent, chaotic, and turbulent time and this affected not only the artists and the art, but also the historiography of art. For in the eighteenth century, there are very few of the expansive and erudite treatises on art which flourished in the seventeenth century, or the steady production of exquisite muraqqas in impeccable taste and style that the earlier Mughal emperors had most felicitously ensured. Instead, in the eighteenth century and then in 1857, the great centres of Mughal art would be raided and destroyed time after time, with a violence that was visceral and all-consuming and the cities of Delhi, Faizabad, Lucknow, Murshidabad would be torn apart, brick by brick, and set ablaze, folio by folio. Art was first 'gifted', then destroyed, looted, and hidden away, and even today, individual folios of beautiful late Mughal art appear on the market, their provenance unknown. Entire collections were seized from their

---

*It is believed that Shuja was the patron of at least two albums including the 'Fremantle' Album in the Chester Beatty Museum and the Small Clive album. It is also thought that there was an album presented to Nathaniel Middleton, now lost.

patrons, taken to the West, and then confusingly rebaptized with the name of the British legator, such as the so-called Clive albums and the Douce albums so that the origins of these works remain shrouded in mystery and etymology. Even within the country, museums in India remain opaque in their dealings, and many priceless collections and paintings are hopelessly and pointlessly beyond the reach of any but the most intrepid scholars. It is, therefore, not surprising that it is difficult to attribute entire muraqqas to individual patrons, or to trace the trajectory of individual artists with certainty. In contrast to this there are the impeccably catalogued, sealed and signed collections of Polier and Gentil, deposited in the safety of European museums, their enchanting images and personalized notes an irresistible counterpoint to the nawab's apparent absence.

What is indisputable is that art flourished in Awadh in the second half of the eighteenth century like it had never done before. Artists experimented with great freedom with themes of naturalism, and detailed backgrounds were now carefully painted in. Calligraphers arrived in Awadh too, including the Persian-born Hafiz, who became a sarkari calligrapher as well a teacher of calligraphy.* Apart from being patrons themselves, the nawabs could also buy muraqqas and folios as soon as they appeared on the market, these gorgeous items of prestige sometimes coming straight from the ateliers of the emperors, as Delhi was despoiled time and again. And though no written records remain of the migration of these Mughal artists, scholars have studied the styles of paintings, to painstakingly piece together the history of some of the artistic legacy of Awadh.

Awadhi artists in the second half of the eighteenth century became deeply interested in light and shadow, and the creation of volume and space. Some of these ideas, naturally, were occasioned by exposure to European art. After all, in the sixteenth century under Akbar and then Jahangir, Mughal artists had studied European art extensively, absorbing ideas about space and depth and naturalism with great subtlety and craft. The presumption was that after this cataclysmic clash of Persianate and European art, Mughal artists would inevitably

---

*Hafiz's calligraphy was so valuable that it was said that people bought passages written by his hand at enormous prices. Rough copies of his work were said to sell in the bazars for one rupee per letter of the alphabet.

follow the path of greater realism in their paintings. This, however, was not the case, and the grumbling criticisms of scholars who found this baffling grew loud. But as art historian Kavita Singh has so peerlessly shown,* there was no smooth transition to European style realism because the Mughal artists chose not to do so and allowed themselves the liberty of using the Persian style, or the European one, or indeed a hybrid of both at once if the painting required it. Some scholars now see the style of artists as visual language, to be 'read' only by the discerning, using a subtle Morse code of signals. Indeed, to be able to correctly understand or 'read' such a painting, explains Kavita Singh, the paintings needed to be understood alongside 'poetry, rhetoric, philosophy and theology—and also astronomy, astrology, music, medicine, physiognomy and mathematics' in addition to the dynastic history and political ideologies of the time. And as it was with the Mughal artists of the sixteenth century, so it was with Awadhi artists in the eighteenth century too.

There were a number of great Mughal artists who were active in Awadh, both in Faizabad and then later in Lucknow, in the mid- to late eighteenth century. Apart from Mehr Chand, there was Faizullah†, Mir Kalan Khan, Nidhamal and Fakirullah, amongst others, who had links to the imperial court at Delhi. The unsuspecting amateur, however, will find themselves assailed by entirely contradictory opinions on the very same artist, by different scholars, at different points of time. And of these names, it is Mir Kalan Khan who is the most controversial, opinion on him veering wildly from the angrily derogative to the subtly appreciative. He has been called one of the 'great oddballs of Indian history', his subjects described as 'demented or fractious'.‡ Others have startlingly claimed that his 'capricious reversals of naturalism for superficial effect seem to cover a personal coldness'.§

Mir Kalan Khan's work is certainly distinctive. He explored firelight and other internal light sources, by night, almost obsessively

---

*All essays by this superlative scholar are treasures, and the interested reader is urged to look at Kavita Singh, *Real Birds in Imagined Gardens: Mughal Painting Between Persia and Europe*, London: Getty Research Institute, Getty Publications, 2017. See also works by Yael Rice, Malini Roy, Molly Aitkin, Friederike Weis.
†Art historian John Seyller has traced the genealogy of Faizullah, who was the son of Faqirullah Khan and the grandson of Muhammad Afzal, all three Mughal artists who worked in Delhi.
‡By Terence McInerney, auctioneer and art dealer.
§Linda York Leach, his most vocal critic.

and his paintings fairly glow with a burning luminescence. Even his figures sometimes appear to flicker with an internal fizzing energy, their tiny limbs askew, ravaged by an invisible filament of energy. In other paintings, within the very same image, there are scenes from different eras or different places; large-eyed ladies from the Rajput tradition and Deccani damsels with their golden robes parlaying companionably with Persian influenced 'moon-faced' beauties. Kavita Singh has described how these are not pastiches at all, or some lunatic inability to form a visually coherent narrative. Instead, the images need to be understood within an immense repertoire of artistic knowledge, both Persian and Indic, past and present.* And this was something that the cultured and refined nawabs of Awadh would have been entirely aware of.

Art historian Isabelle Imbert has brought to light some interesting conclusions about Awadhi art and indeed even about Awadhi society. There is a phenomenon that is unique to Faizabad and Lucknow, Imbert points out, and that is the inclusion of full-page delicate flower paintings in large numbers. There were flower paintings earlier too, but never in the quantities seen in Awadh, where half a muraqqa might be just flower paintings. There was also the disappearance of pages of calligraphy in the albums, so that the flower images represented a replacing of Persian poetry with visual poetry. Together, these clues seem to point to a greater democratization of art and painting, with a knowledge of calligraphy no longer necessary. Scholar Friederike Weis meanwhile has shown that there were an increasing number of women in the images,† singly or in groups, in albums made for Shuja and for the Europeans. Intriguingly, this greater visibility of women could indicate the patronage of women. After all, women like Bahu Begum might well have had muraqqas in their trousseaus which they brought with them from imperial Delhi and been patrons of artists as well. And then there were the European wives of EIC

---

*For this fascinating new reading of Mir Kalan Khan, see Kavita Singh's 'Elephants in a Landscape: Dakhi Poetry and the Poetic Imagination of Mir Kalan Khan', Prahlad Bubbar's website, 2017 and *Real Birds in Imagined Gardens*, and Molly Aitken, 'Parataxis and the Practice of Reuse, from Mughal Margins to Mīr Kalān Khān.' *Archives of Asian Art*, Vol. 59, 2009, pp. 81–103.

†These were images of women in terrace scenes, enjoying a hookah, watching a performance, or at their toilette, riding horses, feasting in the harem, etc.

agents, who could also have sponsored artists.

And finally there is the art of Faizullah who, like the culture of Awadh itself, is unlike anything else at all. Art historian Stuart Cary Welch has infamously written of this great late Mughal master that 'European "scientific" perspective struck Faiz-ullah...with the force of a custard pie'. Striking though that metaphor is, it is once again a tired criticism of Faizullah's unique and shocking use of aerial perspective in his landscapes. In some of his most famous paintings, Faizullah has multiple dizzying vanishing points, worlds within worlds, and an astonishing clutter of buildings and activities within paintings which seem to stretch on forever into the distance. These 'terrace paintings' of Faizabad were analysed by Kavita Singh, who offers an altogether more nuanced appreciation of these extraordinary paintings, by placing them firmly within the historical events that shaped them. The paintings were being made at the same time as Shuja was reshaping the very horizon of Faizabad, replacing the semi-permanent structures of his predecessors with grand buildings—palaces, forts, mausolea, mosques and more—all gleaming white limestone and gold. The earlier nawabs, Saadat Ali and Safdar Jang, had commissioned their grandest havelis and buildings in Delhi, which a scholar describes as 'the greatest Indo-Islamic style domestic edifices ever commissioned during the history of Mughal architecture'. But Shuja would shape the landscape of Faizabad instead.

This maelstrom of activity signalled to everyone that the nawabs of Awadh were there to stay, no longer feudatories of crumbling Mughal overlords. The nawabs would now claim their own built legacy, which Faizullah demonstrated in the excessively ordered and delineated cityscape of a fairy-tale garden city. While the foreground of these paintings is luminous with the honeycomb white terraces and endless earthly delights of Faizabad, in the distance there are tiny marching soldiers, faint elephants with emperors on them and minuscule forts which look suspiciously like the Qila-e-Mualla in Delhi. There are also elements from these paintings that are exact replicas from the great *Padhshanama*\* which was at this very time in the library of Shuja. This, explains Singh, represented the history of violence and anarchy that

---

\*Illustrated history of the reign of emperor Shah Jahan. Shuja-ud-Daula had acquired this painting and it would remain the property of the nawabs until it was gifted to Governor General John Shore in 1799 by Nawab Saadat Ali Khan.

had been the legacy of Delhi for the past few decades, and especially during the catastrophic Buxar episode. This, then, was troublesome Delhi, with its refugee king, its storm winds, and abraded veneer, which Shuja now wanted no part of, and which Faizullah had discreetly relegated to a hazy, distant set-piece (image 12).

# FATHERS AND SONS

Mirza Amani, a rotund, soft-limbed and splutteringly gregarious young person, must have long laboured with the desire to compete with a dashing and handsome father whose idea of a fine time was to 'risk his life in riding a most unruly horse or elephant, in hunting a ferocious tiger with the sword or lance and in swimming across a river more mighty than the Ganga during the rainy season and infested with dangerous reptiles'. A man, moreover, who was charming and suave, and who had the great gift of making every person he met feel personally singled out and cherished. Growing up in the intimidating presence of such a father, it was not surprising perhaps that Nawab Shuja-ud-Daula's eldest son was always found sadly wanting. Historian Mohammad Faiz Baksh was particularly stinging in his description when he wrote that 'while he was sitting, he seemed to be a young man of tall stature but when he stood up his head only reached the waists of those around him. From his childhood he was obese; his fat ears, neck and double chin were one fleshy mass'.

Tilly Kettle's portrait of the nawab and the twenty-four-year-old Mirza Amani belies this harsh description, at least to some extent. In the portrait, the young Mirza does indeed suffer in comparison to the stately figure of the nawab, appearing apologetically hunched and turtle-like with his rounded back and short limbs. Nonetheless, if the nawab was exceptionally tall, almost 6 feet, then the mirza would have stood around 5 feet 4 inches, which was almost exactly average for an Englishman of the late eighteenth century, for example\*, so the navel-gazing imp of Faiz Baksh's description was a snide exaggeration. What the portrait does betray is a sort of anxiety, in the way the mirza looks up at the nawab, and in his plump hand that clutches his cummerbund, as if desperately gathering himself together in the presence of his father. Where the nawab grasps a katar in one hand and a sword in the other, Mirza Amani holds no weapons, and instead wears a decadent satlara string of pearls. Even his small, scratchy moustache looks apologetic compared to the resplendent whiskers of the nawab.

An incident that occurred when the mirza was a teenager betrays

---

\*The average height for an English male at the end of the eighteenth century was 5'5".

this anxiety to please his father, a hopeless desire that was destined to be constantly thwarted. On one occasion the nawab was returning to his capital and was organizing the crossing of a bridge by his large retinue which included Bahu Begum and her entourage. There was a great crush of elephants, horses, camp-followers, baggage bearers, all waiting to cross the river when Mirza Amani suddenly lumbered into the melee on an elephant. Apparently blithely unaware of the pandemonium he was causing, Mirza Amani struggled to control his elephant in an effort to make the animal bow down on its knees to salute the nawab, who was watching in growing annoyance. Finally, the young mirza had to content himself with simply saluting his father, his gallant gesture quite ruined, while the nawab smoothed his moustaches in anger.

The nawab on the other hand was a master of the swashbuckling gesture. An English guest wrote of being entertained by the nawab in 1773 by a display of horsemanship and dexterity during which the nawab and his sons thundered down a course on horses at full gallop, shooting at targets and throwing lances, 'with great strength and agility'. It is not certain that Mirza Amani was one of the sons riding on this occasion, for the nawab had a great many other sons too. Most accounts state that the nawab had close to fifty children, and thirty or so sons.* One of those other sons was Mirza Mangli,† closest to Mirza Amani in age and particularly adored by their grandmother, Nawab Begum. Mirza Mangli was an intelligent and subtle young man and Modave provides an anecdote that points out another intriguing difference between the brothers. When Shuja tried encouraging Mirza Mangli to learn English, he apparently refused because 'my brother is learning this language, and I prefer to learn French.‡'

Mirza Amani, with his graceless rolls of fat, charmless silhouette and thick neck, appeared even more gauche in comparison. Perhaps in retaliation, Mirza Amani seemed to seek out the most disreputable companions to have by his side, all of whom delighted in bawdy

---

*Modave says fifty-seven children and Foster's number is fifty.
†The nawab's third son was Mirza Jangli, continuing the pleasing tradition of rhyming names.
‡Mirza Mangli seems to have cherished a fondness for all things French even later in life, for during a visit by the traveller Viscount Valentia to his court in 1803, after he had become Nawab Saadat Ali Khan, the viscount noted that a breakfast of 'tea, coffee, ices, jellies, sweetmeats, French pies and other dishes both hot and cold' had been prepared by the nawab's French cook. The wife of a French officer, Colonel Galliez, a Frenchwoman from Chandernagore, is believed to have taught the young prince French during her stay at Faizabad.

humour and easy laughter. 'From his boyhood,' sighed Faiz Baksh, 'he used to laugh unseasonably, fling derisive abuse at others and desire derisive abuse in return from them.' Whereas about Shuja, Modave wrote that 'he was a generous and kind man. It is said he never lost his temper, and those vulgar obscenities which are common among the nobility in this country were absolutely unknown to him.' The noisy, intemperate, and foul-mouthed Mirza Amani appears to have done everything he could possibly do to provoke his impeccably mannered and impossibly charismatic father. As for the nawab's one flaw—his scandalous weakness for beautiful women—Mirza Amani was able to outdo him since, by all known accounts, he was a homosexual.

But as Bahu Begum's beloved only son, the mirza was nonetheless cossetted and favoured above all the nawab's other children. He was tutored, albeit unwillingly, by the best minds in the land, at the end of which Faiz Baksh would only admit that to his one good quality of innate generosity, the mirza had added excellence in archery. Despite Faiz Baksh's ill-tempered criticisms about Mirza Amani's indolence, it is clear that Shuja kept the young man constantly occupied once he came of age. He headed the nawab's cavalry when he went on tours, was appointed in lieu of his father during the nawab's absence, and the nawab even had him deputed to the establishment of the imperial princes at Allahabad. In this fractured and tense relationship between the nawab and the mirza, there is much that is reminiscent of another tragic father and son dynamic—that between Padshah Akbar and his son Salim who ruled as Jahangir.

Finally, in 1770, when the mirza was twenty-two years old, Shuja arranged for his wedding. Mirza Amani was meant to have married the daughter of Siraj-ud-Daula of Murshidabad but the Battle of Plassey put an end to those projects and he was finally married to Shams-un-Nisa Begum, the granddaughter of Qamar-ud-Din Khan,* once wazir to Emperor Mohammad Shah. In November 1770, sachaq was sent to the house of Sholapuri Begum, the widow of Qamar-ud-Din Khan, in a long procession of uniformed officers and horsemen, while the bridegroom's presents were laid out for the population of Faizabad to admire: five thousand vessels, several thousand trays full of sweets, bottles of perfumes, costly apparel, and jewels and ornaments. A few

---

*He was from an orthodox Sunni Turani family.

days later, the young bride entered the palace on a gilded palanquin, as silver coins were thrown in great handfuls over it and into the outstretched hands of the beggars below.

Gentil, who was invited to the wedding, writes of a most magnificent ceremony called the Saawan, in which Bahu Begum felicitated her daughter-in-law to mark the first monsoon of her married life. On the chosen day, an enormous cortege of horsemen, elephants, soldiers, servants, and charioteers conveyed Bahu Begum and Nawab Begum to the palace of Shams-un-Nisa Begum*. The musicians of the naubat played their trumpets lustily as the elephants swayed through the streets of Faizabad, the nawab's pennant with its three red fish on a white background fluttering in the cool monsoon winds. Dozens of servants carried trays of clothes, as well as sweets and fruits, while three elephants carried the long poles required to set up the swing in the garden of the bride. Troupes of dancing girls and singers twirled and spun outside the walls of the palace, entertaining the waiting noblemen, for only Shuja and his son were allowed into the ladies' palace where the women waited, smoking their hookahs and greeting the presents with appreciative murmurs. But despite all the ostentatious ceremony and the 24 lakh rupees Shuja was said to have spent on the wedding, the union was not a happy one and was apparently never consummated†. Choosing to deal with whispered rumours about his son's lack of performance in the bedchamber in his usual forceful style, the nawab decided to put the blame on the mirza's unsavoury companions, throwing some of them in jail while others were quietly drowned.

But the nawab had preoccupations other than his son's sexual misdemeanours. By 1770, the Marathas, who had disappeared for almost a decade after their bruising encounter with Ahmad Shah Durrani, had marched up once again into Hindustan, causing considerable disarray amongst the powerful factions now acting independently in north India—the Rohillas, the Jats, and the English. But one man was ready to parlay with them—Emperor Shah Alam. By this time the

---

*After the death of Asaf-ud-Daula, Shams-un-Nisa would continue to live in Lucknow, under the next nawab, and the protection of the English, a rich woman occupying herself with arranging the marriages of her nieces and nephews.
†It was from the report of the khawajasara of the zenana that Shuja was informed about the lack of intimacy on the bridal night.

besieged emperor had come to understand his utter powerlessness at Allahabad. The English had prevaricated endlessly over their promise to accompany him back to his capital, never intending to reinstate him at all, preferring to keep him close to their zone of influence at Calcutta. The Marathas, meanwhile, had seized their chance upon the death of Najib-ud-Daula to confront his unruly son Zabita Khan and had captured Delhi. For the Marathas to have the Mughal emperor indebted to them would give them much needed legitimacy. One of their main generals was Mahadji Shinde,* a man who carried upon his body the mark of the disastrous Maratha defeat at Panipat—a pronounced limp resulting from a broken thigh. Modave considered him 'the greatest of the Marathas—his personal valour, his humanity, his sincerity and his generosity' making of him a most famous man.

In accepting the help of the Marathas to regain his capital, Shah Alam knew he was replacing one set of masters with another, but he was now desperate to get back to his begums, his heir, and his elderly mother. Having submitted to endless indignities perpetrated by the English, 'the emperor dissimulated the outrage he felt, but which he never forgot' and which made him especially amenable to parlaying with the Marathas. When threatened by the English that the Company's Allahabad troops would be withdrawn if he left, Shah Alam declared he would rather die by suicide than stay any longer at Allahabad. So, on 9 April 1771, Emperor Shah Alam left Allahabad after thirteen long years in exile. He would have known now, as perhaps he did not before the Battle of Buxar, that he was a pawn to be fought over by the rapacious and the ambitious. Shuja would not be accompanying the emperor back to Delhi. Instead, the nawab set off from Faizabad to meet the emperor at Sarai Alam Chand. Since it was Muharram, the nawab and his entourage rode all day, dressed in the black and green robes of mourning, followed by attendants carrying the tazias, the alams, the standards, and all the accoutrements of the occasion. Every evening they would observe the different stages of mourning, gathering within themselves the grief of their recollection in memory of Imam Hussain. Upon meeting the emperor, the nawab gave him 12 lakh rupees, 100 transport carts, a hundred camels, horses, tents, muskets, cannons, and soldiers, and bid goodbye to his glorious and vexatious guest.

---

*Better known as Mahadji Scindia or Madhav Rao Scindia.

# A NABOB IN DELHI

At the end of the year 1772, three Bretons were part of a magnificent cavalcade that made its way towards the barbican* of the Qila-e-Mualla of Delhi, preparing to meet the newly returned Emperor Shah Alam in grand durbar. In the middle of a cortege of splendidly dressed cavalry, grenadiers, guards, and Mughal noblemen swayed five richly caparisoned elephants. On one of the elephants sat the fifty-year-old Persian commander, Mirza Najaf Khan, recently promoted to Mir Bakshi of the Mughal empire and next to him on his elephant sat an awestruck René Madec in his best regimental uniform, quite overcome. 'I may declare without exaggeration that I entered the capital of India more like a monarch than as a mere individual and subject of the emperor' admitted the Breton proudly. The once scrappy, penniless youth from Brittany now found himself a man of substance, alighting from the elephant in front of the naubat khana of the Qila of Delhi, where the musicians immediately burst into triumphant, acclamatory music. Madec made his way slowly down the marble paths, shadowed by the memory of long-dead emperors and their magnificent daughters. Next to the marbled fountains, courtiers flew kites nonchalantly, impervious to the grandeur of the moment. Madec stopped in front of the diwan-e-khas, where there was a press of supplicants waiting to see the emperor. Among them was his compatriot and fellow Breton, Daniel du Jarday, dressed as a Mughal and passably incognito. Alongside Madec was another Breton officer, de Kerscao, a nobleman from the French colony of Reunion Island.

At last the emperor appeared, sitting upon a simple wooden throne borne upon a palanquin and preceded by stout guards striking the ground with their sticks, and loudly proclaiming the glory of the emperor. After Madec had presented his nazr (seven silver coins) to Shah Alam, he was given a khillat which he was made to wear in the emperor's presence. Finally, the emperor removed his own sword from his side and presented it to the Frenchman. 'I could barely believe

---

*The barbican had been added in front of the main Lahori gate of the Qila-e-Mualla by Aurangzeb, and was criticized by Shah Jahan, who had built the fort, as 'a veil drawn across the face of a beautiful woman'.

this was not a dream', wrote Madec, very moved by the emperor's gesture. Madec was also given a respectable brace of titles,* enough to call himself a nawab, or nabob, henceforth.

Madec had had a rambunctious career in Hindustan ever since Shuja had been forced to let him go after the Battle of Buxar.† Along with his party of 400 trained soldiers, he had fought for the Rohillas, and then the Jats, and had established a reputation for valour and military skill. He also got married to the young Marie-Anne Barbette‡ in a ceremony that lasted several days, during which 10,000 people were fed every day. Despite the truly Hindustani opulence of the wedding, Madec seems to have been disappointed by his young bride's lack of charms, for he wrote rather regretfully that 'the Catholics in this country follow the traditions of the locals. One may only see one's wife after the marriage ceremony...and one may thus discover a Lea instead of a Rachel.' A portrait of Marie-Anne Barbette does indeed depict a snub-nosed, pleasantly chubby woman with an unremarkable face, but Madec would console himself by taking a second, presumably comelier, Muslim wife.

Madec was most pleasantly established as a profitable mercenary when he received an unexpected summons from the Governor of the French trading post at Chandernagore. Governor Jean-Baptiste Chevalier has been described by a French historian as an 'ardent patriot' and a man with 'grand dreams' who used his abundant energy to plague the French ministry with a flood of letters, offering inventive ways through which to regain French influence in India.

Once Shah Alam had been reinstated in Delhi, Chevalier was electrified by the possibility of gathering a substantial force around the emperor, one that could be used to attack the British in their stronghold in Bengal. To this aim, Chevalier had initially pleaded with his government in Versailles to send 4,000 troops who would be placed under Madec to help the Mughal emperor regain Bengal. But the French government did not want to be seen to be provoking the English and so instead Chevalier decided to gather as many independent French partisans to the emperor's cause as possible, in the hope that they might counter English interests. Indeed, French

---

*Shams-ud-Daula, Bahadur, Imad-ul-Mulk.
†The terms of the treaty with the English specifically ordered the removal of 'traitors' from the Company army, referring to Sombre and Madec, from within the nawab's domains.
‡Thirteen at the time of her marriage.

policy at this point was to consistently oppose the English in the three main theatres of conflict—North America, the Caribbean and, increasingly, Asia. Agents were sent from France in the guise of civilians to gather intelligence in Indian states deemed likely to oppose the English, such as Mysore, Hyderabad, Lucknow, and the area around Delhi. And if French efforts to thwart the English had now gathered momentum, then the English themselves were facing a potentially disastrous situation, both in Bengal and in America. In Bengal, a 1773 Select Committee* found that an astounding 2 million pounds had been removed from the Bengal treasury and distributed as 'presents', almost all to local EIC employees. And while these obscene sums of money were being confiscated by employees, Bengal itself convulsed in the throes of a dreadful famine, exacerbated by the actions of the Company. When questioned, Clive would respond, with the chilling sangfroid of a true sociopath, that his allegiance was to the shareholders of the EIC, not the people of Bengal. But the 3 million deaths caused by the famine annihilated the productivity of Bengal, bringing the EIC to the edge of bankruptcy. In response, the government in London decided to raise taxes in their colonies in North America, by passing the Tea Act in 1773,† to fund the bail out of the EIC in India. The resulting rage of the American settlers would lead to the Boston Tea Party and, within a few years, to the American War of Independence. The EIC would pay its debt for Bengali blood on American soil.

Meanwhile, in India, Chevalier was intent on securing the support of René Madec. 'What could possibly interest you, sir,' harangued Chevalier, 'other than gaining a good name among your compatriots by attaching yourself firmly to France's cause?' But there was much else that interested the pragmatic, avaricious Breton, namely money. 'I fail to see,' protested Madec, 'how I may be of service to my nation. I simply wish to return to Europe to enjoy the fruits of my actions.' 'You are brave,' encouraged Chevalier undeterred, ignoring his protests.

---

*The resulting 1773 Regulating Act was created to try and control large-scale corruption, and forced the EIC to restructure its management hierarchy, and bring in a Governor General. Hastings would become the first Governor General, with four advisers to rule over the EIC's affairs.

†In 1773, the British government also passed the Regulating Act, giving it for the first time considerable control over the Company, while the Company also had to agree to a Governor General with precedence over regional governors in India.

'The princes of Hindustan want you by their side. In your position, you could bring about a revolution capable of shaking our nation out of the state of torpor where it finds itself today in India.' By now, with the Marathas having aligned themselves with the Mughal cause, Chevalier was conjuring a glorious vision in which France played a leading role against the English, just as she was beginning to do in the American colonies, and reconquered Bengal for the emperor. Finally, giving in to the flattery as well as to some subtle blackmail,* Madec agreed. 'I will sacrifice my desire to return to France to my great zeal to serve my King. I give you my word that if France decides to march to Bengal, I will join the cause with ten thousand men, at my expense.' And so it was that this one-time ship's apprentice† found himself in the Mughal capital wearing a splendid turban and tunic, appointed a sapt-hazari,‡ and preceded by a troupe of musicians permitted to lustily announce his arrival (image 13).

For a short while in Delhi, René Madec found himself an incongruous courtier at the court of the Mughal emperor. He let his beard grow out, like the other Mughal lords, and took up the suitably aristocratic pastimes of polo and archery. The coat of his favourite horse was festooned with floral designs drawn in henna, and he vaulted with his usual enthusiasm into all the courtly activities—camel, ram, and antelope fights, fireworks, and even poetry competitions in the emperor's mushairas§. Madec also had intimate tête-à-têtes with the Mughal emperor who, encouraged by letters from the dogged Chevalier in Chandernagore, 'exhibited a strong desire to begin a correspondence with the French king, to obtain his help so as to enable him to earn the respect of his own subjects.'

But in these churning days in Delhi where every warlord and raja was setting himself up as an independent force, the emperor was quite besieged. He had initially appointed the talented general Najaf Khan to regain the territories around Delhi that had been seized by the Rohillas and Jats during his long absence from the capital.

---

*Madec feared Chevalier would block his promotion to officer rank.
†Madec began his career on the seas as a 'mousse', a young ship's apprentice, who were often recruited as young as 8 or 9, and did the most dangerous jobs such as clambering up the rigging to serve as lookouts.
‡A mansab or rank of 7,000 horses.
§A gathering of poets.

Najaf Khan raised money from his estates to hire soldiers, including as many Europeans as he could entice, and proved a charismatic and capable general, inspiring undying loyalty in his men. But Najaf Khan's energetic efforts threatened the power of these rebellious factions who soon enough formed a coalition with the Marathas to protect their interests. Forsaken, Shah Alam no longer knew who he could trust, and gradually began to suspect everyone around him, even the all-powerful Najaf Khan. As a result, Shah Alam was paralysed by indecision and distrust, as articulated by Modave:

> Ever since his return to Delhi, the Mughal emperor has lost almost all authority, as much because of his own weakness as from the general chaos in Hindustan. Even though this prince has many good qualities—intelligence, kindness, acuity—his weakness of character spoils everything. He remains at ease amongst his women-folk leading an effeminate and limp existence, not bothering with anything other than gathering some pitiable revenues. He has this in common with other weak princes that is to hate the men they are forced to promote. This is how it is with his general Najaf Khan.

The emperor's growing paranoia was woefully self-destructive, for Najaf Khan was the one man capable of restoring some semblance of Mughal order. By 1781, his army was estimated at '30 battalions of disciplined sepoys, 73,000 cavalry and infantry and 5000 rocket-men'. All of this in addition to 300 mounted and 400 unmounted guns, making this the strongest force between Bengal and the north-west regions.

The distrust, it would appear, was mutual, for Modave recounts the farcical situation that arose when food was to be sent from Najaf Khan's kitchen, as was tradition, to the emperor.

> It is a tradition to send prepared dishes to the emperor and this monarch does the same to those he wishes to honour. The dishes for the emperor are put on big trays which are enclosed in a cloth sack on which the seal of the sender is affixed. The emperor has the dishes sent from Najaf Khan thrown secretly into the Yamuna. When Shah Alam sends him back a meal, the general receives it with much ceremony and prostrations but as soon as the servants

who have brought the dishes have left, he gives these dishes to his servants who then eat them.

But there were forces far deadlier to the emperor's cause than Najaf Khan. While the Maratha general Mahadji Scindia would always remain loyal to the Mughal emperor, he now found himself required in his own fief and returned to the Deccan, leaving the other Marathas to ally with Zabita Khan and his Rohillas against Delhi. 'The Maratha army passed like a lightning strike between my forces and the city,' wrote Madec, of his efforts to hold back the ravaging Marathas. Despite being abandoned by the Mughal cavalry, the two Bretons—Madec and de Kerscao—quickly formed a square (carre creux) of their infantry which prevented the Marathas from entering the city. They repulsed the repeated attacks of the Marathas from dawn to dusk, for nine hours, demonstrating such exceptional gallantry that the next day, an emotional emperor honoured them in open durbar and removed two shawls* from around his own shoulders to present to Madec. But this was simply a temporary reprieve for Delhi and there was no longer any future for Madec in the beleaguered Mughal capital with its embattled emperor. And so, gathering his remaining soldiers, retinue, and baggage, and preceded by his indomitable 'fleur de lys' lily banner, he rode out of Delhi in search of a new patron†.

---

*From the time of Akbar, when a system of grading and storing of different shawls was instituted, shawl distribution remained a widely accepted way to bestow honour.
†He would serve a number of patrons, including Mahadji Scindia, Shuja-ud-Daula, and the Jat raja of Gohad before returning to France in 1777 with Marie-Anne Barbette and a huge fortune. In France he was knighted, and he settled in his home province of Brittany, where he gained something of a reputation as an Indian 'nabob', dying peacefully in his bed there in 1784.

# THE WORLD ON FIRE

While Delhi burned, Shuja kept conspicuously out of fatally dangerous Delhi politics, just as Mir Kalan Khan's paintings had repeatedly shown. From the beginning of the post-Buxar period, he focused on keeping Awadh safe and prosperous, and he always objected strenuously to duty-free trade by English merchants. He obtained a ban in 1767 against English merchants and when duty-free trade was reinstated in 1771, without his consent, he forcefully objected, explaining that English agents used violence to carry out their trade independently of all control. He also prohibited the export of gold, silver, and other metals from Awadh, and maintained the balance of trade in his province's favour. Grain, clothing, and other goods were found to be much cheaper in Awadh than in the territories controlled by the Company.

In 1773, the newly appointed Governor General Hastings was sent to Benaras to meet with the nawab. Despite being impressed with Hastings's fluency in Persian, the nawab refused to budge on the matter of trade and Hastings had to promise that 'no English gentleman should reside in his country and that I would never interfere in any disputes between the English gumashtas and his people.' The nawab was thus able to create a trade barrier that prevented the EIC from carrying out its commercial activities in Awadh. Exemptions were made for individual Europeans, and Hastings would quite cynically use this to allow only his friends to make personal fortunes in Awadh through trade. Hastings appointed as the first ever Resident to the court of Awadh, an agent who was his close friend, and also a famously corrupt man—Nathaniel Middleton, of whom Modave had this to say:

> This young man does not lack intelligence, he has fine features, many talents, and intellectual qualities which would make of him an exceptional man, if all these good qualities were not besmirched by an insatiable greed, which has made him the most impudent trader the English have ever sent to Bengal.

Indeed Middleton was called the uncrowned King of Awadh by another Company council man, and he established his own saltpetre monopoly through which he accumulated such a vast fortune that he would return to found a London banking house. In India, his presence was the first intimation of the means through which Britain would one day establish a stranglehold in the country—intelligence gathering. Perched on the eastern edge of the country, the EIC at this stage had very little knowledge of the workings of the hinterland. But in a very short while all this would change through the posting of these Residents who would function as spies, and who were accurately described as standing 'at the cutting edge of British expansion'.

By now Shuja was acutely aware of the danger of the English presence. He hustled, charmed, and postured so that his country and his rule would be considered one of the great powers in India. There is evidence that he emulated some of the grander gestures of the English. He made public appearances wearing English suits, and ordered artillery salutes and fanfares. He had finally gauged the threat the British ultimately represented to such regional powers as his own. When a minor victory by the EIC over Hyder Ali of Mysore and the nizam of Hyderabad was reported to him, his reaction was one of stammering dismay. The English officer who recorded the moment had this to say:

> In all my life I never saw dejection so strongly painted in any man's countenance. He could not disguise himself and was obliged twice or thrice to tell me, 'There is fine hunting hereabouts,' in order to recover himself.

Shuja equally vehemently resisted English demands to only keep with him Frenchmen without arms, and he continued in his efforts to strengthen his artillery. Realizing that the English needed him as a buffer against the unpredictable and violent Maratha incursions, Shuja played his cards expertly. He used English troops to aid him in the subjugation of his troublesome neighbours, including the Jats and the Rohillas, from whom he seized Rohilkhand in 1774. His next project was meant to be a campaign against the Marathas, 'to extract vengeance on all the ravages these people had let loose upon Hindustan.' But his campaign against the Rohillas would be the last in a life filled with the most spectacular battles and reversals of fortunes. The nawab sustained a suppurating injury in this campaign which forced him to return to Faizabad at the end of 1774. By now he was too weak to ride a horse or an elephant and was borne home in a palanquin, where he was given a hero's welcome. The shops of Faizabad were decorated to celebrate the return of the city's most prodigal son, and the merchants and the bankers threw coins and silver flowers along the nawab's passage. A fretting clutch of physicians was immediately summoned to the nawab's bedside but to no great effect. Finally, a resident French doctor was summoned, but the side effects of his treatment proved so deleterious to the nawab that Salar Jang and the ladies of the harem begged that the treatment be stopped.*

By the time a final French traveller arrived at Faizabad to meet the nawab, Shuja was so weak that he had to receive his guest lying down. This was the fifty-year-old Comte Louis Federbe de Modave, on his second foray into Hindustan, whose highly entertaining and knowledgeable memoirs would greatly enliven accounts of those times. An aristocratic man from an ancient lineage, he had the peculiar knack of failing spectacularly at almost every enterprise he attempted. A historian has called his misadventures 'pathetic', and the man himself 'vain and arrogant about his noble birth'. Modave belonged to the old school of military men for whom the officers could only ever be aristocrats. For the 'adventurers' he encountered in Hindustan, men who were making fortunes based solely on their wits and greed, with no pedigree to speak of, he felt nothing but undiluted contempt. About René Madec, whose warm hospitality and frankness he had initially appreciated, Modave quickly grew critical. At their last meeting, Modave sniffed that he felt himself 'obliged to tell him (Madec) that he was but a vile peasant and an insolent rascal whose fortune had gone to his head and he deserved only contempt and loathing.'

Modave was received by the nawab on a cold December evening in his palace, where he was lying on a bed surrounded by two of his brothers-in-law while khwajasaras stood sombrely in attendance. Modave presented his nazr to the nawab, who pulled himself up and embraced the Frenchman. The two men began a long conversation which lasted for over two hours, during which the nawab spoke of his conquests, his country, and his increasing worries concerning English

---

*The French doctor was Visage, and he prescribed liniment of mercury, used for the treatment of syphilis. Mercury can cause poisoning however and the nawab experienced salivation and swelling of the mouth, dysentery and weakness.

ambitions and designs. 'He told me quite openly,' wrote Modave, 'that he could not but worry that his engagements with the English would have unfortunate consequences for himself, and for them; that he would always stand by his own promises but that if the English tried to take advantage of his decency, he knew how to make them pay.' Modave in turn warned the nawab about the great greed, rapacity and arrogance of the English. He had had unpleasant dealings himself on his route to Faizabad, and so spoke from experience. Modave had initially thought that his French compatriots were exaggerating when they had warned him of English spies posted everywhere to prevent French travellers from entering Awadh, but having journeyed to the region himself, Modave realized that this was entirely true. 'The English are so possessive as to prohibit as much as they can, all travel from Bengal to this part of Hindustan (Awadh),' he wrote, quite outraged. 'Declarations have been put up in Cassembazar and Patna, prohibiting all Europeans from going beyond this last city, especially the French.' Modave criticized the English to the nawab and his relatives with so much vim and energy, bitterly excoriating their greed and their selfish interests, that one of the men in the room, quite overcome by the count's dramatic account, sprang up with a great shout and approved Modave's tale using such obscene and colourful language that the count demurred from writing down the exact phrases in his memoirs, to our great loss.

When Modave asked about the possibility of more Frenchmen being employed by the nawab, Shuja confessed to his guest that he hoped 'that within two years, the French would have no more enemies in India'. Modave noted in his dairy that the nawab 'was beginning to tire of the enormous weight of his alliance with the English. He had thought the alliance useful in controlling his enemies, but he was beginning to realise that it would be very difficult for him to control allies who were so powerful, so greedy and so suspicious.'

But the nawab did not have two more years left to him, and he would be dead* within a few days, in Bahu Begum's palace at Faizabad where the clear January air throbbed with the chants of the Hindu

---

*According to Nathaniel Middleton, British Resident at Faizabad, the nawab died from blood poisoning contracted during the Rohilla war. According to Modave, it was due to a syphilitic ulcer.

priests and the Muslim holy men who had been desperately summoned by the begums to pray for his recovery. The nawab died at the age of forty-five, surrounded by his many wives and children, comforted by the fluttery cooing of his beloved pigeons. Despite the repeated protests by the English Council, the nawab had obstinately retained the services of 150 Europeans, mostly French, including Gentil, Polier, and, for a time, Madec. His European-trained army numbered 100,000 smartly uniformed men, his artillery was considered as fine as any in Europe and his lands were more extensive than they had ever been.*

When the nawab died, wrote Gentil, 'all appeared to have lost their father. Everyone thought that ruin had come to him; the merchants, the workmen of all kinds quitted their shops; their women and children ran lamenting through the streets, asking one another, "Where shall we find a prince like him, a veritable father? We have lost all". The devastated people wandered the streets helplessly, tearing at their hair and clothes. 'The grief and the despair were worst in the zenana,' wrote Gentil. 'It was as though the world had been set on fire. All night these scenes of desolation continued, and the next day was worse still.'

One Harcharan Das, who lived during the nawab's lifetime, wrote that 'there was abundant prosperity during his reign; people lived in satisfaction and the towns and markets were full of life. From the day of his death prosperity, happiness and brilliance have departed from the world'. Polier wrote that 'it is difficult to find words to express the sorrow and grief of almost all his attendants and in general of every inhabitant of this place at this event which makes, in my opinion, no bad apology of a prince who with many faults and foibles must yet be acknowledged to have been not only the first and the greatest man in Hindustan, but also endowed with many good and worthy qualities.' The nawab's body was taken to the river Sarju for the ritual wash according to Shia rites, and then placed on a bier. A long procession of attendants and dignitaries followed the bier in a procession as the body was carried to the grave. The nawab's many sons and officers,

---

*At his death, the lands held by the nawab were 'bounded in the north by the hills and forests of the Himalayan Terai, in the north east by the upper course of the Gandak; in the east by a line drawn from the gandak to the walls of the towns of Chaprah and Buxar and by the Karamnasa; in the south by the Karamnasa, the Sone and the Yamuna, and in the west from the Yamuna a little below Agra. See Hamid Afaq Qureshi, *The Mughals, 1722-1856 the English and the Rulers of Awadh*, p. 114.

the Europeans in his service including Polier, Galliez, and Gentil all followed the slow cortège, as the townsfolk openly wept, tore at their clothes and thumped their chests in despair.

The nawab was laid to rest in the Gulab Bari, where his father's body had once lain before being buried in its grave in Delhi. The nawab's main officers and attendants including Hasan 'Hasnu' Reza Khan, Umrao Giri, the Gossain chieftain, the great khwajasaras, Bahar Ali Khan and Jawahar Ali Khan, all removed their fine courtly attire, put on the tattered, coarse clothes of dervishes, and sat in desolate, forlorn groups around the grave of Shuja. There was great grief, naturally, for the commanding, charismatic man who had always appeared larger than life and utterly indestructible. But there was something else also that filled these men with malaise, and made them hunker down in the cold January days in miserable huddles. It was fear and a dreadful uncertainty about their future, because their very lives now depended on the mercurial whim of a very different sort of man altogether—the dissolute, loud, and brash Mirza Amani, now Nawab Asaf-ud-Daula.

BOOK II

# THE LIONS OF GOD
(1775–1785)

# THE ROAD TO LUCKNOW

It must have been fairly galling for Asaf to realize that even his grandmother was set against his becoming the next nawab of Awadh. According to Faiz Baksh, who is the closest we will ever get to a fly on the wall of the zenana, a conversation took place immediately upon the death of Shuja between Asaf's grandmother, Nawab Begum, and his mother, Bahu Begum:

**Nawab Begum**: Your son Asaf-ud-Daula is now twenty-six years old, but up to this time he has devoted himself to amusements unbecoming and inconsistent with his position, and he has neither manners, presence, nor knowledge of business, and he is absolutely incapable of supervising or comprehending administration... all the wealth of your husband will in a short time be dissipated.... place him nominally in the chair of state and appoint Mirza Saadat Ali, who is acute and intelligent, as his minister.

**Bahu Begum**: I have had but the one son in my whole life; bad or good, he is my sole treasure. In your eyes all the sons of Shuja-ud-Daula are equal.

**Nawab Begum**: You can do as you please. It is your affair and you are responsible.

And though Asaf may not have been privy to this exact conversation, he would certainly have been well aware of the less than glowing opinion of him among some sections of society, especially those who had been Shuja's chosen ones. For them, Asaf would always be the pampered, volatile, and intemperate Mirza Amani—cossetted only son of Bahu Begum. His half-brother, Saadat Ali,[*] meanwhile, was by all accounts beloved of his grandmother and would not have endeared himself to his brother by the infuriatingly blameless reputation he enjoyed, of being 'the most promising of the whole family, well-educated, fully trusted by his father, Shuja, and without a single vice', especially as the young Asaf was something of a connoisseur

---

[*]Mirza Mangli would later reign as Nawab Saadat Ali Khan and is referred to as Saadat Ali henceforth. Saadat Ali, twenty years old now, was in charge of Rohilkhand at this time, with 20,000 troops at his command.

and collector of vices himself.

Modave himself gave us a most stinging critique of the twenty-two-year-old nawab, though it must be conceded that being a man with a prickly sense of honour, Modave was mortally offended when Asaf was forced to dismiss the Frenchman because of relentless pressure from the British. As a result, Modave's description is fairly virulent in its assessment.

> (The new nawab) is grotesquely overweight, so that he cannot ride a horse.* One could not conceive in Europe that depravity could be taken so far. This young man has long been married, but he has never touched his wife. It is said he is impotent, which does not stop him from daily scenes which are horrifying and scandalous beyond imagination.

What the aristocratic Frenchman found himself unable to spell out, but which sent horrifying chills down his spine, was no doubt the nawab's accepted homosexuality. While Shuja's libertinage was almost chucklingly accepted, Asaf's homosexuality was usually a matter of muted disquiet. For such an apparently reckless, feckless, and dissolute young man, however, Asaf seems to have demonstrated a very realistic and acute awareness of the problems he was about to face. The nawabi of Awadh had, after all, only recently become 'hereditary', rather than appointed by the pleasure of the emperor, and there was still considerable volatility around the issue. From the life of indulgent leisure that he had led in the largely peaceful domains of his father, Asaf would now have to contend with several powerful forces—the English, poised like vultures at his borders; the clashing claims of his father's other sons; and the powerful presence of the two great begums of Awadh. Faced with so much ferocious opposition, Asaf marshalled all his charm and energy, demonstrating clear-sightedness, vigour, and a keen understanding of human nature. His many critical biographers would, in fact, judge him to have been exceedingly hasty and impolite in the speed with which he acted at this time.

A few days after the death of Shuja, therefore, Asaf had himself invested with the title of nawab of Awadh and rushed to the Gulab

---

*This charge is blatantly untrue, as we will come across many instances of the nawab riding a horse late into his life.

Bari, where his father's many retainers were sitting in huddled and miserable groups around the grave of Shuja, their dervish clothing and open grief an accusation and a solemn rejection of the change of guard that Asaf represented. He personally walked up to every important courtier and genially bestowed upon the men expensive robes of office and gave them fine presents, considerably impressing the men with his quick and warm generosity. He also handed out salaries and increased the pay of his officers and soldiers and cleared their arrears, all of which were canny methods designed to quickly secure their loyalty. This excessive demonstration of nawabi largesse meant that Asaf was soon in dire need of money himself, and so he went to the one person who controlled the greatest wealth in the province, his mother Bahu Begum. But the begum, devastated by the loss of Shuja, and also supremely conscious of the power of her wealth, was in no mood for maternal profligacy. She sent a message to her son via her brother Salar Jang, duly noted down by the gossipy Faiz Baksh: 'Ten days have not yet passed since your father's death and I am in mourning; what a want of respect and how inopportune is this request! Have you not time to shed a tear?'

This sharp interaction between mother and son provided the perfect opportunity for Nawab Begum to sigh and mutter darkly to her daughter-in-law: 'This is the first return for your love. Sweeter recompense yet you will taste for your care.'

Despite her stated misgivings, Bahu Begum agreed to give the nawab 6 lakh rupees at this point. She also gave her son additional sums of money as gifts, to help him establish himself, and then wrote to Company officials and military figures to ensure their support of Asaf. But the next time a person was deputed by the nawab to ask for more money from the begum, it was not one of her trusted brothers, but a most controversial and notorious character—Murtaza Khan, recently promoted to 'Mukhtar-ud-Daula'*. One of the first political actions carried out by Asaf was to elevate men from among his inner coterie, thereby instantly alienating all the old nobility carefully nurtured by Shuja, and causing grievous outrage to historian Faiz Baksh. In his signature doomsday style, Faiz Baksh had this to say about the companions that Asaf chose to promote: 'There was no low or low-

---

*Selected for power in the realm.

minded class, barbers, green-grocers, butchers, fuel-vendors, elephant-drivers, sweepers and tanners, but some of them rose to opulence and rode proudly through the market-places in fringed palankeens, on elephants with silver litters or on state horses. The sight of it was enough to make the sky fall and the earth quake and dissolve in the water.' And of all these renegade characters, the most loathed by the begums was Murtaza Khan.

There was ancient animosity between Murtaza Khan and the nawab's family, particularly Nawab Begum, and Shuja had banished that entire clan from his lands. So it would have appeared an outrageous act of provocation to the begums when Asaf made Murtaza Khan one of his most senior officers, naming him a 'haft-hazari'*, a rank higher than any in the history of Awadh. He was awarded a gorgeous robe of honour, a special palanquin, an elephant with a covered howdah of silver and, most galling of all, the right to bear the Awadh insignia of greatest honour, the mahi maratib.† When Nawab Begum's khwajasaras rushed to tell her about these great honours awarded to Murtaza Khan, she was enraged and shouted at them to confiscate all these objects from Murtaza Khan at once. Nawab Begum also summoned her grandson, whom she harshly criticized for this elevation of her detested enemy. But when Asaf left the zenana after politely listening to his grandmother's rebukes, he forbade the khwajasaras from taking any action against Murtaza Khan and it was clear that an impasse between the nawab and the zenana was about to be reached.

For Asaf it was imperative that he surround himself at this dangerous time with trusted and loyal men. 'Throughout his reign,' writes scholar Karen Chancey, 'he preferred to advance men of insignificant origins who would owe their elevation solely to him and who could be destroyed as easily as they had been elevated.' This gave Faiz Baksh the opportunity for further horrified criticisms when he described with pungent dislike the 'naked rustics, whose fathers and brothers were with their own hands guiding the plough, and were enrolled in the regiments as regulars.' This tactic had ancient precedence, however, and had been carried out by Akbar's son, Salim, for example, for almost

---

*A mansab or rank of 7,000. In the time of Akbar, this was the highest rank that any non-imperial person could attain.
†The fish and scales.

identical reasons. In the aftermath of Shuja's very unexpected death, it was his own nobility and soldiers who were the greatest threat to the unproven Asaf.

All of these changes meant that when Murtaza Khan swaggered up to Bahu Begum's palace a few months after the death of Shuja, demanding more money for Asaf, she was ready to face this new boorish insolence with rigid anger. Murtaza Khan certainly did not try and ingratiate himself to the begum, and in fact seemed to go out of his way to infuriate her. He did not present a nazr to her, as would have been expected for a woman of her rank, and the eunuch he sent into the begum's zenana was armed, another flagrant breach of protocol. The minute she saw the dagger in the eunuch's cummerbund, Bahu Begum rebuked him sharply, and declared loudly: 'I have no money, and any that I have is the gift of Shuja-ud-Daula.' Bahu Begum then ordered a dozen of her khwajasaras to arm themselves and to station themselves inside her palace walls, and the atmosphere quickly became explosive. The begum's brothers also joined the dialogue, at which point a frustrated Bahu Begum lashed out: 'Through you I have lost rest and sleep. You are always bringing messages from those men (Murtaza Khan) and you never answer them. When men are like this, women stand a bad chance.' Finally the British Resident John Bristow[*] also got involved, and advised the begum to pay a sum of money so as to be rid of Asaf, 'who was beside himself through thoughtlessness and drunkenness, and who ignored courtesy, civility and social distinctions', once and for all. At last the begum relented and agreed to give the nawab 60 lakh rupees from the treasury. But first she made him sign the following deed[†]:

> Hereafter I, Asaf, have no claim or demand on or business with, money or valuables accumulated in the time of Shuja-ud-Daula, or on slaves, male or female, or eunuchs, or the mahals in the jagirs or ought else; if ever I again make any such claim or demand, I shall be a sinner in the sight of God and the Prophet and the Imams.

The manner in which the 60 lakh rupees was gathered also reflected

---

[*] John Bristow was appointed Resident in 1775, replacing Nathaniel Middleton.
[†] This deed would be repeatedly violated in the following years, when the Company put relentless pressure on the nawab to extract more money from Bahu Begum, eventually leading to the impeachment of Hastings.

the opulence of the begums' lifestyles. While 24 lakhs were paid in cash, the remainder 36 lakhs were given in the form of 70 elephants, 860 Nagori bullocks, an inlaid hookah worth 70 thousand rupees, a saddle with gold mounting, 40 jewel-studded hookah-covers, pearl necklaces, precious cloths, velvets, and tents.*

While later chroniclers, and especially the British, would noisily berate the begum for impudently withholding from Asaf (and thereby the Company), wealth that was purportedly his inheritance, it is clear that for the begum the wealth in her possession was almost entirely due to unalienable gifts the nawab had made to her in his own lifetime, and therefore quite exempt from inheritance her son was entitled to. She was also very articulate about the fact that Shuja only possessed Awadh in the first place because of her own financial contributions at the critical time of Buxar. In a letter she sent to Warren Hastings in 1775, Bahu Begum reminded him that 'everything paid to the English gentlemen by the late nawab (in 1765 i.e. after Buxar) had been taken from me'. Faiz Baksh too made this fact quite clear in a note he made in the margins of his history of Faizabad:

> Every item the begam possessed, apart from her bridal trousseau, etc., were gifts from a (legitimate) giver, that is her husband. Neither Asaf-ud-Daula nor any other of Shuja-ud-Daula's descendants had any claim, right or share.

And while the British regarded Bahu Begum's wealth as 'state funds' that she had no right to own, contemporary Indo-Persian chroniclers were equally clear in viewing this wealth in familial and personal terms. Even a foreigner like Modave was quite aware of one of the begum's sources of wealth: 'According to most contemporary sources, (the nawab) deliberately deposited with Bahu Begum all surplus revenue sources in exchange for her contribution towards the restoration of his authority.'

It was understood that a price was required of Bahu Begum in return for control of the nawab's treasury. As khaas mahal, the honour of the nawab's family and the prestige of his lineage depended on

---

*Some of these objects would have been from the Begum's dowry, additional gifts given to her over the years, and also possibly objects from the household of Mir Qasim, confiscated by Shuja at the time of Buxar.

the begum's absolute and unquestionable 'purity'. It meant physical seclusion, sexual chastity, and a life of utter blamelessness. This would be visibly demonstrated by Bahu Begum through extravagant gestures of austerity—from the time of Shuja's death, for example, Bahu Begum ate only one meal a day, and slept on a bare wooden bedstead. She also spent money generously on maintaining the symbols of the nawab's sanctity: she ensured the maintenance of his tomb with carpets, lights, and the reading of the Quran at his tomb. Anything less than impeccable blamelessness would have incurred the wrath of witnesses, present and future. Through her spotless reputation, she would retain the right to control all her wealth—her bridal trousseau, her mehr, her revenue-generating jagirs, her earnings, and her gifts, and she would use it to uphold the rule of her son as long as her stature was respected.

But Asaf's family and supporters were not the only interested party involved as he fought to establish himself in the nawabi of Awadh. The insidious and relentless fiscal pressure of the EIC would also profoundly affect the way in which Asaf would rule Awadh, though in these early years this threat would have been obscured by his many fractious rivals and relatives. Shuja had died in debt to the Company, due to their assistance in his Rohilkhand wars as well as the subsidies he owed to the permanent troops they had imposed on him in Awadh. Upon the accession of Asaf, the Company instantly declared all treaties between the EIC and Awadh nullified, citing Mughal precedence, and they began renegotiating a treaty to impose inflated subsidy payments on the nawab. In the treaty they negotiated in 1775, they increased the subsidy required by Asaf for the British-led sepoy troops stationed in Awadh 'for the protection of the nawab' from 210,000 rupees to 260,000. Asaf was also forced to concede Benaras to the English, a concession the begums were stoutly opposed to and which began the erosion of Awadh's territorial integrity. Bahu Begum even offered to pay the Company a large sum of money to retain this wealthy district so troublingly close to her own eastern borders. But Asaf was desperate to prove his political legitimacy and would not have wanted it known that his mother was also equally interested in political affairs.

Far away from vibrant Faizabad, in the crumbling Mughal capital of Delhi only recently restored to emperor Shah Alam, there were two men who were also keenly watching the succession travails of Asaf, and covertly working to influence matters concerning the nawabi even while remaining more than 400 miles away. Modave has written a poignant account of the grand old Mughal city as it appeared at this time. 'Wherever you look,' he wrote with pitying horror, 'you are confronted only by ruins, even under the windows of the emperor's apartments. Large swathes of the city are entirely destroyed, the materials lying dispersed everywhere. The court is no longer magnificent at all. The extravagant spectacles conjured up by Bernier about Aurangzeb's court have been replaced by the strangest parsimony, born of real poverty. The bearers of silver clubs who used to maintain public order have been replaced by a hundred beggars armed with large sticks.... (The Peacock Throne) in solid gold encrusted with a fortune of precious stones has been replaced by a chair of gilded wood which must be a constant reminder to this slumped prince of the visit of Nadir Shah.' Such were the 'fruits of anarchy,' concluded Modave sadly.

The most powerful man at the court of this unfortunate 'slumped prince' was the Persian commander of the imperial forces—Najaf Khan. A celebrated general and a military genius, Najaf Khan was a man of action and of the battlefield. He was also outspoken, charismatic, and indefatigable. Polier tried to explain the undying loyalty he inspired in his followers: 'he keeps them happy with promises and seduces them with kindness. They are allowed to openly criticize his conduct in front of him, to give him advice, from the most humble of the Mughals, they seem to treat him as an equal rather than a superior. He puts up with all this with great patience and even with good humour, and this is why his men love him.' Najaf Khan's greatest rival at the Delhi court was a very different sort of man. Abd-al Ahad Khan* was a Kashmiri Sunni minister who had assiduously courted the emperor till he became his closest confidant. Though he had been introduced to the emperor by Najaf Khan, he became in time the general's most implacable enemy. A refined and unctuous courtier with a fine white beard and fluttery manners, the elegance of his person was disfigured by an ugly birthmark that covered most of his left eye. He was, according to Polier, 'prudent and clever, full of feints and of bad faith, which he

---

*Sometimes known by his honorific title Majd-ud-Daula (glory of the state) while in English correspondence he is sometimes called 'Abdullah Khan'.

knows how to hide behind a generous exterior'. Modave added with admittedly heartfelt bitterness that 'Abd-al Ahad Khan is more polite in his ways that one usually is in this country. He speaks with great affection, which makes one think him less of a liar than the other grandees of Hindustan, next to whom the most insolent imposters of Europe are but novices and school children. But in the end, he is no better than the others and I may even add that the Kashmiris are the Normans* of Hindustan.'

Najaf Khan was extremely interested in the affairs of Awadh for several reasons. He owed his status at the Delhi court in part to Shuja's favours and was, therefore, always loyal to the memory of the nawab, a fellow Shia. Closer to home, he was also related by blood to the nawab's family, since his elder sister Khadija Begum, had married the older brother of Safdar Jang, Mirza Mohsin†. This connection through his sister to the zenana of Safdar Jang meant that Najaf Khan maintained extremely warm and cordial relations with Nawab Begum and this intimate relation with Shuja's widow must bring us to the piquant conclusion that, like her, Najaf Khan too supported Saadat Ali's cause after the death of Shuja. The fact that Nawab Begum preferred the studious, refined Saadat Ali to the rambunctious Asaf was an open secret. Even Modave, who spent just a little time at Faizabad, was clear that 'the mother of Shuja-ud-Daula had greater affection for (Saadat Ali) than for any of her other grandsons. She would send him money for his household and Najaf Khan had promised her to give some thought to his situation.'

As for Abd-al Ahad Khan, it would appear that wishing to counter Najaf Khan's influence, he cannily encouraged Emperor Shah Alam to support Asaf as long as the young nawab severed all links with Najaf Khan. Modave wrote that 'the animosity of the emperor towards (Najaf Khan) was suggested, or at least greatly encouraged, by Abd-al Ahad Khan.' As for Najaf Khan, 'he maintained an attitude of the greatest disdain for them'. This majestic hauteur came from a place of untouchable confidence for, as Modave pointed out, Abd-al Ahad Khan's innate strengths, 'his duplicity and his talent for intrigue, could hardly influence the course of events of this troubled period, and the

---

*Normans in France suffer from the prejudice of being deceitful and two-faced.
†The *Seir Mutakherin* also maintains that one of Shuja's daughters was betrothed to Najaf Khan.

real power lay with Najaf Khan the commander of the army'. It would not have been difficult for a supremely subtle courtier like Abd-al Ahad Khan, however, to stoke the emperor's paranoia. Shah Alam had spent a lifetime gauging the hearts of men, and what he found there must have been bleak indeed as one man after another betrayed him or used him abominably for his own means. Far, far worse was in store for Shah Alam than the machinations of his insinuating minister but, for the moment, Najaf Khan was cautiously ostracized.

A curious incident early in the reign of Asaf has long baffled the observers of Awadhi history. Very soon after he claimed the nawabi of Awadh, Asaf moved away from the city of Faizabad, to eventually settle in Lucknow by October of 1775. Most commentators blame this on Bahu Begum's overbearing personality, her unfeminine greed for power, and her meddlesome interference in the nawab's affairs. And, it is undoubtedly true that Bahu Begum always intended to remain in control of her wealth, and to remain a vocal defender of her rights and privileges. Indeed, after feeling harassed by Murtaza Khan's constant wheedling requests for money, Bahu Begum wrote to the British Resident John Bristow peremptorily stating her intention to travel to Karbala to inter the remains of Shuja as per his wishes. When he found out about this request, Asaf was mortified that his mother was seen to be acting independently and wrote to the Resident about his desire 'to have the custom of his country and Hindustan adhered to, and not to see the begum supplying a connection independently to him.' But as an elite noblewoman and a widow, Bahu Begum could not have spent her treasure in any other manner than the advancement of Awadh and her son, the new nawab, just as she had done after Buxar for Shuja. Asaf was, after all, her beloved only son, one she had moreover defended against Nawab Begum, and the source of her prestige in Awadh. It seems unfathomable that she would have been considered dangerous to Asaf, or someone he had to physically remove himself from in a fit of pique. Instead, there were far more lethal forces at play between Delhi and Awadh, forces that would make Asaf fear for his very life.

There are letters in Polier's *Ijaz-i-Arsalani* that give some intriguing clues about the convoluted web of intrigue that was set in motion immediately after Shuja's death, in which Polier had the role of intermediary between Awadh and Delhi. 'As your sincere friend,' wrote

Polier to Abd-al Ahad Khan in Delhi just four days after the nawab's death, 'I desire that there should be a cordial relationship between you and Nawab Asaf-ud-Daula.' A few days later, Polier wrote again to Abd-al Ahad Khan to warn him that he had brought his letter to the nawab's notice and urging the utmost secrecy saying that 'it will be impolite and undiplomatic to divulge (these matters) to any other person. Take all possibly caution regarding this.' Polier also wrote to Shah Alam at the same time, confirming that he had shown Asaf the letter sent by Abd-al Ahad Khan. 'Things will be done as you wish,' Polier assured the emperor and then, finally, on 9 March 1775 Polier sent a letter to Abd-al Ahad Khan victoriously proclaiming that '*since you wanted Asaf to depart*\*, I have requested him to leave Faizabad and we have reached Mahdighat and are camping on the banks of the Ganges.'

From these extraordinary letters, it would appear that the fractured court of Delhi, itself in the throes of phantasmagorical paranoia and suspicion, encouraged similar fears in Asaf about the one person who seemed to dangerously threaten the masnad, or throne, at this point of time—his brother, Saadat Ali. Asaf had every reason to believe Saadat Ali could challenge him with the backing of Nawab Begum and Najaf Khan, and indeed even have him murdered†. Nawab Begum had always maintained that Asaf was the incompetent and depraved son of his noble father. The appointment of the detested Murtaza Khan, whose family had besmirched the name of Nawab Begum in the past, may have made the situation intolerable for the older begum, who could count on the powerful support of Najaf Khan. The English Resident had noted that when the situation had become particularly fraught, 'Nawab Begum had repeatedly written to the emperor in Delhi asking him and Najaf Khan to come to their relief with a force of Mughal troops.' Abd-al Ahad Khan, as delighted as a smirking, trouble-making imp by this opportunity, found a reason to alienate Najaf Khan by further poisoning the relationship between Asaf and the zenana of Faizabad, and masterminding the removal of the young nawab from Faizabad, and the sphere of influence of Najaf Khan.

---

\*Emphasis mine.

†There were rumours that Nawab Begum gave the orders to have Muhammad Quli Khan, Shuja's cousin, murdered when he was considered a challenge to the nawab.

And so Asaf left Faizabad, prodded by a Frenchman, manipulated by distant Mughal puppeteers, and outmanoeuvred by the implacable will of the two begums. For the begums were not behaving like a cantankerous coven of crows, commentators sneeringly assumed. Both of them were independently wielding their power, parlaying at the highest levels and across vast distances, from within the strictest purdah. They were operating with as much finesse and diplomacy as the most seasoned courtiers, for the advancement of their own cause, and the protection of their power.

After five months camped on the banks of the river, Asaf finally left the city that Shuja and his zenana had created like a dream on the Ghaghara, and moved to Lucknow with his court. Perhaps it was just as well at this time that Asaf was not aware that far away in Chandernagore, French governor Chevalier was also intriguing against him, writing to Madec to dramatically claim that 'the honour of the (French) king was at stake, the interest of the French nation depended only on Madec, that he would be lost if the son of Shuja was made Wazir of the empire'—all this French angst simply a play to oppose whatever it was the perfidious English were in favour of.* In Lucknow, however, Asaf would finally be master of his own destiny, and he would create a city of beauty and light equal to that of his great father, away from the shadow of Mughal Delhi.

---

*The English had accepted the legitimacy of Asaf's claim to the masnad as Shuja's eldest son.

## ALL FRENCHMEN MUST LEAVE

It is, of course, fashionable to blame a stepmother for most of the misfortunes of the world, but Frenchman Claude Martin's stepmother appears to have inspired in him a veritable obsession: 'Go, you obstinate one,' she is believed to have told him, when at the age of sixteen he insisted on joining the French East India Company in Lyon, 'but don't ever come back unless you are in a carriage.' Claude Martin would obey this injunction dutifully, becoming arguably the richest European in North India in the eighteenth century. Sadly, as he never returned to France, his stepmother would not have the satisfaction of seeing him ride through Lyon in a gilded carriage.

The forty-year-old syphilitic and painfully gaunt ex-deserter from the French army who made his way to Lucknow in 1775 had very little in his baggage by way of a fortune. Having escaped the destruction of Pondicherry in 1760, Martin had immediately deserted to the British EIC and had enjoyed a lacklustre career since then. Chronically ill,* Martin had by now a haggard, lupine face which accentuated his large hook nose, an effect softened somewhat by inquisitive brown eyes (image 14). The only treasure he possessed were some holy relics and manuscripts he had pillaged from temples during a Company expedition into Bhutan. And yet, within a very short time in Lucknow, he would own extensive property throughout the province and would become the richest man in Awadh, able to lend the nawab a quarter of a million pounds. The source of Martin's wealth, far exceeding his paltry Company salary, has never been fully explained.

One of the fortuitous acquaintances Martin would make right away in Lucknow, and one that would partly explain his fortune, was the notoriously corrupt Resident, John Bristow, an arrogant maverick who would be later disgraced for his extreme venality. Bristow was the protégé of a Calcutta council man, Philip Francis, and had replaced Hastings's man Nathaniel Middleton as Resident, even though he lacked even the basic prerequisite of speaking Persian. The system of

---

*Rosie Llewellyn Jones believes that by this time Martin suffered from urethral ulceration due to venereal disease, an enlarged prostate and chronic kidney stones, a condition which would eventually lead to the kidney failure that would eventually kill him.

patronage, corruption, and rewards was rife at this period, and since the Company was not able to take part in trade in Awadh directly, officials used their influence to have their acolytes appointed to lucrative posts in Awadh in return for financial rewards or gifts of some kind. And because of the wealth of Awadh and its nawab, Lucknow was considered a particularly attractive posting for a Resident. Later, when questioned, Francis would rail against his government 'which does not allow Bread and Water to Men in a station, where a Fortune might be made in a Day.' 'If you knew the value of this place,' insinuated Claude Martin quite shamelessly to Philip Francis in 1780 about Lucknow, 'and having it in your power as you have at present, I think that you could not give it except to a person entirely devoted to you, as Bristow is... and you will not have an opportunity to regret it.'*

Philip Francis, John Bristow, and Claude Martin would soon become enmeshed in a web of patronage and corruption that would make them all very wealthy. And one of the most lucrative ways in which they were to make money was by persuading Asaf to hand over control of part of the arsenal of Awadh to the Company. Asaf was naturally very reluctant to do this, wanting to keep it under the control of his boyhood friend, the daroga Imam Baksh[†], and finally after much discussion, it was decided to leave half the arsenal in the control of the nawabi, and the other half in the control of the Company. Bristow then had Martin appointed superintendent of the new arsenal, from which post he received a commission on all purchases made.[‡] One of the reasons the arsenal was to prove so lucrative was that Asaf had been obliged to station in Awadh two more battalions of Company troops, all of whose expenses the nawab was to bear, including salaries and equipment. Bristow then noted that, rather conveniently, the nawab lacked good arms in his arsenal, and 'no muskets by him (Asaf) fit for service and no people capable of making them properly'.

It is mystifying that the nawab's arsenal, only recently praised by Modave as being outstanding, and as good as any in Europe, should have apparently fallen into disrepair so rapidly. However, the third

---

*Bristow was Resident from 1774 to 1777 and then reappointed again later in 1782.
†Imam Baksh was one of the youths that Shuja had had thrown in prison when trying to remove all boorish influences from around his son.
‡Martin estimated his earnings from the arsenal at 3 lakhs a year and he continued to supply materials for the arsenal almost up till his death, long after he had retired.

clause of the 1775 treaty that Asaf was forced to ratify stated that the nawab was to dismiss all Frenchmen in his service. 'The Nawab,' Hastings told Bristow, 'must make his election between the French and the English as he cannot be in Amity with one of these nations without bearing an Enmity to the other.' At this time in Awadh, there were some 150 Europeans in non-official roles including thirty-five working for Asaf. When the nawab tried to object to this clause, he was threatened with the withdrawal of the Company brigade, which would have left his borders defenceless.

And so the injunction that Shuja had opposed so valiantly finally came into effect, and Asaf was forced to dismiss the Europeans in his service. Madec had already been let go by Shuja and had immediately jumped into the fray that was the north Indian battlefield. When Gentil's collection of French soldiers was dismissed en masse, they all went to Madec for help. Delighted, Madec rushed to Najaf Khan's court where he 'presented, one after the other, all these Frenchmen numbering more than 60, including a cook whom he had kept in his own service.' Najaf Khan immediately raised Madec's rank but the minute Madec received this promotion, he dismissed all the Frenchmen, leading Modave to pronounce him a 'vile peasant'.

Polier, despite not being quite the renegade that Madec was, in English eyes, was nonetheless forced to leave Awadh for the Delhi court. Gentil, already devastated by the death of Shuja, found he no longer had the heart for service in India. He had gone to visit Asaf three days after the death of Shuja, and had been received with great warmth by the young nawab. Asaf assured Gentil that he would pay the English 10 lakh rupees if they would allow Gentil to remain with him in Lucknow. But a week later, he summoned Gentil and told him with great regret that the English had threatened to raise one of his brothers to the mansab if he did not dismiss Gentil. Emperor Shah Alam then made Gentil an offer to join his court at Delhi but Gentil believed that 'this Prince lacked the force of character which is necessary for the execution of such a project.' Regretfully, Gentil would decline the emperor's offer and would bow out of the history of Awadh, sailing back to France with his Indo-Portuguese wife, their three children, and a treasure of books, manuscripts, paintings, and other valuable objects. As for Modave, the touchy aristocrat was furious that what had been a bracing meeting with Shuja on his deathbed now became, at the hands of his son, a cold dismissal. 'Asaf-ud-Daula was exteriorly a very polite man,' admitted Modave. 'It is said he lacked neither intelligence nor courage. But if he has these two good qualities, they were drowned in so many vices that it is impossible not to hate and despise him,' he railed, before confessing that 'as soon as his father was dead, he changed his manner towards me as he did towards the others.'

Another Frenchman who was dismissed at this time, having spent five years in Faizabad, was the architect Charles-Emmanuel Canaple. He had been sent by the French court to help Shuja strengthen his artillery and he also began work on a huge, star-shaped fort, on which 30,000 men worked daily, destined to rival Fort William in Calcutta. In the five years that Canaple was employed by Shuja, he built 'thirty-six thousand guns', established a 'large cannon foundry, and cast 74 pieces of cannon of different sizes'. By 1773, only the outer wall and covered path remained to be completed and, according to Gentil, the English were furious that the construction of such a fortress had been allowed.

The one Frenchman who did remain was Claude Martin, who made another felicitous meeting in 1775 of a more unusual nature. He bought a young nine-year-old runaway girl from a Frenchman, who had in turn bought the girl from her abusive father. 'Luck made her fall to my lot,' wrote Martin disingenuously, about the girl he would name Boulone Lise. Martin then groomed the young girl carefully—he educated her and 'with all the tenderness of a father, took proper people to learn her principle of her religion, and learned her great modesty and decency, and to read and write'. Apart from the idiosyncratic grammar, what is disturbing is that while Martin claims to have cared for Boulone as a father would, he would soon proceed to take the young girl to his bed, as he would other children in time. The 'lucky' encounter Martin mentions may also allude to the fact that Boulone was from an elite Lucknow family and would later gain him access to nawabi society. And so, the young Indian girl and the middle-aged French roué settled into a rented place in Lucknow called Old Lakhypeera where Martin, like a tenacious limpet, would resist all efforts to have him extirpated and would spend the rest of his life in glittering Lucknow.

## THE BEGUMS AND A RAJA

By the monsoon season of 1775, Awadh had a new capital city. After five months camped at Mehdi Ghat, Nawab Asaf-ud-Daula and all his retinue settled into the Yakh Mahalla of Lucknow, thereby altering the destiny of that city forever. Faizabad was not abandoned, however, for the two great begums remained in residence with their treasure and their enormous entourages, conducting their affairs as before. Bahu Begum maintained a force of 10,000 men to collect taxes in her estates and also kept a personal army of 2,000 mounted soldiers to guard her palace. This was in addition to the begums' personal khwajasaras, their female attendants, their singing and dancing girls, the harried cooks, the animals and their keepers, the tradespersons and all the grand melee of people, objects, and animals that made up their textured and busy lives (image 15).

But the shearing apart of what had been one glorious tightly enmeshed culture into two halves naturally caused a fraying at the edges. In Lucknow, Asaf began petitioning Emperor Shah Alam to grant him the title of wazir, as had been done for his father before him. But he found the emperor strangely reluctant. Encouraged by Abd-al Ahad Khan, wrote Modave, 'the emperor was determined that (Asaf) first sever all links, whether written or of common interest, with Najaf Khan.' At one point, the emperor even made the extraordinary request that Asaf travel to Delhi for the negotiations for the wazirat, accompanied by Bahu Begum. Mortified by the continued influence of his mother, especially as the English Company was gauging his every move, Asaf declined the invitation.\* On another occasion, when it became known that his unhappy grandmother, Nawab Begum, had asked for a relief force from Najaf Khan and the emperor, Asaf irritated beyond endurance, informed the emperor that he would pay his tribute as usual that year but that he would come to Delhi accompanied by his entire Awadhi force to do so. Suitably cautioned, the emperor retreated into a terse silence.

Nonetheless, once the matter of the peshkash (offering)† had been

---

\*Asaf-ud-Daula would eventually receive the wazirat in November 1775.
†A nazr was also an offering, but usually a more modest one, whereas a peshkash would be

satisfactorily settled, Asaf was thrilled to hear that the Mughal emperor had sent the precious khillat of the wazirat to Lucknow. The nawab rode three miles out to a tent specially set up for the purpose of receiving this gilded symbol of Mughal authority. In a grand ceremony, the nawab was clothed in the robes of state sent for him, and ordered a royal salute fired. 'The Vizier expressed more satisfaction on the occasion than ever I saw him,' agreed an English witness.

In Faizabad, meanwhile, released from absolute sequestration by her widowhood, Bahu Begum now began a voluble correspondence with the EIC officials. On one occasion, this proud, self-reliant and least defenceless of women used the gendered language of female distress to beg of Hastings that he 'exert yourself effectually in favour of us helpless women', to protect her from her son's incessant monetary demands. On another occasion, seeking the replacement of one of Asaf's loathed ministers with one of her own men, she assured the council that revenues would be collected promptly, 'and whatever sums are due to the English chiefs, I will cause to be paid'. But the council men at Calcutta, all proud upholders of the patriarchal framework existing at the time in England, were thoroughly appalled to come across a woman who owned property, exercised her right to control it, and who presumed to challenge a man and her own son, over this right.* 'I cannot conceive that she has the least right to interfere in the nabob's government,' sputtered one such council man,† before piously adding that 'in a country where women are not allowed a free Agency in the most trifling domestic affair, it seems extraordinary that this Lady should presume to talk of appointing ministers and of governing Kingdoms.' Even more worrisome for the nawab and for the Company were the begums' regular threats that they would remove themselves to Mecca, as Nawab Begum threatened to do in 1777. Asaf was worried that the begum would leave her wealth to Najaf Khan, whom she regarded as a son, while the Company was equally anxious that neither woman leave with what interested them most—their valuables.

In 1776, the nawab's deepest fear materialized when a group of disaffected nobles formed a plan to assassinate him and proclaim

---

more substantial.
*In eighteenth-century England, for example, husbands had sole control of their wife's property; women had no rights over their children, and they were largely illiterate and uneducated.
†Philip Francis.

Saadat Ali the nawab in his place. Asaf had offended a great many people from Shuja's own guard by naming his particular favourites to high posts. These disgruntled officers now dreamed of a return to the old ways in which their power was unquestioned, and they rallied to Saadat Ali. Leading this rebellion were the incendiary Gossains and their fearsome naked Naga troops who had been removed from their lucrative Doab territories. Encouraged by the Gossains and fearing for his own life, Saadat Ali proceeded to Agra to Najaf Khan, gathering all the rebellious parties around himself.

When Saadat Ali arrived at Najaf Khan's court, Modave wrote that the Khan 'received him like the son of the man to whom he owed his fortune. He promised him many things which were not in his power, and possibly never in his intention, to provide him.\* While Najaf Khan was prevailed upon to keep Saadat Ali safely away in Agra, the Company finally stepped in to help Asaf in April 1776, sending a brigade to oppose Saadat Ali during an engagement in which 500 of his troops were killed in battle. After this disastrous defeat, Saadat Ali was removed to Benaras, suitably chastised, where he would cause no further trouble. Asaf would never forgive his brother for having raised the terrifying threat of rebellion and ruin upon him at this vulnerable stage of his reign. A full year later, the Resident was writing to Hastings to tell him that 'I am sorry to remark that his excellency's suspicions and jealousies of Saadat Ali render him extremely averse to any accommodation with him. He declares publicly that Saadat Ali has long sought his life and that by his conduct he has cancelled every claim he could have to his countenance and support.'

Early on in his nawabi, Asaf had every reason to believe the English alliance very advantageous to him as he grappled to deal with the insurgencies from among his own nobility and family. He could use Company troops to safeguard his borders and quell trouble, while he shored up his own tenuous alliances with men loyal to him. Men like Hasan 'Hasnu' Reza Khan, the illiterate khan-e-saman (superintendent of the household goods) from Faizabad who had 200 relatives in the city to act as bulwark, Imam Baksh, his riotous boyhood companion, Ilich Khan, the devoted Afghan carpet spreader, Jhau Lal, 'a man of low extraction', and other such men of dubious pedigree who would

---

\*Nawab Begum continued to send him money to finance his household expenses.

be written about with sincere detestation by both English and native observers. As would, indeed, the young nawab himself. He would be written about with corrosive distaste even and especially by his supposed allies at this time, the Company men. Musing about the chances of the nawab suddenly dropping dead sans heirs early in his reign, Bristow wrote musingly to the council to say 'it is not that the Nawab's state of health in the least makes me apprehensive of his Death at the present Juncture, yet owing to his amazing Corpulency and as by his former mode of life he is totally debited with respect to women. The possibility of heirs unless his constitution should take some very extraordinary turn is precluded by the latter circumstance and by the former we have great reason to think him liable to a sudden Death.' Even a modern historian has called him a 'pampered, lazy, impulsive, crude and wilful youth.'

There is no question that compared to his strapping, cultured, and suave father, Asaf suffered with his immoderate appetites, gaudy humour, and questionable lifestyle. Where Shuja had been sometimes subject to arched criticisms due to his philandering ways, that was still acceptable for his times, and Shuja was excused as being a man's man. But Asaf preferred the company of men, often young men, and that was something the English at first didn't quite realize, for they began by chastising him for the many women in his harem. Later criticisms would become fairly breathless with disgust, as they trumpeted on about 'unnatural appetites' and vague, licentious ways.

Meanwhile, back in Faizabad, the two begums were beginning to realize that the Company was proving to be a duplicitous friend, indeed. Instead of standing by their pledges to guarantee the begums' rights and privileges vis-a-vis the nawab, the Company appeared increasingly interested in assessing and accessing the begums' wealth themselves, despite pious sermons to the nawab about the sanctity of motherhood amongst other things.* By 1780, the pressure on the begums to hand over jagirs and wealth to the nawab, and the Company, became incessant and intolerable and then, in 1781, Hastings made the calamitous decision to levy an additional tax on the begums' neighbour, Raja Chait Singh of Benaras.

---

*The pledges bound the nawab to pay for the marriages of Shuja's other children, pay the servants at the Gulab Bari, refrain from asking either begum for loans, pay the pensions of retired servants from Shuja's harem, etc. See Richard B. Barnett, *North India Between Empires: Awadh, the Mughals, and the British 1720–1801*, New Delhi: Manohar, 1987, p. 196.

Benaras had been unwillingly ceded to the Company by Asaf in 1775 and since then, was increasingly desperate for money, Hastings had already been imposing an arbitrary 'war subsidy'* on the young raja to help fund the overseas wars that Britain was getting embroiled in. In 1775, insurrection in Britain's prized North American colonies had led to civil war within the British empire, with Britain suddenly reacting to exert control over its thirteen colonies. But, in 1777, British general John Burgoyne surrendered to the American forces at Saratoga, New York, and within days, King Louis XVI of France decided to support the Americans in a formal alliance and what had been a local conflagration in America suddenly mutated into a global conflict once again. With war calamitously declared, Britain found itself having to divert resources to North America in addition to its other theatres of conflict with France including the English Channel, the Mediterranean, the Caribbean, and India. Money, in 1778, became an obsession for the EIC officials too. In a later submission, Hastings would admit that 'on the first intelligence of the war with France in July 1778, it was resolved in Council that Raja Chait Singh should be required to contribute an extraordinary subsidy for the expense which this new exigency had imposed on our government'.

Modave had sensed the motivations behind rapacious EIC behaviour in 1777 itself, writing that:

> It is a monstrous thing that a simple corporation, as they say in England, possessed so much exclusive power, without being subject to any control by the 'grand conseil' of the nation. It seems clear to me that, crumbling under the weight of the enormous national debt, the British ministry, quite helpless, looked to the Indian acquisitions of the EIC as a miraculous resource that could save England.

And so it was that in Benaras, the young raja was being made to pay for events that were taking place 3,500 miles away—the deeply humiliating losses incurred by legendary British generals like Charles Cornwallis and Gerard Lake, who would soon arrive upon Indian shores profoundly scarred by these American defeats. The raja meanwhile paid this subsidy dutifully for a couple of years but when

---

*This amounted to 5 lakh rupees annually.

a further tax was levied in 1780–81 to fund the second Anglo-Mysore war, Raja Chait Singh struggled to raise funds. This was a time of deep uncertainty and fear for the British, as the EIC forces led by Captain William Baillie had just suffered a catastrophic defeat at the Battle of Pollilur in September 1780 at the hands of Hyder Ali and Tipu Sultan of Mysore. Hastings was now belligerent about gathering ever more money and resources to fund these wars. Faced with the raja's reluctance, Hastings reacted with astonishing arrogance. He wrote a particularly harsh letter to the raja in early 1781, saying that 'frequent representations having been made to me of the want of punctuality in the payment of your malguzary; and it having at this time more than any other, a bad and suspicious appearance; I do peremptorily order that all arrears of whatever kind be paid up within 24 hours after the receipt of this parwana or you must expect that bad consequences will follow.' When the raja wrote to Hastings asking for the tax to be stayed or delayed, Hastings did not show him the courtesy even of responding. 'It was his duty to obey them,' wrote Hastings about his orders with icy fury during his later deposition about his demands. 'Not to waste my time with letters of excuse.' Enraged by the raja's inability to pay these outrageous and incessant sums of money, and deciding to view this as 'criminal contumacy and disobedience', Hastings marched to Benaras himself in the summer of 1781, 'resolved to draw from (the raja's) guilt the means of relief to the Company's distress, and to exact a penalty which I was convinced he was very able to bear'.

The English painter William Hodges accompanied Hastings on his travel from Calcutta to Benaras, to 'indulge his curiosity as a man and as an artist'. During their halt at Patna, Hodges described the jostling throngs of people lining the roads and leaning over balconies to catch a glimpse of the Governor General. Everyone appeared 'struck with the simplicity of (Hastings's) appearance' wrote Hodges indulgently, imagining that 'they could not but contrast this appearance with that of their nabobs, whom they had never seen except mounted on lofty elephants, and glittering in splendour'. Hodges had quite misunderstood the Indians who did not in fact appreciate drab simplicity in a ruler, and for whom an amply festooned monarch was instead an auspicious tribute to the people themselves. By the time they arrived in Benaras, all Hodges's plans for painterly activities and the contemplation of 'pure Hindoo manners, arts, buildings and customs, undepraved by any intermixture with the mahomedans', were rudely interrupted by 'the unhappy events' that immediately unfolded.

As the English party set sail from Patna in an almost bucolic spirit, Raja Chait Singh came up to Buxar from Benaras, accompanied by his guard of 2,000 men to lay his turban on Hastings's knees as a sign of supplication and submission, but he was coldly received. Hastings refused to discuss matters until they reached Benaras. In Benaras, the English party camped in a spacious estate in the suburbs of the city known as Mahadeo Das's gardens, and then Hastings made the provocatively insulting decision to have Raja Chait Singh placed under arrest in his own palace, with orders that no one was to visit him. This outrageous imprisonment of the raja in his own watan jagir had an electrifying effect on his troops, who swarmed to the palace where he was being held and slaughtered the sepoys guarding him, including the English officers*. The raja jumped down to the river by means of a rope made of turbans tied together and escaped by boat, followed by his triumphant, riotous soldiers.

'If Chait Singh's people, after they had effected his rescue, had proceeded to my quarters at Mahdoodas' garden instead of crowding after him in a tumultuous manner, as they did, in his passage over the river,' wrote Hastings, 'it is most probable that my blood and that of about thirty English gentlemen of my party would have been added to the recent carnage for they were above 2,000 in number, furious and daring from the early success of their last attempt; nor could I assemble more than 50 regular and armed sepoys for my whole defence.' These few sentences that Hastings wrote in his deposition betray the utter terror that must have instantly replaced Hastings's fury when it appeared that the entire town had erupted into a heaving, baying crowd, utterly alien suddenly in its lust for retribution and anarchy. For in what must have seemed like an instant, the town was swirling with the raja's men, barricading the lanes and firing weapons. Rumours fizzed with as much velocity as the bullets ricocheting off the narrow lanes and when Hastings heard news of an attack being prepared at neighbouring Ramnagar, he fled from Benaras to the fort of Chunar,

---

*On 16 August 1781.

abandoning the wounded sepoys,* and losing all baggage, provisions, and palanquins in the great confusion of his escape. As the beleaguered English party leaped into boats and scrambled upriver, they could see armed rebels massing along the banks firing indiscriminately and jumping into all passing boats. Most fortuitously, Hodges was able to save his drawings and a few changes of linen.

This incendiary reaction was not limited to Benaras, for it spread like wildfire in every direction. As Hastings made his desperate flight from Benaras to Chunar,† triumphant rumours proclaimed the Governor General's massacre, and witnesses made wild-eyed claims of having seen 'his head and right hand suspended over the gateway of Chait Singh's fortress'. Across the country of Awadh sepoys deserted their posts, zamindars huddled together in secret communications and European settlements were seized with panic. In Lucknow, the Resident Nathaniel Middleton along with Claude Martin fortified their quarters and placed cannons defensively for the furious mobs they were assured would appear at any moment while 'the European inhabitants of Patna believed everything they heard and fell into a piteous state of panic', and prepared to abandon the city.

A conflagration of the sort that was witnessed in Awadh in the torpid monsoon season of 1781 could not have occurred without the knowledge and concerted efforts and encouragement of the most powerful force in the country, the begums of Awadh. The begums had begun to greatly resent the constant demands for money the Company made and, more insufferable yet, the violent and venal methods used by Company appointed revenue farmers on lands that the begums claimed as theirs.‡ 'These traders,' Edmund Burke would later accuse during Hastings's trial, 'appeared everywhere; they sold at their own prices, and forced the people to sell to them at their

---

*They were left in the care of Saadat Ali, who had been housed at Benaras after his failed rebellion. He looked after the sepoys with care, giving them money and provisions, and calling for native surgeons to look after them.
†An important defensive fort 30 miles upriver from Benaras which had been the residence of Sher Shah Suri, and was captured by Akbar in 1575. The nawabs of Awadh owned it in the eighteenth century till the British took it in 1764.
‡This was the period of the greatest rapaciousness amongst EIC men. In Bengal, the weavers were now working under such appalling conditions organized by the Company to extract maximum profit that popular anecdotes claim the weavers would cut off their thumbs so that they were no longer employable by the Company.

own prices also.' They appeared 'more like an army going to pillage the people under pretence of commerce than anything else.' The Company, in short, operated under standards that looked 'more like robbery than trade'.

The most notorious of these characters was Alexander Hannay, personally appointed by Hastings to illegally take over the districts of Gorakhpur and Bahraich, an enormous tract of forest land with rich timber harvesting revenues*. Nawab Asaf-ud-Daula had challenged Hastings over this arrangement, but the Governor General had forced the issue, all the while insisting on complete secrecy, because the contract was contrary to Company policy and was, in fact, fraudulent. 'This is a private arrangement,' was the description in the contract, 'and must not in any case be referred to the Supreme Council (of Calcutta).' Alexander Hannay used Hastings's 'gift' with such violent zeal that he 'dropped off gorged', some 300,000 pounds richer,† using the military force he commanded as a tax collector to terrorize and plunder, allegedly imprisoning hostages and beheading recalcitrant landowners.‡

So thoroughly detested was Hannay that when it was rumoured that he was later to be reinstated in Awadh, Asaf wrote to Hastings to say in most uncharacteristically forceful terms: 'If, by any means, any matter of this country dependent on me should be entrusted to the Colonel, I swear by the holy Prophet that I will not remain here, but will go from hence to you.'

The enormous resentment and anger towards men like Hannay and other extractive revenue farmers like him meant that when the revolt at Benaras sparked off, there were many zamindars and farmers primed to explode into ferocious, retributive violence against the English presence. 'No sooner had the rebellion of this zamindary manifested itself than its contagion flew to Fyzabad and the extensive territory lying on the north of the river Dewa, and known by the names of Gorukhpur and Bahraich.' Some 4,000 tenants and employees of Hannay's were massacred as the revolting forces swarmed Gorakhpur,

---

*This was the fourth largest ijara with revenue assessment of 220,000 rupees. The ijara system, introduced by Jahandar Shah (r. 1712–1713), was a revenue farming system whereby the task of collecting the revenue for an area was sold to the highest bidder.
†According to the accusation made by Burke at the trial for Hastings's impeachment.
‡The situation was similarly dire in Bengal and Bihar, where Company monopoly was accused of producing 'universal poverty and depopulation'.

and Hannay was besieged at Faizabad, from where he sent frantic appeals for help to the Resident.

'In the city of Faizabad,' wrote Hastings, 'Nawab Aliya and (Bahu Begum), the mother and grandmother of the Nabob, openly espoused the party of Chait Singh, encouraging and inviting people to list for his service, and their servants took up arms against the English.' By this stage, continued Hastings, 'one half of the province of Awadh was in a state of as complete rebellion as that of Benaras. ...Even the wretched subjects of Nepal dared to seize by force some villages to which they had a claim'. It was widely acknowledged by the English that the begums' khwajasaras, especially Jawahar Ali Khan and Bahar Ali Khan, acted for the begums and recruited troops in the bazars of Faizabad, stopped provisions from being sold to the English, disabled the postal relay system of the English, and commanded the attack on isolated Company contingents. By mid-September, bands of 10,000 rebel soldiers were attacking the reinforcements arriving from Bengal. Nor was the violence confined simply to the cities, as the rural population also attacked incoming sepoy soldiers. A British officer leading reinforcements into Lucknow complained that he 'was insulted by every village I passed... The followers of the Camp were plundered, and at Lucknow my men were insulted by every dirty fellow in the place. I could not get any straw or grass for the...Cattle without fighting for it.' Faiz Baksh also agreed that 'whenever the villagers saw a red-coated regular, they harried him'.

For men like Alexander Hannay, sending increasingly frantic dispatches from his desperate position in Faizabad, the driving force behind this ferocious uprising was very clear:

> The conduct I have related...is a concerted plan for the extirpation of the English. *The people who are daily sent to him (Chait Singh), horse and foot, from Fyzabad,* and the seat of rebellion I have before named, is *very great*. The begums have *almost themselves*[*] recruited for him. The old begum does, in the most open and violent manner, support Chait Singh's rebellion and the insurrection; and the Nabob's mother's accursed eunuchs, are not less industrious than those of the Burra (elder) Begum.

---

*Emphasis in original.

By September 1781, when Hastings ordered Hannay to march to his relief at Chunar, Hannay was writing that 'this town (Faizabad) has more the appearance of belonging to Chait Singh than the Wazir. The begums have placed Guards to prevent any of my people going to the bazar in it.' He wrote of forces of thousands of men being raised in Faizabad to march to Benaras, of cannon being fired all through the days, of Company forces being attacked and massacred, and of rivers being guarded to prevent access to the English. He wrote about the Khwajasara Jawahar Ali Khan standing in the chowk of Faizabad asking 'every man who bears the appearance of a soldier why he goes not to Chait Singh for service'. As for Hannay himself, he was unable to proceed to Hastings' help, for 'it is impossible in the general insurrection which now reigns almost universally for me to get the force together...or to force my way to you.' The one person who did ride up to Chunar to offer help to Hastings in the middle of the uprising was Asaf. The nawab must have thought carefully about the advantages* he would gain by making this gallant decision, for he was forcefully opposed in this by his own family. Bahu Begum, her brother, Salar Jang, and the begum's two main khwajasaras all believed by now that Hastings had been either routed or killed. 'Mr Hastings and all the English have been disposed of,' they assured Asaf. 'What necessity is there for us to get ourselves into trouble?'

Hastings, alive but terrorized, was himself conflicted about this offer, admitting that the nawab's forces, 'rabble' though they were, could be useful to him but loathing the idea that accepting his help 'would invert the relation of our alliance and give him a superiority' in their power dynamic. Hastings finally did welcome the nawab, and it might not be entirely coincidental that Asaf had also made 'an offer of a very considerable sum of money (10 lakh rupees)' as a present to Hastings, which the Governor General 'accepted without hesitation and gladly', a decision that would later come to haunt him.

The snarling virulence with which Hastings would extract

---

*Asaf re-negotiated a new treaty in 1781, the Treaty of Chunar, by which the temporary Fatehgarh brigade was removed, reducing his monthly subsidy to half, the withdrawal of the English Resident at the court of Asaf's tributary at Farrukhabad, the resumption by Asaf of Faizullah Khan's jagir in Rampur, no more English troops on Asaf's account and, finally, the resumption by Asaf of the Begums' jagirs in return for cash equivalent.

vengeance once the revolt was suppressed after two long riotous months was a reflection of the humiliating and terrifying vulnerability he experienced after the arrest of Raja Chait Singh. Forced to flee Benaras in ignominious fashion, Hastings found himself stranded in the fort of Chunar, a desolate and isolated place very far from the genteel security of Calcutta. An alien place of intolerable heat and bare rocks, the great heat accentuated by 'the reflection and glare of the light grey rock, the light grey castle, the light grey sand, the white houses and the hot bright river'. This was a bleak place indeed for Hastings, deep inside a country that must have seemed suddenly overwhelming in its foreignness, with all that he loved very far away from him. For the single, obsessive worry for Hastings was the fate of his wife at Patna. He sent a flurry of tiny letters, rolled up and pushed inside a quill and carried behind the ears of messengers so as to pass unmolested by the raja's forces, to Marian Hastings. 'I am at Chunar,' he wrote repeatedly. 'I entreat you to return to Calcutta, I have no fears but for you.'

The furious revenge Hastings would extract after the suppression of the revolt was the equal measure of the arrogance with which he viewed his role in Hindustan. This was not the blustery and showy arrogance of a Robert Clive, for example, but one that hunkered behind a veneer of sombre and spartan rectitude. It was the sort of arrogance which led him to equate the fate of his own person with that of the British empire itself, notwithstanding his grey, bloodless persona. 'Let it not be thought that I attribute too much consequence to my own person', he was anxious to tell the Council, 'when I suppose the fate of the British Empire connected with it.' At the same time, these would be the actions of a particularly deeply felt personal grievance for as a contemporary essayist noted—'few men loved or hated as did Warren Hastings.'

As soon as the revolt was suppressed, Hastings recalled his one-time friend and protégé Alexander Hannay, stripped him of his post and sent him to Calcutta in disgrace, where he would die a year later, possibly by suicide. Ramnagar, Raja Chait Singh's capital, was razed to the ground on Hastings's particular orders while the raja himself would never be reinstated in his city. Floggings and tortures were inflicted by British officers upon villagers as they slowly stamped out the uprising. But by far the greatest punishment would be inflicted on the most unlikely targets of an English gentleman's wrath—women and eunuchs.

# PUNISHING A BEGUM

Bahu Begum was always supremely conscious that it was her extraordinary wealth and her exemplary behaviour as an elite Shia noblewoman which granted her a status and reckoning far beyond that of any other single woman in North India. This child of the court of Delhi, raised at the knee of Muhammad Shah Rangeelay himself, had the presence, and the power, that would now bring her into inevitable confrontation with the rising power in India at the time, the East India Company.

In 1780, by the age of around fifty,* Bahu Begum was at the centre of a depleted but still impressive court. Decades of patronage had attracted nobility and gentry from Delhi, now older and slightly scuffed, but still a nostalgic symbol of a gilded and endangered way of life. There were people like Nawab Bani Khanam Sahiba, widow of Bahu Begum's older brother, Najm-ud-Daula, and once a favourite of the Mughal emperor, who was so pious and chaste that she maintained a practically impenetrable purdah. When her own brother came to visit her, she would first bind her hands and feet so that nothing was visible of her save her face. Rustling with secret decadence was a most precious relic in her trousseau—the coronation robe of Mohammad Shah Rangeelay himself, which he had presented to her husband, a glittering thing of beauty covered with flowers made of rubies, emeralds, and diamonds. She employed her own guards and escort, and maintained many relatives who had all fled to her side to escape the chaos of Delhi. Young women, especially, were sure to be able to count on her generosity when they were in need of help. There were a number of similarly celebrated widows and matrons who also lived with grandeur and elegance in Faizabad. And then there were all the relatives and descendants of Saadat Khan Burhan-ul-Mulk and their entourages, who had also gathered at Faizabad, generating work for all the artisans of the city for their filigree lives of refinement and beauty. Even Bahu Begum's maidservants lived with the greatest decorum, prohibited from mingling with any male servants.

Lending a further layer of enamelled sheen to Faizabad were the

---

*According to Mohammad Faiz Baksh's account, she would have been born approximately in 1729.

great khwajasaras of Nawab Begum and Bahu Begum, who by now were well established men with grand retinues of their own, sometimes comprising thousands of soldiers and innumerable servants and hangers-on. When Jawahar Ali Khan rode out of the city for hunts, for example, he was accompanied by a glittering and colourful procession of soldiers—there was a Bundela unit in red turbans and belts, a 'Sabit Khan' unit in mango-green livery, irregulars in black livery, regulars in red, Mewatis in white—this procession preceded by heralds on horses loudly shouting out the Khan's glory.

The severity of the purdah Bahu Begum observed brings us to the piquant question of her appearance. There are, of course, no known portraits or likenesses among the thousands of works commissioned, indeed no contemporary chronicler had the temerity or indecency to mention anything about her appearance at all. 'The adab or etiquette of society' wrote a historian, 'demanded that they remain confined'. The closest likeness we might observe are the portraits of her brother, Salar Jang, to whom she was particularly close. In Zoffany's* famous portrait he is a golden-complexioned, elegant, and well-proportioned man, with an expressive and sensitive face. Interestingly, we know more about that most intimate of a purdah-bound woman's feature— her voice. For a veiled woman, not only was a glimpse of her features absolutely forbidden, but the very timbre of her voice was also never to be heard by any male outside the zenana. When communication was necessary, the begum would be seated behind a heavy curtain which would muffle all sound, and she would interact with the outsider via a khwajasara, or a woman attendant. The message spoken by the man sitting in front of the curtain, though perfectly audible to all, would be relayed to the waiting begum by her intermediary, and she would then whisper her response back to the woman servant or khwajasara. But, when overcome by emotion, usually fierce anger, Bahu Begum sometimes dispensed with these niceties, and so we know she had a strong, loud voice which carried like that of a general's in a war room. During the protracted imprisonment of her khwajasaras in 1782, she once sent for her brother Salar Jang to present himself to the door of her zenana for an explanation. Salar Jang was described by an Englishman as 'not brilliant but experienced...mild and just in (his) administration

---

*Colonel Mordaunt's Cock Match.*

and beloved by all'. Entirely unequal to the task, therefore, and aware of the power of his sister's fury, Salar Jang reluctantly presented himself and Bahu Begum 'spoke to him with so loud a voice that everyone anywhere near the door could hear her.' Salar Jang was so shaken that he was unable to utter a response, and 'left in a few minutes trembling and alarmed, while the Bahu Begum shouted to his retreating back: "You may go; all that I looked for from you, I hope my God will do for me."'

Faiz Baksh also gives us an entertaining account of the Bahu Begum's surprisingly robust and stinging language which she used when in high temper. Unlike the more cultured and refined Nawab Begum, Bahu Begum was illiterate and needed a letter writer to put her sometimes tempestuous thoughts to paper. During the time when she was sequestered in the Moti Bagh with the older begum, Asaf wrote to her, accusing her khwajasara Jawahar of fomenting some trouble. Bahu Begum's initial reply to this charge, which she denied with vehemence, was to say: 'Whoever says so tells a lie. Beat him with your shoe, and drive him out of the city.'* Faiz Baksh, the letter writer at the time, was alarmed by this language which had more the cadence of the sellers in Chowk Bazar than of the genteel and elegant ladies of the nawab's zenana. Faiz Baksh went on to replace the begum's language with that of a court gallant, and instead castigated the nawab in a most delicate manner, asking the nawab whether, as a Muslim, he had forgotten the Quran in which it was said 'Say thou not unto them (thy parents) even "uff"!'

After Hastings's debacle at Chunar, it was decided to deal with the Company's fiscal problems† with a solution which would also carry out the vengeance that Governor General Hastings was quite desperate to bring about against the begums of Awadh and their khwajasaras—the seizing of their jagirs. It is clear from both English and Indian accounts that Asaf himself was extremely loath to take over the begums' jagirs which they had long controlled and managed with the help of the khwajasaras. Asaf was not a man who was comfortable with such violent and open acts of confrontation with the great begums, as

---

*A phrase very reminiscent of Akbar's insult when incensed by a courtier that he was to be beaten with a shoe filled with excrement.
†The Company debt was calculated as being 15,000,000 rupees at this point.

his actions in 1775 had also shown. The Resident, Middleton, found himself having to coax, wheedle, and threaten an increasingly reluctant and unhappy nawab. 'The resumption of all the jaghirs, so much against his inclination,' wrote Middleton to Hastings, had cast a paralysing gloom upon Asaf. 'A settled melancholy has seized upon the nawab and his health is reduced beyond conception.' But Hastings was now imperious in his vengeance against the women and eunuchs who had so unmanned him. Somehow his earlier pious sermons to the nawab about the sanctity of motherhood were quite forgotten. Instead, Hastings insisted that the nawab be forced to follow through on these orders but, in the end, nothing would induce Asaf to sign the papers and Middleton himself had to do so, enforced by military posturing.

Simply announcing the resumption of the begums' jaghirs and actually physically taking over these possessions was an entirely different matter as the Company soon found out. When an officer was sent to take charge of the lands, he quickly found himself surrounded by 900 of Bahu Begum's revenue police and 5,000 ominously armed villagers, and the man hastily turned about. Finally, Asaf and the Resident arrived on the outskirts of Faizabad on 8 January 1782, accompanied by the Lucknow forces. They found the city a hive of angry retainers, armed and with cannons deployed, ready to be used. Instead of taking up his residence near Bahu Begum's palace in the Moti Mahal, which was his habit, Asaf encamped instead at the Asaf Bagh garden, two miles away from the Chowk. The nawab, accompanied by Salar Jang, paid several visits of courtesy to Bahu Begum, presented a nazr of 101 gold pieces, exchanged some pleasantries while saliently ignoring the matter at hand. Only when his minister Haider Beg Khan arrived from Lucknow with more forces did Asaf send the hapless Salar Jang to his mother to say, casually and almost incidentally, that he owed a crore of rupees to the English and would she please give him the money.

Like good bazar bargain-hunters, Hastings and the nawab had previously agreed upon a sum that could conveniently be extracted from the begums to repay the nawab's outrageously high debt to the Company. Sixty lakhs, it was understood, would cause no real harm to the begums while contributing substantially to reducing the nawab's debt of 150 lakh rupees*. Even the begums, it is believed, had heard rumours of the 60 lakh rupees that had been agreed upon earlier.

When the begum confronted the nawab the next day, he flatly denied having made any such claim, and instead was relieved to agree to a loan of six lakh rupees from his mother and it seemed as if disaster had been averted. But Haider Beg Khan, the nawab's minister, convinced Asaf that he would be ridiculed all over the city for accepting such a paltry sum. 'We shall lose our good name,' he murmured to the nawab, and suggested instead that her two khwajasaras be used to put pressure on the begum, since they controlled her finances. And so the nawab sent a message saying that he was planning to come to his baradari near the begum's palace, and requested the begum to have her numerous soldiers leave Faizabad for a few days so as to accommodate all his troops. Immediately rumours, contradictory orders, and inflammatory voices began fizzing through Faizabad as the volatile city threatened to turn explosive.

Furious at the fracas caused by Asaf's orders, Bahu Begum reacted with impetuous haste, and decided to vacate her palace within the fort and go to Nawab Begum's Moti Bagh† in the Chowk Bazar. As soon as her servants and retainers saw her leave in such a rage, none dared remain within the fort, and her entire armed force, some 2,000 strong, and all her khwajasaras with their entourages, every last dependent and servant, all followed her in a great jumble of hastily grabbed arms and baggage. Forty carts filled with anxious women attendants followed the begum's palanquin as it trundled out of the gates of the fort. The atmosphere quickly became tense, as all the begum's soldiers hustled to line the road leading to the Chowk, their matchlocks loaded, holding burning fuses at the ready.

It is difficult to know if the begum was simply reacting in pure anger when she left in such a furious show of defiance, or whether she hoped to shame and humiliate her son into seeing the utterly unacceptable nature of his requests. The begum's one great flaw seems to have been a sometimes soaring temper, especially when she felt

---

*This figure is quoted by Barnett, while another figure fixed the debt at 136 lakh rupees. This was a difficult to verify sum, which was constantly changing.

†The reader will remember that Bahu Begum's quarters within the Qila, or Fort, of Faizabad was the Moti Mahal, while Nawab Begum's residence near the Chowk was the Moti Bagh. Bahu Begum left the fort on 10 January 1782.

her honour threatened. And perhaps, even through her anger, the begum gambled that Asaf was not the sort of man who would so easily be estranged from his own mother. Once her anger had subsided somewhat, she kept murmuring to herself that Asaf was her only son, and that he had been led astray by others, as he had so often when he was a volatile young man. That he would return to the path of reason and obedience, surely. And whether or not this was a carefully judged act of spectacular theatre, it very nearly worked.

When the nawab heard the news of his mother's furious departure from her own residence, he was dismayed and started to rush to her side immediately to apologize and persuade her to return home. For a man who had shown unshakeable deference to his indomitable mother, it would have been shameful indeed to be seen in her own city as a plundering, ungrateful son. But Asaf was prevailed upon by his advisers to not interfere. 'She is only going to the Nawab Begum's,' said one soothingly, 'that too is her home.' While another warned that 'things have gone too far,' and whispered in the nawab's ears news about the angry soldiers, the burning fuses, and the armed entourage.

The precipitous exit of Bahu Begum from her secure fort with her entire complement of servants and soldiers was a godsend to the Company. Their soldiers immediately took over the fort and placed soldiers and cannons at every gateway. In retaliation, some of the begums' khwajasaras and servants also placed cannons in the middle of the Chowk, provocatively facing the direction of the Company guns. The Tripolia gateway was bristling with soldiers, some 200 men, standing with muskets and lit fuses ready to face down any soldiers who arrived from the direction of Lucknow. Meanwhile, alerted to the situation with Bahu Begum, jagirdars, landholders, and collectors, 'who were well satisfied with the good administration', all grabbed arms and rushed to Faizabad and along with the Faizabad contingent lined the main road leading out from the fort for a distance of two miles. Sensing this easily combustible mood, shopkeepers wisely shut down their trade and lurked in doorways, waiting for the inevitable denouement. More enterprising onlookers in the Chowk Bazar placed their beds and tables in front of their shops for a better look at this promising scene. The narrow lanes were crowded with tense, watchful men, some 5,000-6,000 strong, by some estimates perhaps 10,000, on this cold January day. In front of the Moti Bagh palace itself were some five hundred gentry, men of rank, and the begums' khwajasara bodyguards, also armed and ready, while the inner gate leading to the begums' residence was crowded with guards. By the next day, the wealthy townsfolk had also gathered to show their support to the begums, as had the friends of the two great khwajasaras, all those 'who remembered that they were residents of the city and that the begums were their patrons and the khwajasaras were their friends.' The entire city had risen together in a single day, 'ready to share the danger and sacrifice their lives' to defend the honour of their begums.

Asaf now found himself in a terrible quandary. Any move by his soldiers would have instantly resulted in an unpredictable tumult and he would never have risked that. So he sent a messenger to the begums, asking with faux naivete what dangers the begums faced that they had summoned all their soldiers in this manner; he gallantly offered to fight those enemies himself. According to Faiz Baksh, after hearing this disingenuous message, Nawab Begum turned to Bahu Begum, with the extraordinary proposal that the two begums ride into battle to fight Asaf themselves. 'Let us get into our litters and go out,' she said. 'And though the rest of the old army has perished, there are still some who are aware of our rank and station, and they are dissatisfied with your son, so probably his hopes may be blasted.' Indeed so high were tensions at this point that it was commonly believed 'that the two Begums would come out together and the old soldiers (would) join them and mutiny, and the villagers would side with them.'

But Bahu Begum was horrified at the suggestion. Suddenly the uproar outside the palace walls—the men brandishing swords and muskets, the feverish mood, and the intolerable crush of all the women huddled into Nawab Begum's palace must have seemed overwhelming now that her raging temper had cooled a bit. And so she turned to the two most vulnerable people inside the zenana—not women at all, but the great khwajasaras Jawahar Ali Khan and Bahar Ali Khan, and said bitterly: 'This whole excitement and misunderstanding is due to you. You are (Asaf's) father's slaves. If he will punish you, submit to it, for it is no disgrace to you. Expect nothing from me.'

In the eighteenth century, eunuch slaves or khwajasaras formed part of the political elite of Awadh. Even though they were legally 'owned' by their patrons, and many had been bought from slave traders as young boys, they were often highly educated and cultured men who became military commanders, managers of nawabi households, and government officials. Indeed, owning a particularly capable and intelligent khwajasara\* became a mark of prestige among the elite. Bahu Begum's most important khwajasaras were her general agent, Jawahar Ali Khan, forty years old now, and her treasurer, Bahar Ali Khan. Interestingly, unlike the European perceptions of eunuchs, and unlike the situation in the Ottoman empire, Awadhi khwajasaras were considered manly and powerful. Where the Europeans emphasized the effete androgyny of eunuchs, Faiz Baksh instead talks of the khwajasaras in terms of their robust physicality and modest, austere habits. Jawahar had joined the service of Shuja's harem† when he was a promising youth, displaying 'intelligence, dignity, and all good qualities' and he was described as having 'a manly appearance', and was 'a shapely, well-made and well-proportioned man, erect, but of middle height, who wore his clothes to advantage'. Since he represented the Bahu Begum, and in a sense reflected her enormous prestige, Jawahar Ali Khan conducted himself with style and elegance. He always rode on an elephant or in a palanquin within the city, and developed a great reputation for generosity and largesse. When nazr was offered to him by the many people seeking favours, he simply touched the coins or gifts lightly and left them on the ground with superb indifference and walked away, while his grateful servants hurriedly scrambled to pick them up. He was known to be an expert archer, and a consummate horseman, galloping so violently that none of his escort could keep up with him. He also enjoyed hunting and hawking and his clothes, though sober, were of the very best materials and he would wear them for only one season, gifting them away at the end of the year.

Paradoxically, because they had no kin of their own and were legally the 'property' of their owners, khwajasaras were also extremely vulnerable. As soon as the Bahu Begum renounced them, and even though the two khwajasaras were highly eminent and respected men with fortunes and establishments of their own, they were

---

\*Some were born eunuchs, most were emasculated when young.

†Jawahar was from a Hindu cultivator family and had been captured by the administrator of Khairabad who enslaved the children of Hindus whose families had resisted his rule, and emasculated the boys.

entirely undone. 'They were astounded,' wrote Faiz Baksh about the khwajasaras' reaction to the begum's orders, 'but dared not make any reply.' Jawahar Ali Khan, however, had a moment's revulsion at the idea of submitting to the nawab and of the complete public ignominy which would necessarily follow. This most proud of men, cultured and refined, who was used to holding candle-lit majlis in the evenings of Muharram in his house, now slipped out of the Moti Bagh with a small bundle of clothes and two hundred gold coins. Standing with his arm around his favourite horse, he contemplated galloping away from the terrible conundrum he found himself in. He would either inspire the soldiers outside to join him, as he had done so many times before, or die in the attempt, which would be a far kinder fate than the one he now faced. But Jawahar Ali Khan was finally dissuaded against any rash action and persuaded to present himself to the nawab. And so both the khwajasaras quietly accepted their fate, bound up their hands in the old sign of submission, and stood humbly with heads bowed before the nawab in his tents in the Asaf Bagh.

When Asaf saw before him these two servants who had been his father's greatly accomplished soldiers and agents when he was just a boy growing up, he rushed up to them and undid the cloths around their hands himself and led them kindly into his apartment. This encounter might have been almost as embarrassing for Asaf as it was for the two khwajasaras. These were men who had commanded enormous respect when Asaf was still the bumbling and foolish Mirza Amani. Jawahar Ali Khan was a man who had with quiet confidence considered himself the equal of any nobleman of Faizabad and Lucknow, and who was not required to stand up for any grandee of Awadh. In many ways, the two men conducted themselves in exactly the opposite manner to the irrepressible Asaf. They were humble, dignified, and reserved, where the young Asaf had been brash, posturing, and loud. For Asaf was the heir to the nawabi of Awadh, son and grandson of celebrated soldiers and leaders, while the khwajasaras had no family, no name, and no lineage.

It was all a terrible misunderstanding, Asaf told the khwajasaras, and rushed over to Middleton's tents to announce to the Resident that he had decided to let the khwajasaras return to the begum. But Middleton and Haider Ali Khan had already decided that the khwajasaras were the perfect conduit to the begum's wealth. A tent had been specially prepared with their immediate imprisonment in mind, and soldiers with matchlocks had been placed around it. So when Middleton strolled out of his own tent with a steaming cup of tea in his hand, and gestured wordlessly to the khwajasaras to enter the chosen tent, what they were effectively entering was a prison cell. When the khwajasaras' agents realized what had happened they were devastated. They ran to Bahu Begum and fell at her feet, sobbing, and there was disbelief and shock at the outrage that had been committed against the representatives of the begums themselves.

That Hastings and Middleton had decided much earlier to exact vengeance upon the begums and their khwajasaras is clear from Company records. By December of the previous year, Middleton was writing to Hastings, grumbling about the 'Nabob wavering in his determination about the resumption of the jaghirs'. Asaf had begged Middleton for another interview with him, but Middleton had peremptorily written that 'the result of our interview whatever it may be, nothing shall prevent the orders (for the resumption) being issued tomorrow'. As for Bahu Begum, Middleton wrote of the 'reluctance with which the ministers and even the Nabob himself interfere with any concerns of the Begum.' The begum's expectation of support from the English was 'unreasonable' thought Middleton, despite the many professions of support, and the treaties signed between the British and the begums. 'She denounces death and destruction to the most trifling opposition,' wrote Middleton with horror, about this purdah-bound 'native' woman who dared to loudly proclaim her right to her autonomy, independence, and wealth, with most unladylike verve.

As for Hastings, he had written to a friend in February 1782, clearly already discomfited by the violence of the actions he had ordered at Faizabad, and putting forward the reason for this behaviour. 'On the revolt of Chait Singh,' he wrote:

> (Bahu Begum) and the old Begum Shuja-ud-Daula's mother raised troops, caused levies to be made for Chait Singh, excited all the zamindars of Gorukhpur and Bahreich to rebellion, cut off many parties of sepoys and the principal amil and a favourite of the younger begum openly opposed and attacked Captain Gorden. Let this be an answer to the men of virtue who may exclaim against

our breach of faith and the inhumanity of declaring war against widows, princesses of high birth and defenceless old women. The old women had very nigh effected our destruction.

Where the khwajasaras were concerned, Hastings had betrayed his sullen discomfort with their role in nawabi politics a year earlier. Bahu Begum had sent Bahar Ali Khan to negotiate with Hastings in Calcutta in 1780, to plead against the jagirs being seized. When the khwajasara walked into Hastings' room, the Governor General gestured towards a rolled-up curtain, which was then unrolled. To Bahar Ali Khan's surprise, he saw Shuja's countenance embroidered on it. As the tearful khwajasara bent low to bow before the image of his old master, Hastings sighed and said: 'Since the day that man died, my peace of mind is gone.' The manly Shuja was a ruler he could interact with, Hastings seemed to be implying, not women and eunuchs. Bahar Ali Khan may have been distracted at this point by the sight of Marian Hastings playing with some kittens in the room. She had a large bowl full of priceless pearls into which she placed the kittens, amused at the way in which the little creatures slipped among the clinking jewels. Bahar Ali Khan also noticed her stunning earrings, which he estimated were worth 50,000 rupees.

When at the end of his bemusing stay, Bahar Ali Khan returned the robe which Hastings had wanted to bestow on him, saying he was not worthy of it because he had not accomplished his mission, Hastings grew enraged. He shouted at the shocked khwajasara in front of the assembled crowd that 'these provinces were bestowed upon Shuja-ud-Daula by the company after his defeat, and as long as he lived he was careful to observe respect towards us. How has this eunuch, who is only a slave of his, the audacity to treat a gift of ours as if it were nothing and refuse it!'

Asaf has often been blamed by both English and Indian writers for being a grasping, profligate son, humiliating his female relatives. But the truth is that he baulked at the idea of forcing anything on the women and their khwajasaras, and that the English harried and coerced every action from him, using him as a pawn in their insatiable lust for money and their desire for vengeance. As soon as Bahu Begum had moved out of the fort, Hastings had written to Asaf to encourage him to 'mete out exemplary punishment to all rioters and aggressors such as the two eunuchs and Shamsher Khan, the Faujdar of Tanda, if their guilt is proven.' But Middleton, who had a great deal more experience of the power structure of Faizabad, counselled against such violence, writing that 'no further rigour than that which I exerted could have been used against females in this Country, to whom there can be no access'.

The nawab tried to suggest conciliation at every turn, and was clearly horrified at the idea of using force even against the khwajasaras. The English would also claim that no violence was used against the khwajasaras, but of course it was. Indeed it was violence of the most deplorable sort for men like this, for it was violence against their prestige and standing in the world, the very fabric upon which their fragile power was constructed. The two khwajasaras were imprisoned for almost two years, occasionally in fetters, and denied their opium[*] to break their will. No public disgrace or humiliation could possibly have been more complete.

Meanwhile in Faizabad as black clouds gathered in the bleached January sky, cold winter rain fell on the fearful citizens of the city, as public criers roamed the city, beating on drums, and proclaiming that any servant of the khwajasaras found bearing arms would be punished immediately. The unseasonal rain and this ominous proclamation caused terror and men fled the city. Some sought sanctuary in the dargahs, while others 'climbed up trees and some fled to the surrounding villages'. The begums' collectors, all elite men used to travelling on horseback and comfortable in their authority, now ran barefoot to the city, their feet slipping on the dirty, muddy lanes, where their erstwhile friends slammed their doors on them and turned them out into the cold rain.

The fragility of the khwajasaras' power was demonstrated in the way in which men and servants fled their service the moment they were imprisoned. One Aqalmand, Jawahar's favourite young apprentice, slipped away the very next day following the khwajasaras' imprisonment and joined the service of Hasan Reza Khan in Lucknow. Over the next few days, there was a veritable deluge of ambitious and talented young khwajasaras in the service of Jawahar and Bahar who left

---

[*] Bahar Ali Khan preferred his opium dissolved in a little milk and sugar. When he was allowed his opium again, it was only in the unsatisfactory pellet form.

Faizabad for Lucknow. As did many of the Bahu Begum's maidservants and soldiers. Only the oldest and most loyal servants remained, those whose lives were inextricably linked with that of the begums'. For the khwajasaras' wealth was ephemeral; as enslaved men it belonged to their owner and would revert to them at the time of their death.

Six months later, Nawab Begum's jagirs were seized too. Humiliated, the Nawab Begum wrote to her old ally at Delhi, Mirza Najaf Khan. Faithful till his last days to the begum, Najaf Khan sent a message to the Resident at Lucknow to say that 'the old begum had resolved rather to put herself to death than submit to this disgrace intended to be inflicted on her; that if such a circumstance should happen, there is not a man in Hindoostan who will attribute the act to the Wazir, but every one will fix the odium on the English.' He gallantly added that 'if the Wazir so little regarded his family and personal honour or his natural duty as to wish to disgrace his father's mother for a sum of money, let him plunder her of all she has, but let him send her safe upto Delhi or Agra, and poor as I am, I will furnish a subsistence for her, which she shall possess with safety and honour though it cannot be adequate to her rank.' But the great general had only a few weeks to live himself, and this would be his last act of generous support to Nawab Begum.

To achieve her ends, and to protect her prestige against the violent waves of aggression that she faced entirely alone, Bahu Begum was prepared to go to great lengths. When months went by and the begums remained cloistered in the Moti Bagh, with no way of collecting revenue and paying their retainers, servants came to the begum to plead for money. 'Unless the jagirs be restored,' was the cold reply sent to the hapless servants, 'the Begum can do nothing.' When the elephant keepers, the stable heads and the cowherds came, crying that their animals were dying of hunger, the answer was: 'If they are dying, let them die. I have not a copper myself.' The stark fact was that if the begum disclosed the treasure available to her, the rapacious English Company would quite simply seize it, as it had done with the jagirs as soon as the list of revenue-generating lands had been made accessible to them. Knowledge of possessions and treasures was the most important asset the English could obtain. And without her wealth, Bahu Begum would lose everything—her status, her prestige, her revenue-collecting abilities and the employment of the thousands upon thousands of soldiers and servants who depended on her. 'To have their village included in the Begum's jagir,' a historian has written, 'was about the greatest stroke of good fortune that could befall the inhabitants thereof, for they thus obtained protection from the extortions of the revenue farmers and other leeches who harassed and drained the greater part of Awadh.'

After a tense stalemate of almost a year, Bahu Begum agreed to pay the sum of 60 lakhs to Asaf so that he could pay off the arrears on the subsidy he owed the Company. She authorized Bahar Ali Khan to gather together whatever cash he had in his house to which Bahu Begum added a glittering array of treasures so that in addition to 24 lakhs in cash, there were bullock carriages, gold-inlaid horse saddles, jewelled hookahs, pearl necklaces and velvet tents. Asaf and the Resident decided that the full debt had not been paid,* so the khwajasaras remained imprisoned for almost a year and were removed to Lucknow in bullock carts. For men who had ridden only elephants and horses, this was a keen humiliation. In Lucknow, the minister Haider Beg suggested that the khwajasaras be tortured and when Bahar Ali Khan saw the torturer arrive with his brutal instruments, he tried to hang himself. When Faiz Baksh and his few remaining friends heard of this, they 'went into a small dark room, threw our arms on one another's necks and wept'.

After many months, Bahu Begum was persuaded by the English commander at Faizabad† to pay the remainder of the money, to which he would add another lakh, to entirely make up the deficit. Bahu Begum moved back into her Moti Mahal palace in the fort, and agreed to pay only when the khwajasaras were returned to Faizabad, and had their fetters removed. When the two men were led into the begum's presence after so many months, they lowered themselves onto the floor in front of her and wept in shame and relief. In two days, the treasure chambers in the fort which had remained sealed since the death of Shuja were opened, and an endless series of bundles were removed every day, and placed upon the baradari overlooking the river. These

---

*Asaf arranged to have the jewels and gold coins undervalued, and a balance of Rs 650,000 was declared to justify the imprisonment of the khwajasaras.
†Major Martin Gilpin.

bundles contained the treasures that had been confiscated by Shuja from Mir Qasim many decades previously. These treasures, and some cash collected from Nawab Begum and from the khwajasaras, were handed over to the British commander who took the money to Lucknow. Now, at last, the 60 lakh rupees that Hastings and the nawab had decided to extract from the begums when they first began hostilities against Faizabad were deemed paid. In one final act of perfidy, the British commander did not pay the one lakh rupees he had promised to pay and, for good measure, took the khwajasaras back to prison in Lucknow, where they would remain under house arrest till Hastings arrived in Lucknow in February 1784.

Despite more than a year of intense pressure and constant negotiations, the begums' fortunes were left largely untouched. A total of 75 lakh rupees in all was recovered from them, most of it from Qasim Ali Khan's treasure seized at the time of Buxar. Almost all of Bahu Begum's jagirs were eventually restored to her, and she held them till her death in 1815 as a very old lady.* The khwajasaras were returned to their mistresses in 1784, and they lived long, prosperous lives in Faizabad with their possessions largely untouched.†

Hastings, however, would face ignominy and disgrace, and a ruinously long trial for impeachment‡ for the 'despoliation' of the begums.§ His attitude towards the begums, and especially the younger Bahu Begum, was one of impenitent fury. Perhaps if she had been a

---

*Faiz Baksh writes that she was eighty-six at the time of her death.
†Jawahar Ali Khan died in 1799, at the age of almost sixty. During his imprisonment, he still had 12 elephants, 30 horses, and 100 servants as did Bahar Ali Khan.
‡In 1788, Hastings's trial for impeachment for 'high crimes and misdemeanours' against the people of India began. Apart from the mismanagement and corruption that Hastings was accused of, there was also the notorious case of the Raja Nandakumar, who had brought charges of corruption against Hastings, and who was then later himself accused of forgery by Hastings, for which he was hanged. This case continues to be closely studied, and is now considered by some as the first instance of judicial murder by the British in India. The presiding judge who declared Nandakumar guilty of forgery, a crime punishable by death in Britain, was Elijah Impey, a close friend of Hastings, who would later face trail for impeachment himself. Hastings himself was acquitted in 1794.
§Among the many charges brought against Hastings was that he violated a treaty with an independent prince, the raja of Benaras, Chait Singh, by compelling him to pay excess tribute and when he refused to pay, drove him from his throne. That he inspired the nawab of Awadh to rob his own mother and grandmother, the begums of Awadh of 5 million pounds, all their treasure, and divided the loot. And that he had accepted valuable presents and bribes from the native begums and princes.

simpering sot, a more 'gentlemanly' attitude may have been assured. But Bahu Begum was aggressive, outspoken, impetuous, and fiery. Whereas to her own people and soldiers, Bahu Begum was quite simply the ruler, to Hastings she was a mere woman. Interestingly, quite a different standard was used when judging a European woman at the same time—Marian Hastings. During the debacle at Chunar, when she convinced the European population of Patna not to flee in terror from the city, she was praised in the most hyperbolic terms, described as 'a Woman as I really believe no Country ever before produced, or will again. She is, without a Compliment, the Glory of her Sex'. The same compliment was not, however, accorded to the 'native' begums of Awadh.

Fuelling Hastings's inexcusable behaviour and staggering rapacity was paranoia over a British conflict entirely unconnected to Awadh and the begums—the global war for dominance between England and France.

# FROM YORKTOWN TO AWADH

On 10 September 1780, one of the most extraordinary defeats of the British took place at the Battle of Pollilur. During this highly significant battle the forces of the kingdom of Mysore under Hyder Ali and his son, Tipu Sultan, destroyed the EIC forces led by William Baillie. The entire British detachment was either killed or captured and Colonel Baillie was captured along with almost 4,000 of his troops. This occurred during the second of the four Anglo–Mysore wars and Tipu Sultan commissioned a huge mural on the walls of his palace at Daria Daulat Bagh to commemorate this famous victory. Historian William Dalrymple has described this painting as 'arguably the greatest Indian picture of the defeat of colonialism that survives'. And whereas the British would carry out a vicious campaign of vilification against Tipu Sultan and were hysterically loud in creating visual celebrations of their later victories against the 'Tiger of Mysore', they were mysteriously silent about the Battle of Pollilur which would thus become the most notorious defeat of the British EIC to be almost entirely forgotten.

Almost exactly one year later, on 19 October 1781, all the way across the world, the forty-three-year-old gruff, plain-speaking general Lord Charles Cornwallis surrendered his troops to George Washington in Yorktown, Virginia, in the country that would become the United States of America. So ignominious and catastrophic was this defeat for the British that Cornwallis feigned illness to avoid the ceremony of capitulation. Instead, General Charles O'Hara* had the unpleasant duty of leading the red-jacketed British troops between a gauntlet of blue coats—the French regiments lined up on one side and their American allies on the other. Few could have imagined the repercussions the British defeat would have on a land and its peoples many thousands of miles away. But what Cornwallis's defeat signified was quite simply the end of the American Revolutionary War, prompting the British prime minister to exclaim, with dramatic flair, 'Oh God, it is all over!' For with this defeat Britain finally lost all its thirteen colonies in North

---

*Charles O'Hara had the dubious distinction of surrendering both to George Washington and to Napoleon Bonaparte (in 1793 at Toulon).

America, thereby losing a huge part of its global empire at the time, after three years of bitter war.*

In both these encounters, in North America and in Mysore, the French played a very decisive role against the British. Almost all Indian sovereigns had believed that post the Treaty of Paris of 1763, France no longer had the will to oppose the British in any significant way. But this was an error based on the lack of accurate intelligence arriving from the west. Instead, France under Louis XV and his minister Étienne François de Choiseul began a 'guerre de revanche'[†], to restore French power after the humiliating defeat of the Seven Years' War[‡]. Ever since the end of that war, mourned Choiseul, France had had 'no money, no resources, no navy, no army, no generals and no ministers.' Choiseul bemoaned the fact that, obsessed by the land wars within Europe, public opinion had ignored the power of the navy and the potential of America. 'Revolution will come from America,' he declared, 'and that will reduce England to a state of such feebleness, that Europe will no longer have to fear her.' And Choiseul was quite prescient about the fact that trouble would indeed come for Britain from America.

After the Seven Years' War, which it had ostensibly won, England found itself almost bankrupt[§]. France, meanwhile, modernized her army and increased the size of her navy and determined to oppose the British in a global effort to curtail her power. The aim of the 'revanche' was primarily to maintain peace in Europe by restoring the balance of power between the British, grown too strong, and the other European nations. To do this, France strengthened her continental alliances, focused on commercial gains in the Caribbean,[¶] and increased her influence in North Africa and the Middle East. This European peace was now to be obtained overseas, through colonial and maritime global wars

---

*The loss of America caused a spate of memorable rebuffs amongst the British, with King George III coldly informing his resigning prime minister: 'Remember, my Lord, it is you who desert me, not I you'.
†Literally, a war of revenge.
‡Historian Sudipta Das describes the Seven Years' War as the most disastrous defeat France had undergone in modern times. French trade with the colonies fell off to less than a seventh of what it had been. Huge debts were incurred that successive ministries up to 1789 were unable to balance.
§England had a deficit of 137 million pounds at the end of the Seven Years' War.
¶Saint-Domingue (today known as Haiti) in the Caribbean, sugar cane plantations of powered by an enslaved population, was the richest colony in the world at this time.

since it was well known that England derived huge revenues from her possessions in America and India. Revenues that were used to build her arms and drive her wars. Already by 1777 France was surreptitiously helping the American revolutionary forces by sending them money and French officers, effectively conducting a war by proxy against her old enemy. On 6 February 1778, France and the American colonies signed an agreement recognizing the independence of the thirteen colonies and further agreeing not to make peace with Britain until the independence of the American States was recognized. Suddenly, what had been seen by the British as a skirmish caused by disenchanted settlers became a global war.* Across the world in India, the EIC reacted immediately, and by October of 1778 had occupied all five French trading posts in India†. There were even rumours, by 1779, not in the least unfounded,‡ that France and Spain were planning an invasion of Britain.

Even the Comte de Modave had sensed the undercurrents of intrigue and ambition by 1777:

> No reasonable person would doubt the fact that it is the English, alone today on this grand theatre, who are getting ready in secrecy and silence to extend beyond any limits the important role they are playing today ever since we (French) are no longer anything. All their actions, their opinions, their plans are towards this grand objective. Using terror, intrigues, kindnesses, promises, and menaces, they are subjugating one after the other all the forces of India. Every day they advance by a few feet towards their ultimate goal and it seems to me beyond any doubt that within a few years, their objective of invading Hindustan and their entire trade with Asia will offer to them in recompense for what they are losing in America. It is impossible to explain their demands in any other way. I do not know if in France they are aware of the reality and the possibility of this project. No doubt it is in Europe's general interest to not let this plan be executed in its entirety; for it will no doubt occur within ten years if we do not take preventive measures.

---

*Because Spain had already signed a treaty with France, they were also pulled into the Franco-British conflict in America.
†Trading posts, at Karaikal, Masulipatnam, Chandernagore, Pondicherry, and Mahe.
‡At one point 60,000 soldiers were mobilized in readiness for the invasion of Britain.

In 1781, as Britain became increasingly entrenched in the morass of the American War of Independence, the French government decided to open a new front against Britain in India to recover their trading posts and to offer support to Hyder Ali of Mysore. Ever since Hyder Ali had seized power in Mysore from the Wodeyar kings in the 1760s, he had been carefully following the fortunes of the French. He had had the opportunity of studying their techniques in battle during the protracted Carnatic Wars that Dupleix had waged against the British, and he had tirelessly worked to recruit French soldiers and men ever since, all while keeping diplomatic channels open with the French government in France.

A flotilla was sent under the French naval commander Pierre André de Suffren de St Tropez, followed a few months later by a land army led by the great hero of the India campaigns of the 1750s,* the Marquis de Bussy, now an old and rather frail man. French ambitions in India by this stage were not to establish a land-based empire, but specifically to balance commercial aims with limited territorial ones, all while blocking and thwarting British ambitions. In minister Choiseul's words: 'If we succeeded only in interrupting Britain's trade, you may depend on it that the resultant alarm and despondence will be as great as if we had landed in some part of the island.' De Bussy's instructions from the French king were equally explicit:

> The Marquis de Bussy is warned that the intention of the King is not to keep any lands which his armies may win through conquest; he must make his intentions to the local Princes very clear, that his Majesty will return to the original inhabitants any lands won from their enemies.

As the global wars between France and Britain picked up momentum between 1777 and 1781, complicated negotiations were also carried out between the Marathas at Poona and the French, through a

---

*The French trading posts of Chandernagore and Pondicherry had grown greatly in strength and power with the arrival of France's most ambitious Governor General, Jean Francois Dupleix, who began training Indian recruits and formed sepoy troops. Succession disputes in the Carnatic and then Hyderabad allowed Dupleix to intervene successfully, aided by his military general, the Marquis de Bussy. When the Seven Years' War broke out in Europe in 1756, pitting the French against the British, both countries sent armies to South India to continue the struggles there for pre-eminence. While the French were initially successful, and de Bussy practically ruled Hyderabad for seven years, the British eventually prevailed.

number of French intermediaries and spies. In 1777, a murky and shifty character, one of whose names was the Chevalier de St. Lubin,* arrived in Poona bearing a letter from the twenty-three-year-old periwigged King Louis XVI† of France. 'Maharaja of the Marathas,' wrote young Louis XVI to the Peshwa, 'I do not wish to possess any lands in Hindustan. I know that Hindustan belongs only to the Marathas, as France belongs to me.' Notwithstanding the irony of the words of this monarch, who would before long not even own his own head, the king went on to assure the Maratha that 'all I desire is the establishment of an equitable commercial enterprise between your subjects and mine, equally beneficial to both.' The 'king' that St. Lubin presented this letter to was the three-year-old Peshwa Sawai Madhavrao‡. The child was sitting on a velvet throne, armoured in pearls and precious stones, and he received the Frenchman with great dignity. 'What a child!' exclaimed the charmed St. Lubin. 'He is the most beautiful I have ever seen in my life. White as a lily and red like a rose.' The teary Frenchman kissed the young child on the forehead and presented him with all the gifts he had brought from France, including twin portraits of Louis XVI and Marie Antoinette. Smelling of roses after having had perfume sprinkled on him, St. Lubin then carried on an edifying conversation with the king's minister, the elderly Sakharam Bapu Bokil. The minister, it appeared, was curious about French women.

'When you die,' asked Sakharam Bapu, 'do they burn with you?'

'No, on the contrary,' replied the hot-blooded Frenchman, 'our women burn for their husbands when they are alive!'

Having thus reassured the Brahmin, St. Lubin continued on his mission. The fervent hope was that with the gift of the port of Chaul that the Marathas had bestowed upon the French, a powerful commercial hub could be created as a counterforce to the British trading post at

---

*According to Indologist Guy Deleury's *Le Voyage en Inde: Anthologie des voyageurs français 1750–1820*, Bouquins, 2003, p.7, 'The knight Pallebot de Saint-Lubin was probably neither a knight, nor a Saint-Lubin. His trade was wig-maker, he was an excellent watch-maker, and he joined Lally Tollendal's expedition as barber in Pondicherry...he plays the role of triple agent between Hyder Ali, Law de Lauriston and the English. Law has him arrested and sent to France in irons.'

†Louis XV had died in 1774 at the age of 64, when his grandson became Louis XVI at the age of 20.

‡The child was the posthumous son of Narayanrao Peshwa, who was murdered in 1773.

Bombay. Even the feted French Indologist Anquetil-Duperron found himself distracted from his more cerebral investigations to dream of an ecstatic situation in which Bombay was thus neutralized by the French and the Marathas, so that 'the Princes of (India) rise up against the English which then also loses the Diwani of Bengal', leading to a total crumbling of British power, and the restoration of the old French commercial trading posts.

A tenacious French narrative was that France would act as the liberator of the Indian states, which would sooner or later come to bitterly resent the yoke of the British. Historian Kate Marsh has shown that from de Bussy to Law de Lauriston and to a later governor of Chandernagore, the ardent belief was that the freedom to trade in India for France would go hand in hand with freedom for Indians from the oppressive control by the British. 'I believe...that the constitution of the French government precludes the idea of wanting to become a territorial power in India,' wrote de Bussy in 1783. 'The princes of Asia, the emperor himself, suffer impatiently under the yoke of the English, that is true; they are waiting for an event which will break their chains and put them once more in possession of their property and their authority.'

By 1782, French hopes were particularly feverish. Admiral Suffren won a series of electrifying naval battles against the British in the Indian Ocean while 'Hyder Ali had made alliances with several Indian rulers' wrote one enthusiastic Frenchman, 'and everyone was determined to unite against their oppressors, and to not lay down arms until they were destroyed'. Hyder Ali and the nizam of Hyderabad had decided to attack the Carnatic together; the Marathas had determined to surround the British at Surat and in Gujarat; while the raja of Berar would attack Bengal. 'It would have spelled the end of the English', the Frenchman claimed, 'if only this coalition had held'. But the British expertly fractured the coalition, and removed the nizam and the raja from this dangerous equation. And then, at the very end of 1782, just as he was besieging Madras, calamitously, Hyder Ali died. 'Hyder Ali Khan was the most astonishing prince ever to appear in Asia', wrote the despairing French ambassador to India at that time—Piveron de Morlat. 'From nothing, he formed a vast empire simply by the strength of his arms. Through his military genius he was able to hold on to his lands till the end and he died the terror of the whole of India, and of the English nation.'

In early 1783, Tipu Sultan learnt that the EIC forces had invaded his territories on the Malabar coast to force him to retreat from the Coromandel. Though he quickly instructed his governors to surrender to the British, Anantapur held out and the British commander General Richard Matthews decided to make an example of the city and execute everyone. The resulting 'carnage was such, and the attacks against young girls and women so horrible, that the news of the rapes, the murders and the suicides of many young Indian women reached the English press, which reacted with indignation.' British lieutenant John Sheen wrote to his father about 'four hundred beautiful women, all bleeding with wounds from the bayonets, and either dead or expiring in each other's arms, while the common soldiers, casting off all obedience to their officers, were stripping them of their jewels and committing every outrage on their bodies. Many of the women, rather than be torn from their relatives, threw themselves into a large tank and were drowned.' This letter was leaked to the press in England and to counter the outrage of the reaction, the story was denied and quickly buried. However, James Scurry, who was captured by Suffren and who remained a prisoner of Hyder Ali and then Tipu Sultan for ten years, affirmed that the wanton and savage treatment of the people of Anantapur 'was fresh in Tippoo's memory' and a reason for his detestation of the British. And while Anantpur was quickly forgotten, when Tipu would later carry out severe punishments against a captured Matthews, this behaviour would be vociferously paraded in Britain as an example of the Mysore ruler's 'savagery'.

As for the French negotiations with the Marathas, in the end, the alliance fell apart because of the divergence of aims of the two parties. The Marathas were ardently invested in founding a large empire at any cost, for which they were willing to negotiate with the British and the Mughals at Delhi, in addition to the French. The French, meanwhile, were committed to an alliance with Mysore, since Hyder Ali and then his son Tipu Sultan were the only rulers actively resisting British expansion in the Carnatic, where the French had their factory at Pondicherry. Mysore and the Marathas being established enemies, this made a unified French alliance with Indian rulers practically impossible. More pragmatically, enthusiastic French involvement in the American War of Independence had bankrupted* the country, having cost France an estimated 1 billion pounds.

There were also innumerable contretemps with regard to logistics, clashing egos, and intemperate communications. One acid-tongued commentator had this to say about the admittedly elderly de Bussy, who was commanding the French land troops, and who, astonishingly seemed to have perfected an early face-lift of sorts. 'M de Bussy was a sort of powdered caricature, weighed down by military braids. This dithering old man was only interested in formalities, costumes, wigs, and most especially in a sort of mechanism which pulled the skin of the face towards the back of the head, thus smoothing out the wrinkles.' Nonetheless, the lost opportunity was bitterly regretted by many French officers, one of whom wrote that 'Hyder Ali Khan had gathered 40,000 men who ceaselessly harried the English troops. It is certain the English would have succumbed, and retired to Bengal, if the French had sided with Hyder Ali.'

After the capitulation of Cornwallis at Yorktown, the English were haunted by the fear that India would follow the way of America and rid itself of her extortionist colonizers. This fear and paranoia would foment many excesses and would be used repeatedly to justify violence and repression. The coffers of Bengal had finally run dry due to financial mismanagement and asset stripping, leaving a land devastated by famine. At the same time, the British national debt grew from 74 million pounds in 1775 to 224 million pounds in 1780 due to its imperial excesses, more particularly the American War. For the first time in a quarter century, bullion began flowing once again from England to India, to make up for this glaring deficit[†]. For the next twenty years, this money would have just one aim—to raise a military

---

*The total cost of the American War to the French is estimated at 1.6 to 2 billion pounds.

†The EIC's plunder of Bengal began after the Battle of Plassey following which 75 ships laden with silver made their way from Murshidabad to a triumphant reception at Calcutta. The revenues from Bengal post the signing of the Diwani of 1764 were used to fund the buying of merchandise by the British as well as funding an enormous sepoy force. Britain, therefore, no longer needed to send cash, or bullion, to India. However, by 1784, the cash cow of Bengal had been bled almost to death and Britain had to resume sending bullion to India. (André Christophe Louis Piveron de Morlat and Jean-Marie Lafont (ed.) *Piveron De Morlat: Mémoire Sur L'inde (1786): Les Opérations Diplomatiques Et Militaires Françaises Aux Indes Pendant La Guerre D'indépendance Américaine.* Paris: Riveneuve éditions, 2013, p. 27)

force with which the Company could 'extract the riches from those parts of India not yet under its sway, thus assuring the steady financing of Imperial British needs'.

The French in India, meanwhile, would struggle to convince local leaders about the great role the French had just played, through military assistance and diplomacy, in the American War of Independence. Most Indian courts did not possess the information required to deconstruct ceaseless English propaganda that presented the French as 'braggarts and boasters'. Only Tipu Sultan kept himself accurately informed about these great overseas behemoth encounters that could impact his small state of Mysore. Tipu Sultan would never abandon, in his diplomacy and in his dreams, the fervent hope that the French nation would stand by him. But, by 1783, peace had been signed through the Treaty of Versailles between France and England, after the independence of America, and France could no longer carry out large-scale military operations in India against the English. This cessation of all hostilities between the French and the English just as de Bussy had landed and a great deal of groundwork had been carried out reinforced the notion with Indian leaders that the French were vacillators and prevaricators. Writing in 1800, the Naval Commissioner, Launay, was aghast when he wrote about the Treaty of Versailles as deeply 'humiliating':

> It was, I tell you, in 1783, a glorious time for the French nation in India, that there was concluded in Europe a peace treaty so humiliating for the French, who were triumphant on the Coromandel coast, where the English were humiliated.

'All we had left,' wrote a Frenchman, 'were 3 or 4 trading posts, flying the flag, shameful reminder of our second-class commercial status, ever at the pleasure of the English.'

It was Modave, once again, who with his usual sensitive appraisal of the motivations of men and countries wondered how different, if at all, the future might have been for France and India:

> It was only commerce that attracted us to the immense territories of a peoples who had practically all our culture and also knew about our military technology. We know how we were treated. Traders who were first so humble and peaceful, having gauged the innate easy-going gentleness of the Indians, and their absolute

inability to resort to arms, became at the first opportunity insolent usurpers, greedy oppressors, and finally insolent and greedy conquerors. Of the four European nations, none is innocent of these charges. France is probably less guilty than the others of all these horrors, but who knows what we might have been capable of if fortune had favoured us? What is for certain is that businesses based solely on convenience, oppressions, monopolies, are certainly not rare occurrences in the history of our dealings in India.

Ever since Buxar, where René Madec and other Frenchmen deserted the EIC to join the Mughal forces, Hastings and other officials were intransigent about the French menace, not hesitating to create an almost hysterical sense of danger about the possible involvement of French officers and soldiers. Now with the loss of the American colonies, the grip of the British on their Indian possessions would become a vice, and the French presence intolerable. For the revolutionary liberal ideas that had conceded liberty to the newly minted Americans would not be deemed valid for Indian peoples. According to historian Nick Robins, 'one of the great "might have beens" of history is to imagine the application of the ideals of the American revolution to that other problem province of the British empire, India. But India was not modern, European or Christian and so was ultimately subjected to a second-class settlement, treated as a piece of property rather than a living community of people.'

# THE GHOST OF THE MUGHAL EMPIRE

By the early 1780s, money was greatly on Hastings's mind. With demands for cash from the Calcutta council growing ever more strident, Awadh was seen as a fortuitously wealthy province and convenient cash supplier. Four years after Shuja's death, the cash demand on Awadh had tripled to 12,386,694 rupees amounting to more than 50 per cent of the entire state revenue. By 1780, a year in which the autumn harvest had failed, the Company demands had increased to 13,612,189 rupees. Asaf's tone towards these demands, as noted by historian Richard Barnett, changed from one of generous largesse towards his kind 'father' Hastings, to one of increasingly wounded incredulity, and finally to despair and hopelessness. He realized, as his own father had done, that there was no satisfying these friends who were 'so powerful, so greedy and so suspicious'. By 1780, Asaf was writing to the council with almost sarcastically dramatic flair that 'in the Country no further Sources remain, and I have no Means for a subsistence. Alas! I have elephants, horses and houses, and if they will serve the purpose of my friends, they are ready for them.' The mould had been cast; subsidies had been set so high that Asaf would always struggle to fulfil them, leading the English to brand him a profligate and incompetent ruler, unequal to his nawabi.

During the imprisonment of the khwajasaras and the begums, Hastings had championed the use of the greatest possible force to extract the treasure from the begums. But Middleton was a great deal more pragmatic about the pressure that could be exerted on the begums. His more light-handed approach infuriated Hastings, who wrote that 'my orders were that Middleton should not allow any negotiation or forbearance in securing the begum's treasures. These were absolute orders...' and had him recalled in September 1782, replacing him with the infamous John Bristow. Hastings warned Bristow that his main target in Lucknow to ensure revenue collection should be the minister Haider Beg Khan because 'either the Resident must be the Slave and Vassal of the Minister, or the Minister at the absolute Devotion of the Resident.'

Bristow took to his new powers with gusto, immediately

requisitioning all the accounts of the state, including the nawab's private household records. Bristow then demanded the official seal of the nawab, so that all his orders for the streamlining of troops and expenses could be immediately put into effect, and thereby took full control of the nawab's private expenses, becoming in name at least, 'the dictator of Awadh'. Faced with all this humiliation, Asaf reacted in the only way he could—he left the city to go hunting.

It had always been Asaf's habit to undertake two tours of his provinces every year, so he set off at this time with all his entourage and followers and stopped first at Faizabad. This was the first time Asaf was returning to see his mother after all the unpleasantness of 1781, and he brought a peace offering with him—his adopted young son, Wazir Ali, who was meeting these ladies for the first time. The begums would have surely been enchanted with their little visitor, because an English painter who would soon make a portrait of him was delighted and impressed with his superb manners. 'He received me,' wrote Ozias Humphry, charmed, 'with all the ceremony of the Shahzada.' Though Asaf had been a crass and noisy pupil himself, he was taking every care to educate his son in Persian and Arabic, and to ensure he had the best tutors an elite education could offer. By introducing Wazir Ali to the begums, the nawab was also proclaiming him his heir, and ensuring that his young son would have the support of these powerful matriarchs, when the time came for him to succeed to the nawabi of Awadh. Equally welcome for the begums would have been the confirmation that Asaf would restore all their jagirs to them. Now that Bristow was threatening to take all power away from him, and that the English had proved such violent 'friends', Asaf would have realized that the begums remained his most powerful and trustworthy allies.

Bristow, meanwhile, was realizing that it was one thing to proclaim himself master, but quite another to have people act accordingly. Slowly, a sort of torpor spread over the province and all revenue collections dried up. Haider Beg Khan became master of the flippant excuse, effectively bringing all functions to a grinding halt. Law and order seemed to have collapsed and in May 1783 a group of 250 'banditti' prowled around the city, thoroughly terrorizing and almost killing one of the remaining English private traders. When Bristow wrote to Asaf in some urgency that he return to take charge of the administration, Asaf replied with admirable hauteur that 'it is a matter of great astonishment to me that my people should consider your orders as equivalent to mine.' And, as he had not finished hunting, 'for some short time I shall not return.' Finally, by the time the entire Awadh army began rioting for want of their salaries, Bristow must have realized that the nawab and his minister had outflanked him. Hastings, who had been receiving angry letters from the nawab, suddenly performed a lively verbal volte-face regarding his orders to Bristow and accused the Resident 'of perverting (his instructions) and neglecting to obey "their obvious and intended meaning"'. He finally understood that he would have no option but to travel to Lucknow himself, to try and restore some semblance of order.

Hastings set off on his journey in a mood of gloomy despair. He had been suffering from poor health for a while and was convinced he would not survive the scourge of another monsoon in Calcutta. His beloved Marian had already left for England, causing a paralysing lassitude that he was barely able to stir from. And then there was the recently fraught state of Awadh itself, and the memory of his humiliating and terrifying escape from Benaras to Chunar. Now, travelling back to Awadh after those ragged months, and all the censure that his subsequent behaviour had elicited, in addition to the terrible anarchy of Bristow's tenure, he was filled with dread. On 17 February 1784, therefore, suffering from 'great languor,' Hastings handed over his will to an agent and set off for Lucknow by river.

The nawab reacted entirely differently on hearing the news of Hastings's imminent arrival a few weeks later. He wept openly with joyous relief, cheerily proclaiming to all that 'his Friend, the brother of his father', would surely favour him with great kindness. He then set about preparing for Hastings's reception with his customary immoderate generosity and hospitality so that when Hastings arrived at Handia, outside Allahabad, he found gorgeously decorated tents waiting for him while the eager nawab rushed forward delightedly to greet his guest.

The poet Mir Taqi Mir, who was present at the time, has left a description of the spectacularly opulent reception the nawab organized:

> At every stage of the journey, a new and different feast was offered;
> new tents; elegant meals; Turkish and Arab horses; towering

elephants; trays of precious robes and jewels; delightful drinks; various fruits of the best kind; fine gifts of local specialities; southern and western swords and bows from Chach.

All the way back to Lucknow, the two parties travelled together, feasting and celebrating, and Hastings found it unfathomable that the nawab's retinue and entourage were all so impeccably gracious to the English party. He noted in his diary, practically in disbelief, that 'the men and baggage were always intermixed on the march. I have since made very particular enquiry whether any disputes had arisen between the people and follower of the two camps and have received the most convincing assurances that...there were none. The utmost harmony on the contrary prevailed between both.' Hastings agreed that the great good nature and warmth of the nawab had a lot to do with the peaceful proceedings. 'His manners are in an extraordinary degree polite,' wrote Hastings no doubt with considerable relief, 'and I do not know a better tempered or a better humoured man.'

When they arrived in Lucknow itself, the nawab proudly showed Hastings all his palaces, buildings, and gardens. Fresh coats of limewash made the buildings gleam white like marble while soft, rich carpets furnished all the floors. The niches in the walls of the buildings were artfully piled with ripe fruit, and crystal vases filled with flowers from the nawab's gardens added to the heady atmosphere. Rose water had been sprinkled around the palaces and pavilions, and golden incense burners were placed in the corners of the rooms. Intricate bamboo screens had been set up in the garden pavilions for evening dance performances in the balmy nights. Asaf set a relentless pace of entertainments and banquets, breakfasting with Hastings almost every day. He introduced his son and heir to Hastings, the little Wazir Ali, and organized spectacular fireworks for the child's fourth birthday.

As for the food, if ever the visitors felt peckish, there were 'roasted almonds, pistachios, and firangi titbits' as well as bowls of faluda of many colours. There were heaps of ice in bowls, more 'pleasing to the sight than molten silver' in the rising heat of April. But for the serious business of Awadhi banqueting, perhaps only a poet[*] could do justice to their descriptions.

---

[*]Mir Taqi Mir.

There was every kind of bread—nan I badam (almond bread) of utmost delicacy; shirmal and baqar khani that would put the sun to shame; nan I javan (youthful bread) so soft and warm that if an old man were to eat it he would act like a youth, nan I varaqi (paper bread) of such a quality that I could fill a whole book with its praise; nan I zanjabil (ginger bread) so flavourful that Tase itself grows happy thinking of it. In the middle were placed varieties of qaliya and do-pyaza so much that the guests were all delighted and satisfied. And the kebabs...kabab I gul (floral kabab) full of bloom and flavour; perfectly salted kabab I hindi stole every heart; kabab I sang (stone kebab) brought relief to those who were tired from the hardships of the journey; kabab I varaqi (flaky kabab) was of such an amazing recipe that it delighted everyone. Ten large plates of food were placed before every single guest. There were pulaos of all kinds and wonderful soups of every type.

No doubt Hastings would have been offered some delicious bread to accompany his kebabs, since Lucknow took great pride in its bread. According to Sharar, because Hindus fried their unleavened bread in ghee, Muslim bakers had the inspired idea to add ghee to their leavened bread and to cook it on a griddle instead of in a tandoor, giving rise to the paratha. It is perhaps not surprising that under this assault of ghee and cream-rich foods and extended entertainments, Hastings's constitution quailed. He often admitted to being overcome by 'languor' and suffered frequent headaches, requiring naps. Fifty-two years old now, unhealthily thin, his brow a corrugated crease of worry, he mentioned the weather daily, with terse notes about the 'violent heats' and the 'close and sultry' days. He stuck rigorously to a most un-nawabi timing, rising at 6 in the morning to have a bath in ice-cooled water, suffering from languor, lassitude, and inactivity till he had another bath and took himself to bed by 10 p.m., dreaming of 'a hard frost and (his) own fireside', at which time the loud acclamations of 'wah wah', and 'subhanallah' would be erupting from the nawab's quarters where the poetry and dance recitals were just getting started.

The nawab, he also noted, remained resolutely enthusiastic. The nawab brought his own 'cookery' sometimes when he stayed with Hastings for a meal, wisely trusting to the skills of his own great chefs. Indeed, a little note in Hastings's diary points to what would increasingly become a common habit among the elite of Lucknow. When invited for a meal, noblemen would take along all the equipment for making some part of the meal, usually a costly affair, so as not to inconvenience their humbler hosts. One such nobleman would take all the ingredients for the preparation of the paan, and a hundred or more hookahs for his appreciative guests, as well as the elaborate equipment for cooling drinking water. And on 15 July, a day set to the sound of the crashing rain, Asaf 'brought the ingredients for making "Kabaub Khataee", and caused it to be prepared before us as we breakfasted'. Hastings carefully noted down the recipe for the kebabs (image 16) as the men companionably ate together.

There were also a number of Europeans at Lucknow whose company Hastings indulged in when not requisitioned by the nawab or his courtiers. There was Claude Martin, in whose house Hastings stayed for some time while in Lucknow. This was the famous Chateau de Lyon on the Gomti,* later rebaptised Farhat Baksh, which served as Martin's main residence. Martin had built it in neo-classical French style, and in such a way that the basement would flood with the waters of the Gomti during the monsoon and cool the entire building. It had been heavily fortified, with a moat on three sides, a drawbridge, and cannons. Huge, iron-hinged doors within the building could be slammed shut in times of volatility, and it was here that the terrified Europeans had gathered during the riot surrounding Chait Singh's revolt.

Hastings may have encountered his old friend, the painter William Hodges, who had so nimbly escaped from Benaras along with Hastings three years prior, losing everything save his drawings. The painter was poorly, for 'the heats and fatigue I had suffered brought on a violent dysentery, and a palpitation of the heart, from which I was long in recovering'. The artist had first stayed with another European, Antoine Polier, but 'my indisposition, however rather increasing than abating, his house being a large bungalow, was consequently very hot and therefore Col. Martin, who had a large brick house, had the goodness to invite me to his, where by his great and most friendly care and the administering of proper remedies I gradually recovered.' There was

---

*Rosie Llewellyn Jones recently identified the faded inscription on the building, proclaiming its old name 'Chateau de Lyon'.

Antoine Polier himself, returned to Lucknow in 1782 largely due to the good efforts of Hastings, whom he had first met in Bengal in 1761. After his forced eviction from the profitable court of the nawab of Lucknow by the British in 1775 Polier had been obliged to offer his services to the emperor at Delhi where he had found himself considerably poorer after his interlude at the Mughal court. 'This officer had amassed a large fortune because of Shuja-ud-Daula's largesse,' chastised Modave, 'but he spent it as soon as he earned it so that he was often short of money.... he was forced to sell one after the other all the jewels and the objects that he had collected during his time at Faizabad.' Polier had bombarded Hastings with requests to have him returned to lucrative Lucknow in Company service and he was at last promoted to the rank of Lieutenant Colonel, and sent back to Lucknow in 1782. Polier might have given Hastings an exquisite engraved emerald for Marian Hastings at this point in time, in gratitude.* And there was the Anglo-German, scandal-ridden, satisfyingly louche artist, Johann Zoffany, who had arrived in India the previous year and whom Hastings had invited to Lucknow.

An activity that greatly enthused both the Europeans and the Indians at Lucknow, and which Hastings would have witnessed, was cockfighting. Shuja had already been an enthusiastic supporter of the sport, and now under Asaf it had become an obsession. A great many court officials and noblemen, including Salar Jang and Haider Beg Khan, were enthusiasts, as were Europeans like Claude Martin, who was particularly adept. The owners of fighting birds would massage them tenderly, tend to their beak and claws, and feed them by hand lest their beaks get damaged. The favoured nawabi diet for these prized birds was a mix of saffron, almonds, pearl dust, and gold foil. To keep the combat slightly less bloody, these miniature warriors had their claws tied together, but their beaks were carefully sharpened. When they were released into the cockpit, the agitated owners would stand behind their gallant gladiators and shout out encouragingly: 'Well done my boy, shahbash!'. Hastings noted in his diary that he

---

*Marian Hastings' engraved emerald ring looks identical to Polier's, but a calligrapher would need to confirm this. Polier had some of the best craftsmen of Lucknow working for him, including the lapidarist famous for engraving seals and other gemstones called Muhammad Salah Khan, who had been Shuja's court lapidarist. Excellent calligraphers were particularly difficult and expensive to hire, usually only the prerogative of the nawab.

had attended a cockfight organized by Asaf's master of ceremonies, Colonel Mordaunt, and he may have been the one to commission a famous painting of the same name by Zoffany (see image 17).

In May 1784, the entire court was electrified to learn of a most illustrious visitor and exile heading towards the court of Lucknow: Mirza Jawan Bakht, the thirty-five-year-old eldest son of Emperor Shah Alam II. The nawab and Hastings both hurried some distance outside the town to greet the shahzada on bended knee. His situation, remarked Hastings, was extremely impoverished, but when they tried to offer him some gifts, 'he scorned them all, while his father continued in the wretched state which he had represented him. The presents of a pecuniary nature tendered to him, he earnestly begged might be remitted to Delhi. He would not share in any luxury whatever, while his royal father remained in his present necessitous condition.' The next day, an elaborate ceremony of welcome lasting several hours was organized by the nawab to formally conduct the shahzada into Lucknow. One of the nawab's royal elephants was richly caparisoned, and the shahzada sat in the howdah while the nawab himself sat on the seat behind him while Hastings followed on horseback. The nawab may have wondered at the strange workings of fate, that a governor of Awadh was offering sanctuary to Mughal royalty, completely reversing the old balance of power.

The political situation at Delhi had become a great deal more tumultuous since the death of the supremely capable Najaf Khan in 1782. Afrasiab Khan, a relative through marriage of Najaf Khan, was now Mir Bakshi but his position was extremely insecure. Early in 1784, he renewed a treaty with Scindia, which greatly alarmed the watching British, and which tightened the control the Marathas now had on Delhi. Mirza Jawan Bakht managed to escape the close watch kept over him at Delhi by the Marathas, by rather daringly climbing down from a window with the help of a rope. Jawan Bakht was the oldest son of Shah Alam, though it was his much younger brother, the twenty-four-year-old Mirza Akbar Shah, who was by far the favourite of their father. 'He resembled Shah Alam in every way, so was his preferred son,' agreed Polier, about Mirza Akbar Shah. 'They slept in the same room, ate out of the same plate; if one fell ill the other did too. In short nothing can equal the love and affection they bear to each other.' But Polier also maintained that the emperor did not openly grant his younger son any special privileges, which remained with his eldest heir. And though Shah Alam sent peremptory messages to the nawab at Lucknow to have his son returned immediately, a secret message was also sent, from the emperor and from his zenana, confirming their blessing for this dangerous venture which had to be kept secret from the Marathas.

Hastings, meanwhile, was utterly charmed by the romance of the situation he found himself in. To be able to show munificence and largesse to Mughal royalty banished all his headaches and energized him with a sense of destiny. These were the occasions which brought out the very best in Hastings. Here before him he found a descendant of the great Akbar, the magnificent Shah Jahan, all names that he was familiar with through his love of the Persian language and Indian history. This was the very year, after all, in which the Orientalist William Jones created the Asiatic Society of Bengal, with Hastings becoming a founding member. The image of the mighty Mughal empire brought low in the shape of this charming and erudite young man, pleading for help, was one that Hastings was in thrall to, entirely without irony. He would countenance no fault whatsoever in his description of the Shahzada:

> I cannot abandon a person of such eminence who, on the credit of my will and ability to serve him, has voluntarily encountered so many difficulties to get to me; unfortunately his character gains, instead of losing, by acquaintance. His faults are trivial, and all grow out of his good qualities, and the best of these is his temper, which is incomparably cheerful and accommodating to every situation that he is placed in. Was he mean, or arrogant, or petulant or unfeeling, or a fool, or vicious, I could easily let him shift for himself. As he is the reverse of all this, I must either contrive to restore him, 'with credit and safety' (these are the Boards' instructions) to his father or leave him here, or be loaded with him to Calcutta.

Hastings, writing to the board, admitted that he found the prince 'gentle, lively, possessed of a high sense of honour, of a sound judgment, uncommonly quick penetration and a well-cultivated understanding with a spirit of resignation and an equality of temper almost exceeding any within reach of my own knowledge or recollection.'

Modave had noted ten years prior the great reverence and charm that the name of the Mughal emperor evoked in all the peoples of Hindustan:

> Despite the terrible anarchy that has overtaken the Mughal empire, everyone maintains some sort of contact with the Delhi court, so that a certain vestige remains of the old order. This desire to maintain the old order shows the depths to which imperial root go in the hearts of people, for one cannot doubt but that the Marathas and the other great soubedars would do away with these remaining formalities if they believed they could do so without consequences. The respect for the name of the emperor, no matter how minimal, maintains in the hearts of the people the ghost of the Mughal Empire.

Polier, who had known the shahzada in Delhi as well as in Lucknow, was somewhat more tempered in his description.

> Mirza Jawan Bukht...is middle sized, strong and well made, of a pleasing open countenance, full of fire; mixed with sweetness, rather too free and unreserved in his deportment. He does not always maintain that dignity he ought, and discovers his sentiments on affairs perhaps too freely for his future welfare. He has however of late put on a greater reserve, no doubt in consequence of some admonition from his well-wishers. He is much attached to the king who places great confidence in him. He is also very fond of pleasure and women and much inclined to indulge himself freely in the pursuit of them.

Hastings had Zoffany paint a portrait of the shahzada almost immediately. Perhaps the most startling thing in the painting is what is missing from the portrait—jewellery. At a time and place where elite men always wore magnificent jewels, this absence is striking, lending him a stark humility which is all the more poignant. The prince wears a simple white muslin jama and a plain green and gold cummerbund and green turban,* but no earrings, no turban ornament, no rings,

---

*The prince was entitled to the green turban and cummerbund as a sayyid, or descendant of

and no arm bands. His jama is stretched tightly over a robust but somewhat portly frame that speaks of a confined life, a sense that is accentuated by his soft, pale hands which hold a sword without much conviction. The prince is clean shaven except for a pair of fine sweeping moustaches and his eyes are large and luminous, with a direct gaze whose expression borders on sadness. Only his full lips, with a whisper of a smile, counter the overall feeling of loss, lending a gentle, sensuous charm (image 18).*

The only vexatious happening occurred, rather unexpectedly, over the prickly matter of an Englishwoman's charms. When leaving Lucknow after five months, Hastings was accompanied by Mirza Jawan Bakht, and the two men attended a welcome parade at the fort of Chunar. Here, to Hastings' enormous discomfiture, the prince was 'allowed' to see two ladies—a Mrs Achmuty and a Mrs Showers, who were not perhaps the greatest examples of ravishing English beauties. The prince must have muttered a sniggering aside to this effect, for Hastings was greatly embarrassed, saying he had been caught unawares, and 'privately apologized', for this lack of English perfection, and urged the prince not to form his opinion simply going by these two ladies.

Meanwhile, alongside the merry gatherings in Lucknow, the more doleful business of Awadh's management and finances had to be resolved. Bristow had already been recalled to Calcutta but Haidar Beg Khan was now able to show Hastings that he had absconded not only with the Residency accounts but with the sum of 14 lakh rupees for his personal use. In his petty desire to inflict as much chaos as possible, Bristow had stolen the very carpets, cushions, and curtains from the house that the nawab had lent to him.† Hastings was forced to write off this enormous sum against the nawab's debt, and several more concessions were made, all of which reduced the nawab's debt by a substantial 50 lakh rupees. When Middleton heard that the debt had been resolved to everyone's satisfaction, he expressed his great relief that catastrophe had been averted, for the nawab 'deficient as he is in

---

the Prophet Muhammad.
*This portrait would later hang at the Hastings's home at Daylesford House.
†Many concessions were made to the nawab, including the writing off of these 14 lakhs against his account. Moreover, the rate of exchange for payments to Calcutta having been hugely inflated, when the rate of exchange was then revised, the total sum owed by the nawab was found to be much lower.

the requisites of business, has a large portion of courage, and a principle of resentment.' Hastings too seems to have been entirely won over by the nawab's disarmingly warm personality for 'he contrived to convert the Governor-General from a violent and imperious taskmaster into a warm advocate.' For two years, noted an English commentator, the nawab's explanations 'had been treated with contempt or indifference; they were now listened to and complied with, and for a brief space he was treated with respect.'

One of the vital and tense issues that Hastings had to address with Asaf was the matter of the begums' jagirs, which both the begums as well as Salar Jang had written to Hastings about as soon as they learnt of his arrival. And so on a day of 'violent heats'* in June, Hastings wrote in his diary that the nawab was to go to Faizabad 'to present the Begums their jaghirs'. He also visited with Asaf 'to commission him to make my peace with his mother.' This was, after all, a woman he had hounded and personally despised for years, for having refused to quietly hand over her wealth when he had demanded it of her. As the black monsoon clouds gathered over Awadh, Asaf set off for Faizabad before dawn, preceded by his kabootar khana. With the jagirs now restored to the begums, both parties were enormously relieved and Asaf went to great lengths to win over the ladies with extravagant demonstrations of his affection and care. He invited them to Lucknow to attend the wedding of his daughter, and 'sent them each 10 elephants, 10 piebald Tanghan ponies, and 10 bullock coaches for their maids and slaves and 50,000 rupees each for their servants on the road.' As the begums set off from Faizabad, they found that the nawab had thoughtfully set up rich tents at each station on the road, where the fragrant smell of spices announced the presence of pulaos and kebabs that he had instructed be kept for the women. Asaf himself hurried some distance outside Lucknow to accompany his relatives into his capital, where the ladies would have observed the many changes Asaf had made to some of the old structures. Nawab Begum sniffily commented that her son's elegant structures at the Macchi Bhawan had been quite ruined by her grandson's new-fangled additions. Asaf moved out of the Panch Mahal so that Bahu Begum could reside there, while Nawab Begum was given the Baoli Palace.

---

*This is the term Hastings used repeatedly in his diary.

Delighted by the presence of these formidable ladies in his capital, Asaf had a proclamation sent out throughout Lucknow:

> Asaf-ud-Daula is the viceregent of his mother and grandmother, of these dominions and cities small and great they are rulers, the subjects in this city are their subjects; if their servants commit any oppression or cruelty, no one can expect any redress from me.

The marriage festivities for the nawab's daughter were carried out in great style, and after a long stay of many months, Bahu Begum returned to Faizabad by 1786. Nawab Begum remained in Lucknow a few more months, and further alliances between the two nawabi clans were arranged, for which Asaf was now invited to Faizabad in turn. As Asaf participated in all these ceremonies with his usual generosity and good humour, he might have reflected with some satisfaction upon the way in which the resilience of the political system of Awadh had been proven. For now, the insatiable appetites of the British had been neutered, though it would not be very long before there would be a reckoning.

# ZOFFANY AND A MUGHAL ZENANA

On an oppressively hot day in April 1786, two British artists fairly tumbled over each other in their haste to be the first to arrive in Lucknow. In the end, Charles Smith, the oil painter, arrived just sixteen hours before Ozias Humphry, the miniaturist. In any event, both the nawab and his royal guest, the shahzada, were so bored at the idea of the sittings that the painters were obliged to paint their exalted patrons at the same time. Wah! Wah! exclaimed Asaf encouragingly, watching the two perspiring firangis painting the shahzada. To pass the dull hour that had been promised to the painters, the nawab and the shahzada recited Persian couplets to each other but despite the genial show of appreciation by the nawab, very little payment was forthcoming, either for the shahzada's portrait or for the nawab's. For Ozias Humphry, 'neurotic, unstable and enigmatic', this was a bitter disappointment. By the month of June he was finding the rising heat of summer intolerable, and hopelessly wrote in his diary that 'we sit in darkness and perspiration all day long'.

Despite the pained angst of the European painters, these were years of blessed respite in Awadh. Following the tribulations of Hastings, a new regulating act had been signed in 1784, Prime Minister William Pitt the Younger's India Act, also known as Pitt's India Act. This Act brought in a system of dual control in which the directors of the EIC were in charge of the daily commercial exercises but there was also now a Board of Control to supervise political activities. Aggressive wars were now not to be encouraged and a new, more pragmatic Governor General was en route to India. In France, meanwhile, civil war was looming and the monarchy itself was on the brink of a bloody precipice, and the travails and fortunes of the French EIC were a distant dream.

All of which meant that the wealth of the nawab of Lucknow and the relative peace in the area proved irresistible to European artists, just as they had done for so many Indian painters, poets, and artisans. Lured by the fortune made by Tilly Kettle under a different nawab and the sparkling tales of Zoffany's commissions, Humphry's arrival in Lucknow had promised a great deal,* especially after his experiences of Calcutta. Not only had he found that the 'restrictions and impoverishments' imposed by the Company's India house made quick fortunes impossible, he was further distressed to find British painters already ensconced in Calcutta. Most troublesome was a popular young woman painter, a Mrs Hill,† 'a young pretty widow with two small children', about whom he wrote that he would 'rather have had all the male painters of England landed in Bengal than this single woman'. But in Lucknow, he had been hospitably greeted by a band of Indian musicians striking up a stirring tune and Humphry had been galvanized in the 'heart and centre of India to hear the English marches sounding on the drum'. Minister Hasan Reza Khan‡ had greeted him personally, in 'full gala', and had conducted him to the nawab who had embraced him warmly before leading him to his circle of friends. But the nawab, it would appear, enjoyed the appearance of patronage rather more than the paintings themselves. When presented with the finished portraits, he would usually gift them away, for the nawab much preferred the Indian miniature paintings in his own collections. Professor of Persian Francis Gladwin described in 1785 the stunning collection of Indian miniatures that Asaf owned:

> His excellency's collection of Indian pictures is considerable, and preserved in large portfolios. From the common daubings of the present country painters, no adequate conception can be formed of these. Most of them are antique productions; and though the figures are generally small, yet is the drawing often correct, and the colouring admirable. In many a story is told, with clearness and precision instantly discernible...and the festoons, foliage and specimens of Arabic writing illuminating the pictures, are altogether excellent.

---

*Humphry had been told by Sir John Macpherson, the Governor General, that a stay of 3-4 months in Lucknow would earn him the absurd sum of 10,000 pounds from the nawab—see *A Man of the Englightenment: Letters of Claude Martin*, p. 175.
†Probably the painter Diana Hill.
‡Hasan Reza Khan had risen since from superintendent of kitchens for Shuja. That was always a post for a man of confidence, since death by poisoning had long been a fear of rulers in India.

Hasan Reza Khan was rather more appreciative of the English painter, accompanying him to his own house on his elephant, and sitting for him for an hour. When the painter returned home, Hasan Reza Khan sent back an elegant dinner for him, 'all dressed'. That the dinner would have been well presented is not surprising, given Hasan Reza Khan's earlier career as superintendent of kitchens for Shuja. During a second sitting, Humphry was invited to breakfast with the minister before the sitting, and was amazed to note that if he 'looked no further than the tea table, I could persuade myself I was in London'. When he questioned the minister, he was told that 'for some years past their interest had been so connected and interwoven with the English that they endeavoured in all matters that they could with propriety to accommodate themselves to their manners'. Hasan Reza Khan had risen high in the nawab's administration, proving himself a well-liked and loyal minister. He had appointed another man, Maulvi Fazal Azim, to the delicate task of supervising the kitchen and it was the maulvi who now carried the trays in to Asaf's dining quarters. Hasan Reza Khan himself now lived in some style in his new house, Hasangary, that he had built across the Gomti in a new quarter that he had founded (image 19). The minister Haider Beg Khan was not so accommodating and having promised to sit for the two painters together, pleaded a fever, though gallingly he was seen the same afternoon at another Englishman's house, in excellent health.

Humphry, therefore, was left sweltering in the heat and torpor of summer in Lucknow, grumbling that 'my spirits have been and still are greatly depressed'. He did, however, appreciate the accountant John Wombwell's lodgings which comprised a bungalow on a mound overlooking the Gomti. Humphry stayed with Wombwell through May, admitting that it 'provided a comfortable existence...in the violence of this season where house and enclosures bring to one's mind the comforts of England with trees and lawns forever green whilst all the lands surrounding Lucknow seem like an Arabian desert'. Perhaps, also, Humphry had found other ways of cheering himself up, for after he had returned to England, (bearing vials of attar of roses to gift to his lady friends), Claude Martin had written to him the following lines, accompanied by a rather suggestive sketch of a dancing girl with large breasts:

> Remember I am to be in the description if you make any for your portfolio of 'Les loisirs de Chevalier Humphry, des beauties des Indes orientales ou des vierges de l'Est.'*

The situation was just as dire for the oil painter Charles Smith. He had left England possibly because he was rumoured to have 'violently expressed political opinions', because of which he was struggling to obtain patrons at home. In the end, as Asaf showed little sign of paying either painter, they both left by July, headed in different directions, bitterly aggrieved†.

In all fairness to the nawab, both Humphry and Smith were easily overshadowed by the skill and reputation of the European painter in residence already at the court of Lucknow, Johann Zoffany.‡ Over fifty years old at the time of his arrival in India, Zoffany usually appeared in his self-portraits painted in macabre hues, accentuating his unhealthy bluish pallor, eerily pale eyes, and thinning grey hair (image 20). Zoffany was a celebrated artist of the 'conversation piece' genre in his lifetime, and a founder member of the Royal Academy, so there is some speculation about why he chose to travel to India. Just before he left for India, a friend had said that Zoffany 'anticipates to roll in gold dust', so perhaps prosaically money was an attraction for the famously profligate painter. But scandal may have played a part in his decision too. The last work that he painted for his royal patron, Queen Charlotte, the Tribuna of the Uffizi, was considered so offensive that the Queen's husband apparently refused to show it to his wife§. He also had the habit of indulging in the dangerous practical joke of introducing real people—those he disliked—into his compositions 'without the permission of the original and often in unflattering guise', usually to settle a score. There is also in his earlier works, and even in some of his conversation pieces, a sense

---

*'The pleasures of Gentleman Humphry, the Beauties of the East Indies or the Virgins of the East.'

†Humphry had rather greedily charged the nawab double his usual price for miniatures. In the end, the nawab paid him Rs 5,000 and a bond for the rest that was owed.

‡According to Elijah Impey, chief justice at the time in Calcutta, Zoffany made some £10,000 on commissions within a few months of his arrival in India.

§Many figures are of actual persons living at the time, including one particularly notorious character. The men are standing in groups looking with more lascivious interest at the nude sculptures than might have been thought decent for a queen's painting.

of underlying violence, and also something scurrilous or lewd, and sometimes both*.

Zoffany first arrived in Calcutta, where he might have found the notoriously lumpen English society somewhat stifling. An EIC writer described a typical evening in 1775 in Calcutta:

> ...the evening was stupid enough, and the supper detestable... With respect to conversation, we have had three or four songs screeched to unknown tunes; the ladies regaled with cherry-brandy, and we pelted one another with bread-pills *a la mode de Bengal*.

In Lucknow, Zoffany settled into Claude Martin's house, the Chateau de Lyon, and embraced Lucknawi life with merry abandon. He stayed for six months in the summer of 1784, and would return the following year, spending a total of two and a half years in Lucknow. He set up a studio in one of Claude Martin's rooms in the Chateau de Lyon, where he began working on his numerous commissions.† Despite having a wife and child in England,‡ Zoffany also had two bibis in Lucknow, with whom he had a number of children. It is easy to imagine these two Europeans, Zoffany with his thick German accent, Martin with his whimsical, scattershot English and darting speech that he often eagerly punctuated with 'do you see?' and 'what do you call it?' Both men were also slightly on the margins of British society in India—one vaguely disreputable and the other subject to smirking snobbery. Both were also Freemasons, discussing their common love of art, objects, and curiosities but also of gossip, of ridicule, of the esoteric, and of the erotic. It was at this time that Zoffany put Martin in contact with Charles Townley, who was a prominent member of the Society of Dilettanti. About membership to this somewhat scandalous club, English writer Horace Walpole had tartly observed that 'the nominal qualification (for membership) is having been in Italy, and the real one, being drunk'.

The Society had been founded in 1734 by young British gentlemen, all of whom had gone on the Grand Tour in Italy,§ with the object of

---

*See *Self-portrait as a Monk*, with condoms in the background hanging next to a rosary.
†Including forty-seven drawings and sketches for Claude Martin.
‡There appears to be some slight confusion about whether his two previous wives were alive at the same time, making him a bigamist.
§The Grand Tour formed a part of wealthy young men's education in the eighteenth century. The focus was mainly on the painting and sculpture of Italy. These men often brought back

bringing the pleasures of classical antiquity to a larger audience by forming collections, sponsoring expeditions, and publishing books on the subject. There was a definite ribald element to the club, with one notorious pamphlet produced being *A Discourse on the Worship of Priapus*,* supposedly inspired by the discovery of a phallic cult in Italy. For Martin, it meant the shipment to Lucknow by Townley of 'drawings, prints, bronzes, marbles, medals, coins...and the cultivation of their common interest in the theories surrounding the relationship between classical and Indian mythology and their attendant sexual practices.'

One of the rare women to be included in this society of European men was Elizabeth Plowden. She was the young wife of Captain Richard Plowden, who commanded the nawab's bodyguard. Elizabeth Plowden visited Lucknow several times in the 1780s, and instantly charmed this circle of men with her lively enthusiasm and her musical abilities. Zoffany was so delighted by her young sons that he exclaimed he would paint them for free. Plowden had developed a fondness for Hindustani music and had learned to sing some of the songs herself. Martin gave her a small portrait of himself copied from Zoffany and also a harpsichord, to accompany her singing. He also wrote her the only letter to a woman in his voluminous correspondence.

> I assure you my dear Mrs Plowden, I never passed more happy day in my life but when you was in Lucknow. Those happy days, I never can forget, your company enlivened the place tho there was many other family in the place, your lively and amiable manner attracted everybody to your home. Your house was my magnet I never visited so much, as I did to you we have had many good lady here, but none that I visited with so real pleasure as I did you.

There is a certain ring of truth to these lines, and it is as though, despite the ceaseless activity of his churning days, Martin may have been lonely in his personal life. The men he most seemed to envy were the ones who returned to Europe, and then married charming European women like Elizabeth Plowden. And yet there were women in Martin's life too, though they were Indian women. For one woman that Zoffany met at this point was the girl that Martin had raised

---

important works of art including statuary from Italy.
*The god of male sexual potency.

since around the age of nine, and who was now his bibi, among six others. The eighteen-year-old Boulone was now a butter-skinned, dark-browed beauty, and Zoffany painted an intimate painting of the young woman with a young boy, Zulfikar* (image 21). Boulone was to be the most faithful of Martin's bibis, and the only companion he seemed to value, staying with him till the end of his life. His relationship with this young woman he would explain in a 1789 letter to Humphry, writing that though many of his good friends had returned to Europe, 'still I think I have some good ones yet in India. I don't mean among the blacks peoples except my amiable girl (Boulone), which I do not rank among the blacks, she being whiter than me, and having had as good an education as an European.' This alabaster complexion that Martin seemed to value above everything else, making her 'white' in his eyes, earned her the sobriquet Gori Bibi.

Zoffany would paint a number of famous paintings of the society he found at Lucknow. They have been carefully analysed and there are conflicting theories about whether or not they depict a genuinely egalitarian and friendly interaction between the Europeans and the Indians. In some of the paintings, Zoffany has painted himself into the groups too, his watery eyes looking out at the viewer, a wisp of an expression, a calculating and penetrating leer, challenging us to decipher the world he has created. Despite the swirling movement and distracting colour in most of the paintings, there is also a faintly disturbing and disquieting sense of the people being pinned to the paper, like butterfly specimens in a case, presented for our amusement. There is one image,† however, an unfinished group painting, which appears far less ambiguous and is painted with charming intimacy. It is a painting of the zenana of William Palmer, who was the confidential agent of Hastings in Lucknow. Included in the painting is Palmer's bibi, Faiz Begum, their three children, and some women attendants. Seated next to Faiz Begum is her sister, Noor Begum, who was about to meet another visiting European, Benoit de Boigne (image 22).

De Boigne was from the Savoy region in what is modern-day France, but in the eighteenth century was still the independent Duchy

---

*Zulfikar 'James' Martin was bought by Martin as a young boy, and was then adopted by Boulone.
†This painting was first attributed to Zoffany, then to the Italian artist Renaldi, and then re-attributed to Zoffany by Mildren Archer.

of Savoy. A soldier first for the French in their Irish Brigades, de Boigne joined the British when he arrived in India and quickly climbed the ranks of the EIC. De Boigne would later find fortune and glory raising an army for the Marathas but in the 1780s, having met Hastings, he came to Lucknow to learn Persian and Urdu and received a khillat from the nawab. 'More than six feet tall with the build of a giant, well-formed limbs and piercing eyes', de Boigne would have cut quite a dash when he arrived in Lucknow and met the Europeans living there. In his thirties at this time, obsessively hard-working, driven and focused, he met the young Noor Begum* who was living with her sister in Palmer's house. Noor Begum would have been around sixteen years old at this time, and was later described as 'a beautiful, fair complexioned, compliant woman of respectable manners and a good education'—she could read and write both Persian and English. Indeed Faiz Begum and Noor Begum were from a respectable family of Lucknow.† Palmer was one of the very rare elite European men who seemed to really view his bibi as his wife, even though they were never legally married. Faiz Begum would always remain by his side and in his will she was described as 'his devoted companion of more than 30 years'. She retained her elite status, and in 1796 the Mughal emperor presented her with a sanad (deed) granting her the title begum. In his future correspondence with de Boigne, after the Savoyard had taken Noor Begum as his bibi, Palmer would always add courteous messages of love and respect to his sister-in-law: 'Send my love to the Begum and hug the little baron for me,' he wrote in 1792, after Noor Begum had had a son. And also: 'All here desire their kindest regards to you, make my affectionate salaams to my Sister the Begum.'

Perhaps it was the exceptional quality of this relationship that made Zoffany paint such a startling and moving image of this Anglo-Indian family, instead of reducing the Indian women to exoticized objects of desire, or introducing an element of caricatural humour. For the other European men like Martin, Polier, and Zoffany himself, the women they had as companions were usually bought, and were

---

*Also sometimes referred to as Halima Begum.
†They are believed to be the daughters of a Persian cavalryman who obtained employment with Shah Alam II, and then relocated to Lucknow where he entered the services of Asaf-ud-Daula. The family would then remain in Lucknow. The mother is believed to have been from a respectable, perhaps even a noble family of Lucknow.

therefore enslaved, the relationship always uneasily off-kilter and provoking social anxiety. When Elizabeth Plowden was invited to a party in Lucknow that included Palmer, Polier, and Zoffany, there were no other women included, European or Indian, though all three men had Indian companions.

Zoffany would finally leave Lucknow, and India, in 1788, leaving his bibis and children in Martin's care. Back home in Europe he would make an additional album—a collection of fifty-three drawings exclusively for Claude Martin in Lucknow. In these drawings, there are many of the phantasmagorical preoccupations of his earlier works. In them, themes of grotesque violence, rape, prurience, and nightmares are mixed in with scenes of more classical leanings. One of the sketches, titled *A Dream*, presents a nightmarish vision of a naked old witch carrying out some form of incantation, while hovering over her head are demons, one of whom appears to be riding the figure of Asaf. This appears to be a sort of exorcism to compel the nawab to pay his debts, in keeping with Martin's repeated accusations that Asaf did not like to pay European men. Made specifically for Martin, this sentiment was poor recompense indeed towards the nawab who would make of him the richest 'nabob' in northern India in the eighteenth century.

# THE CHAMELEONS OF LUCKNOW

When the Orientalist and jurist William Jones created the Asiatic Society of Bengal in 1784, a number of Lucknow regulars became founder members including Antoine Polier, Warren Hastings, and Claude Martin. A focus of the Asiatic Society was the study of Sanskrit and, through it, the understanding of the sacred writings of Hinduism. Apart from purely academic incentives, there was a more pragmatic official reason for the existence of the society. Founded at a time of great upheaval in the fortunes of the EIC, following the fracas with Hastings in Awadh, it was understood that the Company's new presence as ruler of Bengal would require a knowledge of the languages and the laws of the country, in addition to Persian. The collection of land revenues and the administering of justice required an understanding of both Hindu and Muslim law codes. 'It was not by accident', writes a scholar, 'that many of the leading Sanskrit scholars held important judiciary posts,' including William Jones himself. A famous Sanskrit scholar living in Calcutta at the time stated his complaint more baldly, writing to his father that Hastings had brought to the country only unscrupulous 'harpies, who (had) adopted one pursuit—a fortune'.

Surrounded as he was by Brahmin and Kshatriya advisers, there was a bias in the way William Jones approached the subject. There was a disproportionate emphasis on the importance of Brahmins, and the Laws of Manu, stemming from the fact that Brahmins greatly revered the ordinances of Manu and Jones therefore believed these to be equally revered by all Hindus 'whereas most of them had probably never heard of the book'. William Jones's biographer also noted that he did not 'have any way of knowing that the book was probably a Brahmanic compilation in much the same way as the Old Testament', since such a suggestion 'would have been blasphemous to his associates', the Brahmin scholars. And through this web of half-truths and misrepresentations, these Laws of Manu would then become the primary document providing the laws used by the EIC to govern Bengal.

Sensing immediately the ebb and flow of academic currents, and always closely allying himself with the fate of the Company, Polier now stepped away from his long patronage of Persianate art and writings and enthusiastically pursued Sanskrit oeuvres. Almost overnight, he shed his Persianate nobleman avatar and adopted a new one—that of the dedicated Sanskritist. With the help of an Indian scholar named Ramchand, Polier transcribed all the epic poems, stories, and mythologies of the Hindu religion. Polier's final coup was to obtain a copy of the Vedas, historically deemed almost impossible. 'It is known that many attempts had been made to obtain the Vedas, on the Coromandel Coast, in Bengal and even in Benaras. But all these efforts only brought to light certain shastras, commentaries on the Vedas.' He obtained manuscript copies of the Vedas from Jaipur, through the help of the Portuguese physician at the court of Raja Pratap Singh. 'Once I possessed this treasure, which I only desired so that I could send it to those whose knowledge of Sanskrit would enable them to make sense of it, I sent a copy immediately to William Jones in Calcutta, at that time the only European in India who could read Sanskrit.'

Before his re-invention as a Sanskrit scholar, Polier had lived for decades as a Persianate nobleman both in Lucknow and Faizabad. Across the river Gomti about 5 miles outside Lucknow he had built a large Hindustani-style bungalow modestly named Polierganj. William Hodges had suffered through his illness in Polier's bungalow for five months, which he deemed much too hot. Polier's bungalow house, Hodges explained, was built on one storey, with a large central room for eating and relaxing, and rooms at each corner for sleeping.* The bungalow had a thatched overhanging roof with open verandas on every side, and was consequently much warmer than the house of the other European in residence—Claude Martin. There were additional buildings that served as guest houses, as well as a zenana for his two bibis and children. In his sprawling bungalow complex, his wives would squabble in uneasy intimacy and his children would grow up being treated by unani doctors and encouraged to visit with Claude Martin. As in his bungalow in Faizabad, there would have been his favourite mango pickles, his hookah, his attar,† and his spices, and the sound

---

*No sign of Polier's house can be traced today, though some ruins of his house at Faizabad remain.
†While Polier had a fondness for the popular attar of roses, other fragrances included kamal (lotus), chameli or juhi (jasmine), champa (magnolia), kewra (pandanus flower), and chandan (sandalwood).

of music from his dancing girls endlessly practising their evocative stances. Polier also grew roses from which he made attar, and he noted that the perfume produced was of a different colour depending on the day the flowers were harvested. 'I have obtained this year (1787) beautiful emerald green attar, fluorescent yellow attar, and reddish attar, from roses from the same field but collected on different days.' Polier was a popular host and Hastings was a visitor to the bungalow in 1784 as were de Boigne and Zoffany (image 23).

Ozias Humphry witnessed a dance, or 'nautch', for the first time at Polier's bungalow. 'The grace of attitudes of his principal dames,' wrote a charmed Humphry, 'were exquisitely beautiful, surpassing all things of the kind I have ever seen.' The one criticism Humphry noted was that 'the practice of dyeing the teeth and the gums...is odiously disgusting to one unaccustomed to it.' The women also had henna on their hands and feet, which accentuated each perfect flick of the wrist, and each tapping toe. 'I was seated with Colonel Polier upon a sofa, to whom the dancers would direct their songs of love,' continued Humphry. 'Eight of the girls, some very young, sat by to look on.' There exists a painting of an interaction between Polier and some of these 'nautch' dancers (image 24). It is believed to be based on a lost Zoffany painting, and shows a dancer, possibly the famous Kashmiri dancer Khanum Jan herself,* demonstrating a particular dance movement to a watchful Polier. The dancer wears a layered long white angarkha and odhani and an elaborate headdress with a curving plume. Polier himself lounges against bolsters, in a long jama, cloak, and nawabi headgear, his hookah coiled by his side. Outside the covered veranda a tent flutters, and a fountain gurgles over a long-necked heron. Polier is shown in this painting as a discerning patron of music and dance, training his singers and his dancers much as an ustad would have done at the elite courts.

The Chateau de Lyon that Martin built on the banks of the Gomti in Lucknow was vastly different in style from Polier's bungalow, reflecting the owner's far more fraught relationship with India. It did, however, provoke great admiration in visiting Europeans, and persistent envy in Asaf. 'Our Nabob is building everyday houses, palaces, gardens and copy everyone's house,' wrote Martin to Elizabeth Plowden, smugly,

---

*Identification proposed by musicologist Katherine Butler Schofield.

'but I don't think he will ever be able to copy mine. He often demanded plan of my present house on the water.'* And, undoubtedly Chateau de Lyon was a unique and striking building. Martin built it on what was at the time an extensive, isolated, and wooded bit of land by the river. Once over the moat and through the drawbridge, the visitor would have been confronted with a somewhat eclectic arrangement of European Palladian style buildings topped with turrets. Inside the building, the visitor would have admired large, handsome halls while the most striking apartment was built right over the river so that, as a guest wrote, 'boats passed under the room in which we dined'.

The rooms were filled with 'every European curiosity and contraption he could get his hands on: telescopes, steam engines, an oxygen pump and the makings of hot air balloons. (Martin) acquired prints and caricatures by the hundred...an inventory of Martin's possessions at his death in 1800 ran to nearly 80 pages'. As Martin spent his growing fortune on collecting objects and curios in an almost orgiastic manner, and then filling his house with them, the effect could be overwhelming. The two large rooms 'were covered with glasses, pictures and prints; in short, you could see no walls three feet from the floor', noted a visitor, so laden were the walls with objects and paintings. There was a billiard table in one room, a Herschel telescope in a turret, more than a hundred oil paintings, scientific equipment (noted in some bafflement in his inventory as 'electrifying machines'), plaster busts including ones of Louis XVI and Marie Antoinette, Hastings, and Cornwallis, an organ and guitars, 17 beds and 124 chairs, copies of Chippendale furniture, books, mirrors, candles, candelabras and more.

The majority of these objects point to the fact that the interiors of Martin's homes were furnished almost exclusively in a haphazard Western style. There were no Mughal or nawabi wall hangings, paintings, or floor coverings just as Martin would never adopt Indian dress. There are no paintings of him in Indian clothes, or any mention of them in his inventory. Instead, the inventory of Chateau de Lyon lists European clothes—great coats of scarlet cloth, white breeches, jackets, a waistcoat of 'scarlet cloth regimentals', shirts, and silk stockings. Two

---

*Martin would have been furious to know that the next nawab, Saadat Ali Khan, would buy Chateau de Lyon and re-baptise it Farhat Baksh in 1802.

years before his death, Martin was writing to de Boigne, asking for a smart Hussar* uniform: 'I also wish very much to have a complete saddle in the hussar style for riding, covered with a nice bearskin or that which the Hungarian hussars use... and a full costume with cap, boots etc...a good sabre *a la hussarde*† will be well received.'

Martin was a generous and hospitable host, always pleased to entertain visiting Europeans to his chateau. But the welcome to his table, wrote a visitor, although it 'was always a hearty one, it could have offered no attractions to any but persons whose purses were so scantily furnished as to render a gratis dinner an object of importance. It was served in a careless slovenly manner, and with most abominable viands, more resembling the green and yellow dinners of a Spanish or Portuguese ambassador, or the ordinaries of French or Italian tables d'hote, other than the neat comfortable repasts of an English officer.' Apart from a suspect fondness for 'neat' English fare, this anonymous writer does suggest that Martin's steward, Spaniard Joseph Quieros, was at least partly to blame for the regrettably European concoctions. Many of the other servants in Martin's busy household, meanwhile, were enslaved locals, bought when they were children. As for his zenana, there were seven women and children listed in his will. Apart from Boulone, whom he had bought when she was nine, there were Boulone's two sisters, and Sally, the presumed illegitimate daughter of Resident Gabriel Harper, who was only fourteen by the time Martin died at the age of sixty-five. There were also a further three named women in the zenana. There were no biological children of Martin's listed in his will, as he himself was unable to father any children.

Martin's numerous mistresses, and the fact that they were bought as very young children, was what earned him the most opprobrium from other Europeans. The following criticism was quite typical of the opinion many held him in:‡

> A more infamous or despicable character than the late General Martin never existed. He had not a single virtue, though he

---

*The quintessential cavalryman since the Middle Ages.
†This sudden desire for a hussar-style uniform might have been a result of the short-lived unit of Hussar cavalry that entered the Madras and then the Bengal units of the EIC in the late eighteenth century.
‡George Annesley, 2nd Earl of Mountnorris, also known as George Viscount Valentia, was a British traveller, writer, and politician (1770–1844).

laboured to assume the appearance of several. He took the female orphan children of two of his friends, declaring that he would educate and provide for them both, but when they reached the age of 12, they unwillingly became his concubines.

Indeed some sense of this same unease regarding the ethics of having forced these girls into concubinage pervades Martin's will too:

> I had them when in their childhood and I had them educated as virtuously as I could, they have fulfilled my intention to my great satisfaction. God may give them their reward they are innocent of any Guilt I am capable on the Sin if they have committed any by having partook my bed they owed Compliance to my Command as their Duties...

As for the education that Martin fondly hoped transformed Boulone into a 'virtuous' woman, as scholar Dubra Ghosh points out, 'in affirming her virtue, her education and her piety, Martin's account rewrote the slave origins of Lise, remaking her into a respectable, educated and more equal and appropriate partner for him'. Neither 'black' then, nor enslaved, Boulone thus became an acceptable companion for Martin.

Martin also inherited Zoffany and Polier's bibis and children. The fate of Polier's son worried him especially. He was, he wrote to Elizabeth Plowden, 'a fine stout boy whom I will endeavour to send to his wife as the education of India is so bad that I never would advise anybody to let their children receive it in such a country, where they learn every kind of evil by (from) black servant.'

In a letter to the artist Ozias Humphry written in 1789, Martin ruminated on the many anxieties that increasingly haunted him. In India, he wrote, 'he can't enjoy peace of mind...security to one's property, which is here at the mercy of many causes.' And then in addition, 'the worst of all is of losing a friend, constantly, as well as by the fatal strokes of death, or going home.' As for the people that remained in India, 'I cannot say that there is a great deal of sincerity existing among one another, and much worse among the amicable fair.' Always despised by the French as a deserter, scorned ever so subtly by the British for his haphazard English, his grasping parvenu attitude, and his embarrassingly large gifts, Martin was the quintessential outsider. As for the Indians who surrounded Martin, in his home and at his work, he claimed rather outrageously to Humphry that 'I have lived very little among them really! Their company I have always avoided...' As for the notion that there could have been any imbalance of power in these interactions, Martin was clear that only the threat of force kept a dangerously simmering violence at bay. 'Tho it is fashion to call us India gentlemen "the murderers of thousands! The plunderers of these poor innocents creatures..." I wish to see those great orators at the mercy of those "innocent creatures" without the support of any powers, then I have no doubt that they would speak differently.' In 1780 he had criticized a visiting British general* for his 'fundamental kindness and the good opinions that he has of the Blacks (that) allows him to overlook everything...' This almost pathological fear and distrust† Martin extended even to the man who had enabled him to prosper so spectacularly, the nawab himself. 'For what I know of his character,' Martin wrote ominously to Humphry, 'I think it such that if one could read in his heart he would perceive it loaded with many dark sinister intentions and as you know those who compose his Court, you then ought to know what man he is.'

Perhaps Martin dreamed of the only family he could claim—a family of Freemasons, living in style and safety in Constantia,‡ the enormous fortified structure that he began building in 1795 but never completed, and which has been described§ as a 'wedding-cake in brick, a Gothic castle and a baroque folly.' In a letter to de Boigne in Europe, Martin wrote that 'when you return I hope that you will bring me about a thousand or two of nice curiosities from Europe, things of little value, but in great numbers, bringing me also several books on the (Free) Masonry with jewels of the orders in gold or silver, the ribbons and other things connected with this subject so that we can establish a (lodge) here when you arrive where you can serve as the Grandmaster in my new chateau, which has not yet been baptised,

---

*Eyre Coote.
†This attitude, and fear, is similar to that which was being experienced by white enslavers in British colonies like Jamaica at this very same time, in which the overwhelmingly large population of enslaved blacks was used to justify extreme, brutal violence.
‡Today known as La Martiniere College, Lucknow.
§Martin himself admitted it was 'an unnecessary thing that I could do without' in a letter to de Boigne.

and I hope that you will be the godfather.'

Martin would die in the Chateau de Lyon in 1800, surrounded by his extensive collection of silver and gold jewellery, watches, medallions, china, glassware, and firearms and a silver service* from Europe that cost over 3,000 pounds†. He was embalmed, as per his will, and buried in the centre of the basement room at Constantia, still unfinished at the time of his death. He left behind jewels inscribed with his name and date of death for Boulone and his other bibis to wear, as well as mourning rings for his friends. He lies there to this day, watched over by four life-size wooden sepoys, their arms reversed in mourning.

As for Polier, in 1788, the year in which he finally left India after thirty years, a letter was received by the Provost and Fellows of King's College Cambridge, from Patna. An alumnus of the college in India had 'acquired a collection of Persian manuscripts amounting to more than 550 volumes', and was sending these manuscripts back to England.‡ This was almost the entirety of Polier's enormous manuscript collection, the largest collection of Indian manuscripts in the late eighteenth century, including all his precious Indo-Persian texts, paintings, and manuscripts, which he had sold before he left India. Upon his return to France, he sold another section of his collection, keeping just a small selection with himself, including a copy of the Vedas.

The collection he thus sold included the majority of the paintings now attributed to the great artist Mehr Chand, produced over thirteen years. Polier's collection included gorgeous bound volumes of Awadhi paintings, and also older seventeenth century works of Mughal and Deccani origin. Scholars have praised his muraqqas as being among the finest produced at that time, with a symmetry in frontispiece and distinctive borders which make them instantly recognizable (image 25). After a lifetime of living like a Persianate Mughal nobleman in India, and then a short interlude as a Sanskrit Oriental scholar, Polier shaved his nawabi moustache and sloughed off his habits, his art, and his Indian family. He exchanged his muslin clothes and jewelled turban for a powdered wig and scarlet uniform. He returned home

---

*Martin described the service as 'an excess of vanity' on his part.
†More than a quarter of a million pounds today.
‡The manuscripts were divided between King's College and Eton. Cambridge University library now has 550 Polier documents, called the Pote Collection.

with a large fortune to find a young wife* in post-revolutionary France, and left Arsalan-e-Jung (Lion in Battle) far behind in the fine dust of Lucknow.†

---

*The present day Polier family are descended from Anne Berthoudt, Polier's European wife.
†Polier would not long enjoy his wealth and his young wife. He would be murdered in France by a mob in 1795, presumably for his pro-royalist leanings.

BOOK III

# THE TIGER AND THE FISH
(1785–1794)

# THE GLORY OF LUCKNOW

It was with particular enthusiasm and extravagance that Nawab Asaf-ud-Daula celebrated Holi during the spring of 1787. The stifling grip of the EIC demands had loosened considerably after years of tense posturing and now Bahu Begum had come to Lucknow at Asaf's express invitation to celebrate this auspicious festival. Faiz Baksh was not entirely appreciative of this penchant the nawab had for these festivals when he wrote that 'the Nawab used to associate freely with Hindus and had a great fancy for such displays. He used at this festival to give a public entertainment and spend large sums of money'. Bahu Begum, he added, 'remained a month there (in Lucknow) to please her son and then returned to Faizabad'. The aristocratic writer Abu Talib* meanwhile was even more direct in his criticism when he wrote that 'during the whole of Phagun at the Holi, in the Wazir's carnival and marriages and illuminations, each year five or six lakhs are spent for these customary celebrations.' So spectacular were the Holi celebrations of the nawab that a painting was made by an artist from his studio, the master Mir Kalan Khan, early in the reign of the nawab. In it, a young Asaf makes his stately way through a gold-drenched courtyard in which groups of women are draped in dappled layers of purple and lilac and are singing and playing on the drums while outside the palace all is night.

Because English criticism of Asaf and all the later nawabs of Lucknow was so relentless and shrill, it is easy to misunderstand the way in which the nawab spent his resources from this time onwards on the patronage of art, music, dance, architecture, and in all the forms of etiquette that would form the great chimaera culture of Awadh. The EIC deplored this spending which they viewed as extravagance because it did not end up directly in their coffers.† They wanted the nawab to

---

*Mirza Abu Talib's father had been in nawabi employ, but Abu Talib soon decided that the rising power of the EIC was a better bet and moved to Calcutta in 1795. Unable to find any permanent employment, he decided to journey to London to open a Persian language school, convinced by an EIC agent. In London he was celebrated as 'the Persian Prince' and he wrote a highly entertaining account of his journeys through England, France, and the Middle East.
†Following the debacle of attempts at direct control of Awadh in the early 1780s, and the dire state of the Bengal finances, the EIC at this time decided to step away from Awadh, preferring

focus on revenue collection, which could then be spent paying back bottomless 'debts' to the Company, or for ruinous garrisons stationed in Awadh. Anything that was not spent in this manner would come to be described as 'effeminate, 'debauched', 'profligate' and generally suspect by both the English as well as locals like Abu Talib who were working for the English.

When Cornwallis was appointed the new Governor General by the Company and arrived in Calcutta on 1 September 1786,* Lucknow was still in a state of tense anticipation, keenly awaiting Cornwallis's next moves after the past fraught years. But with the spectre of Hastings's scandalous attempts at forcible and violent measures to control Awadh still painfully vivid, Cornwallis strongly opposed any interference in the nawab's government. He immediately worked to reduce Lucknow's financial burden, slashing the salaries paid out to the Company's servants at the Lucknow Residency, and all other claims upon the nawab.† Haider Beg Khan, meanwhile, was tenacious and indefatigable in his demands for a diminution of the nawab's financial liabilities and went to Calcutta to parlay with Cornwallis in 1787 and to valiantly fight the nawab's corner. Palmer, writing from Calcutta to his disgraced patron Hastings in England, admitted as much when he reported that 'they (the Awadhi party) wish to be relieved from the expense of the Fatehgur (sic) Battalion which they think useless and burdensome',‡ before adding that 'they want to prevent all European influence in their country whether by statesmen, soldiers, or merchants. But they will relinquish the first to obtain the rest though reluctantly, and the minister (Haider Beg) will make a pretty stout defence even in that article.' And though Cornwallis had wanted the maintenance of the ruinously costly Fatehgur Brigade, the nawab forcefully stated that 'the two Brigades, the establishment of the Company's servants at Lucknow, the stipend of Saadat Ali Khan and the Rohillas shall not altogether exceed the sum of fifty lakhs annually.'

---

to allow the nawabi structure to continue with revenue collection and administration.
*He replaced Sir John Macpherson.
†Including the allowance to Saadat Ali Khan, the Rohilla stipend, and the military subsidy for two brigades, the total amounted to a lump sum of Rs 5,000,000 per year.
‡Meant to be a 'temporary' brigade, the Fatehgarh brigade in effect became permanent with a yearly cost of Rs 3,700,000 to the nawab. See Barnett, *North India between Empires* p. 157, Table 2.

Palmer himself was in a dispirited frame of mind since Cornwallis was refusing to employ anyone who had been associated with Hastings's tainted government in any way whatsoever. As for Haider Beg Khan, Palmer was nettled enough to note that the minister's 'conduct to me has been so unjust and cruel that neither my honour nor my feelings, or of my being the channel of conveyance...' were taken into account at all.* It seems clear that with the arrival of a new Governor General, the nawab and his ministers were determined to rid themselves of all the parasitic Europeans who had lived off the largesse of Awadh,† and to keep English interference to an absolute minimum. Cornwallis himself would promise Asaf that no resident would be allowed to interfere in his government, and in a letter to his directors reasoned that it was better to 'bear deficiencies of no great importance on the part of his Excellency with a little patience rather than attempt to renew the species of interference in the details of his government through the medium of our Resident which has been so judiciously reprobated by your Honble Court.'

Other interested parties also made their way speedily to Calcutta to woo the new Governor General. Leading the charge was Claude Martin, desperately anxious to retain his lucrative posting in Lucknow. Arriving in Calcutta, Martin assiduously sent 'gifts' to Cornwallis's private secretary Alexander Ross, to whom he sent attar of rose and a 'pair of pistol, shawl handkerchief and Mughal jewellery', as well as 'two (flintlock muskets), a pair of pistol, production of my office...a small vial of genuine oil of rose...two large handkerchief (shawls) and a (Cashmere) blanket' for Cornwallis himself. A few weeks later he sent for Cornwallis via Ross 'unprocurable coin', of a sort 'which his Lordship may remain 20 year in India and may not be perhaps able to collect such a number, they were struck by the famous Nur Jahan Begum.' Martin's fondest hope, as he wrote to Hastings in January 1787, was 'to be appointed a full colonel and to command the Vizier's troops'. In the end, his persistence, or perhaps simply the gifts, proved irresistible, for he returned to Lucknow a few months later, entirely delighted. He later sent Ross 'a small private seal' of

---

*In a happier time, Middleton had written to Hastings that 'Hyder Beg Khan appears to me to possess talent and a knowledge of business far beyond any other man now about the court'.
†Palmer's salary, paid by the nawab, was Rs 19,000 per month.

his name in gratitude, and named a 30-pound cannon in Cornwallis's honour.* It may have helped Martin's cause that Cornwallis was also a Freemason, and Grandmaster of the six Calcutta Lodges. Polier, also in attendance at Calcutta, appears not to have been as successful, for he followed Hastings to Europe in just a couple of years, delayed only by his outstanding debts with the nawab.

Perhaps upon Martin's triumphant return to Lucknow the nawab was made to believe that the great concessions that Cornwallis had accorded to him had partly been due to Martin's efforts. For it was at this very time that the nawab gave Martin an extraordinary gift—a sword whose hilt was made of white jade, jewel-encrusted, and whose blade was inscribed in gold with Martin's name.† This was an object of the most exquisite workmanship and value, and yet there was never any suggestion that the nawab was ever especially friendly with Martin. There was always a sense that the nawab tolerated Martin for the sake of expediency and because Martin clung on to the rich province like a barnacle-encrusted limpet.‡ Martin, for his part, had nothing but suspicious contempt for the nawab, which he was not shy of stating in his letters. As for the nawab, though he was usually unfailingly gracious to the Europeans in his city, Martin was never on the list of Europeans attending the nawab's hunts, nor was he favoured in any way, despite being such a fixture in Lucknow. The sort of man preferred by the nawab was of a different temperament entirely, exemplified by his favourite British courtier—Colonel Mordaunt.

John Mordaunt was the illegitimate son of an earl, who had proved fiercely resistant to all attempts at an education. Though practically illiterate, he was a lively, suave, and handsome man, with a tall, svelte figure which his besotted biographer described as being as striking as a Roman god's. And while he could barely write, he spoke with an elegant turn of phrase and learnt both Hindi and a smattering of Persian. Asaf was delighted with his natural grace and easy manner, and spent a great deal of time hunting and attending cock-fights organized by him. An anecdote recounts that when Cornwallis had told Mordaunt

---

*The Cornwallis cannon can be found now upon the terrace of La Martiniere School, Lucknow.
†'By the order of His High Excellency Nawab Asaf-ud-Daula, to be given to General Martin of the East India company, the year of 1201 of the Hijra (1786-87)'.
‡In a later letter, Martin writes that the nawab used to visit him in his house, the Chateau de Lyons, but stopped doing this later.

*Top*: Shuja-ud-Daula enjoyed wearing a Persian inspired jacket with a fur stole around his neck, which recalled the Persian origins of the nawabs of Awadh.

*Bottom*: Completed by Benjamin West long after Robert Clive had died, this is a highly romanticized image of the moment Emperor Shah Alam II handed over the diwani of Bengal to Clive and the EIC.

*Top*: Dilkusha, Faizabad, in ruins today.

*Bottom*: Culinary etiquette reached extraordinary heights under the nawabs of Awadh, with food being sent to Shuja from six separate kitchens.

*Top*: Emperor Shah Alam was forced to remain in Allahabad for more than twelve years, being undermined and bullied by the EIC.

*Bottom*: Loyal, sincere, and honest to a fault, Jean-Baptiste Gentil remained by Shuja's side till the death of the nawab.

*Top*: The subah of Ajmer, in the *Gentil Atlas*.

*Bottom*: Image from a Polier album showing two Awadhi noblemen, one of whom might be Antoine Polier himself in the yellow jama, enjoying a song and dance entertainment.

*Top*: Polier's spectacular table-cut emerald ring with his title—Arsalan-e-Jang—engraved in the finest nastaliq script.

*Bottom*: Polier built himself a handsome haveli-style residence at Faizabad, the ruins of which lie half buried.

Tilly Kettle's oil paintings of Shuja, his sons, and courtiers would prove very influential, inspiring many copies.

*Top*: Awadh artist Faizullah used dizzying multiple perspectives to show the terraced houses and gardens of Faizabad.

*Bottom left*: René Madec painted during his lifetime, wearing the turban that Shah Alam had presented to him.

*Bottom right*: Chronically ill and gaunt, Claude Martin's lupine face was softened by his inquisitive brown gaze.

15

16

*Top*: The busy world of the Awadhi zenana, where elite women play chess surrounded by khwajasaras and attendants, while children play and paan is passed around.

*Bottom*: A page from Warren Hastings's 'Lucknow diary' of 1784, noting down the recipe of a kebab made by Asaf's cooks.

he may be required to return to his regiment, he had smoothly replied: 'Indeed my lord, I can't do you half the service there that I can in keeping the nawab amused while you ease him of his money.' Just as Asaf had always preferred to keep his own loyal and familiar childhood companions close to him, in the same way, he preferred the Europeans who genuinely shared his tastes. And Mordaunt* was the European who pleased him most, finding new ways to entertain and amuse him, joining in the revelries without ever descending into over-familiarity and disrespect. When Mordaunt tried to recover some of the money Asaf owed him, he replied: 'No, no, my dear Mordaunt: if I were to pay you, you would go to England, which must not be. I cannot part with you; everything in the world that you can wish, you shall have'. Despite these extravagant assurances, Asaf was becoming increasingly canny about the British who were so avid in their demands. Initially hired at the absurdly high salary of 3,000 rupees per month as bodyguard to the nawab, Mordaunt soon found his wages falling behind, and scrambled desperately to have his debts paid. And it was not only Mordaunt, but practically all the Europeans in Lucknow who had their loans interminably extended. Polier, for example, was unable to leave the country while huge sums of his money were tied up in debts which the nawab simply ignored.

Meanwhile, regarding the nawab's apparently sudden assumption of impenitent inflexibility vis-à-vis Company demands, Palmer betrayed a perplexed bemusement in his letters as he attempted to decode the people responsible: 'I am of the opinion,' he wrote sourly to Hastings, 'that his Excellency has been excited to it† by the Begums.... You know their intriguing dispositions and inveterate hatred to the English name.' When one of the surviving Gossain brothers, Himmat Bahadur, asked for protection from the nawab, Palmer grumbled that 'he has, I hear, received permission to repair to Lucknow with 50 attendants and I think he will not fail to improve his situation in concert with his old friends the Begums to the cost of the Vizier and the Company,' once again blaming the begums.

While it is interesting to note the continued influence attributed to

---

*When Mordaunt died of a fever in Kanpur in 1790, Asaf attended the funeral and wept over the death of his dear friend.
†Refusal to allow an EIC agent to raise and command troops.

Bahu Begum in the affairs of Lucknow, it is remarkable that the EIC agents constantly underestimated the nawab and dismissed him as a malleable fool. They mistook his generosity for profligacy, his calm good humour for a cowed timidity, and his curiosity for venality. When an EIC surgeon (Daniel Johnson) had noted, however, that Asaf was 'of a moderate stature, rather corpulent, with a handsome face and sharp penetrating eyes', he had added that 'he possessed much activity of body for a man of his size'. It was this intelligence that was easier to dismiss because of the distracting corpulence that hinted at comfort and debauched excess. The surgeon had noted this dissonance between the gentle rolls of fat, so unlike his strapping father, and the entirely unexpected vigour and energy. And it was with endless energy and activity that Asaf would direct his intelligence, his enormous resources, and his discerning taste into creating a legacy he could be proud of.

The paintings of the nawab made by his contemporaries show a commanding and grave figure, in expensive but largely unadorned and sober muslin or jamdani, often grasping a sword or a musket (image 27). With no father to now stand toweringly over him, the nawab's girth lends him substance and anchors him solidly within his space, the occasional priceless string of pearls alluding to royal wealth. There is no trace of simpering effeminacy at all. In a more informal quick sketch by Zoffany, the nawab looks out of the painting, his intelligent gaze sharp and almost unsettlingly gauging (image 28). But the British would expend a great deal of vitriol, and reams of letter paper, to portray the nawab as an effeminate and debauched buffoon. The subtext to these rants would be to unsubtly crystallize the case against the suitability of such a nawab to rule a vast and rich province such as Awadh.[*] Unable to defeat such a ruler on the battlefield, since this nawab had displayed such generous acts of friendship, and unable to effect a direct takeover as the bloody attempts by Hannay had shown, the British would instead become relentless in their efforts to undermine the nawab's character, and the way in which he chose to spend the revenue from his province.

Asaf had been sixteen at the time of Buxar, and would certainly have remembered the utter desolation visited upon his indestructible father by the forces of the EIC. Now there would be no more armies

---

[*] I am grateful to Professor Veena Talwar Oldenburg for helping me to consolidate these views.

raised in Shah Alam's name, no noisome martial gathering under the couchant lion standard of the emperors of Hindustan, as Shuja had once done so long ago. None would rally to Mirza Jawan Bakht's battle cry, and the heir to the Mughal throne would remain in Lucknow, and then Benaras,\* dependant on the stipend (50,000 rupees) that Asaf generously paid out to him. He would die in 1788, undone by fate, and largely unmourned. And Asaf would stake his claim to immortality by rivalling the Mughals in Delhi in the great Indo-Persianate culture they had gifted to the world, in all its harmonies, colours, and graces.

In the interlocking courtyard, gardens, and terraces of his Macchi Bhawan palace, Asaf created a lifestyle of beauty and elegance, sweeping in his train the entire elite society of Lucknow. On the roofs of the palaces were fluttering flocks of pigeons bred for their beauty, and kept according to the colour of their plumage. They were trained to fly, swoop, and swerve at a whistle from the boys tending to them. In the monsoon season, the tumbling pigeons had the company of the nawab's kites, which were decorated with 5 rupees worth of gold and silver tassels, glittering against the gunmetal skies. If the nawabi kites were lost and brought back, the victor was awarded the 5 rupees. The nawab's stables were filled with elephants, horses, and hunting dogs, in numbers too baffling to contemplate.† He was said to possess the tallest elephant in Hindustan, and possibly in the world, as well as an English dray-horse so overfed it could barely walk. His horses, especially, were the envy of Englishmen who grumbled that 'this attachment of (the nawab's) to horse flesh is peculiarly unfortunate for the English, for he does not scruple to lay his hands on all passing through his dominions, and as he invariably picks out the best and gives any price to the dealer, it seldom happens that horses of any real value or good quality can reach Calcutta.' His carriages and palanquins were upholstered in cloth of gold and brocade, while his crocodile, peacock, and elephant-prowed boats glided proudly down the Gomti. And the Gomti itself was ceaselessly

---

\*Asaf-ud-Daula was insulted when Mirza Jawan Bakht left for Delhi to summon his relatives without informing the nawab. The two fell out over this issue and the prince left Lucknow for Benaras.
†1,200 elephants, 2,000-3,000 horses and 1,000 dogs according to Abu Talib ibn Muhammad and William Hoey (tr.), *History of Asafu'd Daulah, Nawab Wazir of Oudh: Being a Translation of 'Tafzihu'l Ghafilin', a Contemporary Record of Events Connected with His Administration*, Allahabad: Pustak Kendra, 1885, p. 37.

plied by boats carrying 'rhinoceros from Assam for the Nawabs' zoos, shire-horses from England, barrel-organs...huge look-glasses from France, musical clocks and trinkets from Switzerland, crockery and silver from England and room-sized chandeliers from Bohemia.'

All the objects that celebrated his refined and opulent lifestyle were crafted with the greatest care and delicacy, the enamelled metalware in particular. The paan-daans for the paans spiked with gold and pearl powder were made of enamelled silver, the hookah bases in enamelled glass, the wine decanters in bidri-ware (image 26). Not only did these objects become extremely sophisticated, but the type of decorations used were unique to Lucknow. Whereas the Mughals had perfected the use of the single, still flower as decorative motif, Lucknawi crafts showcased vibrant and effervescent patterns with blooms of irises, lilies, poppies, and roses twirling in luscious glory on jugs, rose-water vials, ewers, as well as scabbards, shields, and sword handles. Another very popular floral imagery was the scrolling split-acanthus[*] vine, and the great nawabi symbol—a pair of fish. Lapidary arts thrived, and elegant emerald and stone seals were produced, with exquisite engravings.[†] According to art historian Stephen Markel, the decorative arts of Lucknow during the reign of Asaf 'exhibit an elegance of form and material sumptuousness rivalling those produced during the heyday of the great Mughal emperors in the 17th century'. So lavish was the patronage of arts and crafts by the elite of Awadh that by the mid-nineteenth century, two-thirds of its population were artisans.

And if Claude Martin's guests in Chateau de Lyon had to contend with garishly coloured indifferent dishes, then the nawab's dastarkhwan was becoming ever more refined and elaborate. As the wealthy elite of Lucknow became interested and knowledgeable connoisseurs of gourmet food, the highly skilled and valued rakabdars (chefs) became increasingly specialized, honing their skills in the preparation of a single magnificent dish. An anecdote about Asaf confirms the great respect that these specialists were held in, and the quasi-magical quality of their food. One particular expert was hired by Asaf to cook only dals, at a salary of 500 rupees a month. The rakabdar insisted on a number of

---

[*]In use in western art as early as the seventh century BCE on Corinthian capitals, the split acanthus leaf was assimilated into South Asian art and was used in the Mughal period too.
[†]A famous lapidarist called Muhammad Salah Khan had been living in Awadh since the time of Shuja-ud-Daula.

conditions, namely that the nawab not let the food get cold and stale before tasting it. When the nawab was late to the dastarkhwan one day, the furious cook threw the pot of dal at the foot of a withered tree and disappeared from Lucknow while the tree, unexpectedly, bloomed.

Food became a place of contestation too, between Mughal Delhi and nawabi Awadh. Since Delhi was famous for its biryani, Lucknow cultivated a taste for the more subtle pulao. And so the humble pulao itself became a thing of great refinement, with an almost infinite variety, including the gulzar (the garden), the noor (the light,) koku (the cuckoo) and chameli (the jasmine) pulaos. A particularly ingenious pulao was the moti (pearl) pulao. This was created by beating 200 grams of silver foil and 20 grams of golden foil into the yolk of an egg, which was then fed to a hen. The slaughtered hen was then delicately seasoned and carefully cooked, and when sliced into, would produce shining 'pearls' which were then mixed with meat and rice.

A distinctive Awadhi kebab, meanwhile, was said to have been invented by the nawab of Kakor, just outside Lucknow, in an act of pique. When a British officer sniffed that the kebabs he had been served were coarse, the furious nawab demanded his chefs create a more refined version, and the kakori kebab was born, made from minced tendon from a leg of mutton, khoya, white pepper, and a secret blend of spices.* Another food that became synonymous with Asaf was the creamy layer formed on the top of milk. In Lucknow, the milk would be gently heated in trays and the cream skimmed off the surface and placed in several layers one on top of the other. Asaf was especially fond of this malai, which he proposed be re-named 'balai'.†

In his personal style, Asaf preferred a refined and elegantly understated style. The nawab favoured the angrakha or jama in the lightest of muslin or jamdani, worn with payjamas‡. This very fine

---

*The galauti kebab, even more delicate, was created for Wajid Ali Shah in the nineteenth century after he had lost many teeth. They were made of finely ground meat and cream, shaped into patties, and fried in ghee. The original version was said to contain more than 100 aromatic spices and flower essences.

†For the Persian word for 'above', bala, since it came from the top of the milk. Lucknow became very famous for its sweets, and the sweets for the general population were made by Hindu moiras while the upper classes preferred those made by Muslim halwais.

‡In the nineteenth century, these payjamas would become extremely wide, called the farshi payjama or kalidar payjama (panelled).

muslin was called Sarkar-e-ala*, and his creamy white angrakhas were often edged with patta gota† in burnished gold at the border, while the sleeves were crinkled, using a sophisticated technique called chunnat, achieved with the help of a particular stone. The jamdani cloth from Tanda became very popular in Awadh at this time, where the nawabs preferred white on white patterns of jamdani. A master artisan from Jais called Bika once presented a kurta and pagri of his finest jamdani, interwoven with the nawab's name and praises to Asaf. Another innovation, originally from Bengal,‡ was chikan work. This fine white-on-white embroidery on plain muslin became a veritable craze under the nawabs of Awadh in the eighteenth century. In Lucknow, it was almost exclusively patronized by the elite, and was appreciated for the tiny, tidy stitches which produced delicate, barely perceptible patterns. At its height, chikan work would be characterized by thirty-two distinct stitches, of which only six are in use today. A turban or cap was always indispensable and the nawab wore a turban of fine white muslin called a dastar, embellished with a goshpech.

While the very luxurious accoutrements were favoured by the elite, in Lucknow the general populace also began taking pride in always being fashionably dressed. A certain type of fashionable gent called a Banka, or dandy, was soon to evolve. The Banka was not only an honourable man of his word, but he could be recognized from a distance by his stylish net shaluka that he wore under his muslin kurta, his turned up ghatela shoes (long and shaped like an elephant's trunk, curving over the feet in a large spiral) long hair, neatly trimmed moustache, hint of kajal at the eyes, and a smear of henna on the tip of his little finger.

This great style was not kept only by the nawab, but by all the courtiers at his court as well as the wealthy citizens of Lucknow. In 1788, Elizabeth Plowden wrote about a sumptuous breakfast that Hasan Reza Khan gave for some of the British women in Lucknow as part of his daughter's marriage celebrations. After an excellent banquet of both Indian and English dishes, the minister gave gorgeous presents to his guests, including gold and enamelled bottles of rose

---

*This was said to be so fine that it could be passed through a ring.
†Embroidery with gold or silver ribbon and lace.
‡Bengal being the great centre for textile production, it is likely that chikan work originated there. It is possible that master embroiderers were invited to Lucknow by the nawabs.

water, embroidered shawls, and necklaces of pearls. The afternoon of the wedding, an elaborate nine-course dinner was also sent to the home of each one of the guests.

The important Hindu festivals like Holi were marked by the entire court in great style. Elizabeth Plowden wrote about a play that was enacted by some of the nawab's 'nautch women' in March of 1788, clearly to celebrate Holi*. 'They were newly draped in Hindoo drapes,' she wrote, 'and there were two superior figures draped in high caps and more superbly than the rest, around which the others sang and danced.' Plowden was surprised to note that there were very few 'black persons' invited to the celebration, and decided that it was because 'the nabaub having entertained himself all the forenoon playing the Holi in which occasion his courtiers attended and perhaps had leave of absence'. Indeed, the giddy effervescence with which one particular courtier chose to play Holi one year provoked the ire of even the genial Asaf. Using the pretext of the bacchanalia of Holi, one Sharaf Ali Khan burst a large water balloon on the back of the Mughal prince Azfari† himself, greatly offending his host the nawab. So annoyed was the nawab that Azfari had to intervene to placate him, reminding Asaf cordially that 'etiquette and regard and respect for elders are all set aside in playing Holi'.

The great begums in Faizabad too held enormous celebrations and festivals, during which scores of artisans were employed. In 1786, writes Faiz Baksh, 'a year was spent in making silver vessels and building houses and preparing carpets, curtains and other necessary furniture' for a wedding. Between the nawab and his ministers, the Europeans at Lucknow attended either a breakfast, banquet, or some other entertainment with a Lucknow notable every week. Elizabeth Plowden described an evening in 1788 during which the Resident Edward Ives played the harpsichord and sang to entertain the nawab. The nawab had also requested that Elizabeth Plowden sing a Persian

---

*Holi fell on 22 March in 1788 so the date would correspond with this Hindu festival.

†The Timurid prince Muhammad Zahiruddin Mirza Ali Bakht, known as Mirza-i-Kalan (the Big Mirza), lived for years in the salatin quarters of Shahjahanabad, from where he escaped first to Lucknow, before ending up in the territory of the nawab of Arcot, where he would die in 1818. He wrote his memoirs under the title *Waqiat-i-Azfari*. By the time of his death, Azfari had reconciled himself to giving up any claim to sovereignty he might have earlier held, and indeed had come to see the benefits of British rule under the EIC!

song to an audience which included his two principal ministers.

This extravagant style was adopted not simply by the citizens of Lucknow who could afford it, but some who could not as well. Grumbling as per his wont about the gaudy profligacy of Lucknow, Abu Talib complained that 'men of position in Lucknow are not so affected by slenderness of income as to feel themselves thereby straitened, for if they are close handed in matters of clothing and on occasions of weddings and funerals, they are reckoned among the lower orders of society.' The unshakeable logic of the times seemed to be: if they spend money, they must have money.

The nawab appeared to have understood the sort of entertainments that would appeal to his European guests, most of whom would not understand the nuances of classical Kathak dance and music, an Urdu majlis, or a piece of theatre. Instead, he organized elephant fights, cock-matches, or mime and puppet shows. It is telling that when Europeans were invited to an evening usually the only other Indian courtiers attending were only his two ministers, his eldest son, Wazir Ali, and one of his cousins. The carnival of 1788, for example, organized especially for the Europeans, began with a breakfast of tea, toast, and passion fruit while the guests were entertained by nautch dancers and a set of mime artists, one of whom 'emulated a monkey exceedingly well'. The day progressed as follows:

> The Nawab conducted his visitors to a terrace overlooking the water where they were seated at tables covered with white linen and flowers and lit with candles in green and white cut-glass shades. In front of them a cavalcade of beautifully decorated and illuminated boats drifted slowly down the river, while fireworks in the form of peacocks, tigers, flowers and bears illuminated the embankments. The evening's entertainment was largely in the form of circus-type acts, puppet shows, animal tricks and acrobats. The only intellectual offering was an elaborately staged play which Sophie Elizabeth Prosser, the British diarist who recorded the event, found dull since she could not understand it, although she did note the beauty of the costumes.

These entertainments in turn would earn him a reputation as a dilettante and a simpleton among the Europeans themselves. But among the cognoscenti, whispers of the nawab's prodigal wealth and refined discernment had reached Delhi, and the poets, Kathak dancers, painters, and musicians arrived in numbers to the sparkling court of Lucknow. Musicians from Delhi and elsewhere had already been given patronage at Faizabad and Lucknow from the time of Shuja, who had loved music. Asaf in turn greatly increased the retinue of musicians at his court, prompting a dazzled witness to exclaim that 'Lucknow's lamp was lit by that of Delhi.'

Asaf was prodigiously generous with the enormous resources at his disposal. He employed an army of attendants, his household servants including '2000 farrashes (carpet spreaders), 100 chobdars (mace-bearers) and khidmatgars (waiters), and 4000 gardeners and hundreds of cooks. His cook-room costs Rs 2000 or 3000 per day, and the loose and idle characters whom he has with him on his tour, carrying baggage, camp furniture, and tents, amount to a thousand, who receive their daily bread as wages.'* 'The vast sums expended by Asaf-ud-Daula,'† wrote a later English traveller, 'brought to Lucknow merchants of large property from all parts of India.... The town rapidly increased in extent and prosperity.' He used his generosity as a weapon, challenging men to outspend him if they could. He once sent 60,000 rupees along with a letter of congratulations to King George III on the king's recovery from a bout of madness, half to be given to the king's physician, the other half to be distributed as charity in England.‡ He welcomed every deserving artist, artisan, craftsperson, and talented worker to his great capital, to create a cultural centre (markaz) that could equal anything in the world at the time. The most popular saying associated with Asaf in folklore is the affectionate dictum 'Jis ko na de maula, us ko de Asaf-ud-Daula' (He to whom God does not give, to him will Asaf-ud-Daula give). He was also charming and urbane. Elizabeth Plowden wrote about how he would ask her many questions

---

*Since these figures are provided by Abu Talib, always critical of Asaf, a slight exaggeration is to be assumed.

†More than 6,912 servants are listed for this year 84/85, with a combined salary of 540,790 rupees. This amounted in 1784 to 21 per cent of the gross revenues of Awadh for that year. See Fisher, p. 76.

‡It is now believed that this king suffered from a condition resembling bipolar disorder. When in a manic state, the king would be described by witnesses as suffering from 'incessant loquacity' talking until the foam ran out of his mouth. He also suffered from convulsions, to the extent that his pages had to sit on him on the floor, to prevent him from harming himself or others.

about her children, once exclaiming that little William was so comely and fair, he could not possibly be made of flesh and blood and was surely made of wax and cotton. On another occasion, during an evening of entertainments, he bent down to put a garland of yellow marigolds around her little daughter's neck himself. When Plowden asked the nawab about the words to a song he had composed, he offered to send her a copy of the song right away. Not unsurprisingly, the nawab then gained a reputation among the British for being 'mild in manners, polite and affable in his conduct'.

The prosperous state of Awadh was noted decades later by the English traveller and writer Fanny Parkes in 1831. She greatly admired Lucknow and wrote that 'The subjects of his Majesty of Oude are by no means desirous of participating in the blessings of British rule. They are a richer, sleeker and merrier race than the natives in the territories of the Company.' These views were in exact opposition to the repeated remonstrations that the Company men would make about the mismanagement of Awadh by the nawabs, and the debasement of the Awadhi subjects. But the warp and weft of Asaf's life was spun out of music and dance, and such ephemera stood little chance against the violence of EIC recordings.

# THE BARA IMAMBARA AND A LIGHT DIVINE

On a stiflingly hot evening in 680 CE, a middle-aged man pitched his tents on the sands within sight of the great Euphrates River. There didn't seem to be anything distinctive about this scholarly man and his seventy-two tired and threadbare companions. And yet, over the next ten days, in an elegy of pain and suffering, all the men save one would be dead, in a cascading series of events that would forever be remembered in grief and keening mourning. Each event would be described in haunting detail, year after year, century upon century. The young bridegroom in his wedding finery, 'pearls swinging from his ears', the first to be cut down by the enemy. The mighty warrior, two white egret's plumes unfurling from his helmet, cut down in the night as he tried to bring back water for the children dying of thirst in the camp. And when it didn't seem possible for sorrow to get any darker, there was the tiny, whimpering infant boy, shot through the neck while in his father's arms. And then finally, on the last day, the middle-aged man put on a plain white robe and declared simply, 'We belong to God and to God we shall return.' For the man was Imam Hussain, Prophet Muhammad's grandson, and he was preparing to die on that sacred battlefield on the last day of Muharram, which would come to be known as Ashura.

The massacre of Imam Hussain and almost every last one of his followers[*] at Karbala[†] at the hands of soldiers sent by the Umayyad Caliph Yazid, was the bloody central tragedy that would seed centuries of retributive violence between the Shia and the Sunni followers of Islam. Since the time that Prophet Muhammad had died without a son or a nominated heir in 632 CE, leaving behind an enormous legacy that bound all the tribes of Arabia together, the schism was already foretold. For a small number of Muslims only Ali, the Prophet's cousin and son-in-law, and his family members, could ever conceivably be the legitimate inheritors of the Prophet's sacred authority, carried in the bloodline. These were the Shias. But for the vast majority of Muslims,

---

[*]The single male survivor was Hussain's teenage son, Ali Zain al-Abidin, who was lying sick with a fever during the battle.
[†]In present-day Iraq.

the Sunnis,* successors were to be chosen by elite members of the Islamic community. In the end, the Sunni won the issue of succession and named Abu Bakr, the Prophet's close friend, the first caliph or leader in Islam and Ali would eventually become the fourth caliph. After the tragedy of Karbala, what had been a fault line fractured into a deep crevasse so that for the Shia, there could be no reconciliation any longer with the corrupt Sunni Umayyad caliphs†.

When Hussain had made that fateful journey to Karbala from his home in Mecca, it was to reclaim the role of caliph from the Syrian Umayyad Caliphs, who had had Ali assassinated, and bring it back to its rightful place within the family of Muhammad himself—the Ahl al-Bayt. But terrorized by the brutality of Yazid's rule, the support that the city of Kufa‡ had promised Hussain never materialized. Instead, Hussain and his seventy-two warriors faced an army of thousands, and every one of them was killed and decapitated over the course of those torrid ten days. For Yazid, this was meant to be the final end to all challenge to his leadership, the family of the Prophet ground into the bloody sand of Karbala. Instead, it was only the beginning.

Just four years after the murder of Imam Hussain, pilgrims would begin to assemble on the anniversary of the battle which they had named Karbala.§ Here, where villagers had buried and marked the grave of the seventy-two headless warriors, millions would one day gather, for the memory of Hussain's martyrdom and his ultimate sacrifice in the name of justice would reverberate down the ages in a rising tide of passion and piety. Almost 300 years after Hussain's martyrdom, Ashura¶ was observed in Baghdad for the first time in 963 CE, 'with intense and emotional devotions. The markets closed and the citizens circled the city in dishevelled and torn black clothing, weeping and wailing as they walked.' And over the years, these emotions would be conjured again and again, in city after city, till it could truly be said that 'Every day is Ashura, every land is Karbala'.

More than 1,100 years later, and over 2,000 miles away, Nawab

---

*From Sunna or tradition. The Sunni centre their faith primarily on the Quran.
†The Syrian Umayyad caliphs held political power at the time.
‡In present-day Iraq.
§'The place of trial and tribulation'.
¶Ashura means ten in Arabic. For Shia Muslims it marks the tenth day of the Battle of Karbala, during which Imam Hussain was martyred.

Asaf-ud-Daula began work on a building in Awadh which would commemorate these tragic events with all the majesty and awe they deserved. The commemoration of Imam Hussain's martyrdom on the day of Ashura became the beating heart of Twelver Shia* remembrance all over the world. In India, the Shia community had always longed to make the pilgrimage to the sacred site of Hussain's tomb, and to be buried near that beloved figure. But Iraq was a long way away and so earth was brought back from Karbala and sprinkled over local burial grounds, transforming those lands into that long ago place of sacred sorrow. Next, a way was devised to bring Hussain's mausoleum to India too, through ephemeral models in bamboo, glass, and paper, to symbolize that mausoleum. And so the tazia† of India came into existence. Since ritualized, collective mourning was a central part of Twelver Shiism, a place was required to hold these gatherings of remembrance, or majlis, and to deposit the tazias and so Asaf decided to build such a place in Lucknow. The imambara‡ was a South Asian innovation, and had existed since the sixteenth century, first in the Deccan, where they were called Ashurkhanas§. But the Bara Imambara that Asaf built was much grander than any that had been built till then, and was by far the largest in the world at the time. Viscount Valentia deemed it 'certainly the most beautiful building I have seen in India'. At a time when Mughal Delhi was gently crumbling into the dust for want of funds, this would be an eloquent statement of Awadh's wealth and confidence.¶ No longer would the Shia rituals be held in diffidence and obscurity, as they had in the past.

The Bara Imambara was built as a series of three vast arcaded enclosures (image 29), linked by gateways with the surviving Rumi Darwaza gateway a magnificent and singular example (image 30).

---

*Twelver Shias form the largest branch of Shiites in the world. They believe that Ali, the first imam, was followed by eleven divinely ordained imams. Twelver Shias believe that the last, or twelfth, imam is the Mahdi, who has disappeared into a mystical realm, and will return at a future date to establish social justice. There is thus an element of the occult in Twelver Shiism.
†In Iran, however, the word tazia refers to the plays devoted to the tragedy of Karbala.
‡The term imambara and the layout of the building in Lucknow were probably taken from Murshidabad, where the oldest known imambara exists, though it was destroyed and then largely rebuilt in the nineteenth century.
§In Central Asia they are called tazia khana and husayniyas, in Pakistan, imambargas.
¶The annual cost of the imambara and its accompanying mosque was put at 20 million rupees by the project accountant, averaging 4 million a year over a 5-year period, roughly 30 per cent of the annual gross revenue of Awadh, according to Hussein Keshani.

Because Lucknow was far from the stone quarries that supplied Mughal Delhi, the imambara would be built using thin Lakhori bricks, baked from clay excavated along the banks of the Gomti, covered in malleable stucco. The stucco was used in robust, confident style to create lush, sinuous foliage decorations, as well as the emblematic fish of Awadh. The Rumi Darwaza, meanwhile, would also have a unique crowning of stone roses like the diadem of a queen. 'From the brilliant white of the composition, and the minute delicacy of the workmanship', wrote an admiring traveller, 'an enthusiast might suppose that Genii had been the artificers.' Such dynamic innovation would have been impossible in a Mughal context, asserts historian Catherine Asher, where decorations had crystallized, perhaps even ossified, into staid, single-flower elements. The surface of the Rumi Darwaza, like the imambara, was covered in exuberant leaf, flower, and fish motifs in gleaming white three-dimensional stucco.

Scholar Holly Shaffer has pointed out that the Bara Imambara's majestic and pillarless central sail vault was constructed to magnify light. The nawab had ordered two massive glass chandeliers from England at a cost of 1 lakh rupees, and lamps enough to require lamp oil costing at least 4 lakhs a year. During Muharram commemorations, more standing candelabras, some more than 5 feet in height, made of decorated porcelain, coloured glass or metals, crowded the floor, lighting up the shadowed halls of the imambara in a blaze of luminescence. Many of these chandeliers and candelabras were donated by wealthy citizens, as acts of merit.* The nawab himself, to Abu Talib's lasting irritation, used the building in a most excessive way:

> Every year since its completion four or five lakhs of rupees have been spent on the decoration of the Imambara. Hundreds of taziyas, big and small, are made of gold and silver, and the number of glass chandeliers with and without glass shades, plain and coloured, and candelabras of gold silver and brass with drum-shaped and bell-shaped shades, which are purchased defies computation. The halls, large as they are, have their floors and ceilings filled with them, so that the caretakers can with difficulty perform their duty.

---

*Many of the best and most exotic items would be stolen from the imambara during the uprising of 1857, including a pair of life-size green glass tigers from China.

In Lucknow, the first intimation of the season was the hush that fell upon the city on the first day of Muharram. The traders in the bazars languished, the kothis of the courtesans fell silent, and people replaced their gorgeous clothes with black, green, or grey ones, loosened their hair and put aside their jewellery. Then, from the second day onwards, people started visiting the tazias in friends' homes, and in the Bara Imambara which, during this period, would have been glittering with lights and decorations. In Awadh in the eighteenth century, Muharram commemorations lasted ten days and included poetry recitations, dirges, and lectures on the themes of mourning in gatherings called majlis, and a procession of people carrying alams, or standards, and various other symbols recalling the events at Karbala. On the tenth day of Muharram, the day marking the martyrdom of Imam Hussain, all the tazias would be carried from peoples' homes, and from the imambaras in a long procession to be buried in a Karbala, or offered to a river. Visible and emotional mourning for the imams was an integral part of Muharram commemoration and was 'based on the medieval philosophical principle of imitation, or "making a resemblance"'. By their grief, the mourners were 'pulled nearer to those who suffered at Karbala'. The lectures recited during the majlis were preceded by the sombre chanting of dirges, or soz khwani, and elegies, called marsiyas. Marsiya poetry, which conjured up the suffering and transcendental heroism of Hussain and his family, became an increasingly important genre of poetry in Lucknow at this time. Poets of marsiya used all their talent to evoke the greatest emotions in the listeners using the most elegantly charged language, so that the expression of grief itself became a form of art. These thrumming laments pulsed through the nawabi halls, and the gullies and the lanes of Lucknow, until the entire city hummed with the shared recollection of almost unbearable grief (image 31).

In the zenana quarters of the women of Lucknow, Muharram was marked with equal, if not greater, fervour. The word 'shahadat' which means 'self-sacrifice', or martyrdom, also has another meaning which is 'bearing witness'. And in the tragic tale of Karbala, if Hussain was the prince of martyrs, then the women were the witnesses, and none was more moving in her fierce grief than Zainab, Imam Hussain's sister. For had there been no women to bear witness, and to translate into words the impossible courage and sacrifice of Hussain, and of all the seventy-two, then those deeds would have blown away with the east wind, that dark wind of trial and tribulation. 'Do not let Satan take away your courage,' Hussain had warned his sister Zainab on the last night he had left in the world. So when Yazid's men had stormed the tents, she had covered her nephew's fever-hot body with her own, and even Yazid's killers quailed at the thought of assassinating the Prophet's granddaughter. And then as Zainab was led away in chains along with the surviving women and children, preceded by the horror of Imam Hussain's head on a spike, 'her words of grief...would haunt Islam through the centuries':

> 'Oh Muhammad, Muhammad, may the angels of heaven bless you!' she wailed. 'Here is Hussein in the open, stained with blood and his limbs torn off. Oh Muhammad! Your daughters are prisoners, your progeny are killed, and the east wind blows dust over them.'

Then when the women were dragged through the streets of Kufa, the city whose courage had failed it when Hussain had asked for help, Zainab gathered her grief into a spear of accusatory words so powerful that the people of Kufa wept. This, according to Shia belief, was the very beginning of azadaari, or mourning.

An Englishwoman[*] who had married a Muslim nobleman in the early nineteenth century, and who had lived in Lucknow for twelve years, witnessed the commemoration of Muharram in the zenanas of Lucknow[†]:

> The expressions of grief manifested by the ladies are far greater, and appear to me more lasting than with the other sex. Indeed I never could have given credit to the extent of their bewailings without witnessing, as I have done for many years, the season for tears and profound grief return with the month of Moharram. In sorrowing for the martyred Imams, they seem to forget their private griefs; I have had opportunities of observing this triumph of religious feeling in women, who are remarkable for their

---

[*] Mrs Meer Hassan Ali. Her identity and her first name are yet to be discovered.
[†] A series of letters written by Mrs Meer Hassan Ali have been compiled under the title *Observations on the Mussulmauns of India*.

affectionate attachment to their children, husbands, and parents—they tell me, 'We must not indulge selfish sorrows of our own, whilst the Prophet's family alone have a right to our tears.'

The construction of an elaborate and highly visible Shia architecture in Lucknow by Asaf was a clear proclamation to the Sunni Mughals in Delhi of the extent of his glory and independence. The Mughals had long been sympathetic to the minority Shias in India since the time of Akbar, who had declared that they could openly mark their rituals, instead of doing so in hiding. Under Aurangzeb, this trend had been reversed,* but the later Mughals again grew tolerant of Shia practice, as elite Shia Persian immigrants drifted to the Mughal court from neighbouring Safavid Persia. Under the nawabs of Lucknow, beginning with Asaf, this Shia presence would be wrought in architecture and celebrated through culture like never before in India. Asaf also marked the Shia power of Lucknow through patronage of sites abroad: 'He paid for a canal to bring water to Najaf, which is still known as Asafiya or Hindiya Canal;† a hostel for Indian pilgrims; and a library with 700 manuscripts in the same city. His government also restored a mosque in Kufa; the gates and market in Kazmain; and sent funds to support religious teachers and the poor in Karbala‡.' In return, the nawab welcomed skilled builders from Najaf and Karbala who were employed in building Shia monuments in Lucknow, and whose descendants continue to live in the city.

Soon, all the people of Lucknow were caught up in the rapture of Muharram, the fervour of their passion sweeping along rich and poor alike. 'Amongst the poorer classes of the people,' wrote Mrs Meer Hassan Ali, 'those who cannot compass the real splendour of an Imambara are satisfied with an imitative one in the best hall their habitation affords; and, where mirrors and chandeliers are not available, they are content to do honour to the Imambaras with lamps... of pretty shapes, curiously painted, and ingeniously ornamented with cut paper.'

---

*Tavernier writes that at this time the Shia 'had no scruples about conforming...to the cult and customs of the Sunnis'.
†Built at Karbala at a cost of half a million rupees.
‡Interestingly, Abu Talib, who visited Najaf and Karbala at this time, described a 'handsome cenotaph' erected in Karbala by Nawab Asaf-ud-Daula's wife.

Mrs Meer Hassan Ali described the tazias of Lucknow in 1832 as 'formed of every variety of material, according to the wealth, rank, or preference of the person exhibiting, from the purest silver down to bamboo and paper'.

The deeply universal story of Imam Hussain and his family willing to die at the hands of an evil tyrant in search of justice and dignity appealed to large swathes of the population of Awadh. That ancient grief of a mother for a child, of a father for his son, of a clan for their home, required no translation. As witnessed by a resident:

> Urban and rural Hindus venerated Husain and incorporated his cult into their rituals. They offered flowers and sweets at local 'Karbalas', participated in processions, decorated and kept tazias and sought Husain's intercession in disease and calamity. The Imam's trials and tribulations inspired faith in a universal nemesis ensuring justice for oppressed souls. In popular belief he was Ram of Ayodhya carrying his crusade into the wilderness; his brother Abbas personified Lakshman, devoted, energetic and brave; his sister Zainab and wife Um-I Kulsoom were cast in the image of Sita, caring, dutiful and spirited. Yazid, the Umayyad ruler and Husain's persecutor was Ravan, greedy, corrupt, ambitious, cruel and ruthless.

Empathetic crowds lined the streets of the city during the matam processions, in which self-flagellants hit or whipped themselves, offering water or sherbet to the impassioned, bloodied participants. The tazias themselves were versatile, and could look like Mughal tombs, just as they sometimes looked like temples and straw huts. 'Hindus even, on approaching the shrine, bow their heads with much solemn gravity,' noted Mrs Meer Hassan Ali, perhaps mistaking the glittering tazias for little temples.

Patronized by the wealthy and powerful nawab himself, Shia rituals quickly became widespread among the nobility. They built imambaras in their taluqqas* in the countryside, where mourning rituals were conducted. Amongst the Hindus, the Saxena and Shrivastava Kayasthas, as well as the Khatris, who had long associations with Muslim rulers,

---

*Administrative subdivision.

and were thus considered 'hum-pyaala I hum-niwala',* also adopted aspects of the azadaari. The nawab's minister, Jhau Lal, 'adopted Muslim customs, dress, and prayer and Ramzan fast', and also built an imambara, as did Raja Nawal Rai and others. 'Local chieftains and zamindars' writes scholar Madhu Trivedi, 'also adopted azadaari and performed it with great precision and ostentation, to the extent that Muharram became the living symbol of the Shia culture and attained the colour of Iranian processions and the grandeur of the Dussehra festival†.' The marsiyas were particularly popular among Awadhi residents and 'thousands of Hindus also chanted these dirges'. Even beggars in Lucknow up until the twentieth century would supplicate passers-by with the phrase 'Khuda gham-i-Husain ke siwa koi gham na de.'‡

Europeans were particularly taken aback at this joyful integration of cultural markers. Mrs Meer Hassan Ali explained it as follows: 'This pompous display is grown into a habit by a long residence amongst people who make a merit of showy parades at all their festivals. Foreign (Muslims) are equally surprised as Europeans, when they visit (Hindustan), and first see the Tazia conveyed about in procession, which would be counted sacrilegious in Persia or Arabia; but here the ceremony is not complete without a mixture of pageantry with the deeply expressed and public exposure of their grief.'

Modave, meanwhile, was more critical about the colour and pageantry that had entered Muslim rituals: 'This lukewarm attitude in the Muslims of India derives in part from the fact that Islam was never taught there with the same care that Muslim priests take in Persia and in Turkey in instructing the faithful. Islam in India is infected with many superstitions which obviously came from the practice of Hindus and is full of a number of popular traditions which can appear ridiculous...'

Asaf would be relentlessly criticized by the British for his profligacy and financial mismanagement. But the truth was far more subtle. Asaf understood very clearly the limits of his powers, with the British presence so inexorably poised at his border, their rapacity insatiable.

---
*Those who eat and drink together, close friends.
†Though shocking to orthodox Muslims, a number of Hindu rituals such as Durga Puja and the Jagannath festival had a major influence on Indian tazia rituals.
‡Except for the grief of Imam Hussain, may God save you from all grief.

He had seen his titan of a father defeated at Buxar, and would have known that his skills would need to be used in a far more versatile manner. Scholars have shown that there were only three areas in which he could have reduced spending—his personal and household expenditure, which was no more than any monarch at the time. Expenditure on pensions to family and retainers, many of which were in fact imposed by the EIC, including Saadat Ali Khan's, and which the nawab did try and control. And, finally, the army, which the British wanted reduced to a minimum. Asaf insisted on maintaining an 80,000-man force, and kept it as a separate entity to the British-led forces. As for his lands, they were well managed, as were the extensive properties of the begums in Faizabad. The annual revenue of Awadh increased notably under Asaf. From 1 crore 15 lakh rupees per year at the time of Shuja's death in 1775, it had increased to 2 crores 20 lakhs by 1784-85.

Consequently, Asaf may have felt that whatever money he could spend on his city, his projects and the arts, was money that the Company at least would not appropriate. It was also money that stimulated the Awadhi economy and gave employment to thousands of craftspeople, while celebrating all the symbols of his rule. In spending lavishly on the arts of his city, Asaf was emulating the Mughals, and the Indo-Muslim rulers' use of conspicuous consumption as a deliberate policy. Cultural patronage created political authority, and the nawab was as aware of this as the Mughals were. This would make of Asaf a beloved and generous patron to his own people, remembered long after his death, despite the endless character assassination by the British. As noted by scholar C. A. Bayly, 'the Company in its time was celebrated only for the construction of jails and courthouses.'

For such an important monument as the imambara, it is surprising that no clear date has been noted for the beginning of its construction.* The only written account is for the date of completion, since Abu Talib notes that the imambara had been completed by 1791. Popular accounts state that it was begun in 1784 as a famine relief measure for the great famine of that year†. Rumour had it that work continued

---

*Popular lore claims that the architect was Kifayatullah, a Delhi-based architect who won the commission through a competition. There are no records to support this.
†Many rumours have been associated with the building of the imambara. In true 'noblesse oblige' style, one account claimed that the nobility would work on the imambara at night, so

on the Imambara during the day time, and then it was torn down at night, so as to continue endlessly thus providing work for the hungry. It is claimed that as many as 40,000 people were employed in these enormous works and were paid for in food.* Another popular anecdote has the Imambara as the site of the genesis of a hugely popular cooking technique—the 'dum' (Persian for steamed) style. According to popular lore, the thousands of workers for the Imambara were also fed daily at a communal kitchen. The food was cooked in giant pots sealed with dough and kept warm in huge ovens. One day Asaf sampled the food himself, and found it so flavourful that he ordered a similar oven be made for use at court banquets, thus giving rise to the 'dumpukht' method of cooking. A number of vegetarian dishes were created too, dishes like arbi kebab and kathal kebab, while a meat kebab known as galauti kebab was rumoured to be made out of 160 masalas including crushed roses, pearls, gold and silver foil.

Despite these beguiling anecdotes, since Hastings had visited Lucknow for five months during the summer of that year, making copious notes on the intemperate winds, he would surely have noticed if such an enormous and expensive enterprise were underway. It is more likely that the project began around 1785–1786, when the begums were residing in Lucknow, perhaps even with the blessings of those devout ladies. Even in 1788 Elizabeth Plowden had noted that the Imambara being built though very fine, was 'at present in an unfinished state'.†

If the creation of a resurgent Shia culture in Lucknow was a visible counterpoint to the Mughals in Delhi, then it was also surely a statement against the threatening British. As he continued to charm

---

that no one would see their reduced circumstances. This may not have been entirely fanciful, because a similar attitude existed even a hundred years later, during the famine of 1878. At that time, it was said that a group of Muslim gentlemen formed a committee to raise money for the help of impoverished purdah-bound respectable women who would have felt too ashamed to ask for money publicly. It is in fact impossible to obtain statistics for the relief measures because recipients would not let it be known that they had received public charity, but the sums were believed to be considerable.

*The great famine of 1784 began when the lateness of the autumn rain caused the kharif crops to fail. 1785 was a poor year for rain too and 1786 had excessively heavy rain which ruined the spring crops. This led to several years of famine due to scarcity of grain, during which people were said to have subsisted on seeds, grasses, and the bark of trees. Gram sold at the unprecedented price of 8 sers for the rupee in Faizabad.

†Given the speed of construction at that time, it would have been completed had it begun in 1784.

the European residents with breakfasts, elephant fights, and 'exotic' entertainments, the nawab simultaneously directed his energies towards the creation and fostering of a culture that was completely alien to the Europeans, and quite hidden from them. The Ganga-Jamuni tehzeeb* that would include all the people of Lucknow, through Holi, Muharram, marriages, and celebrations, would be regarded by the Europeans with incomprehensible distaste and increasingly even with a sort of abhorrence.

Even physically, the nawab appeared to be edging away westwards, as other Europeans moved eastwards,† away from the Residency of Lucknow where the English would create an increasingly strait-laced enclave of Britishness. Ten years after he had shifted the capital to Lucknow and had extensively remodelled the old Macchi Bhawan palaces, Asaf began to build an entirely new palace complex—the Daulat Khana. The centre piece of the Daulat Khana was the Asafi Kothi, built within a formal garden and with a private mosque, a sheesh mahal, and the famous 'aina khana', the nawab's museum. 'The Vizier possesses several palaces, some of them immense piles of building,' agreed an English traveller in 1787, 'yet he prefers to all these princely residences a small bungalow on the river, the enlarging of which employs a good deal of his time and attention.'

But to the west of Lucknow next to the Bara Imambara the Daulat Khana would be, for a time, a place where 'bonds of friendship and understanding remained intact because Shias and Sunnis of all classes shared a language and literature and a cultural heritage.' And where 'no one in Lucknow ever noticed who was a Sunni and who a Shia'.‡

---

*The expression is a reference to the rivers Ganga and Yamuna which converge at nearby Prayag. 'The essence of the expression is that when the rivers, each having its own colour (the Ganga being turbid and light yellow and the Yamuna being green), amalgamate and flow into each other, the integration is so seamless such that no difference can be noticed.' From Sushama Swarup, *Costumes and Textiles of Awadh: From the Era of Nawabs to Modern Times*, New Delhi: Roli, 2012, p. 19.
†Martin would build Constantia far to the east of the city, and Polier's buildings, though their exact location remains unknown, are also believed to be east of Macchi Bhawan.
‡In the nineteenth century, it became part of Muharram commemorations to recite Tabarra, which is the vilification of the first three caliphs before Hazrat Ali, regarded as usurpers. The Sunni Muslims found Tabarra deeply offensive, since they revere these caliphs along with Hazrat Ali. This would give rise to tensions and sectarian conflicts between Shia and Sunni Muslims in Lucknow. Under the influence of the later nawabs of Awadh, Muharram commemoration rituals lasted for forty days, and then up to two and a half months, the longest anywhere in

# ART IN CHAOS

At the same time that Asaf was building a city of light in Awadh, in Delhi, the world was turning dark for Emperor Shah Alam II. The death of Najaf Khan in 1782 had announced the final descent of Delhi and her emperor into ruination and tragedy. For ten years, this most indefatigable commander had fought valiantly to regain Shah Alam's territories and with his death, the malevolent forces that Najaf Khan had been holding at bay swept through the city like a dark tide. Even as rival factions among Najaf Khan's own generals clamoured to take over as leader, the usual suspects rose up in revolt outside the city—the Sikhs, the Jats, and the Rohilla Afghans. Quite helpless, paranoid, and utterly vulnerable, Shah Alam had little choice but to appeal to the Maratha general Mahadji Scindia for protection once again.

In 1784, the emperor met with the Marathas at their camp outside Mathura, accompanied by six of his sons, and a favourite seven-year-old daughter. An English traveller witnessed the sadly reduced state of the emperor of Hindustan, the Shadow of God on Earth, when he examined the gifts that had been sent to the English party on behalf of the emperor:

> The royal gifts of a horse, an elephant, a princely dress and a tiara of jewels sound very grand, and as a part of the formula of the introduction of eminent visitors at the Mogul court, were not to be despised; but on examination, the diamond and emerald sepeych was found to be composed of green glass and false stones; the horse was worn out, and in the last stage of existence; and the elephant, upon taking off his trappings, discovered a long ulcerated wound on the back from the shoulder to the tail, the whole was emblematical of the fallen state of the unfortunate monarch, or rather the shadow of a prince, by whom they were represented.

---

the world. In India, the self-mortification is also more extreme. Flagellants attach razor blades to chains with which to lash their backs. In India also began the practice of walking barefoot on burning coals, and this would be done in the huge platform of the Bara Imambara. The alams used are somewhat smaller than in Iran.

Delhi at this time was as ruinous as her emperor—the storied havelis were neglected or entirely abandoned and the canals had run dry. The large avenues had lost their majesty, crowded as they were with mean hutments, clustered along the sides of the road. In the salatin quarters the lives of the princes were more wretched than ever. Whenever they heard the voice of the emperor, these starving cousins were wont to shout out: 'Send someone to slit our throats! It would be a far sweeter death than the one you make us suffer!'

The Marathas had fared much better than the emperor, whose authority they continued to undermine, having gone from strength to strength in the previous decade. In the Deccan, they tussled with Tipu Sultan for supremacy and were fighting to recover all the lands that Tipu had initially wrestled from them. For, after the death of his father, the thirty-two-year-old Tipu Sultan had established himself as ruler of Mysore with assured panache, abandoning altogether the pretence of ruling in the name of the Wodeyar kings. He refused to maintain the charade of submitting to the Mughal emperor, and took on the title of Padshah, one of the emperor's own titles, becoming the first Indian ruler to do so in 1786. The year before, in 1785, Tipu had looked overseas for further sanction of his claims to sovereignty—he had sent an embassy from Mysore to the Ottoman Caliph in Istanbul to back his claims in addition to proposing trade links and assistance in fighting the British. In 1787 he followed this with another embassy, to the court of Louis XVI of France, demonstrating his unique understanding of the geopolitics of the time, and the breadth of his ambition for the state of Mysore. For Tipu realized that to consolidate the territories his father had conquered for Mysore, it was not the feeble Mughal emperor who was a threat, but the three other powers in the Deccan—the Marathas, Hyderabad, and the British.

Meanwhile, in Delhi, though Mahadji Scindia swore loyalty to the emperor once again, he was missing from Delhi four years later in 1788 when the twenty-year-old Rohilla Ghulam Qadir realized that the gates to the city were undefended, and decided to wreak vengeance on the Mughals and their city. The slavering violence of the young Ghulam Qadir had its genesis in events fifteen years prior when, in 1772, Shah Alam had made a valiant attempt along with Najaf Khan and the Marathas to reclaim his inheritance upon his return to Delhi from Allahabad. In the fracas that followed, Ghulam Qadir's father, Zabita Khan, had been defeated, and the Marathas had plundered the Rohilla train, raping many of the women and despoiling the tomb of Ghulam Qadir's grandfather, Najib-ud-Daula. Ghulam Qadir, then just a child, had been taken hostage and kept at Delhi's Qudsiya Bagh, where the emperor grew extremely fond of the boy. 'He was given servants and guards, and fed magnificently 3 times a day'—rumours would swirl in later years about the unnatural interest the emperor took in the comely boy, who was deemed a handsome youth with fine large eyes despite his truly diabolical nature. Others whispered that, on the contrary, he was castrated for being a threat to the royal women. Or perhaps it was simply the dishonouring and defeat of his father that spurred the young man but the fact remains that when Ghulam Qadir and his 2,000 soldiers entered the Qila of Delhi in August 1788, the ferocity of their violence was truly cataclysmic. People were tortured and murdered, royal women stripped and raped, the Mughal princes humiliated, and Emperor Shah Alam blinded. Some accounts even claim that Ghulam Qadir cut out the elderly emperor's eyes himself.* Having assaulted Shah Alam and his family with savage focus, Ghulam Qadir temporarily instated Mughal prince Bidar Bakht† as a puppet emperor.

Ghulam Qadir then ripped through the Qila and the city, looking for jewellery and cash and, in the mayhem of his plunder, the great Mughal library was sacked and many of the gorgeous album paintings, or muraqqas, were seized. A witness to these troubled times wrote that Ghulam Qadir's relatives now sold Shah Alam's 'paintings and books like they were vegetables and crops'. In addition to Mahadji Scindia and other local rulers, Nawab Asaf-ud-Daula was one of those who bought single folios and albums and was thus 'able to protect early Mughal paintings and albums...from further degradation in the open market, a space (comparable) to the sorrow and pain one feels in remembering the death of Hussain'. Asaf was a knowledgeable and enthusiastic collector of art and had been buying great Mughal

---

*See Dalrymple's extraordinary account of this incident in *The Anarchy*, London: Bloomsbury Publishing, 2019.

†Bidar Bakht was the eldest surviving child of another emperor, Ahmad Shah. He was titular emperor for a few months till Mahadji Scindia reinstated Shah Alam. He was allegedly killed on the orders of Shah Alam in 1790.

artworks for some time, occasionally for phenomenal sums. He had a copy of the exquisite Mughal *Padshahnama* manuscript, which he had bought for 12,000 rupees*. He had also bought a folio showing Jahangir as an elephant driver for which he had paid 3,000 rupees. Asaf thus rather neatly added to the Rohilla-origin collection, already part of his library,† inherited from his father. When Shuja had defeated the Rohilla leader Hafiz Rahmat Khan in 1774, the nawab had also acquired a large part of his art collection.‡ Asaf was well aware of the quality of his collection, and Hastings had observed that 'part of the books (from Shah Alam's library) had been purchased at Lucknow, that is by the vizier (Asaf), and upon enquiry found this to be the case, for his Excellency produced some of them to the English Gentleman boasting that they were the 'King's'.

Many of the single-leaf folios that the nawab collected at this time were bound into volumes, or muraqqas, known today as the Asaf-ud-Daula Albums.§ The seventeenth-century folios of portraits and calligraphy specimens were carefully placed within new margins, and arranged into discreet sections, with Asaf's seal on each folio. A very interesting section contains paintings made for Mirza Salim, when he was mounting a rebellion against his father Emperor Akbar, at Allahabad in the early seventeenth century¶. Six of these paintings even contain the treasonous dedication to 'Padshah Salim', from the artist 'Nanha Ghulam'. With Akbar reigning as Mughal emperor from Agra, Mirza Salim, of course had no business calling himself 'Padshah'. Asaf

---

*This precious volume remained in Lucknow till Saadat Ali Khan offered it to the British in 1799, no doubt to secure his nawabi. He also sent five other volumes along with the *Padshahnama* to George III, where they were made part of the king's library.

†By the late eighteenth century, the great Lucknow library was reputed to contain 300,000 volumes, only 700 of which came from the libraries of Mughal kings. Because the Lucknow library was plundered by the British post 1857, its books now form part of impressive 'Persian manuscript collections in London, Paris, Oxford, Cambridge, Dublin, Glasgow, Berlin, and even in Aberystwyth', relocating to the West knowledge systems which were once integral parts of busy libraries in India.

‡The Rohillas seemed to have operated a lively 'recycling' economy of sorts, after their campaigns of plunder. As Bayly describes it: 'the plundered goods, such as jewels and clothes... they sold all these things at low prices. Cloth goods worth ten rupees they sold for one rupee and those worth one rupee for eighty tankah.'

§They are today part of the Royal Collection Trust.

¶Between 1600 and 1604, Mirza Salim set up an almost independent court at Allahabad, and lured some important courtiers and painters to this subversive court. He proclaimed himself Padshah Salim, and challenged Akbar's power from Allahabad.

would have known about this troubled time in Mughal history, when the great Emperor Akbar was struggling to control his talented but intemperate and impatient son. It is tempting to wonder whether this episode in history resonated personally with Asaf, who had also once been the gauche son of a superhuman father. Moreover, the album appears to contain a small sample of writing in Salim's own distinctive hand, carefully cut out and pasted into the album, almost like a talisman. There are also six beautiful portraits of persons belonging to the Mughal royal family, kneeling on namdar rugs, including Babur, Humayun, and Mirza Kamran, but none of Akbar.* In fact, there are no portraits of Akbar in Asaf's albums at all.

Even before the unspeakable depredations of Ghulam Qadir, the nawab had gathered an impressive collection of paintings. A British art collector in Lucknow at the time also agreed that the nawab had 'many persons employed in collecting and copying books.' Canny courtiers and applicants would also compete to offer paintings as gifts to the appreciative nawab. A khwajasara once presented a painting to the nawab who was so pleased that he paid 2,000 rupees for it†. At other times, the nawab would bestow gifts in return for the paintings. These could include guns and swords, as well as robes and jewellery, though the receiver would have occasionally been perplexed by the present of a parrot or a deer. The contents of Shuja's and Asaf's libraries were celebrated in their own time and yet it is almost customary to think of nawabi paintings of this time as 'provincial', and somehow more rustic, meagre, and unrefined compared to the Mughal high art of Shah Jahan's time. In 1848, an assessment of the Awadhi collection was made by the British, no doubt eagerly anticipating that the books would become part of EIC collections. This indexing showed that there were 10,000 volumes in the nawabi library. Most of these would disappear from Lucknow post 1858, either destroyed in the uprising or stolen as loot, leaving behind a flickering shadow of what had been a most glittering collection.

The nawab was not the only elite patron encouraging the arts in

---

*I am grateful to Friederike Weis for inviting me to the seminar on the Polier albums held in Berlin in September 2021, where I was able to hear Emily Hannam give a lecture on the RCT Asaf-ud-Daula albums.
†The price paid for paintings ranged from Rs 300–3,000 for individual folios and Rs 2,000–12,000 for complete albums.

Lucknow, for there would be many distinguished guests from the besieged Mughal family who would find solace in Asaf's generous hospitality. Apart from Mirza Jawan Bakht, another royal prince—Mirza Ali Bakht—also arrived in Lucknow in the early 1790s. This prince was the poet who went by the pen name Azfari, and whose refined sensibility baulked initially at Lucknow's narrow, clattering lanes. But the nawab went to great lengths to make these impoverished princes feel honoured. He gave them generous stipends and, despite his own great status, always treated them with lavish deference. The nawab would never sit on the masnad or allow the use of the ruler's fly-whisk in the presence of the princes, graciously telling his guests that 'I feel embarrassed that I use a fly whisk in the presence of such high stature people such as yourselves.' Instead, Asaf 'commanded that an ordinary rumal (handkerchief) be used to swat flies for him.' Indeed the prestige and the great allure of the Timurid name was still magnetic, even though the actual power of the Mughals was entirely a mirage. When Azfari had first escaped from his salatin quarters prison, he was received by the rajas of Jodhpur and Jaipur, who had prepared a royal takht and parasol especially for him. Azfari was similarly delighted with his interactions with the rest of the Lucknow aristocracy, and came to appreciate the city's great charm and refinement. Along with his cousin Mirza Jalal-al-din, he spent happy hours engaging in archery contests with Asaf, and had to admit that the nawab was by far the best archer of them all.

Another prince was Mirza Sulaiman Shukoh,* who had arrived in 1788, also a great patron of poetry, and who patronized the émigré poets Mushafi,† Insha,‡ Rangeen, and Jurat§. Many erstwhile 'Dihlavi' poets would have had their bitter exile somewhat comforted by the patronage of these enduring symbols of past Mughal glory. Like his brothers before him, Mirza Sulaiman Shukoh migrated to Lucknow along with his wives, children, and entourage, and maintained his own court. All these royal guests kept a court with poets, artists, and scholars, and adopted over time the cadence of the language of Awadh, along with their customs and etiquette.

---

*Other princes in Lucknow included Mirza Ilahi Baksh and Mirza Husain Baksh.
†Shaikh Ghulam Humdani.
‡Insha Allah Khan 'Insha'.
§Shaikh Qalandar Baksh 'Jurat'.

Into this rarefied atmosphere of art and refined manners, the gruff and ruddy-cheeked Cornwallis arrived from Calcutta in 1787. A practical, soldierly man, he was wont to begin his dinner parties in Calcutta with the pragmatic command, 'Off coats!', so that his gently sweating guests could rid themselves gratefully of their absurd jackets in Calcutta's clammy heat. Certainly Cornwallis appears not to have accepted his posting in India with joy in his heart, for he wrote about his appointment in a letter to say that 'much against my will, and with grief of heart, I have been obliged to say yes and to exchange a life of ease and content, to encounter all the plagues and miseries of command and public station.' Cornwallis had arrived in India determined to slash away at the entrenched and corrupt system of patronage, and one of his more successful initiatives was to increase the salaries of Company men, and thus make them less susceptible to bribes. Unfortunately, he also blamed Indians in the Company's service for most of the excesses he saw, commenting on one occasion that 'every native of Hindustan (I really believe) is corrupt.'\* According to a scholar, though he 'was sparing in punishing Europeans who had committed fraud or taken graft, believing that they could be reformed, he dismissed all Indians from important positions in the service whether suspected of misconduct or not, and in 1790 barred them from ever holding an office worth 500 pounds or more.' He was especially critical of Anglo-Indians, who were not only tainted by their 'Indian-ness', but were also loathed 'settlers'. When Cornwallis had surrendered to the American and French forces at Yorktown, where England lost her American colonies, he had developed a pathological hatred for the settlers who had risen up against the mother country. In India, this hatred would translate into the exclusion of Anglo-Indians from employment in the Company, and reinforce a sense of superiority in 'pure-bred' Company men.

Cornwallis's expedition to Lucknow included a traveller, the Englishman Charles Madan, who would make copious notes about the long voyage which betrayed many of the evolving prejudices and attitudes of the British at this time. The party travelled from Bengal mainly by boat, and Madan noticed that the Hindu members of their

---

\*In 1790 he would bar Indians from ever holding an office worth 500 pounds a year or more and disqualified sepoys from any hope of rising to commissioned status.

crew waited till they were ashore to eat their meals. 'The Muslims are not so strict,' he wrote to his father, 'and pay more attention to the cravings of nature than the religious half-starved Hindoo!' When they stopped at Murshidabad, where the nawab and the begums graciously held 'an elegant entertainment in the English style', he noted snidely that the begums remained in purdah, a custom 'which rendered the ceremony rather a subject of mirth.' Madan continued in this bigoted manner, writing of 'ridiculous fakirs', and the 'black skulls' of the boatmen, whom he seems to have viewed as somehow sub-human, able to withstand the most glaring sun, unlike the pale-skinned and delicate firangis. At the same time, Madan was extremely conscious of being a stranger in a strange land, very far away from all 'civilization' and safety. Finding himself hundreds of miles away from the familiar enclaves of Calcutta, floating on an immense river, he wrote that 'any of them (rivers) in any other country, would be termed immense! it is curious to cast an eye over the map and at this very moment, to find ourselves with a fleet of large vessels, in the very heart of the country.... The scale of this part of Asia is certainly beyond all measure, grand! And extensive! Our own little island would lose much, nay, would sink to nothing, by a comparison!'

It is perhaps this deeply hidden terror at being in a vast, dangerous, and incomprehensible land, that promoted the constant denigration and occasional loathing. For when Cornwallis and his party met with Mirza Jawan Bakht in Benaras, Madan was positively crowing in his description of how the Mughal heir had been diminished in the four years since he had famously met Hastings in 1784:

> When Mr Hastings saw the Prince in 1784, he was obliged to undergo several disagreeable forms and ceremonies, nay, I may say indignities, for a governor general to yield to—such as going into the presence with his shoes off, sitting behind the prince on his elephant, and fanning him etc. All this was omitted upon the present occasion; his lordship went into the imperial presence with his shoes on, and his family in boots, nor did he drive away the flies from the princely visage; the form we observed was literally the following—3 salaams, nazrs of 50 gold mohurs, 3 more salaams. Short conversation between the two in Persian, then the Prince took off his own coat and put it over the governor's....

The robes that the prince gifted to Cornwallis were deemed 'more calculated for an effeminate Asiatick than an Englishman', beginning the inevitable and vicious questioning of Indian male masculinity and virility. Cornwallis felt the need to explicitly insult the prince by stating that if he visited Calcutta, he would be treated with respect but that the honours that Hastings had assiduously made sure were given to him as a descendant of the House of Timur would no longer be his[*]. Even when the English party visited with the Mughal prince to dine with him, they sent their own cooks ahead, 'not choosing to trust entirely to Hindustan cookery', an attitude of suspicious superiority far removed from Hastings's careful noting of Asaf's 'kabaub recipe'. Not for Cornwallis, then, extravagant sighs over the suffering of this tragic prince like Hastings had once experienced. Not for him nostalgia over a lost Mughal past, and a painting to mark the occasion.

---

[*]Intensely annoyed, Jawan Bakht went to Delhi to try and join forces with the Rohillas, then retired to Benaras where he would die of a fever in May 1788.

## COURTESANS AND POETS

In the intoxicating and nargis-scented air of a balmy Lucknawi evening in 1789, a glittering ensemble of people gathered together for an intimate majlis held by Nawab Asaf-ud-Daula. The nawab would have been resplendent in a gleaming white jamdani, surrounded by some of his favoured courtiers, lying back on gold-fringed, embroidered bolsters. Among them was Hasan Reza Khan, grown comfortably portly, the doleful folds of his cheeks belying his easy-going good humour and Haider Beg Khan, still handsome despite his forbidding manner (image 32). Also present were some of the European adventurers as well as some Company officials, all seated on the crisp white chandani farash. There were even a few women, including the irrepressible music enthusiast Elizabeth Plowden. The room was lit with brass lamps and the light from the candles was reflected in the mirrors on the walls and the glass of the chandeliers till the room of the majlis glowed with the trembling luminescence of a thousand flames. The guests murmured in pleasurable anticipation as the soft burbling of hookahs* provided a pleasing backdrop, and the fragrant paan-daan was passed around. Outside the space of the majlis, the nawab's many pigeons had quietened at last, in a final feathery settling of a thousand wings. From the courtyard, there might even have been a single, heart-breaking roar from the nawab's caged tiger.†

Suddenly, there was a quickening of interest and a hushed silence fell among the spectators as the first breathy notes of a sarangi cut through the air. There was a rustling of clothes and a whispering of anklets as the music gathered itself into the warm air and filled all the spaces of the room. Then there was a woman gliding into the room, her henna-tipped fingers appearing to part the perfumed air around her as she made her entrance into the majlis, her odhani a hazy halo around her beautiful face and sloe-black sparkling eyes. This was the famous courtesan, Khanum Jan, whose reputation for matchless

---

*Hookahs became more elaborate at this time. The cords were made of silk and kalabattun, and used to be 3 metres long but for the nawabs the cords could increase to a length of 30 metres.
†Thomas Twining, visiting Lucknow in 1794, described 'a tiger of extraordinary size confined in a small wooden cage' in the courtyard of the nawab's palace.

song and dance performances had made of her a celebrity in Calcutta. Now in Lucknow she performed for Asaf, gazing straight at him in the intimate, charged atmosphere of the majlis to sing with almost unbearable longing, her voice artfully breaking:

> Oh cupbearer! It is the season of spring—let's celebrate!
> The wine is brought before us, so pour it out—let's celebrate!
> Bring the cup to the lip and the flask to the breast:
> Your kisses and embraces are as heady as wine—let's celebrate!

Musicologist Katherine Schofield has described the enchanting Khanum Jan as follows:

> Khanum Jan* was the star of an elite troupe of courtesans that traversed the major north Indian courts and British cantonments. Her Kashmiri ethnicity is debatable; any fair-skinned courtesans from the north west, especially from Punjab, miraculously turned into 'Kashmiris' when they arrived on the plains of Hindustan because Kashmiri courtesans were esteemed as great beauties and thus commanded more prestige and higher fees. Whatever the case, as an elite courtesan Khanum was highly trained in Hindustani music, singing, Persian and Urdu poetry, courtly etiquette, wit and of course the arts of seduction; courtesans generally did not marry but had sexual relationships on their own terms with their most ardent patrons.

Khanum Jan and her group of kalawant, or hereditary artists, travelled from court to court in northern India.† The troupe often lived in tented encampments and the patrons of the greatest durbars courted Khanum Jan with lavish gifts. For a famous courtesan was not a mere entertainer, but could seduce an entire gathering in the space of an evening with music, and elegant and teasing repartee, with the crackling use of puns and metaphors, with Urdu couplets recited at just the right moment,

---

*I am extremely grateful to Dr Katherine Schofield, Head of Music at Kings College, London, for sharing the manuscript of the book which was yet to be published at that time: *Music and Musicians in Late Mughal India: Histories of the Ephemeral, 1748–1858*, Cambridge: Cambridge University Press, 2023.
†Sometimes called 'deredar' courtesans, or tawaifs of the dera, or the camp, travelling the land and camping wherever a rich man took a fancy to one of them, and entertaining the nobles of the area.

and especially with languid glances from under her dark lashes which made every single participant believe that she had eyes only for them. It was the art of seduction, whose essence was poetry and music. An earlier British woman traveller had observed about courtesans that it was their 'languishing glances, wanton smiles, and attitudes, not quite consistent with decency, which are so much admired'.* The Lucknawi courtesans in particular gained such a reputation for the most exquisite and refined manners that the young sons of the gentry were sent to the salons of the best known tawaifs† for lessons in etiquette, in comportment, and the proper appreciation of Urdu poetry. The salons of the leading courtesans, many of them supremely wealthy women, 'were centres of the high culture of the era, with poetry readings, concerts, and daily social gatherings of the city's most urbane aesthetes.' As for her sexual favours, an accomplished courtesan would form an attachment with a wealthy nobleman or courtier, usually for a long period, and might only have two or three such liaisons over the course of her entire career.‡

What Khanum Jan looked like we cannot really know§ though she was esteemed very beautiful, with 'speaking eyes'. For a certain idea of female beauty appreciated at the time, we have the intrepid traveller Fanny Parkes's account of a 'native gentleman's' idea of beauty at the time: 'Bara bara naak, bara bara aankh, moonh jaisa chand, khoob bhari aisa',¶ stretching out his arms as if they could not at their fullest extent encircle the mass of beauty he was describing!' Nonetheless Khanum Jan, as an entertainer and a dancer, would not have been quite as portly as to satisfy this gentleman's idea of female perfection. The most subtle art of a skilled courtesan was the nakhra, or pretence. In her elaborate game of seduction with her patron, a courtesan needed to use every art she possessed to obtain rewards, jewels, adoration, and loyalty. Feigned indifference, a sudden headache, an unexplained rage

---

*Jemima Kindersley writing in 1767.
†The word 'tawaif' originated in the nineteenth century. In the eighteenth century these women were referred to as 'bai-jees'. The word tawaif has become loaded over time, and some scholars like Saleem Kidwai prefer the term ganewali—singing ladies.
‡During the course of her fieldwork scholar Veena Oldenburg discovered that the closest sexual relationships the courtesans had were with other women.
§Katherine Schofield has posited that the image of 'Polier watching a nautch' depicts Khanum Jan, image 24.
¶A very, very large nose, very, very large eyes, a face like a moon; very very portly, thus!

or a fit of apparent jealousy could all be used with the utmost realism to extract the most out of an unsuspecting and lovestruck patron.

Elizabeth Plowden herself was utterly charmed by Khanum Jan. She would write in her diary that the courtesan was 'superior to anything I have seen in the country. She sings the Kashmirian airs and dances these dances in the best style.' Plowden was a voracious collector of Hindustani songs, which she would transcribe with the help of a Goan musician called John Braganza.* The songs that Plowden collected from Khanum Jan and her musicians were sung in a whole repertoire of Hindustani languages—Persian, Urdu, Brajbhasha, Punjabi and more. Asaf was so delighted with Plowden's rare enthusiasm for Hindustani music and for her 'exceptional devotedness, and rare fidelity, high titles and honourable address', that he obtained a farman from the Mughal emperor Shah Alam II giving Elizabeth Plowden the formal Mughal title of Begum.

For the highly celebrated Lucknow tawaifs like Khanum Jan, being an accomplished singer added immeasurably to their cachet. If the tawaif had had an exemplary training in music, especially from an established music ustad, or teacher, then it made her a highly prized entertainer. Tawaifs were trained in ghazals, thumri, ragini, and dhun. Of these styles, all considered 'light'† as opposed to more sombre classical genres like dhrupad, it was thumri which became the iconic Lucknow genre. The training of the tawaifs had been described as follows:

> The artistic training of the best tawaif was a rigorous affair, starting around the age of five, and continued for ten years or more. This talim was generally imparted by males, either family members or from the same community as the tawaif. Sometimes taught by well known ustads employed by courts, who belonged to hereditary lineages of music specialists such as kalawants and qawwal bachche.

In the numerous salons of Lucknow, and in the mushairas held in the homes of noblemen, of Mughal princes, and of the discerning wealthy

---

*The manuscript is now in the Fitzwilliam Museum, Cambridge. MS 380 Plowden Album.
†The 'lightness' comes from the idea that the raag may be sung in an interpretive manner, rather than a set manner, with less emphasis on the alaap.

citizenry, the very language of poetry itself—Urdu—was morphing into something exquisite and refined, shedding all traces of its more robust and pedestrian origins. Because Persian had long been admired as the language of sophisticated poetry par excellence, Persian phrases and idioms were self-consciously inserted into Lucknawi Urdu poetry, a process known as islah-i-zaban*. And so another aspect of Lucknawi life became uniquely elegant in the cauldron of its patrons' intense, searing gaze. The Urdu master Mushafi described this slightly ambiguous and admiring relationship between Persian and Urdu as follows:

> Mushafi put Persian on the shelf:
> Now is the time for Hindavi (Urdu).

Indeed, the Persian language retained its magical lustre for a long time, even at a time when the regional languages and Urdu were in clear ascendancy. It was a particular compliment to admit fluency in Persian and Arabic in a poet and, conversely, to cast suspicion on their mastery of Persian was to fatally risk a poet's intellectual reputation entirely.

For the women confined within the zenanas of Lucknow, musical entertainments were of a somewhat different nature. Not for them the languorous seduction of a courtesan's mehfil. Only one particular community of performers was allowed access to both male and female spaces—the domnis and dhadinis, whose main instrument was the frame drum or dhol. The women would sing dhrupad, sohila, or auspicious and merry songs on the occasions of festivities that particularly occupied the zenana—births, marriages, celebrations, Eid, and so on. The women performers were chosen for their modesty, chastity, and good character, and naturally would not be expected to perform any sexual role. Domnis became very popular in Lucknow households, all the elite families employing a troupe of these women. As for courtesans or 'naatch women', agreed diarist Mrs Meer Hassan Ali, 'no respectable Mussulman would allow these impudent women to perform before their wives and daughters'. Perhaps Mrs Ali had not listened to the entire domni repertoire, for Fanny Parkes, noted that 'during weddings, these women, the domnee, played and sang abusive bridal songs. The songs for the domnee are indecent beyond the conception of a European.'†

---

*Literally 'correction of language'.
†Even today, songs sung among women to celebrate upcoming nuptials in India are satisfyingly

Just as the Urdu language used in Lucknow became increasingly refined, so did the sentiments conjured by the language. Emotion itself was shorn of all things sordid, and developed what would become the calling card of Lucknawi expression—its delicacy or nazakat. Verse upon verse would describe the sublime agony of separation, or unrequited love, using imagery subtle as shadows and language as delicate as a lover's sigh. A popular adage of the fastidious lengths to which Lucknawi delicatesse could extend to was Lakhnau ki nazakat hai ki rasgulle bhi chhil ke khaye jate hain.* And the poetic genre par excellence to capture this mood became the Urdu ghazal. In time this delicacy of sentiment would be deemed excessive and wanton, its proponents similarly derided as effeminate and decadent. But in the late eighteenth century, these evenings of exquisite music and dance in Lucknow would become so famous that a saying was created: Subh-e Benaras, Shaam-e Awadhwa, Shab-e Malwa.†

And yet the first wave of poets who migrated from Delhi to Lucknow would not be entirely complimentary about their adopted city. Indeed, they were sometimes bitter in their vitriol, and scathing about the brash new city they had moved to, especially when compared to the remembered grandeur and elegant decrepitude of the grand old Mughal city of Delhi. 'Far better than Lucknow the ruins of Delhi,' mourned Mir Taqi Mir, the finest ghazal writer of his time, with unvarnished scorn. 'Would that I had died back there / than let my madness lead me here!' Mir would live the rest of life in Lucknow, and would make an art form of his prickly truculence regarding Lucknow and its citizens, and would go out of his way to belittle everyone around him. When the Lucknow cognoscenti asked Mir to recite his poetry for them, the scornful poet demurred, saying that it would be quite beyond their understanding for 'to get my poetry you need to understand the language that is spoken at the steps of Delhi's Jama Masjid,‡ and that

---

teasing and ribald in nature.
*In Lucknow, even the rasgullas must be peeled (the sub-text being that the non-existent 'skin' of the rasgulla would be too rough for the Lucknawi).
†Mornings in Benaras, with their bathing ghats, are the best, evenings in Lucknow, and night-time in Malwa with its clear, cloudless skies.
‡The best Urdu, it was said, could be heard at three places: at the court and army bazar of Delhi, at the flower-sellers' market on the Yamuna, and at the tomb of the saint Shah Madar in Etah district, 'a resort of horse-sellers, harkaras, palankin-bearers and other common people': C. A. Bayly, *Empire and Information: Intelligence Gathering and Social Communication in India*,

you do not.' Mir struggled to reconcile himself to a changing order, one in which his unfashionably sober clothes were gently mocked, and the brash and brassy confidence of the Lucknow elite was an grievous insult. The best known story about his introduction to this sparkling new world was when he entered a mushaira for the first time, his frayed dignity wrapped tightly around himself, and no one recognized him for the great poet from Delhi that he was. When it was his time to recite a poem, these are the verses he pronounced:

> Why do you mock at me and ask yourselves
> Where in the world I come from, easterners?
> There was a city, famed throughout the world,
> Where dwelt the chosen spirits of the age;
> Delhi its name, fairest among the fair.
> Fate looted it and laid it desolate,
> And to that ravaged city I belong.

Mir was around sixteen years old when his beloved city was devastated by Nadir Shah, and he would never recover from the horror of that desecration, and the nostalgia for all that he had lost:

> This age is not like that which went before it.
> The times have changed, the earth and sky have changed.

On one occasion, when Asaf failed to pay sufficiently respectful attention to Mir while he recited a ghazal, distracted by the fish in his pond, the poet was quick to show his displeasure. But the nawab cheerily refused to be insulted, and continued to pay the poet his stipend till the end of his life. The nawab could console himself with the knowledge that Mir had insulted the emperor himself, when he was in Delhi. The emperor had once rather impetuously claimed that he himself was such a good poet that he could churn out verses while performing his ablutions in the morning. 'Yes, and they smell like it,' was Mir's stingingly predictable rejoinder. In Lucknow, Mir's 'deeply emotional and sincere verse', wrote a scholar, 'appeared old-fashioned in Asaf-ud-Daula's court, yet his mere presence brought fame to it.'

Another great Delhi poet who made Lucknow his home was Mirza Muhammad Rafi 'Sauda'. Sauda was given an annual grant of 6,000

*1780–1870*, Cambridge: Cambridge University Press, 1996.

rupees by Asaf and he lived in the city, with rather less angst than Mir, till his death in 1781. Nevertheless he too delighted in satirizing the nawab and when he heard that Asaf had killed a lion during a hunt, composed the following couplet:

> See, Ibn-i-Muljam comes to earth again
> And so the Lion of God once more is slain

When he learnt of these lines the nawab was understandably startled. The 'Lion of God' was one of the titles of Imam Ali himself and Ibn-i-Muljam the name of the man who had killed him. 'Mirza, I hear you have compared me to the murderer of the Lion of God?' he asked the irreverent poet who answered laughingly, 'well it was a fair comparison. The lion was God's, not yours or mine.'

Perhaps even more galling for Asaf would have been the lines of the other great Delhi émigré poet, Mir Hasan. For Mir Hasan revolted against the physical fact of the city of Lucknow itself:

> When I arrived in the land of Lucknow
> I saw no pleasure in that town.
> Grief had so besieged my soul,
> I felt I could never take to this place,
> Even if there are many pious people here,
> What shall we do if the place itself is bad?'

One of the features of Lucknow that caused such turmoil in Mir Hasan's sensitive Delhi poet's soul was its undulating nature, with its gentle rises and dips. 'This country is settled on bumpy ground, so that its paths wind all up and down.' He huffed about the narrow alleys: 'Each lane is so narrow here, that it's scarcely possible to take a breath.'

As for another great émigré poet, Mushafi, the critique appeared personal to the point of insult:

> Lord, you've robbed me of my city
> Brought and sat me in this wilderness
> What can there be between me and these Lakhnavis?
> Dear God, what have you done to me?

So even while the artists in their paint-splattered ateliers were producing the perfectly ordered and paradisiacal stepped terraces and courtyards typical of this age, the poets were hinting at a more disorderly reality. From the sheer quantity of construction activity begun by Asaf at this time, it is certain that there would have been heaps of rubble and debris, as well as the elegant terrace buildings that would be immortalized in paintings and later poetry. Nonetheless, perhaps with an abashed eye upon the source of his patronage, Mir Hasan* himself admitted piously that Asaf had much to be praised about:

> May Asaf-ud-Daula be kept safe forever
> For he made the plans for his stay in this place
> He put an end to all the dirtiness here
> And gave a real shape to Lucknow.

It must have been a great trial upon the nawab's patience to withstand the many barbs of these Delhi poets. And yet when one of the Mughal princes also used poetry to deliver a veiled castigation, the nawab reacted with his usual good humour and charm. On one occasion during the Holi celebrations, Azfari felt that his royal cousins had not been treated by Asaf with quite the deference they were owed, and this prickly Mughal scion extemporized a few verses to this effect. On hearing this poetic complaint, Asaf smiled and promised to assure the cousins a proper stipend too, a promise which he held till the end of his life.

Perhaps Mir's most devastating critique would be of Lucknawi poet Jurat's ghazals which he called 'not poetry, but descriptions of kissing and licking' (chumachati). This particularly colourful insult is believed to have been caused by Jurat's use of a notorious Lucknawi innovation—Rekhti. If the lofty Urdu ghazal used the normative masculine Rekhta voice, then Rekhti arose as the self-consciously playful and feminine anti-ghazal. Instead of the cerebral themes of ghazals, Rekhti provocatively presented the quotidian and the feminine, while adopting the voice of a woman: 'the travails of burdensome husbands; the annoyances and quotidian spats between housewives and their domestic servants; the rivalries among co-wives; and the lascivious shenanigans of illicit liaisons—including within the zenana itself'. The idiom of Rekhti is sometimes called 'begamati

---

*Mir Hasan would dedicate his famous Urdu Masnavi *Sihr-ul-Bayan* (1785) to Asaf-ud-Daula.

zubaan' (language of the respectable women) though, paradoxically, poet Rangeen, who is credited with inventing Rekhti, claimed to have acquired an understanding of the idiom during an ill-spent youth in the company of tawaifs. Rangeen adopted a woman's name, Anvari, dressed up in women's clothes and exhibited feminine mannerisms when he recited his poetry. Rekhti had much in common with the Bhakti mode of song and poetry in which the poets identified as women and sometimes dressed up as women while singing to their beloved Krishna. In time, this aspect of Lucknawi poetry would also be used by the British to question the nawabs' masculinity.

Despite the unshakeable nostalgia for Delhi, however, almost all of the great Delhi poets flocked to Lucknow.* It was said that there were more Urdu poets in Lucknow than lived in the rest of India. And since the grandeur of a court in India was gauged by the excellence of its poets, Asaf brought blinding brilliance to his own court while simultaneously dimming the lustre of the Mughal court.

Mir 'Soz', a Delhi poet outstanding for his ghazals, was appointed ustad, or poetry teacher, to the nawab. Not only was the nawab a poet himself, but 'at least one of his wives, most of his successors, and many of his prominent courtiers and officials were poets in their own right, some of recognized quality even today'. Asaf was considered a passably competent poet, Mir himself writing graciously about the nawab's poetry. One of Asaf's verses was as follows:

> Oh Asaf, the story of this life is so delicate,
> That it ends in a jiffy.†

In time the great Delhi poets would die out, their place taken by a confident new generation of Lucknawi born and bred poets, the most famous of whom would be Shaykh Imam Baksh 'Nasikh' and Khwaja Haider Ali 'Aatish'.

Perhaps some of the disgruntled Delhi poets were mollified by the fact that the Mughal poet prince Azfari held mushairas twice a month at his court, and would respectfully send his own mace-bearers to escort them to his gatherings. These mushairas began to

---

*Only Khwaja Mir 'Dard', of the major Delhi poets, remained in the old Mughal city.
†With grateful thanks to poet and soz singer Askari Naqvi, for sourcing and translating this verse for me: Qissa-e-jan gudaz ai 'asif'/Thodi si baat men tamam kiya.

be held very regularly, in Sufi khanqas, in the houses of poets or in private homes, in addition to the courtly durbars of aristocrats. An invitation would be sent, sometimes including a line of verse, which the attending poets would then have to incorporate into an original poem. The gatherings began at the 'aristocratic time' (between 9 p.m. and 10 p.m.) and poets would indulge in the dangerous pastime of trying to humiliate and outdo each other through their acidic verses. But first there was the potentially incendiary task of drawing up the seating arrangement, giving senior poets a more prominent position. This delicate job was given to the nazim, or presiding poet, a man of taste and urbanity who conducted the evening following strict rules of etiquette. A candle would be placed in front of the nazim when the evening began, then the candle would be moved in front of each poet in turn as they recited. The evening usually began with the youngest poets, and ended with the most accomplished poets. The poets could either recite their poems, or chant them in a melodious manner though this method could backfire, when poets might be accused of sneaking in inferior verses camouflaged by a charming singing voice.

As each poet recited their verses, the listeners would react with elaborate courtesy, politely exclaiming 'wah wah' or 'subhanallah'* at a particularly exquisite or clever line, muffled sometimes by the paan being chewed. A particularly effective line would be musingly repeated by the listeners, while a high-voltage moment of charged appreciation would be marked by the poet being asked to repeat a particularly excellent line. The poet in turn elegantly acknowledged the praise by salaaming to the crowd. As the candle, or shama, was passed around the circle of poets, the night sky of Lucknow faded into the early dawn, when finally the poets bowed to each other, extinguished the candle, and left the assembly.

Apart from the poets, the artists and the courtesans, Delhi musicians arrived in Awadh too, and joined in the great creative cauldron of the late eighteenth century in Lucknow.† Hindustani musicians of the time

---

*'Jazak Allah', 'mukarrar irshad', and 'mahraba' were other accepted phrases.
†Delhi musicians who made new homes in Awadh in the 1750s–80s included the great kalawant Rahim Sen and his young relative, Musahib Khan; Taj Khan Qawwal's sons, the important khayal singers Jan Muhammad Khan 'Jani', Ghulam Rasul, and Jivan Khan; Ghulam Rasul's even more famous son, Ghulam Nabi Miyan 'Shori', who transformed the tappa vocal genre; several of Anjha Baras' disciples including his cousin's grandson, Muzaffar Khan; Adarang's key

set both Persian and Urdu ghazals to the north Indian ragas and talas. A genre of song called the tappa became very fashionable at the nawabi court at this point, though Elizabeth Plowden was less than enchanted by it, writing that it was 'a sort of Wild Harsh Music without any air'. Miyan Ghulam Nabi Shori, son of famous Delhi qawwal Ghulam Rasul, is credited with making the tappa genre, with its 'complex and abrupt rhythm and fast tempo' extremely popular in Lucknow. It must have also been due to the particular patronage of the nawab that tappa became such a rage at this time and it is easy to imagine Asaf with his fizzing energy and effervescent enthusiasms being charmed by this quicksilver musical style. Asaf's clear preference for Hindustani styles of music and recitation is demonstrated by an anecdote noted by Azfari in his memoirs. On one occasion, the court was being regaled by the slow, sonorous Persian recitations of one Shah Husain, who had arrived from abroad (wilayat). When one of the courtiers leaned over to the nawab to praise the 'distinguished' visitor and his 'beautiful and attractive voice', the nawab, clearly taxed, sighed excessively and said that 'perhaps you say this on account of your knowledge. This banda (meaning himself) is totally illiterate in this art.' Silently acknowledging the rebuff, the wilayati visitor gathered his robes and left the court, never to return to India. 'He did not listen carefully to the songs of Hindustan,' noted Azfari sagely. 'When he heard Indian songs, however...he accepted that the real music is what the people of India sing.'

The Shia resurgence that Asaf was actively promoting through architecture and culture also influenced the basic forms of Shia elegies that were performed. These elegies were transformed by innovations and influences which made them uniquely Awadhi. One important innovation was to set the texts of the marsiya and soz to popular raags, including the 'ragini' Bhairavi, which was a major departure from orthodox practice. But it was 'precisely this', notes a scholar, 'which contributed to the greater accessibility of the majlis and opened up the music to a wider audience, including women in purdah, thereby adding to the popularity of Shiism*.' Some women, including courtesans,

---

disciple in Lucknow, Chajju Khan, who was reputed to be his son; the descendants of fêted Delhi qawwals Shaikh Moin-ud-din, Shaikh Kabir, Allah Banda, and many others.

*According to one estimate, up to 85 per cent of Lucknow tawaifs were Shia by birth or conversion.

became expert in the singing of soz and marsiya and memoirist Sharar describes an occasion during which '...at Muharram, thousands of enthusiasts came to Lucknow from other places and sat hopefully in Haidar's imambara waiting for the courtesan Lady Haidar to commence her song of lament (soz).'

Despite the fact that the fine arts remained the prerogative of the elite classes, there is some indication that the famous Lucknawi refinement and musicality did not leave the other classes indifferent. According to Sharar, 'sometimes bazar boys have been heard singing bhairvin, sohni, behag* and other ragas with such excellence that those who heard them were entranced and the greatest singers envied them.'

And if there were women who might have been proficient in one or the other aspect of Lucknawi culture, it was only the tawaif who commanded a complete mastery of all aspects of this intricate and nuanced world. This, after all, was a time and place in which very little time or money was invested in the education or culture of ordinary women. Abbe Dubois, the enlightened French missionary†, has described the abysmal state of neglect in which most women in India were kept at the time‡:

> (Women) in India do not occupy a place much higher than that of a slave. Destined only to satisfy the physical needs of men, they are judged incapable of acquiring any degree of mental capacity which would render them useful in the daily intercourse of life. It is generally understood that a woman can only exist in state of utter dependence, and that she may never become mistress of her own destiny. Because of this attitude, the education of women is completely neglected. In no way is the understanding of young girls cultivated, even though many of them are naturally ingenious, and would shine under the advantages of education.

---

*Classical ragas or melodic modes.
†This Catholic missionary was the first European to carry out a comprehensive survey of the manners and customs of the Hindus.
‡The dichotomy between the 'cultivated public woman and the domestic wife is founded on customs long prevalent in traditional India. Until colonial times, there does seem to have been a split between females who are keepers of culture and females who are keepers of the home. The former are considered to be unmarried, unchaste, attached to a matrilineal kin group, economically independent and educated to a degree; the latter are recognized as being married, chaste, embedded in a patrilineal kin group upon which the wife is economically dependent and uneducated in spheres unrelated to the home.' *The Courtesan's Arts*, pp. 164–65.

Because of the state of utter degradation that women are kept in, it is thought quite sufficient in India that a woman can grind and boil their rice or attend to the other household concerns, which are neither numerous nor difficult to acquire. Courtesans...are the only ones allowed to learn to read, to sing and to dance....
A modest woman would be ashamed to admit she could read.

Given the lack of companionship from conjugal life that was encouraged in most homes, it is not surprising that many elite men would be utterly captivated by courtesans who could quote poetry, sing, and dance enchantingly, and expertly engage in piquant conversations with the men. Women, moreover, in whom the art of seduction was so fine as to appear entirely natural and who could speak openly and laughingly about love and longing. It is amusing, if tragic, that Abbe Dubois quotes an instance in which a young married man tried to show some affection to his wife in public. The outraged young woman complained that 'such behaviour covers me in shame. Has he become a firangi, and does he think I too am of a similarly vile condition?'

But 'by the end of the nineteenth century,' writes scholar Saleem Kidwai, 'tawaif had become an impolite word not used in genteel conversation; in the popular mindset the tawaif was equated to a whore.' The awestruck appreciation of some of the eighteenth-century Europeans would harden very soon into contempt. Victorian ideals would classify these women as indecent, and Indian society would turn its back on what had once beguiled and fascinated it. The brutal elision of these women and their contribution to Indian society would be complete. Almost nothing remains of the writings of the most educated women of their times. Dancer and scholar Manjari Chaturvedi points out that while society appropriated all the elements of their artistry—the thumri and the ghazal, the jewellery, the farshi pants, kathak dance—the tawaif herself would be deemed a 'fallen woman' while her male counterpart was acknowledged as an ustad. But in the late eighteenth century, armed with her husky voice and molten gaze, the tawaif of Lucknow was preparing to break a million hearts.

# THE ROOSTER AND THE TIGER

At the very time that Asaf was beginning to commemorate Muharram in the largest imambara in the world, a very different scene was playing out at the distant court of King Louis XVI of France. On a sultry day in August 1788, three men walked side by side into the majestic Hercules Salon in the Chateau de Versailles outside Paris. Renovated by Louis XIV in 1736, the Hercules Salon was a celebration of opulence with its fine marbles, luminous gilt, elaborate bronzes, and large oil paintings including an immense painting on the theme of *The Apotheosis of Hercules* that covered the entire vaulted ceiling. The men would not have had much time to admire the paintings, however, for waiting for them on a throne placed against the fireplace at the end of the room was the king of France himself—the cherubic, portly and benign Louis XVI. All around the king were his great courtiers and the first noblemen of the land and on both sides of the room, clustered within specially constructed enclosures, were members of the royal family. To the left waited Marie-Antoinette, queen of France, slim, pale face overshadowed by a towering wig powdered gun-metal grey and quivering with ostrich feathers. With her was Madame Elizabeth, devoted sister of the king, pious and uncompromisingly royalist, and the little Mousseline (Marie-Thérèse Charlotte), ten-year-old daughter of Marie-Antoinette and Louis XVI*.

As they entered the room, the three men bent to salaam the king, bringing their right hand to their head. They then walked to the middle of the room and salaamed once again in the saturated light as the ladies fanned themselves and leaned forward breathlessly in a rustling, clinking mass of silks and pearls to admire the jewels the men wore and the fine, gold-lit muslin of their clothes that trailed ever so ephemerally the scent of roses. One of the men then advanced up to the throne of the king and salaamed a third time, at which point Louis XVI took off his tricorne to greet his guests for these three men were the ambassadors† of the mighty Tipu Sultan of Mysore, son of the great Hyder Ali Khan

---

*The entire family, except young Mousseline, would be guillotined within a few years after the French Revolution.
†This was the first embassy sent by an Indian ruler to a European nation.

and long-term ally of the French. After the king had accepted a token gold mohur from each of the men, the interpreter read out the letter that the chief ambassador, the handsome and elegantly white-bearded Darwesh Khan, handed to him. The letter reminded the king that Hyder Ali had been 'the most faithful ally' of the French king, and had died in battle 'for the cause of the French'. His son, Tipu Sultan, now wished 'to strengthen the bonds of friendship that had lasted more than 30 years' between France and Mysore*. The king politely replied that he 'would never forget the constancy and the greatness of the late Hyder Ali Khan, faithful ally, and that he recognized the same virtues in his son Tipu Sultan.' Royal pleasantries exchanged, the three men took a moment to admire the perfumed, periwigged, and shimmering and whispering crowd in their glinting lightweight silks, before taking their leave of the king.

Much had changed in the previous decade to unsettle the long-standing alliance between Mysore and France. With the signing of the Peace of Paris in 1783 at the end of the American Revolution, Louis XVI had agreed to a peace treaty with the British with the immediate cessation of all hostilities everywhere in the world. This also meant that the French had to stop waging war in India against the British, a decision which enraged Tipu Sultan. The French crown was moreover crippled with mounting debt after French involvement in the American Revolution and was leery of further military engagements on distant shores. Many French officials were dismayed by this result, especially since the most famous naval commander of the eighteenth century, Admiral Suffren, had had to stop engaging with British naval forces in 1783 just as he had won a series of devastating battles against the British in the Indian Ocean. Not long before his death, Hyder Ali had lamented that 'I can defeat them (the English) on land, but I cannot swallow the sea.' It was widely held that had the eccentric and redoubtable Suffren—admiringly nicknamed Admiral Satan by those who witnessed his quasi-demonic energy during battles—been allowed to continue fighting the British 'English power would probably have received a terrible blow in India.'

But the French were keen to re-establish commercial relations

---

*Despite assertions of friendship, no formal alliance or treaty was ever signed between France and Mysore, as the Treaty of Versailles in 1783 had put an end to all attempts to do so.

with Mysore, especially for the Indian cotton which was so prized in Europe. And Tipu, though he was furious that the French had withdrawn military aid, 'was seeking to transform Mysore into a global economic power based on the production and exchange of Indian cotton and silk textiles, pearls and other goods, and he saw the value of trading with France'. As for trading with the British, Tipu had explained to French merchant and captain Pierre Antoine Monneron all the measures that he was taking to prevent them from plundering the riches of his country. 'I prohibited the export of linen from my states by the Carnatic route because I know that the English are doing considerable business with it and I do not want to contribute to their profits (or richness).' Nor had Tipu entirely given up hope that the French might help him militarily against the English and it was to carry out these various missions that the sultan had decided to send an embassy to the court of Louis XVI.

The three men chosen for the mission were Muhammad Darwesh Khan, Akbar Ali Khan, and Muhammad Ousman Khan and in addition to creating an alliance, they were charged with procuring French artisans and engineers, gardeners and physicians, manufacturers of porcelain, glassware, clocks, weapons, and wool. Because the British representation of Tipu Sultan would focus so overwhelmingly on his battles, and then on his death in battle, it is easy to forget that Tipu worked tirelessly to transform Mysore into an economically vibrant country. Scholars have shown that ferocious confrontations with the British forcibly brought about huge improvements in Mysore in 'agriculture, commerce, manufacture and technology'. Tipu understood that it was trade and industry which had given such an advantage to the countries of western Europe and resolved to power his country into prosperity through the same means. He sent embassies and agents to Burma, Persia, Oman, and China, carrying spices, clothes, jewels, and ivory. From France he asked for craftsmen to be sent to Mysore for the manufacture of muskets and cannon-pieces, clockmakers, producers of Sèvres porcelain, makers of glass and mirrors, astronomers, physicians, wool-carders, textile-makers, weavers, physicians, and more. Darwesh Khan and his companions would have been pleased to find in the entourage assigned to them in Paris an old India hand—Jean-Baptiste Gentil who had served Shuja for twelve years. Gentil accompanied the

Mysoreans everywhere, and served as their translator.

The ambassadors were particularly amazed by the factories they visited, especially the wallpaper manufacturers, the printing press, and the mint. They attended banquets held by the factory owners and told Gentil that they were taken aback by the great wealth accumulated by the merchants in France. 'A banian in France is worth as much as a raja in India,' they exclaimed. 'His factory is as well run as a small province. M Reveillon* is like a governor, and the workers are the inhabitants.' They were also charmed by the French women they encountered, many of whom came out in great numbers at the banquets and on the streets to meet these exotic visitors. When one of these ladies asked Akbar Ali Khan what he thought of France, the gallant Mysorean replied: 'Madame, France is like an immense and magnificent garden, in which you are the flowers.'

Some sense of the fascinating exoticism of these men can be gauged by the reaction of French painter Elisabeth Vigée Le Brun. This celebrated painter of the French queen Marie-Antoinette was astounded when confronted with the Mysorean delegation at the Opera. 'I saw these Indians at the opera', she wrote, 'and they appeared to me so picturesque that I thought I should like to paint them. But as they communicated to their interpreter that they would never allow themselves to be painted unless the request came from the King, I managed to secure that favour from his Majesty.' Vigée le Brun convinced the ambassadors to sit for their portraits, and went to visit them armed with large canvases and paints. She was taken aback to have rose water sprinkled on her but greatly admired the 'superb physiognomies' of the two men, despite their 'bronze complexions'. Darwesh Khan struck a pose with such natural grace and confidence that Vigée le Brun painted him just as he chose, standing majestically against the draperies, sword in hand. The resulting portrait (image 33) is an extraordinary statement that combines virile power, exotic otherness, and luxurious excess. Darwesh Khan stands proud and assured in his rich white muslin robes sprinkled with gold flowers, intelligence and humour shadowing his face. Their appearance on the great boulevards of Paris similarly caused a frenzy of excitement among the people, 'whose interest is always piqued by novelty, and

---
*Owner of the famous French wallpaper factory.

who were more interested in the exotic costumes of these foreigners than the important mission they were charged with'.

For a short while, Tipu Sultan would become an unlikely fashion icon and cultural celebrity in Paris, his ambassadors besieged by adoring crowds wherever they went. Writing in 1801, Joseph-François Michaud admitted reprovingly that:

> The arrival of the 3 Indians in Paris was a spectacle for the capital, they filled all the conversations, were the object of all attention, and the name of Tippoo-Saib enjoyed a moment of celebrity amongst a superficial people, who were struck more by the originality of the Asian costumes than by the importance of our possessions in India.

The naval minister agreed that 'they cannot take one step outside without it being general gossip'. Throngs of curious people crowded the underground kitchens to watch, agog, the ambassadors' 'spicy food' being prepared, while in the city of Brest, where they were to set sail for India, the ambassadors were dazed by the riotous cheers of the schoolboys who had gathered to wave them home.

Interest in Tipu Sultan's affairs was feverishly high in France in these years, aided in no small measure by the drama that was taking place across the channel. The impeachment trial of Warren Hastings had begun in February 1788 and so impassioned was the oratory of the minister bringing the charges against Hastings, Edmund Burke, that women were being carried out fainting from Westminster Hall, quite overcome. When the charges were brought in on behalf of the begums of Awadh, spectators paid 50 pounds a seat to enjoy the full unfolding of the drama in court. Across the channel in France, the fact that these high voltage events were taking place in the country of their traditional enemies spiked the interest of the French in affairs in India in general, and in Tipu in particular.

Tipu's embassy to France resulted in a flurry of representations of the Sultan and his men, including paintings on porcelain, etchings, and engravings. While the British would depict the Sultan as a snarling, deranged megalomaniac and despot, French representations showed the Mysoreans as dignified, stately, and powerful, on an equal footing with their European counterparts. Jasanoff has shown that it was precisely Mysore's close ties with their dreaded enemy France that made of Tipu Sultan and Hyder Ali 'such potent figures of villainy' in Britain. Tipu Sultan, who understood very well the power of symbols and imagery, would have been well pleased. The sultan's personal idol, and the patron of his empire after the death of his father, was Imam Ali, prophet Muhammad's son-in-law. Prophet Muhammad had honoured Ali with the title 'Lion of God' because he had fought with such faultless valour for the Prophet. Tipu too had been forged in the fire of the battlefield from a very young age and had proved his heroism in battle time and again. In India the word 'Asad', or lion,* can also be translated as 'sher', or tiger and Tipu would use the symbology of the tiger to cleave to himself its terrifying power and charisma. Tipu, unlike his illiterate father, Hyder Ali, was born a prince and educated in all the nuances of the multi-layered world he had inherited. His banner had a stylized calligraphic tiger mask that read Asad Allah ul-Ghalib—the Victorious Lion of God. The symbol of the tiger stripe was present everywhere in Mysore and flickered like fire on the cloth of Tipu's tents, and on the uniforms of his soldiers. His glittering throne was fashioned in the shape of a life-sized tiger. Above Tipu's arms were letters which spelt the initials: The Lion of God is the Conqueror. Tipu might have been less impressed with the symbol of his allies, the Bourbon kings' lineage that Louis XVI belonged to—the rooster. Nonetheless this unassuming creature, sign of hope and faith, would come to represent French identity within a year, at the time of the French Revolution.

The regiment of French soldiers that Tipu had dreamt of commanding himself at Seringapatam never did materialize, for the timing of the Mysore embassy was catastrophically wrong. Many of the simmering tensions that had erupted into the American Revolution in 1778 were mirrored in France, a decade later. Class inequalities and dissatisfaction, with both countries focusing their angst and anxieties on a hated monarch, whether George III of Britain or Louis XVI of France. Moreover, many of the key French players in the American Revolution brought those revolutionary ideals back to France, most notably the Marquis de Lafayette†.

---

*Similarly, the word Hyder also means lion, translated as tiger in India.
†Lafayette would go on to draft the *Declaration of the Rights of Man and of the Citizen* with

French society was in the throes of severe anxiety about France's place in the global economy and the resulting risk to French culture and domestic trade. There was anxiety, also, about the threat to French textiles from the influx of British imported textiles which were primarily plain and printed Indian cotton. This Anglomania had flooded the French market with dresses 'a l'anglaise', undermining French textiles. The opulence of the Mysorean embassy, and the possibility of oriental excess and decadence that they could be said to represent was also troublingly associated with the growing aversion in French society to the excesses of French royalty, symbolized by the despised 'foreign'* Queen Marie-Antoinette. The French government was also uncertain about how the embassy might be viewed by their great rivals, the British. All these factors led to terminal indecision by the monarchy, and Louis XVI vacillated endlessly about the way in which to interact with Tipu and his ambassadors. In the end, rather than send a mighty army, Louis XVI 'preferred to strengthen the Mysorean bond by sending 98 artisans, a Sevres porcelain service, and some plants, seeds and bulbs for the Jardin du Roi'.

---

the help of Thomas Jefferson
*Marie-Antoinette was the Archduchess of Austria, and as her unpopularity grew, she came to be considered increasingly as a foreign influence.

# CLAUDE MARTIN IN MYSORE

Assailed on all fronts by waves of dissatisfaction and rage that threatened to gather into an overwhelming force, Louis XVI reacted in the only way he knew how—by seeking comfort in the mechanical objects that were his abiding passion. As spring turned to summer in Paris in 1789, his usual lassitude deepened into melancholia because of the death of the young Dauphin,* and the king ignored the clamouring, desperately hungry crowds and the gargantuan fiscal problems brought about by France's wars. The staccato rhythms of his clocks might have brought the gentle Louis XVI some solace, but they were to be his undoing. The king's lethargy and inertia would have well-known catastrophic results for the monarchy in France, but they would also have disastrous consequences for Tipu Sultan of Mysore.

Not only did Louis XVI's unwillingness to sign a military alliance with Mysore leave Tipu isolated and surrounded by enemies, but it also propelled the forces of the EIC into an angry offensive. After the loss of the American Colonies, Britain had been forced into a reckoning about its place in the world and the righteousness of its cause. Part of that moral reckoning would result in the trial for impeachment of Hastings, in which one man would stand trial for the evils of the British empire. The loss of the American Revolution would cause a crisis about the competence of the British ruling classes in general, but 'it would be madness to imagine that simple reasoning would cure Europeans of the gangrenous evil of conquests, invasions etc.' wrote French philosopher Anquetil-Duperron. 'There are tribunals for petty criminals; but the great, like the lion, can break those chains.' It was clear that the empire itself could not fall and instead France would be thwarted in every attempt to foment trouble in India, the nightmare of Yorktown exorcised once and for all.

France had tried to maintain a semblance of a united front between the three strongest powers in the Deccan—the Marathas, the nizam of Hyderabad, and Tipu Sultan—against their common enemy, the British Company. But with Louis XVI vacillating and France in the throes of

---

*In France, the eldest son of the king, the heir apparent, was called the Dauphin, the Dolphin. Louis XVI's eldest son, Louis Joseph, died at the age of seven of tuberculosis in June 1789.

revolution that uneasy alliance, always fragile, was exploited by the British and soon crumbled. Instead, it was the British Company that benefitted from the alarm that Tipu's energetically expansionist policies excited in his neighbours—the Marathas and the nizam of Hyderabad—and in 1790 they signed a Tripartite Treaty with both these powers. The Company was also 'in the unusual position of being at peace in both Europe and India', with the further comforting knowledge that three new regiments of European soldiers had arrived at Bombay. The Company had further aligned itself with the raja of Travancore, Rama Varma, and when news arrived that Tipu was preparing to invade Travancore in 1790, they found the perfect reason to attack the sultan in turn, hostilities that would launch the third Anglo-Mysore war and change the fate of Mysore and its sultan altogether.

In the beginning, the Third Anglo-Mysore War proceeded as per plan for Tipu, with the sultan moving at lightning speed right up to Trichinopoly in December 1790, decimating the Company forces he met along the way. But Cornwallis, 'regarded by many as responsible for the loss of the American colonies', was not about to be cowed by this demonstration of military power. Cornwallis, that brusque old soldier and veteran of the catastrophic defeat in America, was ready to use any reason to attack Tipu, with or without the support of the Calcutta council. According to historian Jean Marie Lafont, Cornwallis's unofficial mandate was 'to prevent the French from doing in India what they had done in America, and to protect the principal source of finance (India) for the English to carry out their world politics'.

And it was Cornwallis himself who would personally lead the charge against Tipu, after an initial encounter led by Captain William Medows ended in defeat. With just such a victory could Cornwallis hope to redeem his humiliation at having surrendered to the French at Yorktown. Cornwallis had been sent to India with even more power than Hastings had had, and with the complete backing of the British king and prime minister.* With the board of the EIC hustling to assert itself over the Company's directors, Cornwallis 'did not hesitate to act independently...in making war in Mysore.' Cornwallis had already

---

*Parliament granted Cornwallis full powers without prior reference to London or the supreme council in India. He was appointed commander-in-chief of the armies, regular and company.

prepared his case against Tipu, writing about him that he was:

> A Prince of very uncommon ability and of boundless ambition, who had acquired a degree of power in extent of territory, in wealth, and in forces that threatened the Company's possessions in the Carnatic and those of all his other neighbours with imminent danger.

Historian Kate Brittlebank, however, writes that 'unlike the British, Tipu regarded the treaties he signed as binding', and that it was instead the Company that worked tirelessly to undermine the Sultan's power among his neighbours. Duperron agreed that 'when the English offered aid to an Indian Prince against another Prince, it was always because of a quarrel that they have incited themselves.' And while no help would be forthcoming for Tipu from France, the French Governor of Mauritius,* Cossigny, was planning to help the sultan with 'good advice'. When Tipu wrote to the governor for help against the Company, Cossigny was deliberately vague about what he could do. 'The French are making big preparations of war since one year,' he wrote to Tipu, mysteriously adding that 'I cannot now tell you everything about it but be sure that they (the French) have understood what you told me.' When Tipu requested a force of 5,000 troops, Cossigny offered him the following advice:

> Do not engage in big battles but attack your enemies as often as possible to fatigue them. Do not allow them to have food or fodder... write to the Marathas and the Nizam; tell them your interests, that your enemies are also theirs... the time has come to get rid of all those enemies. Make big monetary sacrifices, trust in what I tell you... what is the use of money? I hope your fame will surpass your father's, your father showed the way to Delhi.

In private, Cossigny was rather more circumspect about Tipu's chances against the famed military Governor General of the EIC.

---

*Mauritius was first colonized by the Dutch in 1638, who named the island in honour of Prince Maurice of Nassau. They then abandoned the colony in 1710, and the French claimed it in 1715, renaming it Mauritius. It became a prosperous colony under the French EIC, with the French government taking it over in 1767. It served as a naval base for the later Napoleonic Wars but the British would seize it in 1810.

(Tipu) is quite intelligent and knows quite a lot of things, but he is ambitious and longs for glory. He is quite gifted for war and takes his position in a country he knows very well. He works hard and detests pleasure. That is quite all right, but Cornwallis also is a big man and he has gathered at this instance the strength of four presidencies. It is very much against the prince who has recently established his power, who is more feared than loved.

Riding to war alongside Cornwallis as his ADC was a most unlikely figure—the fifty-six-year-old, chronically ill Claude Martin of Lucknow. It is not known if Martin was asked to accompany Cornwallis but it is more likely that he bought his way to what was undoubtedly a prestigious honour. Martin had already ingratiated himself to Cornwallis and his secretary Ross through innumerable gifts and now he organized a troop of horses to be sent to Madras, a gift that he would later insistently invoke as a reason to be rewarded with a promotion. Nawab Asaf-ud-Daula also helped out the Company by sending horses* for their war against Mysore, and 'loans and donations in kind were solicited by the Company from wealthy Indians and Europeans throughout India.' The British themselves appeared somewhat perplexed by the presence of the eccentric and excitable Frenchman, one man noting that 'though at an advanced age and independent in his fortune,' he chose to be present at this dangerous theatre of war.

The war was a protracted and desperately fought one, and more than once hung in the balance. In February 1791 Cornwallis led his troops right into the heart of Tipu's country, and seized the city of Bangalore and prepared to ride even further before becoming dangerously bogged down during the monsoon by lack of supplies, disease, and attrition. But it was at this grim moment that their Maratha allies arrived with supplies and provisions to rescue the starving Company soldiers. De Bussy had written in 1778 about the Marthas' extraordinary ability to keep provision lines open even in battle. 'To ensure the success of an expedition,' he had written, 'it is essential to ally oneself with a power who can procure all the provisions of a market place, and who can provide all the necessary essentials such as bullocks, horses, camels etc; the Marathas are today masters of this

---

*The nawab also provided 200 baggage elephants.

in the entire Mughal empire.' Rested and regrouped, the Company forces, bolstered also by their Hyderabadi and Maratha allies who had joined them, rode out in January 1792 to attack Tipu in his fortress city of Seringapatam. When the combined forces of the three armies arrived at the walls of Seringapatam in February 1792, Cornwallis attacked immediately, taking Tipu completely by surprise. Even as the city was besieged and attacked relentlessly, the Company forces were astonished by the sheer majesty and beauty of Seringapatam and its gardens: '...the sun then shone bright upon its ramparts, and the many sumptuous buildings they surround, and his rays glittered upon the gilded domes of the palace of the Sultan', wrote a young colonel in Cornwallis's army, before admitting 'what satisfaction to return to Calcutta with my sacks of Pagodas.'

And sacks of pagodas there would certainly be. Deserted by his French allies, Tipu was beaten by the Company for the first time and surrendered in February 1792. Cornwallis would then personally oversee the dismemberment of Hyder Ali's once mighty empire. Tipu was forced to concede half of his territories. In addition, the enormous sum of 3 crores and 30 lakh rupees was imposed as 'compensation'* to the Company, for effectively invading his lands. Much against his will and that of his family, Tipu was forced to send two of his young sons as hostages to Cornwallis for the foreseeable future to guarantee his 'good behaviour'. Endless delays over the final peace settlement were caused by the heart-breaking decision the sultan's family had to make over which of his two sons to hand over to their dreaded enemy. Later, the English party were surprised to hear a 21 gun-salute booming out from the Seringapatam fort and were told that it was in gratitude for the kind reception given by Cornwallis to the two boys, by their desperately worried father.

Elderly, ailing, and almost constantly in pain from kidney stones and venereal disease, the eccentric figure of Claude Martin was by the side of Cornwallis when Tipu Sultan surrendered. While Martin may not have participated in any military skirmishing, he did get the

---

*Wellesley's wars were financially ruinous for the Company. Between 1799 and 1807, the Indian debt increased from 10 million pounds to 26 million pounds, leading to his reputation as a military maverick with no regard to costs. (*Richard Wellesley and the Fourth Anglo-Mysore War*, by Ryan Campbell, The Histories, Vol 15, Issue 1, Article 9). The territories ceded to them assured them an income of 40 lakhs.

opportunity to indulge in a favourite hobby—botany. He noted the various kinds of plants that grew in the region, and was interested in a long grass that thrived and was eaten in great quantity by cattle. He sent a specimen plant and some seeds to the superintendent of the Botanic Garden at Calcutta at the time, William Roxburgh; in characteristic excessive manner Martin had not simply observed the plant and its seeds but had even tasted them, writing to Roxburgh that 'if you taste these (seeds), you will note that though they are old, their taste is exceedingly bitter'. He would then successfully grow these plants in Lucknow. He had also observed that Hyder Ali had used the 'Mysore thorn' to grow attractive prickly bushes around his forts and took this plant back with him and introduced it to Bengal, where it became widespread. That Claude Martin was an enthusiastic amateur botanist and a patron of natural history paintings is often overlooked because of his more colourful activities, but in fact he patronized one of the earliest and most extensive collection of such art in India. His entire collection* of paintings would number some 600 plants  Nothing at all on this scale had been commissioned before, and this represents 'the very first attempts by a European to seriously catalogue India's flora and fauna. William Roxburgh noted in his *Flora Indica* that Martin had sent him six plants, one of which he named 'Andropogon Martini' in honour of the Frenchman.

In the Lucknow botanical paintings of Claude Martin, the Mughal visceral emotivity and colour is combined with a European sense of volume and controlled scientific precision. There are flowering plants depicted alongside their fruits, and seeds, for example, showing an overall scientific sensibility, quite apart from the Mughal decorative one. Many of the botanical drawings in the Martin collection are of exceptional quality, though not all are equally luminescent and the collections are clearly the work of a number of artists, all unnamed. They are of typically Indian and South East Asian plants, many of them 'useful' in some way—medicinal, edible, commercial etc. They include paintings of trees, bushes, grasses, garden plants as well as

---

*At some point, Martin's plant and animal drawings were given to, or purchased by, Gore Ouseley, a merchant who was working for the nawab when Martin was living in Lucknow. Ousely left the drawings to his son, and they eventually were purchased for the Royal Botanic Gardens, Kew, where they now remain in their archives.

medicinal plants, like aloe vera and cannabis. This practical aspect resonates perfectly with the patron, who harangued his gardeners constantly about the market price of the fruit trees he grew on his farm at Najafgarh, like mulberry, quince, and pomegranate. Most of the drawings were identified and labelled by Roxburgh, but not everything could be identified and native names appear, in words still familiar today—ganga, urad dal, lobia, matar, amrood, dhaniya, and imli. These original Urdu/Persian native names represent a rare collection of Indian flora before they were claimed and 'colonized' by the West and their Latin nomenclature. These paintings are almost the crucible within which those changes coalesced, and we can sense it happening by reading a letter from the Lucknow physician Dr Robert Bruce, pasted alongside one of the paintings.

> My dear Martin,
>
> The flower is very well done. It is called in botany by a pompous name, the gloriosa superba and is, I fancy, the most beautiful of the Lily tribe. The paper is infinitely superior to the country kind for covering drawings.

On the painting itself, Martin has added with his eccentric spelling that the 'flowers when young, they are tinged with a greenish clour and older with yellow and Read and when above old strong scarlate colour more old the colour incline on Deep crimson and deep bulls Blod'.

Martin had had a painting commissioned, and not knowing its name, sent it for identification to the British doctor living in Lucknow. And so did the agnishikha, the incomparable flame lily, transform into the *Gloriosa superba* on a single sheet of paper (image 34).

There is also a substantial collection of paintings of birds and animals, clearly made in Lucknow, including gorgeous birds whose intricate symmetry of feathers draws in the gaze. The patronage of these drawings is uncertain, as there is nothing that ties them in with certainty to any particular connoisseur. It is possible that some of these birds and animals would have been painted from nature, from the specimens in Asaf's menagerie for example. We know from Abu Talib's extravagant grumblings[*] that the nawab kept a great number of

---

[*] About the money spent on these exotic creatures, including that one pair of snakes was capable of eating up to a 'maund' of flesh.

animals—elephants, rhinoceros, wild buffaloes, horses, dogs, pigeons, roosters, sheep, deer, monkeys, scorpions, snakes, and spiders and much more. Claude Martin also kept some animals on his Najafgarh estate, though far fewer. He notes, for instance, that the storks and the peacocks he kept were allowed one pomegranate a day, and was extremely annoyed when his songbirds died suddenly.

In 1792, as he rode back to Lucknow, Claude Martin would have been well pleased. The Third Anglo-Maratha War had been concluded to the satisfaction of Cornwallis, Martin was richer by 968 pounds* and in his pockets he carried the seeds of the mystifyingly bitter grass. After he returned to Lucknow, he would commission a second set of botanical drawings,† and he would entertain his friends with his accounts of the war. One of the recipients of his Mysore letters, his great friend and one-time Lucknawi, Benoit de Boigne, was meanwhile involved in warfare, under his new patron, Mahadji Scindia.

---

*After military campaigns, the loot seized by the Company from the conquered ruler was divided up amongst the soldiers who participated in the campaign, according to a strict hierarchy of rank. The money the EIC soldiers got was called the prize money, and the total amount of prize money that the EIC obtained in this particular campaign in cash was 45 lakh rupees.
†This set, painted in the 1790s, is now part of the Kew Gardens Archive.

# DE BOIGNE AND THE ARMIES OF HINDUSTAN

On 1 June 1793, Benoit de Boigne, who was making for himself a glorious name as one of the great heroes of the Hindustani battlefield, found himself dangling off a tree in the middle of a battle in a most unmartial manner. 'Do you remember,' he later wrote ruefully to another Frenchman,* 'how I climbed a tree to reconnoitre the enemy and at the exact same time a cannon ball cut off part of the branches of the tree I had climbed on, and killed 4 or 5 ensigns standing next to you.... One must admit that we were lucky that day; the whole enemy army was destroyed and the carnage was awful. Over 18 miles, the road was littered with corpses.'

The bloody confrontation which found de Boigne in this inelegant situation was the Battle of Lakheri in Rajasthan, which he was fighting on behalf of the Maratha warlord Mahadji Scindia against Tukoji Holkar.† After his interlude in Lucknow in the 1780s, de Boigne had joined the service of Scindia and had created the French Brigades of Hindustan, which soon gained a formidable reputation throughout the country. He raised ten infantry battalions‡ of 750 men each, all highly disciplined and trained in the British manner, with Europeans as officers. He also had a train of particularly dashing cavalry, the men in striking green jackets and red turbans, the folds of which were highlighted by silver wire. At full strength, the French Brigades would number 10,000 men under arms, superbly disciplined, and by far the greatest fighting troops raised in India till then. In 1791 Scindia asked de Boigne to create a second brigade, placed under the command of Frenchman Pierre Cuillier-Perron,§ and the regular troops now numbered 18,000 soldiers. When riding to battle in these distant fields, de Boigne's troops unfurled the banner of the white cross of

---
*The future General Perron.
†After the Battle of Panipat in 1761, the hereditary ministers or peshwas lost total control over the Maratha state which then became a confederacy of five chieftains under the nominal leadership of the peshwa. These chieftains, including Scindia and Holkar, were very rarely united, and were often at war.
‡Of these, seven were known as the Telingas, and the other three were Najibs, recruited from among the Pathans.
§French military adventurer (1753–1784), would later become famous as General Perron.

Savoy against a red field, rather than the new tricolour of the French republic.* As for his matchlock men, their command to engage was shouted out in Irish, a quirky reminder of de Boigne's early days in the Irish battalions of France.

With France officially neutral after the conclusion of the American Revolution and the Treaty of 1783, many Indian states had scrambled to recruit the remaining dispersed French officers to train their soldiers against aggressive neighbours, or the EIC. 'The Indian states,' confessed a Frenchman modestly, 'believe that the French are very brave soldiers. And that 1,000 Frenchmen are enough to rout 3,000 Englishmen'. And de Boigne was arguably the most flamboyantly successful of them all in the late eighteenth century. Strikingly tall, with powerful shoulders and piercing blue eyes, the forty-two-year-old de Boigne was a force of nature (image 35). He made up for a somewhat mediocre education with great linguistic skills—he spoke French, Italian, Persian, Urdu, and English fluently—and a truly insatiable and tenacious ambition. He was up at first light to 'visit his arsenal, inspect his troops, enrol new recruits, oversee his 3 brigades, harangue his soldiers, receive ambassadors, administer justice, conduct the affairs of an estate of over 20 lakh rupees.... All this without recourse to a single European, for he was very reluctant to trust anyone.' Leading from the front, and intolerant of the slightest misdemeanour from his men, de Boigne also had the enviable reputation of never having lost any engagement he ever took part in. A Briton he had served with was moved enough to write about De Boigne:

> On the grand stage where he has acted a brilliant and important part for these ten years, he is at once dreaded and idolized. Latterly, the very name of De Boigne conveyed more terror than the thunder of his cannon.... (Najaf Quli Khan) in his last moments advised his begum to resist in the fortress of Cannound, the efforts of his enemies. 'Resist them', he said; 'but if De Boigne appears, yield'.

De Boigne's patron, Mahadji Scindia was a most extraordinary leader. He would be known to posterity simply as the Great Scindia and

---

*A royalist, De Boigne was furious that France had incorporated the Duchy of Savoy into the territory of France post the revolution.

in the last quarter of the eighteenth century, the Marathas were all that stood between the Mughal emperor and desolation. The Maratha general had reinstated Shah Alam on the Delhi throne in 1788 after Ghulam Qadir had blinded him, and had then inflicted prolonged and bloody vengeance upon Ghulam Qadir.* Scindia believed in the need to adapt to European military technology and his trust in de Boigne was complete. De Boigne returned this trust for he was 'religiously faithful to his master, and amidst the most enticing offers to betray he preserved his allegiance unsullied.' This loyalty was deemed to be all the more laudatory for de Boigne was infamously close to his money. In 1792, Scindia was confirmed Naib Vakil-ul-Mulk of Hindustan by the emperor, prompting Palmer to proclaim that '(Scindia) will obtain success in all his other projects with the same ease, as there is no power in Hindustan that can resist him now.'

Following these actions feverishly from Lucknow, de Boigne's friend Claude Martin was quite agog. 'The balance of power will be held by you!' he exclaimed in a letter before continuing, in a vaguely scurrilous tone: 'How glorious to see at your feet the Mughal emperor, Princes and Princesses who seek only your friendship, and God knows what else.' For once, Martin was not exaggerating in claiming that the Mughal royal family was entirely dependent on de Boigne and Scindia's good wishes. Blinded by a once beloved adopted son, betrayed and humiliated, surrounded by enemies, Emperor Shah Alam was a shadow of the young man who had so confidently and proudly ridden out to war to claim his lost inheritance from the British in Bengal. Now he hunkered in the long shadows of the crumbling fort of a forgotten city, writing piteous letters begging for crumbs.

So wretched was the emperor's condition at this point that the Marathas gave him no money at all, and instead simply sent food daily for the emperor and the four† others who constituted his immediate family, while the leftovers were to be scrabbled over by their servants:

---

*Ghulam Qadir was captured by Scindia after his depredations against the emperor. According to a French witness 'he avenged the cruelty he had practised on the emperor by cruelties even more barbarous. He shut him up in a cage, cut off his nose, his ears and his hands, and paraded him on a camel in this condition, prior to throwing his body into a drain.'

†This consisted of the king, his physician, his son and heir, a little favourite daughter, and, by turns, one of his 200 begums at a time.

> Scindhia sets Shah Nizam ud din over the Badshah as the greatest scoundrel they could find... Every day he (Shah Nizam ud din) furnishes the old King with two ser (1.8 kg) of pillaw and 8 ser of meat for himself to get cooked as he likes this, with 2 loaves of bread, about the length each of a cubit, to suffice for breakfast, dinner and supper, and he may get masala where he can.

As for the rest of the extended Mughal family—the queens, concubines, sons and daughters, female slaves and eunuchs—they had to make do with 2 sers a day of barley flour for every three to four persons, to bake into rotis.

In the peaceful, affluent town of Chambery in Savoy, sheltered by the Alps, lies a most extraordinary collection of letters in the de Boigne family archives. There are letters addressed in Persian to Benoit de Boigne from the emperor of Hindustan, as well as from some of the most senior women of the Mughal zenana in the late eighteenth century, including the wife of Emperor Shah Alam and mother of the Mughal heir, Qudsiya Begum* herself. In the 1790s, she wrote to de Boigne to say:

> Since you, my dear son, have taken up my cause, it will all end well. Your devotion is impressed upon my mind. I look upon you as the strength of my right arm. My whole and sole aim is to put the affairs of my son Mirza Akbar in good order. At present there is a rumour of the advance of an army from Persia and Mirza Ahsan Beg, the inveterate enemy of my family. This has taken away my senses. In the event of their approach, take care of us all. Do not leave us alone.

An atmosphere of utter paranoia and distrust soaks through these letters, in which truths lie behind fantasies, and can only be guessed at. The queen sent another letter to de Boigne, hinting that the real secret she wanted to communicate lay within yet another note, secreted inside a sack of almonds and condiments. 'His Majesty (Shah Alam) further gives you positive order,' she then warns, 'not to let the nature of this correspondence transpire upon the mukhtiyar/agent'. This was a season of spies, of betrayals, and degradation. After all, just a few

---

*Not to be confused with the Qudsiya Begum who was the consort of Muhammad Shah Rangeeley and mother of Ahmad Shah Bahadur.

years prior, Ghulam Qadir had stripped naked some of these very women, and had made Mirza Akbar, the queen's son, dress up in drag to dance in front of his jeering, grabbing soldiers.

'My heart burns,' wrote de Boigne in reply to these pleading letters, 'to hear of the straitened circumstances of His Majesty. But at present nothing can be done.' Nonetheless, de Boigne would do what he could to augment the pitiable pension of the royal family, arguing their cause with Mahadji Scindia.

Clues to the tangled threads of de Boigne's history, inextricably woven through the shadowy world of Mughal zenanas and Anglo-Indian liaisons, can be glimpsed at in the travel diary of a British civil servant. In 1794, when Thomas Twining* was travelling through central India, he met a very different avatar of de Boigne when he stayed with him in his jagir in present-day Aligarh.† After staying the night in de Boigne's low bungalow set in the middle of a garden, and dining on 'pillaus, curries, fish, poultry and kid', he attended a durbar that de Boigne held with all the local vakils from the surrounding states. De Boigne's customary, severely upright stance and the sharp planes of his face were softened by the trailing hookah he was smoking, and his unfashionably close-cropped steel-grey hair was hidden by a turban. His young son was sitting next to him, 'dressed much as the child of a prince of the country would have been—a sort of turbaned cap, similar to what his father wore, on his head, a handsome shawl over his shoulders, crossing round his waist, and sandals, worked with gold thread on his feet.' All the chieftains and vakils were similarly handsomely dressed with expensive white, orange and green shawls and turbans. Upon entering the room, each man salaamed and courteously offered a nazr to both de Boigne, and his little son, who unhesitatingly reached out and lightly touched each coin with his right hand, watched fondly by his father.

Twining, sitting in a corner, was astounded by the charm of the ceremony, exclaiming that 'no European court could well display more propriety, more delicate tact and grace than did these noble delegates of Hindustan.' Discussing the general's complicated early career, Twining

---

*Of the tea family fame.
†De Boigne had transferred his headquarters to Aligarh in 1791 and proceeded to make the fort one of the strongest in North India. He administered his jagirs very efficiently and began the cultivation of indigo, helped by his friend Claude Martin.

told him that it was 'generally believed in Bengal that he was a native of France' but de Boigne explained that he was in fact from Chambery, in the independent duchy of Savoy*. When he had joined Scindia's service, the Maratha general had agreed that de Boigne need never bear arms against the English but should he chance to meet them on the field of battle, de Boigne clarified to Twining with a laugh, he would certainly engage them.

What Twining witnessed, therefore, was de Boigne's Anglo-Persianate† avatar, which he slipped into quite easily off the battlefield. The difference between him and other Europeans like Polier and Martin was that de Boigne's bibi, Noor Begum, was an elite noblewoman, with all the accompanying advantages of a politically and culturally important zenana. Zenanas were supremely important sites of gossip and information, of intrigue and network formation. With Noor Begum's sister, Faiz Begum, having been given a title by the Emperor Shah Alam, this family would have had inroads into the Mughal royal family itself. It is not surprising, therefore, that de Boigne carried out secret negotiations with the queen mother, as well as with other elite Mughal noblewomen. In the Chambery Archives there is a fascinating letter from Faiz Begum addressed to de Boigne:

> The money which you entrusted me to present to Moushi she refused it, saying, never mind, it is of no consequence, in the future we shall think about this. My lord, she is an influential person; if the sum had been worthy of her position, she would have accepted it. A purse and that sum are returned herewith. Pray do not be offended. You are a great man, she is likewise very respectable, so it matters not. We shall consult together what to offer.

The identity of this 'Moushi'‡ that Faiz Begum tried to forward a purse and a sum of money to on de Boigne's behalf, remains mysterious. She was someone 'very respectable', and, therefore, may have been a senior Mughal noblewoman. She may also have been the mother of another bibi of de Boigne's, for in 1792, he married an adopted daughter of Najaf Quli Khan, a Mughal nobleman and a lieutenant of General Najaf

---

*Savoy would finally become part of France in 1860.
†Strictly speaking, Euro-Persianate.
‡Mother's sister.

Khan. In 1792, Najaf Quli Khan's younger widow offered de Boigne 'her foster-child, Moti Begum,* who had been brought up in music and dancing' in return for his protection for her family. This marriage was viewed with a somewhat jaundiced eye by Palmer, who seemed to consider it a betrayal of Noor Begum. 'Make my affectionate salaams to my sister, the Begum,' he wrote to de Boigne in 1792. 'How will she bear a rival princess?' he added worriedly.

For men like Claude Martin, Polier, Hodges, Zoffany, Humphry, and countless other Company men, the women they entered into liaisons with were usually bought, and so there would have been a great deal more anxiety over the nature of the relationship.† The unease over the nature of these transactions between white men and enslaved Indian women, by nature deeply unequal, was obfuscated by men like Martin who cloaked them in the language of sentiment and affection, and presented them as 'rescue fantasies'. With the exception of Polier, most of these men could speak barely any Urdu or Persian, so even communication with these women would be cursory and limited.

Noor Begum herself had been leading a quiet, self-effacing life in Lucknow while de Boigne was away on campaigns. When Claude Martin's factotum visited her in 1792, he found her very modest in her lodgings and requirements. 'You have in your lady a Treasure, my good friend,' he wrote to de Boigne, delighted. 'She has no will of her own, and (I have) never heard a woman be contented with so little.' By this time Noor Begum had two small children with her—a daughter Banoo Jaan born in 1789, followed by a son, Ali Baksh, in 1791. Even the factotum, Joseph Quieros, was appalled at the heat in Noor Begum's lodgings. 'I have told her...that she should not be so economical,' he wrote aghast. 'At present she has charge of two dear children of yours, who for the sake of saving a few rupees, ought not to be exposed to the danger of too close lodgings.' 'Only you can save her' cautioned Claude Martin as well, finding the young mother

---

*There seems to be some confusion about the name of this girl whom Jadunath Sarkar names Moti Begum. Rosie Llewellyn Jones writes that it was the widow of Najaf Quli Khan who was called Moti (fat) Begum and her daughter was Mehr-un-Nisa.
†Dubra Ghosh found that a third of the women recognized by British men in their wills were servants or slave girls in their households, imparting a distinct sense of illegitimacy and transgression to these liaisons. *Sex and the Family in Colonial India: The Making of Empire*, Cambridge: Cambridge University Press, 2006.

dispirited and melancholic, a few months after de Boigne's 'marriage' to Moti Begum.

Perhaps Noor Begum was only too aware of de Boigne's tenacious frugality and gambled that her own parsimony would endear her to the general and would make it more likely that he would keep her close to him. And, in 1796, when de Boigne finally sailed back to Europe on the *Cronborg*,* after the death of Mahadji Scindia,† he took Noor Begum and her two children with him to England,‡ a very rare occurrence in firangi-Indian liaisons of the time. He also took a fortune estimated at a colossal 400,000 pounds, and a kingdom of Mughal treasures including a sarpesh or turban ornament bestowed by the Mughal emperor, a 'dugdugee' locket of gold and diamonds also given by the emperor, and a large emerald, a keepsake from the raja of Jaipur. Within a year, however, de Boigne would marry Adèle d'Osmond, a beautiful sixteen-year-old impoverished aristocrat,§ while Noor Begum and her children would be abandoned in a small town outside London called Enfield, with a rather paltry yearly allowance of 300 pounds.¶ That de Boigne felt he might be harshly judged by his old clique in India is clear from Palmer's reassuring letter to him in 1799.

> Be assured my friend that my affection for you is in no degree diminished, nor can ever be impaired. I was truly happy to learn the perfect recovery of your health, and now rejoice to find that your felicity is complete by marriage.

Palmer's own relationship with his Indian bibi, Faiz Begum, was rather unique for the time. For most European men, these women would be charming diversions before they went on to marry European women when they returned home. It was almost always the European men who gained greater advantages from what always felt uncomfortably

---

*After de Boigne disembarked in England, the *Cronborg*, a Danish vessel, continued towards Denmark but sank in the Baltic Sea, with all de Boigne's collection of miniatures, books, armoury, carpets, etc.
†In 1794 Mahadji Scindia decided to go to Poona to meet the Peshwa. He fell ill and died on 12 February 1794, aged sixty-three.
‡De Boigne's health also did not permit him to remain, as he was suffering continuously from fevers and 'the flux'.
§She was the daughter of the Marquis d'Osmond, who had fled France during the Revolution.
¶It was suggested to Noor Begum that she could sue de Boigne, presumably for bigamy, but she declined to do so on account of her children.

like a transactional equation. That there was lingering guilt or a sense of a duty owed for ostentatiously honourable men like de Boigne, at least, can be seen in the names of other men's dependants who are among his fastidious lists of legatees. He financially maintained Polier's children,* and sent money to Polier's bibis in India, including for Ramzan and Shaab-e-Barat. He also sent money to one 'Major Gardiner's' bibi, as well as to the two women he left behind in India, one in Aligarh and one in Delhi.

As for the gentle Noor Begum, she would live out the rest of her life in the wooded village of Horsham outside London, having converted to Christianity and been re-born as Helen Bennet[†]. She would cultivate something of an air of eccentricity, staying in bed till midday, 'a-la-Mughal', smoking hookahs, keeping a menagerie, spending money excessively and wearing flashing rings. She would get her twelve-year-old daughter, Ann[‡], to write letters to the absentee de Boigne saying 'Maman is surprised to have received no news from you. She is expecting a letter any day now.' Noor Begum would also write to de Boigne herself, asking him to clear her debts by using phrases that have the faintest whiff of blackmail—'My dear general,' she wrote to de Boigne explaining her expenses, 'all my comfort to look a respectable appearance which are creditable to you and to your son. Almost everybody knows that you are the supporter.'

When he proposed marriage to the French aristocrat, Adèle, de Boigne had failed to disclose anything to her at all about Noor Begum and her children, clearly not considering himself 'married' in any relevant sense. 'Before I did see you,' he wrote to Adèle, 'I had never entertained a decided preference for a matrimonial state...if I have paid a kind of attention and I may say assiduities to some of the fair, I may affirm its having been more by way of diversion and as an amusement to the mind than from an inclination of heart which remained untouched till now, I offer you free from any engagements whatsoever.' But the two would separate in 1804 and Noor Begum may

---

*The identity of 'George Polier' whose education de Boigne ensured remains a mystery. Llewellyn-Jones believes he might have been the son of a third mistress of Polier, one Durdanna, with whom Polier had a son not long before he left India in 1788.
†She was baptised Helen when she converted. Helen was de Boigne's mother's Christian name, while 'Bennet' was the Anglicized version of his first name, Benoit.
‡Banoo Begum, born in 1790, was christened Ann Bennet.

have had some satisfaction in receiving de Boigne's decidedly bitter letter in 1801 after three years of marriage: 'I will content myself in saying that I am a little more happy than I had been for these three years past' he wrote. Meanwhile, Noor Begum was able to write to de Boigne with some spirit in 1806:

> I sincerely hope you will act like a father toward your son. You know He is your son. You may have many more but you are not sure they are yours.

This son was the little Ali Baksh of Twining's recollection, once a small Persianate nobleman in training, now transformed into the young English gentleman Charles-Alexandre,* studying at a boarding school in England, his memories of India fading into his dreams. When Abu Talib† visited Noor Begum outside London in the 1800s, he was delighted to find her looking well, wearing the high-waisted, loose-flowing English gowns fashionable at the time. She greeted him warmly, and sent back a letter for her mother still living in Lucknow. And when Noor Begum died in 1854‡, long after de Boigne,§ she left behind a lengthy and fairly respectable list of creditors including a jeweller, a boot-maker, a maker of wallpaper, a saddler, a surgeon, a ladies' tailor and, rather like Cleopatra, a supplier of asses' milk.

---

*Noor Begum's son Charles would be recognized as de Boigne's heir, and de Boigne would have no other sons. The current Comte Pierre-Edouard de Boigne is a direct descendant of Charles aka Ali Baksh, and I am truly grateful for his generosity in allowing me access to the family archives in Chambery.
†Abu Talib wrote an entertaining account of his travels to Britain, Europe, and Asia Minor. On his return from Britain, he was known as Abu Talib e-Landani—Abu Talib from London.
‡Noor Begum's grave in the old cemetery of St Mary's in the town of Horsham near London is still visited by curious tourists. Her grave is perpendicular to all the other graves, and faces east-west, in the direction of Mecca, instead of north-south like the other graves.
§De Boigne died in 1830 in Chambery, at the castle of Buisson Rond and his son Charles-Alexander.

# THE AGE OF SPLENDOUR

Every day half an hour before dawn in Faizabad, while the sellers of attar, flowers, paan, and hookahs still slumbered in their quarters above their shops in the Chowk Bazar, a man would slip out of Bahu Begum's Moti Mahal. He walked on silent feet past the slumbering urdubegi women guards, nodded at the yawning infantry guards and then past the Mewatis marching stiffly part the palace walls. He was tall and simply dressed, and climbed into the palanquin that was waiting for him. Shuffling through the gloom, the palanquin would stop in front of a large house, the attendants signalling their arrival with a loud 'Bismillah!' The man's house was fastidiously clean and impeccably decorated, with rich furnishings of carpets, curtains and masses of embroidered cushions in velvet and silk. An hour after sunrise the man was served breakfast—a variety of fragrant meat dishes and spicy pickles laid out on a gleaming white dastarkhwan. As the sun curved through the sky, the man's life unfolded to a strict routine, as he attended to Bahu Begum's durbar, and spent time in prayer, and in sober conversations with erudite and learned men, discussing religious matters or political gossip from Delhi. In the evenings, the man climbed up to the roof of his terrace and practised archery with a few chosen companions. Wherever he went, he was attended by a throng of followers—matchlock men, servants, mace-bearers, soldiers, and friends. Late at night, all duties completed, he would return to spend the night in the most privileged place in Faizabad—Bahu Begum's sleeping chamber, where there would be a woman massaging the begum's limbs, while another spun intricate stories in the fragrant night in a sonorous voice which gently lulled the begum to sleep.

The man who had such exceptional access to Bahu Begum's most private quarters, and who lived a life of such ordered fastness was not a great nobleman of Faizabad, but one of its most famous khwajasaras, Jawahar Ali Khan. After Asaf shifted to Lucknow in 1775, a great many courtiers and noblemen followed him there, leaving Faizabad to become the domain of the begums from the old families, and of the khwajasaras. And the most powerful khwajasara during the lifetime of Bahu Begum was Jawahar Ali Khan. In the glory days of Shuja-ud-Daula, he had had a throng of scholarly and literary men in his entourage, but many had been lured away by Asaf to Lucknow, to that beguiling city of dreams spun in white and gold. But Jawahar had managed to retain two esteemed companions—Munshi Lacchmi Narayan, a khatri from Lahore, who was famous for writing exquisite Persian poetry and prose, and Shaikh Muhammad Khalil, the calligrapher who had mastered eighteen forms of handwriting.

The khwajasaras surrounded themselves with 'chelas', adopted sons or acolytes, followers, petitioners, staff and soldiers, but at their death all their wealth and properties reverted to their masters. And so they spent money with an exuberant ferocity that gilded their reputations as generous men, the most fulsome accolade an Awadhi could ever obtain. An itinerant Iranian peddler once came from Kabul to Awadh, bearing the warm, stolid clothes typical of those cold climates, lured by the stories of the wealth of Awadh. Jawahar bought up all his goods, to the horror of his treasurer who was aghast because 'these clothes are not the sort in fashion here.' But Jawahar reasoned that 'this poor Mughal has travelled a long way in the hope of profit. He has come to Lucknow thinking Hindustan a rich country and its inhabitants wealthy.' But all the Lucknawis, dressed as they were in fashionable and expensive mulmul and kamkhwab, sniggered at the rough, loose robes the merchant sold and so it was for Jawahar to maintain the immaculate reputation for generosity of Hindustan.

The chelas and acolytes were meant to offer some bulwark against an intemperate social order, and the khwajasaras spent money and time to cultivate men of culture and education. Faiz Baksh wrote that of all things, Jawahar was most fond of 'companions, servants and cavalry'. A scholar has pointed out that 'the conspicuous consumption of followers also fulfilled a function in absorbing labour and providing employment outside the agrarian economy. This was itself a mark of royalty...'

But if the khwajasaras secured their reputations by ostensible acts of largesse and extravagance, then they were limited by the wealth and prestige of their masters. And so there was always simmering tension between the khwajasaras of the two great begums of Faizabad, since Bahu Begum's khwajasaras were a great deal more wealthy than those of Nawab Begum. Similarly, when important courtiers like

Hasan Reza Khan or indeed Asaf himself visited from Lucknow, the begums' khwajasaras were prickly with the perceived slights to their status. On one occasion, on a cool winter morning, a discussion on theology was organized between two opposing maulvis at one of Bahu Begum's khwajasaras'* spacious house. Word spread through town and hundreds of townsfolk rushed to listen to what promised to be a satisfyingly fiery discussion. Between the khwajasaras' servants and followers, the townsfolk and curious onlookers, some fifteen hundred people were crammed in and around the courtyard and arched verandas of the house, while others milled around outside in a noisome mass. As the discussion got increasingly heated, and was punctuated by loud acclamations and shouts from inside the house, the armed followers of the khwajasaras thought that some great injury had happened to their master. Mischief-makers added to the confusion by pulling off peoples' turbans and throwing them into wells, while another group of louts brandished swords and daggers and whirled and jumped around, furiously stabbing the air. 'It was a marvellous tumult', wrote Faiz Baksh, which threatened to disintegrate into mayhem. Since Jawahar had by far the greatest number of armed men present, some five hundred in all, they were the most dangerous and he had to push through the crowd and scramble onto the roof so they could see him, and satisfy themselves that he had not, in fact, been murdered by another khwajasara's servants.

Aside from these minor diversions, wrote Faiz Baksh, 'in Faizabad during the days of the Bahu Begum, her employees and servants, great and small, enjoyed peace and security. They had neither the hardships of a campaign, nor the griefs of war and battle to undergo. They drew their salaries month by month, paid to them even in advance, in full and without deduction and drawback. And every man lived happy and contented night and day.'

And with no war to occupy these men, a lot of the entertainment was procured by elaborate and posturing demonstrations of power between the various rival khwajasara gangs. A great deal of effort was spent in horse-riding, archery, and hawking. One famous practitioner could ride down the fields standing on two horses galloping side by side, urging the frothing beasts to greater speed. Another arresting trick

---

*Bahar Ali Khan.

he performed on a galloping horse was to clamber down the horse's belly and climb back on to the saddle from the other side. Yet another khwajasara, Mahbub Ali Khan, was said to be 'free and easy going and very fond of music and singing'. Whenever a professional singer was known to be in Faizabad, he insisted with presents and persuasion to have them perform at his house. He used his charm and smooth talking to get away with the most flagrant offences, including leaving Bahu Begum's durbar without permission. He would be arrested and brought back, wrote Faiz Baksh with some bitterness, but never punished as he deserved to be.

A great deal of Faizabad's panache was thus built on elaborate chicanery of one kind or another. The khwajasaras, though emasculated, were the equivalent of virile and elite noblemen; illiterate acolytes were mistaken for smooth-talking, eloquent, and erudite Persian speakers; swelling entourages and teeming servants were left unpaid for months, an illusion of largesse and excess carefully created. When Bahu Begum ordered goods from the bazar, for example, she would imperiously name a price she thought fair. Her agent would then pay the shopkeepers a much higher price, absorbing the difference himself. Another courtier was famous for not paying Nawab Begum's staff for six months at a time due to lack of funds, but did so in such a charmingly sincere manner that the staff came away well pleased, comforted by his endearing apologies.

Interestingly, the art of elaborate artifice entered the highly competitive domain of food as well. As Lucknawi cuisine became ever more elaborate, a celebrated element became the art of dissimulation and surprise. Sometimes, an entire meal was prepared using a single ingredient, cooked in enterprising ways, a technique called a pehle, or riddle. Almonds, for example, were painstakingly shaped to look like rice in a pulao dish, or a sweet dish like murabba was presented to look like a savoury qorma. A Kashmiri dish that became popular at this time was the shab degh, a slow-cooked stew of minced meatballs and turnip, wherein it was impossible to tell the two main ingredients apart.

Nonetheless, Bahu Begum had loosened by a fraction the ferocious grip she had maintained on the hierarchy of respect owed to her. For a long time, no inferior wife or concubine of Shuja's was allowed anywhere near her presence. But, after many years, these unfortunate women whose lives had been circumscribed by the walls of the Khurd Mahal, begged Bahu Begum that they be permitted to attend upon her and be allowed to enjoy the gardens too. The begum's relenting betrayed an edge of cruelty for while she rode on ahead in a magisterial sedan, preceded by drummers astride camels and horses, these lesser wives lumbered behind her on hired bullock carts, a most humble means of transportation. This rath they travelled in consisted of a seat the size of a large bed, with a dome-shaped roof and curtains hanging from all four sides. And, when in her presence, these women could never sit down, but had to remain standing quietly in front of her, while the begum sat at her ease amidst bolsters and cushions draped in pearls, jewels, and embroideries. And only now, after Shuja's death, were some of his other sons like Mirza Mangli and Mirza Jangli* allowed to visit her.

The reduced circumstances of the concubines and lesser wives of Shuja was noted by Abu Talib† who roundly blamed Haider Beg Khan, since it would have been his job to apportion suitable pensions to these women from the nawab's treasury, even while Nawab Begum gave these women a certain stipend. Even the other sons of Shuja were not being paid their pensions of 1,000 rupees and were 'starving owing to his breaches of faith, his doings and his affronts'. As for the women at Faizabad

> (they) are sometimes so overpowered by hunger, because of the delay in paying their allowances, that a hundred or two hundred females make a raid from the haramsara, loot the bazar and carry back with them grain and other necessaries. Up to the present (1799) no one has arranged for the marriage of any of his daughters, because funds are not found.

Nonetheless, these instances were recorded as having occurred early in the reign of Asaf-ud-Daula, and the nawab soon arranged for these women to have a more regular pension.

When they visited Bahu Begum, these lesser wives would have been careful to wear the most conservative of clothes. Not for them the

---

*Mirza Jangli had left Faizabad in 1779 for want of funds to join the service of Mir Jaffer's son, Mubarak-al-Daula. He remained with that prince till his death in 1794, then returned to Lucknow.
†It must be remembered that Abu Talib did not prosper at Asaf's court, and would later join British service and actively encourage the assumption of power by the Company.

increasingly fitted and revealing angiyas and clothes that the Lucknawi women were flaunting, influenced in some part by the popularity of the courtesans' elaborate costumes. In Faizabad, the two great begums maintained the decorum reminiscent of the older Mughal days of Delhi, when elite Muslim women had worn loose, layered clothes similar in style to the men. Whenever they left their home, they covered themselves with a thick chador over their head and across their shoulders. No doubt they would have muttered disapprovingly about the new Lucknawi styles—the tight, figure-hugging peshwaz, the outrageous, transparent odhanis and the ridiculous farshi pyjamas which were getting ever wider and longer. As for the colours, a range of scandalously bright hues reflecting the Awadhi countryside was being paraded by the Lucknow nobility—amrasi or saffron yellow to recall a ripe mango, jamuni (violet) from the fruit, baigani purple from brinjal, gopi chandani (pale yellow), totai (parrot green), and dhani (paddy fields).

From within their palaces in the Moti Mahal and Moti Bagh, Bahu Begum and Nawab Begum maintained their courts, held majlis during Muharram, kept up a lifestyle that required hundreds of skilled workers, and organized what was the bedrock of elite society—marital alliances. They both had adopted daughters, Bibi Luft-un-Nisa Begum and Bibi Ashuran respectively, and they arranged for elaborate wedding ceremonies with appropriate grooms. Enormous sums of money were spent over months, in the making of furniture, jewellery, clothes, and gifts, as well as for the dances and festivities that were part of the celebrations themselves. Asaf would always travel to Faizabad to attend these weddings, and was regularly petitioned by the begums to bestow allowances on all the parties concerned, which he acquiesced to with his usual generosity.

Nonetheless despite the begums' efforts, as the most affluent nobility left for Lucknow, Faizabad's glory dimmed, and its grand architecture began falling gently to ruin. 'Although the shops of traders and artisans were not to any great extent deserted,' wrote Faiz Baksh about Faizabad after the death of Shuja, 'yet the houses of the cavalry officers and the cantonments, which formed a large part of the city, were forsaken and became ruined.' The deserted lands were taken up by farmers, and turned into cultivated fields. The artist William Hodges, travelling to Faizabad in 1783, had a similar assessment of the city. It was a large and populous city, he wrote, but filled with people 'mostly of the lower class for the court being removed to Lucknow, drew after it the great men and the most eminent of the merchants, bankers and shroffs, or money-changers.' There were still many 'handsome brick buildings,' however, and soon after his arrival Bahu Begum sent a number of 'curries and pulaos' to welcome him to the city. The meal was excellent, though he would have enjoyed 'a glass or two of good wine instead of water'. When he visited the nawabi palaces, Hodges noted that Shuja's Dilkusha had a grand gateway with a naubat on top of the gateway from which drums sounded at sunrise and sunset. The Dilkusha palace itself 'was a vast building, covering a great extent of ground', and was an elegant building on the same plan as the palace at Lucknow, much more richly decorated but with the painting and gilding already starting to fade.

The grandest wedding of them all would be held not in Faizabad, but in Lucknow, with both Bahu Begum and Nawab Begum in attendance. In 1793, Asaf organized the wedding of his son, Wazir Ali, thirteen at the time, to Bano Begum, daughter of a courtier. By all traveller accounts, the festivities surrounding the wedding were of a scale never witnessed before in Awadh. The nawab had decided that all the crafts, skills, luxury, and wealth of Lucknow would be harnessed to create a magnificent spectacle, and to proclaim to the world, and to the Company especially, that Wazir Ali was his true heir. Outside Lucknow on a level field, huge tents[*] had been erected in colourful cloths hung with silk cords. One panel of the tent had a jaali cut out to enable all the ladies in purdah to observe the proceedings. The main tent was ablaze with the light of 200 chandeliers, several hundred mashaals, and endless tall candlesticks in glass covers. 'The glare,' wrote a Company officer,[†] clearly conflicted, 'was dazzling and offensive to the sight.' Inside the tents, a hundred richly dressed dancing girls were performing their 'elegant but rather lascivious dances' as the guests

---

[*] The two largest tents were just under the size of an Olympic swimming pool.
[†] Lewis Ferdinand Smith. Smith's account was clearly written with an eye to entertaining a public eager to hear about 'oriental excess' back in England. In the note in the Asiatic Annual Register which accompanies his letters, the editors breathlessly introduce the letters as 'a more particular, as well as a more pleasing account of the amusements he describes, than has hitherto been presented to the public'.

arrived, while the nawab himself greeted his guests warmly, glittering in his best pearls and jewels.

From the tents, the guests were taken in a magnificent cortège, comprising 120 elephants, to a beautiful garden. The nawab himself sat in a howdah on an enormous elephant which was covered in gold brocade cloth and once all the English ladies and gentlemen as well as the local nobility were seated on their assigned elephants, the procession started its swaying progress. As night fell on the city of Lucknow, it must have appeared to the guests as though a thousand moons were rising from the ground to banish the darkness forever. Both sides of the road were lined with a filigree of bamboo screens lit up with lamps, and with each step the elephants took, fireworks burst from the ground sending slivers of light all around, while hundreds of men carrying mashaals strode along the cortège. In front of the elephants, men carried one hundred platforms each bearing two dancing girls and two musicians, the dancing girls twirling and spinning the whole while and in this extravaganza of music, splendour and spectacle the procession slowly reached the garden.

> The garden...was illuminated by innumerable transparent paper lamps or lanterns of various colours suspended to the branches of the trees. In the centre of the garden was a large edifice, to which we ascended and were introduced into a grand saloon, adorned with girandoles and pendant lustres of English manufacture, lighted with wax candles. Here we had an elegant and sumptuous collection of European and Indian dishes, with wines, fruits and sweetmeats; at the same time above a hundred dancing girls sung their sprightly airs, and performed their native dances.

The spectacle lasted until dawn, and it is no wonder the English party admitted being 'delighted and wonderstruck with this enchanting scene'. The festivities continued for three successive nights, and were estimated to have cost 300,000 pounds.* The nawab himself was extremely pleased by the proceedings, and observed with some satisfaction 'that such a spectacle was never before seen in India and never would be seen again'.

That this was the age of Lucknow was made poignantly clear by

---

*200,000 pounds according to another estimate.

a description of the Delhi court at this very same time, described in a letter to Hastings.

> All the ancient forms of the court (and nothing else remains) are strictly observed. I was received in the dewan khas. Far from the impression of magnificence the durbar struck me as a dismal and gloomy spectacle. The emaciated monarch seated upon the musnud was surrounded, in the place of noble Persians, with a group of mean Mahrattas. Nothing concealed the violence with which the king had been deprived of sight by that Ruffian Gholam Kader. His sons to the number of 36 and grandchildren were seated on each side dressed in coarse maratta chintz such as a menial servant in any decent family would be ashamed to wear.

And while Asaf had perfected the art of fraternizing amiably with the Company men and women, offering entertainments and hospitality with charm, he was utterly resolute about limiting their commercial interests which had proved so harmful in the past. In 1789, the then Resident Otto Ives wrote to Cornwallis that the nawab 'has declared it to be his determination not to allow in future any of the European merchants coming to reside in his country, but to confine their commercial intercourse to the medium of gomastahs (middlemen in trade)' and the reason for this, said Ives was 'the disgust he has conceived against those who are already here.' He was, moreover, perturbed by the English merchants' habit of approaching him directly about their grievances via the Company Resident. The nawab also made an official objection for the first time, and submitted to the Resident that he 'does not think proper to consent to their (the Europeans) erecting houses or other buildings in his Dominions and that they must therefore consider themselves as prohibited from doing so.'

In October 1794, Asaf rode in high spirits in a shimmying cortège of horses to a site 100 kilometres south of Lucknow, near Dalmau on the Ganga. He had heard that the commander-in-chief of the Company forces, Robert Abercromby,* was passing through Awadh on his river expedition from Allahabad to Kanpur. The nawab arranged for a

---

*Robert Abercromby had fought during the American Revolution, and was present at the siege of Yorktown when it had capitulated to the Americans, along with Cornwallis. He was sent to India in 1790, just as had happened with Cornwallis, and was made colonel for life of the 75th Highland Regiment, established to defend British interests in India from the French.

splendid tent to be set up and entertained the British party at breakfast. 'Besides coffee, fish, curries etc,' wrote the young[*] Thomas Twining who was in attendance, 'the table was covered with a profusion of sweetmeats and flowers.' Apart from the fragrant food, Twining was struck by 'the splendour of the dresses worn by the vizier and by his court. Their manners were most dignified and noble.' The nawab sat next to Abercromby, and chatted pleasantly in Hindustani with him, via the interpreter, George Cherry. The table extended the entire length of the immense tent which was full of the nawab's courtiers as well as the British commander's officers. The table, wrote Twining, 'was surrounded by the most splendid dresses, Asiatic and European mixed together, the effect was exceedingly brilliant.'

Asaf had an ulterior motive for the excessively gracious reception given to Abercromby. Faizullah Khan, the Pashtun chief of the Rohillas, who had controlled Rampur as a jagir on behalf of Shuja, had just died after a peaceful reign of twenty years. In his last campaigns Shuja had fought to bring Rohilkhand entirely under his control, but had died before he could complete his project. Now, with Faizullah Khan dead, Asaf was delighted at the thought of realizing his father's dream and seizing Rohilkhand with Company help. Immediately upon Faizullah Khan's death, a tussle for succession amongst his sons had resulted in a younger brother murdering the eldest son and heir, Muhammad Ali. Asaf reacted quickly and asked Abercromby for help in ousting this fratricidal villain and claiming Rohilkhand for himself. After all, the nawab was still paying for the so-called 'temporary' Brigade at Fatehgarh all these years later, at a rate of 400,000 pounds per year. Abercromby agreed instantly and set up regiments to attack the Rohillas. In the end, though he did not get the whole of Rohilkhand, the terms that were worked out with the help of the Company were very favourable to Asaf. Faizullah Khan's large treasury was surrendered to the nawab and to the Company, and the jagir was bestowed upon Muhammad Ali's infant son, and Asaf got direct control of several large districts. Flushed with the successes of the past decade, and distracted by the blaze of Lucknow's effulgence, the nawab may not have noticed that desolation had come calling.

---

[*]Thomas Twining, eighteen at the time, had been just sixteen when he arrived in India two years before.

BOOK IV

# THE LION OF BRITAIN
(1794–1803)

# MEN OF EMPIRE

On a cold January morning in 1793, Citizen Capet prepared to die. Dressed soberly but neatly in a white waistcoat and black silk stockings, his powder-grey hair groomed and tied back, he climbed into a carriage drawn by two black horses, accompanied only by his confessor. The streets of Paris leading to the scaffold were ominous with soldiers and cannon in the thin morning light, while a squadron of horses led the carriage, the heavy clatter of their hooves strangely loud in the tense and waiting streets. When they reached the square* opposite the Tuileries Garden, it was heaving with cavalry and eager women crowding out of every high window, straining to see the dreadful new contraption placed in the square below—the guillotine†. Leaving his weeping confessor to stand forlornly at the bottom of the scaffold, the gently rotund Citizen Capet, not yet forty, climbed up the steps alone, remarkably composed. With terrible haste, Louis XVI's head was severed from his body and brandished aloft by his executioner‡ as the frenzied crowds roared and waved their hats, exulting in the enormity of what they had done.

The execution of Louis XVI flung revolutionary France down a bloody path from which there would be no return. When the revolution had been declared by the storming of Bastille prison in July 1789, it was believed that France would slide comfortably into a constitutional monarchy in the style of Britain, curtailing the monarchy's excessive powers and bringing the aristocracy to heel. There was a great deal of fevered enthusiasm about the ending of the old French feudal order and the rise of the Enlightenment ideals of freedom and equality. After all, the ideals of the Enlightenment had been shown to have successfully sparked the American Revolution, and now there was the electrifying

---

*Place de la Revolution.

†The guillotine was first used in France in 1792 after French physician and member of the National Assembly Joseph-Ignace Guillotin passed a law requiring all capital punishments be carried out by 'means of a machine', rendering the process relatively painless.

‡Charles-Henri Sanson assumed the hereditary role of the chief executioner of Paris in 1778 and thereby became an unwilling participant in the French Revolution. It is claimed that he oversaw the execution of 2,918 people before handing the title to his son, Henri, in 1793. According to Sanson, the last words of Louis XVI were: 'Peuple, je meurs innocent—People, I die innocent'.

possibility of bringing about similar change in France. The American Declaration of Independence* was even used as a template when drafting the Declaration of the Rights of Man and the Citizen in 1789. Many in Britain were particularly galvanized by the sweeping away of the old corrupt order of bishops and aristocrats, with the poet William Wordsworth declaring that 'bliss was it in that dawn to be alive'.

But the bloodbath of the Reign of Terror† and the execution of Louis XVI united all the European governments against France, including Spain, Naples, the Netherlands, Britain,‡ the Holy Roman Empire, and Portugal—all of whom joined together to form the First Coalition. For Britain, as Jasanoff observed, it was a fight against 'the kingless, godless, egalitarian republicanism of the Reign of Terror'. The newly minted United States, meanwhile, refused to enter the war on France's side, despite France's critical help during the American Wars of Independence, and instead signed a Proclamation of Neutrality in 1793. But from the island of Corsica a dark-haired, painfully thin, and fiery-eyed young officer nicknamed 'Le Petit Caporal' was making a name for himself as an enigmatic and courageous leader of men. Napoleon Bonaparte would find these volatile times perfect for his vaulting ambitions, and France would remain at war, and undefeated, almost continually until the Battle of Waterloo in 1815.

These Revolutionary-Napoleonic Wars were vastly different in scale, ferocity, and ambition from those that had preceded them, like the Seven Years' War for example. In sheer gargantuan numbers, Europe had not seen its like before. The French revolutionary government was able to appeal to the nationwide mood of exultant patriotic ardour to conscript hundreds of thousands of Frenchmen through the levee en masse (general conscription) so that by 1794, the French army numbered 600,000, far more than all of its enemies combined. With the

---

*The declaration was the first formal statement by a nation's people asserting their right to choose their own government.

†The increasingly hawkish attitude of the French state provoked several European countries into taking an aggressive stance against the French revolutionaries which in turn provoked 'La Terreur', or 'The Terror', which lasted from 5 September 1793 to 27 July 1794. During this time, in the face of hostile armies surrounding it, the Revolutionary government ordered harsh measures against all 'enemies' of the Revolution (priests and nobility essentially) and there was a wave of executions in Paris. A revolutionary leader, Maximilien Robespierre, became a virtual dictator.

‡Britain joined the First Coalition of 1 February 1793.

monarchy, the state religion, and the old aristocratic order all swept away, this was now a war that would bring in a new world order entirely, and that challenged the very foundation of pre-Revolutionary European societies. The ideological dimension of these wars meant that 'for the French revolutionaries, conquest formed part of an imperial *mission civilisatrice*, or "civilizing mission," designed to spread republican and Enlightenment ideals across Europe.' For the British, with the threat of a French invasion now a terrifying possibility, this would mean that aggressive overseas conquest and empire-building would become essential to blockade French ambitions. Direct territorial conquest in Africa and Asia, now that America was lost, would increasingly come to be seen both by the governing bodies and by the general public in Britain as essential to preserving a Christian and British way of life. More insidiously, as Catholic France was cast as the monstrous 'other', a unifying sense of Protestantism was used to define a sense of Great Britain as a nation.

In Westminster Hall in London, meanwhile, the impeachment trial against Hastings was sputtering to a conclusion. Despite lasting an extraordinary seven years, the trial was waylaid by events of national importance such as the madness of King George III and the French Revolution. Edmund Burke, who was leading the charge against Hastings, used the full power of his oratory—his opening speech itself lasting a full four days—and thundered such fulsome accusations against Hastings as 'I impeach him in the name of the people of India, whose laws, rights and liberties, he has subverted, whose properties he has destroyed, whose country he has laid waste and desolate.'

'By venting concerns about Hastings's particular misconduct,' writes historian Priya Satia, 'the trial redeemed the broader imperial project as something ultimately progressive'. The acquittal of Hastings in 1794 served as a 'cleansing and regeneration of the imperial mission', for it piously allowed the appearance of moral accountability, at least in an individual. 'The personalized scandal around Hastings', continues Satia, 'deflected focus from "the scandal of empire" itself'. The soul-searching that had wracked the national consciousness in Britain after the loss of its American colonies could now be safely set aside as a new challenge to its national identity arose from revolutionary France.

By the time the forty-two-year-old John Shore was named

Governor General\* to India in 1793, he had already undergone a startling refashioning of himself†. Radically different physically from his bluff and hardy predecessor Cornwallis, Shore's 'thin face and delicate features were often drawn with pain from frequent illness'. With pale, rheumy eyes and an uncertain chin in a face dominated by a surprisingly substantial nose, Shore had suffered from ill-health from the time he became a Writer at the age of just eighteen in Calcutta‡. He had suffered a further emotional breakdown, and recurring nightmares, during his tenure as Famine Commissioner in 1784 and had subsequently left for England for the first time in 1785. In his earlier years Shore had cultivated an Indo-Persianate lifestyle and had kept at least two Bengali women as bibis, one of whom§ would bear him four¶ children. Indeed the diaries kept by Britons in Calcutta at the time smirkingly noted that Shore's years there 'contained a riotous blend of alcohol, parties and sexual intrigue.' By the time he returned as Governor General, however, he was a reformed man, accompanied by his respectable English wife Charlotte Cornish and had converted to fervent evangelicalism\*\*. The 1780s were a time of wracking national angst in Britain, following the loss of the American colonies, the horror of the French Revolution, and the economic depression. Political evangelicalism thrived in those troubled waters, when it seemed like a furious God was exacting vengeance for the excesses, cruelties, and hubris of imperial ambitions. Fears of a divine retribution were very real, and powered Protestant Evangelical life. An Evangelical life that tended to be rather severe, puritanical, and inflexible, no doubt exacerbated by the unshakeable

---

\*John Shore was the first non-military man appointed as Governor General. The post of Governor General was a highly lucrative one, the salary of 25,000 pounds a year matched only by the Lord Lieutenant of Ireland in Britain.
†By the nineteenth century, Shore had positioned himself as an imperial statesman, part of the Board of Control of India and founding president of the British and Foreign Bible Society.
‡Symptoms included biliousness, being 'uneasy', racing thoughts, confusion, and sleeplessness.
§Her identity was recently uncovered by scholar Margaret Makepeace. Her name was Chand Bibi, also known as Bibi Shore, and her four children were John, Francis, George, and Martha.
¶John Shore would end up with ten children in two countries.
\*\*John Shore was part of an evangelical Anglican Group of Friends, many of whom lived close to the Surrey village of Clapham, which was fast developing into a London suburb. The contemporary term for them was a somewhat sarcastic 'Saints', which later became 'Sect', leading to the moniker 'Clapham Sect'. Members included Charles Grant, who was Chairman of the EIC, Henry Thornton, Zachary Macaulay and William Wilberforce. They were dedicated to 'practical Christianity' and opposed slavery.

belief that 'humankind was congenitally infected by the Original Sin of Adam', and therefore damned. The very public trial of Hastings,* and the obscene wealth of the earlier returning 'nabobs', had served to highlight this unease. Only a virtuous Christian life, Evangelicals believed, could lead Britons out of these dangerous times.

When John Shore settled into Government House at Calcutta as Governor General, therefore, he introduced a new age of austerity and decorum. On the day he officially took office, Shore piously prayed for grace that he might perform his duties in 'promoting the happiness of Thy creatures not only by my public actions but by my example. And grant that, under my government, religion and morality may be advanced.' Shortly after his arrival in India, Shore was devastated by the loss of two small daughters, a personal grief that strengthened Shore's belief that he was being personally tested and punished by God. 'I murmured not against the Hand that had inflicted my wounds,' he assured Evangelical parliamentarian Charles Grant†. 'The offences of my life have been too many, not to acknowledge the justice of Divine Punishment.'

His wife Charlotte, as Lady Governess, was equally committed to controlling the notoriously frontier-style garrulous and hard-living‡ society of Calcutta, and was herself simple and dignified in her dress and habits. For Evangelicals like the Shores, 'spreading the Word of God as contained in the Bible was not simply an act of beneficence, but a bounded duty' and so the Shores attended church weekly, accompanied by their aides and officers, and Shore promoted Christianity as 'the religion of the state'§ as far as he could within the existing restrictions. He also began assessing Bengali customs with a much more leery eye

---

*John Shore was called on as a witness for Hastings during the trial. He faced the threat of impeachment himself. Burke protested vehemently at Shore's appointment as Governor General, citing it as further proof of the corruption of the EIC.
†Charles Grant made a fortune through silk manufacture in India and returned to England to become director of the EIC (1794–1816) He helped establish the Sierra Leone Colony for freed slaves in East Africa in 1791.
‡Calcutta was known for its balls and masquerades at which liquor flowed, disagreements spilled into all-out fights, and duels were common.
§Promoting Christianity was illegal under the Company charter of 1793. The EIC feared that proselytizing would lead to unrest with the native population because they would suspect the British of forcing Christianity upon them. Charles Grant had petitioned to include a 'Pious Clause' in the renewed 1793 charter to encourage missionary missions to India, as Indians were deemed 'universally and wholly corrupt' and in urgent need of saving.

than he previously had, and in 1795 published an article that would be the first public missive in the *Asiatick Researches* from evangelical sources to criticize Hindu manners, seeking reforms. His pamphlet—*On Some Extraordinary Facts, Customs, and Practices of the Hindus*—roundly castigated the use of dharna to subvert Company authority in Benaras, the use of amulets, astrology, and witchcraft, the depraved and indecent depiction of female nudity, and other edifying remarks*.

Shore had an illustrious predecessor who had written a similarly outraged, and much more influential tract, in 1792—Shore's friend, the powerful EIC administrator and fellow Evangelical—Charles Grant. Grant had returned to Britain in 1790 after a career in India, and had dedicated himself to the spread of missions in India, and the promotion of evangelically minded chaplains to the EIC.† Grant had written a plea called *Observations on the State of Society among the Asiatic Subjects of Great Britain*. In his treatise, Grant rejected the earlier Enlightenment notions of Hindus being 'harmless, kind, peaceable and suffering', instead now railing about the Hindus as 'selfish, cruel, avaricious and tyrannical, completely lacking in truth, honesty good faith, patriotism and concern for the well-being of others.' These fairly astounding character traits Grant further blamed squarely on the religious beliefs and systems of the 'Hindoo code',‡ including horrors such as idolatry and superstition, the 'abandoned wickedness of their divinities' and the 'scandalous legends' that constituted the religious epics. Not surprisingly, Grant primly noted a huge difference between the 'European moral complexion', and the Hindu one, stretching the metaphor to point out that the difference was as marked as the 'difference in colour between the two races'. Nonetheless, Grant proposed that the Hindu, like the enslaved African was a 'potential recipient of Christian redemption which Britain had a duty to dispense...'

At the beginning of his tenure, Shore had shown promising signs

---

*In 1797 Shore's government outlawed dharna, the first company legislation to ban an indigenous custom the Company in India.
†In 1813, the EIC would finally relax its ban on proselytising activity after concerted evangelical campaigns by Charles Grant and William Wilberforce amongst others.
‡Grant is also credited with the term 'Hindooism' to describe the religion of India's non-Muslim inhabitants. This would be extremely influential when later missionaries were describing the overarching system they had to fight against, as one, unified construct.

of following Cornwallis's recommendations for non-interference in Awadhi affairs. In fact, in his letter of introduction to the nawab in 1793, he warmly assured him 'I am happy in the present opportunity of renewing the assurances addressed to you by his lordship (Cornwallis) and myself, that I shall have the sincerest satisfaction in cultivating and improving that friendship.'* He also found in his entourage two young protégés of Cornwallis, enthusiastic and ambitious imperialists—the Persian translator George Cherry and his close friend Neil Edmonstone†. Both these men had joined Company service as teenagers, had acquired excellent language skills, had feistily adopted the habit of keeping both a Bengali bibi and an English wife, and had endearingly high opinions of their own status as Company men in India. Their knowledge of Indian languages and Persian in particular gave them extraordinary powers because they were able to directly access the information of the Persian news writers and increasingly control intelligence networks at the very edges of British power.

In 1793 Shore appointed Cherry Resident of Lucknow, and the twenty-eight-year-old Edmonstone took Cherry's place as Persian translator in Calcutta. Cherry was also accompanied by his wife who was, according to a quixotic description by Claude Martin, 'the most correct Lady I have seen, polite to everybody, neat, clean and an excellent society, only like too stiff in her manner but on the whole a very good Lady...' Cherry's one-point agenda was to extract more money from Awadh—essentially by cutting Asaf's expenses, and having him redirect his resources to paying the bottomless Company 'subsidy'. The thirty-two-year-old Cherry threw himself enthusiastically into the job, and within a year was proud to report that he had managed 'to persuade Asaf to reduce the size of his menageries and to cut down on his kitchen staff.' This was not an inconsiderable saving since cuts to the kitchen staff saved the nawab 14 lakh rupees annually.‡ Cherry also

---

*It is perhaps somewhat less reassuring, and rather more ominous, to realize that the Governor General had written the exact same letters to all the Indian rulers including Tipu Sultan and the raja of Nepal. The interested reader is directed to Add MS 13501, Vol. 1, at the British Library.
†Neil Edmonstone would later become Governor General Wellesley's Persian secretary and the chief intelligence officer in Calcutta.
‡He also persuaded the nawab's minister Tikait Rai to hand over a full account of the nawab's finances, and abolished the nawabi government custom of borrowing money at exorbitantly high interest rates, usually from Europeans like Claude Martin, to pay back existing debts and thereby incurring even more debt.

wrote to Edmonstone, reporting with a certain smug condescension that the nawab 'is not the senseless block he has hitherto been considered'.

But Cherry's ambitions as a newly forged man of Empire, of the generation who had come of age as Britain lived through the national shame of losing her American colonies, were far greater than simply cutting the nawab's household costs. Cherry demanded a role in the administration of Awadh itself, for himself and the Company, and could be brutish, bullying, and serenely implacable in his attempt to bring about these changes. The nawab, for his part, had neither incentive nor intention of reducing his expenses more than necessary, simply to fill the Company coffers. The so-called 'temporary' Fatehgarh Brigade stationed at Awadh was still costing him fully half of the subsidy, whereas he had fought for decades to have it disbanded as promised*. His revenues were needed to create and maintain the sumptuous lifestyle of Awadh he had fostered. He needed it to pay the Mughal princes, the poets, the dancers, the musicians, the craftspersons, and all those who contributed to Awadh's glory. And he needed it also to keep notoriously fickle ministers loyal to him.

After a further frustrating year of amiable stonewalling by the nawab, an increasingly exasperated Cherry decided to force the issue. After all, the aim of the younger generation of political experts like Cherry and Edmonstone was to 'command the politics of the 3 remaining great post-Mughal courts in Madras, Hyderabad and Lucknow using the skills of their harkaras and munshis.' A meteoric rise in Company affairs due to linguistic abilities[†] and the personal mentorship of men like Cornwallis and Shore, had not encouraged humility in the young Cherry. Brash and abrasive, he made the mistake of judging the nawab on his hospitable and genial appearance, and believed him when the nawab shruggingly blamed all administrative problems on his ministers. This was of course entirely untrue. From the time of Shuja's unexpected death, Asaf had used his acute intelligence, his gauging sensibility and his exuberant energy to mould his world and navigate the considerable challenges he had

---

*At this point, the brigade had been in existence for seventeen years despite many assurances, including by Hastings, to have it disbanded.
†Cherry spoke Urdu and Bengali, and some Persian, skills which were still rare in Company men.

to face. He used his warm affability and boundless energy to beguile and distract, to smooth away resistance where other men may have used force. But Cherry had decided that he would control the nawab by installing a malleable minister who was sympathetic to the British cause. When Abu Talib had warned Cherry that trying to control Asaf would be a mistake, Cherry arrogantly replied that 'the Marhattas are notorious for their craft and cunning, and I have managed them. I must be left to deal with these who are nothing to them, and see what the results will be.'

Cherry was in close communication with his friend and ally Edmonstone in Calcutta and clearly the two men were forwarding their ill-humoured complaints to the Governor General. Already in January 1794 Shore was writing to say 'I see no embarrassment from any quarter, excepting Oude, under our existing Engagements with the Vizier. There is great difficulty in restoring the Affairs of his desolated Territories. His Minister and acting Minister, have the most rooted aversion to each other...' The person Shore was addressing his own grumbling letter to was Henry Dundas, Secretary of State for War and the Colonies, who enjoyed the worrisome nicknames 'The Great Tyrant' and 'The Uncrowned King of Scotland'.* A year later, in May 1795, Shore was writing the following missive to Dundas, regarding the thriving cultural capital of Lucknow and its well-loved nawab:

> The Disorders in Oude are so serious, that I fear the necessity of repairing there myself to restore them if possible. The Dominions of Asoph ud Doulah are in the precise situation to tempt an invasion; disaffection and anarchy prevail throughout, and nothing but the presence of our two Brigades prevents Insurrection; the Nabob is in a state of Bankruptcy, without a sense of his Danger, and without a wish to guard against it. The Indolence, and Dissipation of his Character, are too confirmed to allow the Indulgence of any expectation of Reformation on his part....

And yet, despite such strong misgivings about the anarchy and desolation of Awadh, Shore found himself begging the nawab for help in 1796 in his own struggles against the army in Bengal, which was

---

*Henry Dundas was impeached in 1806 for mismanagement of naval funds.

on the brink of armed resistance at the time.* Asaf agreed to send Shore his best soldiers, elephants, and cash. Benoit de Boigne, packing up before leaving Hindustan, was also persuaded to send a regiment of cavalry from the Maratha army, and to sell to the Company his excellent personal bodyguard† of 600 horsemen, 100 camel troops, and 4 artillery pieces. De Boigne had intended to offer his army to the nawab of Awadh but Wiliam Palmer convinced him to give the refusal to the Bengal government first 'so that if an augmentation of the Company's cavalry were intended, Government might have the preference of a very fine corps, fit for immediate service', but also surely to deny Asaf the possibility of owning such a corps. The anarchy and the desolation seemed rather to have plagued the Company at the time, instead of the nawab.

Since the death of Haider Beg Khan in 1792, the nawab's most important minister was Hasan Reza Khan, and his deputy minister was Maharaj Tikait Rai.‡ Cherry now bafflingly proposed an entire re-structuring of the nawab's administration, and even outrageously ordered the effective disbanding of his army. But the nawab swatted aside all the names Cherry put forward, and proposed an astonishing plan of his own. There would be no requirement for any ministers, he argued, since he would attend to his country's affairs himself, aided by his favourite courtier, Jhau Lal. He dismissed both Tikait Rai and Hasan Reza Khan,§ and appointed two of his sons in their place—the fifteen-year-old Wazir Ali and twelve-year-old Raza Ali.

Jhau Lal was a Saksena Kayastha from a family that had a tradition of service to the nawabs. He had worked his way assiduously up the ranks through a series of administrative posts and, in addition, meticulously cultivated the friendship of the nawab himself. He

---

*Disgruntlement in the Bengal Army was rife in the 1790s due to the disproportionate pay between king's army officers and Company officers, and also between the military and the civilian branches of the EIC. The mutiny of the Bengal officers of 1795-96 was extremely worrisome to Cornwallis, who found out that the Bengal army officers were ready to seize the Governor General and the commander-in-chief and to enact a coup, if their conditions were not met.

†Historian Jean-Marie Lafont believes de Boigne's bodyguard may constitute part of the founding units that eventually made up part of the president's personal bodyguards in India today.

‡Tikait Rai was a Srivastava Kayasth who had long been in the service of Awadh. He appointed many family members and dependents to posts under his authority.

§Both the men would then join Company service.

adopted 'Muslim customs, dress, and religious duties such as prayer and the Ramzan fast' and seamlessly fitted into the refined Shia lifestyle of elite nawabi Lucknow. As a result, Asaf had named him his naib, and gave him the title of honorary 'Maharaj'. Maharaj Jhau Lal, fondly known as Lalluji, was now about to distinguish himself with an act of extreme bravery, loyalty, and grit. As Asaf prepared to leave Lucknow at the end of the monsoon season of 1796 on his biannual excursion, the rain continued to fall with such relentless force that gusts of strong wind set the tents of the encampment rippling and the men, elephants, and camels struggled in the slush and mud of the embankments as they prepared to cross the Ghaghara at Faizabad. In the midst of the chaotic confusion, Jhau Lal stationed himself at the ghaat, battered by the pouring rain and the snapping wind, as he organized the crossing of the nawab's enormous cortege. In took five days for the entire encampment to cross the bridge of boats, which swayed and creaked in the treacherously deep river, and a number of men and boats were lost to the deadly waters. Jhau Lal, however, remained steadfastly at his post for the full five days, guiding men and animals. This incident more than any other explains the success of Lalluji, where sheer determination, personal courage, and force of will overcame any lack of brilliance. Asaf would not forget the gallantry of Jhau Lal, especially at a time when so many of his ministers were finding it easier to quietly slip over to the British.

One of the reasons Asaf was so keen to leave Lucknow was that he was by now thoroughly disgusted by Cherry's supercilious and sneeringly disrespectful behaviour. By this stage Cherry had even taken the provocative decision to confront the nawab directly, instead of through one of his ministers, to lecture him about the state of his finances. The liaison officer Tafazzul Hussain Khan had warned Shore that the nawab was careful about his dignity and considered himself 'in every respect as one with the English sirdars'. Even Cherry's secretary grew alarmed at the way the nawab was being treated and reported to Cherry that he had witnessed that 'his Excellency was in a humour and anger that exceeds anything I ever saw of him'. Asaf had angrily insisted he would pay whatever was required of him but he would never relinquish his sovereignty as the sole ruler of Awadh. Cherry could either accept that or allow him to go 'unattended to Calcutta; give me a bit of bread and a little water, and make which of my brothers you please the Master'.

But Cherry's arrogance did not allow him to see the world of the nawab, as Hastings had been able to do in an earlier age. He could not conceive of the nawab's evenings, swirling with the languorous beauty of thumris, and alive with the fierce duelling of the best poets that India would ever produce. For Cherry's generation of Company men were driven by an unshakeable assumption of their superiority, and of the debased nature of indigenous culture. Edmonstone would note that it was Cherry who had taught him 'both by example and precept' not to trust the Indians. And so he dismissed all the warnings and instead rudely declared that he would not attend the nawab's durbar if Jhau Lal were present and, even more provocatively, sent for four battalions of soldiers from Kanpur to protect British interests in Lucknow.

A furious nawab then wrote to Shore to proclaim that he was setting off on a hunting expedition since his country had become odious to him. He complained that Cherry had used language that could only have been 'calculated to disgrace and lower me in the eyes of all ranks of people'. Shore was naturally horrified at the complete fracturing of relations between the Company and a nawab who had always been a genial friend to them. 'By his indiscretion (Cherry) contrived to forfeit all the advantages of my Exertions to prevail upon the Nabob Vizier to establish a better administration,' wrote a terribly worried Shore to Dundas. Cherry was hurriedly removed from Lucknow, and sent as a judge to Benaras*. A new Resident was appointed to Lucknow, James Lumsden, a man of pleasing and gentle manners. Within a month of meeting Lumsden, Asaf wrote to Shore in great good humour, praising Lumsden as he 'has all the qualities of extreme politeness, penetration, wisdom, goodness and abilities'. Disaster, it appeared, had narrowly been averted.

---

*At Benaras, Cherry increased the recruitment of informants from within the mendicants, pilgrims, and merchants of the bustling city, thus strengthening the EIC's intelligence network.

# THE GOLDEN AGE OF AWADH

On an unremarkable afternoon in 1796, Nawab Begum slumped over while performing her prayers, dying as she had lived, in piety and discretion. With the death of Nawab Begum, the daughter of the great Burhan-ul-Mulk himself, an entire way of life came to an end in Faizabad. Her chief eunuch, Matbu Ali Khan, a man who had amassed a considerable fortune in jewels, shawls, weapons, gold, and silver in addition to cash, immediately panicked. He knew that the nawab, or the British, would claim any wealth the Nawab Begum and her eunuchs had owned. And so he hastily gathered all his glittering objects and money, and pressed each item upon the members of his large circle of friends—'the sayyids, Mughals and Shaikhs of eminent piety'—for safekeeping. These were, after all, men who had obsequiously followed him all his life, shouting out 'Bismillah!' and 'subhanallah!' most gratifyingly at each of his utterances. Soon enough, a eunuch arrived from the court of Lucknow to escort the Nawab Begum's eunuchs back to Lucknow for questioning. In Lucknow, Matbu Ali Khan placed his hand upon the nawab's head and swore an oath to the effect that he had renounced all his wealth. Matbu Ali Khan was a greatly respected eunuch who had been in the service of the nawabs since the time of Saadat Khan himself, and Asaf had to accept his word. But by the time Matbu Ali Khan returned to Faizabad, he found his friends suddenly forgetful, feigning a powerful amnesia about his wealth, and Matbu Ali Khan had no option but to quietly spend the rest of his days ruminating upon the fickle nature of his temporal friendships.

The remainder of the Nawab Begum's large retinue found themselves similarly destitute upon her death. Some of her eunuchs gathered at Lucknow, looking for work, while others prepared miserably to perform the hajj. The most wretched were the maidservants, 'who had lived modestly in the seclusion of the harem, now hiding themselves in some old buildings within the fort, huddled together like grain in a pitcher or a sack'. They lived for a while upon a few rupees that Bahu Begum gave them, and then they slowly disappeared from Faizabad like the memory of dreams at dawn. 'The change came in the twinkling of an eye,' wrote Faiz Baksh sadly. 'And not a trace is now left of the nobles and gentry who used to come night and morning to pay court at (Nawab Begum's) door.'

One man who could have been similarly devastated by these changing circumstances, but who instead continued to thrive spectacularly, was the famous khwajasara Mian Almas Ali Khan. He had arrived in Awadh along with Bahu Begum, as part of her dowry, when he was a humble young cup bearer. The little Mirza Amani would always address Almas Ali Khan as 'mamu',* and even when he became nawab, Asaf treated the khwajasara as an equal. As Bahu Begum began accumulating jagirs, she appointed Almas Ali Khan as the manager of all her lands. Almas turned out to be a supremely judicious manager and, in the process, grew fabulously wealthy himself. Unlike the other great khwajasaras of Faizabad, he maintained a decorous and discreet distance from all the fractious jealousies and posturing of the other eunuchs, and was spared the humiliations that his brethren endured in the 1780s. By 1771 Almas had enough money to found his own town in Unnao district called Mianganj. Apart from his commercial dealings, Almas also owned indigo factories and maintained his own military force, one that was larger even than Asaf's. By 1775 when Asaf became nawab, Almas was the single largest revenue farmer in Awadh, controlling almost a quarter of the total revenue collected in Awadh.†

'Miyan Almas', wrote William Sleeman‡ travelling through Awadh in the nineteenth century, 'was the greatest and best man of any note that Oude has produced. He held for about 45 years (Miyanganj) and other districts, yielding to the Oude government as annual revenue of about 80 lakhs of rupees. During all this time he kept the people secure in life and property and as happy as people in such a state of society can be; and the whole country under his charge was, during his lifetime, a garden... He systematically kept in check the Taluqdars, or great landholders; fostered the smaller; and encouraged and protected the best classes of cultivators, such as Lodhs, Kurmis and Kachhis, whom he called and considered his children. His reign over the large

---

*Maternal uncle.
†By 1783 the areas managed by Almas included Kora, Sharah, Jagdishpur, and Etawah, as well as the territories south of Farrukhabad.
‡William Henry Sleeman was a colonial administrator. He was involved in campaigns against the 'thugee' tribes of North India, earning him the nickname 'Thuggee' Sleeman.

extent of country under his jurisdiction is considered to have been its Golden Age.' Fully aware of the fact that his wealth was a mirage, and would revert to the nawab upon his death, Almas spent money lavishly on useful works, on charity, and in a magnificently hospitable lifestyle, all the things that would bring glory to his name long after his death*. Nawab Asaf-ud-Daula himself would sometimes visit his 'mamu' at Miyanganj, staying for up to a month at a time.

When Cherry began his angry tussling with Asaf over the choice of a minister to manage his affairs, an obvious candidate was Almas Ali Khan, and his name was brought up in discussions. But a man who had served the nawabs for almost half a century, with dignified rectitude and impeccable sobriety, was judged to be not sympathetic enough to the British cause. The uncomfortable distaste with which khwajasaras were increasingly viewed by changing British attitudes were reflected in Viscount Valentia's reflections in 1803:

> The person I observed with the most curiosity was Almas Ali Khan... He is a venerable, old-woman like being, upwards of 80, full 6 feet high and stout in proportion. After all the cruel plunderings which he is stated as having undergone, he is supposed to be worth half a million of money...

For all their lofty lectures on the management of the nawab's domains, the British were essentially only interested in remitting revenue into the Company coffers, and sending it back to Britain. They were not interested, as Almas and the nawab were, in building charitable institutions, or even gardens. As Sayyid Ghulam Hussain Khan had written in the *Seir Mutaqherin*:

> So many English that have carried away such princely fortunes from this country, not one of them has ever thought of shewing his gratitude to it, by sinking a well, digging a pond, planting a public grove, raising a caravanserai, or building a bridge; and that even where there are bridges already, they never fail to clog them with a toll if they but make any slight repairs to any of them. These accusations are true, but cannot, however, much affect the

---

*He also built a number of forts, and encouraged his followers to do so too. One fort at Kudarkot was built of bricks, and had 16 bastions, and Almas sometimes held his court here. He also built a new fort at Gangaganj in Miyangunj, with the aim of keeping watch on the Ganga.

national character of the English who being, to a man, occasional sojourners, have no time to conceive an affection for this country.

A great deal had changed in Awadh in the past few decades. The sublime and layered world full of delicacy and grace that the nawabs had created had been adopted by an earlier generation of Europeans, either with passionate enthusiasm or pragmatic ease. But a new breed of British Company men and women would no longer condescend to luxuriate in this refined lifestyle.* Brash with a new confidence about their role in their world and their civilizing mission they would instead impose their ways upon a land far away, whose foreignness had once appeared charming.

---

**In quite a literal sense, the children of European men and Indian women became unacceptable within British society. Cornwallis recommended that they not be allowed to serve in the Company army unless they could prove that they were 'without any mixture of the blood of the natives of India'. In 1790, the Company banned Eurasians from owning land, and these mixed-race children would be viewed as Indian rather than British subjects. See Sarah Pearson, *Making Britain in Empire: John Shore, nation and race in the Eighteenth-Century East India Company world,* Doctoral Thesis, 21 January 2021, pp. 73-74.

# LITTLE ENGLAND IN AWADH

When young Thomas Twining walked through Delhi in 1794, no one looked at him twice. The bazar he passed through was busy with men in white robes and turbans, coloured shawls tied at the waist, all carrying arms of some sort—a wicked blade or a scimitar, or sometimes a black shield. 'All the inhabitants I met in this crowded bazar,' he wrote in his memoirs, 'were perfectly-behaved and civil, not displaying more than that certain degree of curiosity which is not, perhaps, unpleasing to a stranger.' The men simply acknowledged the presence of the pale firangi with a discreet salaam, stepping aside to make room for him as he passed by. No longer were there horrified villagers running away at the sight of these 'white devils', nor curious mobs as there had been a few decades before. Hindustan had changed considerably in the last decades of the eighteenth century.

The sense of dislocation must have been pronounced by the time Twining arrived in Lucknow in 1796. He was immediately swept up into the giddy social scene enjoyed by the British residents there and was moved to remark that 'the style in which this remote colony lived was surprising, it far exceeding even the expense and luxuriousness of Calcutta'. This intimate little band of Europeans spent these winter evenings sitting by a crackling fire, alternately dining at each other's homes. They had organized a large band of musicians for their entertainment at these numerous soirees. 'I had singular pleasure,' sighed Twining, 'on hearing some old English and scotch airs played extremely well. The traveller cannot have much music in his soul who is not moved with the concord of sweet sounds which remind him of his native country.' No longer were inquisitive Europeans moved by the concord of Hindustani music itself, nor the courtesans' husky thumris, as they had in the past. Indeed there was no mention of local women or bibis at all in Twining's account. Instead, young[*] Twining was thoroughly charmed to find himself in the company of a certain Mrs Arnot, who 'enjoyed the distinction of being the handsomest lady in India'.[†]

---

[*] He would have been just nineteen at this time.
[†] One of these merry gentlemen in Lucknow, the merchant Robert Orr, made a hasty exit the

All the Europeans who had once led those brocaded lives were now long gone. Madec, Polier, Gentil, Zoffany, and de Boigne had all left Lucknow, leaving only the increasingly solitary figure of Claude Martin. Martin no longer spoke of returning to Europe himself, perhaps realizing that it was a mirage, best left to the world of dreams. For the fate of many of these men had proved uncertain, and even violent, as in the case of Polier, and had been enormously sobering for Martin. 'I really lament and very much, the fate of Colonel Polier, how unfortunate he has been,' Martin wrote to Elizabeth Plowden in 1796. 'He was an excellent good man, and the life of society where he was.' Writing to de Boigne, he admitted to 'a kind of taciturnity, without being melancholy', which required the frequent society of all available Europeans so as to remain 'always in gay spirits and happy'. He was delighted, and perhaps envious, when he received a portrait of de Boigne with his ethereally beautiful teenage aristocratic bride Adèle. 'As pretty as an angel,' Martin exclaimed, 'being eighteen years old, possessing music and songs in particular to perfection, with unequalled zest and a remarkable gaiety, born of good family...beautiful with all kinds of talents, ho! My good friend! The painting is so beautiful that I envy your sort and should even be jealous...' As for himself, 'I am forced to content myself with the "Beauties of the Indies", who are well below that of the painting that you have sent me.' After a lifetime spent with the charming and beautiful Boulone Lise, it was deeply ungallant of Martin to claim that he was 'forced to content' himself with such company. Clearly this reflected his own anxiety, untethered despite decades in India, in the face of the Company's growing racism and sense of superiority.

Nonetheless, Lucknow was at its most enchanting in the late winter, which Twining would have experienced. In the nawab's Mughal-style gardens, the orange and apple trees would have bloomed and the flower beds would have been thickly planted with luscious marigold, blue larkspur, white and yellow jasmine, and deeply fragrant red and white rose bushes. The nawab went to great lengths to make his European residents feel comfortable and to accommodate their exigencies. An

---

following year leaving 10 lakh rupees in debt behind him, including 40,000 rupees owed to a mortified Martin. Other luminaries in Lucknow included the physician James Laird, a Mr Paul, and Mr and Mrs Arnot.

English employee of Asaf described his easy-going bonhomie:

> He is very fond of the English, and English manners; he eats at table with them without the silly superstitious repugnance of other Mahomedans and he relishes a good dish of tea and hot rolls. Once he was at table and a roasted pig by mistake was placed before him, he smiled and said—though I am forbid to eat that animal I am not forbid to look at it.

Twining himself had been awe-struck by the magnificence of the nawabi cortège when he had witnessed it a few years earlier, and now wrote that 'in polished and agreeable manners, in public magnificence, in private generosity, and also, it must be allowed, in wasteful profusion, Asaf, king of Oude, might probably be compared with the most splendid sovereigns of Europe.'

Most of the houses of the British and European residents of Lucknow were clustered within a site to the east of the Macchi Bhawan and along the Gomti, an area that would later be called simply the Residency. Sometime in the 1770s Claude Martin had bought up a large swathe of land here, while the rest had been bought by the nawab. Houses were sporadically built here which Martin then rented out to the British residents. In 1778 the first Company building was specifically built as a Treasury, and the remaining structures were added haphazardly. The residency thus displayed a mixed character, with mosques, shrines, and zenana structures amongst the gardens and the brick bungalows and larger buildings. Llewellyn-Jones believes these buildings were constructed by order of the nawab and leased to the Resident and his staff for a trifling amount. The nawab was also forced to pay for the upkeep of the Residency staff's houses, as well as the salaries of the employees such as the guards, gardeners, messengers etc.*

And yet there was increasing condescension in the way in which the nawab was viewed, even a sniggering disdain. A British man who confessed that 'Asaf allows me 1800 pounds a year and nothing to do but

---

*Claude Martin had the most profitable interaction with the nawab. He was paid a salary, as well as the arsenal expenses ever since it was set up in 1775. He also charged the nawab a hefty 36 per cent on all cash loans he made to him. In 1794, Martin loaned the nawab 25 lakh rupees, covering half the subsidy amount that was overdue to the Company, again at 36 per cent interest rate. In the end the nawab refused to pay the interest, but paid the principal as a lump sum in 1796. In comparison, the Company was giving 12 per cent interest per annum on loans it received in 1796.

enjoy his frequent entertainments of shooting, hunting, dancing, cock fighting and dinners' wrote about the nawab to his friend in England, to say that:

> Asaf-ud-Daula is absurdly extravagant and ridiculously curious; he has no taste and less judgement... He is...extremely solicitous to possess all that is elegant and rare; he is...a curious compound of extravagance, avarice, candour, cunning, levity, cruelty, childishness, affability, brutish sensuality, good humour, vanity and imbecility; in his public appearance and conduct he is admirably agreeable. In short, he has some qualities to praise, some to detest and many to laugh at.

After this litany of indictments, the writer sheepishly added that 'he is very affable, polite and friendly to me'.

The charge of being 'extravagant and ridiculously curious' was one that many Europeans were beginning to hiss angrily about the nawab. What had once inspired amazement and awe—the nawab's collection of astonishing objects—now increasingly attracted censure and derision. Twining had also visited Asaf's Aina Khana, or 'Mirror Hall' which contained 'English objects of all kinds—watches, pistols, guns, glassware, furniture, philosophical machines, all crowded together with the confusion of a lumber room. The number of clocks and watches was quite extraordinary. Many of them were very beautiful and were said to have cost the Nabob immense sums.' A repeated criticism of the nawab's collection was that 'all were placed without regard to order or reference to their qualities or value. A valuable chronometer...would be suspended next to a common watch of the most ordinary description.'

But as Jasanoff has recorded, collecting 'was part and parcel of the culture of Indian kingship. Kings make collections, and collections make kings. To own rare, precious, sacred or just plain numerous things is a virtually universal emblem of royal power. In many parts of the Muslim world, collecting meaningful and valuable objects enhanced a sovereign's personal charisma, or barakat, and with it, his ability to command the loyalty and admiration of his subjects.'

There was, therefore, an illustrious list of collectors amongst Indian kings to serve as glorious examples to Asaf, some of the most famous being the Mughals. Asaf was intensely aware of the luminous charisma of some of these objects, and the aura of sacred kingship associated with them. He was an avid and proud collector of manuscripts that had belonged to the imperial library in Delhi, including the *Padshahnama* of Shah Jahan himself. The Mughal emperor Akbar was the collector par excellence of Hindustan, acquiring lands, brides, animals, and art to incorporate all of the country symbolically into the king's being. But perhaps the emperor that Asaf identified more closely with was the rebellious, provocative, intemperate, immoderate, and treasonous Mirza Salim who became the expansive aesthete of exquisite taste and refinement as Emperor Jahangir. As a collector, Jahangir had no need for the prosaic and the mundane. He would instead focus on the infinitely rare, even the extra-terrestrial—he had a unique dagger made from a meteorite rock, for example, and he collected albino animals and flightless birds.*

Interestingly, as pointed out by scholar Natasha Eaton, the collection of European objects that Asaf amassed in this haphazard manner in the Aina Khana may have had another subversive meaning. Asaf was already leading two lives—one as the quintessential Indian ruler and aesthete, patron of Hindustani music, dance and art, and builder of magnificent Shia monuments. These activities he indulged in away from prying and judgemental European eyes—the mushairas in the felt Lucknow nights, the Shia remembrance in their separate spaces within imambaras, the art collections enjoyed with discerning patrons like the Mughal princes. Simultaneously he breakfasted on jams and jellies with the Europeans, and produced 'childish' puppet shows, mimic troupes, animal fights, and dancers for their amusement. The nawabs, writes Eaton, 'confined western luxuries to limited spaces in their palaces and public rituals. They developed a carefully coded mimicry that disrupted colonialism's belief in its own supremacy by hanging pictures upside down, letting their portraits rot away, encouraging automata to rust and mirrors to atrophy.' These collections may have been intended to show that Asaf *could* acquire the very best that Britain and Europe had to offer, if he chose to, but that he would invest no further meaning or ritual around these objects. He would not honour them with the

---

*Jahangir's great painter of animals, Mansur, made an image of what was arguably the last living dodo on earth.

semi-sacred ceremony that surrounded the appreciation of miniature paintings, for example, which were to be enjoyed at the right season, surrounded by the appropriate scents and sounds that would stimulate the greatest sensory delight. After all, Asaf had a history of giving away the European portraits that were made of him, and even the famous oil painting by Zoffany was kept negligently in the Daulat Khana, where it was noticed a few decades later by Fanny Parkes. 'The whole of the figures are portraits,' she wrote of this painting of a cock-match. 'The picture excellent, but fast falling into decay.'

The malaise that surrounded some of the re-fashioning that was taking place between Europeans and Indians can be seen in a particularly unsettling episode that took place later at the court of Nawab Nasiruddin Haider of Awadh in 1833. Nasiruddin had a favourite courtesan called Nuna, who was very beautiful and who had a captivating singing voice. 'There was a pathos in her voice in singing—a plaintive pathos,' wrote a British traveller, 'as she sang of the happy valley* where she had been brought up.' One day, perhaps growing tired of the courtesan's charms, Nasiruddin decided to amuse himself by making her dress in a European woman's clothes. When she presented herself at court dressed as an 'English memsahib', the unhappy Nuna cut a sorry figure:

> A more wretched transformation it is hardly possible to conceive. The clothes hung loosely about her in an eminently dowdyish way. She felt that she was ridiculous. All grace was gone; all beauty was hidden. It was distressing to see her disheartened look as she took her place again. The king and the (English) barber laughed heartily at her plight, while hot scalding tears coursed down Nuna's cheeks.

The essence of Indian art and grace, this episode seemed to demonstrate, became an object of ridicule when taken out of context, and swaddled in European attire.

Perhaps Asaf was aware of the liminal space beyond which he could not go without forsaking his identity and his dignity. According to Llewellyn-Jones, though European influence was now more evident in Lucknow, 'the Europeanization of Lucknow remained superficial;

---

*She was said to have come from Kashmir.

*Top*: Johann Zoffany's famous painting of Asaf, his courtiers, and many identifiable Company men at a cockfight has been the subject of many interpretations.

*Bottom*: Crown Prince Mirza Jawan Bakht, eldest son of Emperor Shah Alam II, painted during his stay at Lucknow in 1784.

*Top left*: Hasan Reza Khan rose from humble beginnings to become the highest ranked courtier at the durbar of Asaf, painted here by Zoffany.

*Top right*: Zoffany trailed a slight air of disreputability, a reputation he encouraged through his disquieting self-portraits.

*Bottom*: Bought by Martin at the age of eight or nine, Boulone Lise was painted by Zoffany alongside her adopted son, Zulfikar.

*Top*: The most intimate of Zoffany's works, this painting shows William Palmer and his bibi, Faiz Begum, as well as her sister, Noor Begum.

*Bottom*: Polier examining the produce from his gardens, painted alongside friends Martin, John Wombwell, and the artist Zoffany.

*Top*: Polier dressed in Awadhi style watching a dance performance, after a lost Zoffany painting. Katherine Schofield believes the main dancer to be Khanum Jan.

*Bottom left*: Two beautiful women enjoying wine on a terrace, from a Polier album.

*Bottom right*: The hookah bases of the nawabs were made of intricate bidri-ware, engraved in silver.

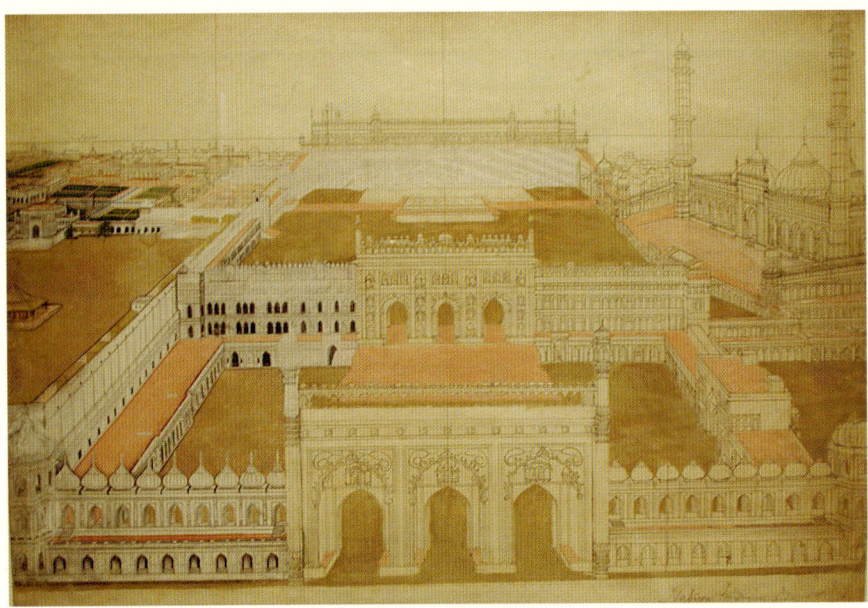

*Top left*: An unusually candid sketch of Asaf by Zoffany in which the nawab's glance betrays his canny intelligence.

*Top right*: Asaf painted by Zoffany in 1784, in his favourite white muslin, wearing strings of magnificent pearls and jewels.

*Bottom*: An unusual European style topographical painting of the Bara Imambara by an unknown artist.

30

31

*Top*: The Rumi Darwaza was covered in exuberant leaf, flower, and fish motifs, and had a crown of stone roses.

*Bottom*: Asaf and his courtiers in the Bara Imambara, during a Muharram remembrance.

32

33

34

*Top left*: Ozias Humphry painted this fine miniature of Asaf's courtier Hyder Beg Khan, but he struggled to get paid for his works.

*Top right*: Darwesh Khan formed part of the embassy sent by Tipu Sultan to Paris in 1788, where the men caused a stir due to their exoticism and elegance.

*Bottom*: The *Gloriosa superba* botanical drawing with comments in Martin's distinctive scrawl.

*Top*: An obsessively driven and hard-working man, Benoit de Boigne was a spectacularly successful military commander working for the Marathas.

*Bottom*: Asaf-ud-Daula's simple grave inside the Bara Imambara.

native life continued to revolve around the inner courtyards and zenana apartments of traditional houses, whether or not these houses had European features.' While the Europeans huddled around the fires in bungalows that evoked a faraway green and frosty 'home' in the Residency, the nawab moved further away to the west and to the Daulat Khana, with the sacred space of the Imambara separating him from the Residency. In the great Imambara Asaf kept the European objects that had true value to him—the giant mirrors and chandeliers that illuminated and magnified with incandescent power the divine light that was at the very heart of his great Shia renaissance.

But Europe was about to crash with violence and intemperance into the genteel world of Awadh the nawabs had created with all their wealth and imagination. The Revolutionary Wars of France had picked up momentum and France, under the tempestuous leadership of Napoleon Bonaparte, had overrun Belgium, western Germany and, in 1796, Italy too. With their great imperial rival threatening their powers and their colonies everywhere in the world,* Britain was determined to protect and consolidate their richest remaining colony—India. Any power that threatened British interest in India would not be tolerated at all, and a larger army in India was needed for which even more money was to be extracted from Awadh. And so the directors of the EIC sent John Shore an ominous missive, and informed him that 'we deem it your indispensable duty to interfere (in Awadh) whenever it shall be deemed necessary', and to increase the subsidy paid to the Company. No force, however, was to be used, only 'advice... (and) remonstrance.' And so, sighing under the weight of such responsibility, John Shore set off on his first expedition to Lucknow.

---

*An incendiary source of conflict had lately occurred in 1791 in the slave worked sugar islands in the Caribbean, during the revolt of Toussaint Louverture in French St Domingue (today Haiti), with the danger that this revolutionary flame could spread to nearby British-owned Jamaica, the most profitable colony that Britain possessed at the time.

# MAKING AN ETHIOPIAN WHITE

In January 1797, John Shore set off from Calcutta to Lucknow by boat, accompanied by his Persian translator Neil Edmonstone. The journey was slow and could take several weeks as the boats slowly slipped along the Ganga. When the wind dropped, or blew against them, the boatmen had to jump into the shallows and slowly tug the boats along, heaving laboriously at the heavy ropes. Dozens of boats would have been needed, as the party included all the luggage, horses, food, and stores the travellers would require, while palanquins for later use were strapped to the roofs of the boats. The men disembarked at Benaras, where Shore and Edmonstone decided to visit Qutlugh Sultan Begum,* the widow of Mirza Jawan Bakht who had died almost ten years before, and her two sons. The begum and her children were living on a pension generously† accorded to them by Asaf, but their circumstances were still terribly tattered. Writing to his wife about this visit, Shore was acutely aware of the complete transformation that had occurred both in the conditions of the imperial family, and in those of the Company, as he beheld their withered lives:

> These poor descendants of Imperial dignity maintain the forms of royalty: and we mutually acted parts inconsistent with our real characters; I, the Representative of our Power, professing humility and submission before the dependants on the bounty of the Company; whilst they, who are the objects of charity, and feeling their situation, thought it incumbent on them to use the language of Princes.

The old familiar ceremony was carried out, in which a sword, shield and turban were given to Shore who felt 'caparisoned' with these objects and when the young mirzas took off their jackets to bestow it on the Governor General, a 'sense of ridiculous character' he was acting assailed him. It was not the indigenous ceremony itself that he bristled at—in Calcutta, Shore was in the habit of holding a 'native levee' himself, during which paan was distributed and Shore

---

*She would die in Benaras in 1818 and was buried in the Bagh-e-Fatiman.
†10,000 rupees a month according to John Shore.

sprinkled attar of roses on his guests. But in Calcutta, Shore was the one magnanimously bestowing the honours and now he baulked at being the recipient of it, even from the imperial family itself.

Away from Calcutta, Shore was disquietingly aware of the great freight of the Company name. 'I arrived here without anything,' he wrote musingly to his wife, 'and I have found everything... The name of the Governor-General is a talisman, which will not indeed erect palaces, but give me the use of them; it produces plenty in the midst of wilds, and conveniences in the land of sterility.' Far away from the familiarity of Calcutta, deep into the dark hinterland and in a most overwhelmingly foreign city like Benaras, it was the Company name that brought honours and security, dispelling the terrors of the utterly unfamiliar. It was with some relief that he contemplated his next visit, which was to the raja of Benaras where he hoped to find 'a complete contrast to the misery of yesterday.... [T]oday I expect to find all the comforts of opulence and happy dependence.' Shore clearly anticipated that the grateful plenitude of the raja of Benaras would be a balm to what must no doubt have been painfully guilty feelings regarding the state of the begum and her sons.

In the week that Shore spent in Benaras, he would have had much to think about, aside from the flattering attentions he now commanded as the powerful Governor General of the East India Company. One of the great challenges of this religious-minded Governor General's tenure appeared not in the form of any Indian insurrection or some competing European power, but sprang vociferously from another British Company man—Robert Hobart*. Hobart was the thirty-seven-year-old aggressive governor of Madras, a man who seemed not to favour the path of diplomatic subtlety when braggadocio could be used in dealing with Indian powers. He had been appointed governor in 1793 with no prior experience in India, having served as a soldier in the American Revolutionary Wars and as aide-de-camp to successive Lords Lieutenants of Ireland. During debates in the Irish House of Commons it had been noted that his voice was 'good, clear, full, well-toned' but that rather mystifyingly he affected a 'feminine lisp adopted from his familiar intercourse with pretty ladies and pretty gentlemen.' Nonetheless, with fetching wavy dark hair and an impressive aristocratic

---

*Lord Hobart was the fourth Earl of Buckinghamshire.

lineage he was deemed 'pleasing, sensible and well-looking, (with) the finest teeth possible.' While Shore was criticized for being 'a very cautious and over-prudent politician,' Hobart was his exact opposite—advocating aggressive interference and infamously 'dragooning' the raja of Tanjore into handing over more control to the Company over his administration.* There may have been a further smidgen of class tensions, with Shore prickly about his wealthy but mercantile background† when faced with the over-bearing self-assurance of the aristocratic Hobart.

Hobart had challenged Shore's authority almost from the time he arrived in India, fuming at not having been made Governor General himself. Shore had initially tried to temper Hobart, advising 'persuasion and conciliation', adding that kindly attention from a Company man like Governor Hobart would have 'flattered (the nawab of Arcot's) vanity', and made him amenable. But writing to Cornwallis about Hobart in April 1796 Shore somewhat piteously complained that 'his Lordship chose to address me in terms which I would not have used to any subordinate officer'. Hobart found Shore utterly intolerable and had thundered that he would not remain in India if Shore continued as Governor General, spluttering in turn about Shore's 'diabolical libels' about him. Hobart himself seemed to believe that he was the best replacement for the mild Shore‡ as supreme Company power in India. At the time of Shore's trip to Lucknow in 1797, Hobart's vigorous and intemperate actions were winning him accolades,§ while Shore's moderate and acquiescing style was in danger of appearing weakly placatory.

Shore was quite aware of the criticisms that his tempered actions

---

*Hobart would be recalled in 1798 by the court of directors over criticism about his Carnatic policy, though he had hoped to become the Governor General after Shore. He was compensated for this loss of power by an ample pension of 1,500 pounds per annum.

†When learning of Shore's appointment as Governor General, William Hickey, English lawyer and memoirist in India, had called him 'a man of low origin, without any connexion of weight or influence.'

‡In the end, as a result of the two men's inability to work together, both were recalled to England and Wellesley was appointed Governor General.

§In January 1797, reports were received that largely approved Hobart's measures, and Shore wrote to a friend that 'Lord Hobart is made very happy by an overland despatch dated in August announcing the satisfactory intelligence, that the measures of his administration including his negotiations with the nabob, and his treaties with the Raja of Tanjore, the King of Candia are approved....'

might generate, in the climate of muscular 'interference' that the Company was now exhibiting, and this seemed to sometimes paralyse him with indecision. Writing to Charles Grant, Shore admitted that 'I hesitate when I should have decided without demur.... Languor will occasionally steal upon me, and impede exertion; and the climate has produced an irritability which affects my nerves.... I am almost tempted to regret that I did not retire this season'. To bolster his moral certainty, Shore's recourse was the perusal of religious literature during the only free time he had, which was when his hairdresser was attending to him, during which time he managed to 'read the New Testament through many times, many parts of the Bible frequently, Warburton's Divine Legation, Jortin's Ecclesiastical History, Jortin's Sermons over and over, Paley's evidences and many other books of a similar tenor'.

In addition to Hobart, the Governor General had other worries of a more indigenous nature. A regular source of national anxiety was Tipu Sultan, the most energetic of the Indian leaders and the most committed to the destruction of British influence. A potent source of information on Tipu's 'machinations' was William Kirkpatrick,[*] Resident at Hyderabad from 1793–1797. Kirkpatrick was also a great friend of Edmonstone and Cherry with whom he shared a desire for much greater Company interference in Indian affairs. As Resident at Hyderabad, Kirkpatrick had invested a great deal in expanding his corps of agents and spies, and improving his intelligence network to keep an obsessive check on Tipu's every movement. The Company had been made embarrassingly aware of its acute lack of an intelligence network during the disastrous Second Anglo-Mysore War[†] and had made a great deal of improvements since then. Until then, the Company had been circumspect about the usefulness of the harkara, or courier system, of intelligence gathering and had grossly underpaid their staff, not paying important intelligence officials more than 2 guineas for dangerous work. By the mid 1790s, this had changed entirely, and Kirkpatrick now had a vast communication network of harkaras and dak relays.

---

[*]William's younger brother was James Achilles Kirkpatrick, who features in William Dalrymple, *White Mughals*, New Delhi: Penguin Books Limited, 2004.
[†]Began in 1780 when Hyder Ali attacked the Carnatic and ended with his unexpected death in 1782.

Long used in Indian intelligence and post gathering, harkaras were believed to have been trained through a system of set exercises and competition, similar to that existing in neighbouring Safavid Iran. Runners from Mughal India and Persia regularly ran to each other's empires in the seventeenth century so it is believed that Tavernier's description of Persian runners' training would have been similar to the Indian runners too:

> The young Persian runner began walking practice slowly at the age of six or seven. The next year he began to run a league at a time 'at a handsome trot'. The following year he ran two or three leagues. At the age of eighteen, he was given water bottle, bread pan and other accoutrements.

The best class of harkara were expected to possess an astonishing degree of mental as well as physical accomplishments. Classical knowledge of subjects such as the Vedas, astronomy or astrology,* and, surprisingly, vocal music, was required in addition to five languages, 'Dravid (Tamil), Telang (Telegu), Karnataki (Kannada), Avidhi (Awadhi) and Marathi.' Bodily strength, the ability to disguise oneself and, worryingly, the ability to be 'steadfast in bringing news in wartime' was further appreciated. It was imperative that the harkara be quick-witted and articulate, since for security reasons written messages were only a supplement to a verbal message which he had to deliver accurately. Having spoken his message to the 'Presence' it was destined for, an answer (jawab) was always sought. Throwing a harkara out of the city on a donkey or blackening his face signalled a declaration of war. Unlike the situation in the Ottoman empire or in Central Asia, India did not replace its runners with camel or horse post,† and this harkara system persisted into the mid-nineteenth century.

The question of who could control the intelligence networks that surged and ebbed through the country, deep now into the hinterlands, was one that would play an astonishingly Machiavellian role in the

---

*Lower classes of harkara required less scriptural knowledge, but even they had to know 'three or four languages' and one script, be clever and 'capable of appearing in various guises.' See C.A. Bayly, *Rulers, Townsmen and Bazaars: North Indian Society in the Age of British Expansion: 1770–1870,* New Delhi: OUP India, 2012, p. 64.

†Possibly because of the availability of cheap labour in India, and the difficulty of maintaining horses. Humans could also blend into the population and escape notice more easily.

future of Awadh as Shore made preparations for the overland journey to Lucknow. Kirkpatrick was particularly aggressive in his defence of the most devious and deceitful tactics that the Company was now using against Tipu Sultan. Writing about the Third Anglo-Mysore War (1790–1792) he praised those tactics that had 'obtained dominion over them (Mysoreans) either by Conquest or Circumvention; under the specious name of Aid, that is either by open Force or underhand Fraud.' But Shore himself was relatively sanguine about the sultan, writing to Cornwallis in January of that year that 'the preparations of Tippoo have not been extended in any degree to excite new alarm.' A more immediate concern was the appearance of an old nemesis from across the Hindu Kush—a Durrani warrior from Kabul.

The death of Ahmad Shah Durrani's son Timur Shah in 1793 had been followed by a violent period of palace revolutions. Twenty-four of his sons had fought each other for supremacy as the Afghan empire crumpled around them in a bloody civil war. The twenty-three-year-old Zaman Shah finally claimed the throne and following in the lead of his grandfather Ahmad Shah, had decided to march into India to restore his fortunes. After two failed attempts, it was in late 1796 that Zaman Shah had crossed the Indus and marched on India for the third time with an army of 32,000 cavalry and 1,400 infantry. Zaman Shah had been encouraged in his march by an ambassador sent by Tipu Sultan to his court. In 1797, two men dressed as wandering fakirs and carrying letters of credentials carefully folded into bamboo sticks had made their way to Kabul. 'It is become proper and incumbent upon the leaders of the faithful that uniting together they exterminate the infidels', the note from Tipu Sultan had said. More pointedly, he added that 'the supremacy of the English was the source of evil to all God's creatures'.

To the British themselves, this brawl of ferocious warriors attacking the borders of India was something of a blessing in disguise. If ever Zaman Shah were to reach Delhi, the threat of him plundering Lucknow was very real and could be used as a useful tool to force monetary and military concessions from the nawab. As to the actual threat of the Afghan reaching Delhi, this never seemed likely since Zaman Shah had stopped at Lahore itself. Indeed while en route to Lucknow, Shore wrote to his wife to say, 'I have no fears about Zaman

Shah: he was at Lahore on the 17th of January: and if he come to Delhi this year, he must make haste*. I think the prospective danger alarming; the immediate danger, a very good instrument in promoting my views with the vizier—There are politics for you!' He also confirmed this in a dispatch to Calcutta writing that 'Zaman Shah by the last accounts was still at Lahore, and there was no authentic intelligence that he has dispatched considerable part of his troops in advance.'† Before long Zaman Shah turned towards home from Lahore itself, upon hearing of threats to his throne in Kabul.

As Shore made his way to Lucknow, therefore, passing mango groves and tamarind trees, he was wracked with seemingly impossible and opposite aims to live up to. On the one hand was his need to live up to his ideals of his moral certitude, of Evangelical paternalism and his need to lead by example the life of a righteous man if he was to return to England and the 'Clapham Sect' Evangelical haven. On the other hand, his very career and his future in India were being railroaded by men like Henry Hobart, who demanded aggressive actions. Judging all these shenanigans from Britain was the Secretary of State for War, Henry Dundas‡. Dundas, of furrowed brow and florid face, was described as a man 'of bold and manly spirit', though one member of parliament lamented that he was 'miserably Scottish in his accent, and inelegant in his arrangement and diction'. More pertinent to matters in India than his dismaying Scots accent was the fact that his term as president of the Board of Control of the EIC was described as being one of 'pillage and patronage', demonstrating the extraordinary level of violence and plunder that had been approved by Dundas in the British colonies.

There is enough to show that propelled by these febrile conditions, and despite his reputation for non-interference, Shore had in fact conceded to the need to obtain results in Awadh whatever the means.

---

*It took several months for the journey, and the Afghan would have had to calculate a return journey well in time to avoid the terrible north Indian summer.
†He also wrote to the governor of Madras to say: 'I retain my conviction that he will not advance this season beyond the Punjab.'
‡He was 1st viscount Melville, a Scottish MP, and the first Secretary of State for War in 1796. His legacy is today highly controversial, as he is recognized as being instrumental in deferring the abolition of the Atlantic slave trade, causing more than half a million enslaved Africans to be sent across the Atlantic due to the delay. Slave trading by British ships was not abolished until 1807. He was president of the Board of Control of the EIC from 1793–1801.

'I see no difficulty in combining an effectual interference [in Awadh] directed by the sole object of the Public Good, with an ostensible disavowal of it', Shore had admitted to Cherry the previous year. The notion of what the 'public good' might be in light of the Company's new paternalistic attitude had been hinted at strongly over the past few years. There had been a series of pointed anonymous[*] letters in the Calcutta press, urging the Governor General to take a more robust attitude with regards to Asaf. The reasons given were varied, but some seemed to have been aimed directly at Shore, when writing of the 'paternal care' that the Company needed to exercise to bring good governance to Awadh, and not let 'the happiness of some millions of subjects...be sacrificed to a mistaken and reprehensible delicacy'. With Zaman Shah providing such an unexpected and timely excuse for interference, Shore could take comfort from having such a convenient bogeyman to exert pressure on Asaf. Shore had written to Dundas acknowledging this ruse, saying that 'I hope (the nawab's) fears of Zeman Shah will open his eyes to his true Interests, and enable me to promote the advantage of the Company: for this purpose I promise you all the Zeal and Exertion of which I am capable.'

Despite Shore's bombastic letter to Dundas, it seems clear that he continued to prevaricate about his future course of action. Hobart had also written to Dundas, complaining that Shore was being his usual dithering self in his interactions with Awadh: 'I have heard too, but not with sufficient accuracy to state it, that Sir John Shore is pledg'd and unpledged upon the subject of Oude as disgracefully to himself as injuriously to the honour of his Government.' That Shore was making different promises to different people, or that he was reneging on stated promises was entirely plausible. For while he seemed convinced about the loyalty of Asaf himself, willing to 'pledge my life on his attachment to the Company', he was nonetheless wracked by uncertainty about the best way in which to obtain what he wanted from the rich nawabi of Awadh. 'The two points which I should most wish to obtain from the Vizier,' Shore wrote to Dundas, 'are the possession of Allahabad, and a Tract of Country equal to the tribute; one or the other might possible e'er this have been gained, if I had not attempted the Reform in his Administration.' These were not humble designs that Shore

---

[*]The authors of some of the letters are believed to have been Cherry and Edmonstone.

had decided upon. The fortress of Allahabad, built by Akbar himself, was one of the great strategic fortresses of Hindustan, one which was indispensable to the security and integrity of Awadh. Asaf had already outright refused to hand over this fortress to the Company, and Shore knew that the nawab would be intractable. As to ceding Awadhi territory to the Company, Asaf would have viewed this as untenable.

Though this was his first visit to Awadh, John Shore was already on exceedingly cordial terms with at least one member of the nawabi family: a year before setting off for Lucknow, in February 1796, Shore had granted a personal interview to Asaf's half-brother, Saadat Ali Khan. He also maintained a warmly genial correspondence with Saadat Ali Khan, in which he referred to him as 'my friend', and even declared that 'it is my sincere desire to gratify your wishes upon every practicable occasion'. Ever since his failed coup to seize the nawabi in 1775, Saadat Ali Khan had been biding his time. Living in Benaras on a pension that his half-brother grudgingly had to give him, he cultivated a friendship with the Company officials, and made regular visits to Calcutta to participate in Company festivities. His proximity to the British population at Benaras had clearly influenced Saadat Ali Khan, for a British traveller (Charles Madan) passing through in 1787 had noted that 'if you hunt with him, his pack I'm told is so very well managed that you may fancy yourself with "Lord Fitzwilliam", or "Mr. Mennel". He always rides in cap and boots, leather breeches etc. and upon the most capital horses. If you dine or sup with him, the same appearance of everything "English" strikes you'. These wonderfully familiar trappings of English aristocracy in the ancient and bewildering city of Benaras made Saadat Ali Khan 'much liked by the English'. Now, with the arrival of his 'friend' John Shore, Saadat Ali Khan began to believe that the stars were aligning for him at last.

John Shore first met Asaf outside Lucknow, near Jaunpur, where the nawab had come to ceremonially greet his visitor and escort him back to Lucknow. The nawab would have known at once that this visit was unlike the earlier visits by Cornwallis and Hastings, for amassed outside Lucknow was an ominous battalion of native infantry, the soldiers smartly dressed in their short red jackets, white pantaloons and black boots. This presence of a fighting corps from the Company's army would have sent a clear message to the nawab about the strength of the Company and the status of the Governor General.

The Company party was housed in grand style among the nawab's glittering palaces and fragrant gardens. Initially at least, all was well, as Shore found Asaf to be 'naturally good' and the only deficiency he felt arose from 'bad advisers, mean associates and absolute power'. The men had a private audience soon after Shore's arrival 'from which we separated both much pleased'. But very rapidly, Shore began to demonstrate views suspiciously similar to those of Edmonstone and Cherry. The Governor General had a relapse of his chronic health issues while in Lucknow and suffered 'a fever every night and a headache almost constant and a general depression upon him.' In his feverish and vulnerable state, he seemed to become entirely receptive to the views of the most aggressive of the Company men. Resident Lumsden had written to Shore a few months prior complaining that he saw in Lucknow 'more and more reason to fear that (the nawab's) present Servants are capable of every act of Treachery by which they conceive that our influence may be diminished, and that they might be able to persuade their Master to adopt measures which would prove ultimately ruinous to himself under the pretence of relieving him from Subjection'. As for Edmonstone, he had written to Cherry a few months before to flippantly aver that if other methods failed, 'I should suppose (the nawab) must be alarmed in a different manner. *I presume we ought to exercise the power we possess of frightening him into a concurrence*\* in the measures recommended.'

Within a month of arriving at Lucknow, Shore was writing with distaste about the 'fools, knaves and sycophants, (that) compose the Court of the Illustrious Ruler of millions! Never did I undertake so unpleasant a task.' Though the nawab had ruled his country for more than twenty years, making it one of the most spectacularly flourishing states in India, Shore felt it useful to badger Asaf by 'talking to him on subjects which never entered his imagination—the prosperity of his country, the happiness of his subjects, the improvement of his Administration and the dignity of his character.' The improvement of the administration that Shore desperately wanted to achieve was, of course, the Company's. For all his lofty talk, the Governor General wanted the possession of Allahabad for the company with imperious

---

\*Emphasis added.

urgency. 'If Zaman Shah had advanced,' wrote Shore with vivid regret to Dundas, 'I should have obtained it or have deemed myself justified in taking possession of it, even against the Vizier's consent on the grounds of necessity.'

Asaf, however, remained steadfastly opposed to the relinquishing of Allahabad and with no viable excuse left to seize it, Shore admitted defeat. He did, however, obtain one crucial concession—the dismissal of Raja Jhau Lal, and an additional subsidy of 5.5 lakh rupees per year. 'My time in Lucknow...did not pass in amusement, or even pleasantly,' wrote a pained Shore to the governor of Bombay. 'I was engaged in the very disagreeable attempt of making an Ethiopian white; and I cannot flatter myself that I have made much impression on his complexion.' In these edifying remarks on the nawab's complexion, Shore was quite plainly repeating what Grant had famously claimed, about the difference in moral complexion between the Europeans and the Indians, while also conflating the 'native' moral degradation with that of the African enslaved people. Shore's nightly fevers and headaches may therefore have been a physical manifestation of the emotional turmoil he suffered while aligning his own sense of moral superiority with the vicious and aggressive bullying he was subjecting the nawab to, for he quickly recovered his health as soon as he left Lucknow.

Shore may have believed that he had had little effect on the nawab's temperament or 'complexion', but he was being disingenuous, for his effect on the nawab was to be fatal. When he met Asaf, he was surprised to find him in robust health; 'the age of the Vizier is about 51; his health is vigorous, and has not yet suffered from the habitual use of opium in large quantities.' The nawab appeared to be in buoyant health, with Shore noticing that the nawab's opium consumption did not affect his appetite or his strength. Indeed, though Asaf was five years older than Shore, it was the younger man who suffered from debilitating ill health. 'He enjoys a remarkably good state of health; and is subject, as far as I can learn, to no complaint...' continued Shore, almost against his better judgement. And yet, shockingly, within five months of the Governor General's departure from Lucknow, Nawab Asaf-ud-Daula would be dead.

# DEATH OF A NAWAB

At the beginning of John Shore's visit, in February of 1797, Asaf had reason to be cautiously optimistic. The Governor General had a reputation for clemency and equanimity, and Asaf had, after all, already successfully dealt with the austerely cerebral Hastings and the pugnacious Cornwallis with skilled diplomacy. And apart from the Governors General there had been the Residents, the agents, and the endless grasping European merchants. So many men had trespassed on his hospitality, had feinted and feigned, and still the nawab had parried their incessant attempts to curtail his sovereignty and limit his wealth. As for the strident demands for greater subsidies, Asaf had always managed eventually to wear down the Company men, and have the subsidies written off or reduced. Asaf had begun courting the new Governor General upon his arrival at Calcutta in 1794, tactfully sending him presents of pomegranates and apples, having heard of his anti-corruption drive, and had written to him letters full of warmth and eager pleasure. Shore too, seemed pleased at the beginning of his stay at Lucknow, and wrote that 'the Nabob and myself visit daily, and are in the best humour imaginable with each other.' There was one ominous note, however, and that was Shore's absolute refusal to interact with Asaf's favourite courtier, Raja Jhau Lal.

Ever since the upheaval in the nawab's administration caused by Cherry the previous year, when Asaf had replaced all other ministers with Jhau Lal and with his own sons, the nawab had been very keen to have his favourite approved by the Company officers. He had sent Jhau Lal along with Wazir Ali, his young heir now fifteen years old, to Kanpur, and Jhau Lal had also accompanied the nawab on his tour of Allahabad, Kanpur, and Farrukhabad, 'to show off to the English and his subjects the dignity with which he had invested Jhau Lal'. But the English had 'snubbed' the minister, and the nawab had returned to Awadh with dread in his heart.

In a court fairly fizzing with intrigues, factions, and ever-shifting loyalties, Jhau Lal seemed to have been the one constant in the nawab's life. He had joined the nawab's service in 1775, and had been utterly loyal to Asaf his entire career. His steady loyalty also meant that he was completely opposed to the Company, unlike men of substance like Hasan Reza Khan and Tikait Rai who would view with indulgence the overtures by the British officials. Historian C. A. Bayly has noted that the fiercest opponents of the British in India were people of humbler birth, who had less to lose, and 'a more developed sense of traditional patriotism' and Jhau Lal was a Kayastha of very pedestrian origins. This made him devoted to the nawab who had lifted him out of obscurity, and also 'dangerously anti-British' in his views simply because he would put Asaf's desires before the Company's.

Jhau Lal also possessed a power which the Company was beginning to view with the greatest suspicion—control of the intelligence network. In his time, Shuja had been celebrated as 'the best-informed man in Hindoostan' and he was supposed to have employed 20,000 harkaras in the 1770s* in Awadh alone. Now in the 1790s, as head of intelligence and someone who commanded dozens of skilled harkaras who crossed the length and breadth of northern India, Jhau Lal could amass accurate and early information. He also controlled the Lucknow kotwal chief,† had placed informants strategically in the army, and had deputed agents at Delhi. Shore admitted that 'the dauk, an intelligence department, was very extensive under Jhao Lal', further grumbling that it was a 'source of great oppression as the hercarrahs were much oftener employed as spies and informers for the purpose of extortion than in their proper duties.'

The 'source of oppression' that Shore lamented was that these particular harkaras were working for the nawab, instead of the Company. For it was the Company that now began to control an ever expanding network of informants and spies. Already in the 1770s Modave had been amazed at the intelligence network the Company possessed:

> It cannot be simple curiosity that makes them send lively and intelligent emissaries to all corners, to gather intelligence about the counties and their affaires. The English already know the large territory that separates Bengal from the frontiers with China, as well as the road from Calcutta to Delhi... what other objective

---
*In comparison, the Mughal empire was said to have had 4,000 imperial harkaras.
†The kotwal chief was a certain Bahadur Ali, whose remit was the security of the property and persons of a population of half a million people, according to John Shore.

could there be to their daily activities, regular acquisition of lands, and the hidden and in-depth measures of the English administration in India.

It would become supremely important to the EIC to isolate Awadh from political events outside of the province, by controlling the flow of intelligence. They wanted to maintain a choke-hold on information, by ensuring that the Resident remained the sole conduit of intelligence into and out of Awadh.

In addition to his invaluable role as chief intelligence officer, Jhau Lal was a tireless servant of the state. Even Abu Talib, ever critical of the nawab's favourites, noted that he worked for twelve hours a day, starting his day at 4 a.m. For not only did he need to oversee his spy network, and carry out the functions of the diwan, but the nawab also desired his presence by his side at all times. Almas Ali Khan once chided Jhau Lal for working right through the day, citing the example of Safdar Jang, who had kept a fixed time and place for business. But Jhau Lal pragmatically shrugged and replied 'I know nothing of Safdar Jang, but I know this much... Everyone who refers any matter to me must receive a reply whether it be "yes or no".' Asaf was consequently very dependent on Jhau Lal, and used to say that 'Hasan Reza Khan, Haidar Beg, and Tikait Rai* were all three untrue to me, but Jhau Lal set my house to rights.'

But Shore was unable to disguise his fierce disdain for men like Jhau Lal, and indeed for all of the nawab's courtiers. 'His confidants are the meanest and lowest people,' wrote Shore to his wife and as for the nawab, 'every evening, almost, he stupefies himself with opium'. Confronted with this inflexible rigidity the nawab may have believed that the Governor General, like countless Company men before him, was holding out for other incentives because within a week, he had a private audience with Shore during which he offered him '5 lakhs of rupees and 8 thousand gold mohurs' of which 4 lakhs were for Shore, 1 for his attendants, and the gold was meant for Lady Shore. This offer allowed Shore to enact the charade of the incorruptible Englishman and he 'peremptorily declined' the money. Instead Shore requested from Asaf as a keepsake a small portrait that the Governor

---

*John Shore describes Husain Reza Khan and Tikait Rai's 'attachment to the company' as 'most sincere'.

General had spotted in the Aina Khana that Zoffany had painted of the nawab, though he privately scoffed to his wife that he deemed it a worthless painting.

As for Jhau Lal, whom Asaf was hoping to send to attend upon the Governor General, Shore refused to tolerate his presence, and instead began insisting that the nawab ban him from Lucknow altogether. Shore outlined the reason to the Calcutta Council, as to why Jhau Lal was such a nefarious presence: 'I had the most satisfactory conviction that the ascendency of Jao Lal over the Vizier was systematically directed to oppose and undermine the influence of the Company's government and that the preservation of it was in great measure dependent on the subject of my endeavour to destroy the influence of Jao Lal...' Shore declared that he would not attend the nawab's durbar as long as Jhau Lal were part of his council, a statement the nawab would have seen as a shockingly obnoxious interference in his affairs. Unsurprisingly, during their next meeting Shore found the mood of the nawab much altered, arrogantly writing that 'he is a weather-cock; and to fix him is my task.' Frustrated and furious, Asaf railed at Tafazzul Hussain Khan\* that '(Shore) wanted to turn his house topsy-turvy, and sweep the Augean stable clean'.† But Tafazzul Hussain Khan was the one man that the British trusted, and it was he who 'with masterly eloquence and honour...strengthened and enforced all the dictates' that Shore had laid down. That the British were steadfastly insistent on Tafazzul was no surprise. A subtle and intelligent man with a deep Indo-Persian education and a command of English, he had become very friendly with various Company men, including Shore, since his appointment as ambassador of the court of Awadh to the EIC at Calcutta in 1788.

What John Shore's dictates demanded was that the nawab certainly not be allowed to control his own administration, along with a known 'anti-British' minister like Jhau Lal, who favoured Asaf's privileges

---

\*Allama Tafazzul Hussain Khan Kashmiri, popularly known as the Khan-i-Allama, was from a well-regarded family who had become courtiers to the nawabs of Awadh. Tafazzul had studied at the Firangi Mahal of Lucknow and became a highly reputed Persian savant with a talent for debate, mathematics, astronomy, and Aristotelian logic. He was fluent in Persian and Arabic, able to read Latin and Greek, and had a good command of English.
†A phrase that John Shore uses indicating that he was trying to clean the nawab's administration of corruption.

over the Company's. Instead, it was Tafazzul who was forced through as minister, despite the nawab's stated reluctance,* while Jhau Lal was dismissed from office and banished to Benaras.

As for the issue of Allahabad, which Shore had wanted astonishingly to claim outright for the Company he found 'the reluctance of the Vizier to relinquish the possession of this fortress insuperable by argument or persuasion, nothing but absolute intimidation could overrule him.' Not surprisingly, Asaf viewed this move as 'an attempt for depriving him of his country', and was absolutely determined that he would not allow it. Instead, Shore insisted that Asaf have the fort repaired and allow it to be used as a depot for provisions and military stores, under the command of a British officer 'It was not without much perseverance and a disavowal of any intention to ask for the possession of the fort,' that Shore was able to get the nawab to agree to this egregious plan. Shore also forced Asaf to agree to pay for two regiments of cavalry, one 'native' and one European, which the nawab had categorically refused to do before the arrival of the Governor General.

After more than twenty years of resisting the increasing attempts by the Company to interfere in the governance of Awadh, it can seem astonishing that Asaf gave in to the demands of a Governor General whom posterity has viewed almost consistently as a weak, timid, and vacillating man. There are some clues in the letters he wrote to Henry Dundas that Shore must have used the language of bullying arrogance, as well as the threat of newly acquired Company power to browbeat the nawab into submission:

> I will not pretend to assert that the Concessions of the Vizier were voluntary; he yielded to persevering Importunity, aided by the habitual ascendancy of the Power of the Company over him, and the Weight of my Public Station. In my presence he was ever submissive even to humiliation; he never attempted the Discussion of my propositions or any Reply to the arguments by which they were supported, yet he never would have yielded anything to the language of reason.

---

*The nawab asked for Almas Ali Khan to be installed as minister instead, but Shore refused, apparently unsure about the Company's ability to control such a powerful man. 'His severe, arbitrary and unaccommodating disposition' wrote Shore to the Council, 'which might have led him into opposition or inattention to the recommendations of the President.'

A further hint that Shore's tone to 'native' rulers might not have been quite as graciously patient and conciliating as with his Company interlocutors can be inferred from his letters to the young nazim of Bengal. These letters portray a man who could be 'condescending, threatening and irritable' when the Nazim did not acquiesce perfectly with Shore's demands. And if Hobart's methods were 'overtly coercive tactics', then Shore's letters were deemed to contain 'an undertone of menace with insinuations that something unspecified but terrible would happen if the Nazim did not comply'.

What, then, may have been the tenor of the private conversations that Shore had with the nawab, of which no records exist at all? It is entirely plausible that relentlessly encouraged by eager imperialists like Edmonstone who were his constant companions, terribly aware that his sworn enemy Hobart was expecting his methods to fail, and of his own unsuitability for the task as a non-military man, Shore used the non-existent menace of Zaman Shah and the alarming presence of Company troops to bully, threaten, and intimidate the nawab into agreeing to all of his changes. In his letters to his wife with whom Shore did not need to curate his words, Shore writes almost playfully that he could have, 'upon the dragooning plan' obtained his results with the nawab in five days instead of five weeks. He even told her that Tafazzul had admitted that '"I have done as much as possible since I have been here, unless I had adopted the dragooning plan."—Nous verrons[*]!' 'Dragooning' was of course the exact term that Shore had used to criticize Hobart's methods in forcing a treaty with the raja of Tanjore, as being morally dishonest. These letters to Charlotte Shore prove that a 'dragooning' plan in fact *did* exist in the case of the nawab of Awadh; it was simply that Shore could not be seen to be using it so as to maintain the moral high ground. Instead, bolstered by his new awareness of the intimidating strength of the Company, and a battalion of menacing Company soldiers camped outside Lucknow, Asaf was subjected to the serrated edge of Shore's moods and was cowed enough for Shore to push through his agenda 'against the Vizier's consent on the grounds of necessity'... 'I was, however, obliged to appear somewhat angry with his Excellency,' admitted Shore to the governor of Bombay. 'He has been very angry since I went away, and very submissive.'

---

[*] 'We will see.'

For some days before Shore's departure from Lucknow in April, Asaf appeared reconciled to matters and 'in the best humour,' regaining his old affability. In stark opposition to the Company's churlish and crass behaviour, Shore admitted that the nawab met him with steadfast good humour and 'invariable attention on his part to my care and accommodation'. As soon as Shore had left Lucknow, however, Asaf, faced with the grim reality of all the humiliations he had been subjected to, appeared to fly into a rage and strode into the well-appointed houses he had generously set aside for William Palmer and the Resident, Lumsden, and evicted the men peremptorily from those quarters. Shore saw this as another instance of the nawab demonstrating 'the Passions of a Child'. But clearly this truculence was the frustration and rage of a man who had always done everything within his power to accommodate the bottomless avidity of the Company men, only to be treated with outrageous disrespect, humiliating threats, and the brazen curtailing of his sovereignty.

The reasons that the Company would always advance for their interference in Awadhi affairs would be the lackadaisical disinterest of the nawabs in the management of their province, leading to the impoverishment of the state. But, in fact, the opposite was true. What Shore had observed in Lucknow instead was a fabulously wealthy court with a powerful army and intelligence network, and a nawab who was determined to maintain his sovereignty and his country's integrity. '(The nawab) intends to press the argument of no-interference in the affairs of Oude...and to resist with the utmost force, all connection with the English government except the regular payment of the subsidy' Cherry had written miserably in 1796. And allied to him was Jhau Lal, a man who hated the British and who was a master of espionage, and therefore incalculably dangerous. Shore admitted as much to Dundas after his return to Calcutta:

> (Jhau Lal)'s Power is great, and might be dangerous, if he had the Capacity to improve and exert it; His Revenues notwithstanding the Defalcations from mismanagement are equal to all his Expenses, and even to furnish a Fund for accumulation.

Even Claude Martin, that great detractor of everything the nawab represented, had warned John Shore in 1794 about the potential threat posed by Asaf's wealthy country:

> (The nawab has) a great accumulation of treasure, a large family which our legislators can't do otherwise but to acknowledge, an extensive dominion- with great progress of military science as well in this country, as all the powerful neighbours, the easy methods of making firearms all over India, with the small forces we have in this part not sufficient to defend our own territory...

And this was a policy that the Company had always maintained with regards to Awadh with obsessive anxiety, from the time of Shuja's post-Buxar reign. Back in 1768 the Council at Calcutta had noted with worry the placing of Shuja's dak posts even in the Deccan, 'an indefinite augmentation of his troops, (and) his curiosity concerning our affairs in the Deccan.' Astonishingly, the President already outlined the Company's objective regarding Hindustani powers, declaring that 'I think it ought to be our invariable aim carefully to restrict any one power in Hindustan from rising too high above the general level.' Now with their vastly increased powers and fuelled by their paranoia of French and other foreign aggressions, 'the funds for improving the Company's army could be obtained and a potential rival destroyed, by annexing Awadh.'

For a short while after Shore's departure, Asaf may have believed he could still bide his time, and wait out the tenure of John Shore. Jhau Lal had previously received the information that Shore was due to return to England shortly. But Tafazzul kept an unyielding watch on the nawab, who would have been quite aware of the minister's entirely pro-British loyalties. And in May came a final devastating blow. Jhau Lal was ordered to move with his family to distant Patna, quite beyond the reach of the nawab. It was at this point, finally, that Asaf seemed to give up the will to live.

For all his life Nawab Asaf-ud-Daula seemed to have benefitted from a robustly solid constitution despite his impressive girth. His tireless energy, his enthusiasms and exceeding good humour were often remarked upon. Even Shore had noted that Asaf enjoyed 'a remarkably good state of health'. Shore further noted, in a semi-scientific treatise to no less a luminary than the great Evangelist and abolitionist William Wilberforce, that the nawab did not suffer from the side-effects of excessive opium* consumption, concluding that opium could therefore be taken to great benefit at a later stage of one's life, 'at a period of life when the natural benefits begin'! Nor does the nawab seem to have drunk to excess, as witnessed by his English factotum Lewis Ferdinand in 1797:

> He was once fond of drinking European liquors to excess, especially claret and cherry brandy, but he has lately foresworn it, and now intoxicates himself with large quantities of opium, and a green inebriating leaf called subzee (cannabis)...

Ever since the previous year when Zaman Shah had first begun his aggressive military posturing, Asaf had been filled with malaise and an overwhelming sense of dread. He had told his attendants that 'all the people of this country but me will see the commotion (Zaman Shah's) invasion will cause, I shall not live to see it'. He began to see dark visions in the quiet and dangerous murmurings of soothsayers and holy men and became 'certain that he was going to die'. After Jhau Lal was banished, Asaf's sense of foreboding deepened, surrounded as he now was by ministers who viewed him with the coldly gauging gaze of vultures, assessing where their interest lay. He began to appear in public visibly intoxicated and even, shockingly, during a religious festival. 'He is seldom seen by our Resident,' Shore was writing in early September 1797, 'but in a state of Intoxication and in this situation he exhibited himself lately at a very solemn Mahommedan festival.'

Edmonstone recorded the nawab as suffering 'for a great length of time' from excessive opium consumption, but this could not have been accurate since Shore himself had agreed that the nawab's appetite, energy, and sleeping habits, just five months before his death, were entirely unchanged, which would not have been the case if he had been an opium addict.† Instead, the nawab appeared to have been overwhelmed by a fatal sense of impending disaster and, in a sense, allowed himself to die. In his last weeks, he remained intoxicated and deliberately refused all medication even when he began showing symptoms of opium poisoning.‡ Through these final ravaged weeks

---

*Opium became a Company controlled monopoly in 1798.
†Opium addicts are skeletally thin, since appetite is entirely suppressed. See the famous painting of Inayat Khan—Dying Inayat Khan—a courtier of Jahangir's and an opium addict.
‡Edmonstone described the nawab's condition as follows; '...his limbs swelled, his body wasted

as he felt the night closing in on him, Asaf fiercely refused to let the Resident or Tafazzul witness his spectacular disintegration. Whenever they were nearby, he marshalled the last of his willpower, and strode about talking with his usual jovial ebullience, swatting away all enquiries about his health. But there was one person before whom the nawab had neither the desire nor the will to keep up a façade—his mother.

When she heard the calamitous news about her son's health, a distressed Bahu Begum rushed to Lucknow. As soon as she saw her beloved son mortally ill, Bahu Begum began sobbing and rushed to his side and Asaf allowed himself at last to fall weeping into his mother's arms. Mother and son remained inconsolable for the final weeks of the nawab's illness and Asaf finally died, in the comfort of his mother's embrace, on the afternoon of 21 September 1797.

Nawab Asaf-ud-Daula died much as his father had done, a proudly independent sovereign of a rich and powerful state. But this was about to change dramatically, for even weeks before the nawab's death Shore had been anticipating this outcome and had informed Dundas that the issue of the nawab's succession, now imminent, 'appeared more embarrassing than it appeared from a more distant view'.

---

away, his appetite forsook him—and the latter part of his life was little more than a continual lethargy...' (In M. K. Chancey, *In the Company's Secret Service: Neil Benjamin Edmonstone and the First Indian Imperialists, 1780–1820,* Florida State University. 2003, p. 87)

# THE SECRETS OF THE ZENANA

On a cold January day in 1798, Kothi Bibiapur outside Lucknow was witness to the most extraordinary scenes. Situated 5 miles east of Lucknow on the banks of the Gomti, Kothi Bibiapur was an elegant two-storeyed Indo-European style building which Asaf had built around 1775[*]. Initially used as a hunting lodge, it was a serene structure, with walls of pale gold, elegant columns rising with sober majesty. The kothi was surrounded by extensive parkland, and was often used as a temporary accommodation for Residents and Company officials. But now the quiet parks were ablaze with colour and commotion as a huddle of colourful tents shivered in the cold air. Two tents in particular were distinguished by their brocaded opulence and numerous discreet screens—these were the tents of Bahu Begum, mother of Asaf, and Shams-un-Nisa Begum, Asaf's widow. In addition to these two grand ladies, all the powerful courtiers and wealthy elite of Lucknow including Hassan Reza Khan and Tikait Rai were gathered in fretful groups, in encampments on the grounds. The two great khwajasaras were there too—Bahu Begum's emissary Jawahar Ali Khan, and Almas Ali Khan, the wealthiest landowner of Awadh. Meanwhile, inside Kothi Bibiapur itself, crimson-jacketed British Company men whispered together in belligerent groups. Governor General John Shore, Resident Lumdsen and Edmonstone conducted intense discussions and scrutinized countless messages, working in a fever of intrigue and machination. 'My mind has been worked up to a pitch beyond its strength' exclaimed Shore in a letter to his wife. Nervously gathered around the Governor's party were all the European residents of Lucknow, harried and nervous. For what Shore and his party had come to Lucknow to effect was quite simply a coup d'etat.

The mood of charged anticipation that rippled through the kothi and the tents was proof that this was no celebratory gathering. Roaming the grounds of the kothi and massing in ever-swelling numbers were two battalions of the young Nawab Wazir Ali's soldiers. In an uneasy confrontation with the nawab's men were a troop of sepoys that Shore

---

[*]The identity of the architect remains uncertain. Tandon believes it could have been Charles Marsack, or any one of the European architects working in Lucknow at the time.

had brought with him from Benaras as well as his escort of armed bodyguards, who patrolled the kothi menacingly. On 11 January, the worried young nawab walked into the Kothi Bibiapur unannounced, to speak with the Governor General. Wazir Ali professed ignorance of all the military preparations that had been taking place in Lucknow, 'made unqualified professions of obedience' to the British, swore to follow all of Shore's recommendations and asked him to 'take him by the hand'. To which Shore grandly replied that 'as long as he behaved well, he should not want a protector in me, and at a time when he least expected it.'

When Asaf had died so unexpectedly in September 1797 almost everyone had been taken by surprise. The only possible candidate to succeed him seemed obvious—his son and heir Wazir Ali, barely sixteen at the time. Lumsden, Tafazzul, and all the other courtiers in Lucknow supported this decision and as for Bahu Begum, 'her only wish was that the succession should go in the line of the late nawab (Asaf) and not in that of his father Shuja-ud-Daula.' For Bahu Begum, the idea that a son of one of the lesser wives of Shuja should be made nawab was inconceivable. And so she bestowed the khillat upon the young Wazir Ali, under the benign gaze of Resident Lumsden and Asaf's widow. No doubt all the principal actors were serenely contemplating the malleable nature of such a young ruler. Wazir had also written gratifyingly to Shore, saying 'may the almighty preserve you, whom I consider in the place of my late Father, nay even as the Superior to him, as my respected uncle, as the disposer of me and mine'. Lumsden noted with satisfaction that 'Wazir Ali's disposition is mild and he will be easily advised.' A salute was ordered from Fort William in Calcutta to mark the happy succession and all seemed well.

But alongside these genial events surrounding the wazir, a much more energetic power base was coalescing around the one person in Lucknow whom the British still viewed with the greatest suspicion and fear—Bahu Begum. Immediately upon the death of Asaf, Bahu Begum had seized all the moveable property of her son's that she could—'elephants, tents, animals such as blue antelope, wild buffaloes, and milch cows, which she selected from his stock'. Instead of returning to Faizabad, Bahu Begum set up her own durbar in Lucknow, assisted by Almas Ali Khan, clearly intending to finally control the destiny of

Awadh. Bahu Begum also demanded the return of her confiscated jagirs as had been promised in 1782, as well as all the jewellery and private treasure of Asaf. Together, Bahu Begum and Almas Ali Khan were a formidable presence in Lucknow. These two players controlled huge tracts of land as well as a large army, had years of experience and enjoyed a devoted following[*]. Most of the senior gentry congregated to the begum's court, reassured by a return of the old nawabi system of patronage and power. But the British feared the power that Bahu Begum represented, especially allied with another independent power broker like Almas Ali Khan. The memory of Hastings's bruising battle with the begum and his subsequent trial for impeachment was still uncomfortably resonant, and the British rejected a proposal to make Bahu Begum formally part of the administration of the country. Shore had clarified his attitude in a letter to Dundas before he ever arrived in Lucknow: 'if the Begum perseveres in her opposition to (Tafazzul), or in other words, to the Company, the Question will be briefly this, whether we are to resign Oude to her government and that of Almas and leave the country, or maintain our influence there by force.'

As for Wazir Ali, being just a teenager and entirely unused to serious responsibilities, he behaved much as any youth would have, and bristled at the constant reprimands and haranguing orders that Tafazzul began issuing. The minister grumbled to Edmonstone that Wazir listened instead to the advice of 'the low people that he has about him', and instead of heeding Tafazzul's list of candidates appointed his own favourites to key positions. This was, naturally, no different to what earlier nawabs had done too, to quickly strengthen their vulnerable positions. It was no surprise either that Wazir should be intensely suspicious and resentful of Tafazzul. The minister was deeply unpopular in Lucknow as he was seen as blatantly following British orders and undertaking measures that were destroying the very fabric of Lucknawi society—slashing expenditure at all costs, including the money spent on costly celebrations and festivals like Diwali, and dismissing all staff he deemed superfluous. That Tafazzul was an agent of the British was an open secret. Ever since Tafazzul had become embroiled in Saadat Ali' Khan's[†] rebellion in 1775, he had been treated

---

[*]Hassan Reza Khan and Tikait Rai also supported this alliance.
[†]The learned Tafazzul had been appointed tutor to the young Mirza Mangli by Shuja-ud-Daula,

with genteel disdain by Asaf. As a result, Tafazzul quickly came to realize that his best chance of a glittering career was with the EIC at Calcutta, and had worked there since 1788 where he had become rapidly indispensable due to his robust erudition and language skills. After he had been reluctantly reappointed as minister to Asaf in the late 1790s, he had shown through his actions and especially through his recommendations to the EIC that he was, in fact, more British than the British. Shore had written to his wife during the fraught negotiations with Asaf earlier in 1797 that Tafazzul was peremptory in speaking the unvarnished truth to the nawab and that 'he even speaks plainer to the Nabob than I do'. Now regarding Wazir's behaviour, Tafazzul wrote to Edmonstone recommending 'downright coercion', to remove all the young nawab's favourites from court. Tafazzul would later remonstrate with the British men that 'this is Hindustan, not Europe; and affairs cannot be done here as in Europe', assuring them that notions of honour, loyalty, and decency were to be jettisoned at the borders of the country of Awadh.

Within a very short time, therefore, both Bahu Begum and Tafazzul were casting about for another candidate to the masnad in lieu of the disappointingly wilful Wazir Ali. Bahu Begum's candidate was Mirza Jangli, one of the surviving sons of Shuja while Tafazzul and the British party including Shore and Edmonstone preferred his amenable older half-brother, Saadat Ali Khan. And the reason that alternative candidate names were so breezily bandied about was that there were scandalous rumours regarding the parentage of Wazir Ali. That Wazir Ali was brought up as a prince and as the heir of Nawab Asaf-ud-Daula was incontrovertible. Wazir Ali had once charmed the painter Ozias Humphry with the grace of his impeccable manners even as small child. Unlike his own sputtering career as a schoolboy, Asaf had ensured that his heir 'learnt court manners and was well versed in letter writing, horse riding, sword fighting, archery and the game of polo*.' He had always been careful to present Wazir Ali as his only heir, as witnessed by Elizabeth Prosser and various Residents and Governors General. Wazir Ali's wedding in itself had been a magnificent proclamation of his status and Asaf had sent invitations

---

which explains why he got caught up in the events of 1775 when Asaf ascended to the masnad.
*He also learnt calligraphy from Muhammed Ali, a foremost master of the craft.

to Company officials. As to the fact of the nawab's progeny, no less a gossip than Claude Martin was witness to the fact that Asaf had children, when he wrote a letter to John Shore, recently arrived in India, to say that 'since (Asaf) took in his head to have children, his family (are) very much increased by it, they are of little expense as all his ladies are equally paid from the Sarkar, and receive dress equally, as those women are of low family, very few ready cash is given for their pin money...'

But now there were vicious whispers* being spread that Wazir was not Asaf's son at all, but that his mother was a 'farrash' or carpet cleaner, and that she had been brought into the nawab's zenana, already pregnant, to give birth to the child who was then adopted by Asaf as his own heir. Further proof offered that he was not Asaf's biological son was that, unlike the nawab, he was 'of a dark complexion, and not handsome', and there was 'nothing very princely in his appearance'.

Despite Shore's outraged and grand proclamations that 'no one with honour' could investigate the prurient details behind the hidden world of the zenana, the British were in fact very much doing just that. Their network of informants included 'burains', or old ladies, who worked in zenanas and who were also employed by the EIC as peeping toms who 'kept all India amused with a flow of dirty stories, till more severe morality intervened in the 1830s'. These old crones specialized in the recounting of salacious gossip from within the fabled harem, the more lurid the better. Another source of harem gossip were the khwajasaras. And it was the head khwajasara of the harem, Tehsin Ali Khan, who brought the British the dubious information about Wazir's lowly and duplicitous birth since he claimed to have been the one to have sneaked in the pregnant carpet cleaner into the harem. Apart from Tehsin Ali Khan, the EIC had by now infiltrated every major political faction with their spies. Wazir Ali's head harkara himself was a spy for the British, as was Jawahar Ali Khan, Bahu Begum's chief khwajasara, and Tafazzul had also placed a spy in Almas Ali Khan's camp. 'If strict control of what people can know is one of the hallmarks of the modern state,' writes Bayly, 'then it was between 1790 and 1820 that such a

---

*Interestingly, very similar rumours also surrounded the birth of James Stuart, son of James II of England, with Protestant naysayers claiming he had been snuck into the royal palace in the guise of a bed warmer.

state emerged in India,' and it was the British who masterminded that state. Edmonstone would live by this maxim of information control obsessively for the whole of his Indian career. He knew that they were outnumbered in the country by about 6,000 to 1 and was sharply aware of the vulnerability of the British position in India.

When Saadat Ali Khan had first grumbled to Shore about the gossip concerning Wazir Ali's parentage, Shore had dismissed this matter outright, as not pertinent to the succession. But within a few months, Shore had changed his mind. And so by November 1797 Shore was returning to Lucknow, comfortably reassured by his own assessment that 'in eastern countries, as there is no principle, there can be no confidence. Self-interest is the sole object of all; and suspicion and distrust prevail, under the appearance and professions of the sincerest intimacy and regard.' He was accompanied by Edmonstone who was coldly calculating about the measures that needed to be taken, and had already decided just one month after Wazir Ali's succession, 'to adopt coercive measures and a more direct interference' in the affairs of Awadh. Even Edmonstone, however, had the grace to feel some shame as they travelled to Lucknow, feigning friendship towards Wazir Ali. 'It was rather an extraordinary situation to be employed in a conspiracy against the Prince whose guests we were' he wrote to his sister sheepishly, 'and sounds as criminal as extraordinary'.

But criminal or not, Edmonstone would show a steely determination to oust Wazir Ali who, he claimed, had surrounded himself with 'panderers and low scoundrels' who 'rage of independence from the English.' By the time the British party reached Jaunpur and met with Tafazzul, the minister was waxing nostalgic about Nawab Asaf-ud-Daula, the man he had positively plagued to death: 'Wazir Ali bears no resemblance whatever to Asaf-ud-Daula', he complained bitterly. '(He had) an idea that by bringing out the troops and making a display of power and authority he will get into his own hands the entire control and management of affairs.' By now, Shore himself had decided that the 'Begum must be opposed and the nawab should be under tutelage and be compelled to submit to the direction of the Company through the Resident and (Tafazzul)'. By the time they reached Lucknow in December 1797 trailing a menacing assembly of soldiers and bodyguards, Shore refused to even allow Wazir Ali to meet him, and the young man grew fearful and uncertain. Lacking the diplomatic genius of his father and shackled by his own lack of experience, Wazir Ali alternated between pleading supplications and frustrated displays of military strength. When Wazir Ali called for reinforcements to assemble at Lucknow and Shore suddenly found the city teeming with armed men, the nervous British party decided to leave the city. On 10 January 1798 John Shore decided to escape to the relative seclusion and safety of Kothi Bibiapur, followed rapidly by the rest of the European population of Lucknow, to carry out his coup d'etat. Following the British party were the begums, the courtiers of Lucknow, and Wazir Ali himself, all tensely anticipating the Governor General's next move.

For the British, the farce of Wazir Ali's doubtful parentage[*] was only ever that—an elaborately constructed charade to disqualify Asaf's sons, and thereby remove Bahu Begum from a position of power. Only Saadat Ali would be an acceptable candidate for the nawabi. Saadat Ali, whom the begum detested and who had demeaned himself to the extent of immediately making a promise to the British that 'I shall while I live manifest my zeal for the Interests of the Company on every occasion…in all matters whatsoever I shall incessantly endeavour to manifest my obedience to them.' Saadat Ali, who had been courting the British from his exile at Benaras for twenty years, attending their celebrations at Calcutta, and even buying a second home in Calcutta much against Asaf's wishes. The begum sent a messenger to Shore, dismayed at his choice of candidate, urging him to consider Mirza Jangli who 'was universally liked and Saadat Ali Khan detested'. But Shore shouted at the man 'with a degree of temper' and insisted that only Saadat Ali Khan would do. There remained, however, the problem of Saadat Ali himself. Having spent more than twenty years away from Lucknow, Saadat Ali was unpopular with the people of Lucknow, and deemed 'secretive, parsimonious, and Anglicized'. He had no soldiers, no powerful supporters, suffered the disdain of the begum and was, moreover, 200 miles away in Benaras.

---

*According to Islamic law, Asaf's acknowledgement of Wazir was enough to make him his son. The character and motives of Tehsin were also somewhat questionable; as darogah earlier he had faced many complaints of illegal actions and corruption. And he had moreover had run-ins later with Wazir Ali and had threatened him with violence.

Having trumped up the embarrassing charade of Wazir Ali's doubtful parentage, Shore decided to present the courtiers at Lucknow with a fait accompli. He designed an elaborate ruse to have Saadat Ali brought over from Benaras, laying dak chowkis in every direction from Benaras so that spies would not realize in which direction Saadat Ali was being taken. Cherry organized the complicated deception in Benaras but first he had to make Saadat Ali accept the proposition that Shore had sent for him. In return for making him nawab, Saadat Ali 'had to agree to a stronger subsidiary than had ever been proposed by the Company to an Indian state'. The subsidy amount would be increased to a staggering 76 lakh rupees per annum, Allahabad would be forfeited to the Company, British troops increased to 10,000 while the nawab's army would be drastically reduced. Saadat Ali would not be allowed any interaction with other powers and what he was signing was in effect 'a treaty of vassalage.' For in the end, for the Company, it was never about the legitimacy of the ruler or the best governance of Awadh and its people. Instead, with Saadat Ali, Awadh was simply sold to the highest bidder.*

Early on 19 January 1798, Saadat Ali reached Kanpur and began marching towards Lucknow while in Kothi Bibiapur, Wazir Ali found himself abandoned. One by one all his supporters stepped back into the shadows, leaving Wazir Ali alone in the cold spotlight of British intransigence. As the British moved inexorably to isolate Wazir Ali from all his supporters, the young man shed tears of frustration and rage at all those who had recanted their promises to him. 'What has become of her Oaths, her religion and the Quran!' railed Wazir Ali, about the begum's promises to him. But Bahu Begum had more important matters to attend to than a snivelling man-child and had left Kothi Bibiapur to return to Lucknow to organize a defence of the city which now seethed with tension. Through the night of 20 January armed militia roamed the coal dark alleys of Lucknow. The Lucknow army possessed 300 pieces of ordnance, operated by 1,000 gole andaze, or native artillery men, and 30 pieces of cannon had been lined up. Troops began assembling in noisome groups and tense messages arrived in

---

*Writing in 1817 the English historian James Mill wrote about this episode that it was 'impossible not to confess that (John Shore) decided against the unfortunate Nawab (Wazir Ali) the great question of a Kingdom, upon evidence upon which a court of English law would not have decided against him a question of a few pounds...'

the kothi of the preparations at Lucknow under the begum's watch. In Kothi Bibiapur the wretched Wazir Ali was summoned from his tents by Shore for his own safety to remain within the kothi. Depressed and undone, Wazir sat miserably within a high-ceilinged room full of Company men who shuffled uncomfortably in the presence of a man whose life they had ruined. He spent the night in the grounds of the kothi in a 'gloomy Hindoostani' tent provided by Claude Martin, refusing the bodyguards offered by Shore.

By 21 January Shore informed the begum that Saadat Ali Khan was en route to Lucknow, and no opposition to his accession would be tolerated. Faced with the possibility of bloodshed in her city, the begum then stood down her forces and waited with pragmatic patience for the new nawab. Saadat Ali Khan was brought to Kothi Bibiapur by Edmonstone, where Shore was waiting for him. The exhausted Saadat Ali, nerves jangling from the long journey and the tense uncertainty of the past few days, was placed on an elephant alongside Shore, an unsubtle signal that the Company was now co-ruler of Awadh. As Company troops led the elephant past the kothi and towards Lucknow, there was one lonely figure who watched the procession—Wazir Ali had been told to take possession of the kothi after Shore left it, and 'he was almost deserted, and without the assistance of the English who remained at Bibiapur would not have found servants to prepare the House for his reception.' No longer a nawab and not even allowed the grace of having been the son of the nawab, Wazir Ali had been entirely cast aside and it is not surprising that Shore was convulsed with guilt in his presence. 'Vizier Ali is fallen' wrote Shore to his wife, almost unbelievingly. '[H]is servants forsake him; and I showed him an attention which I never did before.'

The road leading out towards Lucknow was crowded with curious and animated townsfolk who shouted excitedly when they spotted a large elephant lumbering through the hazy winter dust. Saadat Ali Khan and John Shore were seated on the elephant, throwing down silver coins to the cheering crowds, while preceding and following them were a corps of Company troops. The cavalcade made its way to Bahu Begum's palace, where the begum was ready to bestow the khillat upon Saadat Ali Khan. Forty-five years old now, slightly more portly than when he was a young man first vying for the masnad, a dense beard masking his expression, Saadat Ali knelt before the begum and 'laid his head at her feet and asked her to place his turban on his head as a blessing, and he promised to show her such reverence that she would absolutely forget his half-brother Asaf.'

John Shore would be handsomely recompensed for the 'hours, days and nights of anxious doubt and expectation' that he had gone through while definitely interfering in the affairs of Awadh. While he was still at Lucknow, he received a letter from Dundas 'couched in kind and flattering' terms announcing that he had been given an Irish peerage, and accorded the title of Lord Teignmouth. It was at this time, also, that Shore was offered a most precious gift. A grateful Saadat Ali brought out a gorgeous manuscript from Asaf's exquisite collection, and showed it to Shore, insisting that he take the manuscript. The book, Shore exclaimed,* 'was fit for a royal library' and he could only accept it on behalf of the king of Great Britain. Shore thus accepted the fabled *Padshanama* of Shah Jahan, along with five other manuscripts carefully selected by Tafazzul from the nawab's collection, and forwarded them to Europe.† Six weeks after Wazir Ali had been deposed, John Shore, now Lord Teignmouth, with indecent haste set sail, at last, for Britain.

Wazir Ali was soon informed that he would be required to move to Benaras, where Mahadeo Das's house was being readied for him by Cherry. Wazir Ali asked only that he be given enough space for 'a quantity of baggage and a great many people' and he was to be allowed to have his jewels, his family and other friends who chose to remain with him. Left behind in Lucknow to work out the details of Wazir Ali's removal to Benaras, Edmonstone would have been quite unaware of the ominous prescience of his thoughts on the young man's state of mind when he wrote that '(Wazir Ali) does not appear to be much affected by his fall... I think he has rather the feeling of anger and sullenness than of submission and despondency.'

One day while looking out of the windows of her palace in Lucknow, Bahu Begum was witness to a most outrageous sight. Preceded by drummers on camels and horses lustily beating out a noisome fanfare was a magnificent sedan chair bearing the mother of the new nawab, passing provocatively right in front of Bahu Begum's

---

*'I was informed that the deceased Asaf purchased it for 12,000 rupees, or about 1500 pounds' wrote Shore.

†The *Padshanama* remains today in the Windsor Library, the Royal Collection Trust. It has been digitized and can be viewed online.

window. This was the woman whom Bahu Begum had cast out from her presence during the lifetime of Shuja, and who was even later only ever permitted to stand humbly before her, now enjoying her moment in the spotlight. For Bahu Begum, this was worse than any of the other belittling slights that she felt herself subjected to in Lucknow by Saadat Ali—the reduction in her kitchen allowance and the shifting of her cookhouse from its usual place. Many of these changes were due to money-saving measures the desperate nawab was trying to implement but for Bahu Begum they were insulting attempts upon her dignity itself. Her sense of ownership of her own wealth and the legitimate power it gave her was clear when she criticized Saadat Ali, saying about him—'this son of mine is a very base sort. In the first instance, all this wealth (he now possesses) is from Shuja-ud-Daula, and after that from Asaf-ud-Daula, and in actuality it all comes from me.'

Also, despite her stout determination to participate in Awadhi politics through the old nawabi system of co-sharing, Bahu Begum was undone by the British men's craven refusal to accept her claims to legitimacy. Finally, one day, she summoned Lumsden and held a meeting with him at her palace in the Sunehra Burj, with only Jawahar Ali Khan as witness. She spoke to Lumsden directly, dispensing with the niceties of an intermediary and told him that 'God has given me money, jewels, clothes, vessels, furniture and other property... As long as I live, I am mistress of what I have.' What was hers by right, she had now decided, she wanted to leave to the Company upon her death as long as they promised to abide by her bequests and wishes. Having violently resisted Hastings's attempts to acquire her fortune it can appear bemusing that Bahu Begum now decided to leave all her property to the very Company that had so harassed her. But after decades of tussling over what constituted her unalienable property, this was a way to ensure the ownership of her wealth. It was also a pragmatic way in which to guarantee the safety of her property and her endowments under a nawab she could no longer trust.

Saadat Ali was understandably furious when he heard about this meeting, sending the begum an angry message reminding her that 'no stranger had ever heard her voice as long as his father or his half-brother were living, and he would like to know what extraordinary emergency had now arisen that she talked to a stranger, an Englishman, with her own lips and not through another person.' But the begum was not a woman to be cowed in the slightest by this once-exiled son of a lowly concubine, and she sent an even sharper reply to the nawab, 'to the effect that it was his accession that had driven her to this step...that he had been constantly talking to the English night and day, and it was no business of his if she spoke to an Englishman about her own affairs; that she was her own mistress and he had nothing to say to her.'

Both Nawab Begum and Bahu Begum had lived within a fluid system that had recognized the right of the khaas mahal and the widowed mother to participate in a form of co-sharing of political power in Awadh, based upon their independent wealth and the respect they were held in. But the British brought a much more rigid understanding of property and power as only to be inherited by male heirs, and this intractable reluctance to let a woman share power and influence would be demonstrated repeatedly in the struggles following Asaf's death.

Now, faced with the begum's proposal to bequeath her immoveable assets to the Company, the men prevaricated. Finally, years later, the Company refused to recognize the begum's sovereign right to her own property and jagirs, insisting on the patriarchal right of the nawab. Instead of her jagirs and her fortune, they said she could invest one-third of her moveable property in Company bonds, so that the interest could fund pensions for all her dependents. The begum had no choice but to accept the offer, and finally gave up a list of all her moveable assets, a veritable Aladdin's cave of buried jewels, gold mohurs and cash, buried in hiding spaces dug out for that express purpose among the palaces of Faizabad, and carefully covered over so as to be absolutely invisible*.

The begum finally returned to Faizabad at the end of 1798, where she lived for many years in contented if reduced splendour. Slowly all the old familiar faces disappeared from around her, stepping back into the shadows of the night. Her brother Salar Jang had died, as had many of the matriarchs who had contributed to the finely woven texture of elite Faizabadi life. Her dear Bani Begum died as did the

---

*Some of the hiding places included 'in the cellar below the Bara Durree, gold Mohurs and rupees worth 15,38,991, in a small apartment adjoining the Old Kutcherrie, sicca and corah Rupees worth 9,36,641, in a small apartment of the house, in gold mohurs, sicca and corah rupees worth 8,12,015', all of these in Jawahar Ali Khan's house.

steadfast Jawahar Ali Khan. Even Saadat Ali Khan, who had caused her so much indignant fury, died in 1814. On a cold January day in 1815, Bahu Begum was startled by a glimpse of a beloved and almost forgotten image. Perhaps she saw a shadow in the quietened corridors as the raking light moved through the jaali windows. 'Barey Nawab'* had come to get her, she whispered to her worried khwajasara,† as she seemed to see that tall, strapping figure stride purposefully towards her. 'Barey Nawab' she whispered one last time and then her maids rocked their old bodies in grief and wept painful tears as she lay quietly down to die.‡

---

*Shuja-ud-Daula.
†Darab Ali Khan became her chief khwajasara after the death of Jawahar Ali Khan.
‡Bahu Begum died on 7 January 1815, as recorded in Faiz Baksh's Faiz Baksh's *Memoirs of Lucknow and Faizabad* (Muhammad Faiz Bakhsh and William Hoey, *Memoirs of Delhi and Faizábád: Being a Translation of the Táríkh Farahbakhsh of Muhammad Faiz Bakhsh from the Original Persian*, Allahabad: Government Press, North-western Provinces and Oudh, Vol. 2, 1889) at the age of around eighty-five.

## TUMULT IN BENARAS

Benaras in the late eighteenth century was an overwhelming city in every sense*. The narrow wayward lanes were bustling with people† hurrying through the shade of the high stone houses. The air was fetid with an 'intolerable stench' from stagnant waters. The population itself was a somewhat alarming mix of tradesfolk, desultory members of the Mughal royal family, itinerants, and pilgrims, and armed hooligans‡ attracted by the wealth of the city. The presence of this elite population with their own armed retainers always ready to take offence at any slight, perceived or real, made for a volatile and explosive city. The European inhabitants lived in more salubrious conditions in a suburb 5 miles outside Benaras called Secrole. Their houses there were deemed 'handsome', but the area was bare and devoid of trees, for fear of attracting mosquitoes. Mirza Shagufta Bakht,§ Mirza Khurram Bakht, and Mirza Muzzafar Bakht, sons of the deceased crown prince Mirza Jawan Bakht, who had once so charmed Hastings in Lucknow, lived in Benaras, as did some 300 members of the family of Raja Udit Narayan, the raja of Benaras. The raja himself lived in his palace at Ramnagar, and was 'most immoderately fat' and sickly looking, with a malady that rather mysteriously was said to do no credit to his status as a Brahmin and a married man. The raja was clearly used to frequent British visitors who viewed him as something of a curiosity, for he had obliged them by teaching his dancing girls to sing the English folk songs 'The Miller of Dee' and 'Malbrook'. He received a pension of 4 lakh rupees from the British, and had 'nothing to do with the zemindary of Benaras.'

The arrival of Wazir Ali in Benaras in February 1798 with his horses,

---

*By the late eighteenth century, both Benaras and Lucknow supported populations of 200,000, while the imperial cities of Lahore, Delhi, and Agra had gone down from 400,000 in 1700 to about 100,000 by 1800. (Bayly, *North Indian Towns*).
†In 1800 Viscount Valentia estimated 30,000 houses with a population of 58,000.
‡According to Aniruddha Ray 5,200 people were 'local toughs' ready to fight for cash, including 'noted burglars, thieves, notorious gangster, dissolute and abandoned characters ready for action on payment'.
§Mirza Shaguft, aka Mirza Hajji, was the eldest surviving son of Mirza Jawan Bakht while Mirza Khurram Bakht was a younger son, whose mother was the senior widow Qutlugh Sultan Begum.

elephants, armed retainers, acolytes,* and his prickly sense of loss added to this highly charged atmosphere. Having been for a few months the fabulously wealthy nawab of Awadh, Wazir Ali had to now contend with a newly pedestrian reality. Even in his reduced circumstances however, he still lived in grander style than the unfortunate Mughal princes. The three elder sons of Mirza Jawan Bakht had continued to live in Benaras after the death of their father. The elder son Mirza Shagufta was tall and slim, with a 'fierce' expression while the younger Mirza Khurram, an amiable young man, was short and pleasantly plump with a pock-marked face and a straggly beard.† The two brothers were not on friendly terms due to matters of protocol because though Mirza Shagufta was the eldest, his mother was not a woman of consequence while the younger Mirza Khurram's mother was Qutlugh Begum,‡ a Timurid woman and Mirza Jawan Bakht's principal wife. As a result, the two princes avoided ever being in the same place together. This uneasy balance of power had made Mirza Shagufta truculently haughty, extremely sensitive over matters of precedence and honour. It was a threadbare arrogance, however, for this grandson of Mughal emperor Shah Alam lived in scuffed and tattered glory. He had been allotted a measly allowance of 4,000 rupees a month and 'everything (around him) marked poverty', according to an embarrassed visitor. While his furnishings were of richly coloured cloths, they were frayed at the seams, and though his ceremonial clothes were of gold brocade, he had no jewels to wear. Nonetheless the two princes had their elephants, and their palanquins of gold gilt for ceremonial use, and the British accorded them the debatable honour of a gun salute. This strange dichotomy made the Mughal family painfully nostalgic for all they had lost, and 'they praised Agra and Delhi and the magnificence of the buildings' while a visitor sympathized that 'could they do otherwise than recollect that those palaces were once theirs, and that there they had reigned in the plenitude of eastern power; that now, alas, how great the contrast.'

Wazir Ali meanwhile arrived in Benaras with a comparatively generous yearly allowance of 2 lakh rupees and almost immediately

---

*The pension accorded to Wazir Ali by Edmonstone was 2 lakh rupees a year.
†Descriptions of the princes are from Viscount Valentia's travels, when he met them at Benaras in 1803.
‡Mirza Khurram shared a pension of 11,000 rupees per month with his mother Qutlugh Begum.

there were aggressive posturings and displays of power between all these elite men and women. Cherry worried that 'some general rule (was) to be established' to avoid clashes between Wazir Ali, Qutlugh Begum, and Mirza Shagufta while Wazir Ali was confident of his ascendence, primarily due to the excessive assurances given by Shore who had been wracked by guilt and doubt for most of the proceedings at Lucknow. 'I shall on all occasion be happy to promote your responsibility and comfort,' Shore had written to Wazir Ali hastily after he had been removed from the masnad. 'It will not be long before I shall have the pleasure of seeing you at Benaras' he further assured the young man duplicitously, all the while preparing his return to England post-haste, with no intention of ever returning to Benaras nor, indeed, to India

Wazir Ali soon made himself popular in Benaras, spending lavishly and giving expensive presents to people who came to visit him, and helping out generously in organizing the weddings of his followers' children. He settled into life at Benaras in some style, having a naqqara played before him wherever he went, always accompanied by a smart clutch of armed guards. It was noted that Wazir Ali enjoyed a lifestyle far beyond the means of his pension, and he supplemented his spending with the treasures he had brought with him from Lucknow.* The Company men on the ground at Benaras—Cherry and especially a judge-magistrate named Samuel Davies—viewed Wazir Ali with a more jaundiced eye, and ruled that he would be shown no mark of distinction in Benaras, and they moreover reduced his rank so he could no longer claim any privileges of royalty. This would have rankled Wazir Ali terribly, as he prepared to move into the newly restored Mahadeo Das's garden house. Davies grumbled that Wazir Ali's soldiers were dressed in the same manner as the Company sepoys, and that Wazir Ali was recruiting ever more soldiers, spending money extravagantly. He complained to Calcutta about Wazir Ali's 'style of magnificence', his 'numerous and increasing Retinue of armed men', and especially 'the independence he affected upon all occasions'. Rumours began to circulate among the ever paranoid British residents that Wazir Ali was

---

*Included in an inventory of his effects at Benaras were many bundles of precious shawls and cloths, silver plates, turbans, cummerbunds, furs, swords, firelocks, elephant howdahs, rosewater bottles, 10 Gujarat bullocks, 34 drag bullocks, 4 horses, 1 hare, and 12,500 rupees.

preparing to fight to regain his masnad from an unpopular Saadat Ali Khan. Indeed Davies at this point formulated a fear that would soon become a widespread mantra among EIC officials, one that would insinuate itself like poison into the very marrow of India for a very long time—'one measure of precaution', wrote Davies, 'might be to remove from the City and the district all the Mahomedans whose high rank and ample incomes may be supposed to inspire them with ambitious views, and who might possibly be induced to throw their weight into the scale of insurrection.' Edmonstone would spell out the very same fears with crystalline intention when he wrote to his brother at exactly the same time:

> (the Indians) entertain the utmost hatred towards us, especially the Mohammedans whose power has been annihilated by our supremacy. They consider us as polluted beings, as wretches devoted to damnation ... by the tenets of their religion the persecution & murder of Infidels is a merit entitling them to the highest rewards in a future state [;] ... can you wonder that I should detest a country where such a system exists, & must exist in spite of all the benevolent efforts of the ruling power to dispense justice & maintain the rights and religion of its subjects?

Thus did the 'Mohemmedan' become the despised, feared 'other' for the EIC officials, due to the guilt and malaise over the actions they were taking in state after state, deposing ruler after ruler in the most arbitrary and despotic manner. And Benaras housed the most eloquent reminder of great houses brought low—the Mughals and the Awadh nawabs.

Meanwhile Zaman Shah, with predictable regularity, had decided once again to march upon India. Rumours had reached the British by August 1798 and on 25 November, Zaman Shah had marched into Lahore unopposed. The arrival of the Afghan warlord caused considerable commotion in the country. The Company men began once again outlining alliances, real or imagined, between the Afghan and various Indian rulers to throw the British out of the country. Wazir Ali, it was claimed, had asked for Zaman Shah's help in reclaiming the masnad of Awadh. Saadat Ali Khan meanwhile remained so unpopular that he feared for his life and slept with guards at his door. He now began to clamour for Wazir Ali and Mirza Jangli's removal far from Awadh altogether, preferably to Calcutta. Finally on 24 December 1798, an order was issued for Wazir Ali's removal from Benaras to Calcutta.

It would appear that Wazir Ali had been planning some manner of action against the British at Benaras for a while, and that his plans were precipitated by the hasty order to remove him to Calcutta. He had been hiring soldiers and men, was in communication with the raja of Benaras, the Marathas, the Rohilla chief, the raja of Bhutwal, the rajas of Bundelkhand, Tipu Sultan, and Zaman Shah. On 14 January 1799, Wazir Ali had asked to meet with Cherry for breakfast before his removal to Calcutta. He arrived at Cherry's house in Secrole in the morning, accompanied by 200 of his armed attendants, on horse and on foot, who remained conspicuously stationed outside the house while Wazir Ali and four armed men strode into Cherry's dining room. As soon as tea had been served, Wazir Ali appeared 'much agitated and expressed himself with intemperance' over his removal to Calcutta. He angrily challenged Cherry, accusing him of having 'ruined the house of Asaf-ud-Daula' and refusing to leave Benaras. One of his armed companions silently got up to stand next to Cherry who then made the fatal error of threatening Wazir Ali that he would report him to the government. It was only when a furious Wazir Ali lunged at Cherry and grabbed him that Cherry panicked, trying to escape from the dining room. But Wazir Ali's men were waiting outside with guns and swords and Cherry was struck down and killed in the garden of his house, as were two other men. The men then ransacked Cherry's house, and attacked Davies's house, after which Wazir Ali returned to Benaras where he was joined by 2,000-3,000 armed men and declared that he had 'destroyed the English gentlemen and that his authority was now established in the City'.

Despite some sharp skirmishes within the narrow lanes and rooftops of Benaras's crowded alleys, the British were quickly able to suppress the rebellion due to the fortuitous presence of Company troops posted near Benaras in the event of Zaman Shah moving beyond Lahore.* The British troops quickly brought artillery into the city, and subdued the insurgents. Terrified Europeans who had hidden in

---

*The 13th Regiment from Chunar was moved to the city of Benaras.

the high maize fields were able to come out, and then the Company troops marched to capture Wazir Ali at his residence at Mahadeo Das's garden. But Wazir and his men fought fiercely from within the structure which had been stoutly fortified, and by the time the high iron gates were blasted by cannon, Wazir Ali had made his escape. Wazir Ali remained on the run for some time, in the Gorakhpur region of Awadh, and then in Bhutwal. He had the support of some of the zamindars of Benaras and Awadh, mostly Rajputs, and was able to raise some 6,000 troops. In the end, however, he lacked the support of any of the real power brokers—the Marathas, Tipu, the Afghans, the Mughal royals, etc.—and Wazir Ali's supporters began deserting him. He was finally lured and handed over to the EIC in December 1799 by a Rajput chieftain, Raja Pratap Singh of Jaynagar, in return for the promised prize of 50,000 rupees.*

Wazir Ali was captured and brought through Benaras exactly twelve months after his revolt, with 'a sword, a bow, a red velvet gold embroidered quiver containing 36 arrows'. He sailed by boat to Fort William in Calcutta where he was locked 'in a room built to resemble an iron cage'. The terms of his imprisonment were draconian, and he was kept in solitary confinement, closely guarded, with no contact with the outside world. He remained in prison till his death in 1817. The expenses for his funeral were listed as costing 70 rupees, a stark contrast from his wedding twenty years earlier during which 30 lakh rupees had been spent. In Benaras, the courtesans of the city would long remember his generosity and would provocatively sing out songs in his praise whenever they noticed a 'firangi' passing through the shadowed alleys.

When Edmonstone heard of the news of the massacre of his 'more than friend Cherry', he was profoundly devastated. He wrote to his brother to say that 'so closely connected as I was with all the transactions which led to (the murder) and so interested as a private man in the shocking catastrophe...I never think on it without horror and I have long endeavoured to drive it from my thoughts but it is forever returning to my mind.' The fear and vulnerability that the

---

*For this betrayal of hospitality due to a guest, Pratap Singh would face bitter censure by scholar and EIC officer James Tod, in his *Annals and Antiquities of Rajasthan: Or The Central and Western Rajput States of India*. United Kingdom: H. Milford, Oxford University Press, 1920. Pratap Singh did, however, insist that Wazir Ali not be killed, or placed in irons.

British had experienced as they moved further into these unfathomable heartlands was sharpened into horrified loathing. Edmonstone was convinced that plans were being made to completely extirpate the British presence from India, and his sense of paranoid suspicion and distrust deepened significantly. He advised the government that the Indians could not be won over by what he called '"the modern French philosophy"—the acknowledgement of their right to have some say in their government.' Instead, the 'natives' were to be controlled at all cost, so as to prevent a rebellion in which a mob 'should cut all our throats'. Listening carefully to Edmonstone's paranoid recommendations was a new Governor General, the most hawkishly aggressive till then, and the dangerous native leader they would now focus their rage and venality upon was Tipu Sultan.

## A TRAP FOR A TIGER

From the start of the Revolutionary Wars between France and Europe, the *Calcutta Gazette*[*] had begun reporting on some extraordinary scenes of national celebrations that were taking place in the capital of the EIC. On important occasions like the New Year, or St Andrew's[†] Day, all official Company men in Calcutta walked into the Writers Building[‡] to the crashing music of 'Rule, Britannia' pounded out by the artillery band. Toasts were made to the king, the queen, the prince of Wales, to the EIC itself, to the army and the navy, as well as to the Governor General and other luminaries. Each toast was accompanied by sufficiently strident martial music such as 'God Save the King', 'Britons Strike Home', and more culinary-inspired ditties proclaiming the merits of exquisite British cuisine such as 'Roast Beef'[§]. In 1793 the *Calcutta Gazette* was breathlessly reporting on a lavish ball that had been held to celebrate the military success of the British over Tipu Sultan, the first such celebration of a military victory in India[¶]. These overtly nationalistic celebrations demonstrated a growing sense of unity and of 'Britishness' within this dislocated society in Calcutta, forged in the furious wars that Britain was engaged in against France. And of all the Indian kings, Tipu Sultan was that most loathed creature—both viciously anti-British and a long-standing French ally.

---

[*] This was one of the earliest newspapers in India, founded in 1784 as a weekly by the EIC officer Francis Gladwin. It remained in publication for over 200 years.
[†] Patron saint of Scotland.
[‡] This building was begun in 1777 by a self-styled builder and erstwhile carpenter Thomas Lyon, to house the clerks (Writers) of the EIC. It was completed in 1780 and was the first three-storey building in Calcutta. It was a utilitarian building, considered an eyesore by British visitors. Much grander buildings would be built such as Government House (now Raj Bhawan) in the early nineteenth century.
[§] This edifying tune includes the lyrics:
   When mighty Roast Beef was the Englishman's food
   It ennobled our brains and enriched our blood
   Our soldiers were brave and our courtiers were good
   Oh! The Roast Beef of old England
   And old English Roast Beef!
[¶] Amongst the florid faces and flaxen haired cheering men in 1793 was a more unusual celebrant—Saadat Ali Khan before he became nawab and was still living in exile at Benaras. He had travelled from his residence at Benaras specially to attend the ball in Calcutta celebrating the defeat of Tipu Sultan along with his 'friend' John Shore. (Pearson, *Making Britain in Empire,* p. 209)

For those who would find this lugubrious fare and depressingly parochial celebrations mystifying, Napoleon Bonaparte was to blame. 'Intolerant Protestantism,' writes scholar Linda Colley, in reaction to the dreaded Catholic menace, 'served as a cement between the English, the Welsh and the Scots, particularly lower down the social scale' and soldered them together in a spirit of shared 'British' values. Throughout the eighteenth century, Britons had good reason to fear France—it was larger and more populous, had a terrifying land army, it was Britain's great imperial rival and, moreover, it was Catholic. All Britons, therefore 'were able to feel an emotional and ideological stake' in protracted encounters with the French. Defeat at the hands of the French during the American Revolution and then the Revolutionary–Napoleonic Wars resulted in a profound malaise about the nature and the essence of the British ruling elite. To ensure cohesive, patriotic virtues in the elite classes, their education would no longer be entrusted to private tutors, as was the case in the early half of the eighteenth century. Instead, from around 1800 onwards, English peers would be sent to public schools*—Eton, Westminster, Winchester, and Harrow—where they 'were exposed to a uniform set of ideas and learnt how to speak the English language in a distinctive and characteristic way'.

Confronted with Napoleon's grandiose vision of Revolutionary France and his high-octane celebrations and constructions to the glory of this vision, Britain reacted in kind. British nationalistic celebrations, it was decided, would be even more splendid, and eye-wateringly extravagant than those taking place in Republican France. And to distinguish these splendid patriotic celebrations from the French ones, British fetes and festivals would instead focus firmly on the monarch.† Moreover, unlike the 'upstart and synthetic contrivances of the French', British ceremonial would underline the antiquity of British traditions, real or invented.

---

*Even in recent years, Boris Johnson, Theresa May, Margaret Thatcher, David Cameron, Tony Blair, and Bill Clinton all went to Oxbridge.

†Twenty-first-century readers might be amused to find a resonance in the everlasting royal celebrations of the last 50 years, from the wedding of Prince Charles and Diana, of Prince William and Kate, the Golden and Jubilee celebrations for Queen Elizabeth II, the prolonged ceremonies around her death and around the coronation of King Charles III. It will be interesting to see how they translate into the reign of Charles III.

In France, the revolution had brought about a number of different, conflicting and often very ambiguous attitudes towards the Indian states. For a revolutionary state that celebrated 'liberty, equality, and fraternity' for all, there was a great deal of equivocation over the granting of these liberties to Indians, and indeed over the very nature of a French empire within a republic. Instead, French officials like the mayor of Pondicherry congratulated themselves on the great benefits the grateful Indians were deriving from their republican ideals, while also arguing that India exhibited a particularly immutable, eternal character to which it would be irresponsible to introduce dramatic and dynamic change. Some of the dichotomy in the French attitude can be seen in Indologist Anquetil-Duperron's remarks about India where, on the one hand, he waxed nostalgically in the following manner about 'eternal India':

> Peaceful Indians, living since antiquity in such a fertile land, you calmly gather its bounty for your needs. Happy with very little only the sky, by withholding the rains, could make you unhappy. Your minor quarrels (and which nation doesn't have these!), soon interrupted by the coming of the monsoon, leave no traces upon your countryside...

In 1778, electrified by the beginnings of the American Revolution, he then urged his fellow French citizens to mobilize to 'liberate' India from the British:

> Let us use all of France's efforts with the greatest confidence for such a great cause, towards the whole of India... 24 years of servitude will surely move a young monarch (Louis XVI) whose first immortal act was to support American independence.

In the revolutionary decade of the 1790s, French political actors were further galvanized by the idea of unifying the Indian states in a charge against British forces, as they had done so successfully in the American colonies. Tipu Sultan was considered a likely partner, but first the new French Republic had the delicate task of informing the sultan, whom they unanimously qualified as a 'despot', that he could no longer address his letters to the king, because 'through the most glorious of revolutions the French nation has been transformed into a Republic'.

Having achieved the admittedly nimble feat of assuring a 'despotic' king that the Republic was his friend, the French were then undone by their own terminal vacillations. Shackled by poor communications between the different parties (Mysore, Versailles, Pondicherry, and the French colony of Mauritius*) and the absence of a unified approach towards its Indian ally, France prevaricated when Tipu Sultan was desperately asking for reinforcements of 6,000 soldiers in 1793.

When news arrived in Mysore early in 1797, therefore, that a French force had landed on the coast, Tipu Sultan was overjoyed. François Ripaud, a Frenchman and second in command of the French colony of Mauritius, had landed on the coast of Mangalore with a battered warship, gallant proof of a recent naval battle. 'Since I had long desired news from your country,' wrote a delighted Tipu to French officials about Ripaud, 'I asked him to come to my capital, and I questioned him on the ongoing war, on your positions, and whether you still remembered your old ally.' Once Ripaud arrived in Mysore, it was soon suspected that he was some manner of imposter—simply an inhabitant from Mauritius sailing on a merchant vessel without any official mandate at all. One of Tipu's ministers was bracingly frank about 'this Ripaud that is come, God knows what ass it is, whence it comes and for what purpose.' At this point, and possibly threatened with imprisonment for imposture, a desperate Ripaud began to indulge in some fairly dramatic and outlandish ceremonies.

Ripaud leapt into his role of republican saviour with considerable panache. He began by lecturing Tipu sonorously on the discipline, loyalty, and good faith of the republican ideals, whipping off his hat and kissing the republican rosette pinned on it to seal his oath. He then organized a meeting every Sunday for a month, in the local church, of all the members of the 'French parti'† in Seringapatam. During these meetings, or 'assemblies', some grandiose political discourses were made, and a few symbolically charged acts were carried out—the old fleur-de-lys flag of France was publicly burnt, and was replaced by the Republican tricolour flag, which was brought out reverentially accompanied by a guard of honour, while cannons and muskets

---

*Since the beginning of the 1790s, French policy on India was being elaborated at Mauritius, further complicating the speed of communications.

†These consisted of French soldiers, as well as some Portuguese and British men.

were fired to further mark this solemn occasion. Attending members embraced each other, publicly demonstrating republican values of fraternity and a 'liberty tree' was planted, topped by that other unlikely symbol of the French revolution—the knitted red bonnet, or cap.*

For a few months in the torpid Mysore summer of 1797, the electrifying ideals of the French republic ricocheted off the whitewashed walls of the palaces of the island city of Seringapatam as Ripaud's dramatic oratory transfixed the gathered French soldiers, and no doubt intrigued the sultan and his ministers too. The freighted symbolism of the French tricolour flag, reverentially accompanied by guards and cannon, would have been immediately recognized by Tipu, whose own tiger stripe 'babri' banners and motifs studded all aspects of his life. That Ripaud was a republican himself is certain, as he proclaimed it openly, and was a member of political clubs. But for the rest, Ripaud was an imposter. He was a Breton privateer based in Mauritius, and he had spent the previous year attacking English ships off the coast of Malabar. And yet despite the reservations he might have had, Tipu Sultan appeared convinced and six months after his arrival, Ripaud was sent back to Mauritius, tasked with representing Tipu Sultan to the French governor, Comte Anne Joseph Hippolyte de Malartic, and to raise an expeditionary force to come to his aid. But the surprised Malartic was in no position to raise the 10,000 men that Tipu requested. Instead, he made a proclamation from Mauritius, calling on volunteers to sign up to join Tipu Sultan. A paltry 100 men signed up, with Malartic adding 15 officers under the command of Brigadier Chapuis, and 'this motley reinforcement of naval, and military, creole, and European' landed in Mysore in June 1798, severely disappointing Tipu. But news of this proclamation reached Calcutta in early 1798, and there would be far deadlier repercussions to this than Tipu could ever have imagined.

---

*The bonnet rouge was a potent symbol of the Revolution, possibly being borrowed from the red Phyrgian cap of classical antiquity.

# THE FALL OF SERINGAPATAM

In 1798 two ships set sail from Europe bearing two very different men whose intertwined destinies would alter the topography and the history of India. In the frigate *La Virginie* sailed the thirty-eight-year-old Richard Wellesley,* an Anglo-Irish aristocrat with penetrating blue eyes staring out from under straight black brows who was replacing John Shore as Governor General of India. Propelled by personal ambition, arrogance, and a robust hatred for the French, Wellesley was described as 'a sublime dandy' and a 'man of staggering vanity, who craved to the end of his days the dukedom which he considered his due. He was idle, domineering, often preposterous, but had outstanding intellectual ability and genuine force of character.' And for his predecessor of sober and vacillating habits, Wellesley had only contempt, describing John Shore as of 'low birth, vulgar manners and eastern habits'. In the warship *L'Orient*, meanwhile, the twenty-nine-year-old dashing and fiery-eyed General Bonaparte stood at the helm, his long dark hair blowing in the briny air as the ship set sail from Toulon, in France. *L'Orient* would have an extraordinary history† and in May 1798 this 118-gun ship was part of an armada of 300 ships that was leaving with 32,300 men‡ from five separate ports in France, Italy, and Corsica,§ all headed for a secret mission to Egypt.

After his spectacular campaigns in Italy the previous year, Bonaparte had carefully contemplated his next moves. The French foreign minister Talleyrand and Bonaparte had desultorily contemplated invading Great Britain, but had finally shrugged off that idea in favour of an invasion of Egypt. The idea of an empire in Egypt had been seducing the French for some time, who saw in its fabled lands and untold riches some consolation for the loss of their possessions in Canada and India. For

---

*Richard Wesley was the eldest son of the 1st Earl of Mornington, but changed the family name to Wellesley in 1789. He was educated at Eton and Oxford.
†She would receive fire from Admiral Horatio Nelson's ships and would blow up spectacularly when the fire reached her powder magazines. Her captain, Luc-Julien-Joseph Casabianca, and his young son both sank with the ship, inspiring the poem *Casabianca* with the famous first line: 'The boy stood on the burning deck'. When Nelson died after the Battle of Trafalgar, he was buried in a coffin made from a plank of wood from *L'Orient*.
‡This included, in fact, 300 women.
§Marseilles, Toulon, Genoa, Ajaccio, and Civitavecchia.

the impatient young Bonaparte, it had the added allure of recapturing Alexander the Great's glory, by evoking that magnificent conqueror's legendary conquests. And perhaps, most importantly, the French believed that by capturing Egypt, they would seriously impede the route to their great rival Britain's trading wealth in India. There may have been the added incentive of using the campaign to get Bonaparte away from Europe, as the post-revolutionary Directory* was growing somewhat leery of this ambitious and charismatic young general. If that was part of the calculation, then it backfired spectacularly.†

Bonaparte's armada included 170 scientists—mathematicians, chemists, geographers—several musicians and a poet. They carried with them hot air balloons, and a printing press, and the Egypt campaign was very much a voyage of discovery as well as one of conquest. And the discoveries that the French scientists would make in Egypt would throw light on the great mysteries of that ancient country for the first time. But this was also a conquering republican army, and they almost incidentally captured the island of Malta en route to Egypt. Bonaparte landed in Alexandria promising the people 'liberation' from the 'usurpers', the Mamelukes. The Mamelukes were originally Christian slaves from the Caucasus, who had been in Egypt since the thirteenth century, and who were still considered foreigners to some extent. At the Battle of the Pyramids, Bonaparte's rallying speech included the electrifying vision that 'from the heights of the Pyramids, 40 centuries look down on us'. Bonaparte led his army to a resounding victory against the legendary Mamelukes, effectively sealing his reputation as an invincible destroyer of mythical foes. And even though these initial successful campaigns were followed by disasters and cruelly violent engagements, Bonaparte was a master of spin and he returned to Europe the following year to a hero's welcome.

The swashbuckling actions of a soldier of genius and an endlessly ambitious Frenchman‡ was the stuff of nightmares for the British in the

---

*The Directory was the French Revolutionary government which lasted from November 1795 to November 1799. It marked the end of the Reign of Terror (September 1793-July 1794), and was followed by the Consulate of Napoleon.

†One month after his return from the Egypt campaign, in December 1799, in a bloodless coup d'etat, Bonaparte seized power and became the ruler of France as Napoleon I.

‡Napoleon Bonaparte's 'Frenchness' was slightly suspect, since he was born and brought up a Corsican.

late eighteenth century. Ever since the deposition of the luxuriously periwigged and Catholic James II of England during the Glorious Revolution of 1688 and his exile in Catholic France, the threat of a 'Jacobite'* invasion of Great Britain remained an unshakeable and ferocious fear. That the heirs of James II would return to claim the English throne and upset the Protestant Reformation, supported by an occupying Catholic French army fuelled much paranoia. 'Most politicians, military experts and popular pundits,' writes Linda Coley about the late eighteenth century, 'continued to see France as Britain's most dangerous enemy, and for good reason'. In a move that predated Brexit by several hundred years all things French, including the language, the wigs, the valets, the food, the refinement, and the luxurious imported goods—were all to be shunned in favour of bland British mercantile goods and stolid habits.

French shenanigans in Egypt meant that by the time Wellesley reached Calcutta in May 1798, he loathed them with all the passion of his intemperate, arrogant soul. He colourfully condemned them as the 'Scourges of the Earth' as well as the 'Dogs of Hell' and in 1798 gave a voluntary donation of 5,000 rupees to aid the war effort in Europe, sighing contentedly 'what a happiness it is for the civilized world that England is engaged in the war'. In Calcutta Wellesley found a kindred spirit in Edmonstone. Edmonstone, the shadowy kingmaker, was now at thirty-five years of age an urbane, sophisticated, and charming man, but he was also intransigent about the British needing to be far more forceful and aggressive in India.

Before he had even set sail for India, in February 1798, Wellesley had pondered the political situation and had already described to Dundas the advantages that could be derived from Zaman Shah's fortuitous incursion into India:

> It is very difficult to form a conjecture with respect to the probability of Zaman Shah's being able to execute his romantic design. That he entertains such a design is unquestionable; and whatever may be the result, it is prudent to be on our guard, and in the meanwhile *to derive every collateral advantage from his declaration.*

---

*This name arose from the Latin name of James II's heir, James Stuart, Jacobus. A Stuart Catholic restoration was considered a real threat to the Protestant government of Great Britain.

By June 1798, Dundas was replying to Governor General Wellesley, urging him to further militarize the Europeans in India since 'in consequence of the menaces and arrogant language of our enemy (France), threatening by an invasion of our own island, at once to strike at the whole vitals of our strength and power a spirit of zeal, ardent loyalty and national pride has been excited to a degree unequalled at any period of our history.' But Wellesley needed no encouragement, and was many steps ahead of the minister for war. Hearing about the landing at Mysore of the pathetically small force of a hundred French soldiers from Mauritius, Wellesley decided that aggression against an outspoken enemy like Tipu Sultan would be justified. In the backdrop of Bonaparte's landing in Egypt, officials in Britain would be far too distracted to pay close attention to Wellesley in India. The enormous war indemnity of 3.3 crore rupees and territorial concessions that Cornwallis had imposed on Tipu by kidnapping and holding his sons to ransom had quite effectively neutralized that ruler's threat. But as a scholar has pointed out, Wellesley was always equally strongly motivated by 'thoughts of the (material) rewards of victory' against Tipu.*

And so Wellesley and Edmonstone began a campaign of treachery and lies, assuring Dundas that Tipu was being asked to explain his actions regarding the small French force, while in fact Edmonstone was writing to the Sultan assuring him of Wellesley's goodwill. The nizam of Hyderabad was quietly persuaded to join forces with the Company, even as news of Bonaparte's landing reached India. A letter fell into British hands en route to Tipu, quite possibly as a deliberate provocation to the British and as part of Bonaparte's scare tactics vis-à-vis France's old foes:

> You will have learnt about my arrival on the banks of the Red Sea, at the head of a large and invincible army, desirous of liberating you from the oppressive yolk of the British. I am keen to learn from you, via the Muscat and Mecca route, your political situation. In case you could send an intelligent person who had your full confidence, to the Suez or to Cairo, to speak with me.

---

*Wellesley had also forced the nizam of Hyderabad, Ali Khan, into a subsidiary alliance with the EIC in September 1798, making Hyderabad the first Indian princely state to enter into a subsidiary alliance with the British.

> May the Almighty increase your power, and destroy your enemies,
>
> Signed Bonaparte

Bonaparte also wrote a second letter to the Sharif of Mecca, assuring him that 'there is not a single Mamelouk oppressor remaining in Egypt, and that the inhabitants can live their lives without fear.' He also rather casually asked the Sharif to forward an accompanying letter to 'our friend Tippu Sultan'. Bonaparte at this stage was most definitely the cavalier agent of chaos, stirring hornets' nests around the world.

This letter and Bonaparte's wars in Egypt allowed Wellesley to ask for reinforcements of 4,000 soldiers and on the last day of 1798, this force landed in Madras. All the while Wellesley and Edmonstone goaded and harassed Tipu, and offered him ludicrously impossible terms,* knowing that he could not accept them without humiliating himself and accepting the complete carving up and destruction of his country. Just as Edmonstone was wrestling with his conscience about how dishonourable it might in fact be to attack Tipu without waiting for his reply to their ultimatums, they received news of Cherry's murder in Benaras by Wazir Ali. All Edmonstone's simmering fears and raging paranoia spiked through his grief. 'The great body of Mussulmen from whom we have wrested the Govt. and whom we now exclude from all situations of extensive trust and power', he wrote to his brother, 'will ever harbor a wish to regain the supremacy. They hate us not only as we are usurpers but as they are bigots. To conciliate enemies of this description is impracticable. We must control them.'

Both Wellesley and Edmonstone were now in perfect concord that the Indians were to be 'controlled', and in the case of rulers like Tipu, this could be understood as 'destroyed'. They presented a final list of risibly insulting terms,† and then the Company force marched upon Seringapatam. That the Company had been working ceaselessly and with a single focus to goad Tipu into battle and never to try and find a peaceful solution can be determined quite simply by the size

---

*In November 1798 they had offered Tipu an ultimatum—to avoid hostilities he was to banish all Frenchmen from his lands, accept a permanent British Resident and surrender his seacoast province.

†The terms meant Tipu would have to surrender half his remaining lands, pay 20 million rupees to the Company, and give up 8 hostages, of whom 4 would be his sons.

of the army they had carefully marshalled and marched to Mysore. This was 'the greatest army* ever assembled in India and relative to its supposed objective, the most complete ever put together possibly in any country.' Riding into battle at the head of the Madras forces was a familiar name, from the very beginning of this story. Edward Clive, son of Robert Clive, had been named Governor of Madras in 1798 no doubt as recompense for his father's earlier muscular actions.†

Even the general‡ sent to lead the Company forces was duplicitous, never allowing Tipu a chance to negotiate. 'I entirely approve of your determination not to negotiate with the Sultaun', Wellesley would congratulate him subsequently. Tipu, clearly never having anticipated war until the very last moment, since he had believed the Governor General was willing to parlay, was completely unprepared. It was only when he heard of the vast army of crimson jackets raising dust upon the horizon that Tipu realized Wellesley's intentions. For the army marching towards Seringapatam was truly awe-inspiring. It marched in two parallel columns, with the British and Madras regiments on the right and the Hyderabad contingent to the left. The cavalry was placed at the front and at the back of the lines, while the supply columns were placed in the centre, the whole forming a procession 7 miles in length and 2 miles wide. The supply column had been carefully prepared because of the fiasco with supply issues that Cornwallis's 1792 campaign had suffered from. Now the soldiers were comfortably buffered by camp followers ten times their number, and by the noisome addition of 100,000 oxen, horses, donkeys, and elephants carrying supplies, ammunition, and ordnance.

Realizing too late the murderous intent of Wellesley's army, Tipu ordered a scorched earth campaign and sent his troops to harass the

---

*The army comprised a Madras contingent of 4,381 European troops and 10,695 Native troops; a Hyderabad contingent of 16,157 European and Native troops, a Bombay army of 1,617 European troops and 4,803 Native troops, a total of more than 37,000 battle-ready troops.

†Edward Clive was accompanied in India by his wife, Henrietta, the daughter of the Earl of Powis. Henrietta brought aristocratic cachet to the Clive name, while the Clives rescued Powis from financial decrepitude. Both Edward and Henrietta would gather considerable loot and money following the fall of Seringapatam, and would take this back to England where it was added to the earlier loot brought by Robert Clive. All these plundered treasures lie today at Powis Castle, the seat of the Powis family, where the fading, hand-written notes accompanying these exhibits are yet to be updated as curator notes pointing to the history of violence and plunder that brought these objects to Britain.

‡General Harris, yet another veteran of the shameful American War of Independence.

advancing soldiers but the lines kept moving inexorably forward. By 7 April all the Company forces had arrived at the island fortress of Seringapatam and the siege of the city had begun. Once Tipu realized that the British had proved duplicitous once again and would not parlay, he defended his capital with such valour and energy that the British themselves were astounded. He 'gave us gun for gun... (and night-time skirmishes were) made with desperate exertion.... Soon the scenes became tremendously grand; shells and rockets of uncommon weight were incessantly poured upon us from the SW side, and fourteen pounders and grape from the North face of the Fort continued their havoc in the trenches.' Finally by 1 May the British forces had hauled their 'unprecedented quantities' of artillery, some forty 18-pounders up to the walls of Seringapatam.

On the morning of 4 May Tipu visited his Brahmin astrologer, as he was wont to do before all his battles. The omens were not on his side, he was informed, as the smell of gunpowder filled the air and the guns rumbled outside the walls of his city. Tipu gave the priests 'three elephants, two buffaloes, a bullock and a she-goat' and an iron pot full of oil. As he bent over the iron pot and looked upon his reflection in the dark liquid, Tipu appeared, at last, to have found peace. So many times since his defeat in 1792 he had wrestled with his fate. He had been haunted by the thought that he had failed his God, that his defeat had been a sign of divine displeasure. Now, at last, a reckoning had arrived. 'I am entirely resigned to the will of God, whatever it may be', he said, and prepared himself to die.

That whole day the giant British guns pounded the walls of Seringapatam despite a fierce defence by the besieged soldiers. The final charge against the walls was led by a Scottish captain who had skin in the game, for he had once been held captive by Tipu within those very same walls—the 'brawny and beloved' David Baird. At 1 p.m. on 4 of June, at the hottest time on a blistering day, Baird climbed out of the trenches and led the charge across the rock-strewn Kaveri River and through the breach in the wall, under intense firing from muskets and rockets. The first flag planted by the British forces was struck down by furious firing from the inner wall but Company soldiers kept swarming across the river and through the breach and at last the flag was planted. As they stormed Seringapatam, the first soldiers the

Company men encountered were French ones, many Mysorean officers having been bribed by the British to stay away. Against all expectations, even when the French king and then the French government had failed their old ally, Tipu's French soldiers stood by him to the last. Chapuis, the elderly brigadier sent with 100 soldiers from Mauritius, displayed exceptional gallantry and fought to the end till he was taken prisoner* by the British who sourly admitted he 'had something of the military veteran in his appearance'. The Sultan's remaining French troops, some 450 men, also did honour to the friendship that Tipu had always shown them, and to the sultan's own, perfect bravery. During the siege of the city, on 22 April, the small French corps marched out to face the British guns, the Republican rosette jauntily waving, and fell almost to a man.

Hearing the boom of cannon and the screams of men, Tipu rushed out of a small gateway where he had been having a quick lunch, strapped on his sword, grabbed his guns and leapt onto a rampart. He reached a transverse wall near the breach from where he flung himself into the action, bellowing to his men and 'encouraged them by his voice and example to make a determined stand.' Following their leader's example, the Mysore men fought with desperate bravery. At the end, when his men began to flee and unable to rally them any longer, Tipu found himself with just a small band of his most faithful followers. Tipu and his last remaining men jumped from one transverse wall to the next, as the huge mass of Company men kept filling the breach, pushing the defenders back. At each wall, Tipu and his men grabbed the reloaded weapons that their servants thrust at them and fired upon the attackers. As the bullets and cannonballs smashed into stone and screaming flesh all around them and the endless stream of attackers howled into the fort, Tipu's very last servant pleaded with his master to surrender and be taken alive. 'Are you mad?' shouted Tipu Sultan over the noise of war, swinging up his musket one last time. 'Be silent!'

In the evening, Tipu Sultan's body was discovered near the Water Gate of the fort, lying under 'a vast heap of the slain'. The sultan's body

---

*Chapuis was kept as a prisoner for two years at a prison in Portsmouth, and then returned to France where he would give a report of the battle to Napoleon, as he had promised the four sons of Tipu Sultan.

was identified by Baird and even in death Tipu appeared so charged with life force that his enemies struggled to believe he was indeed dead. His body was still warm, they later claimed, and his large and luminous eyes were open. He had been bayoneted thrice, and killed by a shot to the head. A grand total of 120 motley French men were discovered in Seringapatam and the tricolour flag that had caused such devastation was captured and eventually presented to George III.*

As the British forces streamed into the breached fortress, they indulged in an unprecedented orgy of violence and loot. Indian losses on that single day numbered more than 9,000, while British losses were only 1,500 for the entire duration of the Mysore campaign. Wellesley's younger brother Arthur Wellesley† wrote to his mother about the scale of the carnage:

> Scarcely a house in the town was left unplundered, and I understand camp jewels of the greatest value, bars of gold etc etc have been offered for sale in the bazaars of the army by our soldiers, sepoys and followers. I came in to take command of the army on the morning of the 5$^{th}$ and with the greatest exertion, by hanging, flogging etc etc in the course of that day I restored order...

Lady Henrietta Clive, daughter-in-law of Robert Clive, wrote rather more gleefully of all the plunder and loot that was being distributed:

> The plunder of Seringapatam is immense. General Harris will get between £150,000 and £200,000. Two of the privates have got £10,000 in jewels and money. The riches are quite extraordinary. Lord Clive has got a very beautiful blunderbuss...that was Tipu's and much at Seringapatam. I should like to have the pickings of some of the boxes. There was a throne of gold, which I'm sorry to say they are breaking to pieces and selling by parts. Lord Mornington (Richard Wellesley) has presented me with one of the jeweled tygers *(sic)* from the throne.

---

*Richard Wellesley was made Marquess Wellesley in the Peerage of Ireland in 1799 for his role in the Mysore campaign, but he was bitterly disappointed. He had hoped to receive the much more prestigious Order of the Garter for his service in India. He contemptuously referred to his Irish peerage in a letter to Pitt as a 'double-gilt potato'.

†Arthur Wellesley would have by far the more glorious career of the two brothers, and would be known to posterity as the Duke of Wellington.

The violence of the British forces had something primeval about it, as though they wished to bury the very name and memory of the hated Tipu into the bloody mud. They exorcised their shameful fear through a ritualistic degradation of his objects and palaces*:

> Shortly after Tipu's defeat, British soldiers occupied the Lal Bagh Garden, the site of his father's mausoleum. They made firewood of the ornamental Cypress trees that had surrounded the tomb; exercised their horses on the manicured lawns; used the buildings and monuments for target practice; used areas set aside for meditation as latrines; and buried their dead in the flower-beds. This desecration and destruction was within site of the Royal Palace where Tipu's family was imprisoned before being transported to Vellore.

This visceral desecration and obliteration of Tipu Sultan's memory would continue in the iconography and memorabilia that the EIC produced post 1799. After the war, the Governor General awarded to every British and Indian soldier the EIC medal, known as the Seringapatam Medal. It featured the British lion trampling the tiger of Tipu Sultan, with the Urdu motto—Asad Allah al-Ghalib—The Victorious Lion of God. This was, of course, Tipu's very motto, one that was inscribed on his guns, his swords, and his helmets. Tipu's tigers, which were discovered by the British in the palace courtyard, were shot.

Amongst Tipu's private papers were a number of Persian and French documents relating to Tipu's diplomatic exchanges of the past few years. They included letters to the French, particularly to the French governor of Mauritius, to Indian princes such as the nizam of Hyderabad and to the Marathas. Wellesley decided that these were 'documents of great importance, explanatory of the nature and the connection between Tippoo Sultan and the French Republic'. What these papers would be 'explanatory' of instead would be the actions of Wellesley, in attacking and killing a sovereign prince who was communicating with the Company and ready to negotiate a treaty.

---

*An exactly identical fate awaited the Bara Imambara after the Uprising of 1857. Scholar Veena Oldenburg notes that 'British troops ate pork, swilled alcohol, trampled the sacred hall in regimental boots, and manifested every other kind of contempt for the religion of the old rulers of the province.'

For Wellesley needed to find a smoking gun to justify his actions, to prove Tipu's inveterate hatred for the British by demonstrating a solid alliance with the dreaded French revolutionary forces. The papers were translated into English, and then printed rapidly in Madras on Wellesley's orders before being forwarded to Calcutta post-haste. And included in this large sheaf of papers was what would turn out to be an outright forgery by Company officials.

In addition to Tipu's correspondence, the officials had found the minutes of the privateer Ripaud's colourful Republican meetings of 1797. They were written by a French clock-maker employed by Tipu, as a heartfelt description of the joyously charged meetings in a text littered with spelling errors and patriotic emotion. But for the Company men, the papers would become proof of a dangerous 'Jacobin' presence in Mysore, ready to lead the conquering revolutionary Republican armies of Bonaparte to India. To drive home this point, the Company men quite simply inserted an inflammatory title to these meetings, which now became 'Copy in the French Language together with a Translation of the Proceedings of a Jacobin Club formed at Seringapatam, by the French Soldiers in the Corps commanded by M. Dompart'. With the insertion of the dreaded spectre of 'Jacobinism', the Company launched its propaganda campaign to justify the destruction of Tipu and the plunder of Mysore. Very soon, the idea would be picked up and sentiments like the following put forward: 'The wicked principles of the mother-country had, in a very early stage of the French Revolution, infected the colonies of Pondicherry and Chandernagore and the capture of those places by the English had dispersed some of the most zealous propagators of mischief among the courts and armies of the native Princes of India.' According to scholar Blake Smith, 'the counter-revolutionary press across Europe seized on the improbable image of a Citizen-Sultan at the head of a regicidal army'. Meanwhile, the violent truth of 'British aggression against Mysore disappeared, concealed by the legend of Tipu's Jacobin club'.

A few months after the fall of Seringapatam, Governor General Wellesley wrote to Henry Dundas anticipating conquests using terms that evoked the visceral eating and consuming of Indian territories, including Awadh, fully half a century before Dalhousie infamously spoke of Awadh as a cherry that was about to drop into British mouths.

> If you will have a little patience, the death of the Nizam will probably enable me to gratify your *voracious appetite for lands and fortresses*. Seringapatam ought, I think, to stay your stomach awhile; not to mention Tanjore and the Poligar countries. Perhaps, I may be able to give you a supper of Oudh and the Carnatic, if you should still be hungry.

Wellesley was true to his promises. By the time he visited Saadat Ali Khan in Lucknow in 1801, a very great deal had changed. When he stopped en route at Benaras where he visited Qutlugh Sultan Begum and her sons, Wellesley went out of his way to humiliate them. Unlike the Governors General who had passed through before him, Wellesley refused to be bestowed with the khillat by the royal family, objecting to this age-old Mughal ceremony 'as too degrading'. Instead he appeared resplendent before this ruined family, standing stiffly in his crimson jacket with its flashing gold braiding and high collar, and received the khillat laid out in trays.

As for Nawab Saadat Ali Khan, the relentless pressure that Wellesley and Edmonstone had maintained on him to give up his country to the Company had made of him a broken man in just a couple of years. In 1801 Wellesley suggested he allow the annexation of the entire province of Awadh, to which the nawab objected strenuously. He began drinking heavily, and his mood veered from 'bouts of "unusual gaiety" interspersed with deep dejection', and sudden episodes of tearful frustration so reminiscent of Asaf in his last year. By the time Wellesley sailed towards Lucknow in 'an ornate green and gold vessel that had at its "head a spread eagle gilt; its stern a tiger's head and body"'... paddled by '20 natives dressed in scarlet habits with rose coloured turbans' to make a brutish show of force in late 1801, Saadat had signed a revised treaty which agreed to the disbanding of almost all his troops[*] and the cession of half of the territory of Awadh.[†] Since the original treaty Saadat Ali had signed to get to the throne had deprived him of so much of his army and revenue, he was in no position to block the aggressively acquisitive object of men like Wellesley and Edmonstone. All of which spoilation happened even while Saadat was

---

[*] The remaining army was a tenth of what it had been.
[†] This included Rohilkhand, the agriculturally rich lands in the Doab that had been under his control, and Gorakhpur, which supported the greatly increased Company army.

a perfect friend to the British, and paid all of his subsidies promptly on time. For Saadat there would be no room for manoeuvre at all and he, like all the subsequent nawabs, would retreat ever deeper into the warm seduction of courtly entertainments, arts, and music, till finally, in 1856, a second treaty of annexation brought the entirety of Awadh under British rule.

By the time Viscount Valentia was travelling through Lucknow a year after Wellesley's visit, he could sense that all the old glory of Lucknow was teetering on the verge of a genteel decrepitude. Muharram was now commemorated in a muted manner, Saadat Ali Khan having melted down some of the great gold and silver standards. The Muharram procession itself was halted when Valentia expressed a desire to examine the ceremonial horse of Imam Hussain, the horse led to him while the participants waited around in abashed silence. Asaf had been buried in one of the pavilions of the Imambara (image 36), his tomb covered by a rich canopy of gold which was now sadly faded. Asaf had also left an endowment of 100 rupees per day so that forty priests would read the Quran over his grave, but Saadat had had to reduce that number to ten.

'His hair is now grey, and he had lost many of his teeth, but the fire and intelligence of his eye still lightens up his countenance' Valentia wrote of the nawab, with whom he spent many a congenial evening. The Company officials also missed no opportunity to humiliate the nawab and sneer at his dignity. 'The lowest European gentleman seems to consider himself as on an equality with his highness, and does not always treat him with that respect, which is his due' noted Valentia sadly. Instead of attending the nawab's durbar, so as to participate in the ceremonial of court and enhance the nawab's prestige, the Resident Colonel Scott instead insisted on conducting business at breakfast with him. With the thirty-two-year-old Valentia, who was passing through as an independent traveller sympathetic to the nawab, Saadat Ali Khan was impeccably gracious and hospitable. He sent him ice and fruit every morning when told he would accept no larger presents, and sent foragers into the woods to bring back rare birds and plants when he found out Valentia was a naturalist.

Wellesley, meanwhile, had returned to Calcutta where he would hold court in the new Government House in a style very different from John Shore's earlier, austere example. Sitting high upon a gilded chair and stool placed upon a 'musnud of crimson and gold, formerly composing part of the ornaments of Tippoo Sultan's throne', Wellesley now outshone the Mughal emperor himself. Pinned to his breast would be the star and badge of the Order of St Patrick, which General Harris had had made for him from Tipu's jewels, and above his head hung a magnificent state canopy, which had cost 820 pounds. Below him in a semi-circle were the members of his council, the chief justice, the judges, and on each side of the room, on blue satin chairs, sat the wives of the Company men in their glittering jewels, looking up at the most powerful man in the country. All the old tigers of Hindustan had disappeared, and there was now a brash new lion on the throne.

# THE BATTLE OF DELHI

In October of 1801, astonishingly ecstatic reactions to French envoys were celebrated throughout Great Britain. People clamoured to view the French diplomats clattering past in their carriages in London while throughout the country, jubilant bells rang out and illuminations were organized in great relief and joy. The reason for this most rare moment of détente between these ancient enemies was the Preliminary Treaty that had been signed, soon to be followed in 1802 by the definitive Treaty of Amiens, bringing to an end almost a decade of continuous conflict. The Revolutionary Wars that had begun in 1792 had brought enormous financial strain to Great Britain, and the people were overjoyed that peace had at last been declared.

The British diplomats, however, were less sanguine about this treaty. There were familiar figures in the grey northern French city of Amiens to ratify the treaty in 1802. Representing Britain was the old soldier Cornwallis, now Marquess Cornwallis while the French sent Joseph Bonaparte, Napoleon's brother. British politicians felt they had paid a high price for peace, having had to concede most of the colonial gains they had made*. The French, for their part, had agreed to evacuate their forces from Egypt. Napoleon had left Egypt at the end of 1799 to return to a hero's welcome and the chance to effect a bloodless coup and become leader of France. Napoleon's army had remained in Egypt, however, and the British had landed a force to attack them and secure their trade links to India. David Baird landed in Egypt in 1801 with an Anglo-Indian relief force raised in Bombay. French forces eventually surrendered at Alexandria on 31 August 1801, being forced thereby to hand over all Egyptian antiquities they had discovered including, incidentally, the Rosetta Stone. In this manner the Egypt campaign, which had caused so much trouble to Tipu in a different corner of the world, finally came to an end and France gave up her dreams of a Middle Eastern empire. But both Napoleon and the British politicians were equally leery about the trustworthiness of the other, and the peace turned out to be simply a moment of bated breath before war resumed once again, declared by Britain just fourteen

---

*Only Trinidad and Ceylon were left with the British.

months after the Treaty of Amiens was ratified.

'All the affairs of this world are inter-connected' wrote a far-sighted French officer* in 1799. 'What might have occurred in Europe if Tipu had survived a few years. He would certainly have kept the British in India occupied, and they would not have become as strong or as prosperous in India. They would therefore not have thought so seriously of troubling Europe, and of instigating wars, by giving their allies huge subsidies.' For war would not only continue in Europe, subsidized by Britain's Indian empire, but would become bloodier, vaster, and ever more devastating in the shape of the Napoleonic Wars.

Meanwhile in India, the increasing power of the British Governor General was inversely proportional to that of the emperor of India. Now seventy-five years old, Shah Alam's beard was snow-white and his unseeing eyes were shut tight against the pain in his world. Under the graceless watch of Mahadji Scindia's successors, Shah Alam and his family had scarcely more freedom than the unfortunate residents of the dank salatin quarters, some 500 descendants of past emperors. Their lives were now circumscribed within the walls of the Qila and every missive and scrap of paper sent to the salatin quarters or to the emperor himself was first seized peremptorily and decoded for any information that could be of interest to the Marathas, or their commander, the French general Pierre Perron. For after Benoit de Boigne had left India in 1795, the command of his formidable Brigades of Hindustan had been handed over by the Marathas to Perron,† while another Frenchman, Louis Bourquien, had command of the 3rd Brigade which now guarded the Qila at Delhi. Bourquien was a soldier of humble origins‡ and was affectionately known in the country as Louis Sahib. He had under his command other French soldiers but he also had a number of Anglo-Indian officers. Because of Cornwallis's 1791 ruling disallowing 'country-born gentlemen', otherwise known as Anglo-Indians, from a military, civil, or naval career with the EIC, many ambitious and talented young men joined the Brigades of Hindustan, including one James Skinner§.

---

*Brunet, a young French EIC surgeon.
†A few prodigious battles previously had endeared Perron to the emperor, who had conferred upon the Frenchman the title of Haft Hazari, Nasir-ul-Mulk, Intizam-ud-Daula, Bahadur, Muzaffar Jang and also bestowed upon him the mahi and maatib standard as well as the naubat.
‡Originally a pastry chef by some accounts.
§James Skinner had a British father and a Rajput mother, and would become enormously

Now in 1802 Richard Wellesley decided that having finally neutralized the Mysore menace, the Marathas and their irksome French commanders would need to be vanquished too. The Marathas by the early nineteenth century were a most formidable foe. Their empire consisted of '40 million people, with the combined armies of the chieftains totalling 210,000 cavalry and 96,000 infantry'. Most of the infantry was under European officers, drilled and formed in the same manner as the British Indian army and their cavalry was widely acknowledged to be the best in India, 'with excellent horses, medium sized but strong, of a distinctive dark bay color.' In battle conditions, the Maratha cavalry presented a stunning display of fluttering banners of various colours, their horses fearsome and magnificent with their henna-dyed tails, their manes elaborately plaited through with ribbons and silver roses, and their bridles glinting with various decorations.

Wellesley was fortuitous in his timing, however, for there was trouble brewing in the Maratha Confederacy. The young Daulat Rao Scindia, who had succeeded the Great Scindia, was unproven and volatile, yet enormously powerful. This had made the nominal leader, the new peshwa\* at Poona Bajirao II,† extremely uneasy. At this fractious and uncertain time, one-eyed Jaswant Rao Holkar‡ decided to attack Poona, since the peshwa and the Scindia had opposed his succession, and he inflicted such a decisive defeat upon them that Bajirao II fled Poona altogether and reached Bassein, near Bombay, where he sought the help of the EIC in regaining his throne. The British could not have been more delighted to be in a position to 'help' the young refugee peshwa. They forced him to sign the Treaty of Bassein which effectively reduced the Peshwa to a British vassal. The peshwa was made to cede territory worth 2,600,000 rupees which

---

successful, raising a squadron of Light Cavalry called Skinner's Horse which became the first regiment of the Bengal Lancers, and later of the British Raj. Interestingly, Doon School, the equivalent of Eton or Harrow in India, still retains a playing field called Skinner's Field.

\*The peshwas were the nominal heads of the Marathas but succession disputes from 1772 onwards progressively eroded the Peshwa's authority.

†Bajirao was twenty-seven at this time and Daulat Rao Scindia twenty-three. Bajirao II is not to be confused with Bajirao I, subject of the Bollywood film *Bajirao Mastani*. Daulat Rao became chief of the Scindias at just fifteen.

‡The Holkars were the Martha rulers of Indore. In addition to the peshwa, the Maratha Confederacy included four chieftains, one of which was the Holkar family. Jaswant Rao had been wounded many times in battles, the loss of one eye being the most visible battle scar.

would support over 6,000 British troops within the Maratha lands.

The Maratha Confederacy quite rightly decided that such a fearsome foreign force within the peshwa's lands were a threat to their independence and so Daulat Rao began gathering his forces together and, by August 1803, war had broken out between the Marathas and the Company. Wellesley realized that the board of the EIC in Britain, already unhappy about the killing of Tipu and the huge expenses of the war with Mysore, would need to be convinced about the need to engage with the Marathas. And so he sent a force to Delhi, to 'liberate' the elderly Mughal emperor from the control of the Marathas, and persuade him to accept British protection instead. Almost a hundred years after the death of the last of the 'great Mughals', the name of the emperor, tattered and faded though it was, still held some lustre. Having been usurped at different times by the Marathas, the Rohillas, and the Afghans, now it was finally the time of the 'firangis'.* Having defeated all the other pretenders, it would be the British who would now appoint the emperors of India, and who would rule in his name.

The man chosen for this delicate operation was Gerard Lake, a sixty-year-old veteran of the American Wars. Fastidious about appearances, Lake was 'known for appearing in full uniform, with all his buttons done up and perfectly powdered wig in place' even at the ungodly hour of 2 a.m. But Wellesley did not leave things entirely to the battlefield. Wary about the skill of the deadly French-led brigades, he issued a Proclamation on 6 August 1803 offering every Anglo-Indian and French officer in the French Brigades 'the same grade in the English army that they had in the French Brigades with the same salary without obligation of service, or a pension for life if they decided to retire'. It was a huge incentive to defect and indeed this proclamation led to 'a massive desertion of the Anglo-Indian† officers', effectively destroying the integrity of the Maratha's French Brigades. Historian Jean-Marie Lafont also asserts that there very probably was a 'gentleman's agreement' between Lake, Wellesley, and the French general Perron, to the effect that Perron's wealth and

---

*In 1857 the rebel forces of the Indian sepoys would do the same thing during the Indian Rebellion, rushing to the Red Fort from different corners of the country, to fight in the name of Padshah-e-Hind Bahadur Shah Zafar.
†Lafont writes that 'it would be naïve to believe Skinner' when he claimed to have defected to the English side with his 2,000 men only after the battle.

family would be assured if he left the country before hostilities began. General Perron did indeed desert at the beginning of the war, along with a substantial number of officers. Bourquien, however, remained gallantly at his post in Delhi and on 11 September 1803, the Battle of Delhi took place at Patparganj. With the Brigades under Bourquien thoroughly destabilized by the desertion of their officers, victory was assured for Britain, and Lake entered Delhi* on 14 September and seized the treasure from the Qila to share with his troops. Having thus 'liberated' the elderly emperor from the Marathas, Lake appointed David Ochterlony the first British Resident of Delhi, and that grand old capital city finally fell to the British.

Wellesley also sent a force under his brother Arthur Wellesley to destroy the remaining Maratha forces under Daulat Rao†. The Battle of Assaye that was fought on 23 September was described by Arthur Wellesley as 'the most severe I have ever fought in India'. In the last battle, fought on 1 November at Laswari, Lake engaged what remained of de Boigne's troops. De Boigne's old soldiers fought to the last man, having to be bayoneted as they stood at their gun posts, refusing surrender. 'I never was in so severe a business in my life', wrote Lake to Wellesley the next day, aghast. 'These fellows fought like devils, or rather heroes...' 'The decisive victory,' clarifies Lafont, 'was possible because of the devastation caused by the Proclamation of 6 August.' Daulat Rao was later forced to sign a treaty ceding to the EIC all his territories in Hindustan. Finally in 1805, a treaty would be redacted between Holkar and Calcutta too. More than fifteen years of constant aggressions by the EIC, vociferously using both the real and imagined presence of French threats, would result in a great empire for the British. Hopelessly bogged down by the crisis of revolution and then the Napoleonic Wars, France would pose little actual threat in India but that was entirely irrelevant to the Company men, many of whom had been scarred personally by the humiliation of Yorktown and the American Revolutionary War.

As David Ochterlony settled comfortably into the Dara Shukoh haveli in Delhi and prepared to take his thirteen Indian bibis out

---

*Britain would control Delhi for 144 years, till the Independence of India in 1947.
†Holkar had decided to remain neutral at this juncture, while the Gaikwar of Baroda had been encouraged by the British to stay out of the battle. Holkar would later conduct a lightning raid to recapture Delhi but David Ochterlony defeated him and he surrendered in 1805.

for evening elephant rides, there remained but one real force to be reckoned with for the EIC at the dawn of the nineteenth century—the Sikhs. And just as it seemed like the perfidious French had finally been ousted, a new spectre emerged from the still blazing embers of French ambition. In 1807, Napoleon signed the Treaty of Tilsit with Tsar Alexander I, making allies of France and Russia, and dividing Europe between the two countries. From that time onwards the spectre of British nightmares would have a new name—Russia. The British would become obsessed by the possibility of Russia taking over their empire in India by marching through Afghanistan and this, in turn, would ignite the complicated spy shenanigans of the Great Game whose effects in Central Asia can be felt to this day. In 1815, Arthur Wellesley, now Duke of Wellington, used the battle techniques he had used in India and especially against Tipu Sultan's forces to defeat Napoleon at the Battle of Waterloo, finally bringing to an end twenty-three years of constant global warring with France.

But even the death of Napoleon, the menace who had kept Britain in his thrall for more than two decades, did not becalm the endless nightmares of the India Company men. Ochterlony went to his grave in 1825 still warning the British about 'the risks of a French invasion of India, an invasion he waited for and was preparing himself to repel, but which never came'. But the French never did return and little remains today of the French dreams that obsessed generations of men for more than 100 years. There are small spaces of Gallic beauty in unexpected places—Antoine Polier's collection of gorgeous manuscripts in the Museum of Islamic Art in Berlin, and Jean-Baptiste Gentil's Atlas in the Bibliotheque National de Paris, for example as well as some bemusing structures like René Madec's Manoir des Indes in his hometown of Quimper, and an extraordinary 'Fountain of Elephants' in the alpine town of Chambéry, celebrating Benoit de Boigne's luminous career in India. In India, against all odds and all notions of decency, perhaps the most extensive bequest to have survived are the schools established posthumously in the name of that most curmudgeonly and waspish Frenchman—Claude Martin. Today there are seven 'La Martiniere' schools across the world that bear his name and legacy, including one in Lucknow built at Constantia.

# EPILOGUE

In 1848 a thirty-six-year-old small, pale, sickly man landed in Calcutta. Hunched over from pain when he walked, the youngest Governor General ever sent to India did not seem like he would survive a season in India, much less alter the course of its history. '(He) has an affection of the kidneys and could not leave the house,' an English politician would write worriedly before his departure for India. 'I do not like the appearance of his health at all.' The man himself admitted that he 'landed in Calcutta an invalid, almost a cripple'. But crippled or not, James Andrew Broun Ramsay, 10th earl of Dalhousie and now Governor General of India, would demonstrate a positively gargantuan appetite for the territories of India.

The East India Company's power as a maverick autonomous, military, and political force had been shackled in the nineteenth century through consecutive parliamentary acts in Britain,* till it had become a largely administrative body. Nonetheless, this was no deterrent to Dalhousie who was driven by a quasi-religious zeal to subsume ever more land under British rule, and he immediately dreamt up a policy called the 'Doctrine of Lapse'. In India, where it had long been a custom for rulers without natural heirs to adopt a child, who in turn became the legitimate ruler, the British had imposed their right to be consulted on this choice of heir. Now, Dalhousie decreed, if the British refused the choice of the ruler, the region would instead conveniently 'lapse' to the Company upon the death of the ruler. In this manner, Dalhousie began to incorporate ever more territories at a furious rate into British controlled lands.† In 1849 Dalhousie captured the state of Punjab, and looted young Maharaja Duleep Singh's Kohinoor diamond, which would later be presented to Queen Victoria. Then he turned his attention to Awadh.

In 1847, just a year after Dalhousie landed in India, Wajid Ali Shah, arguably the most famous of the nawabs, became king of Awadh at twenty-five. Like so many of the nawabs before him, Wajid Ali

---

*Apart from Pitt's India Act in 1784, further restricting Acts were passed in 1817, 1833, and 1854.
†The Company took over the princely states of Satara (1848), Sambalpur (1849), Baghat (1850), Udaipur (1852), Jhansi (1854), Nagpur (1854), Tanjore and Arcot (1855).

immediately tried to take control of his kingdom and was eager to bring in changes to his administration. But any such show of independence was harshly curtailed by the all-powerful Resident, and Wajid Ali would instead direct his creative energy and his refined aestheticism to building a truly unique culture of music, dance, and theatre for the nine years that he was allowed to be nawab. He built the architectural marvel that was the Kaiserbagh Palace where he created and performed in operas described by poet Ranjit Hoskote as 'an ensemble performance that wove dance, music, theatre, mime, scenography and architecture into a grand multi-media presentation'.

But Dalhousie would not see an energetic and cultured ruler, beloved to his people. Instead Dalhousie wrote to say: 'The king of Oude seems disposed to be bumptious. I wish he would be. To swallow him before I go would give me satisfaction. The old king of Delhi is dying. If it had not been for the effect folly of the court, I would have ended with him the dynasty of Timur'. Since there was no possibility of using the Doctrine of Lapse here, Dalhousie used the pretext of maladministration to annex Awadh. Wajid Ali was deposed in February 1856 and then exiled to Calcutta taking with him his mother, Mallika Kishwar. The people of Lucknow were so distressed by the exile of their beloved Jan-i-Alam—Life of the World—that weeping citizens followed him all the way to Kanpur. The neighbouring city of Benaras would not celebrate Diwali that year, in grief for the nawab, childhood friend of the raja of Benaras. All the nawab's beloved animals were sold at auction for ludicrously low prices, as the British were keen to be rid of what was for them a superfluous expense. Heartbreakingly, the kotwal of Lucknow bought all the nawab's pigeons, hoping to give them to him when he returned. But Wajid Ali would never return, and would instead die in Calcutta after an exile of thirty-one years. Mallika Kishwar would travel to Britain to make a desperately brave appeal, from one queen to another, to ask Victoria to reverse the annexation of Awadh. Mallika Kishwar would die on the journey back to India, heartbroken, and lies buried in the Père Lachaise Cemetery in Paris. In 1877, Queen Victoria would be proclaimed empress of India. Dalhousie left India in 1856, and died four years later.

With the deposition and removal of Wajid Ali Shah, the British were completing the voracious consuming of Awadh that had been foretold all those years ago at the beginning of this story, when Shuja had so confidently and foolishly decided to fight the EIC on behalf of the Mughal emperor at Buxar. Having glimpsed the immense wealth that the nawab and Bahu Begum owned, Awadh had always been a marked country. But Dalhousie and the other officials did not realize how deeply they were alienating the sepoys of their armies and the people of the conquered territories by their disregard and antipathy for local customs, their religious interference, and their alienation of the traditional gentry of the country. The Bengal Army of the EIC was composed primarily of soldiers from Awadh and the egregious deposition of Wajid Ali was entirely offensive to them. In May 1857, soldiers in Meerut first revolted at the orders to use animal-greased cartridges, as it offended their religious sentiments. Almost instantly, what began as a mutiny against the officers at Meerut spread throughout the north of the country, becoming a full-blown uprising which included the sepoys and the general populace. A full 139,000 of the 169,000 sepoys of the Bengal army rose up, pouring into Delhi and Lucknow, and Lucknow would be the most violently contested city of the Uprising. When British forces finally recaptured Lucknow in 1858, they completed the process of bloody consumption by indulging in an orgy of plunder and destruction of buildings, manuscripts, and papers that would almost erase the memory of the nawabs and begums of Awadh from the face of the world.

But that culture proved far less fragile than it had appeared, and it survives, still, in the culture of nazakat—elegance and refinement—which flows like water through Lucknow and Faizabad's shadowed alleys. It endures, despite all odds, in Lucknow's grand but crumbling mansions, and in its tumbling ruins. It thrives, even today, in the Ganga-Jamuni culture that all Lucknawis so proudly embody in their effortless acceptance of varied customs and traditions, despite endless assaults. And it flourishes, especially, in the grace of the people—in their language, their food, their music and poetry and most especially in their boundless generosity reminiscent of so many of the nawabs, most notably Asaf-ud-Daula himself. As for Asaf's exquisite and unique vision, his great Imambara still survives in all its glory, containing within its magnificent, arcaded silence, the quiet grave of the nawab himself.

# ACKNOWLEDGEMENTS

This book would not have been possible without the encouragement and support of writer and historian Rana Safvi. I owe Rana an incalculable debt, for not only did she help me throughout the writing of this book, with insights, suggestions and feedback, but she also introduced me to her wondrous circle of family and friends at Lucknow, all of whom welcomed me into their homes and lives with unmatched generosity and love.

In Lucknow, I am grateful beyond words for the hospitality of Sheeba Iqbal Jairajpuri, who organized a magical evening of music with a mirasan troupe, and a lavish Lucknawi style banquet in her charming haveli. I am grateful also to the late nawab Jafar Mir Abdullah who served us an elaborate tea in the Aladdin's cave enchanted environment of the Shish Mahal. Carlyle McFarland graciously opened the grounds of La Martiniere's Boys' College so that we could visit it, while we stayed in the College guest house. I am further extremely thankful to Mehru Jaffer, the late Salim Kidwai, Roshan Taqui, Askari Naqvi, Madhavi Kukreja, Farah Naqvi, Zohra Chatterjee, Shubhangie Mishra, Syed Husain Afsar, Himanshu Bajpai, Danish Wasi, and Professor Ali Khan Mahmudabad.

As always, I am immensely grateful for the generous help of scholars, friends, and acquaintances, who responded to queries, suggested avenues of research, and helped in countless ways little and large—Rosie Llewellyn Jones, Veena Oldenburg, Maya Jasanoff, William Dalrymple, Amin Jaffer, Paul Abraham, Nidhin George Olikara, Manu Pillai, Paul Abraham, Marcus Thompson, Pramod Kumar, Deepthi Sasidharan, Charles Andrew Greig, Henri Noltie, Emily Hannam, Axel Langer, Katherine Schofield, Deniz Erduman, Malini Roy, Professor Syed Akhtar, Comte Pierre-Edouard de Boigne, Asif Khan Dehlvi, and Julia Buckley.

I am particularly indebted to art historian Friederike Weis, who invited me to a workshop on the Polier Albums in Berlin and who has, ever since, been so generous with her time and her expertise. The great art historian Kavita Singh passed away during the writing of this book. I will always be grateful for her warm encouragement, and the humility and grace of her brilliance will remain a beacon in the dark.

A great deal of this book was possible due to the archives stored with loving care in some of the great museums of the world. I owe a very great deal to the atmosphere of quiet erudition in these spaces and to the patience and enthusiasm of the staff of collection curators, in particular the British Museum, London, the Archives Municipale de Chambery, France, the Museum for Islamic Art, Berlin, and the Bibliotheque Nationale de France.

To my wonderful publisher David Davidar, and the Aleph team who toiled with so much patience on this book—Pujitha Krishnan, Amrin Naaz, Bena Sareen.

To my daughters Yashoda and Devaki, for existing in this world, to Air Marshal B. D. Jayal and Manju Jayal, and to Mohit Jayal, the best of my love.

# IMAGE CREDITS

Map of Faizabad 1775 on p. x courtesy Bharat Kachroo.

Image 1: Shuja-ud-Daula enjoyed wearing a Persian inspired jacket with a fur stole around his neck, which recalled the Persian origins of the nawabs of Awadh. Courtesy Wikimedia Commons.

Image 2: Completed by Benjamin West long after Robert Clive had died, this is a highly romanticized Image of the moment Emperor Shah Alam II handed over the diwani of Bengal to Clive and the EIC. Courtesy Wikimedia Commons.

Image 3: Dilkusha, Faizabad, in ruins today. Courtesy Akash Joshi.

Image 4: Culinary etiquette reached extraordinary heights under the nawabs of Awadh, with food being sent to Shuja from six separate kitchens. Courtesy Staatliche Museum für Asiatische Kunst, Staatliche Museen zu Berlin/Martin Franken/Public Domain.

Image 5: Emperor Shah Alam was forced to remain in Allahabad for more than twelve years, being undermined and bullied by the EIC. Courtesy Wikimedia Commons.

Image 6: Loyal, sincere, and honest to a fault, Jean-Baptiste Gentil remained by Shuja's side till the death of the nawab. Courtesy Wikimedia Commons.

Image 7: The subah of Ajmer, in the Gentil Atlas. Courtesy Bibliothèque Nationale de France.

Image 8: Image from a Polier album showing two Awadhi noblemen, one of whom might be Antoine Polier himself in the yellow jama, enjoying a song and dance entertainment. Courtesy Museum für Asiatische Kunst, Staatliche Museen zu Berlin/Martin Franken/Public Domain.

Image 9: Polier's spectacular table-cut emerald ring with his title—Arsalan e Jang—engraved in the finest nastaliq script. Courtesy Rare Book Society of India.

Image 10: Polier built himself a handsome haveli-style residence, the ruins of which lie half buried. Courtesy Danish Wasi.

Image 11: Tilly Kettle's oil paintings of Shuja, his sons, and courtiers would prove very influential, inspiring many copies. Courtesy Wikimedia Commons.

Image 12: Awadh artist Faizullah used dizzying multiple perspectives to show the terraced houses and gardens of Faizabad. Courtesy 'The David Collection, Copenhagen'. Inv. number 46/1980. Photograph Pernille Klemp.

Image 13: René Madec painted during his lifetime, wearing the turban that Shah Alam had presented to him. Courtesy Wikimedia Commons.

Image 14: Chronically ill and gaunt, Claude Martin's lupine face was softened by his inquisitive brown gaze. Courtesy Wikimedia Commons.

Image 15: The busy world of the Awadhi zenana, where elite women play chess surrounded by khwajasaras and attendants, while children play and paan is passed around. Courtesy British Library, Painter Nevasi Lal, 1760–1775.

Image 16: A page from Warren Hastings's 'Lucknow diary' of 1784, noting down the recipe of a kebab made by Asaf's cooks. Courtesy British Library.

Image 17: Johann Zoffany's famous painting of Asaf, his courtiers, and many identifiable Company men at a cockfight has been the subject of many interpretations. Courtesy Tate Britain, Google Arts and Culture.

Image 18: Crown Prince Mirza Jawan Bakht, eldest son of emperor Shah Alam II, painted during his stay at Lucknow in 1784. Courtesy Wikimedia Commons.

Image 19: Hasan Reza Khan rose from humble beginnings to become the highest ranked courtier at the durbar of Asaf, painted here by Zoffany. Courtesy British Library.

Image 20: Zoffany trailed a slight air of disreputability, a reputation he encouraged through his disquieting self-portraits. Courtesy Wikimedia Commons.

Image 21: Bought by Martin at the age of eight or nine, Boulone Lise was painted by Zoffany alongside her adopted son, Zulfikar. Courtesy Wikimedia Commons.

Image 22: The most intimate of Zoffany's works, this painting shows William Palmer and his bibi Faiz Begum as well as her sister Noor Begum. Courtesy British Library.

Image 23: Antoine Polier examining the produce from his gardens, painted alongside friends Claude Martin, John Wombwell, and the artist Zoffany. Courtesy Wikimedia Commons.

Image 24: Polier dressed in Awadhi style watching a dance performance, based on a lost Zoffany painting. Katherine Schofield believes the main dancer to be Khanum Jan. Courtesy Museum Rietberg, Zurich, Photo: Rainer Wolfsberger.

Image 25: Two beautiful women enjoying wine on a terrace, from a Polier album. Courtesy Museum für Islamische Kunst, Staatliche Museen zu Berlin/Christian Krug.

Image 26: The hookah bases of the nawabs were made of intricate bidri-ware, engraved in silver. Courtesy Wikimedia Commons.

Image 27: An unusually candid sketch of Asaf by Zoffany in which the nawab's glance betrays his canny intelligence. Courtesy Royal Collection Trust.

Image 28: Asaf painted by Zoffany in 1784, in his favourite white muslin, wearing strings of magnificent pearls and jewels. Courtesy British Library.

Image 29: An unusual European style topographical painting of the Bara Imambara by an unknown artist. Courtesy The Metropolitan Museum of Art.

Image 30: The Rumi Darwaza was covered in exuberant leaf, flower, and fish motifs, and had a crown of stone roses. Courtesy Wikimedia Commons.

Image 31: Asaf and his courtiers in the Bara Imambara, during a Muharram remembrance. Courtesy British Library.

Image 32: Ozias Humphry painted this fine miniature of Asaf's courtier Hyder Beg Khan, but he struggled to get paid for his work. Courtesy Wikimedia Commons.

Image 33: Darwesh Khan formed part of the embassy sent by Tipu Sultan to Paris in 1788, where they caused a stir due to their exoticism and elegance. Courtesy Wikimedia Commons.

Image 34: The *Gloriosa superba* botanical drawing with comments in Martin's distinctive scrawl. Courtesy the Board of Trustees of the Royal Botanic Gardens, Kew.

Image 35: An obsessively driven and hard-working man, Benoit De Boigne was a spectacularly successful military commander working for the Marathas. Courtesy Wikimedia Commons.

Image 36: Asaf-ud-Daula's simple grave inside the Bara Imambara. Courtesy British Library.

# NOTES

## PROLOGUE

xxx     'with dishevelled hair and dress': J. Frederick Price and K. Ranga Achari (eds.), *The Private Diary Of Ananda Ranga Pillai*, Vol. 3, India: Government Press, 1914, p. 95.
xxx     'baggage, horses, oxen, rams,': Ibid.
xxx     'The rout was so general': Ibid.

## INTRODUCTION

xxxiii     'pall of smoke' that spread over Delhi: Cahal Milmo, 'Revealed: How British Empire's dirty secrets went up in smoke in the colonies', *The Independent*, 29 November 2013.
xxxiii     remembered with 'fondness and respect': Ian Jack, 'The History Thieves by Ian Cobain review– how Britain covered up its imperial crimes', *The Guardian*, 6 October 2016.
xxxiv     'British expansion was hotly contested': Maya Jasanoff, *Edge of Empire: Lives, Culture, and Conquest in the East, 1750–1850*, New York: Knopf, 2005, p.8
xl     'this great country, once so flourishing, has descended into complete anarchy': Jean Deloche (ed.), *Voyage en Inde du comte de Modave, 1773–1776: (nouveaux mémoires sur l'état actuel du Bengale et de l'Indoustan*, France: École française d'extrême-orient, 1971, p. 232.
xlii     'an imbalance...' writes Jasanoff: Jasanoff, *Edge of Empire*, p. 8.
xliii     described by Winston Churchill as 'the first world war': Charles Royster, 'The War to Begin All Wars', *New York Times*, 13 February 2000.
xlvi     'The English papers said many horrible things': Guy Deleury, *Le Voyage en Inde: Anthologie des voyageurs français 1750-1820*, Bouquins, 2003, pp. 986-987.
xlvii     'if we are to de-centre...': South Asia Archive and library group, Blog of Friday 9 october 2015

## BOOK I: THE FISH OF HINDUSTAN (1720–1775)

### 1764: SOMEWHERE BETWEEN BIHAR AND BENGAL

3     'We were not leaving the English like vile deserters': Max Vignes, *L'histoire du nabab René Madec*, France: Terre de Brume, 1995, p. 50.
3     'Had one firelock gone off by accident or otherwise': Sir Evan Cotton, 'The Journals of Archibald Swinton', *Bengal, Past & Present*, Journal of the Calcutta Historical Society, Vol. 31, Part 1, 1926.
3-4     Their leader, Frenchman René Madec, later wrote: Ibid.
4     'Let all those who love me': Vignes, *L'histoire du nabab*, p. 50.
5     Indeed Shuja was delighted: Ibid., p. 55.
5     'The prince was gracious: Ibid., p. 56.
6     'the most handsome person I have ever seen in India': Henry Crossley Irwin, *The Garden of India: Or, Chapters on Oudh History and Affairs*, United Kingdom: W. H. Allen, 1880, p. 85.
6     'dastardly son of a Persian flea market salesman' Jean Baptiste Joseph Gentil, *Mémoires sur l'Indoustan: ou Empire Mogol*, France: Petit, 1822, p. 293.
6     'strength and skill in all physical exercise': Deloche, *Voyage en Inde*.
6     'of average height, quite dark, with fine features': Vignes, *L'histoire du nabab*.
6     'The English had made': Deloche, *Voyage en Inde*.
7     'Sweet friendly talk': Ashirbadi Lal Srivastava, *Shuja-ud-daulah*, Vol. 1, India: S.N. Sarkar, 1939, p. 173.
7     Former Kings of Hindustan, by exempting the English Company: Ibid., p. 182.

| | |
|---|---|
| 7 | 'the hope that I entertained to contribute': Vignes, *L'histoire du nabab*. |
| 8 | A veritable temporary city made of reeds: Ibid., p. 62. |
| 9 | 'who were a race of most valiant': Srivastava, *Shuja-ud-daulah*, Vol. 1, p. 84. |
| 9 | 'had often proved that he lacked neither': Deloche, *Voyage en Inde*, p. 269. |
| 9 | 'I had always fought in this country': Vignes, *L'histoire du nabab*, p. 63. |
| 10 | 'an uneducated Arab soldier of fortune': William Dalrymple, *The Anarchy*, London: Bloomsbury Publishing, 2019, p. xviii. |
| 10 | 'intimidated by the Wazir's numbers': Seid Gholam-Hossein Khan, *The Seir Mutaqherin*, Vol. 2, India: Inter-India Publications, 1986. |

## WHEN AWADH WAS A HARDSHIP POSTING

| | |
|---|---|
| 12 | 'The prince, adorned by all': Khan, *The Seir Mutaqherin*, Vol. 1, p. 278. |
| 12 | 'beautiful slave-boys and young men': Ibid. |
| 13 | These war bands or misals: Richard M. Eaton, *India in the Persianate Age: 1000–1765*, UK: Penguin Books Limited, 2019, p. 360. |
| 15 | Finally in 1735 Saadat Khan engaged the zamindar: H. M. Elliot, *The History of India, as Told by Its Own Historians: The Muhammadan Period, Vol. 8*, United States: FB&C Limited, 2016, p. 52. |
| 15 | Indeed so distracted was the Mughal court: Khan, *The Seir Mutaqherin*, Vol. 1, p. 308. |
| 16 | 'The Indian warriors, sayyids': Elliot, *The History of India*, p. 61. |
| 17 | According to one Dutch account: Dalrymple, *The Anarchy*, p. 42. |
| 17 | 'carrying the pick of the treasures': Ibid., p. 44. |
| 17 | The paltry present of seven horses: Elliot, *The History of India*. p. 65. |
| 17 | 'For the ten years that he survived this disaster,': Deloche, *Voyage en Inde*, p. 237. |
| 18 | Court painters experimented: Malini Roy, *A Reign of Tyrants*, Unpublished PhD Thesis. |
| 19 | (Safdar Jang) had with him over ten thousand horse: Ashirbadi Lal Srivastava, *The First Two Nawabs of Awadh*, New Delhi: Life Span Publishers and Distributors, 2022, p. 104. |
| 20 | On the day of the sachaq: Srivastava, *Shuja-ud-daulah*, Vol. 1, p. 6. |
| 20 | 'You are now the most promising': Khan, *The Seir Mutaqherin*, Vol. 3, p. 276. |
| 20 | 'full of levity, and (who) carried a head': Ibid., p. 286. |
| 21 | 'was not a man of great intellect': Elliot, *The History of India*, p. 112. |
| 21 | 'who had in the days of the former sovereign': Ibid., p. 113. |
| 22 | 'a woman of uncommon genius and courage': Khan, *The Seir Mutaqherin*, Vol. 3, p. 303. |
| 22 | When Safdar Jang reached Delhi: Ibid., p. 304. |
| 22 | His dismembered head: Jadunath Sarkar, *Fall of The Mughal Empire*, Vol. 1, New Delhi: Orient Longman, 1991, p. 234. |
| 23 | For the Turani faction: Srivastava, *The First Two Nawabs of Awadh*, p. 255. |
| 23 | 'Every business was transacted': Sarkar, *Fall of The Mughal Empire*, Vol. 1, p. 290. |
| 23 | One day, finding the guns: Ibid., p. 292. |
| 24 | 'Imad-ul-Mulk', admitted French officer Jean: Jean Law de Lauriston, *Mémoire Sur Quelques Affaires de l'Empire Mogol, 1756–1761*, United States: FB&C Limited, 2018. p. 178. |
| 24 | Imad ul Mulk needed allies: Ibid. |
| 24 | 'the lust of battle fired': Sarkar, *Fall of The Mughal Empire*. |
| 24 | 'Safdar Jang became heart-broken': Ibid., p. 307. |
| 25 | So thorough was the Jat destruction: K. Islam and R. Russell, *Three Mughal Poets: Mir, Sauda, Mir Hasan*, New Delhi: OUP India, 1994, p. 28. |

## SHUJA-UD-DAULA, WARRIOR KING, AND NAWAB BEGUM

| | |
|---|---|
| 28 | 'So, huzoor, it is you': Khan, *The Seir Mutaqherin*, Vol. 4, pp. 66-67. |
| 28 | 'whose private life was marked by a high standard': Srivastava, *The First Two Nawabs of Awadh, p. 241.* |

| | |
|---|---|
| 28 | The reasonable thing for Shuja-ud-Daula: Lauriston, *Mémoire Sur Quelques Affaires*, p. 181. |
| 29 | He was of a kind and generous nature: Deloche, *Voyage en Inde*, p. 157. |
| 29 | In 1757 the Maratha envoy: Srivastava, *Shuja-ud-daulah*, Vol. 1, p. 51. |
| 31 | Every day there is a new master: Neelam Khoja, *Sovereignty, Space and Identity*, Unpublished Dissertation, Harvard University, 2018, p. 129. |
| 32 | 'was overcome by such an unexpected scene': Khan, *The Seir Mutaqherin*, Vol. 2, p. 287. |
| 32 | These unfortunate victims of a stupid: Deloche, *Voyage en Inde*. |
| 32 | He finally reached Awadh: Srivastava, *Shuja-ud-daulah*, Vol. 1, p. 57. |
| 34 | 'it may be so for other music': Khan, *The Seir Mutaqherin*, Vol. 3, p. 382. |
| 35 | on 'the impropriety of unrestrained kafirs': Richard B. Barnett, *North India Between Empires: Awadh, the Mughals, and the British 1720–1801*, New Delhi: Manohar, 1987, p. 57. |
| 35 | 'They had stripped the (Diwan-e-Aam)': Khan, *The Seir Mutaqherin*, Vol. 3, p. 385. |
| 36 | 'the finest mobile artillery of that age in Asia': Sarkar, *Fall Of The Mughal Empire*, Vol. 2, p. 324. |
| 36 | 'a starving army mounted on sorry famished nags': Ibid., p. 324. |
| 36 | 'eight thousand miserable Maratha refugees': Srivastava, *Shuja-ud-daulah*, Vol. 1, p. 104. |
| 36 | Indeed Surajmal, 'a man of middle stature': Sarkar, *Fall Of The Mughal Empire*, Vol. 2, pp. 453-453 |
| 36 | 'very much wanted to stuff these officers' corpses': Barnett, *North India Between Empires*, p. 57. |
| 36 | 'the permanent Muslim residents of India': Srivastava, *Shuja-ud-daulah*, Vol. 1,, p. 105. |
| 37 | 'Thousands of wretches': Roy, *A Reign of Tyrants*. |

## A BATTLE AT BUXAR

| | |
|---|---|
| 39 | 'the most dramatically successful war': Linda Colley, *Britons: Forging the Nation, 1707–1837*, London: Yale University Press, 2005, p. 101. |
| 40 | 'It is notorious,': Khan, *The Seir Mutaqherin*, Vol. 2, p. 287. |
| 40 | 'he was overawed by the very name': Ibid., p. 303. |
| 40 | 'The various generals behaved towards him': Lauriston, *Mémoire Sur Quelques Affaires*, p.457. |
| 41 | 'Alas! It is all the same for me': Ibid., p. 458. |
| 41 | 'I was still serving my nation': Ibid., p. 426. |
| 42 | What surprised me the most: Ibid., p. 334. |
| 42 | 'if so were we Arabs, Tartars, Pathans': Ibid., p. 366. |
| 43 | 'was a man of a great deal': Deloche, *Voyage en Inde. p.* 151. |
| 44 | 'Like all men of rank in Asia,': Gentil, *Mémoires sur l'Indoustan*, p. 303. |
| 44 | The nawab 'was so full of himself': Khan, *The Seir Mutaqherin*, Vol. 2, p. 528. |
| 44 | And indeed the nawab seems: Ibid., p. 549. |
| 44 | 'The Vizier crossed the karmnasa': Cotton, 'The Journals of Archibald Swinton'. |
| 44 | 'The English themselves, affected': Khan, *The Seir Mutaqherin*, Vol. 2, p. 558. |
| 45 | 'I fancy that had': Barnett, *North India Between Empires*, p. 64. |
| 45 | 'and even though my troops': Vignes, *L'histoire du nabab*, p. 65. |
| 45 | 'the whole army of the Nawab was a heterogeneous crowd': Uma Shanker Pandey, *European Adventurers in North India: 1750–1803*, United Kingdom: Routledge, 2020, p. 35. |
| 45 | 'The (Shahzaada), who was sick: Khan, *The Seir Mutaqherin*, Vol. 2, p. 536. |
| 46 | 'it is a truly unbelievable thing': Deloche, *Voyage en Inde. p.* 23. |
| 46 | 'For a time,' wrote Madec: Vignes, *L'histoire du nabab*, p. 65. |
| 46 | 'blinded by the pomp and glory': Ibid., p. 69. |
| 46 | 'thought it derogatory to his dignity': Khan, *The Seir Mutaqherin*, Vol. 2, p. 573. |
| 46 | 'I was beyond consolation,': Vignes, *L'histoire du nabab*, p. 69. |
| 47 | 'I have a lot to discuss with you about this war': Gentil, *Mémoires sur l'Indoustan*, p. 242. |
| 47 | '(Gentil) had demonstrated to the English': Vignes, *L'histoire du nabab*. |
| 47 | 'It will in my opinion,': Srivastava, *Shuja-ud-daulah*, Vol. 2, p. 6. |

| | |
|---|---|
| 48 | 'you (were) before unacquainted with our customs': Letter of Shuja-ud-Daula to Carnac, British Library, Manuscript Collection 19 May 1765. |
| 48 | 'Gentil assured Shuja-ud-Daula that the need': Deloche, *Voyage en Inde*. |
| 49 | 'vicious asset-stripper': Dalrymple, *The Anarchy*. |
| 49 | 'an unstable sociopath and a racist': Adrija Roychowdhury, ' Robert Clive: An 'unstable sociopath and a racist', hated both in India and England', *Indian Express*, 12 June 2020. |
| 49 | 'almost overnight (Clive) became one': Peter Frankopan, *The Silk Roads: A New History of the World*, London: Bloomsbury Publishing, 2015. |
| 49 | 'The English gentlemen took off: Srivastava, *Shuja-ud-daulah*, Vol. 2, p. 6. |
| 50 | 'Shah Alam changed colour': Barnett, *North India Between Empires*, p. 74. |
| 50 | 'and even resentment, upon the hardness': Srivastava, *Shuja-ud-daulah*, Vol. 2, p. 11. |
| 50 | 'did not stand like the famous throne': Ibid., p. 12 |
| 51 | 'as we intend to make use of his Majesty': Dalrymple, *The Anarchy*, p. 207-208. |
| 51 | with 'breach of faith': Srivastava, *Shuja-ud-daulah*, Vol. 2, p. 22. |
| 51 | 'whatever I have is of use to me': Khan, *The Seir Mutaqherin*, Vol. 2, p. 586. |
| 52 | After the disaster of Buxar: C.A. Bayly, *Rulers, Townsmen and Bazaars: North Indian Society in the Age of British Expansion: 1770–1870*, India: OUP India, 2012, p. 116. |
| 52 | 'his best friend and his confidant': Gentil, *Mémoires sur l'Indoustan*, p. 297. |
| 53 | 'so greedy, so powerful and so paranoid': Deloche, *Voyage en Inde*, p. 167. |

## A CITY IS BORN

| | |
|---|---|
| 54 | 'The nabob...is the most formidable nabob': Jemima Kindersley, *Letters from the Island of Teneriffe, Brazil, the Cape of Good Hope, and the East-Indies*, 1777, p. 154-155. |
| 54 | 'Shuja-ud-Daula bred up in all the luxury': Srivastava, *Shuja-ud-daulah*, Vol. 2, p. 57 |
| 54 | 'Till of late he gave little attention': Irwin, *The Garden of India*. |
| 55 | 'Within eighteen months,' writes historian Richard B. Barnett': Barnett, *North India Between Empires*, p. 76. |
| 55 | In India there are many chieftains: Deloche, *Voyage en Inde*, p. 306. |
| 56 | 'The defeat of Buxar': Gentil, *Mémoires sur l'Indoustan*, p. 298. |
| 56 | 'Another great failing,' agreed Modave: Deloche, *Voyage en Inde*, p. 306. |
| 56 | 'spending several hours every day': Srivastava, *Shuja-ud-daulah*, Vol. 2, pp. 332-333. |
| 56 | 'He had 22,000 messengers': Muhammad Faiz Bakhsh and William Hoey, *Memoirs of Delhi and Faizábád: Being a Translation of the Táríkh Farahbakhsh of Muhammad Faiz Bakhsh from the Original Persian*, Allahabad: Government Press, North-western Provinces and Oudh, Vol. 2, 1889. |
| 57 | 'As soon as it was known': Abdulḥalīm Sharar, *Lucknow, the Last Phase of an Oriental Culture*, New Delhi: Oxford University Press, 1989, p. 31. |
| 57 | 'Four miles outside Faizabad': Bakhsh and Hoey, *Memoirs of Delhi and Faizábád*. |
| 58 | 'the greatest fortress erected up to then': Banmali Tandan, *The Architecture of Lucknow and Its Dependencies, 1722–1856: A Descriptive Inventory and an Analysis of Nawabi Types*, India: Vikas Publishing House, 2001. |
| 58 | 'were stored with a variety of curious fishes': Sake Deen Mahomet, Michael Fisher (ed.), *The Travels of Dean Mahomet: an eighteenth-century journey through India*, Berkeley: University of California Press, 1997, p. 88. |
| 58 | On one occasion, Nawab Begum was: Srivastava, *Shuja-ud-daulah*, Vol. 2, p. 49. |
| 59 | 'Employing some 500 persons': Tandon, *The Architecture of Lucknow and Oudh*, p. 66. |
| 59 | Outside Faizabad, the fields: Deloche, *Voyage en Inde*, p. 182. |
| 59 | 'from the south gate of the fort': Tandon, The Architecture of Lucknow and Oudh, p. 66. |
| 59 | 'There is such a great crowd here': Deloche, *Voyage en Inde*. |
| 59 | 'basting kababs over a charcoal fire': Meer Hassan Ali, William Crooke (ed.), *Observations on the Mussulmauns of India*, India: H. Milford, Oxford University Press, 1917. |
| 59 | 'it is the residence of one of the greatest': Deloche, *Voyage en Inde*, p. 144. |

| | |
|---|---|
| 60 | 'would ride out each morning': Bakhsh and Hoey, *Memoirs of Delhi and Faizábád*, Vol. 2, p. 6. |
| 61 | 'certainly the most splendid Monument to the Arts': Tandon, *The Architecture of Lucknow and Oudh*, p. 69. |
| 61 | 'pulao; muzaffar, a sweet saffron-flavoured rice dish': Colleen Taylor Sen, *Feasts and Fasts: A History of Food in India*, London: Reaktion Books, 2014. |
| 62 | The third kitchen, supervised by the khwajasara Bahar Ali Khan: Sharar, *Lucknow, the Last Phase of an Oriental Culture*, p. 156. |
| 63 | 'O Mian! What is there to eat': Aslam Mahmud, *Awadh Symphony: Notes on a Cultural Interlude*, New Delhi: Rupa Publications, 2017, p. 95. |
| 63 | About muslin, poet Amir Khusrau had sighed: *Amir Khusrau: Memorial Volume*, New Delhi: Publications Division, Ministry of Information and Broadcasting, Government of India, 1975. |
| 63 | The gold or silver basins: Sushama Swarup, *Costumes and Textiles of Awadh: From the Era of Nawabs to Modern Times*, New Delhi: Roli, 2012, p. 19. |
| 64 | The dupatta is so transparent it hides not: Fanny Parkes Parlby, *Wanderings of a Pilgrim in Search of the Picturesque*, Manchester: Manchester University Press, 2001. |
| 65 | This lady of ladies...passed: Bakhsh and Hoey, *Memoirs of Delhi and Faizábád*, p. 294. |
| 66 | 'would be loaded with stately grandeur': Sharar, *Lucknow, the Last Phase of an Oriental Culture*, pp. 34-35. |
| 67 | I had barely opened my lips: Swarup, *Costumes and Textiles of Awadh*, p. 21. |
| 67 | 'many of the Eastern women have so much beauty': Carl Thompson (ed.), *Women's Travel Writings in India 1777–1854*, Vol.1. 2020. p. 92. |
| 67 | 'There was such a multitude': Sharar, *Lucknow, the Last Phase of an Oriental Culture*, p. 34. |
| 67 | The terms were accepted: Srivastava, *Shuja-ud-daulah*, Vol. 2, p. 132. |
| 67 | 'She followed the style and fashion': Bakhsh and Hoey, *Memoirs of Delhi and Faizábád*, p. 248 |
| 68 | The Begum, immediately divining: Kidambi Srinivasa Santha, *Begums of Awadh*, India: Bharati Prakashan, 1980, p. 3. |
| 68 | The majority of the population: Gavin Hambly, *Women in the Medieval Islamic World: Power, Patronage, and Piety*, London: Macmillan, 1999. |
| 70 | 'everyone makes a space': Gentil, *Mémoires sur l'Indoustan*. |

## A FRENCHMAN AT FAIZABAD

| | |
|---|---|
| 72 | 'he has so well adopted the habits of the Asian': Gentil, *Mémoires sur l'Indoustan*.. |
| 73 | By Modave's assessment, Shuja by this time: Deloche, *Voyage en Inde*, p. 147. |
| 73 | 'besides several trays full of jewels: Srivastava, *Shuja-ud-daulah*, Vol. 1. |
| 74 | 'because he was very attached to him and because he felt he would: Gentil, *Mémoires sur l'Indoustan* |
| 74 | 'the Emperor began placing his hopes: Ibid.. |
| 74 | 'this prince lacked the force of character': Ibid., p. 291. |
| 75 | The fighting corps was led: Ibid., p. 269. |
| 75 | 'The King resides now with his court': Thompson (ed.), *Women's Travel Writings in India*, p. 73. |
| 76 | 'Do you know, Sir, who is master here': Gentil, *Mémoires sur l'Indoustan*, 259. |
| 77 | 'blessed with an eloquent tongue': Gentil, *Mémoires sur l'Indoustan*. |
| 77 | To keep the Nawab well disposed: Archives Nationales d'Outre-Mer, Aix-en-Provence. |
| 79 | 'among the mass of Frenchmen who visited': Deloche, *Voyage en Inde*, p. 525. |
| 79 | 'watershed in the history of western Indology': Chanchal Dadlani, 'Transporting India: The Gentil Album and Mughal Manuscript Culture', *Art History*, Vol. 38, 2015, p. 758. |
| 81 | 'rigorous planning in the conception of both': Dhir Sarangi, 'Peintures indiennes et transferts culturels', *Synergie-Inde-Revue du GERFLINT*, No. 7, 2016. |
| 82 | 'Adjustments to European tastes': Susan Gole, *Maps of Mughal India: Drawn by Colonel* |

Jean-Baptiste-Joseph Gentil, Agent for the French Government to the Court of Shuja-ud-daula at Faizabad, in 1770,* India: Kegan Paul International, 1988.

82 In a letter to the French King: Letter from Jean Baptiste Joseph Gentil to Louis XVII, 1778, Archives Nationales d'Outre-Mer, Aix-en-Provence.

83 'I was rewarded by the glory': Letter from Jean Baptiste Joseph Gentil asking for a pension, 1778, Archives Nationales d'Outre-Mer, Aix-en-Provence.

83 'despite all their setbacks, it all works out': Archives Nationales d'Outre-Mer, Aix-en-Provence.

83 'I have lost all courage and energy': Gentil, *Mémoires sur l'Indoustan*, p. 425.

## TAILOR TINKER SOLDIER SPY

85 'The embroiderer is a bastard': M. Alam and S. Alavi, *A European Experience of the Mughal Orient: The I'jāz-i Arsalānī (Persian Letters 1773–1779) of Antoine-Louis Henri Polier,* Oxford University Press. 2001, p. 116.

85 'He said he would finish the work': Ibid.

85 'Ask the gardener,' he wrote: Ibid., p. 147.

85 At one point, the man employed: Tandan, *The Architecture of Lucknow and Oudh*, p. 106.

87 'This was not in the fitness': Alam and Alavi, *A European Experience of the Mughal Orient*, p. 159.

88 'a polite but cold exterior': Deloche, *Voyage en Inde*, p. 96.

88 'he always wore a plain coat of English broad-cloth': Khan, *The Seir Mutaqherin*, Vol. 3, p. 354.

88 "Tis Mrs Hastings' self brings up the read!': P. J. Marshall, 'The Private Fortune of Marian Hastings', *Bulletin of the Institute of Historical Research*, Vol. 37, Issue 96, 1964.

89 'when the English acquired Bengal': Deloche, *Voyage en Inde*, p. 97.

90 'wheat bran soaked in water': Alam and Alavi, *A European Experience of the Mughal Orient*, p. 155.

91 'I fail to understand': Ibid., p. 326.

93 'The French have machinated': 'Letter from Polier to Warren Hastings', British Library, Manuscript Collection, December 1776.

94 'border crossers, social climbers, chameleons and collectors': Jasanoff, *Edge of Empire*, p. 52.

94 And while for Polier the façade of the chameleon: Deleury, *Le Voyage en Inde*, p. 185.

94 'uncouth...and his address ungainly': Antoine Louis Henri Polier, Pratul Chandra Gupta (ed.), *Shah Alam II and His Court: A Narrative of the Transactions at the Court of Delhy from the Year 1771 to the Present Time,* India: S.C. Sarkar and Sons, 1947, p. 111.

## PORTRAIT OF A NAWAB

98 'in the beginning at least, artists were lured': Mildred Archer, 'British Painters of the Indian Scene'. *Journal of the Royal Society of Arts*, Vol. 115, No. 5135, (1967), pp. 863–879.

100 'What need have you': Gentil, *Mémoires sur l'Indoustan*, p. 311.

102 'poetry, rhetoric, philosophy and theology': Kavita Singh, *Real Birds in Imagined Gardens: Mughal Painting Between Persia and Europe,* London: Getty Research Institute, Getty Publications, 2017, p. 8.

103 Scholar Friederike Weis meanwhile has shown: Friederike Weis, Marzia Faietti and Gerhard Wolf (eds.), 'Confident Women in Indo-Persianate Albums: Visual Metaphors or Ethnography?', *Motion: Transformation (35th Congress of the International Committee of the History of Arts, Florence 2019)*, Vol. 1, Bologna, 2021.

104 'European "scientific" perspective struck': 'Entertainment in a Harem Garden', Sotheby catalogue, signed by Faizullah, Faizabad, 1765.

104 'the greatest Indo-Islamic style domestic edifices': Tandan, *The Architecture of Lucknow and Oudh*.

## FATHERS AND SONS

106   'risk his life in riding a most unruly horse or elephant': Srivastava, *Shuja-ud-daulah*, Vol. 2, p. 301.
106   'while he was sitting, he seemed to be a young man': Bakhsh and Hoey, *Memoirs of Delhi and Faizábád*, Vol. 2, p. 16.
107   'with great strength and agility': Srivastava, *Shuja-ud-daulah*, Vol. 2, p. 300.
108   'From his boyhood,' sighed Faiz': Bakhsh and Hoey, *Memoirs of Delhi and Faizábád*, Vol. 2, p. 16.
108   In November 1770, sachaq was sent: Srivastava, *Shuja-ud-daulah*, Vol. 2, p. 160.
110   'the greatest of the Marathas': Deloche, *Voyage en Inde*.
110   'the emperor dissimulated the outrage': Ibid., p. 253.

## A NABOB IN DELHI

111   'I may declare without exaggeration': Vignes, *L'histoire du nabab*, p. 121.
112   'the Catholics in this country follow the traditions': Ibid., p. 78.
112   'ardent patriot' and a man: Deloche, *Voyage en Inde*, p. 20.
113   The EIC would pay: Frankopan, *The Silk Roads*.
113   'What could possibly interest you you': Vignes, *L'histoire du nabab*, p. 108.
114   'I will sacrifice my desire to return': Ibid., 110.
114   'exhibited a strong desire to begin a correspondence': Ibid., p. 148.
115   Ever since his return to Delhi: Deloche, *Voyage en Inde*, p. 261.
115   '30 battalions of disciplined sepoys, 73,000 cavalry': T. G. P. Spear, 'Some Aspects of Late Mughal Delhi', *Journal of the Panjab University Historical Society*, Vol. 5, April 1938, p. 3.
115   It is a tradition to send prepared dishes: Deloche, *Voyage en Inde*, p. 445.

## THE WORLD ON FIRE

117   'no English gentleman should reside in his country': Barnett, *North India Between Empires*, p. 87.
117   This young man does not lack intelligence: Deloche, *Voyage en Inde*, p. 164.
118   'at the cutting edge of British expansion': Michael. H. Fisher, *Indirect Rule in India: Residents and the Residency System, 1764–1858*, Oxford University Press, 1991, p. 29.
118   In all my life I never saw dejection: Barnett, *North India Between Empires*, p. 78.
118   'to extract vengeance on all the ravages': Gentil, *Mémoires sur l'Indoustan*, p. 300.
119   A historian has called his misadventures 'pathetic': Jean-Marie Lafont and Rehana Lafont, *The French and Delhi: Agra, Aligarh, and Sardhana*. India Research Press, 2010.
119   'obliged to tell him (Madec) that he was but a vile': Lafont and Lafont, *The French and Delhi*, p. 61.
120   'He told me quite openly': Deloche, *Voyage en Inde*.
120   'The English are so possessive': Ibid., p. 185.
120   Modave criticized the English: Ibid., p. 165.
120   'that within two years, the French': Ibid., p. 167.
121   'all appeared to have lost their father.': Gentil, *Mémoires sur l'Indoustan*, p. 289.
121   'there was abundant prosperity during his reign': Srivastava, *Shuja-ud-daulah*, Vol. 2, p. 311.
121   'it is difficult to find words': *Bengal, Past & Present*, Journal of the Calcutta Historical Society, 1927, Vol. 33, Part 2, p. 136.

## BOOK II: THE LIONS OF GOD (1775–1785)

## THE ROAD TO LUCKNOW

125   According to Faiz Baksh, who is the closest: Bakhsh and Hoey, *Memoirs of Delhi and Faizábád*, p. 12.

| | |
|---|---|
| 125 | 'the most promising of the whole family': Barnett, *North India Between Empires*, p. 100. |
| 126 | (The new Nawab) is grotesquely overweight: Deloche, *Voyage en Inde*, p. 169–179. |
| 127 | 'Ten days have not yet passed': Bakhsh and Hoey, *Memoirs of Delhi and Faizábád*. p. 20. |
| 127 | She also gave her son additional sums: Nicholas Abbott, '"It all comes from me": Bahu Begam and the making of the Awadh nawabi, circa 1765–1815', *Modern Asian Studies*, Vol. 57, 2022, pp. 1-29. |
| 127 | 'There was no low or low-minded class: Bakhsh and Hoey, *Memoirs of Delhi and Faizábád*, p. 24. |
| 128 | There was ancient animosity: For details of the feud, see Ibid., p. 13. |
| 128 | 'Throughout his reign,': Karen Chancey, 'Rethinking the Reign of Asaf-Ud-Daula, Nawab Of Awadh', 1775–1797', *Journal of Asian History*, Vol. 41, No. 1, 2007, p. 1. |
| 128 | 'naked rustics, whose fathers and brothers': Bakhsh and Hoey, *Memoirs of Delhi and Faizábád*, Vol. 2, p. 21. |
| 129 | 'I have no money': Ibid., p. 26. |
| 129 | Hereafter I, Asaf, have: Ibid., p. 26-26. |
| 130 | While 24 lakhs were paid: Ibid., pp. 27-28. |
| 130 | In a letter she sent to Warren Hastings in 1775,: Abbott, 'It all comes from me'. |
| 130 | Every item the begam possessed: Ibid. |
| 130 | And while the British regarded: To understand the details of the matter, see Ibid. |
| 130 | 'According to most contemporary sources: Abbott, 'It all comes from me' |
| 132 | 'Wherever you look,': Deloche, *Voyage en Inde*, p. 233. |
| 132 | 'he keeps them happy with promises': Ibid., p. 273. |
| 132 | 'prudent and clever, full of feints': Ibid., p. 270. |
| 133 | 'Abd al Ahad Khan is more polite': Ibid., p. 269. |
| 133 | 'the mother of Shuja-ud-Daula had': Ibid. |
| 134 | 'to have the custom of his country': Santha, *Begums of Awadh*, p. 68. |
| 134 | 'As your sincere friend': Alam and Alavi, *A European Experience of the Mughal Orient*, p. 232. |
| 135 | 'Nawab Begum had repeatedly written': Santha, *Begums of Awadh*, p. 48. |
| 136 | 'the honour of the (French) king was at stake': Deloche, *Voyage en Inde*, p. 424. |

## ALL FRENCHMEN MUST LEAVE

| | |
|---|---|
| 137 | 'Go, you obstinate one': Rosie Llewellyn-Jones, *A Very Ingenious Man: Claude Martin in Early Colonial India*, London: Oxford University Press, 1999, p. 6. |
| 138 | 'which does not allow Bread and Water': Ibid., p. 63. |
| 138 | 'no muskets by him (Asaf-ud-Daula) fit': Ibid., p. 66. |
| 139 | 'presented, one after the other': Deloche, *Voyage en Inde*, p. 428. |
| 139 | But a week later, he summoned Gentil: Deleury, *Le Voyage en Inde*, p. 33. |
| 139 | 'this Prince lacked the force of character': Gentil, *Mémoires sur l'Indoustan*, p. 291. |
| 140 | In the five years that Canaple was employed: Letter from Jean Baptiste Joseph Gentil, Archives Nationales d'Outre-Mer. |
| xxx | 'Asaf-ud-Daula was exteriorly': Deloche, *Voyage en Inde*, p. 170. |
| 140 | By 1773, only the outer wall: Letter of M. Gentil at Faisabad, Archives Nationales d'Outre-Mer, 26 November 1772, p. 293. |
| 140 | 'Luck made her fall to my lot': Claude Martin, Dernière Volonté Et Testament Du Major Général Cl. Martin, France: Imprimerie de Ballanche père et fils, 1803, p. 14 |

## THE BEGUMS AND A RAJA

| | |
|---|---|
| 141 | 'the emperor was determined': Deloche, *Voyage en Inde*, p. 271. |
| 142 | 'The Vizier expressed more satisfaction': Michael H. Fisher, *A Clash of Cultures: Awadh, the British and the Mughals*, Maryland: The Riverdale Co., 1987, p. 80. |
| 142 | 'exert yourself effectually in favour of us': Anna Clark, *Scandal: The Sexual Politics of the* |

|     | |
| --- | --- |
|     | *British Constitution*, United States: Princeton University Press, 2013, p. 90 |
| 142 | 'I cannot conceive that she has': Ibid. |
| 143 | 'I am sorry to remark': Letter of Nathaniel Middleton to Warren Hastings, British Library, 11 March 1777. |
| 143 | 'a man of low extraction': Abu Talib ibn Muhammad, William Hoey (tr.), *History of Asafu'd Daulah, Nawab Wazir of Oudh: Being a Translation of 'Tafzihu'l Ghafilin', a Contemporary Record of Events Connected with His Administration*, Allahabad: Pustak Kendra, 1885, p. 78. |
| 144 | 'pampered, lazy, impulsive, crude and wilful youth': Barnett, *North India Between Empires*, p. 523. |
| 145 | 'on the first intelligence of the war': Warren Hastings, *A Narrative of the Late Transactions at Benares*, Kolkata: Bangabasi, 1905, p. 4. |
| 145 | It is a monstrous thing that: Deloche, *Voyage en Inde*, p. 286. |
| 146 | 'frequent representations having been made 'harsh letter: Letter from Governor General to Raja Chait Singh, British Library, Manuscript Collection, 17 January 1781, IOR;L/PAR421. |
| 146 | 'It was his duty to obey them': Hastings, *A Narrative of the Late Transactions at Benares*, p. 46. |
| 146 | 'resolved to draw from (the Raja's)': Barnett, *North India Between Empires*, p. 199. |
| 146 | The English painter William Hodges accompanied Hastings: Hodges, *Travels in India*, p. 37. |
| 146 | 'struck with the simplicity of (Hastings's) appearance': Ibid., p. 44. |
| 147 | 'pure Hindoo manners, arts, buildings and customs': Ibid., p. 47. |
| 147 | 'If Chait Singh's people': Hastings, *A Narrative of the Late Transactions at Benares*, p. 48. |
| 148 | 'his head and right hand': Warren Hastings, et al. *The Letters of Warren Hastings to His Wife*. United Kingdom: W. Blackwood, 1905, p. 134. |
| 148 | 'the European inhabitants of Patna': Hastings, *The Letters of Warren Hastings to His Wife*, p. 134. |
| 148 | 'These traders,' Edmund Burke would: T. W. Nechtman, *Nabobs: Empire and Identity in Eighteenth-Century Britain*, Cambridge: Cambridge University Press, 2010, p. 95. |
| 149 | 'This is a private arrangement,': Barnett, *North India Between Empires*, p. 184. |
| 149 | Alexander Hannay used Hastings' 'gift': Irwin, *The Garden of India*. |
| 149 | 'If, by any means, any matter': Ibid., p. 90. |
| 149 | 'No sooner had the rebellion': Hastings, *A Narrative of the Late Transactions at Benares*, p. 63 |
| 150 | 'In the city of Faizabad': Ibid., p. 63. |
| 150 | 'one half of the province of Awadh': Ibid., p. 66. |
| 150 | It was widely acknowledged: Barnett, *North India Between Empires*, p. 200. |
| 150 | 'was insulted by every village I passed': Ibid., p. 201. |
| 150 | 'whenever the villagers saw a red-coated regular': Bakhsh and Hoey, *Memoirs of Delhi and Faizábád*, p. 107. |
| 150 | 'The conduct I have related': Barnett, *North India Between Empires*, p. 200-201. |
| 151 | 'this town (Faizabad) has more the appearance': Letter of Middleton to Hastings, British Library, Manuscript Collection, 17 October 1781. |
| 151 | 'Mr Hastings and all the English have been': Muhammad, Hoey (tr.), *History of Asafu'd Daulah* p. 53. |
| 151 | 'rabble' though they were: Letter of Warren Hastings to Company, British Library, Manuscript Collection, 1782. |
| 152 | 'the reflection and glare of the light grey rock': Hastings, *The Letters of Warren Hastings to His Wife*, p. 136. |
| 152 | 'Let it not be thought': Hastings, *A Narrative of the Late Transactions at Benares*, p. 48. |
| 152 | 'few men loved or hated': Henry Lawrence, 'The Kingdom of Oude', *The Calcutta Review*, Vol. 3, 1845, p. 102. |
| 152 | As soon as the revolt: Barnett, *North India Between Empires*, p. 202. |

## PUNISHING A BEGUM

155 'The adab or etiquette of society': Richard Barnett, Gavin Hambly (ed.), 'Embattled Begams: Women as Power Brokers in Early Modern India', *Women in the Medieval Islamic World: Power, Patronage and Piety*, New York: St. Martins, 1998, p. 532.

155 'not brilliant but experienced...mild and just': Lady Victoria Manners and Dr G. C. Williamson, *John Zoffany, R.A, His Life and* Works, 1735–1810, London: John Lane, The Bodley Head, 1920, p. 93.

156 Salar Jang was so shaken: Bakhsh and Hoey, *Memoirs of Delhi and Faizábád*, p. 182.

156 'Whoever says so tells a lie: Ibid., p. 187.

156 'Say thou not unto them': Ibid., p. 188.

157 'The resumption of all the jaghirs': Irwin, *The Garden of India*, p. 92.

157 When an officer was sent: Barnett, *North India Between Empires*, p. 209.

157 Sixty lakhs, it was understood: Ibid., p. 204.

159 That he would return to the path: Bakhsh and Hoey, *Memoirs of Delhi and Faizábád*, p. 141.

159 'She is only going to the Nawab Begum's: Ibid., p. 133.

159 The Tripolia gateway was bristling: Ibid., p. 142.

160 'who remembered that they were residents': Ibid., p. 140.

160 'Let us get into our litters': Ibid., p. 144.

160 'that the two Begums would come out': Ibid., p. 146.

160 'This whole excitement and misunderstanding': Ibid., pp. 144–145.

162 'They were astounded': Ibid.

162 He would either inspire: Ibid., p. 148.

162 When Asaf saw before him: Ibid., p. 149.

163 'the result of our interview': Letter of Middleton to Hastings, British Library, Manuscript Collection, 6 December 1781.

163 'reluctance with which the ministers': Letter of Middleton to Hastings, British Library, Manuscript Collection, 27 December 1781, IOR/L/PARL.

163 'On the revolt of Chait singh': Hastings, *The Letters of Warren Hastings to His Wife*.

164 'Since the day that man died': Bakhsh and Hoey, *Memoirs of Delhi and Faizábád*, p. 87.

164 Bahar Ali Khan also noticed: Ibid., p. 87.

164 'these provinces were bestowed upon': Ibid., p. 94.

164 'mete out exemplary punishment': Barnett, *North India Between Empires*, p. 213.

165 'no further rigour than that': Ibid.

165 'climbed up trees and some fled': Ibid.

165 The Begums' collectors, all elite men: Ibid., p. 154.

166 'if the Wazir so little regarded': Santha, *Begums of Awadh*, p. 51.

166 'Unless the jagirs be restored': Bakhsh and Hoey, *Memoirs of Delhi and Faizábád*, p. 183.

166 'If they are dying, let them die': Ibid., p. 182.

167 'To have their village included': Irwin, *The Garden of India*, p. 92.

167 'went into a small dark room': Bakhsh and Hoey, *Memoirs of Delhi and Faizábád*, p. 202.

xxx Perhaps if she had been a simpering sot: Barnett, *North India Between Empires*; Bakhsh and Hoey, *Memoirs of Delhi and Faizábád*.

169 'a Woman as I really believe': Hastings, *The Letters of Warren Hastings to His Wife*, p. 148.

## FROM YORKTOWN TO AWADH

170 'arguably the greatest Indian picture of the defeat': Ram Ganesh Kamatham, 'The Battle of Pollilur: Revisiting the Footnotes of History', *The Wire*, 31 March 2022.

170 'Oh God, it is all over!': Alan Taylor, *American Revolutions: A Continental History, 1750–1804*, New York: WW Norton, 2017.

171 'no money, no resources, no navy': André Christophe Louis Piveron de Morlat and Jean-Marie Lafont (ed.): *Piveron De Morlat: Mémoire Sur L'inde (1786): Les Opérations Diplomatiques Et*

Militaires Françaises Aux Indes Pendant La Gue re D'indépendance Américaine. Paris: Riveneuve éditions, 2013, p. 28.
172 No reasonable person would doubt: Deloche, *Voyage en Inde*, p. 548.
173 'If we succeeded only in interrupting': R. E. Abarca, 'Classical Diplomacy and Bourbon "Revanche" Strategy, 1763–1770', *The Review of Politics*, Vol. 32, No. 3, 1970, pp 313-337.
173 The Marquis de Bussy is warned: Marco Platania, 'L'originalite de la politique francaise en Inde, 1750–1783', *Bulletin de l'institut pierre renouvin*, No. 34, 2011, p. 95.
174 'Maharaja of the Marathas,': Deleury, *Le Voyage en Inde*, p. 938.
174 'When you die' asked Sakharam Bapu: Ibid., p. 944.
175 'I believe...that the constitution': Kate Marsh, *India in the French Imagination: Peripheral Voices, 1754–1815*, London: Pickering & Chatto, 2009, p. 134.
175 'Hyder ali made alliances': Deleury, *Le Voyage en Inde*, p. 963.
175 'It would have spelled': Ibid.
175 'From nothing, he formed': Ibid., p. 962.
175 'carnage was such, and the attacks': Morlat and Lafont (ed.), *Piveron De Morlat*.
176 'four hundred beautiful women': Mohibbul Hasan, *History of Tipu Sultan*, India: Aakar Books, 2005.
176 'was fresh in Tippoo's memory': Morlat and Lafont (ed.), *Piveron De Morlat*., p. 232.
177 More pragmatically, enthusiastic French involvement: Ibid., p. 71.
177 'M de Bussy was a sort of': Deleury, *Le Voyage en Inde*, p. 965.
177 'Hyder Ali Khan had gathered 40,000 men': Ibid., p. 966.
177 At the same time, the British national debt: Nechtman, *Nabobs*, p. 98.
178 'extract the riches from those parts': Morlat and Lafont (ed.), *Piveron De Morlat*, p. 75.
178 'braggarts and boasters': Ibid,. p. 67.
178 It was, I tell you, in 1783: Marsh, *India in the French Imagination*, p. 17.
178 'All we had left,' wrote a Frenchman: Ibid., p. 966.
178 It was only commerce that attracted us: Deloche, *Voyage en Inde*, p. 288.
179 'one of the great "might have beens" of history': N. Robins, *The Corporation That Changed the World*, London: Pluto Press, 2012, p. 144.

## GHOST OF THE MUGHAL EMPIRE

180 By 1780, a year in which the autumn harvest: Barnett, *North India Between Empires*. p. 154.
180 'in the Country no further Sources remain': Ibid., p. 161.
180 'my orders were that Middleton should not allow': Ibid., p. 214.
180 'either the Resident must be the Slave': Ibid., p. 216.
181 'He received me,' wrote Ozias: Mildred Archer, *India and British Portraiture, 1770–1825*, Totowa: Sotheby Parke Bernet, 1979, p. 194.
182 'it is a matter of great astonishment': Ibid., p. 220.
182 'of perverting (his instructions) and neglecting': Ibid., p. 222.
182 'his Friend, the brother of his father': Ibid., p. 224.
182 At every stage of the journey: Mir Taqi Mir and C. M Naim (trans.), *Zikr-I Mir: The Autobiography of the Eighteenth Century Mughal Poet Mir Muhammad Taqi 'Mir' 1723–1810*, New Delhi: Oxford University Press, 1999, p. 121.
183 'the men and baggage were always intermixed': Hastings 1784 Lucknow Diary, British Library, Manuscript Collection, ADD MS 29212 f.83.
183 'His manners are in an extraordinary': Hastings, *The Letters of Warren Hastings to His Wife*, p. 301.
xxx 'roasted almonds, pistachios, and firangi titbits': Mir and Naim (trans.), *Zikr-I Mir*, p. 122.
184 There was every kind of bread: Ibid.
184 'a hard frost and (his) own fireside': Hastings, *The Letters of Warren Hastings to His Wife*, p. 323.
185 One such nobleman would take: Sharar, *Lucknow, the Last Phase of an Oriental Culture*, p. 159.

| | |
|---|---|
| 185 | 'the heats and fatigue I had suffered: William Hodges, Travels in India: During the Years 1780, 1781, 1782, and 1783, London: J. Edwards, 1794, p. 143. |
| 185 | 'my indisposition, however rather increasing': Ibid. |
| 186 | 'This officer had amassed': Deloche, *Voyage en Inde*, p. 441. |
| 186 | 'Well done my boy, shahbash!': Sharar, *Lucknow, the Last Phase of an Oriental Culture*, p. 123. |
| 187 | 'he scorned them all, while his father continued': *The Letters of Warren Hastings to His Wife*, p. 286. |
| 187 | 'He resembled Shah Alam': Polier and Gupta (ed.), *Shah Alam II and His Court*, p. 72. |
| 188 | I cannot abandon a person of such eminence: Hastings, *The Letters of Warren Hastings to His Wife*, p. 324. |
| 189 | Despite the terrible anarchy that has overtaken: Deloche, *Voyage en Inde*, p. 225. |
| 189 | Mirza Jawan Bukht....is middle sized: Polier and Gupta (ed.), *Shah Alam II and His Court*, p. 70. |
| 190 | The prince must have muttered: Hastings, *The Letters of Warren Hastings to His Wife*, p. 322. |
| 190 | In his petty desire: Hastings, *The Letters of Warren Hastings to His Wife*, p. 280. |
| 190 | 'deficient as he is in the requisites of business': Middleton Papers, British Library, Manuscript Collection, M.87–172. |
| 191 | 'he contrived to convert the Governor-General': Henry M. Lawrence, *Essays, Military and Political, Written in India*, Lonodn: W.H. Allen, 1859. p. 102. |
| 191 | 'had been treated with contempt': Ibid. |
| 191 | 'violent heats' in June: Hastings 1784 Lucknow Diary, British Library, Manuscript Collection, MSS ADD 39878-79. |
| 191 | 'sent them each 10 elephants, 10 piebald Tanghan ponies': Bakhsh and Hoey, *Memoirs of Delhi and Faizábád* p. 215. |
| 192 | Asaf-ud-Daula is the viceregent of his mother: Ibid., p. 215. |

## ZOFFANY AND A MUGHAL ZENANA

| | |
|---|---|
| 193 | 'neurotic, unstable and enigmatic': Archer, *India and British Portraiture, 1770–1825*, p. 191. |
| 194 | 'a young pretty widow with two small children': George C. Williamson, *Life and Works of Ozias Humphry, R.A.*, London: John Lane, 1918, p. 145. |
| 194 | 'heart and centre of India to hear: Diary of Ozias Humphrey, British Library, Manuscript Collection, EUR 43-1786. |
| 194 | His excellency's collection of Indian pictures: Mary Webster, *Johan Zoffany, 1733–1810*, New Haven: Yale University Press, 2011, p. 491. |
| 195 | 'looked no further than the tea': Diary of Ozias Humphrey, British Library. |
| 196 | Remember I am to be: Rosie Llewellyn-Jones, *A Man of the Enlightenment in Eighteenth-century India: The Letters of Claude Martin, 1766–1800*, New Delhi: Permanent Black in association with The Embassy of France in India, 2003, p. 175. |
| 196 | 'without the permission of the original': Manners and Williamson, *John Zoffany, R.A, His Life and Works*, p. 100. |
| 197 | ... the evening was stupid enough: J. M.,Steadman, 'The Asiatick Society of Bengal', *Eighteenth-Century Studies*, Vol. 10, No. 4, 1977, The John Hopkins University Press, pp. 464-483. |
| 197 | 'the nominal qualification (for membership) is': Timothy Webb, *English Romantic Hellenism, 1700-1824*, United Kingdom: Manchester University Press, 1982. |
| 198 | 'drawings, prints, bronzes, marbles, medals, coins...': |
| 198 | I assure you my dear Mrs Plowden: Rosie Llewellyn-Jones, *A Man of the Enlightenment in Eighteenth-century India: The Letters of Claude Martin, 1766–1800*, New Delhi: Permanent Black in association with The Embassy of France in India, 2003, p. 287. |
| 199 | 'still I think I have some good ones': Ibid., p. 174. |
| 199 | They have been carefully analysed: Griselda Pollock, 'Cockfights and Other Parades: Gesture, Difference, and the Staging of Meaning in Three Paintings by Zoffany, Pollock, and Krasner', *Oxford Art Journal*, Vol. 26, No. 2, 2003, pp. 156-57. |

| | |
|---|---|
| 200 | 'More than six feet tall': Deleury, *Le Voyage en Inde*, p. 985. |
| 200 | 'a beautiful, fair complexioned, compliant woman': de Boigne family archives, Archives Municipal de Chambery, France. |
| 200 | 'Send my love to the Begum: Ibid. |
| 201 | One of the sketches, titled *A Dream*: With thanks to Charles Greig for his thoughts on this album and this painting in particular. |

## THE CHAMELEONS OF LUCKNOW

| | |
|---|---|
| 202 | 'It was not by accident': Steadman, 'The Asiatick Society of Bengal'. |
| 202 | 'whereas most of them had probably': Garland H. Cannon, *Oriental Jones: A Biography of Sir William Jones, 1746–1794*, Asia Publishing House [for] Indian Council for Cultural Relations, 1964, p. 180. |
| 203 | 'It is known that many attempts': Deleury, *Le Voyage en Inde*, p. 725. |
| 204 | 'I have obtained this year': Ibid., p. 279. |
| 204 | 'The grace of attitudes of his principal dames': Diary of Ozias Humphrey, British Library. |
| 204 | 'Our Nabob is building everyday houses': Llewellyn-Jones, *A Man of the Enlightenment in Eighteenth-century India*, p. 287. |
| 205 | Inside the building, the visitor: Ibid., p. 513. |
| 205 | 'every European curiosity and contraption: Manners and Williamson, *Zoffany, His Life and Works*, p. 134. |
| 205 | 'were covered with glasses, pictures': Llewellyn-Jones, *A Man of the Enlightenment in Eighteenth-century India*, p. 513. |
| 206 | 'I also wish very much to have': Ibid., p. 375. |
| 206 | 'was always a hearty one, it could have offered no attractions': Llewellyn-Jones, *A Very Ingenious Man*, p. 147. |
| 206 | A more infamous or despicable character: Ibid., p. 142. |
| 207 | I had them when in their childhood: Ibid. |
| 207 | 'in affirming her virtue, her education: Dubra Ghosh, *Sex and the Family in Colonial India: The Making of Empire*, Cambridge: Cambridge University Press, 2006. |
| 207 | 'a fine stout boy whom I will endeavour': Llewellyn-Jones, *A Man of the Enlightenment in Eighteenth-century India*. |
| 207 | 'I cannot say that there is a great deal of sincerity': Ibid., p. 174. |
| 208 | 'Tho it is fashion to call us India gentlemen: Ibid., p. 174. |
| 208 | 'fundamental kindness and the good opinions': Ibid., p. 32. |
| 208 | 'For what I know of his character': Ibid., p. 172. |
| 208 | 'wedding-cake in brick, a Gothic castle: Rosie Llewellyn-Jones, 'Claude Martin's coat of arms, now the school's', Taj Magazine, June 2001, < https://franpritchett.com/00routesdata/1700_1799/claudemartin/claudemartin.html> |
| 208 | 'when you return I hope that': Llewellyn-Jones, *A Man of the Enlightenment in Eighteenth-century India*, p. 375. |

## BOOK III: THE TIGER AND THE FISH (1785–1794)

## THE GLORY OF LUCKNOW

| | |
|---|---|
| 213 | 'the Nawab used to associate freely': Bakhsh and Hoey, *Memoirs of Delhi and Faizábád*, p. 232. |
| 213 | 'during the whole of Phagun at the Holi': Abu Talib, Hoey (tr.), *History of Asafu'd Daulah*, p. 37. |
| 214 | 'they (the Awadhi party) wish to be relieved': Letters to Warren Hastings, British Library, Manuscript Collections, Add MSS 29170, 1787-89. |
| 215 | 'conduct to me has been so unjust': Letter of William Palmer to Warren Hastings, British |

| | |
|---|---|
| | Library, Manuscript Collections, 12 April 1786 |
| 215 | 'bear deficiencies of no great importance': Chancey, 'Rethinking the reign of Asaf-ud-Daula, Nawab of Awadh, p. 30. |
| 215 | 'pair of pistol, shawl handkerchief: Llewellyn-Jones, A Man of the Enlightenment in Eighteenth-century India, p. 98. |
| 215 | 'which his Lordship may remain': Ibid., p. 102. |
| 215 | 'to be appointed a full colonel': Ibid., p. 100. |
| 216 | This was an object of the most exquisite workmanship: Stephen Markel, et al, *India's Fabled City: The Art of Courtly Lucknow*, Los Angeles County Museum of Art, 2010, p. 220. |
| 217 | 'Indeed my lord, I can't': Manners and Williamson, *John Zoffany, R.A, His Life and Works*, p. 91. |
| 217 | 'No, no, my dear Mordaunt': Webster, *Johan Zoffany*, p. 499. |
| 217 | 'I am of the opinion,': Letter of William Palmer to Warren Hastings, British Library, Manuscript Collections, 12 April 1786. |
| 218 | 'of a moderate stature' rather corpulent: Webster, *Johan Zoffany*, p. 504. |
| 219 | 'If the nawabi kites were were lost': Sharar, *Lucknow, the Last Phase of an Oriental Culture*, p. 131. |
| 219 | 'this attachment of (the Nawab's) to horse': Charles Madan, *Two Private Letters, to a gentleman in England, from his son who accompanied Earl Cornwallis, on his expedition to Lucknow in the year 1787*, [By C. Madan.], United Kingdom: J. Jacob, 1788. |
| 220 | 'rhinoceros from Assam for the Nawabs': Llewellyn-jones quoted in Tereza Kuldova, *Luxury Indian Fashion: A Social Critique*, New Delhi: Bloomsbury Publishing, 2016. |
| 220 | 'exhibit an elegance of form': Markel, et al, *India's Fabled City*, p. 199. |
| 220 | Another very popular floral imagery: Ibid., p. 222. |
| 221 | When the nawab was late to the dastarkhwan: Sharar, *Lucknow, the Last Phase of an Oriental Culture*, p. 158. |
| 221 | And so the humble pulao itself: Ibid., p. 158. |
| 223 | 'They were newly draped in': *Diary of Sophia Elizabeth Plowden*, Asia, Pacific and Africa Collections, British Library, Mss Eur F127/94. p. 58. |
| 223 | 'etiquette and regard and respect': Markel, et al, *India's Fabled City*, p. 195. |
| 223 | 'a year was spent in making silver vessels: Bakhsh and Hoey, *Memoirs of Delhi and Faizábád*, Vol. 2, p. 221. |
| 224 | 'men of position in Lucknow are not so affected': Abu Talib, Hoey (tr.), *History of Asafu'd Daulah*, p. 39. |
| 224 | The Nawab conducted his visitors: Chancey, 'Rethinking the reign of Asaf-ud-Daula', p. 22. |
| 225 | 'Lucknow's lamp was lit': Sharar, quoted in Markel, et al, *India's Fabled City*, p. 244. |
| 225 | '2000 farrashes (carpet spreaders), 100 chobdars (mace-bearers)': Abu Talib, Hoey (tr.), *History of Asafu'd Daulah*, p. 38. |
| 225 | 'The vast sums expended by Asaf-ud-Daula': George Viscount Valentia, *Voyages and Travels to India, Ceylon, the Red Sea, Abyssinia, and Egypt, in the Years 1802, 1803, 1804, 1805, and 1806*, Vol. 1, London: William Miller, 1809. |
| 225 | 'Jis ko na de maula, us ko de': Markel, et al, *India's Fabled City*, p. 104. |
| 226 | 'mild in manners, polite and affable': Chancey, 'Rethinking the reign of Asaf-ud-Daula'. |
| 226 | 'The subjects of his Majesty of Oude: Parlby, *Wanderings of a Pilgrim in Search of the Picturesque*, p. 184. |

## THE BARA IMAMBARA AND A LIGHT DIVINE

| | |
|---|---|
| 227 | 'We belong to God and to God we shall return': Lesley Hazleton, *After the Prophet: The Epic Story of the Shia-Sunni Split in Islam*, United States: Knopf Doubleday Publishing Group, 2009, p. 187. |
| 228 | 'with intense and emotional devotions': Gerda Theuns-de Boer, Rosie Llewellyn-Jones (ed.), 'Monumental Grief', Lucknow: City of Illusion, New York, London, New Delhi: Prestel and |

the Alkazi Collection of Photography.
228 'Every day is Ashura': Hazleton, *After the Prophet*, p. 184.
229 'certainly the most beautiful building: Viscount Valentia, *Voyages and Travels*, p. 157.
230 'From the brilliant white of the composition': Ibid., p. 120.
230 Every year since its completion: Madhu Trivedi, *The Making of the Awadh Culture*, India: Primus Books, 2010, p. 54.
231 'pulled nearer to those who suffered': Holly Shaffer, 'An Architecture of Ephemerality between South and West Asia', *Journal18*, Issue 4 East-Southeast, 2017, <https://www.journal18.org/2054>.
231 The word 'shahadat': Hazleton, *After the Prophet*, p. 181.
232 'Oh Muhammad, Muhammad, may the angels': Ibid., p. 195.
232 The expressions of grief manifested: Ali, Crooke (ed.), *Observations on the Mussulmauns of India*.
233 'He paid for a canal': Shaffer, 'An Architecture of Ephemerality between South and West Asia'.
233 'Amongst the poorer classes of the people': Ali, Crooke (ed.), *Observations on the Mussulmauns of India*.
234 'formed of every variety of material': Shaffer, 'An Architecture of Ephemerality between South and West Asia'.
234 Urban and rural Hindus venerated Husain: Violette Graff, *Lucknow: Memories of a City*, India: Oxford University Press, 1997, p. 119.
235 'adopted Muslim customs, dress': Trivedi, *The Making of the Awadh Culture*.
235 and 'thousands of Hindus also: Sharar, *Lucknow, the Last Phase of an Oriental Culture*, p. 149.
235 'Khuda gham-i-Husain ke siwa: Mahmud, Awadh Symphony, p. 51.
235 'This pompous display is grown: Ali, Crooke (ed.), *Observations on the Mussulmauns of India*.
235 'This lukewarm attitude in the Muslims of India: Deloche, *Voyage en Inde*, p 300.
236 'the Company in its time: Bayly, Rulers, Townsmen and Bazaars, p. 59.
237 'at present in an unfinished state': *Diary of Sophia Elizabeth Plowden*.
238 'The Vizier possesses several palaces: Madan, *Two Private Letters, to a gentleman in England*.
238 'bonds of friendship and understanding: Graff, *Lucknow: Memories of a City*, p. 120.
238 'no one in Lucknow ever noticed': Sharar, *Lucknow, the Last Phase of an Oriental Culture*, pp. 74-75.

## ART IN CHAOS
239 The royal gifts of a horse: James Forbes, *Oriental memoirs*. Vol. 4, United Kingdom: *White, Cochrane & Co.*, 1815.
240 'Send someone to slit our throats: Deloche, *Voyage en Inde*, p. 264.
241 'He was given servants and guards: Muzaffar Alam and Sanjay Subrahmanyam,. 'Envisioning power', The Indian Economic & Social History Review, vol. 43(2), 2006, p. 140.
241 'paintings and books like they were': Natalia Di Pietrantonio, 'Circuits of Exchange: Albums and the Art Market in 18th-Century Avadh', *Journal18*, October 2018, p. 3.
241 'able to protect early Mughal paintings': Ibid.
242 'part of the books (from Shah Alam's library) had been purchased': Emily Hannam, Assistant Curator, South Asia, Royal Collection Trust, from an online talk delivered on 16 September 2021 at the Museum Fur Asiatische Kunst, Berlin.
243 'many persons employed in collecting': Di Pietrantonio, 'Circuits of Exchange', p. 3.
244 'I feel embarrassed that I use': Markel, et al, *India's Fabled City*, p. 195.
244 When Azfari had first escaped: Alam and Subrahmanyam, 'Envisioning power', p. 147.
245 'much against my will, and with grief of heart': Valerie E. R. Anderson, The Eurasian problem in 19th century India, PhD Thesis in School of Oriental and African Studies University, p. 63.
246 'The Muslims are not so strict,': Madan, *Two Private Letters, to a gentleman in England*, p. 8.
246 When Mr Hastings saw the Prince in 1784: Ibid., pp. 26-27.

247 The robes that the prince gifted: Madan, *Two Private Letters, to a gentleman in England*, p.29.

## COURTESANS AND POETS

249 Oh cupbearer! It is the season: (Saqi-a! fasl-I bahar ast Mubarak bashad! Bada pesh arad ke akr-I to Mubarak bashad! Shisha paimana ba-lab qir o surahi ba-kinar: Taba mai busa-kinar-I to Mubarak bashad!); Katherine Butler Schofield, Music and Musicians in Late Mughal India: Histories of the Ephemeral, 1748–1858, United Kingdom: Cambridge University Press, 2023, p. 90.

249 Khanum Jan was the star of an elite troupe: Schofield, Music and Musicians in Late Mughal India, p. 93.

250 'were centres of the high culture: Markel, et al, *India's Fabled City*, p. 248.

250 'Bara bara naak, bara bara aankh: Parlby, *Wanderings of a Pilgrim in Search of the Picturesque*, p. 395.

251 'superior to anything I have seen': Schofield, Music and Musicians in Late Mughal India, p. 85.

251 Asaf was so delighted with Plowden's rare enthusiasm: Ibid., p. 99.

251 The artistic training of the best tawaif: Adrian Mcneil, 'Tawaif, Military musicians and Shi'a Ideology in Pre-Rebellion Lucknow', *Journal of South Asian Studies*, p. 51.

252 Mushafi put Persian on the shelf: (Mushafi farsi ko taq pe rakh/Ab hai ashaar-e Hindavi ka rivaj); Markel, et al, *India's Fabled City*, p. 105–106.

252 The women would sing dhrupad,: Katherine Butler Schofield, 'The Courtesan Tale: Female Musicians and dancers in Mughal Historical Chronicles', *Gender & History*, 2012.

252 'during weddings, these women,': Parlby, Wanderings of a Pilgrim in Search of the Picturesque, Vol. 1, p. 427.

253 'Far better than Lucknow the ruins': (Kharaba Dilli ka dah-chand bahtar Lakhnau se tha/ Wahin ae kash mar jata sarasima na ata yan); Markel, et al, *India's Fabled City*, p. 109.

253 'to get my poetry you need to understand': Saif Mahmood, Beloved Delhi: A Mughal City and Her Greatest Poets, India: Speaking Tiger Books, 2018, p. 133.

254 Why do you mock at me: Islam and Russell, *Three Mughal Poets*, p. 260.

254 This age is not like that: Ibid., p. 22.

254 'Yes, and they smell like it,': Fisher, *A Clash of Cultures*, p. 73.

255 'Mirza, I hear you have compared': Islam and Russell, *Three Mughal Poets*, p. 38-39.

255 When I arrived in the land: Markel, et al, *India's Fabled City*, p. 189.

255 'Each lane is so narrow here': Ibid., p. 190.

255 Lord, you've robbed me: (Yarab shahr apna yun chhuraya tu ne/ Virane main mujh ko la bithaya tu ne/Main aur kahan yih Lakhnau ki khilqat/Ae vae kya kya khudaya tu ne); Markel, et al, *India's Fabled City*, p. 109.

256 May Asaf-ud-Daula be kept safe: Ibid., p. 191.

256 On hearing this poetic complaint: Ibid., p. 194.

256 'which he called "not poetry"': Ibid., p. 109.

256 'the travails of burdensome': Ibid., p. 111.

257 'at least one of his wives': Fisher, *A Clash of Cultures*, p. 73.

258 As the candle, or shama: Ali Khan Mahmudabad, Poetry of Belonging: Muslim Imaginings of India 1850–1950, India: Oxford University Press, 2020, p. 57.

259 'complex and abrupt rhythm and fast tempo': Trivedi, *The Making of the Awadh Culture*, p. 123.

259 'He did not listen carefully': Markel, et al, *India's Fabled City*, p. 196.

259 But it was 'precisely this': McNeil, *Tawaif, Military musicians and Shi'a Ideology*.

260 'sometimes bazar boys have been heard': Markel, et al, *India's Fabled City*, p. 247

260 (Women) in India do not occupy: Jean Antoine Dubois, Moeurs: institutions et cérémonies des peuples de l'Inde, France: Imprimé par autorisation du roi à l'Imprimerie royale, 1825, pp. 475-476.

261 'such behaviour covers me in shame': Ibid., p. 479.
261 But 'by the end of the nineteenth century': Saleem Kidwai, 'The Singing Ladies Find a Voice', *India-Seminar*, <https://www.india-seminar.com/2004/540/540%20saleem%20kidwai.htm>.

## THE ROOSTER AND THE TIGER
263 'the most faithful ally' of the French king: Gentil, *Mémoires sur l'Indoustan*, p. 323.
263 'I can defeat them (the English)': Robins, *The Corporation That Changed the World*, p. 172.
263 'English power would probably have': Meredith Martin, 'Tipu Sultan's Ambassadors at Saint-Cloud: Indomania and Anglophobia in Pre-Revolutionary Paris,' *West 86th: A Journal of Decorative Arts, Design History, and Material Culture*, vol. 21, no. 1, 2014, p. 45.
264 'was seeking to transform Mysore': Ibid., p. 46.
264 'I prohibited the export of linen': Kaveh Yazdani, *India, Modernity and the Great Divergence: Mysore and Gujarat (17th to 19th C.)*, Netherlands: Brill, 2017.
264 The three men chosen for the mission: Martin, 'Tipu Sultan's Ambassadors', p. 46.
264 'agriculture, commerce, manufacture and technology': Yazdani, *India, Modernity and the Great Divergence*.
265 'A banian in France is worth': Gentil, *Mémoires sur l'Indoustan*, p. 328
265 'Madame, France is like an immense and magnificent garden: Ibid., p. 329.
265 'I saw these Indians': Louise-Elisabeth Vigée-Lebrun, Souvenirs of Madame Vigée Le Brun: With a Steel Portrait from an Original Painting by the Author, United Kingdom: R. Worthington, 1879., p. 40.
265 'whose interest is always piqued by novelty': Gentil, *Mémoires sur l'Indoustan*, p. 319.
266 The arrival of the 3 Indians: Marsh, India in the French Imagination, p. 33.
266 'they cannot take a one step outside': Ibid., p. 99.
266 Throngs of curious people: Ibid., p. 36.
267 'such potent figures of villainy': Jasanoff, *Edge of Empire*.
268 'preferred to strengthen the Mysorean bond': Marsh, India in the French Imagination, p. 33.

## CLAUDE MARTIN IN MYSORE
269 'it would be madness to imagine': Deloche, *Voyage en Inde*.
270 'in the unusual position of being': Marla Karen Chancey, *In the Company's Secret Service: Neil Benjamin Edmonstone and the First Indian Imperialists, 1780–1820*, Unpublished Dissertation, Florida State University, 2003, p. 41.
270 'regarded by many as responsible': Lafont and Lafont, *The French and Delhi*, p. 101.
270 'did not hesitate to act independently': Valerie Anderson, Race and Power in British India: Anglo-Indians, Class and Identity in the Nineteenth Century, United Kingdom: I.B.Tauris, 2015.
271 A Prince of very uncommon ability: Kate Brittlebank, *Tiger*: The Life of Tipu Sultan, United Kingdom: Claritas Books, 2020, p. 66.
271 'unlike the British, Tipu regarded the treaties': Ibid.
271 'I cannot now tell you everything': B. Sheik Ali, 'Mauritius Records On The French And The Third Mysore War,' Proceedings of the Indian History Congress, Vol. 18, 1955, pp. 265–67.
271 Do not engage in big battles: Ibid.
272 (Tipu) is quite intelligent: Ibid.
272 'loans and donations in kind': Llewellyn-Jones, *A Very Ingenious Man*, p. 177.
272 'though at an advanced age': Ibid., p. 179.
272 'To ensure the success of an expedition': Deleury, *Le Voyage en Inde*, p. 956.
273 '...the sun then shone bright': Jasanoff, *Edge of Empire*, p. 167.
274 'if you taste these (seeds)': Jean-Marie Lafont, Georges Barale, and Marguerite Yon-Calvet (eds.), 'Le "Major général" Claude Martin, 1735-1800: aux origines de La Martinière ...', *Académie des sciences, belles-lettres et arts de Lyon*, 2019.

| | |
|---|---|
| 274 | He had also observed that Hyder: Llewellyn-Jones, *A Very Ingenious Man*, p. 178. |
| 275 | Most of the drawings were identified: William Dalrymple, Rosie Llewellyn-Jones, et al., *Forgotten Masters: Indian Painting for the East India Company*, United Kingdom: Bloomsbury USA, 2019, p. 32. |
| 275 | My dear Martin: Claude Martin and Victor Martin-Schmets, Lectures d'André Gide: hommage à Claude Martin, France: Presses universitaires de Lyon, 1994. |
| 275 | We know from Abu Talib's extravagant grumblings: Abu Talib, Hoey (tr.), *History of Asafu'd Daulah*, p. 38. |
| 276 | The Third Anglo-Maratha War had been concluded: Llewellyn-Jones, *A Very Ingenious Man*, p. 180. |

## DE BOIGNE AND THE ARMIES OF HINDUSTAN

| | |
|---|---|
| 277 | 'Do you remember': Deleury, *Le Voyage en Inde*, p. 979. |
| 278 | As for his matchlock men: 'Bengal Past and Present', *Journal of the Calcutta Historical Society*, Vol. 33, Part 2, 1927, p. 103. |
| 278 | 'The Indian states,' confessed a Frenchman: Deleury, *Le Voyage en Inde*, p. 978. |
| 278 | 'visit his arsenal, inspect his troops, enrol new recruits: Ibid., p. 985. |
| 278 | On the grand stage where he has acted: James Baillie Fraser, *Military Memoir of Lieut-Col. James Skinner, C. B*, United Kingdom: Smith, Elder and Co., 1851, p. 74. |
| 279 | '(Scindia) will obtain success: de Boigne family archives, 'Letter of Palmer to de Boigne', Archives Municipal de Chambery, France, 2 July 1792. |
| 279 | 'The balance of power will be held': Ibid., 9 November 1789. |
| 280 | Scindhia sets Shah Nizam ud din over the Badshah: Herbert Compton (ed.), *A Particular Account of the European Military Adventures of Hindustan, from 1784 to 1803*, United Kingdom, T. F. Unwin, 1892, p. 83. |
| 280 | Since you, my dear son, have taken up: de Boigne family archives, ', AB II C (annexe) Number 19', Archives Municipal de Chambery, France |
| 280 | The queen mother sent another letter: Ibid., 'Letter no. 80'. |
| 280 | 'His Majesty (Shah Alam) further gives you': Ibid. |
| 281 | 'My heart burns,' wrote de Boigne: Ibid., 'Letter no. 19'. |
| 281 | 'pillaus, curries, fish, poultry and kid': Thomas Twining, *Travels in India a Hundred Years Ago: With a Visit to the United States*, United Kingdom, J.R. Osgood, McIlvaine & Company, 1893, p. 275 |
| 282 | The money which you entrusted me: de Boigne family archives, Archives Municipal de Chambery, France. |
| 283 | 'her foster-child Moti Begum': Sarkar, *Fall Of The Mughal Empire*, Vol. 4, pp. 45-46. |
| 283 | presented them as 'rescue fantasies': Andrea Major, *Slavery, Abolitionism and Empire in India, 1772–1843*, United Kingdom: Liverpool University Press, 2012, p. 114. |
| 283 | 'She has no will of her own': de Boigne family archives, Archives Municipal de Chambery, France. |
| 284 | Be assured my friend that my affection: Ibid. |
| 285 | 'Maman is surprised to have received': Ibid. |
| 285 | 'Before I did see you,': Ghosh, *Sex and the Family in Colonial India*, p. 166. |

## THE AGE OF SPLENDOUR

| | |
|---|---|
| 288 | 'these clothes are not the sort': Bakhsh and Hoey, *Memoirs of Delhi and Faizábád*, p. 56 |
| 288 | 'companions, servants and cavalry': Ibid., p. 51. |
| 288 | 'the conspicuous consumption of followers': Bayly, *Rulers, Townsmen and Bazaars*, p. 60. |
| 289 | Since Jawahar had by far the greatest number: Bakhsh and Hoey, *Memoirs of Delhi and Faizábád*, p. 44-46 |
| 289 | 'in Faizabad during the days of the Bahu Begum': Ibid., p. 222. |

289  Another arresting trick he performed: Ibid., p. 236.
290  Another courtier was famous for not paying: Ibid., p. 237.
291  (they) are sometimes so overpowered: Abu Talib, Hoey (tr.), *History of Asafu'd Daulah*, p. 36.
292  As for the colours, a range of scandalously bright hues: Swarup, *Costumes and Textiles of Awadh*.
292  'Although the shops of traders': Bakhsh and Hoey, *Memoirs of Delhi and Faizábád*, p. 63
293  'mostly of the lower class': Hodges, *Travels in India*, p. 103.
293  'The glare,' wrote a Company officer': Chancey, *In the Company's Secret Service*, p. 69.
294  The garden...was illuminated by innumerable transparent: Lawrence Dundas Campbell, *The Asiatic Annual Register: Or, a View of the History of Hindustan, and of the Politics, Commerce and Literature of Asia*, United Kingdom: Debrett., Vol. 6, 1806, pp. 9–10.
294  'that such a spectacle was never before seen': Ibid, p. 10.
295  All the ancient forms of the court: Hastings, *The Letters of Warren Hastings to His Wife*, p. 433.
296  'Besides coffee, fish, curries etc,': Twining, *Travels in India*, p. 167
296  In the end, though he did not get the whole of Rohilkhand: Chancey, *In the Company's Secret Service*, p. 66.

## BOOK IV: THE LION OF BRITAIN (1794–1803)

## MEN OF EMPIRE

300  'the kingless, godless, egalitarian republicanism': Jasanoff, *Edge of Empire*, p. 118.
300  The French revolutionary government was able: Primary source, volume V issue I, 'Friends, Fellows, Citizens, and Soldiers' by William Scupham p. 24.
301  'for the French revolutionaries, conquest formed': Jasanoff, *Edge of Empire*, p. 120.
301  'I impeach him in the name of the people': N. Robins, *The Corporation That Changed the World*, p. 141.
301  'By venting concerns about Hastings's particular misconduct': Priya Satia, *Time's Monster: History, Conscience and Britain's Empire*, London: Penguin Books Limited, 2020.
302  'thin face and delicate features': Chancey, *In the Company's Secret Service*, p. 58.
302  He had suffered a further emotional breakdown: Sarah Pearson, 'Making Britain in Empire: John Shore, Nation and Race in the Eighteenth-Century East India Company World', *Early Modern Studies*, University of Bristol, 21 January 2021, p. 36.
302  'contained a riotous blend': Ibid., p. 157.
303  'humankind was congenitally infected': Ian Copland, 'Christianity as the Arm of the Empire: The Ambiguous Case of India under the Company, C. 1813–1858', *The Historical Journal*, Vol. 49, No. 4, 2005, pp. 1025–1054.
303  'promoting the happiness of Thy creatures': Henry Morris, *The Governors-General of India*, Vol. 1, Adelphi: The Christian Literature Society, 1894, p. 87.
303  'spreading the Word of God': Copland, 'Christianity as the Arm of the Empire', p. 1026.
303  'the religion of the state': Pearson, 'Making Britain in Empire'.
303  He also began assessing Bengali customs: Ibid., p. 195.
304  'harmless, kind, peaceable and suffering': Major, *Slavery, Abolitionism and Empire in India*, p. 252
304  'European moral complexion': Ibid., p. 252.
305  'the most correct Lady I have seen': Llewellyn-Jones, *A Man of the Enlightenment in Eighteenth-century India*.
305  'to persuade Asaf to reduce the size of his menageries': Chancey, *In the Company's Secret Service*, p. 77.
306  'command the politics of the 3 remaining great post-Mughal courts': C. A. Bayly, *Empire and*

|     | *Information: Intelligence Gathering and Social Communication in India, 1780–1870*, Cambridge: Cambridge University Press, 1996, p. 89. |
| --- | --- |
| 307 | 'the Marhattas are notorious for their craft and cunning: Chancey, *In the Company's Secret Service*, p. 79. |
| 307 | 'I see no embarrassment from any quarter': Holden Furber, *The Private Record of an Indian Governor-Generalship: The Correspondence of Sir John Shore, Governor-General, with Henry Dundas, President of the Board of Control, 1793–1798*, United States: Harvard University Press, 2013. |
| 307 | The Disorders in Oude are so serious: Ibid. |
| 308 | 'so that if an augmentation of the Company's cavalry': Desmond Young, *Fountain of the Elephants*, New York: Harper & Brothers, 1959, p. 177. |
| 308 | There would be no requirement for any ministers: Chancey, *In the Company's Secret Service*, p. 87. |
| 309 | 'Muslim customs, dress, and religious duties': Fisher, *A Clash of Cultures*, p. 69. |
| 309 | Jhau Lal, however, remained steadfastly: Muhammad, Hoey (tr.), *History of Asafu'd Daulah*, p. p. 47. |
| 309 | 'in every respect as one with the English sirdars': Chancey, *In the Company's Secret Service*, p. 80. |
| 309 | 'unattended to Calcutta': Ibid., p. 83. |
| 310 | 'both by example and precept': Ibid., p. 59. |
| 310 | 'calculated to disgrace and lower me': Ibid., p. 83. |
| 310 | 'By his indiscretion (Cherry) contrived: Correspondence of John Shore, (1751–1834), British Library, Manuscript Collection, ADD MSS 13501, Vol. 1. |
| 310 | 'has all the qualities of extreme politeness: Chancey, *In the Company's Secret Service, p. 84.* |

## THE GOLDEN AGE OF AWADH

| 311 | 'who had lived modestly': Bakhsh and Hoey, Memoirs of Delhi and Faizábád, p. 252. |
| --- | --- |
| 311 | 'The change came in the twinkling': Ibid., p. 251. |
| 312 | 'was the greatest and best man: William Henry Sleeman, *A Journey Through the Kingdom of Oude in 1849–1850: With Private Correspondence Relative to the Annexation of Oude to British India, [etc.]*, London: R. Bentley, 1858., pp. 320-322. |
| 313 | The person I observed with the most curiosity: Viscount Valentia, Voyages and Travels to India, p. 135. |
| 313 | So many English that have carried away: *Calcutta Review*, India: University of Calcutta, Vol. 5-6, 1846, p. 438. |

## LITTLE ENGLAND IN AWADH

| 315 | 'All the inhabitants I met': Twining, *Travels in India*, p. 242. |
| --- | --- |
| 315 | 'the style in which this remote colony lived': Ibid., p. 310. |
| 316 | 'I really lament and very much': Llewellyn-Jones, *A Man of the Enlightenment in Eighteenth-century India*, p. 393. |
| 316 | 'I am forced to content myself': Ibid., p. 392. |
| 316 | In the Nawab's Mughal-style gardens: *Diary of Sophia Elizabeth Plowden.* |
| 317 | He is very fond of the English: Lewis Ferdinand Smith in a letter to a friend in 1797, from Mildred Archer, *India and British Portraiture*, p. 191. |
| 317 | 'in polished and agreeable manners, in public magnificence,': Twining, *Travels in India*, p. 311. |
| 318 | Asaf-ud-Daula is absurdly extravagant: Ferdinand Smith in letter to a friend 1797. |
| 318 | 'extravagant and ridiculously curious': Twining, *Travels in India*, p. 311. |
| 318 | 'was part and parcel of the culture of Indian kingship': Jasanoff, *Edge of Empire*, p. 77. |
| 319 | 'confined western luxuries to limited spaces': Natasha Eaton, 'The Art of Colonial Despotism: |

Portraits, Politics, and Empire in South India, 1750–1795', *Cultural Critique*, No. 70, 2008, pp. 63–93.
320 'The whole of the figures': Parlby, *Wanderings of a Pilgrim in Search of the Picturesque*, p. 181.
320 A more wretched transformation: William Knighton, *The Private Life of an Eastern King*, London: Hope and Company, 1855, p. 89.
320 'the Europeanization of Lucknow remained superficial': Rosie Llewellyn-Jones, *Fatal Friendship: The Nawabs Teh British and Yhe City of Lucknow*, New Delhi: Oxford University Press, 1999
321 'we deem it your indispensable duty to interfere': Chancey, *In the Company's Secret Service*, p. 84.

## MAKING AN ETHIOPIAN WHITE

322 These poor descendants of Imperial dignity: Baron Teignmouth and Charles John Shore, *Memoir of the Life and Correspondence of John, Lord Teignmouth*, United Kingdom: Hatchard, 1843., pp. 404-405.
323 'good, clear, full, well-toned': John Robert Scott, *A Review of the Principal Characters of the Irish House of Commons: By Falkland*, Ireland: author, 1789, p. 54.
324 'pleasing, sensible and well-looking': Elizabeth Vassall Fox Holland and Giles Stephen Holland Fox-Strangways Ilchester, The Journal of Elizabeth Lady Holland: (1791–1811), Vol. 1, London: Longmans, Green, 1908.
324 'a very cautious and over-prudent politician': Chancey, *In the Company's Secret Service*, p. 58.
325 'I hesitate when I should have decided: Teignmouth and Shore, *Memoir of the Life and Correspondence of John, Lord Teignmouth* p. 364.
325 'read the New Testament through many times': Ibid., p. 364.
326 The young Persian runner began walking: Bayly, *Empire and Information*, p. 64.
326 Throwing a harkara out of the city: Ibid., p. 65.
327 'obtained dominion over them': Chancey, *In the Company's Secret Service*, p. 108.
327 'the preparations of Tippoo': Teignmouth and Shore, *Memoir of the Life and Correspondence of John, Lord Teignmouth*, p. 398.
327 After two failed attempts, it was in late 1796: Kaveh Yazdani, Foreign relations and semi-modernization during the reigns of Haidar 'Ali and Tipu Sultan,' *British Journal of Middle Eastern Studies*, Vol. 45, No. 3, 2018, p. 11.
327 'It is become proper and incumbent': Birendra Varma, 'Tipu Sultan's Embassy to the Court of Zaman Shah,' *Proceedings of the Indian History Congress*, Vol. 33, 1971, pp. 478-482.
329 'I see no difficulty in combining': Chancey, *In the Company's Secret Service*, p. 59.
329 'the happiness of some millions of subjects': Chancey, *In the Company's Secret Service*, p. 60
329 'I hope (the nawab's) fears of Zeman Shah': Furber, *The Private Record of an Indian Governor-Generalship*, p. 123.
329 'I have heard too': Ibid., p. 195.
329 'The two points which I should most wish: Ibid., p. 117.
330 He also maintained a warmly genial correspondence: Pearson, 'Making Britain in Empire', p. 209.
330 'if you hunt with him': Chancey, *In the Company's Secret Service*, p. 90.
330 The nawab would have known at once: Correspondence of John Shore (1751–1834), 1st Baron Teignmouth, Governor General of India, 1793-98, British Library, Manuscript Collection, ADD MSS 13523.
331 Initially at least, all was well: Teignmouth and Shore, *Memoir of the Life and Correspondence of John, Lord Teignmouth*, p. 407.
331 'a fever every night and a headache': Chancey, *In the Company's Secret Service*, p. 86.
331 'more and more reason to fear': Furber, *The Private Record of an Indian Governor-Generalship*, p. 122.

331 'I should suppose (the Nawab) must be alarmed: Chancey, *In the Company's Secret Service*, p. 82.
331 'fools, knaves and sycophants': Teignmouth and Shore, *Memoir of the Life and Correspondence of John, Lord Teignmouth*, p. 413.
332 'I was engaged in the very disagreeable attempt': Ibid., p. 417.
332 'the age of the Vizier is about 51': Furber, *The Private Record of an Indian Governor-Generalship*, p. 125.

## DEATH OF A NAWAB

333 'the Nabob and myself visit daily': Teignmouth and Shore, *Memoir of the Life and Correspondence of John, Lord Teignmouth*, p. 407.
333 'to show off to the English': Abu Talib, Hoey (tr.), *History of Asafu'd Daulah*, p. 126.
334 'a more developed sense of traditional patriotism': Bayly, *Empire and Information*, p. 88.
334 'the best-informed man in Hindoostan: C. A. Bayly, 'Knowing the Country: Empire and Information in India', *Modern Asian Studies*, Vol. 27, No. 1, 1993, p. 22.
334 It cannot be simple curiosity: Deloche, *Voyage en Inde*, p. 549.
335 They wanted to maintain a choke-hold: Graff, *Lucknow: Memories of a City*, p. 36.
335 'I know nothing of Safdar Jang': Abu Talib, Hoey (tr.), *History of Asafu'd Daulah*, p. 126
335 'Hasan Reza Khan, Haidar Beg, and Tikait Rai': Ibid., 125-126.
335 '5 lakhs of rupees and 8 thousand gold mohurs': Teignmouth and Shore, *Memoir of the Life and Correspondence of John, Lord Teignmouth*, p. 410.
336 'I had the most satisfactory conviction': Records of John Shore, ADD MSS 13523.
337 'an attempt for depriving him': Furber, *The Private Record of an Indian Governor-Generalship*, p. 124
337 I will not pretend to assert: Ibid.
338 'an undertone of menace with insinuations': Pearson, 'Making Britain in Empire', p. 212.
338 '"I have done as much as possible': Teignmouth and Shore, *Memoir of the Life and Correspondence of John, Lord Teignmouth*, p. 412.
338 'against the Vizier's consent on the grounds of necessity': Furber, *The Private Record of an Indian Governor-Generalship*, p. 125.
338 'He has been very angry': Teignmouth and Shore, *Memoir of the Life and Correspondence of John, Lord Teignmouth*, p. 417.
339 'invariable attention on his part': Correspondence of John Shore, ADD MSS 13523.
339 '(The nawab) intends to press the argument': Chancey, *In the Company's Secret Service*, p.
339 (Jhau Lal)'s Power is great: Furber, *The Private Record of an Indian Governor-Generalship*, p. 123.
340 (The nawab has) a great accumulation of treasure: Llewellyn-Jones, *A Man of the Enlightenment in Eighteenth-century India*, p. 250.
340 'I think it ought to be our invariable aim': The President's minute dated 27 July 1768, British Library, Manuscript Collection, MSS Eur G37/6/7 and MSS G37/6/8.
340 'the funds for improving the Company's army': Chancey, *In the Company's Secret Service*, p. 61.
341 'at a period of life when': Teignmouth and Shore, *Memoir of the Life and Correspondence of John, Lord Teignmouth*, p. 415-416.
341 He was once fond of drinking European liquors: Ferdinand Smith in a letter to a friend, 1797.
341 'all the people of this country': Bakhsh and Hoey, *Memoirs of Delhi and Faizábád*, p. 255-256.
341 'certain that he was going to die': Ibid., p. 258.
341 'He is seldom seen by our Resident': Furber, *The Private Record of an Indian Governor-Generalship*, p. 129.
342 'appeared more embarrassing than it appeared: Ibid., p. 129.

## THE SECRETS OF THE ZENANA

343 'My mind has been worked up': Teignmouth and Shore, *Memoir of the Life and Correspondence of John, Lord Teignmouth*, p. 454.
344 'made unqualified professions of obedience': Furber, *The Private Record of an Indian Governor-Generalship*, p. 160–161.
344 'her only wish was that the succession': Aniruddha Ray, *The Rebel Nawab of Oudh: Revolt of Vizir Ali Khan*, 1799, India: K.P. Bagchi & Company, 1990, p. 52.
344 'may the almighty preserve you': Chancey, *In the Company's Secret Service*, p. 88.
344 'Wazir Ali's disposition is mild': Ray, *The Rebel Nawab of Oudh*, p. 52.
344 'elephants, tents, animals such as blue antelope': Bakhsh and Hoey, Memoirs of Delhi and Faizábád, p. 260.
345 'if the Begum perseveres in her opposition': Furber, *The Private Record of an Indian Governor-Generalship*, p. 131.
346 'he even speaks plainer to the Nabob': Teignmouth and Shore, *Memoir of the Life and Correspondence of John, Lord Teignmouth*, p. 412.
346 'learnt court manners and was well versed': Ray, *The Rebel Nawab of Oudh*, p. 57.
347 'since (Asaf) took in his head': Llewellyn-Jones, *A Man of the Enlightenment in Eighteenth-century India*, p. 250.
347 'of a dark complexion, and not handsome': Chancey, *In the Company's Secret Service*, p. 91.
347 'no one with honour' could investigate: Bayly, *Empire and Information*, p. 70.
347 'If strict control of what people can know': Bayly, 'Knowing the Country', p. 30.
348 'in eastern countries, as there is no principle': Teignmouth and Shore, *Memoir of the Life and Correspondence of John, Lord Teignmouth*, p. 440.
348 'to adopt coercive measures and a more direct interference': Chancey, *In the Company's Secret Service*, p. 93.
348 'It was rather an extraordinary situation': Ibid.
348 'panderers and low scoundrels': Bayly, *Empire and Information*, p. 95.
348 'Wazir Ali bears no resemblance': Chancey, *In the Company's Secret Service*, p. 94.
348 'Begum must be opposed and the Nawab': Ray, *The Rebel Nawab of Oudh*, p. 66.
349 'I shall while I live manifest: Chancey, *In the Company's Secret Service*, p. 88.
349 'secretive, parsimonious, and Anglicized': Ibid., p. 106.
350 'had to agree to a stronger subsidiary': Ibid., p. 99.
350 'a treaty of vassalage': Ibid.
350 'What has become of her Oaths': Furber, *The Private Record of an Indian Governor-Generalship*, p. 175.
350 The Lucknow army possessed 300 pieces: Ibid., p. 182.
351 'he was almost deserted': Ibid., p. 180.
351 'Vizier Ali is fallen' wrote Shore: Teignmouth and Shore, *Memoir of the Life and Correspondence of John, Lord Teignmouth*, p. 454.
352 'laid his head at her feet': Bakhsh and Hoey, Memoirs of Delhi and Faizábád, p. 261.
352 'a quantity of baggage and a great many people': Ray, *The Rebel Nawab of Oudh*, p. 71.
352 '(Wazir Ali) does not appear to be much affected': Chancey, *In the Company's Secret Service* p. 103.
353 'this son of mine is a very base sort': Abbott, 'It all comes from me'.
353 'God has given me money, jewels, clothes': Bakhsh and Hoey, Memoirs of Delhi and Faizábád, p. 264.
354 'to the effect that it was his accession': Ibid., p. 264-265.
354 The Begum had no choice but to accept the offer: Charles Umpherston Aitchison (ed.), *A Collection of Treaties, Engagements and Sanads Relating to India and Neighbouring Countries*, Calcutta: Government of India Central Publication Branch, 1929, p. 146–152. (See for details of the valuables and their hiding places).

## TUMULT IN BENARES

356 'most immoderately fat': Viscount Valentia, Voyages and Travels, p. 116.
357 'everything (around him) marked poverty': Ibid., p. 102.
357 'they praised Agra and Delhi and the magnificence: Ibid.
358 'I shall on all occasion be happy to': Ray, *The Rebel Nawab of Oudh*, p. 71.
358 The Company men on the ground at Benares: Ibid., p. 86.
358 He complained to Calcutta about Wazir: Chancey, *In the Company's Secret Service*, p. 115.
359 'one measure of precaution', wrote Davies: Ray, *The Rebel Nawab of Oudh*, p. 99.
359 (the Indians) entertain the utmost hatred: Chancey, *In the Company's Secret Service, p.* 119.
360 It would appear that Wazir Ali had been planning: Ray, *The Rebel Nawab of Oudh.*
360 'much agitated and expressed himself with intemperance': Chancey, *In the Company's Secret Service, p.* 114
360 'destroyed the English gentlemen': Ibid., p. 116.
361 'a sword, a bow, a red velvet gold embroidered quiver: Ray, *The Rebel Nawab of Oudh*, p. 276.
361 'so closely connected as I was with all the transactions': Chancey, *In the Company's Secret Service, p.* 117.
362 'natives' were to be controlled at all cost': Ibid., p. 119.

## A TRAP FOR A TIGER

363 Each toast was accompanied by sufficiently strident martial music: Pearson, 'Making Britain in Empire', p. 45.
364 'Intolerant Protestantism,' writes scholar Linda Colley: Colley, Britons: Forging the Nation, p. 25
364 'were exposed to a uniform set of ideas': Ibid., p. 167.
364 'upstart and synthetic contrivances of the French': Ibid., p. 216.
365 Peaceful Indians, living since antiquity: Deleury, *Le Voyage en Inde.*
365 Let us use all of France's efforts with the greatest confidence: Ibid., p. 955.
365 'through the most glorious of revolutions the French nation': Blake Smith, 'Revolutions en Inde: dimensions coloniales, diplomatiques et culturelles, 1789–1799', *Outre-Mers, Revue d'histoire*, T.103, No. 388-389, 2015, p. 74.
366 Shackled by poor communications between the different parties: Irfan Habib (ed.), *State and Diplomacy Under Tipu Sultan: Documents and Essays*, India: Tulika, 2001, p. 133.
366 'Since I had long desired news from your country': Jean Boutier, 'Les "lettres de créances" du corsaire Ripaud. Un "club Jacobin" à Srirangapatnam (Inde), mai-juin 1797', *Les Indes Savantes*, 2005, p. 5.
366 'this Ripaud that is come, God knows': Ibid., p. 6.
367 And yet despite the reservations he might have had: Ibid., pp. 10–16.
367 'this motley reinforcement of naval, and military: Jasanoff, *Edge of Empire*, p. 162.

## THE FALL OF SERINGAPATAM

368 'a sublime dandy' and a 'man of staggering vanity': M. H. Port, David R. Fisher: *Wellesley, Richard Colley, 2nd Earl of Mornington [I] (1760–1842), of Dangan Castle, co. Meath.* In: R. G. Thorne (Hrsg.): *The History of Parliament. The House of Commons 1790–1820.* Secker & Warburg, London 1986.
368 'low birth, vulgar manners and eastern habits': Chancey, *In the Company's Secret Service*, p. 107.
369 'from the heights of the Pyramids': Philippe Colin, *Face a l'Histoire: Napoleon, l'homme qui ne meurt jamais*, Podcast, 2021.
370 'Most politicians, military experts and popular pundits': Colley, *Britons: Forging the Nation*, p. 25.

| | |
|---|---|
| 370 | 'what a happiness it is for the civilized world': Chancey, *In the Company's Secret Service*, p. 110. |
| 370 | It is very difficult to form a conjecture: Rudrangshu Mukherjee, 'Trade and Empire in Awadh 1765–1804', *Past & Present*, No. 94, 1982, pp. 85–102.; Italics mine. |
| 371 | 'in consequence of the menaces and arrogant language of our enemy': W. S. Seton-Karr, *Selections from Calcutta Gazettes: Showing the Political and Social Condition of the English in India Eighty Years Ago*, Vol. 3, Calcutta: Government of India, 1868, p. 23. |
| 371 | 'thoughts of the (material) rewards of victory': Chancey, *In the Company's Secret Service*, 111. |
| 371 | You will have learnt about my arrival: Joseph-François Michaud, *Histoire des progrès et de la chûte de l'empire de Mysore, sous les règnes d'Hyder-Aly et de Tippoo-Saïb: contenant l'historique des guerres des souverains de Mysore avec les Anglais et les différentes puissances de l'Inde...; ornée de cartes, portrait, plans, etc*, France: Giguet et cie, 1809, p. 377. |
| 372 | 'our friend Tippu Sultan': Ibid., p. 378. |
| 372 | 'The great body of Mussulmen from whom we have wrested the Govt.': Chancey, In the Company's Secret Service, p. 120 |
| 373 | 'the greatest army ever assembled in India': Michaud, *Histoire des progrès et de la chûte de l'empire de Mysore*, p. 207. |
| 373 | 'I entirely approve of your determination': Chancey, *In the Company's Secret Service*, p. 122. |
| 373 | The cavalry was placed at the front: 'Storming of Seringapatam', British Battles, <https://www.britishbattles.com/anglo-french-wars-in-india/storming-of-seringapatam/> |
| 374 | 'gave us gun for gun...(and night-time skirmishes were)': William Dalrymple, *White Mughals*, New Delhi: Penguin Books Limited, 2004. |
| 374 | 'three elephants, two buffaloes, a bullock': Dalrymple, *The Anarchy*, p. 442. |
| 374 | 'I am entirely resigned to the will of God': Jasanoff, *Edge of Empire*, p. 169. |
| 374 | As they stormed Seringapatam, the first soldiers the Company men: Ibid., p. 170. |
| 375 | 'had something of the military veteran in his appearance': Ibid. |
| 375 | During the siege of the city, on 22 April: Dalrymple, *The Anarchy*, p. 349. |
| 375 | 'encouraged them by his voice and example': Chancey, *In the Company's Secret Service*, p. 122. |
| 376 | A grand total of 120 motley French men: Ibid. |
| 376 | Scarcely a house in the town was left unplundered: Dalrymple, *White Mughals*, |
| 376 | The plunder of Seringapatam is immense: Katie Hickman, *She-Merchants, Buccaneers and Gentlewomen: British Women in India*, United Kingdom: Little, Brown Book Group, 2019. |
| 377 | Shortly after Tipu's defeat, British soldiers occupied: Hemant Sane, Vellore Mutiny: The First Major Uprising of the Indian Soldiers of the East India Company's Army, Paper, *Academia.edu*. |
| 377 | 'documents of great importance, explanatory of the nature': Boutier, 'Les "lettres de créances" du corsaire Ripaud'. |
| 378 | 'Copy in the French Language together with a Translation': Michaud, *Histoire des progrès et de la chûte de l'empire de Mysore*, p. 2. |
| 378 | 'The wicked principles of the mother-country had: Ibid., p. 4. |
| 378 | 'the counter-revolutionary press across Europe': Blake Smith, 'The Citizen-Sultan? A Jacobin Club in India', Age of Revolutions, 9 May 2016. |
| 379 | If you will have a little patience: D. Forrest, *Tiger of Mysore: The life and death of Tipu Sultan*, London: Chatto & Windus, 1970, p. 310. |
| 379 | 'bouts of "unusual gaiety" interspersed': Chancey, *In the Company's Secret Service*, p. 141. |
| 379 | 'an ornate green and gold vessel that had': Ibid., p. 146. |
| 380 | 'His hair is now grey, and he had lost many of his teeth': Viscount Valentia, *Voyages and Travels*, p. 172. |
| 381 | 'musnud of crimson and gold, formerly composing part of the ornaments': Ibid., p. 61. |
| 381 | Below him in a semi-circle were the members of his council: Chancey, *In the Company's Secret Service*, p. 147. |

## THE BATTLE OF DELHI

383 'All the affairs of this world': Deloche, *Voyage en Inde*, p. 986.
384 '40 million people, with the combined armies': Chancey, *In the Company's Secret Service*, p. 169.
385 'known for appearing in full uniform': Ibid., p. 167.
385 'the same grade in the English': Lafont and Lafont, *The French and Delhi*, p.102.
385 'a massive desertion of the Anglo-Indian officers': Ibid., p. 103.
386 'the most severe I have ever fought in India': John Pemble, 'Resources and Techniques in the Second Maratha War', *The Historical Journal*, Vol. 19, No. 2, 1976, p. 379.
386 'I never was in so severe': Ibid.
386 'The decisive victory,' writes Lafont': Lafont and Lafont, *The French and Delhi*, pp. 106-107.
387 'the risks of a French invasion of India': Ibid., p. 110.

## EPILOGUE

388 '(He) has an affection of the kidneys': Manmath Nath Das, 'The Marquis of Dalhousie, A Sketch of His Character and Personality,' *Proceedings of the Indian History Congress*, Vol. 20, 1957, pp. 266-74.
388 'I do not like the appearance': Ibid.
389 'an ensemble performance that wove dance, music, theatre, mime, scenography and architecture': Amit Varma, *The Seen and the Unseen*, 'Ranjit Hoskote is Dancing in Chains', Podcast, 8 Jan 2024.
389 'The king of Oude seems disposed to be bumptious': Das, 'The Marquis of Dalhousie'.
390 A full 139,000 of the 169,000 sipahis: William Dalrymple and Anita Anand, *Empire Podcast*, 'Mutiny, Uprising and Rebellion, 23 August 2022.

# BIBLIOGRAPHY

PRIMARY SOURCES
'The Panjab Past and Present', Vol. 6, India: Department of Punjab Historical Studies, Punjabi University, 2006.
Alam M., and Alavi, S., *A European Experience of the Mughal Orient: The I'jāz-i Arsalānī (Persian Letters 1773–1779) of Antoine-Louis Henri Polier*, Oxford University Press, 2001.
Bakhsh, Muhammad Faiz, and Hoey, William, *Memoirs of Delhi and Faizábád: Being a Translation of the Tárīkh Farahbakhsh of Muhammad Faiz Bakhsh from the Original Persian*, Allahabad: Government Press, North-western Provinces and Oudh, Vol. 2, 1889.
Compton, Herbert (ed.), *A Particular Account of the European Military Adventures of Hindustan, from 1784 to 1803*, United Kingdom: T. F. Unwin, 1892.
de Boigne family archives, Archives Municipal de Chambery.
Deleury, Guy, *Le Voyage en Inde: Anthologie des voyageurs français 1750–1820*, Bouquins, 2003
Deloche, Jean (ed.), *Voyage en Inde du comte de Modave, 1773–1776: (nouveaux mémoires sur l'état actuel du Bengale et de l'Indoustan*, France: École française d'extrême-orient, 1971.
Dubois, Jean Antoine, *Moeurs: institutions et cérémonies des peuples de l'Inde*, France: Imprimé par autorisation du roi à l'Imprimerie royale, 1825.
Forbes, James, *Oriental memoirs*, Vol. 4, United Kingdom: White, Cochrane & Co., 1815.
Fraser, James Baillie, *Military Memoir of Lieut-Col. James Skinner, C. B*, United Kingdom: Smith, Elder and Co., 1851.
Furber, Holden, *The Private Record of an Indian Governor-Generalship: The Correspondence of Sir John Shore, Governor-General, with Henry Dundas, President of the Board of Control, 1793–1798*, United States: Harvard University Press, 2013.
Gentil, Jean Baptiste Joseph, *Mémoires sur l'Indoustan: ou Empire Mogol*, France: Petit, 1822.
Hastings, Warren, *A Narrative of the Late Transactions at Benares*, Kolkata: Bangabasi, 1905.
———, et al. *The Letters of Warren Hastings to His Wife*. United Kingdom: W. Blackwood, 1905.
Khan, Seid Gholam-Hossein, *The Seir Mutaqherin*, Vol. 2, India: Inter-India Publications, 1986.
Kindersley, Jemima, *Letters from the Island of Teneriffe, Brazil, the Cape of Good Hope, and the East-Indies*, 1777.
Knighton, William, *The Private Life of an Eastern King*, London: Hope and Company, 1855.
Lauriston, Jean Law de, *Mémoire Sur Quelques Affaires de l'Empire Mogol, 1756–1761* (Classic Reprint), United States: FB&C Limited, 2018.
Martin, Claude, *The Persian Letters of Claude Martin 1785–1796*, British Library, Add. Mss 16,849.
Mir, Mir Taqi, and Naim, C. M, (trans.), *Zikr-I Mir: The Autobiography of the Eighteenth Century Mughal Poet Mir Muhammad Taqi 'Mir' 1723–1810*, New Delhi: Oxford University Press, 1999.
Muhammad, Abu Talib ibn, and Hoey, William (tr.), *History of Asafu'd Daulah, Nawab Wazir of Oudh: Being a Translation of 'Tafzihu'l Ghafilin', a Contemporary Record of Events Connected with His Administration*, Allahabad: Pustak Kendra, 1885.
Polier, Antoine Louis Henri, and Gupta, Pratul Chandra (ed.), *Shah Alam II and His Court: A Narrative of the Transactions at the Court of Delhy from the Year 1771 to the Present Time*, India: S.C. Sarkar and Sons, 1947.
Price, J. Frederick, and Achari, K. Ranga (eds.), *The Private Diary Of Ananda Ranga Pillai*, Vol. 3, India: Government Press, 1914.
Sharar, Abdulḥalīm, *Lucknow, the Last Phase of an Oriental Culture*, New Delhi: Oxford University Press, 1989, p. 31.
Srivastava, Ashirbadi Lal, *Shuja-ud-daulah*, Vol. 1, India: S.N. Sarkar, 1939.
Teignmouth, Baron, and Shore, Charles John, *Memoir of the Life and Correspondence of John, Lord*

Teignmouth, United Kingdom: Hatchard, 1843.

Vigée-Lebrun, Louise-Elisabeth, *Souvenirs of Madame Vigée Le Brun: With a Steel Portrait from an Original Painting by the Author*, United Kingdom: R. Worthington, 1879.

Manuscripts from Berlin Museum and British Library.

BRITISH LIBRARY MANUSCRIPTS:

Correspondence of John Shore (1751–1834), 1st Baron Teignmouth, Governor General of India, 1793-98, British Library, Manuscript Collection.

Hastings 1784 Lucknow Diary, British Library, Manuscript Collection.

Letters to Warren Hastings, British Library, Manuscript Collections.

SECONDARY SOURCES

Aitchison, Charles Umpherston (ed.), *A Collection of Treaties, Engagements and Sanads Relating to India and Neighbouring Countries*, Calcutta: Government of India Central Publication Branch, 1929.

Ali, Meer Hassan, Crooke William (ed.), *Observations on the Mussulmauns of India*, India: H. Milford, Oxford University Press, 1917.

Asher, Catherine B., *Architecture of Mughal India*, Cambridge: Cambridge University Press, 1992.

Bayly, C. A., *Empire and Information: Intelligence Gathering and Social Communication in India, 1780–1870*, Cambridge: Cambridge University Press, 1996.

———, *Rulers, Townsmen and Bazaars: North Indian Society in the Age of British Expansion: 1770–1870*, India: Oxford University Press, 2012.

Barnett, Richard B., *North India Between Empires: Awadh, the Mughals, and the British 1720–1801*, New Delhi: Manohar, 1987.

Brittlebank, Kate, *Tiger: The Life of Tipu Sultan*, United Kingdom: Claritas Books, 2020

Cannon, Garland H., *Oriental Jones: A Biography of Sir William Jones, 1746–1794*, Asia Publishing House [for] Indian Council for Cultural Relations, 1964.

Clark, Anna, *Scandal: The Sexual Politics of the British Constitution*, United States: Princeton University Press, 2013.

Collingham, Lizzie, *Curry: A Tale of Cooks and Conquerors*, United States: Oxford University Press, USA, 2006.

Colley, Linda, *Britons: Forging the Nation, 1707–1837*, London: Yale University Press, 2005.

Dadlani, Chanchal B., *From Stone to Paper: Architecture as History in the Late Mughal Empire*, United Kingdom: Yale University Press, 2018.

Dalrymple, William, *The Anarchy*, London: Bloomsbury Publishing, 2019.

———, *White Mughals*, New Delhi: Penguin Books Limited, 2004.

Deleury, Guy, *Le Voyage en Inde: Anthologie des voyageurs français 1750–1820*, Bouquins, 2003.

Das, Sudipta, *Myths and Realities of French Imperialism in India, 1763–1783*, Germany: P. Lang, 1992.

Desmond, Young, *Fountain of the Elephants*, New York: Harper & Brothers, 1959.

Ghosh, Dubra, Sex and the Family in Colonial India: The Making of Empire, Cambridge: Cambridge University Press, 2006.

Eaton, Richard M., *India in the Persianate Age: 1000–1765*, UK: Penguin Books Limited, 2019

Elliot, H. M., *The History of India, as Told by Its Own Historians: The Muhammadan Period*, Vol. 8, United States: FB&C Limited, 2016.

Fisher, Michael Herbert, *A Clash of Cultures: Awadh, the British and the Mughals*, India: Sangam, 1988.

———, *Indirect Rule in India: Residents and the Residency System, 1764–1858*, Oxford University Press, 1991, p. 29.

Cheema, G. S., *The Forgotten Mughals: A History of the Later Emperors of the House of Babar, 1707–1857*, India: Manohar Publishers & Distributors, 2002.

Hambly, Gavin, *Women in the Medieval Islamic World: Power, Patronage, and Piety*, London: Macmillan, 1999.

Hazleton, Lesley, *After the Prophet: The Epic Story of the Shia-Sunni Split in Islam*, United States:

Knopf Doubleday Publishing Group, 2009.
Hodges, William, *Travels in India: During the Years 1780, 1781, 1782, and 1783*, London: J. Edwards, 1794.
Irwin, Henry Crossley, *The Garden of India: Or, Chapters on Oudh History and Affairs*, United Kingdom: W. H. Allen, 1880.
Jasanoff, Maya, *Edge of Empire: Lives, Culture, and Conquest in the East, 1750–1850*, New York: Knopf, 2005.
———, *Liberty's Exiles: American Loyalists in the Revolutionary World*, United States: Knopf Doubleday Publishing Group, 2012.
Joseph-François, Michaud, *Histoire des progrès et de la chûte de l'empire de Mysore, sous les règnes d'Hyder-Aly et de Tippoo-Saïb: contenant l'historique des guerres des souverains de Mysore avec les Anglais et les différentes puissances de l'Inde...; ornée de cartes, portrait, plans, etc*, France: Giguet et cie, 1809.
Lafont, Jean-Marie, and Lafont, Rehana, *The French and Delhi: Agra, Aligarh, and Sardhana*, India Research Press, 2010.
Leach, Linda York, *Mughal and Other Indian Paintings from the Chester Beatty Library*, United Kingdom: Scorpion Cavendish, 1995.
Llewellyn-Jones, Rosie, *A Man of the Enlightenment in Eighteenth-century India: The Letters of Claude Martin, 1766–1800*, New Delhi: Permanent Black in association with The Embassy of France in India, 2003.
———, *A Very Ingenious Man: Claude Martin in Early Colonial India*, London: Oxford University Press, 1999.
———, *Lucknow, Then and Now*, India: Marg Publications, 2003.
Mahmood, Saif, *Beloved Delhi: A Mughal City and Her Greatest Poets*, India: Speaking Tiger Books, 2018.
Mahmud, Aslam, *Awadh Symphony: Notes on a Cultural Interlude*, New Delhi: Rupa Publications, 2017.
Mahomet, Sake Deen, *Michael Fisher (ed.), The Travels of Dean Mahomet: an eighteenth-century journey through India*, Berkeley: University of California Press, 1997.
Manners, Lady Victoria, and Williamson G.C.,, *John Zoffany, R.A, His Life and Works, 1735- 1810*, London: John Lane, The Bodley Head, 1920.
Markel, Stephen et al, *India's Fabled City: The Art of Courtly Lucknow*, Los Angeles County Museum of Art, 2010.
Marsh, Kate, *India in the French Imagination: Peripheral Voices, 1754–1815*, London: Pickering & Chatto, 2009.
Morlat, André Christophe Louis Piveron de, and Lafont, Jean-Marie (ed.), *Piveron De Morlat: Mémoire Sur L'inde (1786): Les Opérations Diplomatiques Et Militaires Françaises Aux Indes Pendant La Gue re D'indépendance Américaine*, Paris: Riveneuve éditions, 2013.
Nechtman, T. W., *Nabobs: Empire and Identity in Eighteenth-Century Britain*, Cambridge: Cambridge University Press, 2010.
Parlby, Fanny Parkes, *Wanderings of a Pilgrim in Search of the Picturesque*, Manchester: Manchester University Press, 2001.
Ray, Aniruddha, *The Rebel Nawab of Oudh: Revolt of Vizir Ali Khan*, 1799, India: K.P. Bagchi & Company, 1990.
Reid, Stuart, *Armies of the East India Company 1750–1850*, United Kingdom: Bloomsbury Publishing, 2012.
Robins, N., *The Corporation That Changed the World*, London: Pluto Press, 2012,
Santha, Kidambi Srinivasa, *Begums of Awadh*, India: Bharati Prakashan, 1980.
Sarkar, Jadunath, *Fall of The Mughal Empire*, Vol. 1, New Delhi: Orient Longman, 1991
Schofield, Katherine Butler, *Music and Musicians in Late Mughal India: Histories of the Ephemeral, 1748–1858*, United Kingdom: Cambridge University Press, 2023
Sen, Colleen Taylor *Feasts and Fasts: A History of Food in India*, London: Reaktion Books, 2014.
Singh, Kavita, *Real Birds in Imagined Gardens: Mughal Painting Between Persia and Europe,* London:

Getty Research Institute, Getty Publications, 2017.
Srivastava, Ashirbadi Lal, *The First Two Nawabs of Awadh*, New Delhi: Life Span Publishers and Distributors, 2022.
Swarup, Sushama, *Costumes and Textiles of Awadh: From the Era of Nawabs to Modern Times*, New Delhi: Roli, 2012.
Tandon, Banmali, *The Architecture of Lucknow and Its Dependencies, 1722–1856: A Descriptive Inventory and an Analysis of Nawabi Types*, India: Vikas Publishing House, 2001.
Taylor, Alan, *American Revolutions: A Continental History, 1750–1804*, New York: WW Norton, 2017.
Trivedi, Madhu, *The Making of the Awadh Culture*, India: Primus Books, 2010.
Twining, Thomas , *Travels in India a Hundred Years Ago: With a Visit to the United States*, United Kingdom, J.R. Osgood, McIlvaine & Company, 1893.
Vignes, Max, *L'histoire du nabab René Madec*, France: Terre de Brume, 1995
Webb, Timothy , *English Romantic Hellenism, 1700-1824*, United Kingdom: Manchester University Press, 1982.
Webster, Mary, *Johan Zoffany, 1733–1810*, New Haven: Yale University Press, 2011,
Yazdani, Kaveh, *India, Modernity and the Great Divergence: Mysore and Gujarat (17th to 19th C.)*, Netherlands: Brill, 2017.
Zebrowski, Mark, *Gold, Silver & Bronze from Mughal India*, United Kingdom: Alexandria Press, 1997.
Zoffany, Johann, and Orr, Clarissa Campbell, *Johan Zoffany RA: Society Observed*, United Kingdom: Yale Center for British Art, 2011.

## PAPERS

Aitken, Molly Emma, 'Parataxis and the Practice of Reuse, from Mughal Margins to Mīr Kalān Khān', *Archives of Asian Art*, Vol. 59, 2009.
Bayly, C. A., 'Knowing the Country: Empire and Information in India', *Modern Asian Studies*, Vol. 27, No. 1, 1993.
Brown, Rebecca M., 'Abject to Object: Colonialism Preserved through the Imagery of Muharram', *RES: Anthropology and Aesthetics*, No. 43, 2003.
Chancey, Marla Karen, 'In the Company's Secret Service: Neil Benjamin Edmonstone and the First Indian Imperialists, 1780–1820', Unpublished Dissertation, Florida State University, 2003.
Dadlani, Chanchal, 'The 'Palais Indiens' Collection of 1774: Representing Mughal Architecture in Late Eighteenth-Century India', *Ars Orientalis*, Vol. 39, 2010.
Dadlani, Chanchal, 'Transporting India: The Gentil Album and Mughal Manuscript Culture', *Art History*, Vol. 38, 2015.
Del Bonta, Robert, 'Engraving India in 17th and 18th century Europe', *Art in Print*, Vol 4, No. 4.
Eaton, Natasha, 'The Art of Colonial Despotism: Portraits, Politics, and Empire in South India, 1750–1795', *Cultural Critique*, No. 70, 2008.
———, 'Between Mimesis and Alterity: Art, Gift, and Diplomacy in Colonial India', *Romantic Representations of British India,* Routledge, 2006.
Kamleh, Elise, 'Architectural Exchange in the Eighteenth Century A Study of Three Gateway Cities: Istanbul, Aleppo and Lucknow', Doctoral Thesis, University of Adelaide, 2012.
Khan, Vijaya, 'Glimpses into the life and times of the Begums of Avadh', *The India Magazine of Her People and Culture*, Vol. 3, No. 9, August, 1983.
Khoja, Neelam, 'Sovereignty, Space and Identity', Unpublished Dissertation, Harvard University, 2018.
Lafont, Jean-Marie, Georges Barale, and Marguerite Yon-Calvet (eds.), *Le 'Major général' Claude Martin, 1735–1800: aux origines de La Martinière: journée d'hommage tenue le 29 novembre 2018 au Palais Saint-Jean*, Académie des sciences, belles-lettres et arts de Lyon.
Marshall, P. J., 'The Personal Fortune of Warren Hastings: Hastings in Retirement', *Bulletin of the School of Oriental and African Studies*, University of London, vol. 28, no. 3, 1965.
Martin, Claude, and Victor Martin-Schmets, *Lectures d'André Gide: hommage à Claude Martin*, France: Presses universitaires de Lyon, 1994.

Mukherjee, Rudrangshu, 'Trade and Empire in Awadh 1765–1804', *Past & Present*, No. 94, 1982.
Pearson, Sarah, 'Making Britain in Empire: John Shore, Nation and Race in the Eighteenth-Century East India Company World', *Early Modern Studies*, University of Bristol, 21 January 2021.
Platania, Marco, 'L'originalite de la politique francaise en Inde, 1750–1783', *Bulletin de l'institut pierre renouvin*, No. 34, 2011.
Roth, Nicolas, 'Verbal (Re)constructions: Reading Architecture in the Urdu Masnavi', *Journal18*, Issue 11 The Architectural Reference, 2021.
Saha, D. N., 'The Revolt of Raja Chait Singh and Its Repercussions on Oudh and Bihar', *Proceedings of the Indian History Congress*, Vol. 39, 1978.
Sarangi, Dhir, 'Peintures indiennes et transferts culturels', *Synergie-Inde-Revue du GERFLINT*, No. 7, 2016.
Shaffer, Holly, 'An Architecture of Ephemerality between South and West Asia', *Journal18*, Issue 4 East-Southeast, 2017.
Smith, Blake, 'Revolutions en Inde: dimensions coloniales, diplomatiques et culturelles, 1789–1799', *Outre-Mers, Revue d'histoire*, T.103, No. 388-389, 2015.
Weis, Friederike, Marzia Faietti, and Gerhard Wolf (eds.), 'Confident Women in Indo-Persianate Albums: Visual Metaphors or Ethnography?', *Motion: Transformation* (35th Congress of the International Committee of the History of Arts, Florence 2019), Vol. 1, Bologna, 2021.

## PODCASTS
Varma, Amit, *The Seen and the Unseen*.
Collin, Philippe, *Napoleon, l'homme qui ne meurt jamais*.
Holland, Tom, and Sandbrook, Dominic, *The Rest is History*.
Dalrymple, William, and Anand Anita, *Empire Podcast*.

# INDEX

1773 Regulating Act, 113
1773 Select Committee, 113
1775 Treaty, 131
1857 Uprising, xxxiii
Abdali, Ahmad Shah (Durrani), xxv, 31
Abercromby, 295–96
Abercromby, Robert, 295
Abu Bakr, 228
Abu'l Fazl, 81
   *Ain-i Akbari*, 81, 96
Abu Talib, Mirza, xxiii, 213–14, 219, 224–25, 230, 233, 236, 275, 286, 291, 307, 335
Abyssinian officers, 55
Achmuty, 190
Adventurers, xviii, xxxv, xl, xliv, xlviii, 6, 119, 248, 277
   European, 248
   French, xviii, xxxv, xlviii, 6, 277
   military, 277
Adyar River, xxx, xli
Afghanistan, 31, 33, 387
Afghan Rohillas, 29
Afghans, xxv, 13, 16, 22, 30–31, 33–35, 44, 89, 239, 361, 385
Africa, 4, 42, 171, 301, 303
Afzal, Muhammad, 102
Agra, 13–14, 23, 30, 90, 94, 98, 121, 143, 166, 242, 356–57
   siege of, 94
Ahl al-Bayt, 69, 228
Ahmad Shah, Emperor, xxv, 21, 24, 30–36, 44, 70, 76, 78, 109, 241, 280, 327
Aina Khana, 238, 318–19, 336
Aitisam-ud-Daula, 51
Aitkin, Molly, 102
Ajmeri gate, 20
Akbar, Mughal Emperor, 3, 9, 12, 55, 63, 79, 101, 108, 116, 128, 148, 156, 187–88, 233, 242–43, 264–65, 280–81, 319, 330
Aktar, Roshan, 12, *see also* Shah, Muhammad
Alamgir, 67
Alamgir II, Emperor, xxv, xliv, 6, 30–32
   assassination of, xliv, 6, 32
Al-Andalus, xlvii

Albums, xviii, 52, 81–83, 86, 91, 100–101, 103, 201, 241–43, 251
   Asaf-ud-Daula, 242–43
   Clive, 101
   Douce, 101
   Fremantle, 100
   Gentil's, 81
   Large Clive, 52
   Plowden, 251
   Polier, 243
   Small Clive, 52, 100
Ali, Bahadur, 334
Aligarh, 23, 281, 285
Ali Gauhar, Mirza, xiii, xxv, xliv, 6, 31–33, 40
Ali Khan, nizam of Hyderabad, 371
Ali, Meer Hassan, 232–35, 252
Ali, Muhammad, 296
Ali, Raza, 308
Ali, the first imam, 229
Ali Zain al-Abidin, 227
Allahabad, xvii, xxvi, xliv, 10, 25–26, 46–47, 49, 51, 54, 59, 73, 75–76, 108, 110, 182, 219, 241–42, 295, 329–33, 337, 350, 355
alliances, xlii, xlv, 20, 29, 46, 52–53, 74, 78, 120, 143, 145, 151, 171, 175–76, 192, 263–64, 269–70, 292, 345, 359, 371, 378
   continental, 171
   forced, 53
   French, 176
   Indian state and the French, xlv
   military, 269
   subsidiary, xlii, 371
   tenuous, 143
ally(ies), xxi, xxxv, xlvi, 23–25, 30–32, 34–36, 42, 51, 53, 88, 116, 120, 144, 166, 170, 181, 263, 267, 272–73, 307, 363, 366, 375, 383, 387
   American, 170
   English, 88
   French, xxi, xlvi, 263, 273, 363, 387
   Indian, 366
   Maratha, 25, 30, 35, 116, 272, 273
America, xxvi, xlii, xlv, 39, 42, 113, 145, 170–72, 177–78, 270, 301, *see also* United States of America

Franco–British conflict in, 172
  independence of, 178
American
  forces, 145
  revolution, xlvi, 179
  revolutionary forces, xxvi, 172
American Declaration of Independence, 300
American Revolution, 263, 267, 269, 278, 295, 299, 364–65
American Revolutionary War, xx, xxvi, xlvi, 170, 323, 386
American War of Independence, xx, 113, 173, 177–78, 373
Amir Khusrau, 63
Anantapur, 176
Andhra Pradesh, xlii
André Christophe Louis Piveron de Morlat, 177
Anglo-French
  peace, xliii
  struggle, 41
  wars, xxvi, 49
Anglo-Indians, xlvii, 245, 383
  family, 200
  impure, xlvii
  liaisons, 281
Anglo-Mysore Wars, xxi, 11, 146, 270, 273, 325, 327
  Fourth War, 273
  Second War, 146, 325
  Third War, xxi, 270, 327
Anguri Bagh, 59, 74, 78
Annesley, George, 206
Anquetil-Duperron, 79, 175, 269, 365
Antoine, xviii, xxiii, xxv–vi, xliv, xlviii, 87, 94, 185–86, 202, 264, 387
Anupshahar, 34
Anwaruddin, elderly nawab of the Carnatic, xxix, xli–ii
Arabia, 227, 235
Archer, Mildred, 82–83, 98
archery, 15, 108, 114, 244, 287, 289, 346
architects, xxvi, 89, 92, 140, 236, 343
  European, 343
architectural commissions, 34
archives, xvi, xxxiii, xlvii, 274, 280, 286
  family, xlvii, 280, 286
  French, xlvii
*Archives Nationales d'Outre Mer (ANOMA)*, xlvii, 80
*Archives of Asian Art*, 103

Arcot, the capital of the Carnatic, xxx, xli, 98, 223, 324, 388
aristocracy, 12, 58, 244, 299–30
  English, 330
  Lucknow, 244
  military, 12
Armenian officers, 55
*Arsalan-e-Jang* (Lion in Battle), xlviii, 86–87, 210
art and architecture, xviii–xix, xxiii, xxxvi, xlii, xlviii, 19, 58, 61–62, 66–67, 79–80, 82–83, 91, 95, 97–104, 197–98, 203, 209, 213, 220, 231, 233, 241–43, 245, 250, 253, 259, 261, 274, 290, 292, 295, 319–20, 389
  Awadhi, 103
  European, 101
  Indian, xix, 79, 320
  Indo-Islamic style domestic, 19
  Mughal, 19, 104
  Mughal legacy in, xxxvi
  Persianate, 101, 203
Art atelier, xviii, 80
artillery, xxx, 14, 19, 30, 33, 36, 56, 59, 75, 118, 121, 140, 308, 350, 360, 363, 374
  European, 33
  imperial, 19
  native, 350
artisans, 57, 65, 96, 154, 193, 220, 222–23, 225, 264, 268, 292
  French, 264
artists, xviii, xxii–iii, xxvii, xxxvi, 37, 57, 61, 66, 80–83, 91, 98, 100–104, 146, 185–86, 193, 196, 199, 207, 209, 213, 224–25, 242, 244, 249, 255, 258, 274, 292
  Anglo-German, xxii
  Awadhi, 101–02
  British, xxii, xxvii, 98, 193
  European, 193
  hereditary, xxiii, 249
  Indian, 83
  indigenous, 83
  Mughal, 101–02
Asad Allah ul-Ghalib/Assad Allah ul-Ghalib (The Victorious Lion of God), xlviii, 267
Asafi Kothi, 238
Asafiya, 233
Asaf-ud-Daula, Nawab of Awadh, xii–xvi, xx–xxiii, xxvi–viii, xxxv–vii, 20, 34, 62, 109, 122, 125–36, 138–45, 149, 151, 156–60, 162–64, 167, 180–83, 185–87, 191–96, 200–201, 204, 213, 215–23, 225–

26, 229, 233, 235–39, 241–44, 247–49,
251, 254–57, 259, 262, 272, 275, 287–89,
291–93, 295–96, 305–13, 317–22,
329–49, 352–54, 360, 379–80, 390
   collection of Indian miniatures, 194
   death of, xxviii, 109, 344
   embarrassing for, 162
   financial burden, xx
   homosexuality, 126
   orders, 158
   pressure on, 329
   profligacy and financial mismanagement, 235
   reign of, 134, 220, 291
   reputation of, xxxv
   succession travails of, 131
Asher, Catherine, 230
Ashurkhanas, 229
Asia, 36, 44, 113, 172, 175, 229, 246, 286, 301, 326, 387
Asiatic Annual Register, 293
*Asiatick Researches*, 304
Asiatic Society of Bengal, xxvii, 188, 202
Assam, 220
Assassinations, xxxvi, xliv, 6, 17, 32, 228, 236
Astrology, 102, 304, 326
Astronomy, xv, 102, 326, 336
Atlantic Ocean, xlv
Atrocities, xvii, xlvi
   British, xlvi
Attar, 195, 203–04, 215, 287, 323
Aurangabad, 20, 82
Aurangzeb, Mughal emperor, xiii, xxxix, xl, 12–13, 16–17, 111, 132, 233
   death of, xiii, xxxix–xl, 12, 17
Austrian Succession, xxv, xl, xlii, 39
Awadh
   administration of, xxxvi, 28, 306
   affairs of, 133, 348, 352
   anarchy and desolation of, 307
   annexation of, xxxvi, 379, 389
   annual revenue of, 229, 236
   artistic legacy of, 101
   cash demand on, 180
   commercial activities in, 117
   control of, 213
   courts, xv, 18, 20, 117, 336
   cultural renaissance, 37
   culture of, 104, 213
   European imaginings of, 99
   governance of, 337, 350
   history of, xliii, 128, 139
   interference in affairs of, xx
   lifestyle of, 306
   management and finances, 190
   mismanagement of, 226
   nawabs of, xii, xv, xxiii, xxxiv, xlviii, 19, 103–04, 148, 213, 222, 233, 238, 336
   political system of, 192
   revenues of, 225
   security and integrity of, 330
   struggles, xxxvii
   territorial integrity, 131
   visual representation of, 99
   wealth and confidence, 229
Awadhi
   life, 86
   muslin, xviii
   society, 78, 103
Ayodhya, 3, 234
azadaari, 232, 235
Azim, Maulvi Fazal, 195

Babajaan, Anthony, 96
Babur, Mughal empire, xxxix, 12, 15, 243
Baghat, 388
Baghdad, 228
Bahadur Shah, Emperor, 67, 78–79
Bahadur Shah I, 30
Bahraich, xxii, 149
Bahu Begum, mother of Asaf-ud-Daula, xii, xv–xvi, xxiii, xxvi, xxxv–vii, xlviii, 10–11, 20–21, 51–52, 60–62, 65, 70, 79, 103, 107–09, 120, 125, 127, 129–31, 134, 141–42, 150–51, 154–61, 163–64, 166–69, 191–92, 213, 218, 287–93, 311–12, 342–47, 349–55, 390
   conscious of the power of her wealth, 127
   control of her wealth, 134
   court, 345
   durbar, 287, 290, 344
   death of, 355
   expectation of support, 163
   imprisonment of her khwajasaras, 155
   jagirs, 168
   khwajasara bodyguards, 160
   khwajasaras and servants, 159
   Moti Mahal, 60–61, 63–64, 157–58, 167, 287, 292
   overbearing personality, 134
   revenue police, 157
   sovereign right to her own property

and jagirs, 354
wealth, 65, 130
Baillie, Captain William, 146, 170
Baird, David, 374, 382
Bajirao II, 384
*Bajirao Mastani*, 384
Bakht, Bidar, Mughal prince, 241
Bakht, Mirza Ali, 223, 244
Bakht, Mirza Jawan, xiii, xxvii, 36, 187, 190, 219, 244, 246, 322, 356–57
Bakht, Mirza Muzzafar, 356
Bakht, Mirza Shagufta, 356
Bakht, Muhammad Zahiruddin Mirza Ali, 223
Baksh, Ali, 283, 286
Baksh, Didar, 96–97
Baksh, Farhat, 185, 205
Baksh, Imam, 138, 143, 257
Baksh, Muhammad Faiz, xxiii, xlviii, 57, 60, 62, 65, 67, 106, 108, 125, 127–28, 130, 150, 154, 156, 160–62, 167–68, 213, 223, 288–90, 292, 311, 355
Balance of power, 77, 171, 187, 279, 357
Banda Bahadur, brutal execution of, 13
Bangash Afghans, 22
Bangash, Ahmad Khan, 25, 52
Baradari, xxxvii, 158, 167
Bara Imambara, 229–31, 238–39, 377
Barbette, Augustin, 46
Barbette, Marie-Anne, 46, 112, 116
Barey Nawab, 355
Barnett, Richard B., 35, 55, 144, 158, 180, 214
    North India Between Empires: Awadh, the Mughals, and the British 1720–1801, 144
Bastille prison, xxvii, 299
Battle of Buxar, xi, xiii, xviii–xix, xxv, xxxv, xliv-v, 11, 46, 49, 55, 72, 76–77, 110, 112
Battle of Delhi, xxviii, 382, 386
Battle of Elsa, 41
Battle of Karbala, 34, 69, 228
Battle of Lakheri, 277
Battle of Panipat, xxv, 33, 35, 37, 43, 76, 277
Battle of Plassey, xx, xxv, xxxviii, xliii–iv, 33, 39–40, 49, 108, 177
Battle of Pollilur, xxvi, 146, 170
Battle of the Pyramids, 369
Battle of Wandiwash, 41
Battle of Waterloo, xxviii, xxxviii, 300, 387
Bayly, C. A., 236, 242, 253, 326, 334, 347, 356
    *Empire and Information: Intelligence Gathering and Social Communication in India*, 1780–1870, 253
    *Rulers, Townsmen and Bazaars: North Indian Society in the Age of British Expansion*: 1770–1870, 326
begamati zuban, 256, 257
Begums of Awadh, xv, xvii, xx, xxiii, xxvi–vii, xxxiv–v, xxxvii, 13, 23, 29, 58, 61–62, 64–65, 67–70, 110, 121, 126–31, 134–36, 141–42, 144, 148, 150–51, 155–60, 162–63, 165–69, 180–81, 191, 200, 217, 223, 236–37, 246, 266, 278–79, 287–89, 291–92, 322–23, 345, 349–51, 353–54, 390
    jagirs, 156, 157, 166, 167, 168, 191
    treasures, 180
Begum Sombre, 22
Belgium, 321
Benaras, xii–xiii, xvii, xxi–ii, xxvi–viii, xxxv, 4, 8, 15, 28–29, 49, 93, 117, 131, 143–52, 168, 182, 185, 203, 219, 246–47, 253, 304, 310, 322–23, 330, 337, 344, 349–50, 352, 356–61, 363, 372, 379, 389
    ceded to the Company, 145
    insurrection in, xxi, xxii
    revolt in, xii, xxvi, 149
    throne of, xvii
    zemindary of, 356
Bengal, xiii, xviii–xx, xxv–viii, xxxviii, xl, xliv, 3–8, 10–11, 13–14, 18, 25, 30, 33, 36–43, 47–51, 57, 69, 87, 89, 112–15, 117, 120, 148–50, 175, 177, 186, 188, 194, 197, 202–03, 206, 213, 222, 245, 274, 279, 282, 307–08, 334, 338, 384, 390
    annual revenue, xl
    army, xix, xxviii, 308, 390
    British forces in, 41
    diwani of, xx, xxv
    Modave's assessment of the state of affairs in, 89
    pillage of, xliv
    taxes of, xliv
Bennet, Helen, 285
Berar, 175
Bernier, 132
Bhau, Sadashiva, 36
Bhutan, 137
Bibi Ashuran, 292
Bible, the, 302–03, 325
*Bibliothèque Nationale de France*, xlvii
Bidri work, 63

Bihar, 8, 11, 33, 40, 50, 149
Bihar-Awadh border, 8
Bijnor, 34
Bika, 222
bloodless coup, xxviii, 369, 382
Board of Control of the EIC, 193, 302, 328
Bokil, Sakharam Bapu, 174
Bombay, 50, 175, 270, 332, 338, 373, 382, 384
Bonaparte, Joseph, 382
Boston Tea Party, 113
Botanic Garden at Calcutta, 274
Boulone, 140, 199, 206–07, 209, 316
Bourquien, 383, 386
Brahmins, 35, 55, 68, 174, 202, 356, 374
Breach of faith, 51, 164
Brigades of Hindustan, xvi, xx, 277, 383
Bristow, John, xxi, xxvii, 129, 134, 137–38, 180
Britain, xx, xxxiii, xxxviii, xl, xlii, xlv–vi, 3, 7, 10, 39, 41–42, 77, 118, 145, 168, 170–73, 176, 267, 269, 286, 299–302, 304, 306, 313–14, 319, 321, 328, 352, 363–64, 368–71, 373, 382–83, 385–89, *see also* England
   economy, xlii
   loss of its American colonies, 301
   trading wealth, 369
Britain and France/British and French, xvi, xxvii, xxxvii, xlv–vi, 10, 39, 41, 77, 139, 173, 178
   armed global struggle, xxxi
   encounters, xlvi
   engaged in empire building, xlii
   global war for dominance between, 169
   hostilities, xxvii, 33, 39, 41, 178
   incessant fractious dealings, 83
   proxy wars, xlv
   rivalry, xxxvii
   tensions, xvi
   volatile border, xliii
British
   ambitions, 43, 77, 173
   camp, 48
   cause, 307, 313
   character assassination, xxxvi, 236
   defeats of the, 170
   empire, xxxiii, xlviii, 145, 152, 179, 269
   expansion, xxxiv, 118, 176
   forces, xxii, xxviii, 41, 46–47, 365, 374, 376–77, 390
   French threat, xlv, xlvi
   influence, 325
   military victory in India, 363
   national debt, 177
   naval battles against the, 175
   officers, 48, 152
   policies and actions, xxxviii
   power, 43, 175, 305
   pretensions, 44
   rule, xx, 82, 223, 226, 380, 388
   trading post at Bombay, 175
   trading post at Madras, xl
British and the Mughals, 176
British East India Company (EIC), xvi, xix, 39, 137, 170, 269–70, 314, 323, 343
British Indian army, 384
British Madras, xli
Britishness, 238, 363
brocade, 66, 86, 98, 219, 294, 357
Bundelkhand, 360
Burhanpur, 20
Burke, Edmund, 148–49, 266, 301, 303
Burma, 264
Buxar, xi–xiii, xviii–xx, xxv, xxxv, xliv–v, 8–11, 43, 45–46, 49, 52, 54–56, 72, 76–77, 105, 110, 112, 117, 121, 130, 134, 147, 168, 179, 218, 236, 340, 390
   defeat of, 56
   disaster of, 52
   wreckage of, 52
Calcutta, xiv–xv, xxi, xxiii, xxv, xliii, 24, 33, 39, 47, 49–50, 59, 89, 93–94, 98, 110, 137, 140, 142, 146, 149, 152, 164, 177, 180, 182, 188, 190, 194, 196–97, 202–03, 213–16, 219, 245–47, 249, 270, 273–74, 302–03, 305, 307, 309, 315, 322–23, 328–30, 333–34, 336, 339–40, 344, 346, 349, 358, 360–61, 363, 367, 370, 378, 380, 386, 388–89
*Calcutta Gazette*, 363
Calligraphy, 52, 88, 94, 101, 103, 242, 346
Campbell, Ryan, 273
   Richard Wellesley and the Fourth Anglo-Mysore War, 273
Canada, 39, 42, 368
Caribbean islands, 42, 43
Carnac, Captain John, 8, 10, 47–50, 80
Carnatic, xxix–xxxi, xli–iii, 49, 173, 175–76, 264, 271, 324–25, 379, *see also* Karnataka
Carnatic War, xlii, xliii, 173
   First War, xlii
carriages and palanquins, 32, 48, 59, 74, 109, 111, 119, 128, 137, 148, 158, 161,

167, 219, 287, 299, 322, 357, 382
Cartography, 81
Cassembazar, 120
Catholic France, 301, 370
Cavalry, xxxi, xl, xliii, 7, 9, 14, 16, 18, 34, 45, 55–56, 65, 74–75, 108, 111, 115–16, 206, 277, 288, 292, 299, 308, 327, 337, 373, 384
   Indian style, xxxi
   Mughal, xxxi, 7, 116
   Persian, 16
   Persian Qizilbash (red hat), 9
Celebrations, 20, 170, 213, 222–23, 238, 252, 256, 262, 292, 345, 349, 363–64
   marriage, 222
   nationalistic, 363–64
   patriotic, 364
Central Asia, 229, 326, 387
Ceremony(ies), 20, 73, 109, 112, 115, 142, 170, 181, 187, 192, 235, 246, 281, 292, 320, 322, 364, 366, 379
   marriage, 112
   Mughal, 379
Chandernagore, xxv, xxxviii, 5, 33, 40–41, 43, 72, 83, 107, 112, 114, 136, 172–73, 175, 378
   destruction of, 5, 43
Chand, Mehr, artist, xviii, xxiii, xxvi, 91, 96–97, 102, 209
Charlotte, Marie-Thérèse, 196, 262, 302–03, 338
Chateau de Lyons, xlviii, 185, 197, 204–05, 209, 216, 220, 262
chauth, xxxix, 13, 38
Cheema, G. S., xliii
   *Soldier of Misfortune: The Memoirs of the Comte de Modave*, xliii
Cherry, George, xii, xxi, xxviii, 296, 305–10, 313, 325, 329, 331, 333, 339, 350, 352, 358, 360–61, 372
   ambitions, xxi, 306
   arrogance, 310
Chester Beatty Museum, 100
Chevalier, Jean-Baptiste, 83
Chikan work, 222
China, 59, 209, 230, 264, 334
Chowk Bazar, 59–60, 156, 158–59, 287
Christianity, xxi, xlvii, 285, 302, 303
Chunar, 18, 147–48, 151–52, 156, 169, 182, 190, 360
   debacle at, 156, 169
Chunargarh, 15

Civil war, xxv, 23–24, 145, 193, 327
Clapham Sect, 302, 328
Clive Album, 52
Clive, Edward, 373
Clive, Robert, xx, xxv, xxxviii, xli, xliii–iv, 33, 39, 41, 49, 52, 76, 87, 152, 373, 376
   complicated legacy, 49
   duplicity, 50
   expelled from Madras, xli
   seized Calcutta, 33, 39
Clothes/textiles, 5, 12, 17, 19–20, 28, 44, 63–65, 68, 70, 85, 88, 90, 92, 109, 115, 121–22, 161–62, 205, 209, 219, 222, 231, 242, 248, 254, 257, 262, 264, 267–68, 288, 291–92, 294, 320, 353, 357
   ceremonial, 357
   Gulbadan, 85
   gul-i-anar, 85
   jamdani, 98, 218, 221–22, 248
   muslin, xviii, 59, 63, 86–87, 97, 189, 209, 218, 221–22, 262, 265
   production, 222
   qarmizi, 85
   suzani, 85
Cobain, Ian, xxxiii
   *The History Thieves*, xxxiii
Colley, Linda, 364
*Colonel Mordaunt's Cock Match*, 155
Colonialism, 170, 319
   defeat of, 170
Concubines, 8, 29, 61, 92, 207, 280, 291
Cornwallis, Charles, Governor General, xii, xiv, xvi, xx, xxvi–vii, xlvi–vii, 145, 170, 177, 205, 214–16, 245–47, 270, 272–73, 276, 295, 302, 305–06, 308, 314, 324, 327, 330, 333, 371, 373, 382–83
   1791 law, xlvii
   1792 campaign, 373
   attack on Seringapatam, 273
   defeat of, 170
   expedition to Lucknow, 245
   recommendations for non-interference in Awadhi affairs, 305
   seized the city of Bangalore, 272
Coromandel Coast, 39, 41, 176, 178, 203
corruption, xix–xx, 39, 55, 88–89, 113, 138, 168, 303, 333, 336, 349
Corsica, 300, 368
Courtesans, xxiii, 10, 21–22, 29, 37, 66–67, 69, 231, 248–52, 258–61, 292, 315, 320, 361
   Lucknawi, 250

skilled, 250
*Courtesan's Arts, The*, 260
courtiers, xxiii, 40, 46, 55, 77–78, 94, 111, 114, 127, 132, 134, 136, 156, 185, 216, 222–24, 242–43, 248, 250, 257, 259, 262, 287–90, 293, 296, 308, 333, 335–36, 341, 343–44, 349–50, 363
    British, 216
    imperial, 94
    Indian, 78, 224
Court in Damascus, 69
Court of Awadh, xv, 18, 20, 117, 336
Court of Delhi, xxxv, 30, 102, 135, 139, 154
Court of Directors, 47
Court of English law, 350
Court of Faizabad, xv–xvi, 57, 68, 77
Court of Indian rulers, 43
Court of Louis XVI, xvi, xxvii, 240, 264
Court of Lucknow, xix, 187, 196, 225, 311
Court of Nawab Asaf-ud-Daula, xxii, 254
Court of Nawab Shuja-ud-Daula, xiii, xviii, 74, 77, 93, 98–99, 151, 186
Court of Raja Pratap Singh, 203
Court of the Mughal emperor, 114
craftsmen, 57, 186, 264
Criminal contumacy and disobedience, 146
Cuba, 42
cuisine, 62, 290, 363
cultural
    activity, 80
    celebrity, 266
    heritage, 238
    legacy, xxxvi
    memory, xxxiv
    patronage, 236
    practices, xxxvii
culture, xii, xxxiv–vii, xlii, xlvii–iii, 19, 55, 69, 79, 89, 99, 104, 141, 178, 213, 219, 233, 235, 237–38, 250, 259–60, 268, 288, 310, 318, 389–90
    indigenous, 310
    Lucknawi, xxxv, 260
    Shia, xxxvii, 235, 237

Dak-bearers, 85
Dalhousie, Governor General, xxxvi, 378, 388–90
Dalrymple, William, xliv, 170, 325
    Anarchy, The, 241
    White Mughals, 325
Dance, xxxvi, xlviii, 18, 88, 92, 97, 183–84, 204, 213, 224, 226, 249, 251, 253, 261, 281, 292–94, 319, 389
    kathak, 86, 224–25, 261
    performances, 183, 249
Dancers, 8, 18, 57, 65, 67, 80, 86, 204, 224–25, 250, 306, 319
    kathak, 86, 225
Dara Shukoh haveli/mansion, 22–23, 386
Dara Shukoh, son of Shah Jahan, xxxix, 19–20, 22–23, 78–79, 386
    wedding, 20
Daria Daulat Bagh, 170
Dark Ages, xlvii
Darogah-i-bawarchi khana, 62
Das, Harcharan, 121
Das, Mahadeo, 147, 352, 358, 361
Das, Sital, 82
Das, Sudipta, 171
Daulat Khana, 238, 320–21
Dauphin, death of the, 269
Davies, Samuel, 358
Daylesford House, 190
De Boigne, Benoit, xvi, xix–xx, xxii, xxvii–viii, xlvii, 199–200, 204, 206, 208, 276–86, 308, 316, 383, 386–87
    linguistic skills, 278
De Bussy, Marquis, xviii, xlii, 5, 9, 42, 79, 173, 175, 177–78, 272
    Hyderabad campaign, xlii
Deccan, xxxix, xli, xlii, 13, 16, 20, 30, 38, 79, 116, 229, 240, 269, 340
De Choiseul, Étienne François, xlv, 171, 173
*Declaration of the Rights of Man and of the Citizen*, 267
De Kerscao, 111, 116
De Lauriston, Jean Law, 5, 24, 28, 40–41, 43, 174–75
Deleury, Guy, 174
    *Le Voyage en Inde: Anthologie des voyageurs français* 1750–1820, 174
Delhi, xi, xiii–xiv, xvi–xvii, xxii–iii, xxv–viii, xxxiii, xxxv–viii, xl–xliv, 6, 12–13, 15–16, 18–19, 21–25, 29–32, 34–37, 40–42, 46, 50–51, 54, 57, 60, 66–69, 75–78, 80–82, 91, 93–94, 100–105, 110–17, 122, 131–36, 139, 141, 144, 154, 166, 176, 186–87, 189, 219, 221, 225, 229–30, 233, 236–41, 247, 253–59, 271, 279, 285, 287, 292, 295, 315, 319, 325, 327–28, 334, 355–57, 383, 385–86, 389–90
    court, xxxv, 37, 57, 102, 132–33, 139, 189, 295

devastation of, 18
legacy of, 105
political situation at, 187
ravaged, 80
D'Eprémesnil, Jean-Jacques Duval, xxix
De Silva, Khwaja don Pedrose, 95
Dewa River, 149
Dhaka, 57
dhun, 251
Dilkusha palace, 60, 293
diplomacy, xli, 8, 27, 136, 178, 333
diplomatic
  channels, 29, 173
  posturing, 34
  subtlety, 323
*Discourse on the Worship of Priapus, A*, 198
Diwan-e-aam, 35, 50
Diwan-e-khas, 19, 23, 111
Diwani, 175, 177
Diwani of Bengal, 175
Doab, 143, 379
Doctrine of Lapse, 388-89
Doloram, Rae, 42
Dompart, M., 378
D'Osmond, Adèle, xvi, xx, 284-85, 316
Douce albums, 101
dowry, 20, 51, 61, 65, 130, 312
drawings, 81, 148, 185, 197-98, 201, 274-276
  botanical, 274, 276
*Dream, A*, 201
Duchy of Savoy, 278
Dundas, Henry, 307, 328, 337, 378
Duperron, 271
Dupleix, Joseph François, French governor of Pondicherry, xviii, xix-xx, xxx, xxxviii, xl-xliii, 5, 39, 49, 173
  actions against the British trading post at Madras, xl
  ambitions, 49
  deceptive manner, xlii
  the first European nawab in India, xxxviii
Durrani, Ahmad Shah, King of Afghanistan, xxv, 33-35, 44, 70, 76, 78, 109, 327
  camp, 34
  death of, 327
  sartorial sense, 44
  soldiers, 35-37
Dutch, the, 17, 271
dynasties, xl, 12, 389
  hereditary, xl
  Mughal, 12

Earl of Buckinghamshire, 323
Earl of Powis, 373
East India Company (EIC), xii-xiii, xv-xxi, xxiii, xxv-viii, xxxiv-viii, xli-vii, 3-8, 10, 33, 39, 41, 44-45, 47, 49-52, 54-56, 65, 73, 76, 82-83, 87, 93, 95, 103, 110, 112-13, 117-18, 127, 129-31, 137-39, 141-46, 148-51, 154, 156-57, 159, 163, 166-67, 170, 172, 176-80, 186, 193-94, 197, 200, 202, 206, 213-14, 217-18, 223, 226, 236, 243, 245, 248, 269-73, 276, 278, 283, 291, 293, 295-96, 302-06, 308, 310, 313-14, 316-17, 321-25, 327-31, 333-43, 345-51, 353-54, 358-61, 363, 371-75, 377-81, 383-88, 390
  agent, xxii-iii, 94, 117, 174, 182, 199, 213, 217, 345
  agents, 44, 95, 103, 117, 162-63, 218, 264, 325, 333-34
  army, xviii, xliv
  as ruler of Bengal, 202
  camp, 3
  debt, 156
  dominance in India, xxxiv
  entitled to gather all taxes in Bengal, 50
  fiscal pressure of the, 131
  fiscal problems, 156
  incursions of the, xxxiv
  Paintings, xix
  policy, 149
  power, 324, 337
  racism and sense of superiority, 316
  red uniforms, 4
  soldiers, 276
Eaton, Natasha, 30, 319
economic
  depression, 302
  resources, 49
economy, xlii, 236, 242, 268, 288
  Awadhi, 236
Edmonstone, Neil Benjamin, xxi, xxviii, xlvii, 305-07, 310, 322, 325, 329, 331, 338, 341-43, 345-46, 348, 351-52, 357, 359, 361-62, 370-72, 379
Education, 5, 43, 79, 181, 197, 199-200, 207, 216, 260, 278, 285, 288, 336, 364
  Indo-Persian, 336
Egypt, xxviii, 10, 368-72, 382
EIC and Awadh treaties, 131
Ellora Caves, 79, 82

embroidery, 15, 64, 85, 88, 90–91, 222
  metallic thread, 90
  patterns, 90, 91
  zardozi, 64
Emperors of Hindustan, 219
Empire-building, 301
England, xvi, xviii, xx, xxiii, xxvii, 49–51, 88–89, 99, 142, 145, 169, 171–72, 176–78, 182, 194–97, 209, 213–14, 217, 220, 225, 230, 245, 284, 286, 293, 302–03, 318, 324, 328, 340, 347, 358, 363, 370, 373, *see also* Britain
English Channel, 145
English East India Company (EIC), xliii–iv, 3, 141, 166
  militarization of the, xliii
English, the, xxv, xxvii, xxxv, xxxix, xli, xliii–iv, 3, 7, 9, 42–43, 45, 47–50, 54–56, 58, 74–75, 83–84, 87–89, 94–95, 99, 109–10, 112–14, 117–18, 120–21, 126, 130–31, 139–45, 147, 149–51, 157, 163–64, 166–67, 172, 174–78, 180–81, 183, 194–95, 214, 217, 219, 226, 238–39, 242, 246–47, 263–64, 270–71, 273, 282, 294–95, 309, 314, 317, 327, 330, 333, 335, 339, 348, 350–51, 354, 356, 360, 364, 370, 378, 385
  army at Madras, 87
  camp, 3
  displeasure of the, 9
  officers, 49, 93, 147
  soldiers, 46
engravings, 90, 220, 266
Entertainments, 16, 64–65, 67, 183–84, 213, 223–24, 226, 238, 246, 252, 289, 295, 315, 318, 380
Etawah, 93, 189, 299, 312, 365, 380
Ethnicity, 249
Etiquette, 89, 155, 213, 223, 244, 249–50, 258
Eton, 209, 364, 368, 384
etymology, 101
eunuchs, xi, xv, xxiii, xxxv, xxxvii, 21, 52, 129, 150, 153, 157, 160–61, 164–65, 280, 311–12
  androgyny of, 161
  armed militarization and resistance of, xxxv
  elite, xv, xxxv
  European perceptions of, 161
  imperial, xxxv
  slaves, 160

Euphrates River, 227
Europe, xx, xxviii, xl–xlii, xlv, xlvii, 39, 41, 59, 77, 87, 102, 113, 121, 126, 133, 138, 171–73, 178, 198–99, 201, 208–09, 216, 264, 270, 284, 286, 300–301, 316–17, 319, 321, 346, 352, 363, 368–70, 378, 383, 387
European
  armaments, 59
  factories, 56
  moral complexion, 304
  nation, xxxviii, 262
  soldiers, 3, 5, 78, 270
Europeans, the, xiii, xix–xx, xxii, xxx, xxxiii–iv, xxxviii–ix, xli, xliii–iv, xlvii, 3–5, 7–9, 33, 42–43, 45, 55–56, 59, 67, 78–79, 81–83, 87, 91–95, 99, 101–04, 115, 117, 120–22, 137, 139, 148, 161, 169, 171, 179, 185–86, 193, 196–201, 203–06, 210, 214–17, 223–24, 235, 238, 245, 248, 252, 260–62, 266, 269–70, 272, 274, 277–79, 281–82, 284, 294–96, 300–301, 304–05, 314–21, 323, 332–33, 337, 341, 343, 349, 356, 360, 367, 371, 373, 380, 384
Evangelicalism, xlvi, 302
Exoticism, 265

factories, xviii, xlii, 40, 42, 50, 56, 265, 312
  French, xviii, 40
  indigo, 312
Faizabad, xii, xv–xvi, xviii, xxiii, xxvi–vii, xlviii, 14, 18, 21, 26–27, 37, 47, 52, 54, 57–60, 64, 66–71, 73–74, 77–78, 80, 82, 84–86, 89–91, 93, 95–96, 98–100, 102–04, 107–10, 118–20, 130–31, 133–36, 140–44, 150–51, 154, 157–59, 162–63, 165–68, 181, 186, 191–92, 203, 213, 223, 225, 236–37, 287–93, 309, 311–12, 344, 354–55, 390
  courtesans of, 66
  Lal Bagh, 58, 60, 73, 377
  power structure of, 165
  transformation of, 73
  zenana, xlviii
Faizabad School of Art, 80
Faiz Begum, xvi, xxii, 199–200, 282, 284
fakirs, 246, 327
Fakirullah, 102
Famine of 1784, 236–37
  relief measure, 236
farrash, 347

Farrukhabad, 25, 52, 92, 151, 312, 333
Farsh-e-chandani, 86
Fatehgarh/Fatehgur Battalion/Brigade, 151, 214, 306
Ferdinand, Lewis, 293, 341
Feroz Shah Kotla, 20, 24
festivals/festivities, xxxvii, 73, 78, 192, 213, 223, 235, 252, 292–94, 330, 341, 345, 364
    Diwali, 345, 389
    Durga Puja, xxxvii, 235
    Dussehra, xxxvii, 235
    Eid, 252
    Faizabadi, 78, 99, 354
    Holi, 213, 223, 238, 256
    Mahommedan, 341
    marriage, 192
financial resources, 33
Firangi, xxx, xxxvii, 87, 91, 95–96, 183, 261, 284, 315, 361
Firangi Mahal of Lucknow, xv, 336
Firangi nation, xxxvii
Firangi School, 83
First Coalition, 300
Fischer, Michael, 47
Fitzwilliam Museum, Cambridge, 251
Flag of France, 366
Fleur-de-lys, xix, xlviii, 9, 366
food, 32, 48, 57, 61–62, 70, 90, 115, 183–84, 220–21, 237, 266, 271, 279, 290, 296, 322, 363, 370, 390
forces
    British, xxii, xxviii, 41, 46–47, 365, 374, 376–77, 390
    European trained, xx
    expeditionary, xliii, 367
    French, xxviii, 8, 43–44, 245, 382
    Lucknow, 157
    Maratha, xxv, 23, 38, 386
    Mughal, xiii–xiv, xvii, xxv, xxx–xxxi, xxxviii, 15, 45, 179
    revolutionary, xxvi, 172, 378
Forster, George, 44
Fort of Allahabad, 10, 49, 76
Fort of Chunar, 18, 147, 152, 190
Fort of Rohtas, 18
Fort St. George, Madras, xxix, xli
Fort William, Calcutta, xliii, 140, 344, 361
Fort Williams, 10, 33, 99
Fort Williams, Calcutta, 33
France, xvi, xviii–xx, xxiii, xxvi–viii, xxxiv, xxxvii–viii, xl, xlii–iii, xlv–vii, 4, 9–10, 39, 41–43, 49, 72, 77–78, 81–83, 100, 113–14, 116, 133, 137, 139, 145, 169, 171–75, 177–79, 193, 199, 209–10, 213, 220, 240, 262–69, 271, 278, 282, 284, 299–301, 321, 363–66, 368–71, 375, 382, 386–87
    ambitions in India, xlv, 173
    cause, 77
    economy, xlii
    fiscal problems, 269
    Indian factories of, 42
    loss of the American colonies, 179, 270, 302
    offensive against, xlv
    reign of terror in, xxviii, 369
France and England tensions, xviii
France and Mysore friendship, 263
Francis, Philip, xxi, 137–38, 142
Franco–American win, xlvi
Franco-British, xxxvii, xlvi, 172
    conflict, 172
    encounters, xlvi
    rivalry, xxxvii
'Fremantle' Album, 100
French and the Marathas negotiations, 173, 176
French Brigades of Hindustan, 277
French Catholicism, xlvi
French Chandernagore, 33
French colony of Mauritius, 366
*French Compagnie des Indes*, xix, 4
French East India Company (EIC), xix, xli, xliii, 4, 39, 41, 137, 193, 271, 383
    in Hindustan, 39
    travails and fortunes of the, 193
French EIC and the English EIC battles, xliii
French in India, xix, 39, 95, 178
French Pondicherry, xli
French Republic, xlviii, 365, 377
French Revolution, xix, xxvii, xlv, 83, 262, 267, 299, 301–02, 378
    outbreak of the, xlv
French Revolutionary Wars, xlv–vi
French soldiers, xviii–xxx, xliv, 3–4, 73, 139, 173, 267, 366–67, 371, 375, 383
French, the, xii, xvi–xix, xxi, xxv–xxxi, xxxv–viii, xl–xlviii, 3–6, 8–10, 24, 33, 39–45, 47, 49, 55–56, 58–59, 73–74, 77–80, 82–84, 87, 93–95, 107, 111–14, 119–21, 136–37, 139–40, 170–79, 185, 193, 200, 206–07, 245, 260, 262–71, 273, 277–79, 285, 295, 299–302, 321, 340,

362–71, 375–78, 382–87
  adventurers and soldiers, xviii–xxx, xxxv, xliii–iv, xlviii, 3–4, 43, 73, 139, 173, 179, 267–67, 371, 375, 378, 383
  allies, xlvi, 273
  ambitions, 173, 301
  army, xix, 5, 137, 300, 370
  cause, 77
  commercial monopoly in India, xliii
  court, 140
  empire, 365
  enemy of the, xxi
  feudal order, 299
  forces, xxviii, 8, 43–44, 245, 382
  garrison, Madras, xxix, xxx
  government, 112, 173, 175, 268, 271, 375
  guerre de revanche, xlv, 171
  infantry, xxix, xlii
  interest of the, 136, 266
  invasion, 301, 387
  missionary, 260
  officers/officials, xliii, xliv, 5, 40, 43, 45, 77, 172, 177, 179, 263, 278, 365–66
  policy, 77, 112, 366
  regiments, 170
  revolutionary forces, 378
  revolutionary government, 300
  support for the Americans, xlv
  threat, xlv, xlvi
  trade, xli, 171
  victories in South India, xlii
  victory, xlvi
French trading post at Chandernagore, 5, 83, 112
Frigate *La Virginie*, 368

Gaikwar of Baroda, 386
Galliez, Colonel, 107
Ganga-Jamuni tehzeeb, xlviii, 238
Ganga River, xlviii, 15, 46–48, 106, 238, 295, 313, 322, 390
Gardiner, Major, 285
Garrison, xxix–xxx, 47
  French, xxix–xxx
Gastronomy, 61
Gentil, Jean-Baptiste, xii, xviii, xxv–vi, xlii, xliv, xlviii, 5, 8, 10, 40, 43, 45–48, 59, 70–75, 77–83, 91, 93, 95, 99–101, 109, 121–22, 139–40, 264–65, 316, 387
  collection, 81, 83, 139
  Gentil's Atlas, 82, 387
  Indian manuscripts, 83
  marriage, 79
  *Mémoires sur l'Indoustan: Ou Empire Mogol*, 78, 80
  *Receuil sur l'Indoustan*, 74
Gentil, Mossu, 72, 79, 93
George III, King of Britain, 51, 171, 225, 242, 267, 301, 376
Germany, 321
Ghaghara River, 60, 64, 74, 91, 136, 309
Ghazal, 251, 253–54, 256–57, 259, 261
Ghazipur, 15
Ghosh, Dubra, 207, 283
  *Sex and the Family in Colonial India: The Making of Empire*, 283
Gilpin, Major Martin, 167
Giri, Anoop, 26, 36, 46
Giri, Umrao, 26, 122
Gladwin, Francis, 194, 363
Glorious Revolution of 1688, 370
Gole, Susan, 81
Gomastahs, 295
Gomti River, 14, 185, 195, 203–04, 219, 230, 317, 343
Gorakhpur/Gorukhpur, xxii, 149, 163, 361, 379
Gorden, Captain, 163
Gossains, 9, 24, 33, 35, 45, 143
Govardhan II, 80
Graff, Violette, 15
  *Lucknow: Memories of a City*, 15
Grant, Charles, 302–04, 325
  *Observations on the State of Society among the Asiatic Subjects of Great Britain*, 304
Great Britain, 301, 304, 352, 368, 370, 382
  financial strain to, 382
Guerrilla tactics, 13
Gujarat, xxxix, 25, 57, 175, 358
Gulab Bari, 68, 122, 144
*Gulistan*, 86
Gun salute, 273, 357

Haft-hazari, 128
Haidar Beg, 190, 335
Haider, Nawab Nasiruddin, 320
Haiti, 171, 321
Haji Mustapha, 88
Halima Begum, 200
Handia, 182
Hannam, Emily, 52, 243
Hannay, Alexander, xxii, 149–52, 218

Harem, 11, 13, 21, 54, 73, 103, 119, 144, 161, 311, 347
Harkaras, 85, 93, 253, 306, 325–26, 334, 347
Harris, General, 373, 376, 381
Harrow, 364, 384
Hasangary, xiv, 195
Hasan, Mir, 255–56
Hastings, Marian, 88, 152, 164, 169, 186
Hastings, Warren, xii–xiii, xv, xvii, xix–xxii, xxvi–vii, xxxv–vi, xlviii, 87–89, 93–95, 113, 117, 129–30, 137, 139, 142–52, 156–57, 163–64, 168–69, 179–80, 182–91, 193, 199–200, 202, 204–05, 214–17, 237, 242, 246–47, 266, 269–70, 295, 301, 303, 306, 310, 330, 333, 345, 353, 356
  acquittal of, 301
  charges of corruption, 88, 168
  debacle at Chunar, 156, 169
  diary, xlviii, 183–84, 186, 191
  efforts of, 186
  handling of the begums of Awadh, xx
  trial for impeachment, xx, xxvii, 65, 88, 129, 149, 168, 266, 269, 301, 303, 345
  tribulations of, 193
Hawking, 161, 289
Hazrat Ali, 69, 238
Hereditary, xxiii, xl, 7, 14, 25–26, 33, 37, 78, 126, 249, 251, 277, 299
  assignation, 14
  connection, 33, 37
  status, 14
Hickey, William, 324
Hill, Diana, 194
Hindiya Canal, 233
Hindoo/Hindu(s), xxxvii, 22, 24, 26–27, 36, 45, 68–69, 81, 120, 147, 161, 184, 202–03, 213, 221, 223, 234–35, 245–46, 260, 304, 327
  law codes, 202, 304
  processions, xxxvii
Hindoostan/Hindustan, xvi–xvii, xx, xxxiv–vi, 3–10, 13, 15–17, 22, 29–31, 33–34, 37–40, 43–44, 46–47, 50, 54, 57–59, 73–74, 80, 87, 97, 100, 109, 112–13, 115, 118–21, 133–34, 152, 166, 172, 174, 189, 219, 235, 239, 245, 247, 249, 259, 277, 279–81, 288, 308, 315, 319, 330, 334, 340, 346, 381, 383, 386, *see also* India
Hinduism, 202
Hindu Kush, 327
Hindustani
  art and culture, xlii
  cookery, 247
  emperor, 16
  forces, 9, 35, 56
  powers, 340
  rulers and noblemen, 41
Hindutva, xlvii
Historiography, 100
*History of Asafu'd Daulah, Nawab Wazir of Oudh: Being a Translation of 'Tafzihu'l Ghafilin', a Contemporary Record of Events Connected with His Administration*, 219
Hobart, Robert, 323–25, 328–29, 338
Hodges, William, xxii, 61, 146, 148, 185, 203, 283, 292–93
Hoey, William, 219, 355
*Hofstra Law Review*, 88
Holkar, Malhar Rao, 46
Holkar, Tukoji, 277
Holy Roman Empire, 300
Homosexuality, 126
Hookah, 59, 63, 65, 86, 103, 109, 130, 167, 185, 203–04, 220, 248, 281, 285, 287
horses, xxix–xxx, xxxviii, 7–9, 12, 17, 19, 27, 31–32, 35, 54, 60, 66–67, 71, 73, 75, 85, 96, 103, 106–07, 110, 114, 118, 126, 128, 150, 155, 162, 167–68, 180, 182, 219–20, 239, 253, 272, 276, 289–91, 295, 299, 322, 326, 330, 346, 352, 356, 358, 360, 373, 377, 380, 384
  Khurasani, 35
  Persian, 19
  relay system of, 85
House of Timur, 247
Humdani, Shaikh Ghulam, 244
Humphry, Ozias, xxiii, xxvii, 99, 181, 193, 204, 207, 346
Hunhar, 37
hunting, 29, 58, 74–75, 106, 118, 161, 181–82, 216, 219, 310, 318, 343
hunts and excursions, 31, 73–75, 78, 155, 216
Hussain, Prophet's grandson, 34, 234–35, 244, 335
  death of, 34
Husayniyas, 229
Hussain, Ghulam, 12, 21, 40, 44–45, 313
Hussain, Imam, 69–70, 110, 227–29, 231–32, 234, 380
  death of, 241
Hussain's tomb, 229

Hyderabad, xxi, xxvii, xl–xlii, 14, 20, 25, 57,
    62, 113, 118, 173, 175, 240, 269–70, 306,
    325, 371, 373, 377
Hyder Ali, ruler of Mysore, xvi, xxvi–vii,
    xlv, 118, 146, 170, 173–77, 262–63, 267,
    273–74, 325
    attacked the Carnatic, 325

Iberian Peninsula, xlvii
Identity, xxxvii, 68–69, 71, 95, 97–98, 232,
    267, 282, 285, 301–02, 320, 343
    French, 267
    national, 301
    Shia, 69, 71
ideology(ies), xxxvii, xlvii, 102
    Hindutva, xlvii
    political, 102
*Ijaz-i-Arsalani*, 91, 94, 134
Imad-ul-Mulk, 6, 22, 24–25, 30–32, 40, 112
    assassinated Alamgir II, 32
Imambara(s), xxvii, xxxvii, 70, 229–31,
    233–34, 236–39, 319, 321, 377, 380, 390
    decoration of the, 230
Imbert, Isabelle, 103
Imperial
    ambitions, 42, 302
    approval, 15
    army, 23, 40
    artillery, 19
    authority, 15, 17
    buildings, 60
    camp, 76
    courts, 7, 102
    durbar, 20
    dignity, 75
    dreams, xxxviii
    family, 19, 22, 79, 322–23
    forces, 25, 41, 45, 132
    life, 82
    mission, 301
    power, 17
    service, 16
Imperial Delhi, 54, 66, 103
Imperialism, xliii, xlvii
Impey, Elijah, Chief Justice, 89, 168, 196
Impotency, accusation of, xxxvi
Imtiyaz-al-Dawla Iftikhar-al-Mulk, 87
India
    British dominance in, xxxiv
    British interests in, 295
    colonial rivalry in, xliii
    commercial monopoly in, xliii
    conquest of, xxxviii
    courts of, xlv
    French ambitions in, 173
    French influence in, 112
    French involvement in, xxxvii
    French trade in, xli
    French trading posts in, 172
    great powers in, 118
    history of the British in, xlvii
    military operations in, 178
    pre-colonial warfare in, 24
    rising power in, 154
    ruinous wars in, xlii
    territorial power in, 175
    volatility in, xlv
Indian Ocean, 175, 263
Indian(s), xiii, xviii–xx, xxii–iii, xxviii–xxxi,
    xxxiv, xli, xliii, xlv–xlviii, 3, 5, 9–10, 13,
    16, 24, 39, 42–43, 45, 48–50, 54, 72–73,
    78–79, 82–83, 86, 89–91, 95–96, 99–100,
    102, 113, 116, 139–40, 145–46, 156, 164,
    170–71, 173, 175–76, 178–79, 186, 188,
    193–94, 198–201, 203, 205, 208–09, 222,
    224, 233, 235, 240, 245, 247, 249, 259,
    261–66, 268, 271–75, 278, 281, 283–84,
    294, 303, 305, 310, 314, 318–20, 323,
    325–26, 328, 332, 342, 348, 350, 356,
    359, 362–63, 365–66, 371–72, 376–78,
    382–86
    armies, 9
    cotton, 264, 268
    history, xxxiv, xlviii, 79, 102, 188
    insurrection, 323
    kings, 318, 363
    powers, xx, xlvi, 323
    princely state, 371
    rulers, xix, xxxiv, xliii, xlv–xlvi, 5, 10,
        43, 54, 175–76, 305, 359
    sepoys, xxx, 3, 39, 50, 385
    soldiers, 3
    warriors, 16
Indo-British encounters, xxxvii
Indo-Islamic style, 19, 104
Indo-Muslim rulers, 236
Indo-Persianate culture, 89, 219
Indo-Portuguese family, 46, 78
Indus River, 31, 327
Infantry, xviii, xxix, xxxi, xxxix, xlii, 3, 5,
    14, 45, 55–56, 74–75, 115–16, 277, 287,
    327, 330, 384
    native, 330
    regiment, xviii

informants, 93, 310, 334, 347
Insha, Insha Allah Khan, 244
Insurrection, xvii, xxi–ii, xxxv, 145, 150–51, 323, 359
Intelligence, xii, xxi, xxxv, 9, 24, 43–44, 113, 115, 117–18, 140, 145, 161, 171, 218, 265, 305–06, 310, 324–26, 328, 334–35, 339, 380
   gathering, xxxv, 118, 325
   networks, xxi, 305, 310, 325–26, 334, 339
*In the Company's Secret Service: Neil Benjamin Edmonstone and the First Indian Imperialists, 1780–1820*, 342
Intizam-ud-Daula, 22, 383
Invaders, 15, 33
Iranians, 89
Iraq, 227–29
Ireland, 302, 323, 376
Irish battalions of France, 278
Irish Brigades, 200
Irish House of Commons, 323
Islah-i-zaban, 252
Islam, xxxvii, xlvii, 88, 227–28, 232, 235
Islamic Museum of Berlin, xlvii
Islamophobia, xlvii
Istanbul, 240
Italy, 197–98, 321, 368
Ives, Edward, 223
Ives, Otto, 295

Jacobinism, 378
Jagannath festival, xxxvii, 235
Jagat Seths, 33, 42
Jagdishpur, 312
Jaghirs/Jagirs, 20, 65, 129, 131, 144, 147, 151, 156–57, 163–64, 166–68, 181, 191, 281, 296, 312, 345, 354
   confiscated, 345
   resumption of the, 163
Jahangir, Mughal Emperor, xxxix, 12, 101, 108, 242, 319, 341
Jaipur, 203, 244, 284
Jalaluddin, 25
Jalaluddin Haidar, 19
Jama Masjid, Delhi, 253
James II, 347, 370
Jarday, Daniel Du, 111
Jasanoff, Maya, xxxiv, 94
Jats, the, xi, xix, 13–14, 23, 25, 35, 53, 94, 109, 112, 114, 116, 118, 239
   gardi (affliction), 25

rebelled against Mughal emperor Aurangzeb, 13
Jaunpur, 15, 330, 348
Jaynagar, 361
jewellery/jewels, 12, 17–18, 21, 32, 51, 64, 66, 70, 73, 87–88, 108, 164, 167, 176, 183, 186, 189, 208–09, 215, 231, 239, 241–43, 250, 261–62, 264, 291–92, 294, 311, 345, 352–54, 357, 376, 381
Jhansi, 388
jharoka window, xxxix
Johnson, Daniel, 218
Johnson, Richard, 82
Jones, Rosie Llewellyn, 137, 185, 283
Jones, William, xxvii, 188, 202–03
Joseph, Louis, 269
Jurat, Shaikh Qalandar Baksh, 244, 256
Justice of Divine Punishment, 303

Kabaub, 185
kabootar khana, 191
Kabul, 56–58, 288, 327–28
Kafirs, 35
Kamkhwab, 86, 98, 288
Kampani Kalam, 83
Kanpur, 217, 295, 310, 333, 350, 389
Karaikal, 41, 172
Karamnasa River, 121
Karbala, 34, 69, 71, 134, 227–29, 231, 233
   tragedy of, 228–29
Karnataka, xli
Kashmir, 57, 320
Kashmiri, Allama Tafazzul Hussain Khan, xv, 12, 309, 313, 336
Kashmiri Gate, 22
Kashmiris, xv, 22, 94, 132–33, 204, 249, 290, 336
Kaveri River, 374
Kayasthas, xiv, 89, 234, 308, 334
Kazmain, 233
Kenya, xxxiii
Keshani, Hussein, 229
Kettle, Tilly, 98, 106, 193
Khaas Mahal, xv, 11, 30, 130, 354
Khadija Begum, 26, 133
Khairabad, 161
Khan, Abd-al Ahad, 132–35, 141
Khan, Afrasiab, 187
Khan, Akbar Ali, 264–65
Khan, Alivardi, 25
Khan, Almas Ali, xv, 312–13, 335, 337, 343–45, 347

# INDEX

Khan, Ambar Ali, 62
Khan, Ashraf Ali, 37
Khan, Axe, 16, *see also* Shah, Nadir
Khan, Bahar Ali, xv, xxvii, 62, 122, 150, 160–61, 164–65, 167–68, 289
Khan, Darwesh, 263–65
Khandesh, xxxix
Khan-e-saman, xiv, 143
Khan, Faizullah, 102, 104–05, 151, 296
    death of, 296
Khan, Faqirullah, 37, 102
Khan, Ghulam Hussain, 12, 313
    *Seir Mutaqherin, The*, 88, 133, 313
Khan, Hafiz Rahmat, 242
Khan, Haider Ali, 162
Khan, Haider Beg, xiv, 157–58, 180–81, 186, 195, 214–15, 248, 291, 308
    death of, xiv, 308
Khan, Hasan Reza, xiv, 62, 165, 194–95, 222, 248, 289, 308, 334–35
Khan, Hassan Reza, 343, 345
Khan, Hidayat Ali, 32
Khan-i-Allama, xv, 336, *see also* Kashmiri, Allama Tafazzul Hussain Khan
Khan, Ilich, 55, 143
Khan, Inayat, 341
Khan, Ismail, commander of the nawab's forces, 26
Khan, Javed, khwajasara, xi, xxv, 21–22
    *Tarikh-i Ahmad Shah*, 21, 24
Khan, Jawahar Ali, xv, xxvii, 21, 122, 150–51, 155, 160–62, 168, 287, 343, 347, 353–55
    death of, 355
Khan, Lal, 15, 87, 92
Khan, Mahbub Ali, 290
Khan, Mahfuz, xxix–xxx, xli
Khan, Matbu Ali, 311
Khan, Mian Almas Ali, 312
Khan, Mir Kalan, 37, 102–03, 117, 213
Khan, Mirza Ali, 62
Khan, Muhammad Darwesh, 264
Khan, Muhammad Ousman, 264
Khan, Muhammad Salah, 186, 220
Khan, Najaf, xiv, xxvii, 26, 94, 111, 114–16, 132–35, 139, 141–43, 166, 187, 239–40
    death of, xxvii, 187, 239
    influence of, 135
    marriage of, 187
Khan, Najaf Quli, 278, 282–83
Khan, Nawab Murid, 93
Khan, Saadat Ali, xii, xxi, xxvi, xxviii, 104, 107, 125, 205, 214, 236, 242, 330, 346, 348–49, 351, 355, 359, 363, 379–80
    rebellion of, xxvi
Khan, Shamsher, 165
Khan, Syed Hussain Ali, 12
Khan, Tehsin Ali, 347
Khanum Jan, xxiii, 204, 248–51
Khatris, 26, 89, 234, 288
Khillat, 5, 21, 111, 142, 200, 344, 351, 379
Khurd Mahal, 60–61, 291
Khwaja Haider Ali 'Aatish', 257
Khwaja Mir 'Dard', 257
Khwajasaras, xv, xxvii, xxxv, 21, 55, 67, 119, 122, 128–29, 141, 150–51, 155–56, 158–68, 180, 287–90, 312–13, 343, 347
    elite, xxxv
    imprisonment of the, 167, 180
    murder of, 22
Khyber Pass, xl
Kifayatullah, 236
Kindersley, Jemima, 54, 67, 75, 250
King Charles III, 364
King George III, 51, 171, 225, 301
Kirkpatrick, William, 325
Kishwar, Mallika, 389
Kora, 312
Kothi Bibiapur, 343–44, 349–51
Kotwali Chowk, Delhi, 15
Kshatriya, 202
Kufa, 69, 228, 232–33
Kumar, Deepa, xxxvii
Kumar, Raja Nand, 89

Lafayette, 267
Lafont, Jean-Marie, 80, 83, 177, 308, 385
Lahore, 16, 57, 288, 327–28, 356, 359–60
Lahori Darwaza, 19, 23, 111
Laird, James, 316
Lake, Gerard, xxii, 145, 385
Lakhori bricks, 58, 230
Lal Khan ka Lakkad, 15
Lally, Comte de, 41
Lal, Nevasi, xxvi, 80
Lal, Raja Jhau, xiv, 143, 235, 308–10, 332–37, 339–41
    dismissal of, 332
La Martiniere School, Lucknow, 216
land concessions, xlii
Landholders/landowners, xxii, 15, 68, 149, 159, 312, 343
    Hindu, 68
    recalcitrant, xxii, 149

languages, xviii, xxi, xxiii, xlvii, 19, 29, 68, 72, 87, 89, 91, 95, 102, 107, 120, 142, 156, 188, 202, 213, 231, 238, 244, 251–53, 257, 283, 305, 310, 322, 326, 337, 346, 364, 370–71, 390
    Arabic, xv, 83, 181, 194, 228, 252, 336
    Avidhi (Awadhi), xviii, xxiii, 68, 78, 86, 101–03, 134, 141, 161, 183, 209, 214, 221, 226, 235–36, 243, 259, 288, 292, 305, 326, 330, 339, 353
    Bengali, 94, 113, 302–03, 305–06
    Brajbhasha, 251
    Dravid (Tamil), 326
    English, xv, xlvii, 87, 94–95, 200, 364
    French, 79, 94, 377–78
    Greek, xv, 57, 336
    Hindi, 216
    Hindustani, 251
    Indian, 305
    Indic, 103
    Italian, 278
    Karnataki (Kannada), xli, 326
    Latin, xv, 79, 275, 336, 370
    Marathi, xxxix, 35, 326
    Persian, xv, xxi, xxiii, 19, 79, 82–83, 87, 94–95, 103, 117, 137, 181, 188, 193–94, 200, 209, 213, 216, 221, 223, 242, 246, 249, 251–52, 259, 275, 278, 280, 283, 288, 305–06, 322, 336
    Punjabi, 251
    Sanskrit, 13, 79, 83, 202–03, 209
    Telang (Telegu), 326
    Urdu, 15, 25, 72, 83, 87, 96, 200, 224, 249–53, 256–57, 259, 275, 278, 283, 306, 377
    visual, 102
Laswari, 386
Laws of Manu, 202
Library(ies), xlviii, 82, 104, 209, 233, 241–43, 305, 319, 352
    nawabi, 243
    royal, 352
Liddle, Swapna, 15, 19
    *Shahjahahanabad: Mapping a Mughal City*, 15, 19
lifestyle, xiv–xv, xxi, 66, 95, 144, 219–20, 292, 302, 306, 309, 313–14, 358
    Indo-Persianate, 302
Lion of God, xlviii, 255, 267, 377
Lise, Boulone, 140, 316
London, xvi, xxiii, 91, 102, 113, 118, 195, 213, 241–42, 249, 270, 284–86, 301–02, 382

Lord Fitzwilliam, 330
Lord Hobart, 323–24
Lord Teignmouth, 352
Louis XV, French King, xlii, xlv, 171, 174
    leadership of, xlv
Louis XVI, French King, xvi, xxvii–viii, xlv, 83, 145, 174, 205, 240, 262–64, 267–69, 299–300, 365
    execution of, 299–300
Lucknawi
    crafts, 220
    politesse, xxxiv
Lucknow Residency, 214
Lucknow, the capital of Awadh, xii–xv, xviii–xix, xxi–iii, xxvi–viii, xxxiii, xxxvii, 3–4, 15, 18, 32, 34, 37, 46, 48, 54, 57–58, 66, 69, 80, 82, 85, 93, 100, 102–03, 109, 113, 134, 136–42, 148, 150, 157, 159, 162, 165–68, 180, 182–204, 208, 210, 213–26, 229–35, 237–38, 242–45, 248–49, 251–61, 272, 274–77, 279, 283, 286–89, 291–96, 305–07, 309–11, 315–17, 319–22, 324, 327–28, 330–34, 336, 338–39, 342–45, 348–53, 355–56, 358, 379–80, 387, 389–90
    British and European residents of, 317
    British interests in, 310
    courtesans of, 66
    features of, 255
    financial burden, 214
    profligacy of, 224
    Shia architecture in, 233
    Shia monuments in, 233
Luft-un-Nisa Begum, 292
Lumsden, 310, 331, 339, 344, 353
Lutyens' Delhi, 24
Lyon, Thomas, 363

Macchi Bhawan, 191, 219, 238, 317
Macpherson, Sir John, 194, 214
Madan, Charles, 245, 330
Madec, René, xix, xxv, xliii–xliv, xlvii, 3–4, 40, 43, 45–47, 95, 111, 113–14, 119, 179, 387
    camp, 10
    nazr to Shuja, 5
Madonna, oil painting of the, 98
Madras, xviii, xxix–xxx, xl–xli, 39, 41, 50, 87, 175, 206, 272, 306, 323, 328, 372–73, 378
Mahadeo Das's gardens, 147
Mahdi, 229

Mahdighat, 135
Mahe, 41, 172
Mahi Maratib, xi, 13
Mahlaqa Bai Chanda, 22
Mahomedans, 317, 359
Majlis, 69–70, 162, 224, 229, 231, 248–49, 259, 292
Malabar coast, 176, 367
Malguzary, 146
Malwa, xxxix, 57, 253
*Man of the Englightenment: Letters of Claude Martin, A*, 194
Manuscripts, 52, 72, 79, 81–83, 86, 94–95, 137, 139, 203, 209, 233, 242, 249, 251, 319, 352, 387, 390
    collection of, 72
    exquisite, 86
    Indian, 83, 209
    Mughal, 52
map-making, 81
Maratha Confederacy, 384, 385
Marathas/Marhattas/Marathas, xiii, xvi–vii, xx, xxv–vii, xxxix, 13, 23–25, 29–30, 33, 35–36, 38, 40, 42, 53, 57, 109–10, 114–16, 118, 173–76, 187–89, 200, 239, 240–41, 269–73, 276–77, 279, 282, 307–08, 360–61, 377, 383–86
    allies, 25, 30, 272–73
    army, 36, 116, 308
    brigades, xvi
    camp, 239
    envoy, 29
    forces, xxv, 23, 38, 386
    French Brigades, 385
    hegemony, 30
    incursions, 13, 118
    refugee, 36
    state, 13, 277
Markel, Stephen, 220
Marquis de Lafayette, 267
Marriage/wedding, xii, xiv, 20, 78–79, 108–09, 112, 144, 187, 191–92, 208, 213, 222–24, 227, 238, 252, 283–86, 291–93, 346, 358, 361, 364
Marsack, Charles, 343
Marsiya, 71, 231, 259–60
Martin, Claude, xvi, xix, xxii, xxv–vii, xliv, xlviii, 91, 94–96, 137–38, 140, 148, 167, 185–86, 194–95, 197–209, 215–16, 220, 238, 272–76, 279, 281–83, 305, 316–17, 339, 347, 351, 387
    Company expedition, 137

    efforts, 216
    Gloriosa superba, 275
    plant and animal drawings, 274
Masalchis, 85
Masnad, 135–36, 244, 346, 351, 358–59
Masnavi, 256
Massacre at Karbala, 69
Massacres, 17, 69, 148, 227, 361
Masulipatnam, 172
Mathematics, xv, 102, 336
Mathura, 13, 239
Matthews, General Richard, 176
Mauritius, 271, 366–67, 371, 375, 377
McInerney, Terence, 102
Mecca, xxxix, 69, 142, 228, 286, 371–72
Medicine, 59, 93, 102
Mediterranean, the, xlii, 145
Medows, Captain William, 270
Meena bazar, 58
Meerut, 23, 390
*Memoirs of Lucknow and Faizabad*, xliii, 355
Mendec, Lucia, 72, 78
mercenary(ies), 3, 5, 8, 23–24, 45, 55–56, 112
    Austrian, 8, 45
    Breton, 5
    mixed-race, 3
    white, 3
merchants, 5, 7, 10, 37, 49, 56–57, 59–60, 117, 119, 121, 214, 225, 264–65, 274, 288, 293, 295, 310, 315, 333, 366
    European, 295, 333
    Kabuli, 5
Mianganj, 312
Middle East, xxiii, xlii, 42, 171, 213
Middleton, Nathaniel, 100, 117, 120, 129, 137, 148, 157, 162–63, 165, 180, 190, 215
Middleton's tents, 162
Mihr Chand, 91
military
    assistance, 178
    commanders, xvi, xxxv, 161
    posturing, 157, 341
    preparations, 344
    strength, 16, 349
Mill, James, 350
Miniatures, xlviii, 18, 37, 81–82, 86, 98, 100, 186, 194, 196, 284, 320
    Indian, 194
    Mughal, 18, 37, 81, 98
Mir Atish, 19

Mir Bakshi, 16, 111, 187
Mir Jafar, 7, 10, 39, 89
Mir Jaffar, xxv, 42
Mir Qasim, Nawab of Bengal, xviii, xliii, xviii, xliv, 5–8, 43, 49, 130, 168
Mirror Hall, 318
Mir Taqi Mir, 31, 182–83, 253
Mirza Akbar, 187, 280–81
Mirza Amani, 34, 75, 98, 106–08, 122, 125, 162, 312
Mirza Hajji, 356
Mirza Hasnu, xiv, 62, *see also* Khan, Hasan Reza
Mirza-i-Kalan, 223
Mirza Jalal-al-din, 244
Mirza Jangli, 107, 291, 346, 349, 360
Mirza Kamran, 243
Mirza Khurram, xxxix, 356–57
Mirza Mangli, 107, 125, 291, 345
Mirza Mohsin, 26, 133
Mirza Muhammad, 20, 37, 254
Mirza Salim, 242, 319
Mirza Shagufta, 356–58
Misals, 13
Mississippi River, 42
Miyanganj, 312–13
Miyan Ghulam Nabi Shori, 259
Modave, Comte Louis Federbe de, xvii, xxvi, xl, xliii, xlvii, 6, 17, 29, 32, 43, 45, 53, 55–56, 59, 64, 73, 79, 88–89, 94, 107–08, 110, 115, 117, 119–20, 126, 130, 132–33, 138–41, 143, 145, 172, 178, 186, 189, 235, 334
Modave, Louis Federbe de, xl, 115
*Modern Asian Studies*, Vol. 57, 11
Mohammad Shah, Emperor, 17–20, 31, 35, 37, 108, 154
Moharram, 232
monarchy, 193, 268–69, 299, 301
  constitutional, 299
  excessive powers, 299
monopoly, xliii, 4, 117, 149, 341
  African slave trade, 4
  commercial, xliii
  saltpetre, 117
monuments, 233, 236, 319, 377
Mordaunt, Colonel, 155, 187, 216–17
mosques, 61, 68, 104, 229, 233, 238, 317
Moti Bagh, 68, 156, 158, 160, 162, 166, 292
Moti Begum, 283–84
Mubarak-al-Daula, 291
Mubarak Mahal, 60

Mughal
  architecture, xxxvi, 19, 104
  art, xxxvi, 100
  authority, 14, 142
  cause, 58, 114
  court, xxxv, xxxix, 10, 12, 15, 17, 19–20, 22–23, 37, 79, 114, 186, 233, 257, 306
  edifice, xxxix
  empire, xi, xxxix, xl, 3, 6, 13–14, 21, 25, 30, 33, 39, 59, 71, 78, 81, 111, 188, 189, 273, 334
  exchequer, xxxix
  family, xvii, xl, 19, 30, 244, 280, 357
  forces, xiii–xiv, xvii, xxv, xxix–xxxi, xxxviii, xliv, 15, 45, 179
  hierarchy, xxix, xxxviii
  imperial authority, 17
  influence, 18
  kings, 242
  legacy, xxxvi
  legitimacy, 18, 25, 30
  library, 241
  noblemen, xl, 111
  offering sanctuary to, 187
  officers, 16, 27
  royalty, 187, 188
  rulers, xliv
  soldiers, xxix–xxx
  style, 80
  symbols, 9, 18, 25
  throne, xiii, 219
  tradition, 99
  treasury, 30
  wedding, 20
  zenanas, 280–81
Mughal Album, 52
Mughal army, xxx, xl, 43
  defeat of the, xl
Mughal Deccan, 20
Mughal Delhi, 18, 136, 221, 229–30
Mughal emperor, xiii, xvi, xx, xxii, xxxviii–xl, xliv, 4, 6, 8–9, 11–14, 18, 23, 25, 30–31, 37, 43–44, 76, 110, 112, 114–16, 142, 154, 189, 200, 240, 242, 251, 279, 284, 319, 357, 381, 385, 390
  financial ruin of the, xl
  succession of, xliv
Mughal India, 21, 93, 249, 326
Mughals, xi, xiii–xiv, xvi–xvii, xix–xx, xxii–iii, xxv, xxix–xxxi, xxxv–xl, xliv, 3–4, 6–27, 29–31, 33, 36–37, 39–40, 42–46,

52, 55, 58–60, 63, 67–68, 71, 76, 78–82, 85–87, 91, 93–94, 98–104, 110–12, 114–16, 121, 131–32, 135–36, 142, 144, 154, 176, 179, 186–89, 200, 205, 209, 215, 219–21, 223, 229–30, 233–34, 236–37, 240–44, 246–47, 249, 251, 253, 256–57, 273–74, 279–82, 284–85, 288, 292, 306, 311, 316, 319, 325–26, 334, 356–57, 359, 361, 379, 381, 385, 390
  crumbling power of the, xl
  guerrilla tactics to challenge, 13
  offering sanctuary to royalty, 187
  power of the, xl, 13, 244
  violence against the, xvii
Muhammad Shah, Mughal emperor, xi, xiii, xxv, 12–13, 16, 21, 30, 33, 66, 154, 280
Muharram, xxxvii, 34, 67, 70–71, 78, 110, 162, 227, 230–33, 235, 238, 260, 262, 292, 380
  commemorations, 230, 231, 238
  processions, xxxvii, 71, 78, 380
Mukeem, Mirza Abu'l Mansur Mohammad, 14, *see also* Safdar Jung
Mukhtar-ud-Daula, 127
Multan, 57
Munir-ud-Daula, Nawab, 17
Muraqqas, xviii, 91, 100–101, 103, 209, 241–42
Murshidabad, 100, 108, 177, 229, 246
Murtaza Khan, 127–29, 134–35
  honours awarded to, 128
Musaman Burj, 19
Museum of Islamic Arts, Berlin, 52
mushafi, 244, 252, 255
mushairas, 114, 251, 254, 257, 319
music, xlvii, 18, 34, 66–67, 76, 92, 102, 111, 198, 204, 213, 224–26, 248–51, 253, 259, 283, 290, 294, 315–16, 319, 326, 363, 380, 389–90
  Hindustani, 198, 249, 251, 315, 319
  Hindustani styles of, 259
  vocal, 326
*Music and Musicians in Late Mughal India: Histories of the Ephemeral, 1748–1858,* 249
Musicians, 18, 65–67, 76, 80, 109, 111, 114, 194, 225, 249, 251, 258, 294, 306, 315, 369
Mohemmedan/Muslim/Mussulman/Musulmaun, xxxvii, xlvi–vii, 27, 34–36, 42, 45, 68, 69, 112, 121, 156, 184, 202, 221, 227–28, 232, 234–38, 246, 252, 292,

304, 309, 318, 359
  aggressors, xlvii
  as the feared and despised 'other', xlvii
  discrimination in the UK, xlvii
  enemy, xlvii
  Indian, 45
  law codes, 202
  notion of the, xlvii
Mutiny, xxviii, 87, 160, 308, 390
Mutiny of the Bengal army, xxviii
Mysore, xvi, xxi, xxvi–vii, xlv, 10–11, 113, 118, 146, 170–71, 173, 176, 178, 240, 262–64, 267, 269–70, 272–74, 276, 325, 327, 366–67, 371, 373, 375–76, 378, 384–85
  British aggression against, 378
  plunder of, 378
Mysorean officers, 375

Nader Shah/Nadir Shah, xi, xiii, xxv, xl, 9, 15–18, 31, 33, 46, 53, 132, 254
  army, 18, 33
  assassination of, 17
  consequences of entry into Delhi, 16
  invasion of, xl
  Persian cavalry, 16
  proclaimed himself emperor of Hindustan, 16
  sacking of Delhi, 18
  soldiers, 17
Nagas, 9, 24, 26, 33, 35, 45, 143
  eccentric and terrifying style of fighting, 24
  Gossains, 24, 33, 35, 45
  soldiers, 26
  troops, 9, 24, 35, 143
Nagpur, 388
Naib Vakil-ul-Mulk of Hindustan, 279
Najaf Khan, Mirza, 111, 166
Najibabad, 34
Najib-ud-Daula, xvii, 34, 37, 46, 76, 110, 241
  death of, 110
Najm-ud-Daula, 20, 154
Naples, 300
Napoleon Bonaparte, xxviii, xlv–vi, 170, 300, 321, 364, 369, 375, 382, 387
  campaigns in Italy, 368
  death of, 387
  Egypt campaign, 369, 382
  wars in Egypt, 372
Napoleonic Wars, xxviii, xlv, 271, 300, 364, 383, 386

Narain, Raja Ram, governor of Bihar, 40
Narayan, Jagat, 26
Narayan, Raja Lakshmi, 23
Narayan, Raja Udit, 356
Narayan, Ram, diwan of Awadh, 26–27
Nationalism, xlvi
National Museum, Delhi, 16
National shame, 306
Naubat at Allahabad, 34, 61, 76, 82, 109, 111, 293, 383
Naubat instruments, 82
Naubat khana, 76, 111
Nautch, 204, 223–24, 250
    dancers, 224
Naval battle, 366
Nawab Aliya, 150
Nawab Begum, wife of Safdar Jang, xi, xiv–xvi, xxviii, xxxvii, xlviii, 10, 20, 27–29, 58, 60, 62, 67–68, 79, 107, 109, 125, 127–28, 133–35, 141–43, 155–56, 158–60, 166, 168, 191–92, 288, 290–93, 311–12, 354
    death of, xxviii, 311
    discretion and generosity, 68
    jagirs, 166
    wealth of, 311
Nawabi
    court, 79, 259
    employee, 95
    households, 161
    life, 80, 82
    symbol, 220
Nawabi Awadh, xxxiv, 8, 14, 18, 58, 60, 63, 69, 79–80, 82, 85, 95, 126–27, 131–32, 134, 138, 140, 143, 161–62, 164, 180–81, 184, 186, 192, 204–05, 209, 213–14, 219–21, 231, 242–43, 259, 293, 305, 309, 317, 329–30, 345, 349, 353
Nawab of Arcot, 98, 223, 324
Nawab of Bengal, xxxviii, xliv, 5–7, 10, 18, 33, 39
    deposed, 6
Nawab of the Carnatic, xxix, xxxi, xli
Nawabs of Awadh, xi–xii, xiv–xvi, xviii–xix, xxi–iii, xxv–vi, xxviii–ix, xxxi, xxxiv–v, xxxvii–viii, xli, xliv, xlviii, 3–11, 17–20, 23–29, 33–35, 37, 39, 41, 43–52, 54–71, 73–79, 84, 87, 93–95, 98–101, 103–04, 106–10, 112, 117–22, 125–31, 133–39, 141–44, 148–51, 154–60, 162, 165–66, 168, 181–88, 190–96, 198, 200–201, 205, 208, 213–26, 228, 230, 233–36, 238, 241–44, 246, 248, 254–57, 259, 272, 274–75, 288, 290–96, 305–14, 316–21, 324, 327, 329–48, 350–55, 357, 359, 363, 379–80, 388–90
    administration, 195, 308, 333, 336
    army, 47, 350
    collection, 318, 352
    debt, 190
    financial liabilities, 214
    government, 214
    hereditary, 7
    museum, 238
    paintings of the, 218
    private expenses, 181
    private household records, 181
    succession, 342
    troops, 35, 55
    wealth of the, 193
    zenana, 156, 347
Nazr, 5, 27, 40, 47, 74, 111, 119, 129, 141, 157, 161, 281
Negotiations, 8, 16, 50, 141, 168, 173, 176, 180, 282, 324, 346
    complicated, 8, 173
    genial, 16
Nepal, 150, 305
Netherlands, the, 300
New Delhi, 23–24, 144, 238, 325
Newly independent India, xxxiii
New Orleans, 42
New Testament, 325
Nidhamal, 102
nikah marriages, 11, 20
Nizam of Hyderabad, xxi, xxvii, xli–xlii, 118, 175, 269–70, 371, 377
    death of, xlii
Nizamuddin Auliya's tomb, 35
Nizam-ul-Mulk of Hyderabad, xl, 16, 20–22, 24–25
Nobility, 58, 69, 74, 108, 127, 129, 143, 154, 234, 236, 292, 294, 300
Noor Begum, sister of Faiz Begum, xvi, xix–xx, xxii, xxviii, 199–200, 282–86
North Africa, 171
North America, xlii, 42, 113, 145, 171
    colonies, 39, 145
North/Northern India, xvi, xxv–vi, xxxiv, 13, 30–31, 82, 109, 137, 144, 154, 201, 214, 249, 281, 312, 334
Nur Jahan Begum, 215

*Observations on the Mussulmauns of India,* 232

Ochterlony, David, xxii, xxviii, 386–87
Orissa, 11, 25, 50
Officers/Officials
    Company, xlii, 3, 4, 10, 54, 293, 308, 333
    French, xliii, xliv, 5, 24, 40, 43, 45, 47, 77, 107, 172, 177, 179, 263, 278, 365–66, 383, 385
    Mughal, 16, 27
    Persian, 19
oil painting, 98, 99, 205, 262, 320
Old Delhi, 24
Oldernburgh, Veena, 66
Old Lakhypeera, 140
Old Testament, 202
Oman, 264
*On Some Extraordinary Facts, Customs, and Practices of the Hindus*, 304
Operation Legacy, xxxiii
opium, 9, 42, 165, 332, 335, 341
    consumption, 332, 341
Order of St Patrick, 381
Order of the Cross of Saint-Louis, 5
Order of the Garter, 376
ornaments, 12, 52, 108, 189, 284, 381
orphan children, 207
Orr, Robert, 315
Ottoman Caliph, 240
Ottoman empire, 161, 326
Oude/Oudh, 3, 219, 226, 307, 312, 317, 329, 339, 345, 355, 379, 389

paan, 63, 70, 86, 185, 220, 248, 258, 287, 322
paan-daan, 86, 248
*Padhshanama/Padshahnama/Padshanama/Padshanamah*, 81, 104, 242, 319, 352
Padshah Begum, 13
Padshah Salim, 242
pagodas, 273
painters, xxiii, 18, 80–82, 91, 96, 98–100, 146, 181, 185, 193–96, 225, 242, 265, 319, 346
    court, 98
    English, 146, 181, 195
    European, 99, 193
    French, 265
    Indian, 100, 193
    oil, 193, 196
paintings, xviii, xxii, xxxiii, xlviii, 18, 71, 79–80, 82–83, 86, 91, 94, 96–104, 117, 139, 170, 187, 189, 193–94, 196–97, 199, 204–05, 209, 213, 218, 241–43, 247, 256, 262, 266, 274–75, 293, 316, 320, 336, 341
    *Apotheosis of Hercules, The*, 262
    Awadhi, 209
    botanical, 274
    collection of, 243, 275
    conversation piece, xxii, 196
    flower, 103
    Indian, 79
    marginal, 82
    miniature, xlviii, 86, 194, 320
    Mughal, 241
    nawabi, 243
    queen's, 196
Pakistan, 229
Palmer, William, xvi, xix, xxii, 199–201, 214–15, 217, 279, 283–84, 308, 339
Panch Mahal, 191
Panj-hazari, xxxviii
Paris, xxv, xlv, 42–43, 48, 77, 171, 177, 242, 262–66, 269, 299–300, 387, 389
Parkes, Fanny, 64, 226, 250, 252, 320
Parwana, 146
Pathans, 42, 277
Patna, 8, 13, 33, 47, 83, 93, 120, 146–48, 152, 169, 209, 340
patronage, xxiii, xxxvi, 12, 66–67, 69, 103, 137–38, 154, 194, 203, 213, 220, 225, 233, 236, 244–45, 256, 259, 275, 328, 345
    nawabi system of, 345
    system of, 137–38, 245, 345
patrons, xxiii, xxxiv, 18, 63, 66, 80, 82, 87, 100–101, 103, 116, 160–61, 193, 196, 204, 214, 236, 243–44, 249–52, 267, 274–76, 278, 319
peace, xviii–xxix, xliii, 17, 46, 47, 49, 80, 164, 171–72, 178, 181, 191, 193, 207, 263, 270, 273, 289, 374, 382
    proposals, 80
    settlement, 46, 47, 273
Peace of Paris, 263
Peacock Throne, the, 18, 82, 132
Pearson, Sarah, 314
Perceret, Louis, 92
Perron, General, 277, 383, 385–86
Persia, xi, 13, 15–17, 31, 59, 102, 233, 235, 264, 280, 326
Persian, the, xiii, xxiii, 13, 16–17, 35, 61, 79, 101–02, 117, 132, 188, 213, 221, 252, 305
    conqueror, 16
    immigrants, 19, 233

manuscript collections in London, 242
Peshawar, 57
*Peshkash* (offering), 141
Peshwa, Narayanrao, 174
Philippines, the, 42
Philosophy, 81, 102, 362
Physiognomy, 99, 102
Picart, Bernard, 81
    Illustrations de Ceremoies et Coutumes Religieuses de Tous les Peuples du Monde, 81
Pirzada of Ajmer, 82
Pitt's India Act, 193, 388
Plowden Album, 251
Plowden, Captain Richard, 198
Plowden, Elizabeth, 198, 201, 204, 207, 222–23, 225, 237, 248, 251, 259, 316
poem/poetry, 63–64, 66, 78, 80, 85, 102–03, 114, 184, 231, 244, 249–50, 252–54, 256–58, 261, 288, 368, 390
    competitions, 114
    Persian, 78, 103, 288
    recitations, 231
    Urdu, 249–50, 252
    visual, 103
poets, 18, 31, 37, 57, 63, 66, 80, 114, 182–83, 193, 225, 244, 252–58, 300, 306, 310, 369, 389
Polier, Antoine, xiii, xviii, xxiii, xxv–vii, xliv, xlviii, 43, 52, 87–97, 99, 101, 121–22, 132, 134–35, 139, 185–89, 200–204, 207, 209–10, 216–17, 238, 243, 250, 282–83, 285, 316, 387
    allegiances, xviii
    art collection, 97
    manuscript collection, 209
    Persian letter-book, 94
    role of intermediary between Awadh and Delhi, 134
    political affairs, 131
    goals, 24
    integration, 26
    transgressions, xlvi
politics, xi, 6, 19, 72, 117, 164, 270, 306, 328, 353
    Awadhi, 353
    court, 19
    Delhi, 117
    durbar, 6
    Indian, 72
    nawabi, 164

Pondicherry, xix, xxv, xxvii, xxx, xxxviii, xl–xli, xliii–iv, 3–5, 10, 40–41, 43, 137, 172–74, 176, 365–66, 378
    1760 Siege of, xix
    destruction of, xliii, 43, 137
    fall of, xix, 3, 41
Port of Chaul, 174
Portraits, xxiii, 88, 91, 97–100, 106, 112, 155, 174, 181, 189–90, 193–94, 196–98, 242–43, 265, 316, 319–20, 335
Portugal, 39, 300
Pote Collection, 209
power, xiii, xvii, xx, xxviii, xxx–xxxi, xxxiv–vi, xl–xliv, xlvi, 12–15, 17, 18–25, 28–33, 37, 41, 43, 47–48, 50, 54, 56, 61–62, 65, 67–68, 70–71, 75–77, 98, 115, 118, 127, 134, 136, 138, 143, 145, 151, 154, 156, 165, 171, 173, 175, 180–81, 187, 208, 213, 228, 233, 235, 240, 242, 244, 263–65, 267, 269–72, 279, 289, 291, 299, 301, 305, 318, 321, 323–24, 331, 334, 337, 339–40, 344–45, 348, 349–50, 353–54, 357–59, 361, 369, 371–72, 383, 388
    aggressive colonial, xliv
    bases, xxxv, xl, 14, 344
    colonial, xliv
    French, xlvi, 171
    imperial, 17
    indigenous, xxxiv
    local, xxxv
    magisterial, 98
    Mughal, 13, 18, 29, 67
    Mughal Sunni, xxxvi
    political, xlii, 228, 354
    quasi-legendary, xxx
    sacrosanct, xliv
    symbols and imagery, 267
    tussle, 19
Prahlad Babbar's website, 103
Prayag, 238
Prime Minister William Pitt the Younger's India Act, 193
Prince Azfari, 223, 257
Prince/princess, xii–xiii, 5, 8, 12, 19, 31–33, 40, 41–46, 55–56, 74, 76, 80, 107–08, 113, 115, 121, 132, 168, 175, 188–90, 219, 223, 231, 239–41, 244, 246–47, 251, 256–57, 267, 272, 281, 283, 291, 306, 319, 346, 356–57, 363, 377
    Hindustan, 115
    Indian, 377
    Mughal, 19, 223, 241, 247, 251, 256,

306, 319, 357
  Persian, xxiii, 213
  Timurid, 223
prisoners of war, 3
Proclamation of Neutrality, 300
Proclamations, xxxvii, 71, 165, 192, 233, 300, 346–47, 367, 385–86
propaganda, xxxvi, 178, 378
  campaign, 378
  English, 178
Prophet Muhammad, 34, 69, 129, 149, 190, 227–28, 232–33, 267
Prosser, Sophie Elizabeth, 224, 346
prostitutes, 10
Protestant Evangelicalism, xlvi
Protestantism, xviii, xlvi, 301, 364
proxy wars, xlv
Poona, 173–74, 284, 384
Punjab, 13, 31, 33, 37, 249, 328, 388
Puppet emperors, xl, 7, 39, 241
Purdah, 10, 69, 136, 154–55, 163, 237, 246, 259, 293
  severity of the, 155

Qadir Baksh, 96
Qadir, Ghulam, son of Zabita Khan, xvii, xxvii, 240–41, 243, 279, 281
  captured by Scindia, 279
  taken hostage, 241
Qamar-ud-Din Khan, 108
Qasim Ali Khan, 168
Qasim, Mir, xviii, xliv, 5–8, 43, 49, 130, 168
Qila-e-Mualla of Delhi, 12, 19, 23, 31, 35, 50, 104, 111
Qila Faizabad, 60, 74
Qizilbashes, 45
Qizilbash regiments, 33
Qudsiya Bagh, 241
Qudsiya Begum, xi, xxv, 21–23, 30, 280
Quebec, 10, 39
Queen Charlotte, 196
Queen Elizabeth II, 364
  Golden and Jubilee celebrations for, 364
Queen Marie-Antoinette, 174, 205, 262, 265, 268
Queen Victoria, 388–89
Quieros, Joseph, 206, 283
Quli Khan, Muhammad, 26–27, 135, 278, 282–83
Quran, the, 131, 156, 228, 350, 380
Qureshi, Hamid Afaq, 121

Mughals, 1722-1856 the English and the Rulers of Awadh, The, 121
Qutlugh Begum, 357–58
Qutlugh Sultan Begum, the widow of Mirza Jawan Bakht, 322, 356, 379

Racism, xlvii, 316
ragas and talas, 259–60
Ragini, 251, 259
Rahim, Abdur, 55
Rai, Maharaj Tikait, 308
Rai, Raja Nawal, 235
Raja Beni Bahadur, the Brahmin Naib of Awadh, 34–35, 55
Raja of Benaras, xvii, 29, 168, 323, 356, 360, 389
Raja of Berar, 175
Raja of Bhutwal, 360
Raja of Tanjore, 324, 338
Rajas of Bundelkhand, 360
Rajasthan, 277, 361
Rajputs, 13, 15–16, 27, 55, 68, 103, 361, 383
Rakabdars, 62, 220
Rama Varma, raja of Travancore, 270
Ramnagar, 147, 152, 356
Rampur, 151, 296
Ramzan, 235, 285, 309
Rangeeley, Muhammad Shah, xi, xiii, xxv, 12, 18, 37, 66, 280
Rangeen, 244, 257
Rao, Daulat, xvii, 384–86
Rao, Viswas, 36
Ray, Satyajit, xxxiv
  *Shatranj ke Khiladi* (movie), xxxiv
*Real Birds in Imagined Gardens*, 102–03
Red Fort of Delhi, xiii, xxv, xliv, 12, 19, 30, 385
Reign of Terror, xxviii, 300, 369
  egalitarian republicanism of the, 300
  end of the, 369
Reinhardt, Walter, 8, 45
Rekhti, 256–57
Religion, xxi, 29, 81, 87, 140, 203, 301, 303–04, 350, 359, 377
Religious
  beliefs, 304
  duties, 309
  heroes, xxxvii
Residency of Lucknow, 238
Resident of Delhi, xxii, xxviii, 386
Resident of Lucknow, xxvii, 305

Revenues, xv, xxii, xxxix, xl, 7–8, 13–15, 20, 22, 25, 30–31, 50–51, 75, 115, 130–31, 142, 148–49, 157, 166–67, 172, 177, 180–81, 202, 214, 218, 225, 229, 236, 306, 312–13, 379
  assessment, 149
  collection, 180, 214
  collectors, 15
  farmers, xxii, 148–49, 167
  farming system, 149
  generating lands, 166
  land, 202
  tax, xl, 25
Revolt, xii, 149, 152, 163, 185, 239, 321, 361
  Benaras, 149
Revolutionary France, 364
Revolutionary-Napoleonic Wars, 300
Revolutionary Wars, xlv–vi, 382
Reza, Ghulam, 82
Reza Khan, Hasan 'Hasnu', 122, 143
riot, 185
Ripaud, François, xxviii, 366–67, 378
rites/rituals and practices, xxxvii, 11, 36, 68–69, 121, 229, 233–35, 238, 319
  fasting, xxxvii
  Hindu, 36, 235
  Indian tazia, 235
  mourning, 68, 70, 110, 127, 209, 227, 229, 231–32, 234
  Muharram commemoration, 231, 238
  Muslim, 235
  Shia, 68–69, 121, 229, 234
rivalry, xxxvii, xliii, 256
  British, xxxvii
  colonial, xliii
  Franco-British, xxxvii
Roe, Thomas, xxxix
Rohilkhand, xxviii, 31, 118, 125, 131, 296, 379
Rohillas, the, xvii, xix, 29, 46, 53, 109, 112, 114, 116, 118, 214, 242, 247, 296, 385
Rohilla War, 120
Rohilla, Zabita Khan, son of Najib-ud-Daula, xvii, 76, 110, 116, 241
Ross, Alexander, 215, 272
Roxburgh, William, 274–75
*Flora Indica*, 274
Royal
  fortunes, 14
  kitchen, 62
  salute, 142

Royal Collection Trust, 242, 352
Royal Navy, Britain, xl
Royalty, 187–88, 268, 288, 322, 358
  privileges of, 358
Roy, Malini, xxxvi, 91, 102
  Idiosyncrasies in the Late Mughal Painting Tradition: The Artist Mihr Chand, Son of Ganga Ram, 91
Rumi Darwaza, 229–30
rumours, xvii, 22, 76, 109, 135, 147–48, 158, 172, 236, 241, 346–47, 358–59
  Safdar Jang's death, 22
  scandalous, 346
Runnymede Trust, xlvii
Russia, 387

Saadat Ali Khan Burhan-ul-Mulk, Nawab of Awadh, xii, xxi, xxvi, xxviii, 104, 107, 125, 205, 214, 236, 242, 330, 346, 348–49, 351, 355, 359, 363, 379–80
  demoted and exiled, 14
  disastrous defeat, 143
  humiliation of, 386
  the twenty-two-year-old nawab, 26, 126
Saadat Ali, Mirza, 125
Sachaq, 20, 108
Sadr-un-Nisa Begum, xi, xxv, 10, 22, *see also* Nawab Begum, wife of Safdar Jang
Safavid Iran, 326
Safavid Persia, 233
Safavi empire, 13
Safdar Jang, Nawab of Awadh, xi, xvi, xxv, xl, xliv, 14–15, 18–29, 55, 68, 78, 104, 133, 335
  death of, xxv, 28
  left Delhi, xi, 29
  loss for, 24
Safdar Jang's haveli, 23
Saint-Domingue, 171
Salabat Jang, 42
Salar Jang, 60, 62, 119, 127, 151, 155–57, 186, 191, 354
  palace, 60
Salim, Akbar's son, 108, 128
Sambalpur, 388
Samman Burj, 60
Samru, 45, *see also* Reinhardt, Walter
Sarkar, Jadunath, 35–36, 283
  *History of Dasnami Naga Sanyasis, A*, 35
Satara, 388
Sauda, Mirza Muhammad Rafi, 37, 254

# INDEX

Sawai Madhavrao, Peshwa, 174
Sayyid Begum, 92
Sayyid brothers, 12–13
Sayyids, xi, 13
Schofield, Katherine Butler, 204, 249–50
Scindia, xvi-vii, xx, xxvii, 36, 110, 116, 187, 239–41, 276–79, 281–82, 284, 383, 384
Scindia, Daulat Rao, xvii, 384–86
Scindia, Madhav Rao, 110
Scindia, Mahadaji, Maratha warlord, xvi-vii, xx, xxvii, 36, 110, 116, 239–41, 276–78, 281, 284, 383
    death of, xvii, 284
Scotland, 307, 363
Seringapatam, xvi, xxi, xxvii-viii, 267, 273, 366–67, 372–74, 376–79
    fall of, 368, 373, 378
    plunder of, 376
Seven Years' War, xxv, xliii, xlv, 10, 33, 39, 41–42, 49, 77, 171, 173, 300
sexual
    chastity, 131
    intrigue, 302
    misdemeanours, 109
    potency, 198
    practices, 198
    relationships, 249, 250
sexuality, xxxvi
Shaab-e-Barat, 285
Shah Alam II, Mughal emperor, xiii, xx, xxvii, xliv, 6, 9, 33, 36, 40–41, 43, 82, 187, 200, 239, 251
Shah Alam I, Mughal emperor, 78, *see also* Bahadur Shah
Shah Alam, Mughal emperor, xiii, xvi-vii, xxvi-viii, xliv, 7, 33, 40, 45, 50–51, 73–77, 86, 109–12, 115, 131, 133–35, 139, 141, 187–88, 219, 239–42, 279–80, 282, 357, 383
    forced to sign the infamous Treaty of Allahabad, xliv
    Gentil's assessment of, 74
    in exile, 110
    insulted by the Marathas, 40
    rescue of, xxvii
Shahjahanabad, 15, 22, 24, 223, *see also* Old Delhi
Shah, Jahandar, 149
Shah Jahan, Mughal emperor, xxxix, 9, 12, 19, 24, 104, 111, 188, 243, 319, 352
Shah, Mirza Akbar, 187, 280–81
Shah, Nadir, xi, xiii, xxv, xl, 9, 15–18, 31, 33, 46, 53, 132, 254
Shah, Nizam ud din, 280
Shah, Wajid Ali, xxxiv, 221, 388–90
Shahzaada/Shahzada, 6, 40, 45, 181, 187–89, 193
Shah, Zaman, 327–29, 332, 338, 341, 359–60, 370
Shah, Zeman, 329
Shaikhazada, 45, 55
Shaikhs, 16, 311
Shams-un-Nisa Begum, 108–09, 244, 259, 288, 343
Sharah, 312
Sharar, Abdul, 57, 67, 184, 260
Sharif of Mecca, xxxix, 372
Shaykh Imam Baksh 'Nasikh', 257
Shia Muslims, xii, xiv, xxxvi-vii, xlviii, 13, 19–20, 34, 68–69, 71, 121, 133, 154, 227–29, 232–35, 237–38, 259, 309, 319, 321
    legacy, xlviii
    practice, 233
    remembrance, xxxvii, 319
    renaissance, xii, xxxvi, 321
Shia Persian, 19–20, 233
Shiat Ali, 69
Shiism, xxxvii, 69, 229, 259
    expression of, xxxvii
ships, xli, 4, 177, 328, 367–68
    British, 328
    English, 367
    French, xli
Shivdev, Kashiraj, 35, 36
Sholapuri Begum, 108
Shore, John, Governor General, xii, xiv, xxi, xxviii, 104, 301–03, 314, 321–22, 329–30, 333–36, 339–40, 343, 347, 349–52, 363, 368, 381
    grand proclamations, 347
    recommendations, 344
    stay at Lucknow, 333
Shrine of Nizamuddin Auliya, 35
Shuja-ud-Daula, the third nawab of Awadh, xi-ii, xiv-vi, xviii-ix, xxiii, xxv-vi, xxxiv, xxxv, xxxvii, xliv, 4–11, 25–29, 32–38, 41, 43–52, 54–57, 59–68, 70–78, 80–81, 88–89, 91–95, 98–100, 103–10, 112, 116–20, 122, 125–31, 133–36, 138–40, 143–44, 161, 163–64, 167–68, 180, 186, 194–95, 219–20, 225, 236, 242–43, 264, 287, 290–93, 296, 306, 334, 340, 344–46, 353, 355, 390

army, 59
aspirations, 44
as subedar of Awadh and Allahabad, 26
campaigns, 118
death of, xii, xxvi, 65, 125–26, 129, 131, 133–34, 139, 167, 180, 236, 291–92
defeat at the Battle of Buxar, xviii
English reception at Allahabad, 49
European soldiers, 78
forces, 41, 45
grave of, 122, 127
harem, 11, 144, 161
Hindustani forces, 35, 56
inheritance, 27
lack of coordination, 56
Modave's assessment, 73
pastimes of kite-flying and pigeon-flying, 26
portraits of, 99
post-Buxar reign, 340
re-imagining of his capital, 59
reply to the Company, 7
reputation for sobriety, 28
resisted English demands, 118
stay at Lucknow, 37
violation of father's legacy, 28
*Sihr-ul-Bayan*, 256
Sikhs, 13, 37–38, 239, 387
    Khalsa, 13
    warriors, 37–38
Singers, 37, 57, 66, 70, 92, 109, 204, 251, 257–8, 260, 290
Singh, Balwant, raja of Benares, 29, 93
    death of, 93
Singh, Kavita, 102–04
    *Real Birds in Imagined Gardens: Mughal Painting Between Persia and Europe*, 102
Singh, Mohan, 80
Singh, Pratap, Raja of Jaynagar, 203, 361
Singh, Raja Chait, raja of Benares, xvii, xxii, xxvi, xxxv, 93, 144–48, 150–52, 163, 168, 185
    imprisonment, 147
    revolt, 185
    uprising of, xxxv
Siraj-ud-Daula, the nawab of Bengal, xxv, xxxviii, xliii, 7, 33, 39, 42, 108
*Sirr-i-Akbar*, 79
Skinner, 383, 384, 385
slaves, 4, 6, 8, 12, 86–87, 92–93, 129, 160–61, 164, 180, 191, 207, 260, 280, 283, 303, 321, 328, 369
    African, 4
    black, 4
    Christian, 369
    trade, 4, 161, 328
Small Clive album, 52, 100
Smith, Charles, xx, xxvii, xlvi, 99, 140, 145, 170, 193, 196–97, 286, 299, 303, 364
social
    distinctions, 129
    justice, 229
Society of Dilettanti, 197
soldiers or sepoys, xviii–ix, xxix–xxx, xxxv, xxxviii, xliii–iv, 3–5, 7–8, 10, 17, 26–27, 31–32, 35–37, 39, 41, 43, 46, 48–50, 52, 57, 65–67, 73, 76, 78, 87, 94, 104, 109–10, 112, 114–16, 127, 129, 131, 139, 141, 147–48, 150–51, 155, 158–60, 162–63, 166–67, 169, 172–73, 176–77, 179, 200, 209, 214, 227, 241, 245, 267, 270, 272, 276–78, 281, 287–88, 299, 308, 310, 323, 330, 338, 343, 349, 358, 360, 363, 366–67, 369, 371–77, 382–83, 385–86, 390
    Awadh, 148
    begum's, 158
    besieged, 374
    British, 377
    disciplined, 115
    Durrani, 35–37, 78
    EIC, 272, 276, 338, 358, 374
    English, 46
    European, 3, 5, 78, 270
    firangi, xxx
    foot, xxx
    French, xviii, xxix–xxx, xliii–iv, 3–4, 43, 73, 139, 173, 179, 267, 366–67, 371, 375, 378, 383
    Indian, xxx, 3, 39, 50, 385
    local, xxxviii, 5
    Mughal, xxix, xxx
    Naga, 26
    Nawab Wazir Ali's, 343, 358
    Qizilbash, 31
    rebel, 150
    riotous, 147
    trained, 49
Sone River, 121
songs, xlvii–viii, 92, 197–98, 204, 224, 226, 249, 251–52, 257, 259–60, 316, 356, 361
    Bhakti, 257
    bridal, 252

folk, 356
  Hindustani, 251
  Indian, 259
South America, 39
South India, xx, xlii, 173
Sovereignty, xliii, 13, 17, 223, 240, 309, 333, 339
  Mughal, 13
  territorial, xliii
soz khwani, 70, 231
Spain, xlvii, 39, 172, 300
  blood purity laws of, xlvii
Srinagar, 92, 93
Srivastava, Ashirbadi Lal, 23, 93
  *First Two Nawabs of Awadh, The*, 23
St. Lawrence River, 10
St. Lubin, 174
St Thome, xxx, xli
Stuart, James, 104, 347, 370
subah, xxxiv, 3, 14, 23, 33, 65, 81–82
  governorships of, 14
subedar, xxv, 14, 26
subedari, 14, 25
Subh-e Benaras, Shaam-e Awadhwa, Shab-e Malwa, 253
Subsidy, xvii, xxvi, 50, 131, 145, 151, 167, 180, 214, 305–06, 317, 321, 332–33, 339, 350, 380, 383
  alliance system, xlii
  military, 214
  payment of the, 339
  war, xxvi, 145
Succession, xxv, xl, xlii, xliv, 12, 31, 39, 131, 173, 228, 296, 342, 344, 348, 384
  disputes, xlii, 173, 384
  of emperors, 12, 31
Suffren, Admiral, 173, 175–76, 263
Sufism, xxxvii
Sunehra Burj, 353
Sunni Muslims, xxxvi–vii, 19, 35, 68–69, 108, 132, 227–28, 233, 238
  Mughals, xxxvii, 233
  Turani, 19, 108
Sunnism, xxxvii
Supreme Council of Calcutta, 149
Surajmal Jat, 23, 35
  death of, 23
Surat, 175
Swarup, Sushama, 238
  *Costumes and Textiles of Awadh: From the Era of Nawabs to Modern Times*, 238

Swinton, Archibald, 3, 44, 51, 55
Swiss/Switzerland, xviii, xxx, xliv, 3, 87, 95, 220
sword fighting, 346
Sykes, Mark, 42
Sykes-Picot Agreement, 42
symbology, 267

Tajikistan, 85
Takht of Delhi, 31
Talleyrand, 368
Taluqdars, 15, 312
Tanda, 165, 222
Tandon, Banmali, 19, 58–59, 343
Tanjore, 324, 338, 379, 388
Tappa, 259
Tartars, 42
Tavernier, 233, 326
Tawaifs, 249–51, 257, 259–61
taxes, xxii, xl, xliv, 11, 13, 25, 50, 65, 77, 113, 141, 144, 146, 149
  collection rights, 11
  of Bengal, xliv
  revenues, 25
tazia khana, 229
tazia/taziya, 229, 235
Tea Act in 1773, 113
Tensions, xvi, xviii, 160, 238, 267, 288, 324, 350
  British and France, xvi, xviii
  class, 324
territorial
  conquests, xliii, 301
  sovereignty, xliii
The Reunion Island, 111
Thirteen colonies, xlv, 145, 170, 172
  independence of the, 172
Thumri, 251, 261, 310, 315
Timur Shah, the Afghan king's son, 31, 34, 247, 327, 389
  death of, 327
Tippoo/Tipu Sultan, ruler of Mysore, xvi, xxi, xxvi–viii, xlv–xlvi, xlviii, 10, 146, 170, 176, 178, 240, 262–64, 266–73, 305, 325, 327, 360–63, 365–67, 371–78, 381–83, 385, 387
  attacked by Wellesley, xlvi
  campaign of vilification against, 170
  correspondence, 378
  death of, 375, 376
  defeat in 1792, 363, 374
  destruction of, 378

diplomatic exchanges, 377
hatred for the British, 378
killing of, 385
sanction of his claims to sovereignty, 240
scorched earth campaign, 373
surrendered, 270, 273
'Tiger of Mysore', 170
violence and aggression against, xvi
titles
   Arsalan-e-Jang (Lion in Battle), xlviii, 86, 91
   Asaf Jah, 20
   Bahadur, 383
   Bahadur Jang, 13
   begum, 200, 251
   Burhan-ul-Mulk, 13
   Haft Hazari, 383
   hereditary, 26, 78
   Himmat Bahadur, 46
   Intizam-ud-Daula, 383
   Juliana, 78
   Lion of God, 267
   Lord Teignmouth, 352
   Nasir-ul-Mulk, 383
   nawab, xxxviii
   nawab of Awadh, 126
   Padshah, xxvii, 240
   panj-hazari, xxxviii
   wazir, 21, 25, 141
Tod, James, 361
   *Annals and Antiquities of Rajasthan: Or The Central and Western Rajput States of India*, 361
Tollendal's expedition, 174
trade, xviii, xli–ii, 4, 7, 15, 31, 39, 44, 49, 82, 94, 117, 138, 149, 159, 171–75, 240, 264, 268, 295, 328, 382
   barrier, 117
   duty-free, 49, 117
   goods, xlii, 15
   horse routes, 31
   links, 240, 382
   private, xlii
   river, 15
traders, xix, 117, 148, 161, 181, 231, 292
   private, 181
trading companies/centres, xxxviii, 4, 11, 44, 50–51
trading posts, xxv–vi, xxxviii, xxxix–xl, 5, 41, 43, 50, 83, 112, 172–75, 178
   British, xl, 174–75

Chandernagore, 172, 173
commercial, 175
Company's, 50
French, xxv–vi, xxxviii, 41, 43, 172–73, 175
Karaikal, 172
Madras, xl
Mahe, 172
Masulipatnam, 172
Pondicherry, 172–73
travellers, 77, 107, 119–20, 206, 225–26, 230, 238–39, 245, 250, 293, 315, 320, 322, 330, 380
   British, 77, 206, 320, 330
Treasury at Agra, 30
Treaty of Aix-la-Chapelle, xlii
Treaty of Allahabad, xliv
Treaty of Amiens, 382–83
Treaty of Annexation, 380
Treaty of Chunar, 151
Treaty of Paris, xxv, xlv, 42, 43, 77, 171
Treaty of Tilsit, 387
Treaty of Versailles, xxvii, 178, 263
Triangulation surveys, 81
Trivedi, Madhu, 235
troops, xvi, xxvii, xxx, xxxviii, xl–xliv, 6, 9–10, 12, 19, 22, 24, 35–36, 39–41, 45–47, 55–56, 66, 74, 76, 110, 112, 118, 125, 131, 135, 138, 143, 147, 150–51, 158, 163, 170, 173, 177, 181, 215, 217, 271–72, 277–78, 308, 328, 338, 340, 343, 348, 350–51, 360–61, 373, 375, 377, 379, 385–86
   Afghan, 55
   Asaf-ud-Daula, xvi
   at Seringapatam, xxvii
   battle-ready, 373
   British, 170, 350, 360, 377, 385
   British-led sepoy, 131
   camel, 308
   cavalry and infantry, 74
   de Boigne's, 277, 386
   deracinated, 55
   disciplined, xxx
   Durrani, 36, 45, 46
   EIC, xxxviii, 56, 110, 138, 143, 338, 351, 360–61
   emperor's, 41
   English, 118, 151, 177
   European, xli, 45, 373
   European-trained, xliii
   French, xxx, xliv, 10, 39, 45, 177, 375

horses, 272
in Delhi, xvi
Indian, xli
local, 55
Mogul/Mughal, xvi, xxx, 40, 45–46, 55, 135
Naga, 9, 24, 35, 143
Native, 373
nawab's, 35, 55
permanent, 131
Persian, 55
sepoys, 131, 173, 343
Vizier's, 215
Tropez, Pierre André de Suffren de St, 173
Tuileries Garden, 299
Turani, 19, 22–23, 108
    faction, 22–23
    nobles, 22
Turkey, 59, 235
Twelver Shiism, 229
Twining, Thomas, 248, 281–82, 286, 296, 315–18

Udaipur, 388
Udham Bai, 21–22
Umayyad caliphs, 69, 227–28, 234
Ummat-ul-Zohra Begum, 10, 20, see also Bahu Begum, mother of Asaf-ud-Daula
Umm Kulthum, 69
United States of America, 170, 300
Universal poverty and depopulation, 149
Upanishads, 79
Uprising of 1857, xxxiii, 230, 377
Urdu Bazar, Delhi, 15
Uttar Pradesh (UP), 34

Valentia, George Viscount, 107, 206, 229, 313, 356–57, 380
Vedas, 203, 209, 326
Velho, Sebastian, 37, 72, 78–79, 83
Victoria and Albert Museum, 48, 52
Vizier, Nabob, 44, 142, 215, 217, 238, 307, 310, 329, 332, 336–38, 351

Walpole, Horace, 197
War
    against widows, 164
    bands, 13
    camp, 4, 8, 25
    destructive, xlv
    elephant, xxx
    horses, xxix
    indemnity, 16, 49, 51, 371
Warlord, xi, xiii, xvi, xx, xl, 23–24, 94, 114, 277, 359
    Afghan, 359
    Gossain, 24
    imperial, 94
    invasion, xl
    Maratha, xvi, xx, 277
    Mughal, 23
    Persian, xi, xiii, xl
*War of the Austrian Succession*, xxv, xl, 39
Warship *L'Orient*, 368
Wars of empire, xxxviii
Washington, George, xx, 170
Waterloo, xxviii, xxxviii, xlv, 300, 387
Wazir Ali Khan, Nawab of Awadh, xii–xiii, xxi, xxviii, xxxv-vi, 181, 183, 224, 293, 308, 333, 343, 344–52, 356–61, 372
    arrival in Benaras, 356–57
    captured, 361
    death of, 361
    disposition, 344
    insurrection of 1798, xxxv
    parentage of, xii, 346, 348–50
    'style of magnificence', 358
    succession, 348
    wedding, 346
Wazirat, 21, 37, 141–42
    negotiations for the, 141
Weis, Friederike, 102–03, 243
Welch, Stuart Cary, 104
Wellesley, Arthur, 376, 386–87
Wellesley, Richard, Governor General of India, xxi, xxviii, 180, 273, 368, 376, 384
    actions of, 377
    Mysore campaign, 376
West Indies, 4
Westminster, 266, 301, 364
White devils, 315
Wilberforce, William, 302, 304, 340
Windsor Library, 352
Witchcraft, 9, 24, 304
Wodeyar raja of Mysore, xvi, 173, 240
Writers Building, 363

xenophobia, 87

Yakh Mahalla, Lucknow, 141
Yamuna River, 15, 19, 75, 115, 121, 238, 253
Yanam, 41
Yazid, the Umayyad Caliph/Khalifa, 69,

227–28, 232, 234
Yorktown, 170, 177, 245, 269–70, 295, 386
  forces at, 245

Zafar, Padshah-e-Hind, Bahadur Shah, 385
Zainab, Imam Hussain's sister, 69, 231–32, 234
Zamburaks, 36
Zamindars, 14–15, 27, 89, 93, 148–49, 163, 235, 361
Zamindary, 149
Zeenat Mahal, 31
Zenana, xxiii, xxxv, xlviii, 14, 18, 27, 32, 58, 62, 70, 86, 95, 109, 121, 125, 128–29, 133, 135–36, 155–56, 160, 188, 193, 199, 203, 206, 231–32, 252, 256, 280–82, 317, 321, 343, 347
Zenana mahal, 27
Zenana of Faizabad, 135
Zinat-un-Nisa Begum, 13
Zoffany, Johann, xxii, xxvii, 99, 155, 186–87, 189, 193, 196–201, 204, 207, 218, 283, 316, 320, 336
  arrived in Calcutta, 197
  painting, xxii, 199, 204
Zohra Begum, 10, 20